W9-AKV-727

LATIN FOR THE NEW MILLENNIUM

STUDENT TEXT

LEVEL 1

LATIN FOR THE NEW MILLENNIUM
Series Information

LEVEL ONE

Student Text (2008)

Student Workbook (2008)

Teacher's Manual (2008)

Teacher's Manual for Student Workbook (2008)

ANCILLARIES

From Romulus to Romulus Augustulus:
Roman History for the New Millennium (2008)

The Original Dysfunctional Family:
Basic Classical Mythology for the New Millennium (2008)

LEVEL TWO

Student Text (2009)

Student Workbook (2009)

Teacher's Manual (2009)

Teacher's Manual for Student Workbook (2009)

ANCILLARIES

From Rome to Reformation:
Early European History for the New Millennium (2009)

The Clay-footed SuperHeroes:
Mythology Tales for the New Millennium (2009)

ELECTRONIC RESOURCES

(See page 445 for detailed description)

www.lnm.bolchazy.com

Quia Question Bank

Latin-only Villa in Teen Second Life™

Carpe Praedam

LATIN FOR THE NEW MILLENNIUM

STUDENT TEXT

LEVEL 1

Milena Minkova and Terence Tunberg

Bolchazy-Carducci Publishers, Inc.
Mundelein, Illinois USA

Series Editor: LeaAnn A. Osburn

Volume Editors: Elisa C. Denja, LeaAnn A. Osburn

Contributing Editors: Timothy Beck, Judith P. Hallett, Laurie Haight Keenan, Karen Lee Singh, Donald E. Sprague, Rose Williams, Vicki Wine

Historical Timeline: Jayni Reinhard

Cover Design & Typography: Adam Phillip Velez

Cover Illustration: Roman Forum © Bettmann/CORBIS

Other Illustrations: Photo Credits appear on pp. 431–434

Cartography: Mapping Specialists

Indexing: Michael Hendry

Proofreader: Gary Varney

**Latin for the New Millennium
Student Text, Level 1**

Milena Minkova and Terence Tunberg

Bolchazy-Carducci Publishers, Inc.
1570 Baskin Road
Mundelein, Illinois 60060
www.bolchazy.com

Printed in Canada
2010
by Friesens

ISBN 978-0-86516-560-1

Library of Congress Cataloging-in-Publication Data

Minkova, Milena.
  Latin for the new millennium : student text, level 1 / Milena Minkova and
Terence Tunberg.
     p. cm.
  Includes bibliographical references.
  ISBN 978-0-86516-560-1 (v. 1 : hardbound : alk. paper) 1. Latin language--
Grammar. I. Tunberg, Terence. II. Title.

PA2087.5.M562 2008
478.2'421--dc22

                                                                    2008014705

CONTENTS

LIST OF MAPS

FOREWORD

The *aurea mediocritās* of Latin textbooks has arrived! Not a grammar-translation nor a reading approach book, *Latin for the New Millennium* is a blend of the best elements of both.

The key to *Latin for the New Millennium*, Level 1, is the emphasis on reading Latin at the beginning of each chapter and using conversational Latin at the end of each chapter, or, as the authors indicate in the Preface, 'it (Latin) offers you the linguistic key to the minds that shaped European (and therefore American) culture from the time of the Romans to the modern scientific revolution . . . In this book you will learn about the language, step by step by using it.'

The reading passages at the opening of each chapter are based on Latin literature and proceed in chronological order from Plautus to Boethius. Each reading is supported by pre-reading and facing page vocabulary. Grammar is introduced using sentences already seen in the reading passage and, *mīrābile dictū,* there are plenty of exercises. The Vocabulary to Learn, chosen from the adapted reading passage, thus contains some Advanced Placement literature-based words and is reiterated consistently in the exercises and other short reading passages.

Something not seen in most Latin textbooks is the conversational dialogue at the end of each chapter. This will pique the student's interest in the Latin version of modern-day activities and meet certain classical language standards directly. The authors, Milena Minkova and Terence Tunberg, professors at the University of Kentucky at Lexington, are the directors of the hugely popular *Conventiculum Lexintoniense*, the annual summer program that has been running for more than ten years. They are also on the faculty of the *Conventiculum Bostoniense,* a similar program that draws participants to experience conversational Latin in different geographical settings. At the 2007 American Classical League Institute at Vanderbilt University, I participated in a conversational Latin workshop presented by Minkova and Tunberg. Though the participants were seasoned Latin teachers, most were experiencing for the first time the tried and true methods these two experts were using to inspire us to speak Latin. By the end of the workshop, we could converse in familiar Latin phrases and saw how useful this could be for our own students. Tunberg's and Minkova's leadership in these summer programs made them uniquely well suited to design the conversational dialogues in *Latin for the New Millennium* and the copious oral exercises that are contained only in the teacher manual, thus allowing teachers to pick and choose which exercises best meet the needs of their own students.

This book with its range of offerings will appeal to all types of language students and will allow teachers to bring the many facets of the Roman and post-Roman world into the classroom. How wonderful it is to see a passage of adapted Plautus in Chapter 2, a prose adaptation of Catullus' *passer* poem in Chapter 7, of Horace's satire on the boor in Chapter 13, and even of Tacitus' description of the great fire in Rome in Chapter 17. Roman culture is embodied in each of these passages, thus meeting another classical language standard. Accompanying each passage is a quotation or motto, connected to the passage or chapter.

All of this said, *Latin for the New Millennium* is student friendly. Study tips, rhymes, and mnemonics abound in each chapter and little sections called "By the Way" offer additional information for those who always want to know more.

The unit review sections are truly gems! After three chapters, a Latin review chapter provides not just the complete list of Vocabulary to Learn and plentiful exercises but often another piece of adapted literature to read—snippets of Martial or Petronius and more.

But this is not all. A section called "Considering the Classical Gods" offers high-interest readings in both English and Latin on the pantheon of classical gods. Another section, entitled "Connecting with the Ancient World," provides in English additional information on a particular aspect of Roman life contained within the unit.

Capping each review unit is a distinctive essay that explores Roman and modern topics, each written by a university scholar. From the University of Massachusetts to Stanford University, and many places in between, these professors have contributed their special expertise on subject matter related to the chapters. I know of no other book that does this!

There are many useful photographs and maps appropriately placed throughout. The reproductions of fine art and photographs of archaeological sites provide a visual learning experience as well. Needless to say, there are appendices on grammar and syntax and English to Latin and Latin to English glossaries with an added section on various mottoes.

The authors, editors, consultants, and pilot teachers have done a superior job of organizing this book for maximum usefulness and effectiveness. This unique series will include the following: Level 1 Student Text, Level 1 Student Workbook, Level 1 Teacher's Manual, and Level 1 Workbook Teacher's Manual; Level 2 Student Text, Level 2 Student Workbook, Level 2 Teacher's Manual, and Level 2 Workbook Teacher's Manual. Many online and electronic resources will also accompany this series.

Latin for the New Millennium has been thoughtfully designed for and with the twenty-first century student in mind. Please join me in heralding the appearance of this unique new series that will improve and enhance the study of Latin for the twenty-first century.

PAUL PROPERZIO
Boston Latin Academy
2008

PREFACE

Learning Latin helps you learn English and other languages better, and, perhaps even more importantly, it offers you the linguistic key to the minds that shaped European (and therefore American) culture from the time of the Romans to the modern scientific revolution. Latin was the language these people used to express themselves and to record their ideas in permanent form across so many centuries. In this book you will learn about the language by using it, step by step.

CHAPTER COMPONENTS

READING PASSAGES

Each chapter begins with a Reading Passage and notes on the facing page that will help you understand any linguistic elements you have not previously seen. These notes feature vocabulary words in an easy to follow alphabetical listing, providing you the exact meaning needed to understand the reading passage but not the full lexical entries at this point. By reading and seeing these new elements in their natural context, often you will need no explanation to understand how they function, because they appear with words you already know. The Reading Passages are adapted from authentic works of Latin literature, and they are presented in chronological order. As you complete each chapter, you will be tracing the story of Latin as a literary language and the stories of the authors who used it. In addition, you will learn about Roman culture over the periods of time in which the featured reading of each chapter was produced.

VOCABULARY TO LEARN

The Vocabulary to Learn repeats some words encountered in the Reading Passage for each chapter, but in this section the words are listed by parts of speech instead of alphabetically and here the full lexical entry is given. These are words you will need to memorize in order to recognize and use them throughout the remainder of the book. In order to aid you in recognizing connections between Latin words and the English words derived from or related to them, a derivative exercise follows each Vocabulary to Learn.

LANGUAGE FACTS AND EXERCISES

In the body of each chapter you will find simple explanations of the Language Facts featured in the chapter reading passage, along with many different exercises that allow you to *use* all the information you are learning. By doing the exercises in each chapter and in the student workbook, you will not only be reading and writing Latin, you'll be speaking it! Some exercises involve oral exchanges with the teacher and with other students. Because Latin communicates thought, it is a living thing. Therefore, a person who gains an active working knowledge in the language, along with a reading ability, is more likely to progress quickly to a deeper understanding of the language and the enjoyment of its literature. If you have an oral facility and can write in a language, you will not need to be reminded about forms and grammatical rules so often. In this book you will acquire that active facility as a basic part of learning the language.

CONVERSATIONAL LATIN

Toward the end of each chapter there is a Latin dialogue in which a group of modern students are the participants. They discuss, in Latin, situations often encountered in our daily lives. In these dialogues, you will find a bridge between our lives and the thoughts of the ancient, medieval, or renaissance authors who wrote in Latin—a bridge constructed of the same basic language, Latin.

OTHER FEATURES

In each chapter you will find other interesting matter that will help you learn and enjoy Latin.

- *Memorābile Dictū* The first page of each chapter features a famous saying labeled *Memorābile Dictū* (A Memorable Thing to Say), a Latin phrase so well known that it has become an often repeated proverb or quotation. Learning each famous saying will increase your understanding not just of Latin, but of the thoughts and ideas that were important to Romans and have continued to be an integral part of modern life.

- **Study Tips** Each chapter contains sayings, rhymes, mnemonic devices, verses, or other information that will help you remember the various things you are learning.

- **By the Way** You will see this phrase repeated throughout every chapter. When you see this label, you will know that additional information is being presented.

REVIEW COMPONENTS

At the conclusion of every set of three chapters, there is a review containing various components:

VOCABULARY TO KNOW

This is a complete list of all the Vocabulary to Learn words presented in the three chapters, arranged by parts of speech.

EXERCISES

Here you will see many new exercises that will help you review and reinforce the material in the three preceding chapters. In the review exercise section there is often an additional reading passage to help you understand more about Latin literature and its heritage today.

CLASSICAL MYTHOLOGY

This section, entitled *Considering the Classical Gods*, includes passages on mythology, one in English and one in Latin, which tell some of the principal stories about the Greek and Roman gods. These stories reflect many of the main themes seen in literature and art from classical to modern times.

ASPECTS OF ROMAN LIFE

Next you will find a reading in English on an important aspect of Roman daily life. This section, entitled *Connecting with the Ancient World*, will present additional information on a topic encountered in the previous chapters.

EXPLORING ROMAN AND MODERN LIFE

Following the section on daily life, there will be a short essay in English that compares and contrasts some aspect of Roman and American life and illustrates a way in which Latin is a part of our life today. Each of these essays has been written by a university scholar with special expertise in this field of study.

MĪRĀBILE AUDĪTŪ

Each review chapter concludes with a list of Latin quotations, mottoes, phrases, or abbreviations used in English. These sayings relate to one of the unit topics.

The Latin language and Roman culture have not only inspired writers throughout the ages and influenced modern life but have also left their presence in art and archaeology. In this volume, reproductions of paintings, drawings, sculpture, mosaics, frescoes, and other artifacts from antiquity through the present abound with depictions of and references to the stories and lives of the Romans. Likewise, views of archaeological sites remind us of what Rome and its area of influence was like in ancient times. The illustrations throughout the text support the written word in visual form, thus offering you a vivid recollection of the chapter content.

Each author of this book has written different sections of the textbook but both authors have benefited, throughout the composition of the textbook, from continuous mutual advice and support.

M.M. and T.T.
2008

Visit www.lnm.bolchazy.com to see the electronic resources that accompany *Latin for the New Millennium*.

AUTHORS

MILENA MINKOVA

MA and PhD, Christian and Classical Philology, Pontifical Salesian University, Rome, Italy; MA and PhD, Classics, University of Sofia, Bulgaria

Associate Professor of Classics, University of Kentucky, Lexington, Kentucky

Milena Minkova has studied, conducted research, and taught in Bulgaria, Switzerland, Germany, Italy, the Vatican City, and the USA. Minkova has authored three book monographs: *The Personal Names of the Latin Inscriptions from Bulgaria* (Peter Lang, 2000); *The Protean Ratio*, (Peter Lang, 2001); and *Introduction to Latin Prose Composition* (Bolchazy-Carducci, 2007, reprint; Wimbledon, 2001). She has also published numerous articles on Latin medieval philosophy, Latin literature, Latin composition, and Latin pedagogy.

TERENCE TUNBERG

BA and MA, Classics, University of Southern California; Postgraduate researcher, and doctoral student, Medieval Studies, University of London, England; PhD, Classical Philology, University of Toronto, Canada

Professor of Classics, University of Kentucky, Lexington, Kentucky

Terence Tunberg has taught in Belgium and Canada, as well as in the USA. He is a specialist in Latin composition, and an expert in the history of the approaches to writing Latin prose from antiquity to early modern times. His works include an edition of collection of Medieval Latin speeches, commentaries on Latin works, and numerous studies of the history of imitation in Latin writing. In addition, for more than a decade he has offered summer seminars designed to introduce people to the use of spoken Latin.

JOINT PUBLICATIONS BY THE AUTHORS

Minkova and Tunberg have coauthored the following books: *Readings and Exercises in Latin Prose Composition* (Focus, 2004); *Reading Livy's Rome. Selections from Livy, Books I–VI* (Bolchazy-Carducci, 2005); *Mater Anserina. Poems in Latin for Children* (Focus, 2006). They are the directors of the Institute for Latin Studies at the University of Kentucky, in which students study the history of Latin from ancient to modern times, and take part in seminars in which Latin is the working language of all activities. Both Minkova and Tunberg are elected fellows of the Rome-based *Academia Latinitati Fovendae*, the primary learned society devoted to the preservation and promotion of the use of Latin.

EDITORS, CONSULTANTS, AND PILOT TEACHERS

VOLUME EDITORS

Elisa C. Denja
Editor, Bolchazy-Carducci Publishers
Baker Demonstration School, Emerita
Evanston, Illinois

LeaAnn A. Osburn
Editor, Bolchazy-Carducci Publishers
Barrington High School, Emerita
Barrington, Illinois

BOARD OF CONSULTANTS

Virginia Anderson
Latin Teacher
Illinois Virtual High School
Barrington Middle School, Emerita
Barrington, Illinois

Jill M. Crooker
Latin Teacher
Pittsford-Mendon High School, Emerita
Pittsford, New York

Judith Peller Hallett
Professor of Classics
University of Maryland
College Park, Maryland

Sherwin D. Little
1–12 Foreign Language Program Leader
Indian Hill High School
Cincinnati, Ohio

Sherrilyn Martin
Chair, Department of Foreign Languages
Keith Country Day School
Rockford, Illinois

Mary Pendergraft
Professor of Classical Languages
Wake Forest University
Winston-Salem, North Carolina

John Traupman
Professor of Classics
St. Joseph's University, Emeritus
Philadelphia, Pennsylvania

Cynthia White
Associate Professor of Classics
University of Arizona
Tucson, Arizona

Rose Williams
McMurry College, Emerita
Abilene High School, Emerita
Abilene, Texas

Donna Wright
Latin Teacher
Lawrence North and Lawrence Central High
    Schools
Indianapolis, Indiana

PILOT TEACHERS

Jeremy M. Walker
Latin Teacher
Crown Point High School
Crown Point, Indiana

Lanetta Warrenburg
Latin Teacher
Elgin High School
Elgin, Illinois

VOLUME EDITORS

ELISA C. DENJA

BA Marygrove College, Detroit, Michigan; MA Columbia University; MA Loyola University Chicago

Elisa Denja taught Latin at North Chicago High School and Baker Demonstration School in Evanston, Illinois, for many years while concurrently teaching classical mythology at Loyola University of Chicago and in the gifted-distance learning program at Northwestern University. Elisa was awarded the Illinois Latin Teacher of the Year award in 1992 and the Illinois Lifetime Achievement Award in 2007.

LEAANN A. OSBURN

BA Monmouth College, Illinois; MA Loyola University Chicago

While teaching Latin for many years at Barrington High School in Barrington, Illinois, LeaAnn served as both vice-president and president of the Illinois Classical Conference. LeaAnn received the Illinois Latin Teacher of the Year award in 1989, the Illinois Lt. Governor's Award in 1990, and the Classical Association of the Middle, West, and South Good Teacher Award in 1996.

BOARD OF CONSULTANTS

VIRGINIA ANDERSON

BA Loyola University Chicago; MAT St. Xavier University

Virginia Anderson taught Latin for thirty years in private and public high schools and middle schools in the Chicagoland area. In 1999 she was awarded the Lt. Governor's Award for Enhancement of the Teaching Profession and in 2003 was named Illinois Latin Teacher of the Year.

JILL M. CROOKER

BA University of Illinois; MSEd Nazareth College of Rochester, New York

Jill Crooker taught Latin for many years at Pittsford-Mendon High School in Pittsford, New York. She has served as the College Board Advisor to the AP Latin Test Development Committee and in 1996 received the Morton E. Spillenger Award for Distinguished Leadership to the Classical Association of the Empire State. In 2003 she received the ACL Merita Award and in 2006 an Ovatio from the Classical Association of the Atlantic States.

JUDITH PELLER HALLETT

BA Wellesley; MA, PhD Harvard University

In addition to studying at the American Academy in Rome, the Institute of Classical Studies in London, and the University of Maastricht in Holland, Judith Hallett is a former president of the Classical Association of the Atlantic States and Vice-President for Outreach of the American Philological Association. She was named a Distinguished Scholar-Teacher in 1992 by the University of Maryland.

SHERWIN LITTLE

BA University of Cincinnati; MA University of Colorado

Sherwin Little has taught Latin from sixth grade through Latin AP at Indian Hill Exempted Village School District since 1983. Sherwin has received an Ovatio from CAMWS as well as the CAMWS Good Teacher Award and the Hildesheim Vase Award from the Ohio Classical Conference in 1986 and 2007. Sherwin holds National Board Certification in World Languages Other than English and has been both Vice President and President of the American Classical League.

SHERRILYN MARTIN

BA Wilson College; MA, PhD University of Cincinnati

Sherrilyn Martin was named Illinois Latin Teacher of the Year in 1993, was a recipient of the Lt. Governor's Award for Foreign Language Teaching in 2001, and was named a Claes Nobel Teacher of Distinction in 2007. She is a past president of the Illinois Classical Conference and is active in the Rockford Society of the Archaeological Institute of America. Sherrilyn spent a year in independent study at the University of Thessaloniki, Greece.

MARY PENDERGRAFT

AB, PhD University of North Carolina, Chapel Hill

After teaching at UNC-Greensboro and Duke University, Mary Pendergraft began teaching classics full-time at Wake Forest. Mary is a former President of the North Carolina Classical Association and participated in the focus group that wrote the North Carolina Standard Course of Study for Latin.

JOHN TRAUPMAN

BA Moravian College; MA, PhD Princeton University

John Traupman is professor emeritus from St. Joseph's University in Philadelphia where he taught for thirty-eight years. Among his many awards, John received the Distinguished Teaching Award from St. Joseph's University in 1982, a certificate of appreciation from the Pennsylvania Department of Education in 1990, and the Special Award from the Classical Association of the Atlantic States in 1996. John Traupman is especially well-known as the author of *Conversational Latin* and *The New College Latin and English Dictionary*.

CYNTHIA WHITE

BA Chestnut Hill College; MA Villanova University; PhD Catholic University of America

Cynthia White is the Director of the Undergraduate Latin Program and supervises teacher training and K–12 Latin Teacher Certification at the University of Arizona. She regularly teaches at the *Istituto Internazionale di Studi Classici di Orvieto*, the Classics Department's Study Abroad Program in Orvieto, Italy and has studied in Rome with the Papal Latinist Reginald Foster, O.D.C.

ROSE WILLIAMS

BA Baylor University; MA University of North Carolina, Chapel Hill

In addition to postgraduate work in Latin and Humanities at the University of Dallas and the University of Texas at Arlington, on a Rockefeller Grant Rose Williams did research at the Bodleian Library, Oxford University in England and at the University of Pisa. She taught Latin for over thirty years at both high school and university levels in Texas and now is the author of more than ten books about the Classics.

DONNA WRIGHT

BA, MA Ball State University

After teaching Latin at Carmel High School, Donna Wright currently teaches at both Lawrence North and Lawrence Central High Schools in Indianapolis, Indiana. She has been an active member of the Indiana Classical Conference, being named Creative Latin Teacher of the Year in 1976. She has also been active in the American Classical League, sponsoring a JCL chapter, and leading Italy trips for nearly twenty years. Donna also served as an officer, speaker, and board member of Pompeiiana, Inc.

PILOT TEACHERS

JEREMY M. WALKER

AB Wabash College; MA Indiana University

Jeremy Walker has taught Latin at Crown Point High School in Crown Point, Indiana since 1995. He has served as the Co-Chair of the Indiana Junior Classical League and Membership and Public Relations Chair of the National Junior Classical League. In addition to studying in Italy at the Intercollegiate Center for Classical Studies and in Greece at the American School for Classical Studies, he was president of the Indiana Classical Conference. In 2003, Jeremy was recognized as the Latin Teacher of the Year in Indiana, and in 2004 was recognized by the Indiana State Teachers Association as a Torch of Knowledge Recipient.

LANETTA WARRENBURG

BA Indiana University; MAT Indiana University-Purdue University, Indianapolis

Lanetta Warrenburg has taught high school English and Latin for thirty-three years at schools in Indiana and Illinois. Her last twenty-four years of teaching Latin were at Elgin High School in Elgin, Illinois. While teaching Latin there, she served as the Illinois Classical Conference chairperson for Chicago Classics Day, as co-chair for the Illinois Certamen League since 1993, and as state chair for the Illinois Junior Classical League from 1999–2001. Lanetta was honored as the Illinois Latin Teacher of the Year in 2001 and was president of the Chicago Classical Club from 2005–2007.

 # INTRODUCTION

ALPHABET

The Latin alphabet was derived from the Etruscan alphabet some time before the seventh century BCE. The Etruscans were a people in pre-Roman Italy.

Their alphabet owes much to the Greek alphabet. In turn, the Greek alphabet was derived from the Phoenician alphabet. Phoenician traders had spread their system of writing throughout the Mediterranean region. The Phoenician alphabet itself can be traced to the North Semitic alphabet, which was used in Syria and Palestine as early as the eleventh century BCE, and is considered to be the earliest fully developed alphabetic writing system.

An Etruscan couple reclining on a funeral sarcophagus.

Look at the English alphabet in the left column, and at the Latin alphabet in the right one. The Latin alphabet is accompanied by the names of the Latin letters (in parentheses).

English Alphabet		Latin Alphabet		
Uppercase	Lowercase	Uppercase	Lowercase	Letter Name
A	a	A	a	(a "ăh")
B	b	B	b	(be "bay")
C	c	C	c	(ce "cay")
D	d	D	d	(de "day")
E	e	E	e	(e "ĕh")
F	f	F	f	(ef)
G	g	G	g	(ge "gay")
H	h	H	h	(ha "hah")
I	i	I	i	(i "ee")
J	j			
K	k	K	k	(ka "kah")
L	l	L	l	(el)
M	m	M	m	(em)
N	n	N	n	(en)
O	o	O	o	(o "ŏh")
P	p	P	p	(pe "pay")
Q	q	Q	q	(qu "koo")
R	r	R	r	(er)
S	s	S	s	(es)
T	t	T	t	(te "tay")
U	u	U	u	(u "oo")
V	v	V	v	(u consonant)
W	w			
X	x	X	x	(ix "eex")
Y	y	Y	y	(upsilon)
Z	z	Z	z	(zeta "dzayta")

The English alphabet is derived directly from the Latin alphabet. This accounts for the great similarities between the two alphabets. There are 26 letters in the English alphabet and 24 in the Latin. The differences are the following:

- The letter **W, w** (which is the doubled letter **v**) is missing in the Latin alphabet.

- The letter **J, j** is a more recent invention. In fact, it appears in Latin texts written during the Middle Ages and the Renaissance, as well as in many modern editions of ancient Latin texts. It is used to indicate the semi-vowel **i**, sometimes called consonantal **i**. The consonantal **i** is the *i* at the beginning of a word before a vowel, or *i* between two vowels. According to this method, for example, *Iūlius* is written *Jūlius*, and *Āiax* is written *Ājax*. In this book, the letter *J, j* will not be used.

- The distinction between the vowel *U, u* and the consonant *V, v* also belongs to later times. Initially, there was only one letter *V, u* used both for the vowel and the consonant, e.g., *Vrbs*, "The City," (i.e., Rome), or *uictor*, "the winner." However, in accord with the prevailing practice of expressing the vowel with *U, u*, and the consonant with *V, v*, in this book the two letters will be distinguished.

The Latin words *senātus, rēgēs, ūlla, gentēs,* and *prīmus* are engraved on this stone.

Sign from Pompeii carved on stone with Latin letters.

PRONUNCIATION OF LATIN

VOWELS

There are six vowels in Latin and their pronunciation is as follows:

Long Vowel Sound	Short Vowel Sound
ā is pronounced as in "father": *ōrātor* "orator"	*a* is pronounced as in "alike": *amō* "love"
ē is pronounced like the *a* in "rave": *nēmō* "nobody"	*e* is pronounced as in "pet": *bene* "well"
ī is pronounced like the double *e* in "seen": *līmes* "boundary"	*i* is pronounced as in "pit": *nihil* "nothing"
ō is pronounced as in "stove": *videō* "(I) see"	*o* is pronounced as in "often": *rosa* "rose"
ū is pronounced as in "moon": *ūnus* "one"	*u* is pronounced as in "put:" *tum* "then"
ȳ comes from Greek and is pronounced in length somewhere between the *i* in "hit" and the *u* in "mute": *Pȳramus* "Pyramus"	*y* comes from Greek. Its sound, whether long or short, lies in between the sounds of *i* and *u* much as in the French "sûr," but the sound of short *y* is less drawn out than that of long *y* : *lyricus* "lyrical"

BY THE WAY

Everywhere in this book long vowels are indicated by macrons, i.e., *ā, ē, ī, ō, ū, ȳ,* while above the short vowels there are no signs. Sometimes two words differ from each other only in the length of the vowel. For example, *mālum,* with a long *a* means "apple," while *malum* with a short *a* means "bad thing."

▶ EXERCISE 1

Repeat these words aloud after your teacher pronounces them.

1. alō	7. lēnis	13. probō	19. sūtor
2. alumnus	8. sēdēs	14. nota	20. ūsus
3. rāna	9. iter	15. pōnō	21. syllaba
4. rādō	10. timeō	16. dōnum	22. Pȳrēnē
5. teneō	11. nītor	17. ululō	
6. petō	12. mīrus	18. lupus	

DIPHTHONGS

Diphthongs are two vowels combined in one syllable and pronounced together as one sound. There are six diphthongs in Latin:

- *ae* much like the *y* in "sky": *laevus* "left"
- *au* pronounced as *ou* in "our": *aurum* "gold"
- *ei* pronounced as *ei* in "feign": *oiei!* "alas!"
- *eu* pronounced *eoo*, much as if in the two words "grey blue" you were to subtract the "gr-" and the "bl-" and combine the two vowel sounds: *Eurōpa* "Europe"
- *oe* pronounced as *oy* in "boy": *proelium* "battle"
- *ui* pronounced nearly like "we": *hui!* "oh!"

It is believed that quite early, still in ancient times, the diphthongs *ae* and *oe* began to be pronounced as *e.* If you encounter them written *aē* or *aë,* and *oē* or *oë,* this means that they are not diphthongs and the letters should be pronounced separately: *āēr, poēta.*

The diphthongs are always long.

▶ EXERCISE 2

Repeat these words after your teacher pronounces them.

1. aestās	7. seu	13. aēneus
2. aequō	8. moenia	14. poēma
3. raeda	9. neu	15. hei
4. laudō	10. poena	16. huic
5. aut	11. neuter	
6. aula	12. Poenus	

CONSONANTS

- **c** is pronounced as in "come": *clārus* "bright," *censeō* "(I) deem," *cārus* "dear."

- When **b** is followed by **s,** as in *urbs* "city," the sound of **b** approaches that of **p**: a sound we might represent as *urps*.

- **g** is pronounced as in "get": *gaudium* "joy," *gignō* "(I) beget, (I) bear," *grātia* "favor, agreeableness."

- Some think that the Romans of Cicero's time (first century BCE) pronounced the two consonants **ng** as **ngn**: for example, the adjective *māgnus* "great," would have been pronounced in a way that we might represent as *mangnus*.

- **k** is a very rare consonant. In fact, it appears only in two words: *Kalendae* "the first day of every month in the Roman calendar," and in the personal name *Kaeso*.

- **q** appears always in combination with **u** and the combination **qu** is pronounced as in "queen": *quattuor,* "four."

- **v** has a sound similar to **w** (as in the word "wife"): *videō* "I see."

- The consonant **u** in the combination **su** sounds like the English **w** in the following four words: *suēscō*, "(I) become accustomed"; *Suēvī*, a name of a German tribe; *suādeō*, "(I) advise"; *suāvis*, "sweet."

- The letter **r** is trilled slightly. The sound has no exact equivalent in English, but is heard in many other European languages. The best way to make this sound is to pronounce **r** as in "rope," but vibrate the end of the tongue slightly as you say it.

- **x** is a double consonant (equivalent to **cs** or **gs**) that sounds much like the **x** in "six."

- **z** is another double consonant (equivalent to **dz**) and sounds almost like **z** in "zebra." It begins with a slight **d** sound first, so in pronouncing this letter you should hear **dz.**

- **ph** sounds like **p** in "pen," but with the addition of a slight breath of air represented by the **h**; **th** sounds like **t** as in "Tom," but with the addition of a slight extra breathing represented by the **h; ch** sounds nearly like the combination **kh.** These consonants are borrowed from Greek and appear in Greek words: *zephyrus* "western breeze," *chorus* "chorus," *theātrum* "theatre." When **p** and **t** are not accompanied by **h**, this slight aspiration is absent.

- When consonants are doubled, as in the verb *aggredior*, the consonantal sound is lengthened slightly.

▶ EXERCISE 3

Repeat these words after your teacher pronounces them:

1. cibus
2. capiō
3. cumulus
4. crēscō
5. gemma
6. Gallus
7. glōria
8. Zeus
9. bibliothēca
10. philosophia
11. zōna
12. theōrēma
13. phasēlus
14. charta
15. cēlō
16. antīquus

ACCENT

A Latin word is made up not just of letters, but also of syllables. A Latin word has as many syllables as it has vowels or diphthongs (a diphthong works like a single vowel, since it is made up of two vowels pronounced together [see diphthongs, above]).

You will need to know the following terms, when learning about accent.

- ultima   the last syllable in a word
- penult   the second-to-last syllable in a word
- antepenult   the third-to-last syllable in a word

So, in the word *ze-phy-rus* the vowel ***u*** is the ultima, ***y*** is the penult, and ***e*** is the antepenult.

RULES ABOUT THE STRESS ACCENT IN LATIN

1. The stress accent in Latin falls on either the penult or the antepenult.

2. The accent falls on the penult, if the penult is long. If the penult is short, the accent falls on the antepenult.

3. How to determine whether the penult is long or short.

   a. If the penult contains a long vowel (or any diphthong), the penult itself is long. You often need to learn whether the vowel in the penult is long or short as a basic element in learning a new word. A macron above the vowel will tell you that the vowel is long, while the absence of a macron will indicate a short vowel. Pronouncing the word can help you remember the vowel lengths. For example, *vi-de-ō*, "I see," is pronounced *vi´deō*; while *au-rō-ra*, "dawn," is pronounced *aurō´ra*; and *po-pu-lus*, "people" is pronounced *po´pulus*.

   b. If the vowel in the penult is followed by two or more consonants, the penult is long, **no matter whether the vowel in the penult is long or short**, and the accent necessarily falls on the penult. For example, *do-cu-men-tum*, "document," is pronounced *documen´tum*.

BY THE WAY

The consonant ***x*** is double (***cs*** or ***gs***) and counts as two consonants when determining whether the penult is long.

   c. There is one exception to 'b' above. Sometimes, even when there are two consonants between the penult and the ultima, they still do not determine that the penult is long. This happens when the two consonants are a mute and a liquid.

   The mutes are ***p, b, d, t, g, c***.

   The liquids are ***l, r***.

So, in the word *pal-pe-bra*, "eyelid," the antepenult is accented (*pal´pebra*); the vowel of the penult is short, since it is followed by a mute and a liquid. Of course, rule 'a' still applies: in the word *the-ā-trum*, "theatre," the penult is accented (*theā´trum*), since it is naturally long, something we learn from the macron.

▶ EXERCISE 4

Repeat each sentence aloud after your teacher reads it. Pay attention to the pronunciation and stress accent of each word.

What it is Like to Live Over a Bathhouse!
(Adapted from Seneca, *Moral Letter* 56)

Ecce undique clāmor sonat! Suprā ipsum balneum habitō! Prōpōne nunc tibi omnia genera vōcum odiōsa! Fortiōrēs exercentur et manūs plumbō gravēs iactant, cum aut labōrant aut labōrantem imitantur. Gemitūs audiō, quotiēns spīritum remīsērunt. Sunt quoque ūnctōrēs et tractātōrēs. Audiō crepitum manuum umerōs ferientium: sonus quoque ictuum mūtātur: nunc enim manus pervenit plāna, nunc concava. Audiō clāmōrēs, sī fūr est in balneō dēprehēnsus.

Look, there is noise sounding all around! I live above the bathhouse itself! Imagine to yourself now all the hateful types of voices! The stronger ones exercise themselves and swing their hands loaded with lead weights, while they work out—or imitate a person working out. I hear moans, every time they let go a <pent-up> breath. There are also anointers and masseurs. I hear the slap of hands hitting shoulders and the sound of the blows changes: for sometimes the hands come flat, sometimes cupped. I hear shouting, if a thief is caught in the bathhouse.

A pool from inside the Roman Baths in Bath, England.

OVERVIEW OF ROMAN HISTORY

According to legend, Romulus and his twin brother Remus were set adrift on the Tiber River. A she-wolf nursed the boys until a shepherd rescued them. Upon reaching manhood, in 753 BCE, the twins founded a new city near the place where they had been found by the she-wolf, on the basis of an *augustō auguriō*, "a favorable sighting of birds." But Romulus killed Remus in a dispute over who would rule the new city and became its first king.

A view of the Tiber River as it flows through the city of Rome.

Six other kings ruled after Romulus: Numa Pompilius, Tullus Hostilius, Ancus Martius, Tarquinius Priscus, Servius Tullius, and Tarquinius Superbus (Tarquin the Proud). After the last of these seven kings was overthrown in 509 BCE, Rome became a republic, with a representative form of government headed by two consuls, elected annually. By 451 BCE, the first corpus of Roman law, known as the Twelve Tables, was created.

In the last century BCE, the Roman Republic was shaken apart by a series of civil wars. By 31 BCE an autocratic regime headed earlier by Julius Caesar and later by his great-nephew Octavian brought the Republic to an end. The years from 27 BCE—when Octavian assumed the title of *prīnceps*, "chief citizen," as well as the name Augustus—to around 180 CE are known as the early principate, or empire. During this era Rome extended her boundaries to the British Isles in the north, North Africa in the south, Spain in the west, and the Tigris and Euphrates rivers in the east.

From 180 CE onwards, in the period known as the late empire, the Roman state experienced severe economic problems and frequent invasions by Germanic tribes. Responding to the pressure of the first wave of migrations, as well as internal political unrest and economic difficulties, the emperor Diocletian (ruled 284–305 CE) had already divided the Roman Empire into an Eastern and Western half, each under its own emperor—an attempt to make the vast Roman state more manageable.

This political division of the empire actually mirrored a cultural division too: the main language of the West was Latin, while the main language of the East was Greek. Shortly afterwards the emperor Constantine (ruled 312–337 CE) established a new capital for the Eastern empire at Byzantium, which he renamed Constantinople ("the city of Constantine," today called Istanbul). But even after this reorganization, the imperial government ultimately proved incapable of stemming the tide of the migrations, in part because the Roman army was too widely extended and could not be in so many places at once. Indeed many of the invaders were given the status of *foederātī* or "treaty troops." In effect, they were allowed to occupy segments of the empire in return for protecting it. So when Alaric, King of the Visigoths sacked Rome in 410 CE, he actually had a title as a commander in the Roman army!

Rome was sacked again in 455 CE by the Vandals, who had already occupied the Roman province of North Africa. The pillaging of the city of Romulus by the invaders made a profound impression on contemporaries, and to this day the term "vandalism" is a word in several languages for wanton destruction. While the Eastern empire (always more stable and economically prosperous than the West) continued to exist until 1453 CE, the Western empire was extinct as a political entity by 476 CE. In its place were Germanic kingdoms and tribes: Angles and Saxons in Britain, Visigoths in Spain, Ostrogoths in Italy, Franks and Burgundians in Gaul—to name only the major groups. The combination of these new societies with the previous inhabitants, who had been Romanized to varying degrees, would one day provide the basis for the cultures of modern Europe.

But the end of the ancient Roman Empire in the West was **not** the end of Latin. On the contrary, during the next 1200 years Latin not only flourished as the major literary language in the territories of the former Western Roman Empire, the use of Latin was extended to regions the Romans had never occupied, including Ireland, Scandinavia, and even the New World.

BEGINNINGS OF LATIN LITERATURE

Very few complete works of Latin literature produced before the mid-second century BCE (i.e., before 150 BCE) have survived. One reason for this loss was the tremendous popularity of the works produced in the following century by such authors as Cicero, Vergil, and Ovid. Their writings were so widely read and copied in subsequent centuries that the authors preceding them were gradually neglected.

Among the major figures of early Latin literature was a freed slave from the Greek tum named Livius Andronicus, who lived from 284–204 BCE. He was known fc of Greek drama for Roman audiences, and his translation of Homer's *Odyssey* int

THE ROMAN WORLD

BRITANNIA

GERMĀNIA

EURŌPA

GALLIA

ALPĒS MONTĒS

Verōna   ● Patavium

Padus

Mantua

APPENNINUS MŌNS

Rubicō

ETRŪRIA   ĪTALIA

Mare Hadriāticum

Tarquiniī   *Tiberis*

Rōma

CORSICA   Alba Longa   Pompēiī   Brundisi

Vesuvius Mōns

Neāpolis   ▲   Tarentu

Stabiae

HISPĀNIA   *Mare Tyrrhēnum*

SARDINIA   M

Īon

▲ *Aetna Mōns*

SICILIA   Syrācūsae

Hippō   Carthāgō

Rēgius

NUMIDIA   AFRICA   *Mare*

PRŌVINCIA

AFRICA

Pontus Euxīnus

PERSIA →

THRĀCIA

BĪTHȲNIA

PONTUS

ASIA

ACEDONIA

Bȳzantium/
Constantīnopolis

▲ Olympus Mōns

ASIA PRŌVINCIA

Thermopylae

Trōia/Īlium

Mare Aegaeum

Antiochīa

SYRIA

ACA

Delphī

Babylōn

GRAECIA

Athēnae

Sparta

DĒLOS

CYPRUS

CRĒTA

Internum

Alexandrēa

AEGYPTUS

© 2008 Bolchazy–Carducci Publishers

The Romans regarded Ennius (ca. 239–169 BCE) as the father of Latin literature. He wrote many kinds of literary works, including plays. His *Annālēs*, an epic poem about the early history of Rome, was particularly renowned, and perhaps the primary epic read in Roman schools before the time of Vergil. Only fragments of his writings remain.

One of Ennius' contemporaries was the famed Cato the Censor, also known as Cato the Elder (234–149 BCE), a rigidly conservative Roman senator. Most of his treatise on agriculture, called *Dē agrī cultūrā*, survives. It is the oldest work of Latin prose; among Cato's recommendations here are that field slaves be treated similarly to beasts of burden. Cato is also remembered for his statement *Carthāgō dēlenda est*, "Carthage must be destroyed," evidence for the Roman fear of the Carthaginians. The Romans fought three wars, known as the Punic Wars, against the Carthaginians. The first ended before Cato was born; in the second, against Hannibal, Cato served with military distinction; the third ended in 146 BCE, as Cato had demanded, with the destruction of Carthage. On this occasion the victorious Romans were said to have plowed salt into the Carthaginian soil.

Discussions about later authors and adaptations from their writings will be presented chronologically in the chapters of this book.

Ancient ruins at Carthage in Africa.

CHAPTER 1

Parts of Speech; Nouns: Number, Gender, Case (Nominative and Accusative); First Declension Nouns

Oil painting of Romulus and Remus with the wolf. By Peter Paul Rubens (1577–1640).

MEMORĀBILE DICTŪ

SPQR: Senātus Populusque Rōmānus.

"The Senate and the People of Rome."

These four letters form what is known as an acronym, one that symbolized supreme power in ancient Rome.

READING

This story describes how Rome was said to have been founded in 753 BCE. King Numitor of Alba Longa was overthrown by his cruel and ambitious brother Amulius, who not only seized the throne, but so feared that one of Numitor's male descendants might have a legitimate claim on it that he made Numitor's daughter Rhea Silvia a priestess of the goddess Vesta. These priestesses were not allowed to marry during their childbearing years.

RŌMULUS ET REMUS

1   Mārs est deus. Mārs Rhēam Silviam amat. Itaque Rhēa Silvia duōs
    fīliōs habet: Rōmulum et Remum. Amūlius Rhēam Silviam vinculīs
    claudit. Amūlius Rōmulum et Remum in aquam pōnit. Lupa ad aquam
    ambulat. Lupa Rōmulum et Remum bene cūrat et amat. Rōmulus et
5   Remus crēscunt. Posteā Rōmulus et Remus Rōmam aedificant.

Famous bronze statue of the she-wolf and the twins.

READING VOCABULARY

ad aquam – to the water

aedificant – build

*amat – loves

*ambulat – walks

Amūlius – Amulius

*aquam – water

*bene – well

claudit – locks up

crēscunt – grow up

*cūrat – takes care of, cares for

deus – god

duōs – two

*est – is

*et – and

filiōs – sons

habet – has

in aquam – into the water

*itaque – and so

*lupa – she-wolf

Mārs – Mars, the god of war

pōnit – puts

*posteā – afterwards, later

Remum – Remus

Remus – Remus

Rhēa Silvia – Rhea Silvia

Rhēam Silviam – Rhea Silvia

*Rōmam – Rome

Rōmulum – Romulus

Rōmulus – Romulus

vinculīs – with chains

*Words marked with an asterisk will need to be memorized later in the chapter.

COMPREHENSION QUESTIONS

1. Whose sons are Romulus and Remus?

2. What did Amulius do?

3. Who saved the life of Romulus and Remus?

4. What did Romulus and Remus do?

LANGUAGE FACT I

PARTS OF SPEECH

The *parts of speech* used in a Latin sentence determine its meaning, just as in English. While the noun and the verb are the two most important, other common parts of speech are listed below.

Noun: a person, place, thing, idea, action, or quality. Examples: "Romulus," "river," "courage."

Pronoun: a word that stands in place of a noun that has been previously mentioned or is clear from context. Examples: "I," "she," "him," "it."

Adjective: a word that limits or defines a noun or a pronoun. Examples: "little," "strong."

Adverb: a word that limits or defines verbs, adjectives, or (other) adverbs. Examples: "very," "quietly."

Verb: a word that describes an action or state of being. Examples: "go," "stay," "was."

Preposition: a word that begins a prepositional phrase, such as "in," "to," "on," "for," "by," "with." A prepositional phrase is a preposition joined to a noun. Examples: "in the morning," "with a sharp pencil."

Conjunction: a word that connects words, phrases, clauses, and sentences. Examples: "and," "but," "although."

Interjection: a word that expresses emotion. Examples: "wow!"

▶ EXERCISE 1

Review the meanings and identify the parts of speech of the following words. The Reading Vocabulary may be consulted.

1. fīliōs
2. bene
3. aedificant
4. ad
5. ambulat
6. et
7. lupa
8. claudit
9. Rōmam
10. amat

VOCABULARY TO LEARN

NOUNS

agricola, agricolae, m. – farmer

aqua, aquae, f. – water

āthlēta, āthlētae, m. – athlete

fīlia, fīliae, f. – daughter

lupa, lupae, f. – she-wolf

nauta, nautae, m. – sailor

poēta, poētae, m. – poet

puella, puellae, f. – girl

Rōma, Rōmae, f. – Rome

terra, terrae, f. – land

VERBS

amat – he/she/it loves

ambulat – he/she/it walks

cūrat – he/she/it takes care of, cares for

est – he/she/it is

ADVERBS

bene – well

posteā – afterwards

CONJUNCTIONS

et – and

itaque – and so

Aqueducts carried water (*aqua*) to the cities in the Roman world. This aqueduct built in 19 BCE, which stretched across the Gard River, was named the Pont du Gard and brought water to the city of Nîmes in France in ancient times.

BY THE WAY

Each *noun* given in the vocabulary has two forms. The second form is the genitive singular.

A *derivative* is an English word rooted in a Latin word. The English derivative is similar in meaning and form to its Latin source.

STUDY TIP

An English derivative often can help you remember what a Latin word means.

▶ EXERCISE 2

Find the English derivatives based on the Vocabulary to Learn in the following sentences. Write the corresponding Latin word.

1. She shows a considerable filial respect toward her father.

2. Agriculture is a science of cultivating the land.

3. The ship is equipped with all the necessary nautical instruments.

4. We saw all kinds of fish in the aquarium.

5. This is an all-terrain vehicle.

6. When will the athletic competition start?

7. She has a truly poetic nature.

LANGUAGE FACT II

NOUNS: NUMBER, GENDER, CASE (NOMINATIVE AND ACCUSATIVE)

Nouns in Latin show number, gender, and case.

Number: Latin nouns are either singular or plural in number. Number is shown in different ways by different types of nouns, but some ending-patterns are for singular forms, and other ending-patterns are for plural forms.

Gender: Every noun, likewise, is either masculine, feminine, or neuter in gender. You must learn the gender of each noun. In the Vocabulary to Learn lists, the gender is indicated by the common abbreviations *m.* (masculine), *f.* (feminine), or *n.* (neuter).

Case: Latin nouns must have an ending-pattern that displays case. This is quite different from English, in which case is indicated by word position, and not by endings (although case markers are preserved in certain pronouns, such as "he" and "him"). A noun's case reveals what function the noun has in the sentence. There are five common cases: nominative, genitive, dative, accusative, and ablative. Two less frequently used cases are called the vocative and the locative.

STUDY TIP

An easy way to remember the names of the five common cases is to use this mnemonic device:

Never	**N**ominative
Give	**G**enitive
Dogs	**D**ative
Any	**A**ccusative
Abuse	**Ab**lative

Nominative: The nominative case identifies the subject. The subject is a noun or a pronoun that performs the action or exists in a state of being. In the sentence "William is reading," the word "William" is the subject.

> Example: *Mārs . . . amat.* Mars loves . . .

> The noun subject of the verb "love" is the god Mars.

Find more examples of nominatives and their verbs from the reading passage at the beginning of the chapter.

The nominative case *also* identifies the predicate nominative. In the sentence "William is a student," the predicate nominative is "a student." A predicate nominative completes the meaning of the verb "to be." Look at this example from the reading:

> Example: *Mārs est deus.* Mars is a god.

> *Mārs* is the subject and *deus* is a predicate nominative.

Accusative: The fourth case listed is called the accusative; the genitive, dative, and ablative cases will be discussed in later chapters. The accusative case points out the noun (or pronoun) that is the direct object. Remember: direct objects receive the action of the verb. In the sentence "I am writing a letter," the direct object is "a letter."

> Example: *Mārs Rhēam Silviam amat.* Mars loves Rhea Silvia.

> The direct object of "love" is the noun *Rhēam Silviam*.

Find more examples of accusatives and their verbs from the reading passage at the beginning of the chapter.

▶ EXERCISE 3

a. Identify whether the nouns in bold in these sentences are subjects, direct objects, or predicate nominatives. The Reading Vocabulary may be consulted.

b. Label each sentence as *vērum* (true) if it agrees or *falsum* (false) if it disagrees with the Latin reading passage at the beginning of the chapter.

Example: Amūlius est **deus**.
Predicate nominative   falsum

1. **Rhēa Silvia** Rōmulum et Remum cūrat.

2. Amūlius **Rōmulum** et **Remum** bene cūrat.

3. Amūlius **lupam** vinculīs claudit.

4. **Mārs** Rōmulum et Remum in aquam pōnit.

5. Lupa **Rhēam Silviam** cūrat.

6. **Amūlius** ad aquam ambulat.

The power of the city of Rome, founded according to legend by Romulus, is symbolized by these four letters that are prominently displayed in various places within the city.

LANGUAGE FACT III

FIRST DECLENSION NOUNS

A *declension* is a group of nouns that show a certain pattern of word endings. There are five different declensions in Latin. In the reading about Romulus and Remus, these are the forms belonging to the first declension:

Rhēam Silviam   Rhēa Silvia   aquam   lupa   Rōmam

Notice that the text says *Rhēa Silvia* when she is the subject, and *Rhēam Silviam* when she is the direct object.

The first declension is composed of words that characteristically have the vowel *a* at or near the end of the word: *lup**a***.

Below is the pattern that first declension nouns follow to show case and number. Memorize the Latin words in order from the nominative singular down to the ablative singular, and then from the nominative plural down to the ablative plural.

Remember that the endings for a whole group of nouns follow this pattern. Once you learn this pattern, you can recognize the case and number of all the words belonging to this declension.

In this chapter, you have begun to learn about the nominative and accusative cases. The other cases will be explained in later chapters.

First Declension					
Singular			**Plural**		
Nominative	lup**a**	the she-wolf	Nominative	lup**ae**	the she-wolves
Genitive	lup**ae**	of the she-wolf	Genitive	lup**ārum**	of the she-wolves
Dative	lup**ae**	to/for the she-wolf	Dative	lup**īs**	to/for the she-wolves
Accusative	lup**am**	the she-wolf	Accusative	lup**ās**	the she-wolves
Ablative	lup**ā**	by/with the she-wolf	Ablative	lup**īs**	by/with the she-wolves

Dative and ablative plural of the words *fīlia*, "daughter," and *dea*, "goddess" is ***fīliābus*** and ***deābus***. This is to distinguish these forms from the corresponding forms of *fīlius*, "son," and *deus*, "god."

 STUDY TIP

Notice that the ablative singular ending -*ā* has a long mark (macron) above it: this is the only difference between the nominative and ablative singular endings.

Notice that the dative and ablative plural endings are identical.

Here are more words belonging to the first declension:

puella – girl   *fīlia* – daughter   *terra* – land

Most first declension words are feminine in gender, but a few (usually ones that indicate masculine occupations in ancient times) are masculine. Examples are *poēta*, "poet"; *agricola*, "farmer"; *nauta*, "sailor"; *āthlēta*, "athlete."

▶ EXERCISE 4

Identify the case of each singular noun. Then change each form into plural. For some, more than one answer is possible.

Example: filia
nominative   fīliae

1. puellae
2. nautam
3. terram
4. agricola

5. aquae
6. puellā
7. āthlētā

Like the Greek wrestlers portrayed on this ancient bas-relief,
Roman athletes were also fond of the sport of wrestling.

▶ EXERCISE 5

Identify the case of each plural noun. Then change each form into the singular. For some, more than one answer is possible.

Example: puellās
accusative   puellam

1. fīliae
2. terrīs
3. nautārum
4. lupae

5. aquīs
6. poētārum
7. agricolae

BY THE WAY

In all declensions, endings are added to the base of a noun. It is important to know that the base of a noun is found by removing the ending from its genitive singular form. For example, the genitive singular of *puella* is *puellae*. If you remove the *-ae* from *puellae*, what remains is the base of the word, namely *puell-*. For this reason, learning the genitive singular is as important as knowing the nominative singular of the noun.

STUDY TIP

Always learn the genitive together with the nominative, because from the genitive you will know to which declension a word belongs!

A wall painting depicting a Roman farmer (*agricola*) with his sheep.

▶ EXERCISE 6

Translate from Latin into English, and from English into Latin. The most common Latin word order is:

subject – direct object – verb.

1. Agricola terram amat.
2. The athlete loves water.
3. Nauta filiam amat.
4. The poet loves Rome.
5. Agricola terram cūrat.
6. The she-wolf cares for (is taking care of) the girl.

 BY THE WAY

Even though the most common word order is subject – direct object – verb, remember that endings—not word order!—determine which word is the subject and which is the direct object.

TALKING

When we meet one person, we greet her/him with *salvē!* When we meet two or more people, we greet them with *salvēte!* When we bid goodbye to one person, we say *valē!* When we bid goodbye to two or more people, we say *valēte!*

Here are various ways to ask "how are you?" or "how are you doing?":

> *Quōmodo valēs?* or *Quōmodo tē habēs?* or *Quid agis?*
> "How are you?"

Here is a range of possible answers:

> *bene* "well"
> *pessimē* "very bad"
> *optimē* "great"
> *melius* "better"
> *mediocriter* "so-so" or "not too bad"
> *meliusculē* "a little better"
> *male* "bad"

SAYING HELLO

Marīa, Helena et Christīna sunt (*are*) discipulae (*students*).

Marīa: Salvēte, Helena et Christīna!

Christīna: Salvē, Marīa!

Helena: Salvē, Marīa!

Marīa: Quōmodo valēs, Helena? Quōmodo valēs, Christīna?

Helena et Christīna: Bene. Quōmodo tū (*you*) valēs, Marīa?

Marīa: Pessimē.

Helena et Christīna: Cūr? (*Why?*)

Marīa: Timeō linguam Latīnam (*I fear the Latin language*).

Helena: Ego (*I*) linguam Latīnam amō.

Christīna: Et ego linguam Latīnam amō!

CHAPTER 2

First and Second Conjugation Verbs; Principal Parts; Properties of Verbs: Number, Person, Tense, Stem; The Infinitive; Subject and Verb Agreement

This wall painting from Pompeii shows three actors on a stage. At the left is an actor wearing a slave's mask. At the right are two actors, usually men, portraying females.

MEMORĀBILE DICTŪ

Inter sacrum saxumque.

"Between a rock and a hard place," literally "between the sacrificial animal and the rock." (Plautus, *Captives*, 617)

This expression was used by the Roman comic playwright Plautus in his comedies *The Captives* and *Casina* to indicate a difficult situation for which there seems to be no solution. Characters in many of Plautus' comedies find themselves in such difficult circumstances.

READING

The major Latin literary works from prior to 100 BCE are comedies by two Roman dramatists, Titus Maccius Plautus (ca. 254–184 BCE) and Publius Terentius Afer (called Terence in English), who died in 159 BCE. Plautus is said to have written approximately 130 plays. Only twenty-one, however, still survive. He modeled these plays on Greek comedies written in the fourth and third centuries BCE by various Athenian writers.

Still, Plautus writes for a contemporary Roman audience of all social backgrounds, ranging from slaves to the political elite. His comedies allude to current Roman events, and are noteworthy for their inventive and playful use of the Latin language. Here is an excerpt from his *Menaechmī*.

A merchant from Syracuse (a city on the island of Sicily) has two identical twin sons. When they reach the age of seven, he takes one of them, named Menaechmus, on a business trip. The boy gets lost in a crowd and is adopted by local residents. The remaining twin, Sosicles, is renamed Menaechmus in memory of his lost brother. After this Menachmus-Sosicles grows up, he travels without knowing it to the town where his twin brother resides. A long series of misunderstandings occur. Menaechmus' friends and family think Menaechmus-Sosicles is Menaechmus, while Messenio, the slave of Menaechmus-Sosicles assumes that Menaechmus is his master. Because the two men are identical twins, the misunderstandings are not surprising, but because neither twin knows of the other's existence they involve numerous complications. Confusion comes to a head when the two Menaechmi finally meet, each still unaware that the other exists. The slave Messenio is present at this meeting, realizes that the two young men are identical in appearance, and gives voice to his surprise.

DĒ MENAECHMĪS

1   Messeniō: Prō Iuppiter! Quid videō?

Menaechmus Sosiclēs: Quid vidēs?

Messeniō: *(pointing at Menaechmus)* Hic fōrmam tuam habet.

Menaechmus Sosiclēs: Quam fābulam mihi nārrās?

5   Messeniō: Fābulās nōn nārrō. Tū vidēre dēbēs.

Menaechmus Sosiclēs: Papae! *(addressing Menaechmus)* Quōmodo tē vocant?

Menaechmus: Menaechmum mē vocant.

Menaechmus Sosiclēs: Fābulās nārrās! Mē quoque Menaechmum vocant.

Messeniō: Sunt sīcut duae guttae aquae!

10   Menaechmus Sosiclēs: Quam patriam habēs?

Menaechmus: Sum Syrācūsānus.

Menaechmus Sosiclēs: Ego quoque ibi habitō. Itaque tū es frāter meus. Salvē, mī frāter! Diū tē exspectō.

Menaechmus: Salvē, mī frāter! Dēbēmus nunc cum patre habitāre.

READING VOCABULARY

cum patre – with father
*dēbēmus – we ought, must
dēbēs – ought, must
dē Menaechmīs – about the Menaechmi <brothers>
*diū – for a long time
es – are
duae guttae aquae – two drops of water
*ego – I
*exspectō – I am waiting for
*fābula, fābulae, f. – story
*fōrma, fōrmae, f. – form, appearance
frāter meus – my brother
gutta, guttae, f. – drop
habēs – do you have
*habet – has
habitāre – to live
*habitō – live, dwell
hic – this (man)
ibi – there
mē – me
Menaechmī – plural of Menaechmus
Menaechmum – Menaechmus
mī frāter – my brother
mihi – to me
nārrās – are you telling, you are telling

*nārrō – I do tell
*nōn – not
*nunc – now
papae! – wow!
*patria, patriae, f. – fatherland
prō Iuppiter! – by Jove!
quam – what?
quid – what?
quōmodo – how?
quoque – also
salvē! – hello!
sīcut –as
*sum – I am
sunt – they are
Syrācūsānus – from Syracuse
tē – you
*tū – you
tuam – your
*videō – do I see
vidēre – to see
vidēs – do you see
*vocant – do they call, they call

*Words marked with an asterisk will need to be memorized.

COMPREHENSION QUESTIONS

1. What happens between the two Menaechmi?

2. Who is the first to notice the similarity between the two Menaechmi?

3. What serves as a confirmation that the two Menaechmi are brothers?

4. What is the Menaechmi brothers' intention for the future?

LANGUAGE FACT I
FIRST AND SECOND CONJUGATION VERBS; PRINCIPAL PARTS

A *conjugation* is a class of verbs that all follow a certain pattern. There are four conjugations in Latin. In this chapter, you will learn only about the first and second conjugations.

You recognize a verb's conjugation from its *principal parts*, especially from the second principal part.

The principal parts of a verb provide stems for different verb forms. This chapter will concentrate on the first and second principal parts—most verbs have four. You will learn more about the third and fourth principal parts in later chapters.

The *first principal part* is the first person singular of the present active tense verb form. In the case of the English verb "do," the first person singular of the present active tense would be "I do."

The *second principal part* is the infinitive. In English, the infinitive is formed by adding the word "to" to the basic form of the verb: so for the verb "do" the infinitive is "to do."

nārrō ("I tell"), **nārrāre** ("to tell"), nārrāvī, nārrātum

habeō ("I have"), **habēre** ("to have"), habuī, habitum

Look at the second principal part of the verbs listed above. Note that the second principal part ends in a vowel + *-re*. The vowel that precedes the *-re* reveals the conjugation to which the verb belongs. The long vowel *-ā-* shows that *nārrāre* is a first conjugation verb; the long vowel *-ē-* in *habēre* shows that it is a second conjugation verb.

 STUDY TIP

You can easily remember that the vowel *a* is in the first conjugation and the vowel *e* is in the second conjugation, if you know this little rhyme:

A comes before *E*
Even Alphabetical-**ly.**

▶ EXERCISE 1

Determine the conjugation of each verb by looking at the vowel in the second principal part.

1. videō, vidēre, vīdī, vīsum

2. habitō, habitāre, habitāvī, habitātum

3. nārrō, nārrāre, nārrāvī, nārrātum

4. dēbeō, dēbēre, dēbuī, dēbitum

5. cūrō, cūrāre, cūrāvī, cūrātum

6. exspectō, exspectāre, exspectāvī, exspectātum

VOCABULARY TO LEARN

NOUNS

fābula, fābulae, f. – story

fōrma, fōrmae, f. – form, appearance

patria, patriae, f. – fatherland

VERBS

amō, amāre, amāvī, amātum – to love

ambulō, ambulāre, ambulāvī, ambulātum – to walk

cūrō, cūrāre, cūrāvī, cūrātum – to care for, to take care of

dēbeō, dēbēre, dēbuī, dēbitum – ought, must, should; to owe

exspectō, exspectāre, exspectāvī, exspectātum – to wait for, to await, to expect

habeō, habēre, habuī, habitum – to have

habitō, habitāre, habitāvī, habitātum – to live, to dwell

nārrō, nārrāre, nārrāvī, nārrātum – to tell

sum – I am

parō, parāre, parāvī, parātum – to prepare, to get ready

teneō, tenēre, tenuī, tentum – to hold

videō, vidēre, vīdī, vīsum – to see

vocō, vocāre, vocāvī, vocātum – to call

ADVERBS

diū – for a long time

nunc – now

nōn – not

▶ EXERCISE 2

Find the English derivatives based on the Vocabulary to Learn in the following sentences. Write the corresponding Latin word.

1. I read a long narrative about the Second World War.

2. Have you worked with "Habitat for Humanity"?

3. The results exceeded our expectations.

4. This seems fabulous!

5. We are watching a video about the field trip.

6. This group is rather vocal about their rights.

7. Are you paying by credit or debit?

8. Everybody started singing a patriotic song.

9. The preparations for the festival were moving at full speed.

10. The octopus has long tentacles.

11. We heard the siren of an ambulance.

LANGUAGE FACT II

PROPERTIES OF VERBS: NUMBER, PERSON

Number: Latin verbs are either singular or plural in number (depending on the number of the subject noun).

Person: Latin verbs, like verbs in English, may be in the first, second, or third person. The person represents the identity of the subject. The first person is "I" or "we." The second person is "you" (singular or plural). The third person is "s/he/it," or "they."

Six endings in Latin indicate what person is performing the action of the verb. They are in the chart below and must be learned along with the corresponding English pronoun.

Verb Endings				
	Singular		**Plural**	
First person	*-ō* or *-m*	I	*-mus*	we
Second person	*-s*	you	*-tis*	you
Third person	*-t*	s/he/it	*-nt*	they

BY THE WAY

You have seen the first person singular ending *-m* in the word *sum* ("I am"). The first person singular ending *-ō* is seen more commonly on Latin verbs than the ending *-m*.

▶ EXERCISE 3

Identify the person and number of each verb.

Example: aedificant
third person plural

1. nārrās
2. vidēs
3. aedificat
4. habēs
5. dēbēs
6. dēbēmus
7. vocant
8. amat

LANGUAGE FACT III

PROPERTIES OF VERBS: TENSE, STEM

Tense: A verb indicates the time when the action occurs. There are six tenses in Latin, but in this chapter you will be focusing only on the present tense, which shows action happening now.

Stem: The present stem conveys the basic meaning of a word. Find the present stem by removing the *-re* from the second principal part.

To form the present tense of a Latin verb, the personal endings for this tense are added to the present stem of the verb. This is called conjugating the verb in the present tense. Remember: the predominant vowel in the first conjugation is an **-ā-** and in the second conjugation an **-ē-**.

First Conjugation: Present Active

parō, parāre		Singular		Plural	
First person	par**ō**	I prepare	par**āmus**	we prepare
Second person	par**ās**	you prepare	par**ātis**	you prepare
Third person	par**at**	s/he/it prepares	par**ant**	they prepare

Second Conjugation: Present Active

teneō, tenēre		Singular		Plural	
First person	ten**eō**	I hold	ten**ēmus**	we hold
Second person	ten**ēs**	you hold	ten**ētis**	you hold
Third person	ten**et**	s/he/it holds	ten**ent**	they hold

BY THE WAY

Note that Latin pronouns such as *ego* (I) or *tū* (you) are optional, while the personal endings that indicate the pronoun subject are required. Verb forms in Latin are a "package deal" because in one word they include both the meaning of the verb and the subject pronoun.

Translating Latin verbs into English: There are three ways to translate a Latin present tense verb into English. Here are some examples from both first and second conjugation verbs.

> parō: I prepare; I do prepare; I am preparing
> parās: you prepare; you do prepare; you are preparing
> parat: s/he/it prepares; s/he/it does prepare; s/he/it is preparing
>
> tenēmus: we hold; we do hold; we are holding
> tenētis: you hold; you do hold; you are holding
> tenent: they hold; they do hold; they are holding

▶ EXERCISE 4

Give three English translations for each present tense verb.

Example: teneō
I hold/I do hold/I am holding

1. vocās
2. videt
3. exspectant
4. cūrāmus
5. dēbētis
6. habeō

▶ EXERCISE 5

Choose one of three ways to translate each singular Latin verb and write the plural Latin form of each.

Example: exspectās
you wait for *or* do wait for *or* are waiting for   exspectātis

1. vidēs
2. dēbet
3. ambulat
4. habeō

5. tenēs
6. amō
7. habitat

▶ EXERCISE 6

Choose one of three ways to translate each plural Latin verb and write the singular Latin form of each.

Example: parant
they prepare *or* do prepare *or* are preparing   parat

1. habitāmus
2. amāmus
3. tenent
4. nārrant

5. habētis
6. vidēmus
7. exspectātis

LANGUAGE FACT IV

THE INFINITIVE

In the opening of the chapter reading, Messenio addresses his master: *Tū vidēre dēbēs.* "You ought to see." At the end of the same passage Menaechmus tells his brother: *Dēbēmus nunc cum patre habitāre.* "We ought to live with (our) father now."

In English, an infinitive is a verb form preceded by the word "to." In Latin, an infinitive (second principal part) is the verb form that ends with the letters **-re**. The infinitive is unlimited by a specific person: when you say "to read," you are not specifying any person doing the reading—you are just describing the action itself.

Greek mask of comedy.

First conjugation infinitives have the vowel **-ā-** before **-re**, while second conjugation verbs have the vowel **-ē-** before **-re.**

> First conjugation infinitive: **parā-re**
>
> Second conjugation infinitive: **tenē-re**

▶ EXERCISE 7

Translate the infinitive and indicate whether it belongs to the first or second conjugation.

Example: amāre
to love   first conjugation

1. ambulāre
2. habēre
3. nārrāre

4. exspectāre
5. dēbēre
6. vidēre

LANGUAGE FACT V

SUBJECT AND VERB AGREEMENT

The verb *agrees* in number with the subject. This means that if the noun subject is singular, the verb is singular. Likewise, if the noun subject is plural, the verb must be plural.

> Examples:
> *Puella fābulam nārrat.*
> The girl tells a story.

The verb *nārrat* has the third person singular ending **-t**, since the noun subject *puella* is singular (as the nominative singular ending **-a** shows).

> *Puellae fābulās nārrant.*
> The girls tell stories.

The verb *nārrant* has the third person plural ending **-nt**, since the noun subject *puellae* is plural (as the nominative plural ending **-ae** shows).

▶ EXERCISE 8

Make the verbs agree with the subjects in the following sentences. The Reading Vocabulary may be consulted.

Example: Messeniō Menaechmum _____ (vidēre).
Messeniō Menaechmum videt.

1. Menaechmus Sosiclēs et Messeniō Menaechmum _____ (vidēre).

2. Menaechmus Sosicles tells Messenio: "Tū fābulās _____ (nārrāre)."

3. Messenio asks Menaechmus: "Quōmodo ego et Menaechmus Sosiclēs tē vocāre _____ (dēbēre)?"

4. Menaechmus answers: "Tū et Menaechmus Sosiclēs mē Menaechmum vocāre _____ (dēbeō)."

5. After Menaechmus Sosicles asks: "Quam patriam habēs?" Menaechmus exclaims: "Quam patriam ego _____ (habēre)? Sum Syracūsānus."

The Hellenistic era Theatre of Ephesus, which today is in Turkey, was built in the third century BCE into a hillside in the Greek manner. It was enlarged during Roman times in the first and second centuries CE and is said to have accommodated 25,000 spectators.

► EXERCISE 9

Translate into Latin.

1. We ought to wait.

2. You all ought to tell a story.

3. Now they see the fatherland.

4. I take care of the daughter.

► EXERCISE 10

Label each sentence as *vērum* (true) if it agrees or *falsum* (false) if it disagrees with the Latin reading passage at the beginning of the chapter.

1. Menaechmus et Menaechmus Sosiclēs sunt sīcut duae guttae aquae.

2. Menaechmus Sosiclēs nōn est Syrācūsānus.

3. Menaechmus est Syrācūsānus.

4. Messeniō et Menaechmus sunt sīcut duae guttae aquae.

This carving of divinities is on a panel below the stage in the theatre located near the Mediterranean Sea in Sabratha, Libya.

TALKING

In the chapter reading, you encountered the expression:

> *Quōmodo tē vocant?* "How do they call you?"
> *Mē vocant Menaechmum.* "They call me Menaechmus."

There are various ways of asking someone's name in Latin:

> *Quod nōmen est tibi?* "What is your name?"
> *Mihi nōmen est Marīa.* "My name is Mary."

> *Quod vērō nōmen tibi est?* "And what is your name?"
> *Mihi nōmen est Mārcus.* "My name is Mark."

> *Quō nōmine appellāris?* "By what name are you called?"
> *Laura appellor.* "I am called Laura."

This is a list of some common Roman first names and their abbreviations:

A. = Aulus	C. = Gāius	L. = Lūcius
M. = Mārcus	P. = Pūblius	Q. = Quīntus
Ser. = Servius	Sex. = Sextus	T. = Titus

The Roman naming system consisted of *praenōmen* (first name), *nōmen* (family name), and *cōgnōmen* (surname/nickname).

In the name *Titus Maccius Plautus*: *Titus* is the first name, *Maccius* is the family name, and *Plautus* is a surname (it literally means "flat-footed").

In the chapter reading, Menaechmus was asked *Quam patriam habēs?* "What fatherland do you have?" and he answered *Syrācūsānus sum*, "I am from Syracuse."

There are several ways of asking where someone is from in Latin:

> *Cūiās es?* "Where are you from?"
> *Cūiātēs estis?* "Where are you all from?"
> *Unde es ortus/orta?* "Where do you come from (male/female)?"
> *Unde estis ortī/ortae?* "Where do you all come from (male/female)?"

Here are some possible answers:

> *Ortus/orta sum ex Cīvitātibus Foederātīs Americae Septentriōnālis. Americānus/Americāna sum.* "I come from the USA. I am an American (male/female)."

> *Ortus/orta sum ex Californiā, ex Texiā, ex Ohiō, ex Kentukiā, ex Massacusētā, ex Flōridā, ex Novā Caesareā, ex Carolīnā Septentriōnālī, ex Virginiā, ex Indiānā.* "I come from California, Texas, Ohio, Kentucky, Massachusetts, Florida, New Jersey, North Carolina, Virginia, Indiana."

> *Ortus/orta sum urbe* (from the city of) *Novō Eborācō, Bostōniā, Chicāgiā/Sicāgō, Angelopolī, Detroitō, Novā Aurēliā, Atlantā, Philadelphiā, Vasintōniā.* "I come from New York, Boston, Chicago, Los Angeles, Detroit, New Orleans, Atlanta, Philadelphia, Washington D.C."

GETTING ACQUAINTED

Mārcus est discipulus novus. (*Mark is a new student.*)

Marīa: Salvēte! Quōmodo valētis?

Helena et Christīna: Bene valēmus.

Mārcus: Salvēte!

Marīa: Salvē! Quod nōmen est tibi?

Mārcus: Mihi nōmen est Mārcus. Quōmodo tē vocant?

Marīa: Mē vocant Marīam. Cūiās es?

Mārcus: Ortus sum ex Californiā! Cūiās tū es?

Marīa: Ego sum Americāna.

Mārcus: Ego quoque (*also*) sum Americānus. At unde es orta? (*But where do you come from?*)

Marīa: Orta sum urbe Vasintōniā.

Helena: Et ego sum orta urbe Vasintōniā.

Christīna: Et ego sum orta urbe Vasintōniā.

Mārcus: Certē (*certainly*). Schola nostra est Vasintōniae. (*Our school is in Washington, D.C.*)

CHAPTER 3

Second Declension Masculine -us, -er, -ir Nouns; Genitive Case; Vocative Case; Prepositional Phrases

The choreographer and actors are detailed in this mosaic from the House of the Tragic Poet in Pompeii.

MEMORĀBILE DICTŪ

Homō sum: hūmānī nihil ā mē aliēnum putō.

"I am a human being: I think that nothing human is foreign to me." (Terence, *The Self-Tormentor*, 77)

This saying became proverbial, furnishing evidence for Terence's intense interest in human character.

READING

Terence, or Publius Terentius Afer, was born in North Africa between 195 BCE and 185 BCE. He came to Rome as a slave, received a good education, and was freed. He and Plautus are among the most ancient Roman writers whose works have come to us in non-fragmentary form, and their works are the earliest complete examples of Latin comedy. Six of Terence's comedies have been preserved. Terence died in Greece probably in 159 BCE, where he had traveled because of his studies.

Like Plautus, Terence based his comedies on earlier Greek models, but made many changes to these "originals": stating his own views about comedy-writing in the prologues of his plays, emphasizing the humanity of his individual characters, and using refined, elegant language that contrasts with Plautus' distinctive, colloquial, and often bawdy Latin.

Terence loves moral problems that are universal, common to all cultures and ages. That is why his comedies have continuously remained popular until the present day.

The central conflicts between characters in Terence's *Adelphoi*, a comedy whose Greek title means "The Brothers," remain relevant today. The brothers referred to in the title are Demea, a conservative farmer, who believes in imposing rigid limits and tight controls on his children, and Micio, a liberal city-dweller with a more permissive approach to child-rearing. Demea has two sons: Ctesipho, who lives with his father, and Aeschinus, who has been adopted by his uncle Micio. Demea, however, has begun to regret his decision, because he suspects that Micio has allowed Aeschinus to adopt an undisciplined and wild lifestyle. When he pays an unexpected visit to Micio's household, however, Demea runs into Ctesipho, who is spending time with his brother there. Demea insists on exercising his fatherly authority and tries to take Ctesipho away with him. But he has not anticipated being greeted at the door by the trusted slave Syrus.

DĒ DUŌBUS FRĀTRIBUS

1   Dēmea: (*knocking at the door*) Heus, mī fīlī!!!
     Syrus and Ctesipho are inside the house.
     Syrus: Quis vocat? Quis est hic vir?
     Ctēsiphō: Pater mē vocat. Valdē timeō.
5   Syrus: Nōn dēbēs timēre. Dēbēs habēre bonum animum.
     Syrus answers the door.
     Syrus: Quis es tū?
     Dēmea: Salvē, mī bone vir! Ego sum Dēmea, pater Aeschinī et
        Ctēsiphōnis. Habitō in agrīs. Fīlium meum nunc vidēre dēbeō.
10   Syrus: Num ego fīlium tuum habeō? Aeschinus nōn est domī.
     Dēmea: Estne domī Ctēsiphō?

Syrus: Nōn est. Fīliōs tuōs ego nōn habeō.

Dēmea: Estne frāter meus domī?

Syrus: Nōn est.

15 Dēmea: Ubi est Ctēsiphō?

Syrus: Ctēsiphō est cum amīcō.

Dēmea: Ubi habitat amīcus?

Syrus: Prīmum ambulās in viā, deinde in clīvō, deinde vidēs rīvum. Ibi est porta et casa. Ctēsiphō est in casā cum amīcō.

Having sent Demea away on a "wild goose chase," Syrus returns inside to report his success to Ctesipho.

READING VOCABULARY

Aeschinī et Ctēsiphōnis – of Aeschinus and Ctesipho

*amīcus – friend

*animum – spirit, soul, mind

bonum – good

*casa, casae, f. – little house, cottage

Ctēsiphō, Ctēsiphōnis, m. – Ctesipho

*cum amīcō – with a friend

dē duōbus frātribus – about two brothers

*deinde – then

Dēmea, m. – Demea

*domī – at home

*ego – I

es – are

estne? – is?

*fīliōs tuōs – your sons

fīlium meum – my son

fīlium tuum – your son

frāter meus – my brother

heus! – hey!

hic – this

ibi – there

*in agrīs – in the fields, in the countryside

in casā – in the cottage

in clīvō – on the hill

in viā – on the road

mē – me

mī bone vir! – my good fellow!

mī fīlī! – my son!

nōn est – he is not

num? – do I? (negative answer implied)

pater – father

porta, portae, f. – gate

prīmum – first

quis? – who?

*rīvum – brook, stream

salvē! – hello!

sum – am

*timeō – to fear, to be afraid

*tū – you

ubi – where

*valdē – very, exceedingly

*via, viae, f. – road

*vir – man

*Words marked with an asterisk will need to be memorized.

COMPREHENSION QUESTIONS

1. What is the main purpose of Demea's visit?
2. Is Ctesipho happy about his father's visit?
3. What is Syrus' attitude toward Demea?
4. What is the reason for Syrus' behavior toward Demea?
5. What makes Demea go away?

The town of Bosra in Syria was conquered by Trajan's armies in 106 CE. Built in the freestanding Roman style rather than built into a hillside in the Greek manner, the stage and part of the seating area are shown.

LANGUAGE FACT I

SECOND DECLENSION MASCULINE -US NOUNS

In Chapter 1 you learned the first declension, with its characteristic vowel *ā*. In the chapter reading passage above, there are several forms with the characteristic vowel *ō* or *u*: *animum, fīlium, fīliōs, amīcō, amīcus, clīvō, rīvum*.

Nouns that end **-us** in the nominative singular and **-ī** in the genitive singular belong to the second declension. Most of the second declension nouns are masculine with a few feminine and neuter exceptions.

Second Declension Masculine -*us* Nouns

		Singular			Plural
Nominative	amīc**us**	the friend	amīc**ī**	the friends
Genitive	amīc**ī**	of the friend, friend's	amīc**ōrum**	of the friends, friends'
Dative	amīc**ō**	to/for the friend	amīc**īs**	to/for the friends
Accusative	amīc**um**	the friend	amīc**ōs**	the friends
Ablative	amīc**ō**	by/with the friend	amīc**īs**	by/with the friends

STUDY TIP

Notice that the second declension forms look identical in the genitive singular and nominative plural, in the dative and ablative singular, and in the dative and ablative plural. Even though these forms are spelled the same, you can tell the cases apart in context based on their very different functions in the sentence.

▶ EXERCISE 1

Identify the case and number of each noun. For some, more than one answer is possible.

Example: animum
accusative singular

1. fīlium
2. fīliōs
3. amīcō
4. amīcōs
5. animō
6. rīvōrum
7. fīliī
8. animīs

VOCABULARY TO LEARN

NOUNS

ager, agrī, m. – field
amīcus, amīcī, m. – friend
animus, animī, m. – spirit, soul, mind
casa, casae, f. – little house, cottage
domī – at home
fīlius, fīliī, m. – son
puer, puerī, m. – boy
rīvus, rīvī, m. – brook, stream
via, viae, f. – road
vir, virī, m. – man

PRONOUNS

ego – I
tū – you

VERB

timeō, timēre, timuī, —— – to fear, to be afraid

ADVERBS

deinde – then
valdē – very, exceedingly

PREPOSITIONS

cum + ablative – with
in + ablative – in, on

The sign "——" indicates that the verb has no fourth principal part.

► EXERCISE 2

Find the English derivatives based on the Vocabulary to Learn in the following sentences. Write the corresponding Latin word.

1. Better selflessness than egotism.
2. Many small farmers are interested in the new agrarian laws.
3. Being violent is not a sign of virility.
4. You should be more amicable with your colleagues!
5. Let us not be timid, but act with bravery!
6. I flew to Europe via Chicago.
7. Joy and hope animated his face.
8. Do not meddle in the domestic affairs of the others!
9. This is a puerile, not an adult behavior.

► EXERCISE 3

Give the forms indicated in parentheses and an English translation that shows the case, number, and meaning of each noun.

Example: filia (genitive singular)
filiae   of the daughter *or* daughter's

1. rīvus (dative singular)
2. patria (genitive singular)
3. filius (nominative plural)
4. animus (ablative singular)
5. fōrma (accusative singular)
6. terra (ablative plural)

LANGUAGE FACT II

SECOND DECLENSION MASCULINE -*ER*, -*IR* NOUNS

In the chapter reading, you can see the word *ager* in the phrase *in agrīs* "in the fields, in the countryside." Some second declension nouns end -*er* in the nominative singular, instead of -*us*. These nouns decline like *amīcus* in all cases except the nominative singular.

Second Declension Masculine -*er* Nouns			
	Singular		**Plural**
Nominative	ager	the field	agrī	the fields
Genitive	agrī	of the field, field's	agrōrum	of the fields, fields'
Dative	agrō	to/for the field	agrīs	to/for the fields
Accusative	agrum	the field	agrōs	the fields
Ablative	agrō	by/with the field	agrīs	by/with fields

Notice that *ager* loses its *-e-* in all cases but the nominative singular. Nouns like *ager* should be distinguished from a closely related type of second declension *-er* noun that keeps the *-e-* in all cases, such as *puer*.

Second Declension Masculine *-er* Nouns

		Singular			Plural
Nominative	puer	the boy	puer**ī**	the boys
Genitive	puer**ī**	of the boy, boy's	puer**ōrum**	of the boys, boys'
Dative	puer**ō**	to/for the boy	puer**īs**	to/for the boys
Accusative	puer**um**	the boy	puer**ōs**	the boys
Ablative	puer**ō**	by/with the boy	puer**īs**	by/with the boys

STUDY TIP

In order to know what pattern a word ending in *-er* should follow, look closely at the genitive singular. If the *-e-* from the nominative **is not** present in the genitive (as in *ager, agrī*), it will not be present in any of the other cases. If, however, the *-e-* from the nominative **is** present in the genitive (as in *puer, puerī*), it will be present in all the other cases as well.

A distinct second declension noun is *vir* (man), which you encountered in the reading. This noun has the unique nominative singular ending *-ir*.

BY THE WAY

All words in *-er* and *-ir* of the second declension are masculine without exception.

Second Declension Masculine *-ir* Nouns

		Singular			Plural
Nominative	vir	the man	vir**ī**	the men
Genitive	vir**ī**	of the man, man's	vir**ōrum**	of the men, men's
Dative	vir**ō**	to/for the man	vir**īs**	to/for the men
Accusative	vir**um**	the man	vir**ōs**	the men
Ablative	vir**ō**	by/with the man	vir**īs**	by/with the men

STUDY TIP

The spelling of an English derivative often shows whether the *-e-* remains in the stem. For example, the spelling of the English word "agrarian" shows that the *-e-* has dropped from the base Latin word *ager*. Likewise, the English derivative "puerile" reveals that *puer* keeps its *-e-*.

Second Declension Noun Types				
Noun Type	Words in -*us*	Words in -*er*	Words in -*er*	Words in -*ir*
Nominative	amīcus	ager	puer	vir
Genitive	amīcī	agrī	puerī	virī
Other cases	amīcō amīcum amīcō . . .	agrō agrum agrō . . .	puerō puerum puerō . . .	virō virum virō . . .

▶ EXERCISE 4

Identify the case and number of each noun. Then change each form into the singular if it is plural and into the plural if it is singular. For some, more than one answer is possible.

Example: fīliī
genitive singular   fīliōrum   nominative plural   fīlius

1. agrīs
2. lupārum
3. amīcō

4. virōs
5. rīvī
6. animōrum

▶ EXERCISE 5

Give the forms indicated in parentheses and an English translation of the changed form that shows its case, number, and meaning.

Example: puer (genitive plural)
puerōrum   of the boys

1. ager (ablative plural)
2. puer (dative singular)
3. vir (dative plural)

4. puella (genitive singular)
5. fīlius (genitive plural)
6. animus (accusative singular)

LANGUAGE FACT III

GENITIVE CASE

In the chapter reading, Demea presents himself to the slave who opens the door: *Ego sum Dēmea, pater Aeschinī et Ctēsiphōnis.* "I am Demea, father of Aeschinus and Ctesiphon." The forms *Aeschinī* and *Ctēsiphōnis* are genitive. The name *Aeschinus* declines like *amīcus* (Aeschinus, Aeschinī, m.).

A noun in the genitive usually modifies another noun. The genitive often shows possession. A noun in the genitive case usually can be translated using the English word *of*, as in *of the girl*, or by using an apostrophe, as in *girl's*. In the plural, the genitive can be translated as in *girls'* with an **s'**, or by using *of* with a phrase like *of the girls*.

This Roman mosaic of the masks of comedy and tragedy is housed in the Capitoline Museum in Rome.

BY THE WAY

The first declension uses the same ending for the genitive singular and nominative plural: **-ae**. The second declension also uses the same ending for genitive singular and nominative plural: **-ī**.

LANGUAGE FACT IV

VOCATIVE CASE

In the chapter reading, Demea shouts, *mī fīlī*, "my son," and calls Syrus *mī bone vir*, "my good fellow." These forms are in the vocative case. The vocative case is used to address someone.

The vocative case is usually identical in form to the nominative, except for the vocative singular of second declension nouns of the type ending in **-us**. These nouns have the vocative singular ending **-e**.

Example:

Nominative: amī**cus**   Vocative: amī**ce**

Vocative Case, First and Second Declensions			
	First Declension	**Second Declension Masculine -us Nouns**	**Second Declension Masculine -er, -ir Nouns**
Singular	puella	amīce	ager, puer, vir
Plural	puellae	amīcī	agrī, puerī, virī

BY THE WAY

The Latin word for "son," *filius*, has an irregular vocative *filī*, as do all second declension nouns that end in *-ius*. The irregular vocative of *meus*, "my," is *mī*.

▶ EXERCISE 6

Complete each sentence with the correct form of the word in parentheses.

Example: Dēmea _____ (fīlius) vocat.
Dēmea fīlium vocat.

1. Syrus is asking Demea: "Quis es tū, _____ (amīcus)?"

2. Demea is answering: "Habitō in _____ (agrī)."

3. Syrus is saying to Demea: " _____ (fīlius) nōn videō."

4. Dēmea dēbet ambulāre ad casam _____ (amīcus).

5. Fīlius nōn est cum _____ (amīcus).

The Theatre of Marcellus was built as a freestanding structure in the Roman style. Julius Caesar began the construction of this theatre in Rome. Augustus completed its construction in 13 BCE and dedicated it to his nephew and intended heir, Marcellus. This theatre held 20,000 seats and until its completion plays in Rome were held in temporary wooden structures.

LANGUAGE FACT V

PREPOSITIONAL PHRASES

In the chapter reading, Demea says: *Habitō in agrīs*, "I live in the countryside." When Demea asks about his son, the servant answers: *Ctēsiphō est cum amīcō*, "Ctesipho is with a friend." Then he gives Demea (false) directions: *ambulās in viā, deinde in clīvō*, "you walk on the road, then on the hill." Finally he repeats: *Ctēsiphō est in casā cum amīcō*, "Ctesipho is in (that) cottage with a friend."

> *in agrīs,*
> *cum amīcō,*
> *in viā,*
> *in clīvō,*
> *in casā*

are all prepositional phrases. A prepositional phrase is a preposition joined with a noun (that may have an adjective with it).

Prepositions are words (usually small words) that denote a relationship between a noun or a pronoun and another word. The word "preposition" comes from the Latin verb *praepōnere*, which means "to place in front." In Latin, the preposition usually precedes its object noun or pronoun. Prepositions require a particular **case** of the noun object.

Note that the preposition *in* used with the ablative case can mean "in" or "on," and the preposition *cum* used with the ablative means "with."

This ancient Roman road, called the *Via Sacra*, leading towards the Arch of Titus in Rome, shows the enduring, yet worn nature of the polygonal blocks of stone that formed the top layer of Roman roads.

BY THE WAY

When you are talking about someone's home and you want to express "at home," you say *domī* without any preposition.

▶ EXERCISE 7

Supply the preposition that makes sense. Then translate the sentence.

Example: Ambulō _____ aquā.
Ambulō in aquā.   I am walking in the water.

1. Puer _____ puellā nautam exspectat.

2. _____ fābulā lupa puerōs cūrat.

3. Habitāmus _____ amīcīs.

4. Vir est _____ viā.

5. Lupa est _____ agrō.

▶ EXERCISE 8

Label each sentence as *vērum* (true) if it agrees or *falsum* (false) if it disagrees with the Latin reading passage at the beginning of the chapter.

1. Ctēsiphŏ est domī.

2. Ctēsiphō est in casā amīcī.

3. Syrus est pater Aeschinī et Ctēsiphōnis.

4. Syrus fābulās nārrat.

TALKING

Hoc est conclāve scholasticum. "This is the classroom."

Cōnsīdās in sellā! "Sit down in your seat!"

Cōnsīdātis in sellīs! "Sit down (plural) in your seats!"

Surgās et ad tabulam scriptōriam veniās. "Get up and come to the board."

In tabulā scriptōriā scrībō. "I am writing on the board."

Scrībō crētā. "I am writing with a chalk."

Scrībō calamō coāctilī. "I am writing with a board marker."

Ēiice hoc in scirpiculum! "Throw this into the garbage can!"

Nōlī susurrāre! "Do not whisper!"

Nōlīte susurrāre! "Do not whisper (plural)!"

Favēte linguīs! "Silence!"

Licetne mihi īre ad locum secrētum (or lātrīnam)? "May I go to the bathroom?"

Licet/nōn licet. "You may/you may not."

Licetne habēre mappulam chartāceam (nāsutergium)? "May I have a kleenex?"

IN THE CLASSROOM

Magistra: (*teacher [female]*) Salvēte, discipulī! (*Hello, students!*)

Discipulī: (*students*) Salvē, magistra!

Mārcus: Heus (*hey*), Marīa, Helena! Estne magistra bona? (*Is the teacher good?*)

Magistra: Ssst! (*Shh!*) Favēte linguīs! Habēmus novum discipulum. Quod nōmen est tibi?

Mārcus: Nōmen mihi est Mārcus.

Magistra: Surgās et ad tabulam scriptōriam veniās. Dēclīnā (*decline*) "fīlius!"

Mārcus: (TO MARIA) Timeō! (TO THE TEACHER) Licetne mihi īre ad locum secrētum?

Magistra: Nōn licet. Dēbēs scrībere (*to write*). Ecce (*here is*) crēta.

REVIEW 1: CHAPTERS 1–3

VOCABULARY TO KNOW

NOUNS

ager, agrī, m. – field

agricola, agricolae, m. – farmer

amīcus, amīcī, m. – friend

animus, animī, m. – spirit, soul, mind

aqua, aquae, f. – water

āthlēta, āthlētae, m. – athlete

casa, casae, f. – little house, cottage

domī – at home

fābula, fābulae, f. – story

fīlia, fīliae, f. – daughter

fīlius, fīliī, m. – son

fōrma, fōrmae, f. – form, appearance

lupa, lupae, f. – she-wolf

nauta, nautae, m. – sailor

patria, patriae, f. – fatherland

poēta, poētae, m. – poet

puella, puellae, f. – girl

puer, puerī, m. – boy

rīvus, rīvī, m. – brook, stream

Rōma, Rōmae, f. – Rome

terra, terrae, f. – land

via, viae, f. – road

vir, virī, m. – man

PRONOUNS

ego – I

tū – you

VERBS

ambulō, ambulāre, ambulāvī, ambulātum – to walk

amō, amāre, amāvī, amātum – to love

cūrō, cūrāre, cūrāvī, cūrātum – to care for, to take care of

dēbeō, dēbēre, dēbuī, dēbitum – ought, must, should; to owe

est – he/she/it is

exspectō, exspectāre, exspectāvī, exspectātum – to wait for, to await, to expect

habeō, habēre, habuī, habitum – to have

habitō, habitāre, habitāvī, habitātum – to live, to dwell

nārrō, nārrāre, nārrāvī, nārrātum – to tell

parō, parāre, parāvī, parātum – to prepare, to get ready

sum – I am

teneō, tenēre, tenuī, tentum – to hold

timeō, timēre, timuī, —— – to fear, to be afraid

videō, vidēre, vīdī, vīsum – to see

vocō, vocāre, vocāvī, vocātum – to call

ADVERBS

bene – well

deinde – then

diū – for a long time

nōn – not

nunc – now

posteā – afterwards

valdē – very, exceedingly

PREPOSITIONS

cum + ablative – with

in + ablative – in, on

CONJUNCTIONS

et – and

itaque – and so

▶ EXERCISE 1

Decline the following nouns.

1. *terra, terrae,* f. – land

2. *rīvus, rīvī,* m. – stream

3. *socer, socerī,* m. – father-in-law

4. *liber, librī,* m. – book

▶ EXERCISE 2

Conjugate the following verbs. Give the Latin infinitive with its meaning for each verb.

Example: amō, amāre, amāvī, amatum
amāre – to love

amō	amāmus
amās	amātis
amat	amant

1. *habeō, habēre, habuī, habitum*

2. *exspectō, exspectāre, exspectāvī, exspectātum*

3. *dēbeō, dēbēre, dēbuī, dēbitum*

4. *cūrō, cūrāre, cūrāvī, cūrātum*

▶ EXERCISE 3

Fill in the blanks with the correct form of the words in parentheses and translate each sentence.

Example: _____ et _____ videō. (ager) (rīvus)
Agrum et rīvum videō.   I see the field and the river.

1. _____ nārrāmus. (fābula [in plural])

2. Tū amīcum _____. (vidēre)

3. Nōn sum _____. (poēta)

4. Dēbēmus fīlium _____. (cūrō)

5. _____ nōn timeō. (lupa)

6. Fīlius nōn est _____. (nauta)

▶ EXERCISE 4

Choose the appropriate word from the list below to complete the sentence and translate the passage.

cum   et   habeō
dēbet   fīlium   in
est   fīlius   valdē

Dēmea _____ vocat. Syrus Dēmeam convenit (*meets*) _____ dīcit (*says*): "Fīlius nōn est hīc (*here*)." Ctēsiphō autem (*however*) audit (*hears*) et Dēmeam_____ timet. Syrus dīcit: "Fīliōs tuōs (*yours*) ego nōn teneō. Fīliōs tuōs ego nōn _____." Dēmea rogat (*asks*): "Ubi (*where*) _____ Ctēsiphō? Ubi est _____?" Syrus dīcit: "Ctēsiphō est _____ casā _____ amīcō." Itaque Dēmea ad (*to*) amīcum ambulāre _____.

▶ EXERCISE 5

In each pair of nouns, change the second one into the genitive, using the number indicated in parentheses. Translate each phrase.

Example: ager amīcus (plural)
ager amīcōrum   the field of the friends *or* the friends' field

1. animī poēta (plural)
2. aqua āthlēta (singular)
3. terra fīlia (plural)

4. patria puer (plural)
5. amīcus fīlius (singular)
6. fōrma rīvus (plural)

This fresco from the House of the Banker, probably Lucius Caecilius Iucundus, in Pompeii depicts the type of writing utensils that might be used by educated Roman adults and writers like Martial. The scrolls are housed in a typical cylindrical container and a writing tablet is shown.

▶ EXERCISE 6

Translate the following Latin text.

This short poem was written by Marcus Valerius Martialis, known to us as Martial, who lived from ca. 40–102 CE. Born in Spain, he specialized in the literary form of the epigram. Martial's epigrams are renowned for their pointed wit, and for the vivid picture of Roman society that they paint.

The Latin text of this epigram has not been modified or simplified, but presented in the very words that Martial wrote twenty centuries ago.

Nōn amo tē, Sabidī, nec possum dīcere quārē.
    Hoc tantum possum dīcere: nōn amo tē. (Martial 1.32)

hoc – this
nec = et nōn
possum dīcere – I can say
quārē – why

Sabidius, Sabidiī, m. – a personal name, Sabidius
tantum (adv.) – only
tē – you (accusative singular)

Martial's epigram is the source of the famous poem:

> I do not like thee, Doctor Fell,
> The reason why, I cannot tell;
> But this I know, and know full well,
> I do not like thee, Doctor Fell.

MARS

In the initial Chapter One reading, Mars was introduced as the father of Romulus and Remus, the legendary founders of Rome. From an early period, the god Mars was identified with the Greek divinity Ares, who was the son of Zeus, king of the gods, and his wife Hera. Ares, the god of war, was not attractively depicted in Greek mythology. A number of Greek authors portray him as often unsuccessful in battle, and engaging in embarrassing behavior. It is worth noting, therefore, that Zeus' unions with goddesses other than his wife created such impressive divinities as Athena, Apollo, Artemis, and the Muses, but his marriage to Hera produced a son who commanded far less respect.

Yet for the Romans, an extremely military-minded people, Ares, under the name of Mars, ranked as one of the most important and inspiring gods. His name was connected with the origins of their city. Chariot races were held in his honor, and his altar was located in the "field of Mars," the Campus Martius, where military exercises were regularly performed. The wolf was his sacred animal. During the census, the counting of citizens that took place in Rome at five-year intervals, the Roman people gathered around Mars' altar in the Campus Martius and offered him a special sacrifice of a pig, a sheep, and an ox to guarantee the continued military success of the Roman people. The Temple of Mars Ultor was built by Augustus to honor the god after the Battle of Philippi (42 BCE), in which he avenged the assassination of his adoptive father Julius Caesar.

The deities Mars and Venus, who were reported to have had an affair, are on this Roman fresco from the House of Marcus Lucretius Frontinus in Pompeii.

JUPITER (JOVE)

In the reading for Chapter Two, the slave cries out *Prō Iuppiter*! "By Jove!" It was a frequent practice to invoke the god Jupiter as a witness to oaths, or merely in simple exclamations. The Latin name for Jupiter, *Iuppiter*, literally means "sky-father." Jupiter's Greek counterpart is called Zeus, a name that also is associated with the sky.

Like Zeus, Jupiter is the greatest god in the Olympian pantheon, sovereign over heaven and earth, who wields a mighty thunderbolt and causes lightning to strike. Every god on Mount Olympus is his child or sibling. He himself is the son of the Titans Cronus—whom the Romans called Saturn—and Rhea. Cronus, who had previously overthrown his own father Uranus, feared a similar fate from his own offspring and thus devoured each of his children as soon as they were born.

Featuring a portrayal of the head of Zeus, this ancient Greek bronze coin dates from the third century BCE.

But Rhea outsmarted her husband when she gave birth to her last child, and handed him a stone wrapped in baby clothes, saving Jupiter in the process. Later, Jupiter rescued his brothers and sisters from inside their father's body. Although Jupiter married one of these sisters, whom the Romans called Juno, he had love affairs with many other goddesses and many mortal females. The moons circling the planet Jupiter are named after some of these women.

JUNO

Jupiter's wife is Juno, the name given by the Romans to the Greek goddess Hera. Even though she wields power as queen of heaven, she is tormented by jealousy of Jupiter's lovers, and by hatred of the offspring produced

The marriage of Jupiter and Juno on Mount Ida, portrayed on this fresco from Pompeii.

by these unions. Juno is the patron divinity of women, and especially of marriage. The Romans called her by distinctive names that indicated her various functions. *Iūnō Lūcīna*, "Juno who brings to light," was her name as the protector of childbirth. *Iūnō Monēta* (from *moneō, monēre, monuī, monitum*, "to warn") was Juno in her role as giver of advice. A mint was established in the Temple of Juno Moneta at Rome, where coins were made. From this place comes our English word for "money;" indeed, by the time Rome became an empire, the Latin word *monēta, -ae*, f. had come to mean "coined money" or "currency."

Hera's temple in Paestum in southern Italy dates from the fifth century BCE. The Doric-styled temple features 36 fluted columns.

READ THE FOLLOWING PASSAGE

Iuppiter et Iūnō fīlium habent. Fīlius est Mārs. Mārs pugnās valdē amat et pugnās semper parat. Mārs vītam virōrum nōn cūrat. Itaque Graecī eum nōn amant. In quādam pugnā virī deum vulnerant. Deus fugit et Graecī rīdent.

deus, deī, m. – god	quādam – a certain
eum – him	rīdent – laugh
fugit – runs away, flees	semper (adv.) – always
Graecus, Graecī, m. – Greek	vīta, vītae, f. – life
pugna, pugnae, f. – battle	vulnerō, vulnerāre, vulnerāvī, vulnerātum – to wound

The Greek and Roman gods and goddesses were said to live on the cloudy peaks of Mt. Olympus in Greece.

CONNECTING WITH THE ANCIENT WORLD

SLAVERY IN ANCIENT ROME

In the readings for Chapters Two and Three, slaves play a large role in the dialogue. Roman comedy, from which these two reading passages are taken, often features slaves who take charge and solve problems—a comic inversion, perhaps, of the way Roman society actually was. Slavery was extremely visible in ancient Rome, and assumed many forms. Ancient slavery was by no means identical to slavery in more recent periods and countries, such as colonial America. The Romans did not reduce a single race or culture to slavery; rather, slaves came from all over the ancient Mediterranean world, and typically fell into servile status by capture in war. The prices of slaves depended greatly on their qualifications. Many slaves were skilled and educated, often more so than their masters. Slave dealers (*mangōnēs*) both sold and rented out slaves at public auctions. White chalk on the feet indicated that the slave was imported. A tag around the neck gave the slave's name, nationality, and described his character, a guarantee for the buyer that he was making a good purchase.

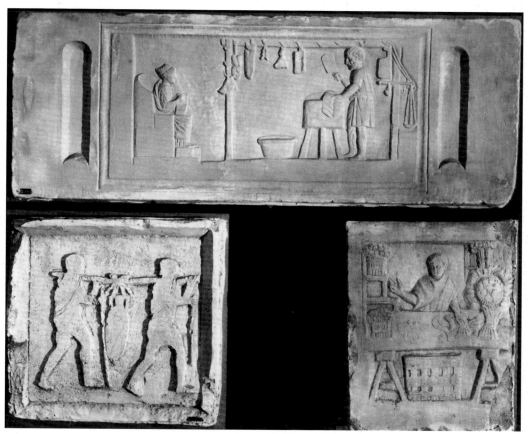

The top relief is of a Roman butcher shop, while the bottom relief at the left shows two slaves carrying an amphora, and the bottom relief at the right depicts a woman selling herbs. From the second century CE.

The experience of slavery differed for different individuals. House slaves might be educated and assigned to train the master's children, or to act as literary or business assistants to the master himself; such slaves might be treated much like personal friends. Tiro, Cicero's secretary, friend, and former slave, invented a system of shorthand to facilitate taking notes. At the other end of the spectrum, however, slaves who worked in the fields and mines might have existences no better than those endured by beasts of burden. Slavery was ordinarily a hereditary condition; children of a slave mother would remain slaves. However, slaves might liberate themselves by accumulating savings (*pecūlium*) and buying their freedom, or be liberated by their masters as a reward for good service (*manūmissiō*). Freedmen were granted citizenship and so were any subsequent children born to them. The playwright Terence himself was a freed slave, who apparently enjoyed close ties to his master. Maltreatment of slaves appears to have been common and those who tried to escape could be whipped, branded with the letters FUG (*fugitīvus*, runaway) on their forehead, or made to wear an inscribed metal collar. The condition of slaves, however, improved somewhat as a result of laws passed during the early imperial period.

Roman workers, probably slaves, are building a wall under the direction of an overseer in this fragment from a painting.

This second century CE Roman mosaic portrays slaves preparing for a festival. The mosaic was found in Carthage.

Each year around the time of the winter solstice in December, the Romans celebrated a festival called *Sāturnālia*. Some say that this happy holiday was the best day of the year. Rules of social conduct and distinctions of social class were reversed on that day, and slaves not only behaved as if they were masters but also acted disrespectfully towards their own masters.

EXPLORING ROMAN COMEDY

ROMAN PRODUCTIONS AND MODERN RENDITIONS

While Roman armies were struggling in Spain and Italy with Hannibal (220–200 BCE), in the city people were developing theatrical forms adapted from Greece, and particularly Roman Comedy offered rich distraction from the anxieties of war. There were two holidays that gave the ordinary people an opportunity for free entertainment at comedies, to laugh away their cares, and to identify with clever slaves who could outwit and out-talk their masters and bring a complex plot to a "happy ending." One of these holidays came in March, as Spring was starting: it was called the *Megalensia* and honored the goddess Cybele. The other was the Roman Games or *Lūdī Rōmānī*, celebrated in September in the Fall. The plays were chosen in competition by junior officials called aediles and staged at public expense. We know the names of several early comic poets (the plays were in verse), but the works of only two have survived: Plautus and Terence.

A theatre mask of comedy from the second century BCE.

Plautus (about 254–184 BCE) freely adapted Greek comedies and added song (*cantica*) and dance to the more sober and "artistic" originals. This combination of dialogue (*diverbia*) interspersed with song is reminiscent of the Gilbert and Sullivan operettas. In the *Menaechmī* there are five such song interludes. Plautus' Latin was colloquial; he made fun of the Greek plots, and he only pretended to be showing a Greek production. The fun for him and the audience came in the obvious Romanization and Latinization of non-Roman situations and half-Roman characters. The crowds loved this kind of theatrics, so much so that we still have twenty-one of his comedies, which were studied and imitated by the first writers of the Italian Renaissance and then by European dramatists like Shakespeare and Molière. The plot lines of Shakespeare's *The Comedy of Errors* are likewise built on coincidences and complications.

One of the most successful modern adaptations of a Plautine comedy is *A Funny Thing Happened on the Way to the Forum* (1966). A combination of two plays (*Pseudolus* and *Mīles Glōriōsus*), this entertaining theatrical play, later made into a movie, combines the favorite characteristics of Roman comedy: disguises, lovers at a loss, deception, slapstick, the clever slave, recognition and recovery, and a happy, if not realistic, ending.

Every time the plot of an ancient play like the *Menaechmī* contains twins, there is an automatic opportunity for one twin accidentally to substitute for the other in good or bad luck, until finally they recognize each other. In the Chapter Two passage chosen from the *Menaechmī*, the twin brothers work out their identity and decide to return home to Sicily.

Even more recently, the movie, *The Parent Trap,* first produced in 1968 and later remade in a modern version in 1998, is another example of mistaken identity and role reversal whereby twin girls try to make their parents reunite rather than rewed. Part of the plot of this movie was reworked into the 2002 TV show "So Little Time," the second TV show in which the Olson twins starred. Likewise in the TV show "Sister, Sister" the twins Tia and Tamera Mowra were separated at birth but at age fourteen met by chance in a Detroit department store. Thus modern TV situation comedies and theatre plays owe much to the continuous comic tradition that runs from Plautus to today.

Terence's dates are uncertain, but we are told that he started life in Rome as a slave, gained his freedom as a young man, and staged his six comedies from 165–160 BCE. He too used Greek originals, but he adapted them with different methods and goals than Plautus. He did not try to make his plays more funny and animated than the Greek, and he often focused on the human

This well-preserved theatre built during Roman times is in Caesarea, a town in Israel and capital of the Roman province of Judaea. After this city had been under the control of Cleopatra, Augustus returned it to Herod the Great who named it in honor of Caesar Augustus.

emotions felt by the characters. The Chapter Three selection from the *Adelphoi* (*Brothers*) would seem from its title to offer humorous opportunities to Terence. Demea, the father of Aeschinus and Ctesipho, has let his brother Micio adopt Aeschinus. The two sons and Micio conspire to fool him and pursue their own pleasures, but that is not so funny now, because Demea is really fond of Ctesipho and anxious to bring him up well. And he disapproves of the way Micio is raising Aeschinus, who in fact has gotten his girlfriend pregnant and not consulted either father about his responsibilities. So we watch a scene here where the slave Syrus is having fun deceiving Demea about where Ctesipho is and what he is doing. Yet what is "fun" for Syrus is sad for Demea, and the audience sees both the fun and the sadness and tends to feel sorry for Demea. This is not simply a trite situation comedy. Both sets of brothers are differentiated by Terence, not exploited for ridiculous games. An audience would come away from a play like this, after two hours, either bored stiff or talking over the moral themes of the comedy: they would not simply be tickled and guffawing at Syrus' confident deceptions. Terence won great success with the crowd that attended his *Eunuch*. On the other hand, he could not hold the audience for either of the first two performances of his *Mother-in-Law*. The *Brothers* was staged at the expense of his friend Scipio Africanus, to honor Scipio's father on the occasion of his death in 160 BCE.

The comedies of Terence were much admired for their moral sentiments, the realistic characters, and the urbane Latin that they spoke; and as a result the plays made him a "school author" throughout antiquity and then in the Renaissance. He had an early admirer and imitator in the nun Hroswitha of Gandersheim, who wrote six pious plays in his manner in the tenth century. Dante quoted and admired Terence; so did Petrarch, who even wrote a biography of him and left an annotated manuscript of the comedies in Florence. In Florence in 1476, the first Terentian play to be staged since antiquity was the *Andria*. In the fifteenth century, continuing to be a "school author," Terence inspired most of the Latin comedies that the humanists attempted. He was read and admired throughout Europe. Molière staged a version of the *Phormio* in 1671.

To conclude, Plautus was more popular with audiences and continues to be performed and performable today, but Terence dominated Roman and Renaissance culture as a "school author." He won the respect of teachers, orators, and religious leaders (like Luther) until late in the nineteenth century. The twentieth century saw Plautus reclaiming dominance (in spite of the adaptation in 1930 of *The Woman of Andros* [*Andria*] by Thornton Wilder), but there are signs in this new millennium that students of Latin comedy are beginning to see that Terence and Plautus each has dramatic and literary merits. The two of them together combine into a superior variety of eminent comedy.

WILLIAM S. ANDERSON
Professor of Classics, Emeritus
University of California Berkeley
Berkeley, California

PHRASES AND QUOTATIONS
RELATING TO THE COMIC TRADITION

PHRASES AND QUOTATIONS

- Drāmatis persōnae. "Characters in a play." An expression indicating the actors in a drama.

- Exit. Exeunt. "S/he exits <the scene>. They exit <the scene>." A way to indicate in a script that an actor or a group of actors are leaving the scene.

- Mīles gloriōsus. "A bragging soldier." This title of a comedy by Plautus also describes a common figure in Roman comedy.

- Nōdum in scirpō quaeris. "You seek a knot in the bulrush, i.e., you find a difficulty where there is none." (Plautus, *Menaechmi*, 2.1.22; Terence, *The Woman of Andros*, 5.4. 38).

- Plaudite, ācta est fābula. "Applaud, the play is over." A typical expression said to the Roman audience at the end of a play. The words "acta est fabula" were allegedly pronounced by Augustus on his deathbed. Suetonius in *The Life of Augustus*, 99, writes that just before dying the emperor asked whether he had played well his role in the comedy of life.

This well-preserved theatre lies in Gerasa, now Jerash, situated just north of Jordan, conquered by Rome in 63 BCE, annexed as a Roman province first of Syria and later of Arabia.

CHAPTER 4

Second Declension Neuter Nouns; Dative Case; First and Second Declension Adjectives; Agreement of Nouns and Adjectives

King Pyrrhus of Epirus fought against Rome twice in the third century BCE. At the top left of the picture is Pyrrhus' name and and at the top right the Latin word *rēx*, "king," and the letters "Epi," which stand for Epirus.

MEMORĀBILE DICTŪ

Aurī sacra famēs.

"Accursed hunger for gold." (Vergil, *Aeneid*, 3.57)

Vergil's words have become proverbial as a concise phrase condemning the insatiable human appetite for money.

READING

Perhaps the greatest of all Roman writers of prose was Mārcus Tullius Cicero (106–43 BCE). Cicero was a great statesman, active in politics (in fact, he was eventually killed upholding the cause of the Roman republic against the absolute rule of powerful dictators in the series of civil wars that shook the Roman state in the last century BCE). He was famous as an orator, and wrote numerous speeches, many of which have survived.

Cicero wrote many letters, which tell us a great deal about the social and political life of his day. He was also a philosopher and the author of many philosophical works, which, though not very original, are highly polished and well designed to transmit Greek philosophical ideas to a Roman audience.

The passage you will now read comes from Cicero's philosophical essay *Dē officiīs* ("On Duties"), where Cicero discusses the relationship between what is morally right *(honestum)* and what is expedient *(ūtile)*. In Book 3.86, he relates an event that occurred more than two centuries earlier.

While Rome had not yet conquered all of Italy in the early third century BCE, it was already the dominant power in the Italian peninsula. Alarmed at Rome's expansionism, the Greek city of Tarentum in the south of Italy made an alliance with Pyrrhus, King of Epirus (a region just west of Macedonia), a kinsman of Alexander the Great and no less greedy for military glory. Pyrrhus' military forces met those of Rome twice, in 280 and 279 BCE. The Greek armies were victorious in both battles. But Pyrrhus had lost so many men each time that he was unable to stop the Romans, and he ultimately had to abandon his ambitions in Italy. To this very day, we call a victory won at an unacceptable price a "Pyrrhic victory." Here is Cicero's version of what occurred just before the Romans met the army of Pyrrhus in open battle.

PROFUGA PRAEMIUM VULT

1　Pyrrhus, rēx praeclārus, bellum cum Rōmānīs gerit. Terram in Ītaliā habēre vult. Profuga ē castrīs Pyrrhī clam fugit et in castra Rōmānōrum ambulat. Nōn timet profuga, sed Fābricium vidēre vult. Fābricius est cōnsul et dux Rōmānōrum. "Dēbēs māgnum praemium mihi dare,"
5　inquit profuga; "sī praemium mihi dās, habeō in animō clam intrāre in Pyrrhī castra et Pyrrhum venēnō necāre." Fābricius autem victōriam dolō habēre nōn vult, sed bellō iūstō. Itaque virōs armātōs vocat. Praemium nōn dat profugae, sed vincula. Iubet virōs armātōs cum profugā ad Pyrrhī castra ambulāre et profugam vīnctum Pyrrhō dare.

READING VOCABULARY

*ad + accusative – into, towards, to

*armātus, armāta, armātum – armed

*autem – however

bellō iūstō – through open warfare

*bellum, bellī, n. – war

*castra, castrōrum, n. pl. – camp (note this noun is one of several that have only plural forms, with a singular meaning)

clam (adv.) – secretly

cōnsul, m. – consul

*dō, dăre, dedī, dătum – to give

dolō – through treachery

*dolus, dolī, m. – trickery, deception

dux, m. – leader, general

*ē (ex before a vowel) + ablative – from, out of

Fābricius, Fābriciī, m. – Fabricius

fugit – flees

gerit – wages

*in + accusative – into, to

inquit – says

*intrō, intrāre, intrāvī, —— – to enter

Ītalia, Ītaliae, f. – Italy

*iubeō, iubēre, iussī, iussum + accusative + infinitive – to order somebody to do something

*iūstus, iūsta, iūstum – legitimate, open, just

*māgnus, māgna, māgnum – large, great, important

mihi (dative case) – to me

necō, necāre, necāvī, necātum – to kill

*praeclārus, praeclāra, praeclārum – famous, distinguished

*praemium, praemiī, n. – reward

profuga, profugae, m. – deserter

Pyrrhus, Pyrrhī, m. – Pyrrhus

rēx, m. – king

*Rōmānus, Rōmāna, Rōmānum – Roman (*Rōmānī* in the masculine plural means "the Romans")

*sed (conj.) – but

sī (conj.) – if

venēnō – by poison

*venēnum, venēnī, n. – poison

victōria, victōriae, f. – victory

vīnctus, vīncta, vīnctum – bound, chained

*vinculum, vinculī, n. – chain, fetter

vult – he wants, wishes

*Words marked with an asterisk will need to be memorized.

COMPREHENSION QUESTIONS

1. With whom are the Romans at war?

2. What does Pyrrhus want in Italy?

3. When the deserter comes to the Roman camp, whom does he need to see?

4. What is the deserter's plan?

5. Why doesn't Fabricius accept the deserter's proposal?

LANGUAGE FACT I

SECOND DECLENSION NEUTER NOUNS

Since Chapter 3 you have already become acquainted with the second declension. You learned the declension of the masculine nouns in **-us**, exemplified by *amīcus* (the largest group of second declension nouns) as well as the declensions of *ager, puer,* and *vir*.

In the text above, you saw another type of second declension noun. These are neuter nouns in **-um**: *bellum, praemium, venēnum, vinculum*. The noun *castra, -ōrum* belongs to the same group, but occurs only in the plural.

These words are declined in the same way as *amīcus* with two exceptions: their nominative, accusative, and vocative are identical to one another; and the ending for the nominative and accusative (and vocative) plural is **-a**.

Second Declension Neuter Nouns				
	Singular		**Plural**	
Nominative	bell**um**	the war	bell**a**	the wars
Genitive	bell**ī**	of the war	bell**ōrum**	of the wars
Dative	bell**ō**	to/for the war	bell**īs**	to/for the wars
Accusative	bell**um**	war	bell**a**	the wars
Ablative	bell**ō**	by/with/from war	bell**īs**	by/with/from wars
Vocative	bell**um**	o, war	bell**a**	o, wars

BY THE WAY

All neuter words in Latin, of whatever declension, always have identical nominative, accusative, and vocative forms, and the *plural* nominative, accusative, and vocative always end in **-a**.

▶ EXERCISE 1

Identify the case and number of each noun. For some, more than one answer is possible.

Example: venēna
nominative or accusative plural

1. praemiīs
2. āthlēta
3. castra
4. vinculōrum
5. dolum
6. fīliī
7. praemiī

VOCABULARY TO LEARN

NOUNS

bellum, bellī, n. – war

castra, castrōrum, n. pl. – camp

dolus, dolī, m. – trickery, deception

praemium, praemiī, n. – reward

venēnum, venēnī, n. – poison

vinculum, vinculī, n. – chain, fetter

ADJECTIVES

bonus, bona, bonum – good

armātus, armāta, armātum – armed

iūstus, iūsta, iūstum – legitimate, open, just

māgnus, māgna, māgnum – large, great, important

malus, mala, malum – bad

praeclārus, praeclāra, praeclārum – famous, distinguished

Rōmānus, Rōmāna, Rōmānum – Roman

VERBS

dō, dăre, dedī, dătum – to give (note the unusual short stem vowel in this first conjugation verb)

intrō, intrāre, intrāvī, —— – to enter

iubeō, iubēre, iussī, iussum + accusative + infinitive – to order somebody (acc.) to do something (inf.)

PREPOSITIONS

ad + accusative – into, towards, to

ē (ex) + ablative – from, out of

in + accusative – into, to, against

CONJUNCTIONS

autem – however

sed – but

A Roman legionary, during the time of the Roman wars with Dacia. This is a relief from Trajan's column, which was built by Apollodorus of Damascus at the command of the Roman senate and was completed in 113 CE. The column was constructed in honor of Trajan's victory over the Dacians and stands in the Forum of Trajan in Rome.

► EXERCISE 2

Find the English derivatives based on the Vocabulary to Learn in the following sentences. Write the corresponding Latin word.

1. These youths are rather bellicose and always fighting.

2. A jussive mood of the verb is a form that conveys an order.

3. This product is premium quality.

4. The venom of the snake was fatal.

5. I received a bonus at the end of the year.

6. The army is ready for a battle.

7. Where is the main entrance?

8. She is a very sweet person, totally devoid of malice.

LANGUAGE FACT II

DATIVE CASE (INDIRECT OBJECT)

In the Latin reading passage you read these sentences and phrases:

> *Dēbēs māgnum praemium mihi dare . . .*
> You ought to give me a great reward . . .

> *Sī praemium mihi dās . . .*
> If you give me a reward . . .

> *Praemium nōn dat profugae, sed vincula . . .*
> He does not give a reward to the deserter, but chains . . .

> *Iubet virōs armātōs . . . profugam vīnctum Pyrrhō dare . . .*
> He orders the armed men to give the chained deserter to Pyrrhus . . .

In each of these sentences the nouns in the accusative case (*praemium, vincula, profugam, vīnctum*) are direct objects—they indicate the entity directly acted upon by the verb.

The nouns in the dative case (*mihi, profugae, Pyrrhō*) indicate the indirect object, i.e., the entity indirectly affected by the verb.

Use the words "to" or "for" to express the indirect object in English.

 BY THE WAY

Indirect objects often occur in sentences that include a verb that means "give," "show," "tell," or a synonym or antonym of one of these verbs.

▶ EXERCISE 3

Fill in the blanks with the dative case of the words in parentheses.

Example: Cōnsul praemium _____ dat. (vir)
Cōnsul praemium virō dat.

1. Fābricius praemium _____ nōn dat. (profuga)

2. Profuga venēnum _____ dare vult. (Pyrrhus)

3. Dux Rōmānōrum vincula _____ parat. (profuga)

4. Fābricius profugam _____ dat. (armātī virī)

▶ EXERCISE 4

Fill in the blanks with the dative case of the words in parentheses and translate each sentence.

Example: Fābulās _____ nārrat. (fīlia)
Fābulās fīliae nārrat.   S/he tells stories to the daughter.

1. Venēnum _____ damus. (lupae)

2. Aquam _____ parātis. (āthlētae)

3. Praemia _____ dēbētis. (nautae)

4. Terram _____ dant. (agricolae)

5. Casam _____ parāmus. (puer et puella)

Modern actors dressed in ancient Roman military and other official garb. Legionaries, ordinary soldiers, served in a legion, usually a group of soldiers about 4,000–6,000 strong. These men served under the direction of a centurion but an *imperātor* or *dux* was in command of the entire legion.

LANGUAGE FACT III

FIRST AND SECOND DECLENSION -US, -A, -UM ADJECTIVES; AGREEMENT OF NOUNS AND ADJECTIVES

Look closely at the following four phrases taken from the passage about Fabricius at the beginning of the chapter: *rēx praeclārus* ("renowned king"), *māgnum praemium* ("large reward"), *virōs armātōs* ("armed men"), *profugam vīnctum* ("chained deserter").

In each instance, a noun is modified by an adjective that describes the noun. An adjective *always* agrees with its noun in case, number, and gender. There are different types of adjectives. In this chapter you will learn adjectives with a masculine form ending in **-us**, a feminine form ending in **-a**, and a neuter form ending in **-um**, e.g., *iūstus, iūsta, iūstum*.

The masculine form is declined like *amīcus*, the feminine form is declined like *lupa*, and the neuter form is declined like *bellum*: i.e., the endings are identical to those you have learned for nouns of the first (feminine) and second (masculine/neuter) declensions.

First and Second Declension -us, -a, -um Adjectives

Singular

	Masculine	Feminine	Neuter
Nominative	iūstus	iūsta	iūstum
Genitive	iūstī	iūstae	iūstī
Dative	iūstō	iūstae	iūstō
Accusative	iūstum	iūstam	iūstum
Ablative	iūstō	iūstā	iūstō
Vocative	iūste	iūsta	iūstum

Plural

	Masculine	Feminine	Neuter
Nominative	iūstī	iūstae	iūsta
Genitive	iūstōrum	iūstārum	iūstōrum
Dative	iūstīs	iūstīs	iūstīs
Accusative	iūstōs	iūstās	iūsta
Ablative	iūstīs	iūstīs	iūstīs
Vocative	iūstī	iūstae	iūsta

Two frequently used adjectives of this type:

> *bonus, bona, bonum* – good
> *malus, mala, malum* – bad

BY THE WAY

An adjective agrees with its noun in case, number, and gender—regardless of the declension to which the noun belongs. So "the just sailor" is *nauta iūstus*, **not** *nauta iūsta*, because the noun *nauta* has a masculine gender.

▶ EXERCISE 5

Make *māgnus, māgna, māgnum* agree with **each** noun in the following sentences and translate the changed sentence.

Example: Ad castra ambulāmus.
Ad māgna castra ambulāmus.   We are walking to the large camp.

1.   In castrīs sum.
2.   Fīliōs habēmus.
3.   Bellum valdē timēmus.
4.   Praemia dēbēs.
5.   Casam poētae cūrāmus.
6.   Agricola ad rīvum ambulat.

▶ EXERCISE 6

Change the noun-adjective pair into the singular if it is plural and into the plural if it is singular. For some, more than one answer is possible.

Example: virōrum Rōmānōrum
virī Rōmānī

1.   iūstō praemiō
2.   agrīs māgnīs
3.   bella mala
4.   nautae armātī
5.   poētae praeclārō
6.   vincula mala

▶ EXERCISE 7

Translate into English.

1.   Dēbēmus nunc praemium exspectāre.
2.   Fābricius dolum nōn amat: victōriam iūstam amat.
3.   In castra Rōmānōrum nōn ambulāmus.
4.   Nōn bellum, sed venēnum timēmus.
5.   Amīcum iubēs Rōmānīs praeclārīs māgna praemia dare.
6.   Amīcōs bonōs habētis.

▶ EXERCISE 8

Fill in the blanks with the accusative case of the words in parentheses, keeping the same number, and translate each sentence.

Example: Virīs armātīs _____ nōn datis. (praemia)
Virīs armātīs praemia nōn datis.   You are not giving rewards to the armed men.

1. Ad patriam _____ vocāmus. (poētae)

2. _____ agricolīs nōn damus. (agrī māgnī)

3. _____ Rōmānīs parō. (praemium iūstum)

4. Bellō nōn dolō _____ habēmus. (victōria iūsta)

▶ EXERCISE 9

Label each sentence as *vērum* (true) if it agrees or *falsum* (false) if it disagrees with the Latin reading passage at the beginning of the chapter. The Reading Vocabulary may be consulted.

1. Pyrrhus dolum parat.

2. Fābricius māgnum praemium habēre vult.

3. Pyrrhus bellum cum Rōmānīs gerit.

4. Profuga Fābricium necāre vult.

5. Fābricius victōriam iūstam habēre dēbet.

6. Rōmānī profugae praemium dant.

7. Profuga est in vinculīs.

A modern re-enactor displays the helmet and body armor of a Roman soldier. A meritorious soldier could rise to the rank of centurion, a non-commissioned officer who usually directed about eighty men from a legion in war.

TALKING

cūr – why

Hoc est pēnsum domesticum. "This is the homework assignment."

locus Cicerōnis – A passage of Cicero

in crāstinum – for tomorrow

ita vērō – yes indeed

Locum in diem crāstinum parāre dēbēmus. "We must prepare the passage for tomorrow."

lexicum, lexicī, n. – dictionary

Licet vōbīs lexicum īnspicere. "You may (i.e., it is permitted for you to) consult a dictionary."

minimē – no

quis – who

DISCUSSING HOMEWORK

Remember that questions are introduced by the little word -ne *attached to another word.*

Marīa: Habēmusne pēnsum in crāstinum?

Helena: Ita vērō. Dēbēmus parāre locum Cicerōnis.

Marīa: Estne locus māgnus?

Christīna: Nōn est nimis (*too*) māgnus.

Mārcus: Quis erat Cicero? (*Who was Cicero?*)

Christīna: Cicero erat philosophus (*philosopher*).

Marīa: Cūr verba (*words*) philosophōrum legere (*read*) dēbēmus? Philosophī dē vērā vītā (*about true life*) nōn nārrant.

Helena: Cicero vēram (*true*) fābulam nārrat dē (*about*) Fābriciō. Fābricius victōriam dolō habēre nōn vult, sed bellō iūstō.

Mārcus: Haec (*this*) fābula nōn est vēra. Virī māgnī victōriam etiam (*even*) dolō habēre volunt (*want*).

Helena: Fābricius autem nōn sōlum (*only*) est māgnus, sed etiam (*also*) iūstus et praeclārus. Virī iūstī victōriam dolō habēre nōn dēbent.

Christīna: Et nōs pēnsum parāre dēbēmus.

CHAPTER 5

First and Second Conjugation Verbs: Present Passive Tense, Present Passive Infinitive; Ablative of Agent; First and Second Declension -er Adjectives

The portrait of a couple on this wall painting from Pompeii is a reminder of Cicero's letters to his wife Terentia.

MEMORĀBILE DICTŪ

STVBEEV

"If you are well, it is well; I am well."

The Romans could send a letter as short as these seven letters, which stand for *"Sī tū valēs, bene est; ego valeō."*

READING

Cicero left a large collection of letters, which tell us a great deal about him as a private person. They not only illustrate the family life of an upper-class Roman of the last century BCE, but also reveal much about the psychology of Cicero as an individual. When Cicero was sent into exile to Greece by his political enemies, he wrote letters full of laments, resentment, and despair. In many of them, though, we detect tender love for his wife Terentia and for his children. Such a letter is presented below.

When the early Renaissance Italian author Petrarch (1304–1374) discovered Cicero's correspondence, he was dismayed to find that Cicero, whom he had earlier known only from his speeches and philosophical essays, was, as a private individual, subject to powerful emotions and plagued by human feelings. Although Cicero had been dead for centuries, Petrarch responded by writing Cicero a letter of his own, full of harsh criticism.

CICERO TERENTIAE SALŪTEM PLŪRIMAM DĪCIT

1   Epistulam tuam, mea Terentia, nunc teneō. Epistulam tamen tuam nōn
     sōlum cum gaudiō, sed etiam cum lacrimīs legō. Nam longē ā patriā,
     longē ā familiā sum miser. Dē tē, dē fīliā et dē fīliō semper cōgitō.
     Animus dolet. Mala cōnsilia ā malīs virīs contrā mē parantur et
5   auxilium mihi ā bonīs virīs darī dēbet. Tē, Terentia mea, valdē amō et
     ā tē epistulās longās exspectō. Sī epistulās tuās legō, tē in animō meō
     videō. Tē ipsam, fīlium, fīliam pulchram bene cūrāre dēbēs. Valē!

READING VOCABULARY

*ā (ab before a vowel) + ablative – by, from

*auxilium, auxiliī, n. – help

Cicero, m. – Cicero

*cōgitō, cōgitāre, cōgitāvī, cōgitātum – to think

*cōnsilium, cōnsiliī, n. – plan, advice

contrā + accusative – against

darī dēbet – has to be given

*dē + ablative – about, concerning, down from

*doleō, dolēre, doluī, —— – to feel pain, to hurt

*epistula, epistulae, f. – letter

*familia, familiae, f. – family, household

gaudiō – with joy

*gaudium, gaudiī, n. – joy

*lacrima, lacrimae, f. – tear

lacrimīs – with tears

legō – I read

*longē (adv.) – far

*longus, longa, longum – long

mē (accusative) – me

meus, mea, meum – my

mihi – to me

*miser – wretched, sad, miserable

*nam (conj.) – for, in fact

*nōn sōlum . . . , sed etiam . . . – not only . . . , but also . . .

parantur – are being prepared

*parō – to design (you already know the meanings "to prepare, to get ready")

*pulchram (accusative singular feminine) – beautiful

salūtem plūrimam dīcit + dat. – s/he greets (someone) (a standard formula for beginning a letter). Literally it means "(s/he) says (i.e., wishes) very much health (the best of health) to . . ."

*semper (adv.) – always

sī (conj.) – if

sum – I am

*tamen (conj.) – nevertheless

tē (accusative and ablative) – you

tē ipsam (accusative) – yourself

Terentia, Terentiae, f. – Terentia

tuus, tua, tuum – your

valē! – good-bye!

COMPREHENSION QUESTIONS

1. Where is Cicero while writing the letter?

2. How many family members does Cicero mention in his letter and who are they?

3. What is Cicero afraid of?

4. How does Cicero feel (according to his own words), when he reads Terentia's letter?

5. What does Cicero ask Terentia to do?

LANGUAGE FACT I

FIRST AND SECOND CONJUGATION VERBS: PRESENT PASSIVE TENSE

In the reading passage you saw the form *parantur*, which you undoubtedly recognized from the forms of the verb *parō, parāre*. Its ending, however, is different from the endings that you already know. This form belongs to the **passive** voice.

Voice: the voice of the verb shows whether the subject is doing the action or is receiving the action.

> **Active voice**:   the subject is doing the action.
> Example: *Malī virī mala cōnsilia parant.*
>   Bad men are designing bad plans.

> **Passive voice**: the subject is not doing the action, but receiving the action.
> Example: *Mala cōnsilia ā malīs virīs parantur.*
>   Bad plans are being designed by bad men.

To form the present passive tense of a Latin verb, the personal endings of the passive voice (see below) are added to the stem of the verb in all persons except the first singular in which the passive ending *-r* should be added to the active first singular form.

Passive Endings

	Singular		Plural	
First person	**-r**	I	**-mur**	we
Second person	**-ris**	you	**-minī**	you
Third person	**-tur**	he/she/it	**-ntur**	they

BY THE WAY

The personal endings for the present passive of first and second conjugation verbs are identical. Just as in the active voice, the only difference between the two conjugations appears in the stem vowel. Remember: the predominant vowel in the first conjugation is a long *-ā-* and in the second conjugation a long *-ē-*.

First Conjugation: Present Passive

	Singular			Plural	
First person	par**or**	I am prepared		parā**mur**	we are prepared
Second person	parā**ris**	you are prepared		parā**minī**	you are prepared
Third person	parā**tur**	s/he/it is prepared		para**ntur**	they are prepared

Second Conjugation: Present Passive					
	Singular			**Plural**	
First person	teneor	I am held	tenē**mur**		we are held
Second person	tenēris	you are held	tenē**minī**		you are held
Third person	tenē**tur**	s/he/it is held	tene**ntur**		they are held

▶ EXERCISE 1

Identify the person and number of each verb and change into the passive voice.

Example: tenēs
second person singular   tenēris

1. vident
2. vocat
3. iubēmus
4. cūrātis

5. amō
6. dēbent
7. das
8. exspectat

VOCABULARY TO LEARN

NOUNS

auxilium, auxiliī, n. – help
cōnsilium, cōnsiliī, n. – plan, advice
epistula, epistulae, f. – letter
familia, familiae, f. – family, household
gaudium, gaudiī, n. – joy
lacrima, lacrimae, f. – tear

ADJECTIVES

longus, longa, longum – long
miser, misera, miserum – wretched, sad, miserable
pulcher, pulchra, pulchrum – beautiful, nice

VERBS

cōgitō, cōgitāre, cōgitāvī, cōgitātum – to think
doleō, dolēre, doluī, ——— – to feel pain, to be hurt
parō – to design (you already know the meanings "to prepare, to get ready")

ADVERBS

longē – far
semper – always

PREPOSITIONS

ā (ab) + ablative – by, from, away from
dē + ablative – about, concerning, down from

CONJUNCTIONS

nam – for, in fact
nōn sōlum . . . , sed etiam . . . – not only . . . , but also . . .
tamen – however

▶ EXERCISE 2

Find the English derivatives based on the Vocabulary to Learn in the list below. Write the corresponding Latin word.

misery   mini-series   malicious   malignant   mall
auxiliary   auction   counsel   constitution   pulchritude
pool   lacrosse   longitude   doll

▶ EXERCISE 3

Complete each sentence with the correct form of the word in parentheses and translate.

Example: Venēnum ā malīs virīs _____. (parō)
Venēnum ā malīs virīs parātur.   Poison is being prepared by bad men.

1. Epistula Terentiae ā Cicerōne (*ablative*) _____. (teneō)

2. Cicero est _____ et Terentia est _____. (miser)

3. Bona cōnsilia ā bonīs virīs _____. (parō)

4. Epistulae longae ā Cicerōne (*ablative*) _____. (exspectō)

5. Terentia in animō Cicerōnis (*genitive*) _____. (videō)

Bust of Cicero from the second century CE.

LANGUAGE FACT II

FIRST AND SECOND CONJUGATION VERBS: PRESENT PASSIVE INFINITIVE

In the reading passage there is a new form of the infinitive: *darī* ("to be given").

> *Auxilium ā bonīs virīs darī dēbet.*
> Help ought to be given by good men.

The present passive infinitive functions in a sentence just like the active infinitive, except that its meaning is passive.

Remember that the infinitive is a verb unlimited by a specific person. In English, the passive infinitive is expressed by putting the English verb form that usually (but not always) ends in *-ed* after the words "to be."

Compare the following active and passive infinitives in English:

Active:	**Passive:**
to love	to be loved
to warn	to be warned
to sing	to be sung
to hold	to be held

In Latin, the passive infinitive of the first two conjugations is formed by adding the ending **-rī** to the stem vowel of the verb.

Present Passive Infinitive

> *parārī* – to be prepared
> *tenērī* – to be held

Compare the present active and present passive infinitives.

	Present Active Infinitive	**Present Passive Infinitive**
First conjugation	parāre – to prepare	parārī – to be prepared
Second conjugation	tenēre – to hold	tenērī – to be held

▶ EXERCISE 4

Change all the active infinitives into the passive and translate the passive infinitives.

Example: parāre
parārī   to be prepared

1. cōgitāre
2. vocāre
3. habēre
4. amāre
5. dēbēre
6. vidēre
7. exspectāre
8. nārrāre

LANGUAGE FACT III

ABLATIVE OF AGENT

Look at this sentence from the reading passage:

> *Mala cōnsilia ā malīs virīs contrā mē parantur et auxilium mihi ā bonīs virīs darī dēbet.*
>
> Bad plans are being designed against me by bad men, and help ought to be given to me by good men (good men have to help me).

With the passive voice, the person who does the action is in the ablative case following the preposition *ā* or *ab*. This ablative is translated with the preposition "**by**."

If the same statement is made in the **active** voice, the ablative of agent becomes the nominative subject and the passive subject becomes the accusative direct object:

> *Malī virī mala cōnsilia contrā mē parant et virī bonī auxilium mihi dare dēbent.*
> Bad men design bad plans against me and good men ought to give me help.

STUDY TIP

Remember the three P's for the ablative of agent: Preposition, Person, Passive.

▶ EXERCISE 5

Change the active verbs into the passive and indicate the doer of the action with an ablative of agent. Translate the changed sentence. The Reading Vocabulary may be consulted.

Example: Puer puellam vocat.
Puella ā puerō vocātur.   The girl is being called by the boy.

1. Vir epistulam tenet.

2. Vir puellam amat.

3. Puer āthlētam nōn videt.

4. Terentia fīlium et fīliam cūrat.

5. Vir agricolae miserō auxilium dat.

6. Nauta fīlium cūrat.

LANGUAGE FACT IV
FIRST AND SECOND DECLENSION -*ER* ADJECTIVES

In the previous chapter you have seen the adjective *iūstus, iūsta, iūstum*, which matches the forms of nouns in the first and second declensions. Adjectives have all three genders because they **agree** in **case**, **number**, and **gender** with any noun they modify. Notice this sentence from the reading passage:

> *Tē ipsam, fīlium, fīliam pulchram bene cūrāre dēbēs.*
> You must take good care of yourself, of (our) son, of (our) beautiful daughter.

The adjective *pulchram* is feminine, singular, and accusative because it agrees with one of the direct objects of the sentence, *fīliam*—also feminine, singular, and accusative.

The adjective *pulcher, pulchra, pulchrum* has endings just like *iūstus, iūsta, iūstum*, except in the masculine nominative singular. It illustrates a sub-type of first and second declension adjectives, in which the masculine nominative singular ends in -*er*, but the -*e*- disappears in all other forms (much as in the noun *ager, agrī*).

First and Second Declension -*er* Adjectives

Singular

	Masculine	Feminine	Neuter
Nominative	pulcher	pulchra	pulchrum
Genitive	pulchrī	pulchrae	pulchrī
Dative	pulchrō	pulchrae	pulchrō
Accusative	pulchrum	pulchram	pulchrum
Ablative	pulchrō	pulchrā	pulchrō
Vocative	pulcher	pulchra	pulchrum

Plural

	Masculine	Feminine	Neuter
Nominative	pulchrī	pulchrae	pulchra
Genitive	pulchrōrum	pulchrārum	pulchrōrum
Dative	pulchrīs	pulchrīs	pulchrīs
Accusative	pulchrōs	pulchrās	pulchra
Ablative	pulchrīs	pulchrīs	pulchrīs
Vocative	pulchrī	pulchrae	pulchra

Another type of first and second declension -*er* adjective keeps the -*e*- in its stem. An example you encountered in Cicero's letter is *miser, misera, miserum*, meaning "wretched." *Miser* can be compared with the noun *puer*, because in both the -*e*- remains present in all forms.

First and Second Declension -*er* Adjectives

Singular

	Masculine	Feminine	Neuter
Nominative	miser	misera	miserum
Genitive	miserī	miserae	miserī
Dative	miserō	miserae	miserō
Accusative	miserum	miseram	miserum
Ablative	miserō	miserā	miserō
Vocative	miser	misera	miserum

Plural

	Masculine	Feminine	Neuter
Nominative	miserī	miserae	misera
Genitive	miserōrum	miserārum	miserōrum
Dative	miserīs	miserīs	miserīs
Accusative	miserōs	miserās	misera
Ablative	miserīs	miserīs	miserīs
Vocative	miserī	miserae	misera

BY THE WAY

The examples *pulcher, pulchra, pulchrum* and *miser, misera, miserum* show that you have to look to the nominative singular form of the feminine (and neuter) to see whether the base keeps its -*e*-. The spelling of English derivatives of -*er* words will also help you remember whether the Latin word keeps the -*e*-. For example, "pul**chr**itude," "mi**ser**y."

STUDY TIP

In -*er* adjectives and nouns
sometimes the word keeps the -*e*-
and sometimes sets it free.

► EXERCISE 6

Make the adjective agree with the noun and translate the new phrase.

Example: cōnsilia (malus)
cōnsilia mala

1. lacrimīs (miser)
2. viam (longus)
3. āthlētārum (pulcher)
4. virō (iūstus)
5. poētā (armātus)
6. patriā (pulcher)
7. vinculōrum (miser)
8. puerī (miser)
9. familiīs (bonus)
10. animus (māgnus)

This sign, attributed to Ciero (*sic*), in Latin *ut conclāve sine librīs, ita corpus sine animā*, may or may not actually be his words but are generally credited to him. It is the motto of the San Francisco Public Library.

► EXERCISE 7

Label each sentence as *vērum* (true) if it agrees or *falsum* (false) if it disagrees with the Latin reading passage at the beginning of the chapter. The Reading Vocabulary may be consulted.

1. Epistula ā fīliā Terentiae tenētur.

2. Cicero gaudium nōn habet.

3. Cicero Terentiam valdē amat.

4. Cicero malam fīliam et malum fīlium habet.

5. Auxilium bonōrum virōrum ā Cicerōne (*by Cicero*) exspectātur.

6. Mala cōnsilia contrā Cicerōnem (*accusative of Cicero*) nōn parantur.

7. Terentia longās epistulās dare nōn dēbet.

8. Fīlius et fīlia ā Terentiā cūrārī dēbent.

TALKING

Quid agis? "What are you doing?"

Quod est mūnus tuum? "What is your job?"

Discipulus sum. "I am a student (male)."

Discipula sum. "I am a student (female)."

Magister sum. "I am a teacher (male)."

Magistra sum. "I am a teacher (female)."

Quod mūnus habēre vīs? "What job do you want to have?"

Volō fierī . . . "I want to become . . ."

mūnus, n . – job

negotiātor/negotiātrix – businessman/businesswoman

custōs pūblicus – police officer

iūriscōnsultus, iūriscōnsultī, m./*iūriscōnsulta, iūriscōnsultae,* f. – lawyer

medicus, medicī, m./*medica, medicae,* f. – doctor (male/female)

artifex, m./f. – artist

DISCUSSING OCCUPATIONS

Marīa: Volō fierī iūriscōnsulta. Nam pater (*father*) est iūriscōnsultus. Iūriscōnsultī māgnam pecūniam (pecūnia, pecūniae, f. – *money*) habent.

Christīna: Ego fierī volō medica. Nōn sōlum iūriscōnsultī, sed etiam medicī māgnam pecūniam habent. Medicī tamen virīs et fēminīs (fēmina, fēminae, f. – *woman*), puerīs et puellīs auxilium semper dant. Ego volō cūrāre puerōs et puellās.

Helena: Ego dē pecūniā nōn cōgitō. Ego sum artifex et dē arte (*art*) cōgitō. Quod mūnus tū, Mārce, habēre vīs?

Mārcus: Ego sum āthlēta. Pater autem est astronauta (*astronaut*). In Californiā in caelō volābat (*flew in the sky*). Nunc Vasintōniae (*in Washington, D.C.*) habet mūnus in regimine pūblicō (*government*).

Puellae: Papae! (*Wow!*)

CHAPTER 6

Present Tense and Present Infinitive of *Sum* and *Possum*; Complementary Infinitive; Transitive and Intransitive Verbs

In Bellini's opera *Norma*, composed in the nineteenth century, the main character was Norma, a high priestess of the Druids and a leader to her people who were in a struggle against the occupying Romans. Norma, however, has secretly borne children to the Roman pro-consul. In this scene, Norma confesses her guilt to the Druids.

MEMORĀBILE DICTŪ

Iacta ālea est.

"The die is cast." (Suetonius, *The Life of Julius Caesar*, 33).

These words were reportedly said by Julius Caesar when he crossed the Rubicon River into Italy with his victorious armies after his conquest of Gaul, disregarding the Senate's order to disband his forces. The saying has become symbolic of the state of mind of a person who has made a fateful decision and is prepared to accept the outcome.

READING

Together with Mārcus Tullius Cicero, Gāius Iūlius Caesar (100–44 BCE) is a chief author of the classical epoch of Roman literature.

Two principal works of Caesar survive: one is his account of his own conquest of Gaul (*Dē bellō Gallicō*, "On the Gallic War"), the region that English speakers now call France; the other is his description of the civil conflicts in which he was the leader of the anti-senatorial faction (*Dē bellō cīvīlī*, "On the Civil War"). Though Caesar emerged victorious, and in virtual control of the Roman state, he was murdered by his enemies at the Theatre of Pompey, where the senate was meeting, on the famous Ides of March, 44 BCE. Caesar's works are a gold mine of information about the late Roman republic, and especially the impressive Roman military machine. He was also an excellent observer of the customs and habits of other peoples. In the passage below he describes the Druids, the high priests who constituted a ruling class in the Celtic society of the Gauls.

DĒ DRUIDIBUS

1   Inter Gallōs sunt virī māgnī quī vocantur Druidēs. Sacra Gallōrum ā
     Druidibus cūrantur. Druidēs ā Gallīs valdē timentur: nam auctōritātem
     māgnam habent, et dē virīs bonīs et malīs iūdicāre solent. Praemia et
     poenae ā Druidibus dantur. Vīta Gallōrum ā Druidibus cūrātur.

5   Propter Druidum scientiam māgnam multī puerī cum Druidibus diū
     manent. Puerī ā Druidibus discunt: Druidēs puerōs docent. Druidēs
     dē sacrīs scientiam māgnam habent, sed librōs et litterās nōn amant.
     Nam sacra Gallīs videntur esse māgna, sī in tenebrīs iacent. Itaque sacra
     Gallōrum nōn litterīs, sed memoriā servantur. Druidēs scientiam

10   māgnam memoriā servāre possunt. Itaque dum Druidēs exempla
     docent et fābulās nārrant, puerī memoriam firmant.

READING VOCABULARY

auctōritātem (accusative singular feminine) – authority

discunt – (they) learn

*doceō, docēre, docuī, doctum – to teach (sometimes both the thing taught and the person being taught are in the accusative case)

Druidēs, m. pl. – the Druids

Druidibus (ablative case) – Druids

Druidum (genitive case) – Druids

*dum (conj.) – while

*exemplum, exemplī, n. – example

*firmō, firmāre, firmāvī, firmātum – strengthen

Gallī, Gallōrum, m. pl. – the Gauls

*iaceō, iacēre, iacuī, —— – to lie down, to be inert

inter + accusative – among

*iūdicō, iūdicāre, iūdicāvī, iūdicātum – to judge

*liber, librī, m. – book

*littera, litterae, f. – letter of the alphabet; pl. literature, letter (epistle)

*maneō, manēre, mānsī, mānsum – to remain

*memoria, memoriae, f. – memory

*multus, multa, multum – much, many

poena, poenae, f. – punishment

*possum, posse, potuī, —— – to be able, can

*propter + accusative – because of, on account of

quī (masculine nominative pl.) – who

sacra, sacrōrum, n. pl. – religious rites

saepe (adv.) – often

scientia, scientiae, f. – knowledge

*servō, servāre, servāvī, servātum – to save, to preserve

sī – if

*soleō, solēre, solitus sum + infinitive – to be accustomed

*sum, esse, fuī, —— – to be

sunt (third person singular of *sum*) – there are

*tenebrae, tenebrārum, f. pl. – shadows, darkness

videntur – note that often (as here) the passive of *videō* means "to seem"

*vīta, vitae, f. – life

COMPREHENSION QUESTIONS

1. Why do the Gauls fear the Druids?

2. Why do many boys among the Gauls attach themselves to the Druids?

3. Why do the Druids make little use of books and writing?

4. How are the sacred rites of the Gauls preserved?

5. What faculty/skill must the students of the Druids develop with special care?

LANGUAGE FACT I

PRESENT TENSE AND PRESENT INFINITIVE OF *SUM*

In the passage at the beginning of this chapter, you met the word *sunt*, which means "they are." This is the present tense, third person singular of the verb "to be."

The forms of the verb "to be" are *sum, esse, fuī,* ——.

In previous chapters you have met other forms of this verb: *est*, "s/he/it is"; and *sum*, "I am."

In Latin, as in many languages, this verb is irregular. But in Latin, as in other languages, you cannot go far without knowing this very important verb. Here are the forms of *sum* in the present indicative, followed by the present infinitive:

Present Tense of *sum*

	Singular			Plural	
First person	sum	I am		sumus	we are
Second person	es	you are		estis	you are
Third person	est	s/he/it is / there is		sunt	they are / there are

Present Infinitive of *sum*

esse   to be

▶ EXERCISE 1

Translate into English. The Reading Vocabulary may be consulted.

1. Druidēs sunt virī māgnī.

2. Estis Druidēs: exempla bona docētis et fābulās nārrātis.

3. Nōn sumus Druidēs.

4. Vir iūstus sum.

5. Ego autem sum māgnus āthlēta.

6. Tū nōn es āthlēta; tū es poēta.

7. Liber est bonus.

VOCABULARY TO LEARN

NOUNS

exemplum, exemplī, n. – example

liber, librī, m. – book

littera, litterae, f. – letter of the alphabet; pl. literature, letter (epistle)

memoria, memoriae, f. – memory

tenebrae, tenebrārum, f. pl. – shadows, darkness

vīta, vītae, f. – life

ADJECTIVE

multus, multa, multum – much, many

VERBS

doceō, docēre, docuī, doctum – to teach

firmō, firmāre, firmāvī, firmātum – to strengthen

iaceō, iacēre, iacuī, —— – to lie down, to be inert

iūdicō, iūdicāre, iūdicāvī, iūdicātum – to judge

maneō, manēre, mānsī, mānsum – to remain

possum, posse, potuī, —— – to be able, can

servō, servāre, servāvī, servātum – to save, to preserve

soleō, solēre, solitus sum + infinitive – to be accustomed

sum, esse, fuī, —— – to be

ADVERB

saepe – often

PREPOSITION

propter + accusative – because of, on account of

CONJUNCTION

dum – while

Latin letters are engraved on this marble slab from Pompeii.

▶ EXERCISE 2

Find the English derivatives based on the Vocabulary to Learn in the following sentences. Write the corresponding Latin word. For some, there is more than one derivative in the sentence.

1. Please send this letter with a delivery confirmation.
2. She works in the conservation department of the museum.
3. We must hear what the essence of the problem is.
4. The garage is adjacent to the main building.
5. This is the largest library in the country.
6. In the past, many people did not go to school and remained illiterate.
7. Have you read the memorandum?
8. One multivitamin a day is recommended for good health.
9. I have a permanent license to park here.
10. There is a very potent agent in this prescription, which can be dangerous in an overdose.
11. They immediately checked for his vital signs in the hospital.

LANGUAGE FACT II

PRESENT TENSE AND PRESENT INFINITIVE OF *POSSUM*

In the text at the beginning of the chapter you also see *possum*, another important irregular verb:

> *Druidēs scientiam māgnam memoriā servāre possunt.*
>
> The Druids are able to preserve a large body of knowledge by means of memory.

The verb *possum* means "I can" or "I am able." Notice that in this sentence *possum* is joined with the infinitive of another verb (*servāre*): in a moment, you will take a closer look at this tendency of *possum* to join up with an infinitive.

Julius Caesar's head along with his name in Latin letters on a modern postage stamp from Italy.

Here are the forms of the present indicative of *possum* and its infinitive:

Present Tense of *possum*

	Singular			Plural	
First person	possum	I can, am able	possumus	we can, are able
Second person	potes	you can, are able	potestis	you can, are able
Third person	potest	s/he/it can, is able	possunt	they can, are able

Present Infinitive of *possum*

posse   to be able

STUDY TIP

The forms of the verb *possum* are nothing more than the root *pot-* (meaning "power-ful") with the forms of *sum* added to it, with *t* changing to *s* before another *s*.

▶ EXERCISE 3

Fill in the blanks with the correct form of *possum*. The subjects are indicated in parentheses. Translate the sentences. The Reading Vocabulary may be consulted.

Example: (Ego) iūdicāre nōn _____.
(Ego) iūdicāre nōn possum.   I cannot judge.

1. (Nōs/we) Puerōs docēre _____.

2. (Tū) Scientiam māgnam habēre _____.

3. (Ego) Memoriam firmāre _____.

4. (Illī/they) Sacra Gallōrum cūrāre nōn _____.

5. (Ille/he) Druidēs (accusative) amāre nōn _____.

6. (Tū) Druidēs timēre _____.

LANGUAGE FACT III

COMPLEMENTARY INFINITIVE WITH *POSSUM, DĒBEŌ, SOLEŌ*

Some Latin verbs, such as *possum*, do not usually appear by themselves.

The most common of these verbs are:

> *possum* – "I am able" (to do something)
> *dēbeō* – "I ought" (to do something)
> *soleō* – "I am accustomed" (to do something)

Such verbs often form phrases with a *complementary* infinitive that "fills out" their meaning.

There are clear examples of such phrases in the passage at the front of this chapter:

> *Druidēs . . . dē virīs bonīs et malīs iūdicāre solent.*
> The Druids are accustomed to make judgement about good and bad men.

> *Druidēs scientiam māgnam memoriā servāre possunt.*
> The Druids are able to preserve a large body of knowledge by means of memory.

BY THE WAY

Verbs (like *possum*, *dēbeō*, and *soleō*) that take a complementary infinitive can appear with either an active or passive infinitive.

For example: *Puella puerō librum dare potest*, "The girl can give the book to the boy," in the passive voice becomes *Liber puerō ā puellā darī potest*, "The book can be given to the boy by the girl."

▶ EXERCISE 4

Translate into Latin.

1. We are accustomed to preserve (our) books.

2. You (plural) ought not to fear the Druids (*Druidēs*).

3. Memory can be strengthened.

4. Stories are usually (are accustomed to be) told by the Druids (*Druidibus*).

5. We can have the rewards: rewards can be given by the Druids.

6. Boys ought to be taught.

LANGUAGE FACT IV
TRANSITIVE AND INTRANSITIVE VERBS

The verbs *sum* and *possum* have no passive forms because they are *intransitive*.

An intransitive verb describes a state of being or an action that takes no direct object (coming, going, and the like). Here are some other intransitive verbs, in addition to those you have already learned: *ambulō* ("walk"), *iaceō* ("lie down"), and *maneō* ("remain").

A *transitive* verb, by contrast, is a verb that takes a direct object and so can be used in the passive voice. Such verbs include: *dō* ("give"), *habeō* ("have"), *videō* ("see").

Julius Caesar writing his commentaries on the *Gallic War* and on the *Civil War*.

▶ EXERCISE 5

Identify the transitive and intransitive verbs in the following sentences and translate into English.

1. Epistulam puellae teneō.
2. In familiā sunt memoriae pulchrae.
3. Virī māgnī saepe in vinculīs iacent.
4. Auxilium ā bonīs virīs datur.
5. Fīliam et fīlium valdē amō.
6. Amīcus in memoriā semper manet.

▶ EXERCISE 6

Change the following sentences into the passive if the verb is active, and into the active if the verb is passive. Translate the changed sentence.

Example: Puer ā puellā exspectātur.
Puella puerum exspectat.   The girl expects the boy.

1. Auxilium ā bonīs āmīcīs datur.
2. Puella fābulam nārrat.
3. Familia ā puerīs amātur.
4. Poētae litterās iūdicant.
5. Mala cōnsilia ā Rōmānīs nōn parantur.

▶ EXERCISE 7

Read and understand the following sentences, then label each one as *vērum* (true), or *falsum* (false). The Reading Vocabulary may be consulted.

1. Inter Gallōs sacra ā Druidibus cūrantur.
2. Druidēs vītam Gallōrum cūrant.
3. Puerī Gallōrum nōn diū cum Druidibus manēre solent.
4. Druidēs sacra Gallōrum librīs et litterīs servāre solent.
5. Puerī ā Druidibus docentur.
6. Gallī memoriam firmāre possunt et dēbent.

The women of Gaul during Caesar's invasion of their country. By August Barthelemy Glaize (1807–1893).

TALKING

probātiō, f. – exam

exāmen, n. – exam

probātiuncula, probātiunculae, f. – quiz

Tollite calamōs. "Take up your pens."

In chartā vacuā scrībite. "Write on an empty piece of paper."

In chartā versā. "On the back of the paper."

In chartā rēctā. "On the front of the paper."

Probātiōnem subībis, subībitis "You/you (plural) will take an exam."

Notam optimam accipiēs. "You will get an excellent grade."

Nōlim in probātiōne cadere! "I don't want to fail the exam!"

PREPARING FOR A TEST

Magistra: Probātiunculam hodiē (*today*) subībitis.

Christīna: Cūr (*why*) probātiunculam hodiē subīre (*to take*) dēbēmus?

Magistra: Quia (*because*) scientiam (*knowledge*) memoriā servāre dēbētis. Nōnne litterās Latīnās (*Latin*) amās? (Nōnne amās? – *Don't you love?*)

Christīna: Litterās Latīnās amō.

Magistra: Itaque locum Caesaris (*passage of Caesar*) discere (*to learn*) dēbēs.

Christīna: In illō (*that*) locō Caesaris sunt multa verba (*words*) nova (*new*). Druidēs nōn sumus. Gallī nōn sumus. Scientiam māgnam et multa verba memoriā servāre nōn solēmus.

Magistra: Locum Caesaris iam (*already*) memoriā tenēs! Es discipula (*student*) bona! Estisne (*are you . . . ?*), discipulī, nunc parātī (*prepared*)?

Discipulī: Parātī sumus.

Magistra: Tollite calamōs. In chartīs vacuīs scrībite. In chartā versā nōmina vestra (*your names*) scrībite.

VOCABULARY TO KNOW

NOUNS

auxilium, auxiliī, n. – help

bellum, bellī, n. – war

castra, castrōrum, n. pl. – camp

cōnsilium, cōnsiliī, n. – plan, advice

dolus, dolī, m. – trickery, deception

epistula, epistulae, f. – letter

exemplum, exemplī, n. – example

familia, familiae, f. – family, household

gaudium, gaudiī, n. – joy

lacrima, lacrimae, f. – tear

liber, librī, m. – book

littera, litterae, f. – letter of the alphabet; pl. literature, letter (epistle)

memoria, memoriae, f. – memory

praemium, praemiī, n. – reward

tenebrae, tenebrārum, f. pl. – shadows, darkness

venēnum, venēnī, n. – poison

vinculum, vinculī, n. – chain, fetter

vīta, vītae, f. – life

ADJECTIVES

armātus, armāta, armātum – armed

bonus, bona, bonum – good

iūstus, iūsta, iūstum – legitimate, open, just

longus, longa, longum – long

māgnus, māgna, māgnum – large, great, important

malus, mala, malum – bad

miser, misera, miserum – wretched, sad, miserable

multus, multa, multum – much, many

praeclārus, praeclāra, praeclārum – famous, distinguished

pulcher, pulchra, pulchrum – beautiful, nice

Rōmānus, Rōmāna, Rōmānum – Roman

VERBS

cōgitō, cōgitāre, cōgitāvī, cōgitātum – to think

dō, dăre, dedī, dătum – to give

doceō, docēre, docuī, doctum – to teach

doleō, dolēre, doluī, —— – to feel pain, to be hurt

firmō, firmāre, firmāvī, firmātum – to strengthen

iaceō, iacēre, iacuī, —— – to lie down, to be inert

intrō, intrāre, intrāvī, —— – to enter

iubeō, iubēre, iussī, iussum + accusative + infinitive – to order somebody to do something

iūdicō, iūdicāre, iūdicāvī, iūdicātum – to judge

maneō, manēre, mānsī, mānsum – to remain

parō – to design (you already know the meanings "to prepare, to get ready")

possum, posse, potuī, —— – to be able, can

servō, servāre, servāvī, servātum – to save, to preserve

soleō, solēre, solitus sum + infinitive – to be accustomed

sum, esse, fuī, —— – to be

ADVERBS

longē – far

saepe – often

semper – always

PREPOSITIONS

ā (ab) + ablative – by, from, away from

ad + accusative – into, towards, to

dē + ablative – about, concerning, down from

ē (ex) + ablative – from, out of

in + accusative – into, to, against

propter + accusative – because of, on account of

CONJUNCTIONS

autem – however

dum – while

nam – for, in fact

nōn sōlum . . . , sed etiam . . . – not only . . . , but also . . .

sed – but

tamen – however

▶ EXERCISE 1

Decline the following nouns.

1. *exemplum, exemplī,* n. – example

2. *gaudium, gaudiī,* n. – joy

▶ EXERCISE 2

Conjugate the following verbs in the passive voice. Give the Latin passive infinitive with its meaning for each verb.

1. *servō, servāre, servāvī, servātum*

2. *firmō, firmāre, firmāvī, firmātum*

3. *doceō, docēre, docuī, doctum*

4. *habeō, habēre, habuī, habitum*

▶ EXERCISE 3

Fill in the blanks with the correct form of the adjectives in parentheses and translate each sentence.

Example: Virōs _____ vidēre possum. (armātus)

Virōs armātōs vidēre possum.   I am able to see armed men.

1. Dē praemiō _____ cōgitāre possumus. (māgnus)

2. Familiae _____ auxilium damus. (miser)

3. Praemium virīs _____ datur. (bonus)

4. Dē fīliā _____ semper cōgitō. (pulcher)

5. Virī _____ memoria librīs servātur. (iūstus)

6. Rōmānōrum _____ vīta litterīs servārī potest. (praeclārus)

Weapons and utensils from the late republican era of ancient Rome. These are the types of weapons with which Roman soldiers of that time would have been armed.

▶ EXERCISE 4

Change the following active sentences into the passive by using the ablative of agent. Translate the changed sentence.

Example: Fābricius virō praemium nōn dat. (Fābricius, Fābriciī, m.)
Virō praemium ā Fābriciō nōn datur.   A reward is not being given to the man by Fabricius.

1. Vir Rōmānus epistulam Terentiae nunc tenet. (Terentia, Terentiae, f.)

2. Fābricius virōs armātōs vocat.

3. Virī malī mala cōnsilia parant.

4. Puerī memoriam firmant.

5. Virī praeclārī patriae auxilium dant.

6. Virī iūstī patriam cūrant.

▶ EXERCISE 5

Translate the verbs in parentheses and change the present tense verb to a complementary infinitive. Translate the changed sentence.

Example: Agrum amīcīs damus. (we can)
Agrum amīcīs dare possumus.   We can give the field to (our) friends.

1. Propter memoriam multa exempla servantur. (they can)

2. Exempla animum firmant. (they are accustomed)

3. Praemium virō nōn datis. (you [plural] ought)

4. Epistulās Terentiae exspectō. (I am accustomed)

5. Poētae praeclārī sumus. (we can)

6. Puerōs docent. (they are accustomed)

▶ EXERCISE 6

After translating this passage, list on paper all the transitive and intransitive verbs.

The following passage is adapted from Cicero's speech *Prō Archiā*. Here Cicero argues that the Greek poet Archias is entitled to Roman citizenship because of his literary merits, extolling the study of literature as well as the special talents of Archias himself.

In librīs sunt exempla multa et bona. Propter litterās bona exempla in tenebrīs nōn iacent. Exempla dantur ā virīs iūstīs quōrum (*whose*) vīta librīs servātur. Dum patriam cūrō, virōs praeclārōs videō, quōrum memoria litterīs tenētur. Propter litterās virī iūstī et bonī et praeclārī in vītā manent et mē vocant. Auxilium et cōnsilia litterīs dantur. Animus litterīs semper firmātur. Litterae nōbīscum (*with us*) domī sunt, sunt nōbīscum in agrīs, manent nōbīscum in viā . . .

Transitive verbs: **Intransitive verbs:**

The remains in the Roman Forum of the Basilica of Maxentius, marked by the three arches seen in the picture. This basilica, built between 308 to 312 CE, served, like most basilicas during ancient Roman times, as a courthouse and meeting hall. Today the word "basilica" usually refers to a church in which the architectural plan is similar to the ones used in ancient basilicas.

As you learned in Unit 1, Jupiter and Juno were children of Rhea and Cronus, who had four more children: Neptune, Pluto, Vesta, and Ceres. All six of these children are regarded as the generation of older Olympian gods. The three male siblings divided the universe among themselves, with Jupiter taking the heaven, Neptune the ocean, and Pluto the underworld.

The famous Trevi Fountain in Rome with a statue of Neptune in its central niche.

NEPTUNE

Neptune, who was known by the Greeks as Poseidon, was the brother of Zeus, lord of the seas. Neptune also controlled earthquakes on land. He is often represented with his three-pronged trident. Neptune was said to inhabit the ocean with his wife Amphitrite, an Oceanid, one of the daughters of the Ocean himself. The depths of the ocean were reported to house many sea creatures. Among them were nymphs called Nereids and the "old man of the sea," named Proteus, who was able to change his form constantly. According to legend, Neptune, together with the mortal Cleito, sired the royal dynasty of the blessed island Atlantis. Ancient tales about the disappearance of this island, an event that ancient authors connect with the spread of human vice, continue to fascinate contemporary archaeologists who still search for it in various underwater locales.

PLUTO AND THE UNDERWORLD

The Greeks imagined a world of three stories: the plain of the earth, surrounded by the river of the ocean; the vault of heaven, which, on the cloudy peaks of Mount Olympus, was the abode of the gods; and the gloomy region of the underworld where dead souls dwelt. They also conceptualized a place even deeper than the underworld itself: a black pit beneath it called Tartarus, where the special enemies of the gods were imprisoned.

It was believed by the Greeks that when people died, their souls descended to the underworld. Near its entrance awaited Charon, a greedy old man who transported the souls in a ferry across the river Acheron (or Styx) to the underworld itself. Since Charon required a fee for this ride, it was customary to place a coin under the tongue of a dead person. The soul of a person who could not pay, or who had not received a proper burial, would wander perpetually without rest.

The ruler of the underworld was Hades, or Pluto, the brother of Jupiter and Neptune. Pluto is represented as a stubborn old man, whose hat could make him invisible, just as the approach of

Sculpture of Neptune in a fountain in the Piazza della Signoria in Florence, Italy. By Bartolomeo Ammanati (1511–1592).

death itself is often invisible. Pluto was thought to reign in the kingdom of the shadows with his wife Proserpina, called Persephone in Greek.

While the souls of most humans, both good and evil, dwelt more or less in the same part of the underworld and endured a similar shadowy existence, a few notorious wrongdoers were doomed to an eternity of punishment. Among them was Tantalus, condemned to stand in a pool of water, with luscious fruits hanging over his head. Whenever he wanted to eat or

Charon rowing his skiff across the river Acheron (or Styx) in the underworld.

drink, the tree with the fruits moved its branches upward, and the water in the pool receded, thereby "tantalizing" him with perpetual thirst and hunger. Similarly, Sisyphus was condemned to roll a boulder to the top of a mountain, only to see it roll back every time he pushed it to the peak. The crimes of these unfortunate individuals involved challenging the power of the gods and attempting to exceed human limitations.

VESTA

In ancient Roman culture, Vesta was the goddess of the hearth and the household, identified with the Greek goddess Hestia. Yet Hestia was a minor deity in the Greek pantheon and had no place among the Olympian gods. By way of contrast, Vesta and her cult were extremely important in Roman society, for she was regarded as embodying the sanctity of family and home. Vesta had a round temple in the heart of Rome, one of the earliest Roman buildings to survive intact.

Her temple contained a sacred flame, symbolic of the hearth, which was carefully tended so it would never be extinguished. A group of priestesses known as Vestal Virgins were in charge of the flame and temple. Girls of good character having both parents living qualified as candidates to enter the service of Vesta. They were chosen by the Pontifex Maximus (highest priest) at no later than the age of ten, and had to swear that they would remain virgins for the next thirty years. Anyone who let the sacred fire go out was beaten, and a violation of the vow of chastity was punished by being buried alive. The Vestals were highly respected, given many privileges, and were very influential when intervening on someone's behalf.

The Vestal Virgins lived in a large imposing house in the Roman Forum itself. The pool in the photograph is part of the peristylium complex of their house. Just beyond the house the three columns in a row are remnants of the Temple of Castor and Pollux while the white building to the right is the reconstructed Temple of Vesta.

CERES

Ceres is the Latin name given to the Greek Olympian goddess Demeter, and she was thought to be a sister of Jupiter and Juno. The English word "cereal" is derived from her name, and a stalk of grain was her symbol. She was a goddess of vegetation, of the earth's creative power, and of agriculture. She is also depicted as suffering painfully over her separation from her daughter, Proserpina. Ancient authors relate that Pluto, the ruler of the underworld, abducted Proserpina when she was picking flowers with other young girls in Sicily, and made her his wife and queen over the dead. For many days Ceres wandered the earth, searching for her daughter in vain, and consumed by deep grief. Finally, the Sun God, who had witnessed Proserpina's abduction, pitied Ceres and told her where her daughter had been taken. Although it was too late for Ceres to get Proserpina

back, for she had eaten some pomegranate seeds in the underworld, a compromise was arranged whereby Proserpina would spend part of each year with her mother, and part with her husband. According to classical mythology, Proserpina's return to her mother brings spring and the rebirth of vegetation, but autumn and the death of the earth's greenery results when she descends back to Hades. In this way the ancients used the myth of Ceres and Proserpina to explain the origin of the seasons.

In this votive relief from 440 BCE Demeter is seen handing a sheaf of grain to Triptolemus, a son of the family who received her kindly during her search. Persephone is also carved on this relief.

READ THE FOLLOWING PASSAGE

Cerēs in terrīs ambulat. Cerēs Proserpinam fīliam vidēre nōn potest et Proserpinam quaerit. Proserpina tamen ā Plutōne in tenebrīs tenētur. Animus deae valdē dolet. Dea terram cūrāre nōn potest et terra est misera.

Tum Iuppiter iubet: "Proserpina per sex mēnsēs in terrā manēre dēbet et per sex mēnsēs in tenebrīs."

Cerēs terram per sex mēnsēs cūrat et terra est pulchra. Dum autem fīlia est cum Plutōne, terra ā deā nōn cūrātur.

quaerit – seeks
Cerēs, f. – Ceres
dea, deae, f. – goddess
per sex mēnsēs – for six months

Plutōne (ablative) – Pluto
Proserpina, Proserpinae, f. – Proserpine
tum (adv.) – then

CONNECTING WITH THE ANCIENT WORLD

ROMAN MARRIAGE

In Chapter 5 you read correspondence between members of a Roman family in the form of a letter from Cicero to his wife Terentia. The Latin word *familia*, from which we derive "family," encompassed not only what we call the nuclear family, headed by the father, or *paterfamiliās* (*familiās* is an archaic form of *familiae*), but also the slaves that they owned. In the privileged households that Roman sources most often describe marriages were arranged for Roman girls in their early teens to young men in their early twenties. When a *paterfamiliās* promised his daughter to a bridegroom, she was said to have become *spōnsa*, "engaged," from the verb *spondeō*, "to promise solemnly." A man who became engaged (*spōnsus*), sent his betrothed a ring, which—like all Roman rings—was worn on the finger next to the little finger of the left hand.

A bride gets ready for her wedding in this fresco from the Villa of the Mysteries in Pompeii, first century CE.

Setting a date for the wedding had its complications, since the ceremonies could not take place during the many Roman festivals, or in the month of May (which was said to bring bad luck). The traditional and most strict form of a Roman marriage was called the *cōnfārreātiō*, which included a ritual consecrating of a special bread—*fār* is a kind of grain—to Jupiter. This most solemn event took place in the presence of the Pontifex Maximus and ten witnesses. Another ritual was called *coēmptiō*, i.e., "buying," which probably reflected the financial arrangements entailed in funding a marriage. *Coēmptiō* was one method by which a Roman wife came under the legal control of her husband, which the Romans called *manus*, "hand." Another was through the process of *ūsus*, in which the wife remained married to her husband for a continuous year.

Various Latin literary works portray the members of a Roman wedding party carrying torches and shouting obscene verses, which were supposed to promote fertility. The bride wore a long white robe and a bright saffron veil. A hair-net and shoes were of the same color. Her hair was fashioned like that of the

Vestal Virgins with three curls hanging down on each side of the face. The Roman historian Livy (*Ab Urbe Conditā*, 1.9) explains the practice of shouting "Talassiō" in his account of how the earliest Romans acquired brides by inviting the neighboring Sabines to a festival, and then abducting their daughters. According to his narrative, one of the Romans abandoned his efforts to seize a particular woman when he heard this phrase: it means "she is reserved for Talassius," the name of another, presumably wealthier and more powerful, man.

After the wedding, once the groom carried the bride over the threshold, under one form of Roman marriage she passed from her father's into her husband's control; the technical expression for this form of marriage was *cum manū, manus* being the Latin term for "hand" or "control." Married Roman women were called *mātrōnae*, which means "women entitled to be mothers of legitimate children." Compared to women in Greek society, particularly those in fifth-century BCE Athens, Roman women had a good deal of autonomy in social and economic matters.

Sculpture of Sabine women being abducted by the early Romans. By Giambologna in 1583.

EXPLORING ROMAN FAMILIES

PARENTS AND CHILDREN THEN AND NOW

In the modern world, there are many laws that protect children from neglect and compel parents to look after their offspring. Fathers and mothers must provide financial support and cannot just abandon babies on the steps of a church or in an alleyway. Parenthood is easy to prove with documents like birth certificates and DNA evidence. But in the ancient world, children were not kept from harm by the state; indeed, they were entirely at the mercy of their fathers, who could choose whether or not to raise them and who could retain complete control over their children, even in adulthood.

When a Roman child was born in the parents' house, the baby was laid at the feet of the father, who would show his acceptance of the child as his own by picking the infant up. If he chose to reject the child, he had no further responsibility; the child might have been fortunate enough to have been raised by the slaves in the household or unlucky enough to be left to die on a wooded hillside outside of the city. There were no formal accommodations, like orphanages or adoptive homes, for unwanted babies, although surely sometimes arrangements must have been made with childless couples. While today citizenship is automatically granted to all people born in the United States, only children born to Roman citizen parents, both father and mother, and accepted by their fathers were Roman citizens from birth.

This funerary bust from Palmyra, Syria, features a husband holding a scroll, and his wife with a spindle and distaff in her hands. The inscription is in Greek.

Much time and effort is spent today deciding on names for babies. Books and websites are dedicated to the possibilities, and every relative and friend has a suggestion to offer. But a Roman baby had no name at first and was called *pūpa* or *pūpus*, girl or boy baby, until the eighth or ninth day after birth (eight for girls; nine for boys). Many babies did not live to see their naming day; in fact, without the type of healthcare the modern world has developed with vaccinations and antibiotics, more than thirty percent of Roman babies died before they were a year old, and children had only a fifty percent chance of living to the age of ten. But if the child did survive to see the *diēs lustricus*, the family gathered to bestow its name and to give the baby *crepundia*, little metal trinkets strung as a necklace that the child would wear around the neck and whose rattling would amuse the infant and might even serve as identification if the child should become lost. No fingerprints or GPS sneakers for the Romans! On this day a child also began to wear a *bulla* (which means "bubble" in Latin), a round locket that contained an amulet to protect the child from evil spirits. If the family was wealthy, the *bulla* would be made of gold, and it clearly marked the child of an important father, and so someone not to be harmed without penalty. Children of the lower classes wore *bullae* made of leather. A boy was also protected by the *genius* (guardian spirit) of the *gēns* (clan), a part of which was born with him and stayed with him for life; in fact, his birthday would be celebrated as a festival of his *genius* to whom offerings of food and drink and flowers would be made to insure his continued presence. A similar spirit called a *Iūnō* watched over a girl.

The firstborn boy of an upper class family would have been given the same three names as his father—a *praenōmen*, the clan name (or *nōmen*) and a *cognōmen*, but all girls were named the feminine form of their clan name—Iūlia, Cornelia, Claudia. Following this tradition, Mārcus Tullius Cicero named his daughter Tullia and his son Mārcus Tullius Cicero. Formal distinctions were made between daughters with the use of *māior* and *minor* for two girls and *prīma*, *secunda*, *tertia*, etc. for more than two; day-to-day confusion must have been avoided by the use of nicknames for the girls and for the son who shared the name of the *paterfamiliās*, just as today a boy named for his father might be called Junior or Buddy.

While Roman parents did have ultimate responsibility for a child's welfare, in a wealthy family daily care was seen to by the child's *nūtrix*, or nurse, who often knew the child better than its parents and was considered a part of the *familia*, much like a nanny might be today. Indeed, the word *familia* in Latin indicates many more people than a modern American family, which generally includes only parents and children, although sometimes grandparents or other blood relatives may live in the same house and share in caring for the children. But a Roman *familia* also consisted of the household slaves, both adults and children owned by the *paterfamiliās*, and perhaps even some of his freedmen.

Young children spent their time at home, learning to read and write along with the other children of the household, both slave and free, and playing with toys, dolls, balls, hoops, dice, and gaming boards or pet dogs, birds, or even monkeys. Cats as pets were late arrivals in Rome (first century CE), following the conquest of Egypt, where they were revered. Roman mothers oversaw this early training, particularly moral instruction, and they made sure that their children were not exposed to any evils that might corrupt their characters.

Sculpture of the head of a young Roman boy.

When boys were seven years old, it was time for more formal education. Unlike modern times when many countries offer education for all children at no charge, Roman schooling was available only to those who could afford to pay the fees, in the same way that parents must now pay tuition if they wish to send their children to private schools. Only boys went to school, but since at seven a boy was too young to go off into the world alone, his parents assigned him a *paedagōgus* (from the Greek word παιδαγωγός meaning "child-guider,") who would take him to and from school and oversee his studies. Even though the *paedogōgus* was a slave, he could punish his charge for failing to pay attention! Once a boy had honed his skills in reading, writing, and arithmetic—the same subjects taught today in elementary schools—he began to study history, philosophy, literature, and rhetoric, all things he would need to know to have a successful political career. Science and mathematics were not part of a Roman education, since these subjects were used only by workmen doing physical labor—constructing buildings, ships, roads, etc.—none of which was considered a suitable career for a well-to-do Roman man. When not in school, a Roman boy spent time with his father, watching how he conducted business and dealt with his clients.

This plaster cast preserves the first century CE body of young man who had worked as a muleteer. Tradition holds that he was found near an entrance gate to Pompeii. The plaster cast of his crouching figure was moved to a building along the forum which protects a variety of finds like the amphorae that surround him.

While educational and career opportunities for women in the United States are virtually the same as those for men, there are many countries even today in which such equality is far from reality. Roman girls had few educational opportunities since they were required to remain at home and learn household management from their mothers—weaving and overseeing the work of the family's slaves. In much the same way, children of the lower classes were trained in whatever trade their parents practiced—as farmers or bakers or fish sellers—and probably began working at the family business as soon as they were physically able to do so. Indeed, all Roman children, wealthy or poor, followed the same life path as their parents, much as in modern times when children are often groomed to work in and eventually take over family businesses.

Childhood for girls often ended rather quickly, since they could marry as early as twelve years of age, although they were more likely to be fourteen or fifteen. A *paterfamiliās* chose his son-in-law, based on the economic or political advantage a union between his household and that of the groom might bring him. On her wedding day, a girl removed her *bulla* and dedicated it along with her toys, the symbols of childhood, to the *Larēs*, the household gods, and left her parents' house to become part of her husband's household (although during the empire, it was not unusual for a woman to remain a part of her father's *familia*, despite her marriage).

Another type of ceremony marked a boy's coming of age: his assumption of the *toga virīlis*. While it could come as early as the age of fourteen, most boys did not make the transition until the age of sixteen. In the morning on the appointed day, just as his married sister had done, a boy placed his *bulla* at the altar of the *Larēs* along with his *toga praetexta* (a bordered toga that marked him as a freeborn male child) and then assumed the white toga of a Roman citizen. A procession composed of family friends, clients, slaves, freedmen, and relatives then accompanied him to the Forum where his name was entered on the role of citizens, much like registering to vote today at the age of eighteen. Today, coming of age means financial and legal independence, but despite his new position as a fully recognized Roman man, a man's father continued to hold formal control over his son's life and finances (if he chose to exercise it) until the day he died, when his son finally assumed the role of *paterfamiliās* of his own household.

JACQUELINE CARLON
Assistant Professor of Classics
University of Massachusetts
Boston, Massachusetts

MĪRĀBILE AUDĪTŪ

PHRASES, MOTTOES, AND ABBREVIATIONS RELATING TO LIFE IN THE TWENTY-FIRST CENTURY

PHRASES

- Annuit coeptīs. "He has nodded favorably on our beginnings." Taken from Vergil's *Georgics*, this inscription is found on the one dollar bill.

- Caveat ēmptor. "Let (may) the buyer beware!" A common warning in commerce.

- Dē factō. "In practice."

- In vitrō. "In a glass."

- Quid prō quō? "What for what?" A favor for a favor, "tit for tat."

- Sine quā nōn. A shorter phrase expressing the concept of *condiciō sine quā nōn*, "a necessary condition," and literally meaning "without which not."

- Status quō. "The condition in which <things are now>."

- Tempus fugit. "Time flees." An inscription often found on clocks.

- Urbī et Orbī. "To the City <of Rome> and to the World." The title of the Pope's address to the world on Easter and Christmas.

- Vice versā. "Conversely," "the opposite."

MOTTOES

- Semper parātus. "Always ready." Motto of the US Coast Guard.

Notice on the one dollar bill the Great Seal of the United States, which contains on top of the eye above the pyramid the Latin phrase *Annuit Coeptīs* and below the pyramid another set of Latin words, *Novus Ordo Saeclōrum*, or "A New Order of Ages."

Written on a blackboard, this Latin phrase that means "Let the buyer beware" should be heeded by all who are about to purchase something.

ABBREVIATIONS

- @ The symbol @, which is used in e-mail addresses, comes from the Latin medieval abbreviation of *apud*, "at," "at the home of."

- etc. An abbreviation for *et cētera*, "and other things."

- P.S. An abbreviation for *post scrīptum*, "written afterwards or below," an item added below the signature to a letter.

This symbol, once used only occasionally in financial matters, is now commonplace and seen in e-mail addresses regularly.

A loving couple on a fresco from Pompeii.

MEMORĀBILE DICTŪ

Ōdī et amō.

"I hate and I love." (Catullus, 85)

The Roman poet Catullus wrote these contradictory words in line one of poem 85 to express his conflicted and painful feelings about his beloved.

READING

Gāius Valerius Catullus (who lived from approximately 84 to 54 BCE) is one of the greatest Latin poets, and the best known among the neoteric, or "new" poets of the first century BCE. They modeled their works and literary personalities on those of Greek writers from the Hellenistic era (third and second centuries BCE). Among them is Callimachus, best remembered for the phrase *Mega biblion, mega kakon,* "a big book is a big evil."

Catullus also places a distinctive stamp on what he writes by giving voice to his own emotions, frankly and often bawdily. Many of his poems treat his passionate and often painful love affair with a woman whom he calls "Lesbia," in homage to the literary achievements and sensibilities of the sixth century BCE Greek female poet Sappho. The name "Lesbia" is evidently a metrically equivalent pseudonym for Clodia, a Roman matron from a politically powerful family.

Several historical figures from the turbulent period in which he lived—Caesar and Cicero among them—figure in Catullus' poems, both those in lyric meters and those in the elegiac couplet.

His elegies greatly influenced the love poetry of Propertius, Tibullus, and Ovid, who wrote during the principate of Augustus (27 BCE–14 CE), and whose work in turn had a major impact on the romantic poetry of the Middle Ages. Like Catullus, they characterize erotic passion as a form of enslavement, referring to the female beloved with the term *domina,* meaning "mistress of slaves." So, too, they emphasize the obstacles to the fulfillment of their desires, ranging from jealous husbands and rivals to locked doors and other forms of physical separation.

DĒ AMŌRE

1   Puella mea passerem habet. Ō, passer, dēliciae meae puellae! Cum passere puella mea lūdit, passerem tenet, passerī digitum dat, digitus ā passere mordētur. Puella nārrat sē passerem amāre. Puella passerem plūs quam oculōs amat. Nam passer est mellītus. Catullus videt

5   passerem esse semper in gremiō puellae. Passer ad dominam semper pīpiat. Catullus tamen vult cum puellā esse et ā puellā amārī. Itaque Catullus passerī invidet. Tū, puella, Catullum amāre dēbēs, nōn passerem. Senēs autem sevērī putant puellam Catullum amāre nōn dēbēre. Verba senum, puella, ūnīus assis aestimāre possumus. Nam vīta

10   nōn est longa.

READING VOCABULARY

ā passere (ablative singular) – by the sparrow

*aestimō ūnīus assis – I do not care a bit (as, assis, m. is the Latin word for a small copper coin)

*aestimō, aestimāre, aestimāvī, aestimātum – to regard, esteem

*amor, amōris, m. – love

Catullus, Catullī, m. – Catullus

*dēliciae, dēliciārum, f. pl. – delight, pet

*digitus, digitī, m. – finger

*domina, dominae, f. – mistress

*gremium, gremiī, n. – lap

*invideō, invidēre, invīdī, invīsum + dative – to envy someone

lūdit – plays

mellitus, mellīta, mellītum – sweet as honey

*meus, mea, meum – my

mordeō, mordēre, momordī, morsum – to bite

nārrat sē passerem amāre – tells that she loves the sparrow

ō (interjection) – oh!

*oculus, oculī, m. – eye

*passer, passeris, m. – sparrow

passerī (dative singular) – to the sparrow

pīpiō, pīpiāre, ——, —— – to chirp

plūs quam – more than

putant puellam . . . dēbēre – think that the girl should . . .

*putō, putāre, putāvī, putātum – to think, consider

*sē (reflexive pronoun, accusative) – she/he (in an indirect statement)

senēs (nominative plural) – old men

*senex, senis, m. – old man

senum (genitive plural) – of the old men

*sevērus, sevēra, sevērum – serious, strict, severe

*verbum, verbī, n. – word

videt passerem esse – sees that the sparrow is

vult – wants

*Words marked with an asterisk will be need to be memorized.

COMPREHENSION QUESTIONS

1. How does the poet feel about the girl's pet bird? Why?

2. Who is in the way of the poet's and the girl's love?

3. What is the poet's reason for his impatience to enjoy love?

LANGUAGE FACT I

THIRD DECLENSION MASCULINE AND FEMININE NOUNS

You have already learned the ending patterns of nouns belonging to the first and second declensions. In the reading passage for this chapter, you saw nouns belonging to the third declension. Their forms are new and distinctive: for example, *amōre, passerem, senum*.

For a noun of the third declension **there is no difference in the case endings between masculine and feminine nouns**. Therefore, the gender of each new noun of this type must be learned along with its meaning.

Third Declension Masculine and Feminine Nouns				
	Singular		**Plural**	
Nominative	passer	the sparrow	passer**ēs**	the sparrows
Genitive	passer**is**	of the sparrow	passer**um**	of the sparrows
Dative	passer**ī**	to/for the sparrow	passer**ibus**	to/for the sparrows
Accusative	passer**em**	the sparrow	passer**ēs**	the sparrows
Ablative	passer**e**	by/with the sparrow	passer**ibus**	by/with the sparrows
Vocative	passer	o, sparrow	passer**ēs**	o, sparrows

STUDY TIP

The nominative singular form of third declension nouns follows no regular pattern, but the stem is easy to find: look at the genitive singular form and remove the ending **-is**. For this reason the genitive singular and the nominative singular should always be learned together.

▶ EXERCISE 1

Find all the third declension nouns in the Latin reading passage. Identify the case and number of each form. If the same noun occurs more than once, write it only once.

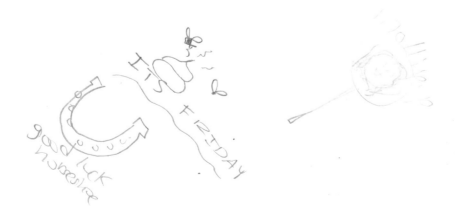

VOCABULARY TO LEARN

NOUNS

amor, amōris, m. – love

dēliciae, dēliciārum, f. pl. – delight, pet

digitus, digitī, m. – finger

domina, dominae, f. – mistress

gremium, gremiī, n. – lap

oculus, oculī, m. – eye

passer, passeris, m. – sparrow

pāx, pācis, f. – peace

senex, senis, m. – old man

soror, sorōris, f. – sister

verbum, verbī, n. – word

PRONOUN

sē (reflexive pronoun, accusative) – s/he (her/him-self)/they (themselves) in an indirect statement

ADJECTIVES

meus, mea, meum – my (a possessive adjective)

sevērus, sevēra, sevērum – serious, strict, severe

stern

VERBS

aestimō, aestimāre, aestimāvī, aestimātum – to regard, to esteem

aestimō ūnīus assis – I do not care a bit

invideō, invidēre, invīdī, invīsum + dative – to envy someone

putō, putāre, putāvī, putātum – to think, to consider

A coin called an *as* was among those that held the least value for Romans. Nero's head is on one side of this coin.

▶ EXERCISE 2

Find the English derivatives based on the Vocabulary to Learn in the following sentences. Write the corresponding Latin word.

1. The whole dinner was delicious.

2. Throughout my college years, I was always a member of the same sorority.

3. Senior citizens can purchase tickets at a discount price.

4. The story is about an amorous relationship.

5. We are equipped with digital technology.

6. A strong pacifist movement developed in the country.

7. Can I have an estimate for this repair?

8. This is the dominion of a dark power.

9. We have a verbal agreement.

10. Don't be so severe with me!

11. I bought myself a new computer.

▶ EXERCISE 3

Decline the following noun.

1. *soror, sorōris,* f. – sister

▶ EXERCISE 4

Translate into Latin.

1. I have beautiful sisters.
2. Many are the tears of love.
3. We do not fear peace.
4. The girl is being taken care of by the sister.
5. The poet envies the sparrow.
6. The old men envy the poet.
7. The poet tells the old men a story.

 STUDY TIP

Note that the rules of agreement for nouns and adjectives apply to any noun, regardless of declension: any adjective modifying a noun of the third declension will agree with the noun in case, number, and gender.

▶ EXERCISE 5

Make the adjective agree with the noun and translate the phrase into English.

1. praemium (māgnus)
2. sorōribus (pulcher)
3. amōrī (miser)
4. senis (armātus)
5. lacrimās (multus)
6. senum (sevērus)
7. passerēs (miser)
8. pācis (iūstus)

LANGUAGE FACT II

INDIRECT STATEMENT: ACCUSATIVE AND INFINITIVE

In the chapter reading you notice some sentences with a new construction.

> *Catullus videt passerem esse semper in gremiō puellae.*
> Catullus sees that the sparrow is always on the girl's lap.

In Latin, **verbs of saying** (e.g., *nārrō* "I report [that] . . ."), **thinking** (e.g., *putō* "I think [that] . . ."), and **observing** (e.g., *videō*, "I see [that] . . .") appear with a construction called an **indirect statement**. While a *direct* statement is an exact quotation of someone's words, perceptions, thoughts, or words, an *indirect* statement indirectly reports these thoughts or words. In English, the conjunction "that" commonly follows such verbs. Classical Latin, however, has no conjunction equivalent to "that." Instead, the subject of the indirect statement becomes the **accusative** (not nominative), and the verb of the indirect statement becomes an **infinitive**.

Look more closely at the previous example. The direct statement would be:

> *Passer est semper in gremiō puellae.*
> The sparrow is always on the girl's lap.

After the main verb *videt* (a verb of observing) introduces the statement indirectly, the nominative subject of the direct statement (*passer*) becomes the accusative subject of the indirect statement (*passerem*), and the verb *est* becomes the infinitive *esse*.

> *Catullus videt passerem esse semper in gremiō puellae.*
> Catullus sees that the sparrow is always on the girl's lap.

If the **subject of the infinitive** is also the **subject of the main verb**, then the accusative *sē* (called a reflexive pronoun because it refers back to the subject) is used as the subject in the indirect statement. For a good example of this, look at another sentence from the chapter reading:

> *Puella nārrat sē passerem amāre.*
> The girl reports that she (herself) loves the sparrow.

The direct statement would be:

> *Passerem amō.*
> I love the sparrow.

In this sentence, the first person subject of the direct statement becomes third person (just as in English) and is expressed as accusative *sē,* which is translated "s/he/they (herself/himself/themselves)." The verb of the direct statement then becomes an infinitive.

If there is a **predicate nominative** in the direct statement, this predicate becomes **accusative** too, in agreement with the subject of the indirect statement. Look at this sentence:

The dove was a bird sacred to Venus, goddess of love. A mosaic from Pompeii.

> *Puella putat passerem esse mellītum.*
> The girl thinks that the sparrow is sweet as honey.

The direct statement would be:

> *Passer est mellītus.*

The predicate nominative *mellītus* becomes accusative *mellītum* in the indirect statement.

BY THE WAY

In a direct statement, the subject of a verb is often expressed in Latin by the verb ending alone (e.g., *damus* for "we give"). But in an indirect statement the accusative subject (e.g., *sē*) is typically expressed in Latin. Why? The answer is simple: the infinitive lacks personal endings, so another word is needed to express the subject!

Find one more indirect statement in the Latin reading passage.

▶ EXERCISE 6

Translate into English. The Reading Vocabulary may be consulted.

1. Catullus videt passerem ā puellā amārī.

2. Poēta nārrat passerem digitum puellae mordēre.

3. Catullus nārrat sē passerī invidēre.

4. Puella putat sē passerem plūs quam Catullum amāre.

5. Catullus putat sē puellam plūs quam oculōs amāre.

6. Catullus putat vītam nōn esse longam.

Sparrows and other small birds in ancient times, like now,
can be quite tame and become like a pet.

▶ EXERCISE 7

Change the following direct statements into indirect statements using the accusative and infinitive construction. The Reading Vocabulary may be consulted.

Example: Puella nārrat: "Passer digitum mordet."
Puella nārrat passerem digitum mordēre

1. Vir cōgitat: "Oculī puellae sunt pulchrae."
2. Poēta nārrat: "Puella ā familiā amātur."
3. Catullus videt: "Puella dēliciās amat."
4. Puella putat: "Passer est pulcher."
5. Poēta cōgitat: "Doleō."
6. Senēs nārrant: "Vīta nōn est semper pulchra."
7. Poēta et puella putant: "Malae fābulae ā senibus nārrantur."

TALKING

Ēsuriō. "I am hungry."

Bene tibi sapiat! Bene vōbīs sapiat! "Bon appetit!" (singular and plural)

Quid comedēs . . . ? "What are you going to eat . . . ?"

Vīsne comedere (+ accusative)? "Do you want to eat . . . ?"

Vīsne bibere (+ accusative)? "Do you want to drink . . . ?"

Volō comedere . . . "I want to eat . . ."

Da mihi, quaesō (a word in accusative) "Give me, please, . . ."

Grātiās tibi agō! "Thank you."

Libenter! "Not at all, gladly done."

Quōmodo sapit? "How does it taste?"

Bene. Optimē. Male. "Well. Excellent. Bad."

Sum bene sagīnātus/sagīnāta. "I ate well (male/female)."

cibus, cibī, m. – food

Mexicānus, Mexicāna, Mexicānum – Mexican

sapidus, sapida, sapidum – delicious

pānis, pānis, m. – bread

pānis īnfersus – sandwich

lac, lactis, n. – milk

īsicium, īsiciī, n. *Hamburgēnse* – hamburger

pōtiō, pōtiōnis, f. *Arabica* – coffee

carō, carnis, f. – meat

piscis, piscis, m. – fish

māla, mālōrum, n. pl. *terrestria* – potatoes

lactūca, lactūcae, f. – lettuce

acētāria, acētāriōrum, n. pl. – salad

pasta, pastae, f. – pasta

placenta, placentae, f. *Neāpolitāna* – pizza

mālum, mālī, n. – apple

banāna, banānae, f. – banana

crūstulum, crūstulī, n. – cookie

thermopōlium, thermopōliī, n. – cafeteria

Romans often bought food or beverages from establishments like this *thermopōlium* in Herculaneum. They would line up at the fast-food counter to make their purchases quickly.

IN THE CAFETERIA

Mārcus: Salvē, Marīa!

Marīa: Salvē, Mārce!

Mārcus: Quid comedēs? Vīsne comedere banānam?

Marīa: Volō comedere nōn sōlum banānam, sed etiam īsicium Hamburgēnse. Nam valdē ēsuriō. Quid tū comedēs?

Mārcus: Ego volō comedere pānem īnfersum.

Christīna et Helena: Salvēte, Mārce et Marīa!

Christīna: (*TO THE WAITER*) Da mihi, quaesō, placentam Neāpolitānam. Grātiās tibi agō.

Mārcus: Quōmodo placenta Neapolitāna sapit?

Christīna: Bene. Quōmodo pānis īnfersus sapit?

Mārcus: Optimē. Cibus est sapidissimus (*very delicious*). Sum bene sagīnātus.

Helena: Nārrās, Mārce, cibum esse sapidissimum. Sed ego volō comedere cibum Mexicānum. Placentam Neāpolitānam et īsicium Hamburgēnse unīus assis aestimō.

Marīa: Hīc (*here*) nōn est cibus Mexicānus.

Helena: Tum tantum crūstula comedere volō. Nam crūstula valdē amō.

Mārcus: (*TO HIMSELF*) Ego tē, Helena, amō. Volō (*I want*) tē esse meam puellam . . .

CHAPTER 8

Third Conjugation Verbs: Present Active and Passive Tense, Present Active and Passive Infinitive; Ablatives of Manner, Instrument, Separation, Place from Which, Place Where; Accusative of Place to Which

This head is a detail from the fifth century BCE statue of Themistocles.

MEMORĀBILE DICTŪ

Melius in umbrā pugnābimus!

"We will fight better in the shade!" (Frontinus, *Stratagems*, 4)

When King Xerxes of Persia invaded Greece in 480 BCE, he was defeated by the Athenians both on the sea and then on land. But this would not have occurred so quickly if not for the Spartan king Leonidas. Warned that the Persians would shoot so many arrows that they would blot out the sunlight, Leonidas replied with this phrase. His tiny band of men held off the Persians in Thermopylae's narrow pass, until an informant showed the Persians a path behind the Greeks' position. Surrounded, the three hundred Spartans died, fighting to the last man.

READING

Cornēlius Nepos (ca. 100–ca. 25 BCE) wrote a book of short biographies about famous Greeks, and some Romans, entitled *Dē virīs illūstribus* ("About famous men"). Nepos' style is simple, and his open-minded attitude is apparent in the preface to *Dē virīs illūstribus*, in which he refuses to condemn certain Greek customs that were not approved of by the Romans.

Here is a passage adapted from Nepos' life of Themistocles, the Athenian leader whose cunning strategy not only helped to advance Athens to leadership in the Greek world in the fifth century BCE, but also helped the united forces of the Greek cities to defeat the immense invasion of Greece by the Persian king Xerxes in 480 BCE. Xerxes had come to Greece with so many soldiers that legend says they drank the rivers dry . . .

THEMISTOCLĒS GRAECŌS SERVAT

1 Themistoclēs est Athēniēnsium dux et homō valdē callidus. Xerxēs rēx
Persārum contrā Graecōs bellum cum māgnā industriā parāre dīcitur.
Xerxēs multōs mīlitēs et multās nāvēs habet et cum multīs virīs armātīs
ad Graeciam nāvigat. Athēniēnsēs bellum timent et ōrācula Pȳthiae
5 petere dēcernunt. Pȳthia Delphīs habitat et cōnsilia Apollinis
hominibus dat. Pȳthia haec verba Athēniēnsibus in templō Delphicō
dīcit: "Athēniēnsēs mūrīs ligneīs servārī possunt." Sōlus Themistoclēs
sē cōnsilium Apollinis intellegere putat. Mūrōs ligneōs esse nāvēs dīcit.
Athēniēnsēs verba Themistoclis esse bona putant. Ā terrā suā fugiunt,
10 sed multās nāvēs aedificant. Tunc nāvēs Persārum māgnā fortitūdine
oppugnant et Persās vincunt. Athēniēnsēs timōre līberantur.

READING VOCABULARY

aedificō, aedificāre, aedificāvī, aedificātum – to build

Apollō, Apollinis, m. – Apollo

Athēniēnsēs – the Athenians

Athēniēnsium (genitive plural) – of the Athenians

callidus, callida, callidum – clever, cunning

*contrā + accusative – against

*dēcernō, dēcernere, dēcrēvī, dēcrētum – to decide, determine (often + infinitive)

Delphicus, Delphica, Delphicum – belonging to Delphi, Delphic

Delphīs – at Delphi

*dīcō, dīcere, dīxī, dictum – to say

*dux, ducis, m. – leader, general

*fortitūdō, fortitūdinis, f. – courage

fugiunt – they flee

Graecia, Graeciae, f. – Greece

Graecus, Graeca, Graecum – Greek (Graecī, Graecōrum, m. pl. – the Greeks)

haec (neuter plural) – these

*homō, hominis, m. – man (i.e., human being); pl. people

industria, industriae, f. – industry, care

*intellegō, intellegere, intellēxī, intellēctum – to understand

*līberō, līberāre, līberāvī, līberātum (+ accusative + ablative) – to free (someone from something)

ligneus, lignea, ligneum – wooden

*mīles, mīlitis, m. – soldier

mūrus, mūrī, m. – wall

nāvēs, f. (nominative and accusative plural) – ships

*nāvigō, nāvigāre, nāvigāvī, nāvigātum – to sail, voyage

oppugnō, oppugnāre, oppugnāvī, oppugnātum – to attack

*ōrāculum, ōrāculī, n. – oracle

Persae, Persārum, m. – the Persians

*petō, petere, petīvī, petītum – to seek, head for, go to, rush at

Pȳthia, Pȳthiae, f. – the Pythian priestess, responsible for uttering the ambiguous oracles at the shrine of Apollo at Delphi, in Greece

*rēx, rēgis, m. – king

sōlus, sōla, sōlum – sole, only

suā – their own (agreeing with terrā)

*tandem (adv.) – at last

*templum, templī, n. – temple

Themistoclēs, Themistoclis, m. – Themistocles

*timor, timōris, m. – fear

*tunc (adv.) – then

*vincō, vincere, vīcī, victum – to conquer, defeat

Xerxēs, Xerxis, m. – Xerxes, the great king of the Persians, who invaded Greece in 480 BCE

*Words marked with an asterisk will need to be memorized.

COMPREHENSION QUESTIONS

1. What are Xerxes' intentions?

2. What do the Athenians do before undertaking anything against Xerxes?

3. Why is Pythia's answer enigmatic?

4. Was Pythia's advice effective?

LANGUAGE FACT I

THIRD CONJUGATION VERBS: PRESENT ACTIVE AND PASSIVE TENSE, PRESENT ACTIVE AND PASSIVE INFINITIVE

Look at the verbs in the Latin reading passage. You will notice that some forms—*dīcitur, petere, dēcernunt, dīcit, intellegere, vincunt*—do not follow the patterns of the first and second conjugations. These verbs belong to the third conjugation.

Remember: the stem of first conjugation verbs ends in *-ā-*, and the stem of second conjugation verbs ends in *-ē-*. The stem of the third conjugation ends in *-e-*, which changes to *-i-* in front of *-s, -t, -m,* and to *-u-* in front of *-nt*. The first person singular passive is formed by adding *-r* to the first person singular active.

Here are the present active and passive forms of the third conjugation:

Third Conjugation: Present Active

		Singular			Plural
First person	petō	I seek		petimus	we seek
Second person	petis	you seek		petitis	you seek
Third person	petit	s/he/it seeks		petunt	they seek

Present Active Infinitive

petere   to seek

Third Conjugation: Present Passive

		Singular			Plural
First person	petor	I am sought		petimur	we are sought
Second person	peteris	you are sought		petiminī	you are sought
Third person	petitur	s/he/it is sought		petuntur	they are sought

Present Passive Infinitive

petī   to be sought

Note that the present passive infinitive of the third conjugation verbs is quite new: the ending *-ī* is attached to the stem minus the *-e*.

STUDY TIP

Note that the *e* before the infinitive ending *-re* in the second conjugation is long (*ē*), but the *e* before the infinitive ending *-re* in the third conjugation is short (*e*).

► EXERCISE 1

Translate into Latin.

1. it is thought
2. we are prepared
3. you (plural) are ordered
4. to become accustomed
5. you judge
6. we teach
7. they understand
8. they are sought
9. you (plural) conquer
10. to be regarded

VOCABULARY TO LEARN

NOUNS

dux, ducis, m. – leader, general

fortitūdō, fortitūdinis, f. – courage

homō, hominis, m. – man (i.e., human being); (pl.) people

mīles, mīlitis, m. – soldier

ōrāculum, ōrāculī, n. – oracle

rēx, rēgis, m. – king

templum, templī, n. – temple

timor, timōris, m. – fear

VERBS

dēcernō, dēcernere, dēcrēvī, dēcrētum – to decide, determine (often + infinitive)

dīcō, dīcere, dīxī, dictum – to say

intellegō, intellegere, intellēxī, intellēctum – to understand

līberō, līberāre, līberāvī, līberātum (+ accusative + ablative) – to free someone from something

nāvigō, nāvigāre, nāvigāvī, nāvigātum – to sail, voyage

petō, petere, petīvī, petītum – to seek, head for, go to, rush at

vincō, vincere, vīcī, victum – to conquer, defeat

ADVERBS

tandem – at last

tunc – then

PREPOSITION

contrā + accusative – against

▶ EXERCISE 2

Match the English word with the corresponding Latin word.

duchy	līberō
fortitude	nāvigō
human	petō
decree	contrā
dictum	intellegō
intelligent	dēcernō
liberated	dīcō
navigation	timor
petition	rēx
contrary	ōrāculum
military	mīles
oracular	homō
regal	dux
timorous	fortitūdō

▶ EXERCISE 3

Conjugate the following verb in the active and passive voice. Give the active and passive infinitives.

1. *intellegō, intellegere, intellēxī, intellēctum*

LANGUAGE FACT II

ABLATIVES OF MANNER, INSTRUMENT (MEANS), SEPARATION, PLACE FROM WHICH

Go back again to the reading passage at the beginning of this chapter and notice the way the ablative case is used in these passages:

A. *Xerxēs rēx Persārum contrā Graecōs bellum cum māgnā industriā parāre dīcitur.*
Xerxes, king of the Persians, is said to prepare war against the Greeks with great care.

Tunc nāvēs Persārum māgnā fortitūdine oppugnant.
Then, with great courage, they attack the ships of the Persians.

In both these sentences an ablative noun describes the way in which an action took place. This is called the **ablative of manner**. The preposition *cum* is very frequently used with this meaning of the ablative: in fact *cum* is always used if the noun is not modified by an adjective (e.g., *cum fortitūdine*), and the preposition is optional if the noun does have an adjective agreeing with it, as in the two previous examples.

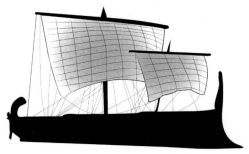

A drawing of a Greek warship.

> **B.** *Athēniēnsēs mūrīs ligneīs servārī possunt.*
> The Athenians can be saved by means of wooden walls.

Here, *with no preposition*, the **ablative of instrument** (also called the **ablative of means)** describes the means or instrument by or with which an action is performed.

Note the difference between this ablative and the **ablative of agent,** which indicates by what *person* something is done. An ablative of agent *always* follows the preposition *ā/ab*.

> **C.** *Athēniēnsēs timōre līberantur.*
> The Athenians are freed from fear.

This type of ablative, the **ablative of separation,** is used with verbal expressions of freeing, lacking, and separation. The ablative of separation usually appears without a preposition, but sometimes the prepositions *ā/ab, dē,* or *ē/ex* are used. Active transitive verbs that take the ablative of separation can take an accusative object as well: e.g., *Athēniēnsēs timōre līberō* (I am freeing the Athenians [accusative] from fear [ablative]). The ablative of separation is closely related in meaning and use to the **ablative of place from which**; the latter, however, almost always appears with a preposition: e.g., *Ā terrā suā fugiunt . . .* (They flee from their land . . .).

BY THE WAY

Because these closely related ablatives describe the circumstances attending/accompanying the action of the verb, they can be called "adverbial," and are all examples of the ablative functioning as the "adverbial" case. The meanings implied in the ablative are more or less conveyed by the English prepositions "by," "with," and "from."

Leonidas and his three hundred men at Thermopylae. By Jacques-Louis David (1748–1825).

▶ EXERCISE 4

Change each sentence by putting the noun in parentheses into the ablative case, keeping the same number. A preposition may or may not be needed. Translate the sentence and identify the type of ablative in each sentence. The Reading Vocabulary may be consulted.

Example: Graecī servantur. (dux)
Graecī ā duce servantur.   ablative of agent   The Greeks are being saved by the general.

1. Praemium meum exspectō. (gaudium)

2. Multōs miserōs senēs vidēre possum. (oculī meī)

3. Nautae fābulam nārrant. (lacrimae multae)

4. Persās exspectāre possumus. (fortitūdō)

5. Animus māgnus nōn vincitur. (tenebrae)

6. Iūstī hominēs līberārī dēbent. (vincula)

7. Ad castra ambulāmus. (casa)

▶ EXERCISE 5

Translate into Latin.

1. We seek the oracles with joy.

2. You are not freed from war.

3. We teach the boys and girls by means of rewards.

4. The wretched people are being held by chains.

5. You are expecting the soldiers of the Persians with great fear.

LANGUAGE FACT III

ABLATIVE OF PLACE WHERE; ACCUSATIVE OF PLACE TO WHICH

You know the ablative of "place from which." Now consider how to indicate "place where" and "place to which." In fact you already have an idea how this is done, since expressions of these relationships have appeared in your readings without comment. Look again at these sentences from the passage at the beginning of this chapter:

> *Xerxēs . . . cum multīs armātīs ad Graeciam nāvigat.*
> Xerxes with many armed men is sailing to Greece.

"Place to which" is expressed by the accusative case, usually with the prepositions *ad* or *in*.

STUDY TIP

Note that the word "to" is used in English with more than one meaning. This word is found where Latin would use the dative of indirect object, as in the sentence "I give the book **to** the boy." But "to" is also used to indicate motion towards a place, as in the sentence "I walk **to** the temple." This distinction in meaning should be kept in mind.

> *Pȳthia haec verba Athēniēnsibus in templō Delphicō dīcit.*
> The Pythian priestess says these words to the Athenians in the Delphic temple.

"Place where" is expressed by the **ablative case** with the preposition ***in***.

A reproduction of the face of the Delphic Sibyl, called Pythia. The original picture was painted on the Sistine Chapel ceiling by Michelangelo.

The remains of the sanctuary of Athena at Delphi.

▶ EXERCISE 6

Translate the following questions. Then choose the best answer for each and translate. The Reading Vocabulary may be consulted.

1. Quō (to/towards what place) ambulant Athēniēnsēs?

> Ad templum Delphicum ambulant Athēniēnsēs.
>
> Ex templō Delphicō ambulant Athēniēnsēs.
>
> In templō Delphicō ambulant Athēniēnsēs.

2. Quō (to/towards what place) rēx Persārum nāvigat?

    Ē Graeciā rēx Persārum nāvigat.

    Ad Graeciam rēx Persārum nāvigat.

    In Graeciā rēx Persārum nāvigat.

3. Unde (from where) rēx Persārum nāvigat?

    Ad Asiam (Asia) rēx Persārum nāvigat.

    Ex Asiā rēx Persārum nāvigat.

    In Asiā rēx Persārum nāvigat.

4. Ubi (where) bellum exspectant Athēniēnsēs?

    In castrīs bellum exspectant Athēniēnsēs.

    Ex castrīs bellum exspectant Athēniēnsēs.

    Ad castra bellum exspectant Athēniēnsēs.

5. Ubi manēre nōn possunt Athēniēnsēs?

    In terrā manēre nōn possunt Athēniēnsēs.

    Ad terram manēre nōn possunt Athēniēnsēs.

    Ē terrā manēre nōn possunt Athēniēnsēs.

6. Quō (to/toward what place) Athēniēnsēs nāvigant?

    In marī (the sea) Athēniēnsēs nāvigant.

    Ē terrā Athēniēnsēs nāvigant.

    Ad nāvēs Persārum Athēniēnsēs nāvigant.

TALKING

merenda, merendae, f. – snack

merendō, merendāre – to have a snack

pila, pilae, f. – ball

tabula (tabulae, f.) *subrotāta* – skateboard

tēlevīsiō, tēlevīsiōnis, f. – television

tēlevīsōrium, tēlevīsōriī, n. – television set

pēnsum domesticum perficere – to do homework

pilā lūdere – to play ball

Quid post merīdiem faciēs? "What are you going to do in the afternoon?"

tabulā subrotātā vehī – to ride a skateboard

tēlevīsiōnem spectāre – to watch TV

tēlevīsōrium accendere – to turn on the TV

tēlevīsōrium exstinguere – to turn off the TV

Vīsne + infinitive "Do you want . . . ?"

Volō + infinitive "I want to . . . ."

AFTER SCHOOL ACTIVITIES

Marīa: Salvē, Mārce! Quid post merīdiem faciēs?

Mārcus: Tabulā subrotātā vehī volō. Quid tū faciēs?

Marīa: Pēnsum domesticum perficere dēbeō.

CHRISTINE APPROACHES.

Mārcus: Salvē, Christīna! Quid post merīdiem faciēs?

Christīna: Tēlevīsiōnem spectāre volō.

Mārcus: Vīsne mēcum (*with me*) tabulā subrotātā vehī? Tēlevīsōrium accendere posteā (*after-wards*) poteris (*you will be able*).

Christīna: Ita vērō! (*Yes indeed!*) Volō tēcum (*with you*) tabulā subrotātā vehī.

HELEN APPROACHES.

Mārcus: Salvē, Helena! Quid post merīdiem faciēs?

Helena: Pilā lūdere volō, deinde merendāre.

Mārcus: Vīsne mēcum et cum Christīnā tabulā subrotātā vehī? Pilā lūdere et merendāre posteā poteris.

Helena: Ita vērō! Volō vōbīscum (*with you*) tabulā subrotātā vehī. Et quid tū, Marīa, faciēs?

Marīa: Pēnsum domesticum perficere dēbeō.

Helena: Heu! Heu! (*Oh! Oh!*) Dēbēs nōbīscum (*with us*) tabulā subrotātā vehī! Pēnsum domesticum perficere posteā poteris.

Marīa: Ita vērō! Bene dīcis. Pēnsum domesticum perficere posteā poterō (*I will be able*). Ubi (*where*) sunt tabulae subrotātae?

CHAPTER 9

Fourth Conjugation Verbs: Present Active and Passive Tense, Present Active and Passive Infinitive; Third Declension Neuter Nouns; Third Declension *I*-stem Nouns

A painting by Cesare Maccari (1840–1919) of Cicero denouncing Catiline in the Senate House.

MEMORĀBILE DICTŪ

Ō tempora, ō mōrēs!

"O, the times, o, the customs!" (Cicero, *Against Catiline* 1.1)

Cicero exclaimed these words in perhaps his most famous speech, in which he denounced Catiline—Lūcius Sergius Catilīna—for having conspired to overthrow the Roman republic.

READING

Gāius Sallustius Crispus (86–35/34 BCE), whom we call Sallust, is the first great Roman historian writing in Latin whose works survive. He wrote *Dē coniūrātiōne Catilīnae* ("About the Plot of Catiline") and *Bellum Iugurthīnum* ("The Jugurthine War"). Catiline was a bankrupt Roman politician who conspired to overthrow the republic. Jugurtha was a usurper of the kingdom of Numidia in North Africa supported by bribed Roman officials. Sallust thought the main source of these upheavals was the decline of Roman morality in the mid-first century BCE. He bitterly describes Rome as "a city for sale and doomed to quick destruction, if it should ever find a buyer."

The following text is an adaptation from Sallust's book about Catiline. The conspirators had planned uprisings and massacres in Rome, supported by their revolutionary army camped in Etruria. Catiline tries to cover up the plot, but he encounters an unexpectedly vigorous accuser . . .

DĒ CONIŪRĀTIŌNE CATILĪNAE

1　Urbs permovētur. In locum pācis et gaudiī veniunt timor et trīstitia. Hominēs miserī ambulant, nēminī crēdunt, valdē timent. Clāmōrēs mulierum in urbe audiuntur.

　　Animus Catilīnae mala cōnsilia parat. Catilīna tamen in cūriam
5　intrat, sellam petit, sē tamquam bonus vir gerit. Tunc Mārcus Tullius Cicero cōnsul longam et lūculentam ōrātiōnem in cūriā habet. Cicero māgnā fortitūdine nārrat Catilīnam esse virum malum et cīvibus Rōmānīs mortem parāre. Cicero dīcit sē posse armīs Rōmānōs servāre et Catilīnam ab urbe Rōmā sēmovēre. Catilīna audit et terram spectat.
10　Tandem Catilīna dīcit patrēs nōn dēbēre verba Cicerōnis audīre. Patrēs tamen verba Cicerōnis audiunt et urbem servāre dēcernunt.

Finally Catiline fled from Rome to his army in Etruria. The army was defeated and Catiline was killed in the battle.

READING VOCABULARY

*arma, armōrum, n. pl. – weapons

*audiō, audīre, audīvī, audītum – to hear, listen

Catilīna, Catilīnae, m. – Catiline

*cīvis, cīvis, m./f. – citizen

clāmor, clāmōris, m. – shout, cry

coniūrātiō, coniūrātiōnis, f. – plot

*cōnsul, cōnsulis, m. – consul

*crēdō, crēdere, crēdidī, crēditum + dative – to believe somebody

cūria, cūriae, f. – senate (building)

*gerō, gerere, gessī, gestum – to carry; sē gerit – s/he behaves

locus, locī, m. – place

lūculentus, lūculenta, lūculentum – splendid

Mārcus Tullius Cicero (Cicerōnis, m.) – Marcus Tullius Cicero

*mors, mortis, f. – death

*mulier, mulieris, f. – woman

nēminī – to nobody

*ōrātiō, ōrātiōnis, f. – speech; ōrātiōnem habeō – make a speech

pater, patris, m. – father, senator (senators were called fathers because they were originally the "elders" of the leading families)

permoveō, permovēre, permōvī, permōtum – to perturb

sella, sellae, f. – seat, chair

sēmoveō, sēmovēre, sēmōvī, sēmōtum – to remove

spectō, spectāre, spectāvī, spectātum – to look at

tamquam (adv.) – as if

trīstitia, trīstitiae, f. – sadness

*urbs, urbis, f. – city (usually the city of Rome)

*veniunt – come

*Words marked with an asterisk will need to be memorized.

COMPREHENSION QUESTIONS

1. What was the situation in Rome during the times Sallust is describing?

2. What were Catiline's intentions?

3. By whom was Catiline discredited?

4. Why was it not easy to discredit Catiline?

LANGUAGE FACT I

FOURTH CONJUGATION VERBS: PRESENT ACTIVE AND PASSIVE TENSE, PRESENT ACTIVE AND PASSIVE INFINITIVE

In the narrative about Catiline there are a number of verbs belonging to the third conjugation: e.g., *crēdunt*, *petit*, *gerit*, *dīcit*. Notice also the form *audit*, which seems similar to the third conjugation verbs, but actually belongs to the fourth. If you look at the infinitive *audīre*, and the forms *audiunt* and *audiuntur*, you will understand that this certainly is not a third conjugation verb.

Here are the present active and passive voices of the fourth conjugation, using the verb *audīre* as an example:

Fourth Conjugation: Present Active

		Singular			Plural
First person	audiō	I hear		audīmus	we hear
Second person	audīs	you hear		audītis	you hear
Third person	audit	s/he/it hears		audiunt	they hear

Present Active Infinitive

audīre   to hear

Fourth Conjugation: Present Passive

		Singular			Plural
First person	audior	I am heard		audīmur	we are heard
Second person	audīris	you are heard		audīminī	you are heard
Third person	audītur	s/he/it is heard		audiuntur	they are heard

Present Passive Infinitive

audīrī   to be heard

STUDY TIP

The fourth conjugation is formed as usual by adding the personal endings to the verb stem. The linking vowel *-u-* appears only in the third person plural, just as in the third conjugation.

BY THE WAY

The verbs of the fourth conjugation are not very numerous, especially compared with the third and first conjugations. Here are three more important verbs:

> sciō, scīre, scīvī, scītum – to know
> sentiō, sentīre, sēnsī, sēnsum – to feel, realize
> veniō, venīre, vēnī, ventum – to come

▶ EXERCISE 1

Find one more fourth conjugation verb in the Latin reading passage. Identify the person and number and whether the form is active or passive.

VOCABULARY TO LEARN

NOUNS

animal, animālis, n. – animal

arma, armōrum, n. pl. – weapons

caput, capitis, n. – head

cīvis, cīvis, m./f. – citizen

cōnsul, cōnsulis, m. – consul

corpus, corporis, n. – body

exemplar, exemplāris, n. – example

mare, maris, n. – sea

mors, mortis, f. – death

mulier, mulieris, f. – woman

ōrātiō, ōrātiōnis, f. – speech; ōrātiōnem habeō – make a speech

tempus, temporis, n. – time

urbs, urbis, f. – city (usually the city of Rome)

VERBS

audiō, audīre, audīvī, audītum – to hear, listen

crēdō, crēdere, crēdidī, crēditum + dative – to believe somebody

gerō, gerere, gessī, gestum – to carry; sē gerit – s/he/it behaves

sciō, scīre, scīvī, scītum – to know

sentiō, sentīre, sēnsī, sēnsum – to feel

veniō, venīre, vēnī, ventum – to come

Roman body armor.

► EXERCISE 2

Find the English derivatives based on the Vocabulary to Learn in the following sentences. Write the corresponding Latin word.

1. There was a heated debate about capital punishment.
2. We insist on keeping our civil rights.
3. What is the meaning of this gesture?
4. The audience received the speaker enthusiastically.
5. He is always buying on credit.
6. I could only find a temporary position.
7. Corporal punishment is banished from our schools.
8. He behaved with exemplary courage.
9. The rate of mortality has dropped significantly.
10. There is urban poverty in this area of the country.
11. Our troops are better armed than our adversaries.
12. You need to apply for a visa at the consulate.
13. This agency works for the protection of animals.
14. Science has made vast improvements in our lives.
15. Let us go to the marina and watch the boats!
16. Cicero was famous for his oratory.
17. The letter I received from my friend was very sentimental.

► EXERCISE 3

Translate into English.

1. scītur
2. venīre
3. sciunt
4. sciuntur
5. venīmus
6. scīminī
7. scit
8. scīrī

▶ EXERCISE 4

Fill in the blanks in the second sentence by using the verb from the first sentence, but change the form to complete the meaning. Translate the changed sentence. The Reading Vocabulary may be consulted.

Example: Hominēs clāmōrēs mulierum audiunt. Clāmōrēs mulierum _____.
Clāmōrēs mulierum audiuntur.   Women's cries are being heard.

1. Catilīna Cicerōnem audit. Cicero ā Catilīna _____.

2. Mulierēs timōrem sentiunt. Timor ā mulieribus _____.

3. Patrēs in cūriam veniunt. Patrēs in cūriam _____ solent.

4. Patrēs verba Cicerōnis audīre dēbent. Verba Cicerōnis ā patribus _____ dēbent.

5. Sciō Catilīnam esse malum hominem. Patrēs _____ Catilīnam esse malum hominem.

The Senate House built by Julius Caesar and dedicated to him after his assassination by his great-nephew Augustus was destroyed by fire in the second century CE. The emperor Diocletian commissioned a new senate house that was built with brick on the very same spot in the Forum. This is the building in the left foreground of the picture.

LANGUAGE FACT II

THIRD DECLENSION NEUTER NOUNS

In Chapter 7 you learned about third declension nouns, either masculine or feminine, that follow the pattern of *passer, passeris*. These words have an irregular nominative, and so the genitive provides their stem.

There are also neuter nouns that belong to this pattern; you have already encountered one of them, *tempora*, in the famous saying at the beginning of the chapter.

These neuter nouns follow the third declension pattern of masculine and feminine nouns with one general exception, which you have already learned in Chapter 4: namely, that the nominative, accusative, and vocative of neuter nouns are always the same; and that the ending for the nominative, accusative, and vocative plural is always *-a*. This general rule applies to all neuter nouns, whatever their declension.

Third Declension Neuter Nouns

	Singular			Plural	
Nominative	tempus	the time	tempora	the times
Genitive	tempor**is**	of the time	tempor**um**	of the times
Dative	tempor**ī**	to/for the time	tempor**ibus**	to/for the times
Accusative	tempus	the time	tempora	the times
Ablative	tempor**e**	by/with the time	tempor**ibus**	by/with the times
Vocative	tempus	o, time	tempora	o, times

▶ EXERCISE 5

Make the adjective agree with the noun in case, number, and gender and translate each phrase.

Example: animālia (māgnus)
māgna animālia   big animals

1. timōrēs (malus)

2. ducī (sevērus)

3. corporis (pulcher)

4. tempus (longus)

5. corporibus (multus)

6. in ōrātiōne (meus)

LANGUAGE FACT III
THIRD DECLENSION *I*-STEM NOUNS

The following pattern is usually called "third declension *i*-stem" because the vowel -*i*- precedes a few of the standard endings of the third declension. In this sub-class of third declension nouns, the -*um* ending (genitive plural) becomes -*ium* and the -*a* ending (neuter nominative, accusative, and vocative plural) becomes -*ia*.

Three types of words are classified as third declension *i*-stem:

1. Masculine and feminine nouns with the **same** number of syllables in the nominative and genitive.

   In the chapter reading you have encountered *cīvis, cīvis,* m./f., a word with the same number of syllables in the nominative and in the genitive:

Third Declension *i*-stem Nouns

(same number of syllables in nominative singular and genitive singular)

		Singular			Plural
Nominative	cīvis	the citizen		cīv**ēs**	the citizens
Genitive	cīv**is**	of the citizen		cīv**ium**	of the citizens
Dative	cīv**ī**	to/for the citizen		cīv**ibus**	to/for the citizens
Accusative	cīv**em**	the citizen		cīv**ēs**	the citizens
Ablative	cīv**e**	by/with the citizen		cīv**ibus**	by/with the citizens
Vocative	cīv**is**	o, citizen		cīv**ēs**	o, citizens

2. Masculine and feminine third declension nouns that have only one syllable in the nominative singular, usually ending in -*s* or -*x*, and have two consonants before the -*is* ending of the genitive singular.

   In the Latin reading passage you encountered the *i*-stem noun *urbs, urbis,* f., which has a one-syllable nominative and a genitive ending preceded by two consonants.

Third Declension *i*-stem Nouns

(one syllable in nominative singular; the base from the genitive singular ends in two consonants)

		Singular			Plural
Nominative	urbs	the city		urb**ēs**	the cities
Genitive	urb**is**	of the city		urb**ium**	of the cities
Dative	urb**ī**	to/for the city		urb**ibus**	to/for the cities
Accusative	urb**em**	the city		urb**ēs**	the cities
Ablative	urb**e**	by/with the city		urb**ibus**	by/with the cities
Vocative	urbs	o, city		urb**ēs**	o, cities

3. Neuter nouns that end in the nominative singular in **-ar**, **-al** and **-e**. These words have the **-ium** genitive ending and the **-ia** nominative, accusative and vocative plural ending, but the ablative singular ends in **-ī**.

Such are the words *exemplar, exemplāris, n.,* "example," *animal, animālis, n.,* "animal," and *mare, maris, n.,* "sea."

Third Declension *i*-stem Nouns
(neuters in **-al**, **-ar**, **-e**)

		Singular			Plural
Nominative	mar**e**	the sea		mar**ia**	the seas
Genitive	mar**is**	of the sea		mar**ium**	of the seas
Dative	mar**ī**	to/for the sea		mar**ibus**	to/for the seas
Accusative	mar**e**	the sea		mar**ia**	the seas
Ablative	mar**ī**	by/with the sea		mar**ibus**	by/with the seas
Vocative	mar**e**	o, sea		mar**ia**	o, seas

View of the Mediterranean Sea (*Mare Internum*) from an Italian coastal town.

STUDY TIP

The only difference between third declension *i*-stem nouns and other third declension nouns is the additional vowel *-i-* in the genitive plural ending *-ium* and in the ending *-ia* for the neuter plural nominative, accusative, and vocative endings, as well as the ablative ending *-ī* instead of *-e* for neuter nouns like *mare, exemplar,* and *animal.*

▶ EXERCISE 6

Change the singular forms into plural and the plural forms into singular. For some, more than one answer is possible. Translate the changed form.

Example: exemplar
exemplāria   examples

1. maribus
2. animālis
3. urbibus
4. exemplārī
5. cīvēs
6. mortium

▶ EXERCISE 7

Fill in the blanks with the correct form of the words in parentheses and translate each sentence. The Reading Vocabulary may be consulted.

Example: _____ mala veniunt. (tempus)
Tempora mala veniunt.   Bad times come.

1. Hominēs _____ intellegunt. (timor)
2. Catilīna in cūriam _____. (ambulō)
3. Cicero _____ Catilīnam arma parāre. (sciō)
4. Cicero dīcit Catilīnam contrā cōnsulem Rōmānum _____ . (sentiō)
5. Verba Cicerōnis ā patribus _____ . (exspectō)
6. Catilīna est _____ malī hominis. (exemplar)
7. Patrēs _____ Cicerōnem bene dīcere. (nārrō)

TALKING

amictōrium, amictōriī, n. – scarf

brācae Genāvēnsēs – jeans (trousers made with fabric from the city of Genova/Genoa)

brācae, brācārum, f. pl. – trousers

calceāmenta āthlētica, calceāmentōrum āthlēticōrum, n. pl. – sneakers

calceāmenta, calceāmentōrum, n. pl. – shoes

camīsia, camīsiae, f. – shirt, blouse

castula, castulae, f. – skirt

digitābula, digitābulōrum, n. pl. – gloves

Exue tunicam. "Take off (your) coat."

Gestābō + accusative . . . "I will wear . . ."

gestō, gestāre + accusative – I am wearing

Indue camīsiam. "Put on (your) shirt."

Lēvigā brācās. "Iron (your) trousers."

perspicillum fuscātum, perspicillī fuscātī, n. – sunglasses

perspicillum, perspicillī, n. – glasses

pilleus, pilleī, m. – cap

Pōne calceāmenta. "Take off (your) shoes."

Pōne pilleum. "Take off (your) hat."

Quid gestābis? "What are you going to wear?"

stola, stolae, f. – dress

subūcula, subūculae, f. – T-shirt

Sūme calceāmenta. "Put on (your) shoes."

Sūme pilleum. "Put on (your) hat."

tībiālia, tībiālium, n. pl. – socks

tunica, tunicae, f. – coat

umbella, umbellae, f. – umbrella

Velim gestāre + accusative . . . "I would like to wear . . ."

vestis, vestis, f. – dress, garment

GETTING DRESSED FOR A PARTY

Marīa: Quid hodiē (*today*) gestābis, Christīna?

Christīna: Castulam et camīsiam pulchram gestābō. Quid tū gestābis, Marīa?

Marīa: Ego brācās Genāvēnsēs velim gestāre.

Helena: Brācae Genāvēnsēs nōn sunt valdē pulchrae.

Marīa: Quid gestābis tū, Helena?

Helena: Ego stolam gestāre velim.

Marīa: Venietne ad cōnvīvium Mārcus? (*Is Marcus coming to the party?*)

Christīna: Ita. (*Yes.*)

Marīa: Nunc intellegō . . . Putō Mārcum Helenam amāre et ā Helenā amārī. Indue, Helena, vestem et tū, Christīna, indue castulam et camīsiam pulchram. Ego autem meās brācās Genāvēnsēs gestāre velim et calceāmenta āthlētica.

Helena: Bene. Nunc parārī dēbēmus. Venītisne? (*Are you coming?*)

VOCABULARY TO KNOW

NOUNS

amor, amōris, m. – love

animal, animālis, n. – animal

arma, armōrum, n. pl. – weapons

caput, capitis, n. – head

cīvis, cīvis, m./f. – citizen

cōnsul, cōnsulis, m. – consul

corpus, corporis, n. – body

dēliciae, dēliciārum, f. pl. – delight, pet

digitus, digitī, m. – finger

domina, dominae, f. – mistress

dux, ducis, m. – leader, general

exemplar, exemplāris, n. – example

fortitūdō, fortitūdinis, f. – courage

gremium, gremiī, n. – lap

homō, hominis, m. – man (i.e., human being); (pl.) people

mare, maris, n. – sea

mīles, mīlitis, m. – soldier

mors, mortis, f. – death

mulier, mulieris, f. – woman

oculus, oculī, m. – eye

ōrāculum, ōrāculī, n. – oracle

ōrātiō, ōrātiōnis, f. – speech; ōrātiōnem habeō – make a speech

passer, passeris, m. – sparrow

pāx, pācis, f. – peace

rēx, rēgis, m. – king

senex, senis, m. – old man

soror, sorōris, f. – sister

templum, templī, n. – temple

tempus, temporis, n. – time

timor, timōris, m. – fear

urbs, urbis, f. – city (usually the city of Rome)

verbum, verbī, n. – word

PRONOUNS

sē (reflexive pronoun, accusative) – s/he (him/herself)/they (themselves) in an indirect statement

ADJECTIVES

meus, mea, meum – my (a possessive adjective)

sevērus, sevēra, sevērum – serious, strict, severe

VERBS

aestimō, aestimāre, aestimāvī, aestimātum – to regard, esteem

aestimō unīus assis – I do not care a bit

audiō, audīre, audīvī, audītum – to hear, listen

crēdō, crēdere, crēdidī, crēditum + dative – to believe somebody

dēcernō, dēcernere, dēcrēvī, dēcrētum – to decide, determine (often + infinitive)

dīcō, dīcere, dīxī, dictum – to say

gerō, gerere, gessī, gestum – to carry; sē gerit – s/he/it behaves

intellegō, intellegere, intellēxī, intellēctum – to understand

invideō, invidēre, invīdī, invīsum + dative – to envy someone

līberō, līberāre, līberāvī, līberātum + accusative + ablative – to free someone from something

nāvigō, nāvigāre, nāvigāvī, nāvigātum – to sail, voyage

petō, petere, petīvī, petītum – to seek, head for, go to, rush at

putō, putāre, putāvī, putātum – to think, consider

sciō, scīre, scīvī, scītum – to know

sentiō, sentīre, sēnsī, sēnsum – to feel

veniō, venīre, vēnī, ventum – to come

vincō, vincere, vīcī, victum – to conquer, defeat

ADVERBS

tandem – at last

tunc – then

PREPOSITION

contrā + accusative – against

▶ EXERCISE 1

Conjugate the following verbs in the present active and passive voice and give the present active and passive infinitives.

1. *gerō, gerere, gessī, gestum*

2. *crēdō, crēdere, crēdidī, crēditum*

Conjugate the following verb in the active voice. Give the active infinitive for the verb.

3. *veniō, venīre, vēnī, ventum*

▶ EXERCISE 2

Decline the following nouns.

1. *cōnsul, cōnsulis,* m. – consul

2. *caput, capitis,* n. – head

3. *fortitūdō, fortitūdinis,* f. – courage

4. *nox, noctis,* f. – night

5. *rēte, rētis,* n. – net, internet

▶ EXERCISE 3

Change the direct statements into indirect statements. Translate the indirect statements.

Example: Pulchram mulierem amō.   Catullus dicit _____
Catullus dīcit sē pulchram mulierem amāre.   Catullus says that he loves a beautiful woman.

1. Passer est dēliciae mulieris.

   Poēta dīcit _____

2. Verba senum sevērōrum ūnīus assis aestimō.

   Catullus sentit _____

3. Amor semper vincit.

   Catullus scit _____

4. Nāvēs Graecōs servāre possunt.

        nāvis, nāvis, f. – ship   Graecus, Graecī, m. – Greek

    Pȳthia scit _____

5. Verba Pȳthiae intellegō.

    Themistoclēs sentit _____

6. Graecī nāvigāre dēbent.

    Themistoclēs scit _____

7. Catilīna mortem cīvium petit.

    Cicero intellegit _____

8. Rōma ā Catilīnā līberārī dēbet.

    Cicero scit _____

9. Cōnsul pācem servāre potest.

    Hominēs audiunt _____

▶ EXERCISE 4

Fill in the blanks with the correct form of the words in parentheses. For some, a preposition may be needed. Translate each sentence.

Example: Cīvēs possunt _____ servārī. (cōnsul)
Cīvēs possunt ā cōnsule servārī.   The citizens can be saved by the consul.

1. _____ dē Catilīnā cōgitāmus. (timor)
2. Catilīna _____ vincī potest. (arma)
3. Virī et mulierēs _____ ambulāre dēbent et nāvigāre. (mare)
4. _____ in agrōs veniunt. (urbs)
5. Passer _____ puellae manet. (gremium)

▶ EXERCISE 5

Translate into Latin.

1. I see with my eyes.

2. We ought to be freed from fear.

3. You should come to the city.

4. You (plural) decide to remain in the city.

5. I hear the words with love.

6. The example ought to be given by the king and by the leaders.

▶ EXERCISE 6

Translate into English.

Catullus sentit sē esse miserum. Nam puella amōrem servāre nōn vult. Catullus dēbet intellegere amōrem servārī nōn posse. Amor in animō puellae nōn manet. Puella Catullum nōn petit. Puella verba Catullī audīre nōn vult. Puella bāsia Catullō dare nōn vult. Itaque Catullus animum firmāre dēbet et ā puellā ambulāre.

bāsium, bāsiī, n. – kiss

vult – wants

CONSIDERING THE CLASSICAL GODS

APOLLO

You have already learned about the older generation of Olympian gods. Let us now turn to the younger Olympians, all of them children of Zeus. Apollo, as he is called in both Greek and Latin, represents the Greek ideal of physical beauty and emotional tranquility: possessing a perfectly proportioned body and rational intellect. He is identified with the sun and with the arts. Apollo is the leader of the nine Muses, who preside over each of these arts: Clio over History; Euterpe over Lyric Poetry; Thalia over Comedy; Melpomene over Tragedy; Terpsichore over Dance; Erato over Erotic Poetry; Polyhymnia over Songs; Urania over Astronomy; and Calliope over Epic Poetry.

Apollo and his twin sister Artemis, known to the Romans as Diana, were the children of Zeus and the goddess Leto. In her capacity as goddess of childbirth and their father's wife, Juno tried to prolong Leto's birth pangs, but eventually, after nine days of labor, she delivered the twins on the island of Delos, which became an important religious center. Its name, which means "bright," is connected with Apollo's role as the god of the sun.

Apollo is often represented with a bow and a lyre, and is also the god of prophecy and healing. The most important oracle in Greece, at Delphi, was associated with his worship. There, his priestess, known as the Pythia, would sit on a tripod and chew bay leaves, working herself into an inspired state from which she would utter obscure prophetic pronouncements. You may remember those prophecies from the reading about the Athenian leader Themistocles. Apollo's son Aesclepius, or Aesculapius in Latin, was the god of medicine.

Replica of a bronze statue of Apollo on the east side of the Temple of Apollo in Pompeii.

Despite his physical beauty, Apollo is not, like his father Jupiter, remembered for his successes in love. Indeed, the best-known story about his romantic interests concerns his unreciprocated desire for the nymph Daphne, whom the gods turned into a laurel tree to spare her from Apollo's embraces. But he remains closely linked with the idea of the rational intellect: the US space expeditions to the moon bear his name.

The ruins at Delos, a site sacred to Apollo.

Contemporary drawing of Daphne as she changes into a laurel tree.

READ THE FOLLOWING PASSAGE

Cassandra est fīlia rēgis Trōiānī. Apollō Cassandram amat, sed ā Cassandrā nōn amātur. Apollō Cassandrae dōnum dat, sī Cassandra Apollinem amāre vult. Dōnum est hoc: Cassandra futūra scīre potest. Cassandra dōnum habet, sed tandem Apollinem nōn amāre dēcernit. Tunc Apollō aliud dōnum Cassandrae dat. Aliud dōnum est hoc: hominēs Cassandrae nōn crēdunt.

Graecī equum ligneum parant et Trōiānīs dant. Tunc Cassandra dīcit Graecōs Trōiānīs mortem parāre. Trōiānī tamen Cassandram nōn audiunt. Equus urbem Trōiānōrum intrat et cum equō mors ad Trōiānōs venit.

aliud (neuter) – another	futūra, futūrōrum, n. pl. – future
Apollō, Apollinis, m. – Apollo	ligneus, lignea, ligneum – wooden
Cassandra, Cassandrae, f. – Cassandra	sī (conj.) – if
dōnum, dōnī, n. – gift	Trōiānus, Trōiāna, Trōiānum – Trojan
equus, equī, m . – horse	Trōiānus, Trōiānī, m. – Trojan
Graecus, Graecī, m. – Greek	vult – wants
hoc – this	

Temple of Apollo in Corinth, Greece.

ROMAN ATTIRE

In chapter 9 and in the essay "Exploring Roman Families," you were introduced to some names for articles of clothing in Latin. Roman clothes were usually woven from wool, and the process of weaving itself—the spinning of woolen fleece into thread, and the production of cloth from the thread—was viewed not only as women's work, but also as the most distinctive and important female activity. An early Roman tombstone inscription praises its occupant with the words *Domum servāvit, lānam fēcit*, "She sustained the household, she made wool." Wealthier Roman women had female slaves to help with the weaving, and such fabrics as cotton, silk, and linen were eventually used to clothe the Romans as well.

Like much else in the ancient Roman world, clothing was a marker of social status. Both men and women wore a simple garment known as a *tunica* under their clothing. On top of the *tunica*, Roman married women wore a *stola*, a long sleeveless robe of undyed wool.

Roman males of the citizen class, however, wore the *toga virīlis*, "dress of manhood," a white garment without any decoration, which they received on the day when their families celebrated their entrance into adulthood. The *toga* was

This fresco from Herculaneum shows a man wearing a toga.

a large piece of heavy woolen cloth, not pinned or fastened in any way, but gracefully draped around the torso. Men who wore the *toga* sometimes kept it from unfolding by pressing their left arm against their body.

While, as many ancient Roman statues attest, the toga symbolized the majesty and dignity of the Roman citizen, it did not permit strenuous physical activity. Those holding high political office wore a *toga* with a large purple margin called the *toga praetexta*. Those who sought political office dressed in a *toga candida*, made of snowy white wool; it is from this garment that we derive our English word "candidate." Triumphant military leaders would wear gold-embroidered garments called *togae pictae*. To clean these garments, the Romans had extensive dry-cleaning facilities, staffed by cleaners called *fullōnēs*.

Roman men wore their hair short, and were clean-shaven. During the imperial period, statues and other works of art portray men with increasingly complicated hairstyles as well as beards. Women always appear to have arranged their hair in elaborate styles; as time went by many also wore wigs and used hairpins. Much evidence suggests that Roman women adorned themselves with different kinds of jewelry, although men usually limited their ornamentation to a signet ring.

These busts show the varying hairstyles of Roman men and women.

EXPLORING ROMAN GOVERNMENT

POLITICS IN GREECE, ROME, AND THE UNITED STATES

Athens in the fifth and fourth centuries BCE and Rome in the third, second, and first centuries BCE are the two best-known, and most influential, ancient examples of popular government. The Athenian democracy (*dêmokratia* meaning "power of the people" in the sense of "the capacity of the people to do things") and the Roman republic (*rēs pūblica* meaning "the public thing" in the sense of "that which is publicly shared") have some important features in common. Both systems were developed as alternatives to government in which all power was concentrated in the hands of an individual: a king or tyrant. When compared to tyranny and monarchy, ancient Greek democracy and Roman republicanism are, therefore, rightly understood as sharing a common set of core values. Most fundamentally, in democratic Athens and republican Rome it was, in principle, the collective will of the citizens (in Athens: *ho dêmos tôn Athênaiôn*; in Rome: *senātus populusque Rōmānus*) that decided policy—not the individual will of an autocrat.

Yet in both Athens and Rome, only adult men were allowed to be active citizens. Women (along with slaves and many free men who had not been granted citizenship) were denied participation rights much like American women who did not have the right to vote until the suffrage movement eventually brought about the passage of the nineteenth amendment in 1919 and its ratification in 1920.

Neither Athens nor Rome employed the familiar modern political principles of representation or separation of powers; neither had a well-developed conception of human rights. This concept was, however, a major issue in the Lincoln-Douglas debates. Presidential candidate Lincoln supported the belief that all men, even slaves, had the "inalienable rights of life, liberty, and the pursuit of happiness." Martin Luther King Jr. in his famous "I Have a Dream" speech anticipates the day when there will be equality among all people.

Athens and Rome, like the United States much later, developed sophisticated sets of political institutions that encouraged public deliberation: that is to say, important policies were made and carried out only after a range of policies had been considered and discussed. As a result, public speeches remained a genuinely important part of political life and political leaders were often skilled orators. Demosthenes, the most famous of the Athenian orators, spoke vehemently against Philip II of Macedon who was planning the conquest of the Greek states. Centuries later in Rome, the well-known orator Cicero delivered several orations against Mark Antony. These were called "Philippics" after Demosthenes' speeches against Philip II. Even today very bitter opposition speeches are known as "Philippics." In the history of the United States oratory also plays a distinct role. Modern political candidates are expected to give public speeches and debate each other on a regular basis. This system of public deliberations in ancient Greece and Rome allowed for competition among would-be leaders, contests that were decided by voting and elections. In these systems there was a rotation of leadership, but also some provision for continuity. In both Athens

and Rome, the political system was complemented by a system of justice that (again in principle) arbitrated disputes and punished criminal behavior on the basis of established law. While both Athenians and Romans spoke with reverence of their ancient lawgivers and the traditional political practices of the past (Athens: *patria politēia*; Rome: *mōs māiōrum*), in fact both systems evolved over time; new institutions and practices were developed in response to new challenges just as in the United States the Bill of Rights and amendments to the Constitution were developed. While Athens made a greater point of free speech, a freedom guaranteed in the United States by the First Amendment, in both Athens and Rome critical dissent by individuals against public decisions was possible and both societies supported a flourishing tradition of political philosophy.

There are, however, substantial differences between the democratic Athenian and republican Roman systems of government. Some of the differences can be explained by scale: Although Athens was among the largest of the Greek city-states, by the third century BCE Rome was already vastly larger than Athens. By the first century BCE, the scale difference was profound. By this time the population of Roman citizens was measured in the millions. By contrast, Athens, at its height, measured its citizen population in the tens of thousands. This scale difference came about because of very different policies on citizen naturalization: Rome was once no larger than Athens, but continually enlarged its citizenship. Roman allies, conquered peoples, even former slaves, found it fairly easy to become Roman citizens. The Athenians, by contrast, jealously guarded citizenship and only occasionally naturalized those who had not been born to Athenian parents. In America, citizenship is a product of birth or naturalization. The limited size of the Athenian citizen population is a primary reason for Athens' eventual failure. Faced by a demographic crisis at the end of the fifth century BCE and by the threat of growing Macedonian power fifty years later, the Athenians consistently refused to follow the advice of politicians who urged enfranchising resident foreigners and freeing slaves in order to expand the citizen body. When, in the later fourth century BCE, the decisive battles were fought, there were not enough Athenians on the battlefield to stop the highly trained and well-led Macedonians.

The scale difference made the experience of popular politics very different in the two societies. In Athens ordinary (male) citizens really did control the government. A citizen, whether rich or poor, whether highly educated or unschooled, expected to vote directly on legislation in the Assembly (*ekklêsia*). A large percentage of all citizens over age 30 had extensive public experience as jurors in the People's Courts, on boards of responsible magistrates, and by serving for a year on the agenda-setting Council of 500 (*boulê*). By contrast, important public offices in Rome were, for the most part, monopolized by a relatively small elite of wealthy and well-connected families. Much of the real work of the government was done at the direction of the Senate. The Senate was a very hierarchical institution, dominated in practice by a handful of highly influential Romans who were invariably former high magistrates (consuls and praetors). The Senate was formally limited to a consultative role, but its advice was typically respected and closely followed—both by individual magistrates and by the voting assemblies. Unlike Athenians, Roman citizens voted on legislative proposals not as individuals, but as members of very large voting-bloc groups. Voting assemblies were divided into "centuries" (in the *Comitia Centuriāta*) or tribes (in the *Comitia Tribūta*). The unequal size and social composition of the voting blocs ensured that, in ordinary circumstances, a wealthy and well-connected minority was able to control the outcome.

Popular government worked well for Athens and Rome. Both democratic Athens and republican Rome were very successful in their own contexts. For most of the 180 years (ca. 507–322 BCE) of its democratic history Athens was the richest, most powerful, and overall most prominent of the ca. 1000 classical Greek city-states. Under its republican government Rome came to dominate not only Italy but the entire Mediterranean region, including the Greek city-states. Although the two best-known popular governments of antiquity were overall successful, both were subject to political pathologies. In the Athenian case the democratic government was dangerously prone to over-ambitious projects and snap judgments. These bad political choices included decisions to launch imperialistic wars (notably, the expedition to Sicily in the later years of the Peloponnesian War) that, by the end of the fifth century BCE led to catastrophic losses of men, economic crisis, and ultimately to civil war. Another well-known, over-quick judgment, carried out after democracy had been restored in the aftermath of the civil war, was the legal conviction and execution of the philosopher Socrates (399 BCE). To their credit, the Athenians never repeated that mistake (Plato and Aristotle flourished in democratic Athens), and the restored democracy instituted legal reforms intended to limit the tendency of the citizen Assembly to make over-hasty judgments.

Political crises in Rome were precipitated by resistance to the Senate's monopoly of power and by increasingly dangerous conflicts between highly ambitious leaders (Marius, Sulla, Pompey, and Caesar are examples) who did not willingly relinquish power at the end of their terms of public service. Their ambitions were fed by the chance of converting independent citizens into obedient clients. Rome's successful wars of expansion had helped to create a large class of impoverished citizens, whose only hope of getting ahead was to join the army. The Roman legionary soldiers increasingly owed their loyalty to their commanders, such as the well-known devotion of Marius' soldiers to him rather than to the political system that offered them neither meaningful chances for political participation nor any meaningful share of the great wealth of empire. The widespread willingness of highly trained Roman citizen-soldiers to follow their commanders into battle with fellow citizens, in violation of Roman constitutional law, was the fuel that fed a long generation of nightmarish civil wars, including the war of Caesar against Pompey and that of Octavian against Antony. The final result was the collapse of the republic at the end of the first century BCE and the creation of the imperial Principate by the first Roman emperor, Augustus. With this change the long history of popular government in antiquity ended—the political forms of republic and democracy would not reappear in human history until the Renaissance (the northern Italian city-state republics of, for example, Florence and Genoa); democracy was not revived as a term for a legitimate national government until the eighteenth and nineteenth centuries, in western Europe and the United States.

JOSIAH OBER
Professor of Classics and Political Science
Stanford, University
Stanford, California

PHRASES AND MOTTOES RELATING TO GOVERNMENT AND DEMOCRACY

PHRASES

- Ē plūribus ūnum. "One <whole> out of more <elements>." This Latin phrase expresses the essence of the federal spirit as conceived by the founding fathers: a group of self-governing units, all parts of an indissoluble whole. It appears on the Great Seal of the United States, as well as on the one-dollar bill.

- Ex officiō. "By virtue of office" held by a particular individual.

The motto of the United States, *Ē Plūribus Ūnum*, can be seen on the reverse side of a penny.

Ē Plūribus Ūnum is shown on this postage stamp.

On the one dollar bill, the reverse side of the Great Seal of the United States is shown with the phrase *Ē Plūribus Ūnum* on banners on both sides of the eagle's head.

MOTTOES

- Audēmus iūra nostra dēfendere. "We dare to defend our rights." Motto of the state of Alabama.

- Ense petit placidam sub lībertāte quiētem. "He seeks with a sword a quiet rest under freedom." Motto of the state of Massachusetts.

- Iūstitia omnibus. "Justice to all people." Motto of the District of Columbia.

- Montānī semper līberī. "The people of the mountains are always free." Motto of the state of West Virginia.

- Salūs populī suprēma lēx estō! "Let the salvation of the people be a supreme law!" Motto of the state of Missouri.

- Sīc semper tyrannīs. "Thus always <it happens> to tyrants." Motto of the state of Virginia. These Latin words aptly describe the outcome of Catiline's plot against the Roman state but are found depicted on the Great Seal of the Commonwealth of Virginia as a female figure representing Virtus stepping on a fallen tyrant.

A Latin motto on the state seal of Massachusetts.

Sīc semper tyrannīs, the motto of Virginia, is on its state seal.

CHAPTER 10

Third Conjugation –*iō* Verbs: Present Active and Passive Tense, Present Active and Passive Infinitive; Third Declension Adjectives; Substantive Adjectives

A modern reconstruction of the Trojan Horse, standing at the archaeological site of Troy in modern-day Turkey.

MEMORĀBILE DICTŪ

Quidquid id est, timeō Danaōs et dōna ferentēs!
"Whatever it is, I fear the Greeks even bringing gifts!" (Vergil, *Aeneid*, Book 2.49)

This is the exclamation that the poet Vergil places in the mouth of the Trojan priest Laocoön, who tries in vain to dissuade the Trojans from bringing into their city the huge wooden horse left, apparently as a gift, by the departing Greeks.

READING

Publius Vergilius Maro (70–19 BCE) wrote perhaps the greatest work of Latin literature: the *Aeneid*, an epic poem in twelve books that celebrates the origins of Rome. In the first six books, Vergil narrates the journey of the mythic Trojan hero Aeneas through the Mediterranean Sea after the destruction of Troy by the Greeks. Its second six books tell of how Aeneas and his Trojan exiles settle in Italy. There the gods ordain that the blending of the Trojans with the local Italian inhabitants produce the people who will one day become the Romans.

Vergil wrote the *Aeneid* as a Roman equivalent of Homer's monumental Greek epic poems, the *Iliad* and the *Odyssey*, to recognize the emperor Augustus' achievements. Chief among them was bringing an end to Rome's civil wars.

The *Aeneid* became the standard Latin poetic text read by schoolboys for centuries to come, not only during the Roman Empire, but also in the Middle Ages and Renaissance, and into later times.

The following passage is adapted from the beginning of the second book of the *Aeneid*. It is the story related by Aeneas himself about the Greek stratagem that caused the fall of Troy. The Greeks had been besieging Troy without success for nine years, trying to recover Helen, wife of the Spartan king Menelaus, who had been abducted by the Trojan prince Paris. Finally, the crafty Greek warrior Odysseus—known in Latin as "Ulixes" and English as "Ulysses"—devised the plan for the Trojan Horse that brought the Greeks victory.

DĒ EQUŌ TRŌIĀNŌ

1   Graecī verba Ulixis audiunt et cōnsilia capiunt. Māgnus equus ligneus ā
    Graecīs aedificātur. Mīlitēs fortēs in equō occultantur. Mala et Trōiānīs
    fūnesta ā mīlitibus Graecīs in equō occultātīs parantur. Tunc equus ad
    urbis portam movētur. Trōiānī equum vident et dīcunt sē bellum nōn

5   nunc timēre: equum esse dōnum; Graecōs equum deīs dare. At Trōiānī
    nōn sunt fēlīcēs. Nam Graecōs abesse crēdunt, nec dē perīculō scīre
    cupiunt. Nunc equus in urbe est. Graecī in equō occultātī noctem et
    tenebrās exspectant. Nox venit. Graecī armātī ex equō in urbem exeunt.
    Trōiānī imparātī contrā hostēs parātōs et ācrēs pugnāre dēbent. Urbs

10 Trōiānōrum servārī nōn potest. Trōia armīs Graecōrum et flammīs
    dēlētur. Paucī fugere possunt.

READING VOCABULARY

absum, abesse, āfuī ,——— – to be absent, away (this verb is composed of *ab* and *sum*)

*ācer, ācris, ācre – keen, fierce

ācrēs (masculine plural) – fierce

*aedificō, aedificāre, aedificāvī, aedificātum – to build

at – but

*capiō, capere, cēpī, captum – to take, adopt, capture; *cōnsilia capere* means "to make plans"

*cupiō, cupere, cupīvī, cupītum – to desire, want

*deus, deī, m. – god

*dēleō, dēlēre, dēlēvī, dēlētum – to destroy

*dōnum, dōnī, n. – gift

*equus, equī, m. – horse

exeunt – exit, go out

*fēlīx, fēlīcis – fortunate, happy

*flamma, flammae, f. – flame

*fortis, forte – brave, strong

*fugiō, fugere, fūgī, ——— – to flee, run away

fūnestus, fūnesta, fūnestum + dative – fatal, deadly (for somebody)

Graecus, Graeca, Graecum (adjective) – Greek

Graecus, Graecī, m. – Greek

*hostis, hostis, m. – enemy

imparātus, imparāta, imparātum – unprepared

ligneus, lignea, ligneum – wooden

mala – bad things

*moveō, movēre, mōvī, mōtum – to move

*nec (conj.) – and not, nor

*nox, noctis, f. – night

occultātus, occultāta, occultātum – hidden

occultō, occultāre, occultāvī, occultātum – to hide, conceal

parātus, parāta, parātum – prepared

*paucī, paucae, pauca – few

*perīculum, perīculī, n. – danger

porta, portae, f. – gate

*pugnō, pugnāre, pugnāvī, pugnātum – to fight

Trōia, Trōiae, f. – Troy

Trōiānus, Trōiāna, Trōiānum (adjective) – Trojan

Trōiānus, Trōiānī, m. (noun) – Trojan

Ulixes, Ulixis, m. – Odysseus, Ulysses (Latin)

urbs – city

*Words marked with an asterisk will need to be memorized.

COMPREHENSION QUESTIONS

1. What was Odysseus' plan?

2. What did the Trojans think about the horse?

3. What happened during the night?

LANGUAGE FACT I

THIRD CONJUGATION -*IŌ* VERBS: PRESENT ACTIVE AND PASSIVE TENSE, PRESENT ACTIVE AND PASSIVE INFINITIVE

In the chapter reading passage you see the verb forms *capiunt* and *cupiunt*. Seeing the vowel -*i*-, you might think that they belong to the fourth conjugation. In fact, these forms belong to a special group of third conjugation verbs whose first principal part ends in -*iō*. These third conjugation -*iō* verbs are distinguished from other verbs of the third conjugation by the additional letter -*i*- that appears before some of the endings. The verb *capiō* ("to take," "to capture") is an example of this class of verb. Notice that the infinitive *capere* has the same form as other third conjugation infinitives (as does the form *fugere* that you encountered in the reading above).

Third Conjugation -*iō*: Present Active

		Singular		Plural
First person	capiō	I take	capimus	we take
Second person	capis	you take	capitis	you take
Third person	capit	s/he/it takes	capiunt	they take

Present Active Infinitive

capere   to take

Third Conjugation -*iō*: Present Passive

		Singular		Plural
First person	capior	I am taken	capimur	we are taken
Second person	caperis	you are taken	capiminī	you are taken
Third person	capitur	s/he/it is taken	capiuntur	they are taken

Present Passive Infinitive

capī   to be taken

STUDY TIP

Third conjugation -*iō* verbs are identical to fourth conjugation verbs in their first person singular forms, active and passive (-*iō* and -*ior*), and their third person plural forms, active and passive (-*iunt*, -*iuntur*).

▶ EXERCISE 1

Translate into English.

1. cupimur
2. cupiunt
3. fugis
4. cupere
5. fugimus
6. cupior
7. cupiminī
8. fugitis

VOCABULARY TO LEARN

NOUNS

deus, deī, m. – god

dōnum, dōnī, n. – gift

equus, equī, m. – horse

flamma, flammae, f. – flame

hostis, hostis, m. – enemy

nox, noctis, f. – night

perīculum, perīculī, n. – danger

ADJECTIVES

ācer, ācris, ācre – keen, fierce

celeber, celebris, celebre – renowned, well-known, crowded

fēlīx, fēlīcis – fortunate, happy

fortis, forte – brave, strong

paucī, paucae, pauca (in plural) – few

VERBS

aedificō, aedificāre, aedificāvī, aedificātum – to build

capiō, capere, cēpī, captum – to take, adopt, capture; *cōnsilia capere* means "to make plans"

cupiō, cupere, cupīvī, cupītum – to desire, want

dēleō, dēlēre, dēlēvī, dēlētum – to destroy

fugiō, fugere, fūgī, ——— – to flee, run away

moveō, movēre, mōvī, mōtum – to move

pugnō, pugnāre, pugnāvī, pugnātum – to fight

CONJUNCTION

nec – and not, nor

▶ EXERCISE 2

Find the English derivatives based on the Vocabulary to Learn in the following sentences. Write the corresponding Latin word.

1. Bats are nocturnal creatures.

2. Celebrities win votes too easily in our political system.

3. Despite the paucity of defenders, the fort held out until relief came.

4. Driving in a dense fog can be very perilous.

5. Gasoline is extremely flammable.

6. In many parts of the country equine sports are still popular.

7. In the second draft of the chapter, many lines were deleted by the author.

8. Many of those who did not lose their lives in the battle were captured.

9. On the accession of a new emperor, Roman soldiers used to receive a donation to keep them loyal.

10. Sometimes simple fortitude is the best remedy for adversity.

11. That lawyer has a pugnacious personality.

12. The cupidity of some politicians is simply amazing.

13. The fugitives hid in the forest and in barns during the day and traveled by night.

14. The governor encountered a very hostile reception in that city.

15. The motion picture industry is still thriving.

16. The outcome was felicitous: I got the job!

17. The post office is an imposing edifice.

▶ EXERCISE 3

Fill in the blanks by changing the verb from the first sentence to complete the meaning of the second sentence. Translate the changed sentence. The Reading Vocabulary may be consulted.

Example: Graecī cōnsilia capiunt. Cōnsilia ā Graecīs _____.
Cōnsilia ā Graecīs capiuntur.   Plans are made by the Greeks.

1. Ulixes dīcit: "Māgnum equum ligneum aedificāre cupiō." Graecī dīcunt: "Nōs (we) māgnum equum ligneum aedificāre _____."

2. Trōiānī contrā hostēs ācrēs cōnsilia capiunt. Trōiānī contrā hostēs ācrēs cōnsilia _____ dēbent.

3. Cōnsilia contrā Graecōs capiō. Cōnsilia ā mē (by me) contrā Graecōs _____.

4. Paucī Trōiānī fugiunt. Dīcō paucōs Trōiānōs _____.

5. Ex urbe Trōiānōrum fugimus. Ego ex urbe Trōiānōrum _____.

After the ruse of the Trojan Horse allowed the Greeks inside the city, they burned Troy. On his way home to Ithaca, Ulysses had himself tied to the mast of his ship in order to be able to hear the songs of the dangerously enchanting Sirens.

LANGUAGE FACT II

THIRD DECLENSION ADJECTIVES

In the passage at the beginning of the chapter, you met some words (*fortēs, fēlīcēs, ācrēs*) that clearly belong to the third declension, based on their endings. They are not nouns but adjectives.

Adjectives are used to modify or describe nouns:

> ***Mīlitēs fortēs*** *in equō occultantur.*
> Brave soldiers are hidden in the horse.

Adjectives of the third declension follow three different patterns. Their differences are seen in the nominative singular.

1. Adjectives with three distinct nominative singular endings (masculine, feminine, and neuter). The genitive is the same as the feminine nominative form.

   > *ācer, ācris, ācre* – keen, fierce

2. Adjectives with two distinct nominative singular endings (one for masculine and feminine, and one for neuter). The genitive singular is the same as the masculine and feminine nominative singular forms.

   > *fortis, forte* – brave, strong

3. Adjectives with one shared nominative singular ending showing masculine, feminine, and neuter gender. Because the nominative form is irregular, these adjectives must be learned with their genitive form.

   > *fēlīx, fēlīcis* – fortunate, happy

 STUDY TIP
The genitive singular ending of all third declension adjectives is the same.

Third Declension Three Nominative Ending Adjectives

Singular

	Masculine	Feminine	Neuter
Nominative	ācer	ācris	ācre
Genitive	ācris	ācris	ācris
Dative	ācrī	ācrī	ācrī
Accusative	ācrem	ācrem	ācre
Ablative	ācrī	ācrī	ācrī
Vocative	ācer	ācris	ācre

Plural

	Masculine	Feminine	Neuter
Nominative	ācrēs	ācrēs	ācria
Genitive	ācrium	ācrium	ācrium
Dative	ācribus	ācribus	ācribus
Accusative	ācrēs	ācrēs	ācria
Ablative	ācribus	ācribus	ācribus
Vocative	ācrēs	ācrēs	ācria

Third Declension Two Nominative Ending Adjectives

Singular

	Masculine and Feminine	Neuter
Nominative	fortis	forte
Genitive	fortis	fortis
Dative	fortī	fortī
Accusative	fortem	forte
Ablative	fortī	fortī
Vocative	fortis	forte

Plural

	Masculine and Feminine	Neuter
Nominative	fortēs	fortia
Genitive	fortium	fortium
Dative	fortibus	fortibus
Accusative	fortēs	fortia
Ablative	fortibus	fortibus
Vocative	fortēs	fortia

Third Declension One Nominative Ending Adjectives

Singular

Masculine, Feminine, and Neuter

Nominative	fēlīx	⟶	
Genitive	fēlīcis	⟶	
Dative	fēlīcī	⟶	
Accusative	fēlīcem		fēlīx (neuter)
Ablative	fēlīcī	⟶	
Vocative	fēlīx	⟶	

Plural

Masculine, Feminine, and Neuter

Nominative	fēlīcēs		fēlīcia (neuter)
Genitive	fēlīcium	⟶	
Dative	fēlīcibus	⟶	
Accusative	fēlīcēs		fēlīcia (neuter)
Ablative	fēlīcibus	⟶	
Vocative	fēlīcēs		fēlīcia (neuter)

BY THE WAY

Aside from the nominative singular forms of these adjectives, all the other case endings follow the general pattern of third declension nouns. But one special point should be noticed carefully: the endings of third declension adjectives are the same as those of the *i*-stem neuter third declension nouns (*-ium* for the genitive plural, *-ī* for the ablative singular *of all genders*, and *-ia* for the neuter nominative, accusative, and vocative plural).

STUDY TIP

The three-ending adjectives walk in three columns: masculine, feminine, and neuter. The two-ending adjectives walk in two columns: masculine and feminine together, and neuter by itself. The single-ending adjectives walk together, until they come to the accusative singular, or to the nominative, accusative and vocative plural. Then the neuter separates into its own column.

▶ EXERCISE 4

Keeping the same case, number, and gender, replace the adjective with the one in parentheses. Translate the changed phrase.

Example: cīvibus iūstīs (fēlīx)
cīvibus fēlīcibus

1. verba māgna (celeber)
2. dominārum pulchrārum (fēlīx)
3. duce sevērō (miser)
4. cīvis malī (fortis)
5. verba bona (ācer)
6. hostī iūstō (fēlīx)
7. mīlitum armātōrum (fortis)

▶ EXERCISE 5

Translate into Latin. The Reading Vocabulary may be consulted.

1. We do not hear the fierce enemies in the horse.
2. You (singular) do not think the Trojans are fortunate.
3. The Greeks capture the city of the Trojans.
4. They are not thinking about the fierce soldiers.
5. We see the city of fortunate citizens.
6. I do not desire the gift of the Greeks.
7. I am captured by the enemies of the brave Trojans.

LANGUAGE FACT III

SUBSTANTIVE ADJECTIVES (ESPECIALLY NEUTER PLURAL)

In the text at the beginning of the chapter, you read this sentence:

> Mala et Trōiānīs fūnesta ā mīlitibus Graecīs in equō occultātīs parantur.
> Bad things and things deadly for the Trojans are prepared by the Greek soldiers hidden in the horse.

Mala is the neuter nominative plural of the adjective *malus*. Likewise, *fūnesta* is the neuter nominative plural of the adjective *fūnestus*.

As this sentence shows, an adjective can sometimes be used by itself, without any noun form. It can be used this way in each of the three genders: in the masculine or feminine, it supposes an implied "man" or "woman," while used in the neuter, it supposes an implied "thing."

So, *bonus* by itself would mean "a good man," *bona* by itself would mean "a good woman" (or "good things," if neuter plural), and *bonum* by itself would mean "a good thing." A frequent use of these **substantive adjectives** is in the **neuter plural**; the noun "things" is always implied with such adjectives. Note that a masculine plural substantive adjective may refer to people collectively, both male and female (e.g., *bonī*, "good people").

▶ EXERCISE 6

Translate into English.

1. Pulchra nōn semper servāmus.
2. Fortēs nōn semper vincunt.
3. Fēlīcēs timōre līberantur.
4. Multī iūsta petunt.
5. Bonī gaudium, malī timōrem sentiunt.
6. Fēlīcia et pulchra petimus, mala timēmus.

▶ EXERCISE 7

Choose the best answer for each of the following questions and translate. The questions pertain to the Latin reading passage. The Reading Vocabulary may be consulted.

1. Cūius (whose) cōnsiliō equus ligneus aedificātur?

    Trōiānorum cōnsiliō equus ligneus aedificātur.

    Deōrum cōnsiliō equus ligneus aedificātur.

    Ulixis cōnsiliō equus ligneus aedificātur.

2. Cūr (why) Trōiānī equum nōn timent?

    Trōiānī bellum nōn timent.

    Trōiānī equum esse dōnum crēdunt.

    Trōiānī sē nōn esse fēlīcēs crēdunt.

3. Cūr Trōiānī nōn sunt fēlīcēs?

    Trōiānī equum vident.

    Equus ad urbem movētur.

    Trōiānī Graecōs abesse crēdunt, sed Graecī nōn absunt.

4. Quālēs (what sort of) mīlitēs in equō occultantur?

    Multī mīlitēs in equō occultantur.

    Paucī mīlitēs in equō occultantur.

    Mīlitēs ācrēs in equō occultantur.

5. Cūr Trōiānī vincuntur?

    Graecī armātī ex equō in urbem exeunt.

    Equus ligneus ad urbis portam movētur.

    Graecī tenebrās exspectant.

An imperial era mosaic showing Vergil, author of the *Aeneid*. The eighth line of the *Aeneid* (*Mūsa, mihi, causās memorā*) can be seen on the scroll on his lap. To the right and the left of Vergil are the muse of history, Clio, and the muse of tragedy, Melpomene.

TALKING

ante + accusative – before

bene māne – early in the morning

bibō, bibere, bibī, —— – to drink

būtyrum, būtyrī, n. – butter

comedō, comedere, comēdī, —— – to eat

difficilis, difficile – difficult

dormiō, dormīre, dormīvī, —— – to sleep

excitō, excitāre, excitāvī, excitātum – to wake up

exeunte hebdomade – on the weekend

expedītē – quickly and easily

hōrologium excitātōrium, n. – alarm clock

ientāculum, ientāculī, n. – breakfast

ientō, ientāre, ientāvī, ientātum – to have breakfast

in studia incumbere – to study

māne – in the morning

omnis, omne – each, every, (in plural) all

ōvum, ōvī, n. – egg

pānis tostus – toast

pōmum, pōmī, n. – fruit

probātiō, probātiōnis, f. – exam

probātiōnem superāre – to pass an exam

pūncta superaddita (plural) – extra points

quandō? – when?

Quota hōra est? "What time is it?"

schola Latīna – Latin class

sērō – late

sīc – so

surgō, surgere, surrēxī, surrēctum – to get up

vesperī – in the evening

vultisne . . . ? – do you (plural) want . . . ?

THE MORNING BEFORE A TEST

Christīna: Quandō, Mārce, surgere solēs?

Mārcus: Sī (*if*) scholās adīre (*attend classes*) dēbeō, bene māne surgō. Tunc hōrologiō excitātōriō excitor. Semper autem cupiō sērō et diū dormīre. Exeunte hebdomade diūtius (*longer*) dormīre possum.

Christīna: Quandō, Marīa, surgere solēs?

Marīa: Semper bene māne surgō.

Christīna: Ego quoque (*also*) bene māne surgere cupiō. Tunc ientāculum bonum parāre possum. Ientāculum amō.

Helena: Ego quoque ientāculum amō. Quāle (*what sort of*) ientāculum parās? Quid (*what*) comedis?

Christīna: Pōma et ōva et pānem tostum cum būtȳrō comedō. Quota hōra nunc est?

Mārcus: Hōra nunc est octāva (*eight o'clock*).

Christīna: Ientāculum bonum nunc parāre cupiō. Ientāre ante scholam Latīnam possumus. Vultisne mēcum (*with me*) ientāre?

Mārcus, Helena: Maximē! (*Yes indeed!*)

Marīa: Tēcum (*with you*) ientāre cupiō, sed in studia incumbere dēbeō. Itaque expedītē ientāre dēbeō. In scholā Latīnā erit (*will be*) crās (*tomorrow*) probātiō. Itaque nōn sōlum vesperī, sed etiam māne in studia incumbō. Parārī dēbeō.

Christīna: Parārī dēbēmus, sed nōn nimium (*too much*) parārī.

Marīa: Nimium parārī nōn possum.

Christīna: Sed magistra (*teacher*) est iūsta. Probātiō nōn erit difficilis. Sīc dīcit magistra.

Mārcus: Sī omnēs probātiōnem superāmus, decem (*ten*) pūncta nōbīs (*to us*) omnibus superaddita dantur. Pūncta superaddita sunt dōna!

Marīa: Dē verbīs Vergiliī poētae cōgitō. In Aenēide (*the "Aeneid"*) Trōiānus dīcit "Quidquid id est, timeō Danaōs et dōna ferentēs."

Christīna: Timēre nōn dēbēs! Magistra est amīca (*friend*), nōn hostis!

Oil painting of Aeneas and Dido hunting. By the Flemish painter Jan Miel (1599–1663).

MEMORĀBILE DICTŪ

Tantae mōlis erat Rōmānam condere gentem!

"It was so much toil to found the Roman race!" (Vergil, *Aeneid*, Book 1.33)

So exclaims the poet Vergil in the *Aeneid*. Throughout the epic, he justifies this assertion by describing the troubles the poem's hero Aeneas meets. Many Romans in Vergil's time saw the stable government established by Augustus, the first Roman emperor, as the ultimate political achievement—in contrast to the preceding civil wars. Yet Vergil never shrinks from making his readers feel the personal and political sufferings experienced by the Trojan exiles who were believed to have been the ancestors of the historical Romans.

READING

In the previous chapter you read part of Aeneas' account of how the wooden horse enabled the Greek invaders to capture Troy. After the horrific destruction of the city, Aeneas and his fellow survivors of Troy sail in search of a new home. Eventually they land at the North African city of Carthage, where Aeneas is welcomed at the court of queen Dido. Book 4 of the *Aeneid* tells how the two embark upon a love affair that ends tragically.

After Dido's brother had murdered her husband, the king of Tyre in what is now Lebanon, she fled to North Africa, founded a new city, and swore never to love again. But after she meets Aeneas, she confesses to her sister Anna *āgnōscō . . . veteris vestīgia flammae*, "I recognize the traces of an old flame . . . ." Our English phrase for a former love interest, "old flame," may derive from Latin passages, such as this one, that represent passion as fire, although Dido is here referring to a totally new love interest. Read what this flame brought to Dido.

DĒ DĪDŌNE RĒGĪNĀ

1   Dīdō rēgīna amōre ārdēbat. Nam Aenēam valdē amābat.

Aenēās et Dīdō in silvā ambulant. Tempestās māgna venit. Dum
tonat et pluit, Aenēās et Dīdō in spēluncā manent. Aenēās sē ā Dīdōne
amārī intellegit dīcitque sē quoque Dīdōnem amāre. Posteā Aenēās et

5   Dīdō Carthāgine saepe ūnā cōnspiciēbantur. Tunc propter amōrem
Aenēās Dīdōque erant fēlīcēs. Sed Iuppiter rēx deōrum Mercurium ad
Aenēam mittit. Mercurius Aenēam iubet Dīdōnem relinquere et terram
novam petere.

Aenēās Dīdōnī dīcit sē manēre nōn posse. Dīdō putat Aenēam male

10   agere. Aenēās Dīdōnī crūdēlis esse vidētur. Sed Aenēās Dīdōnem
relinquit et Ītaliam petit. Dīdō erat mulier fortis, sed dolōrem vincere
nōn poterat. Vīta Dīdōnī mala esse vidēbātur mortemque petere
cupiēbat.

READING VOCABULARY

Aenēās, Aenēae (gen.), Aenēae (dat.), Aenēam/ān (acc.), Aenēā (abl.) – Aeneas

*agō, agere, ēgī, āctum – to drive, lead, do, behave

amābat – she loved (imperfect tense)

ārdēbat – was burning (imperfect tense)

*ārdeō, ārdēre, ārsī, ——— – to burn, be on fire

Carthāgine – at Carthage, in Carthage

cōnspiciēbantur – were observed (imperfect tense)

*cōnspiciō, cōnspicere, cōnspexī, cōnspectum – to look at, observe

*crūdēlis, crūdēle – cruel

cupiēbat – she wished (imperfect tense)

dīcitque – and says

Dīdō, Dīdōnis, f. – Dido

Dīdōque – and Dido

*dolor, dolōris, m. – grief, pain

erant – were (imperfect tense)

erat – was (imperfect tense)

Ītalia, Ītaliae, f. – Italy

Iuppiter – Jupiter

male (adv.) – badly

Mercurius, Mercuriī, m. – Mercury

*mittō, mittere, mīsī, missum – to send

mortemque – and death

*novus, nova, novum – new

pluit – it is raining

poterat – was able (imperfect tense)

*-que – and

*quoque (adv.) – also

*rēgīna, rēgīnae, f. – queen

*relinquō, relinquere, relīquī, relictum – to leave behind, abandon

*silva, silvae, f. – forest

*spēlunca, spēluncae, f. – cave

*tempestās, tempestātis, f. – storm

tonat – it is thundering

*ūnā (adv.) – together

vidēbātur – seemed (imperfect tense)

*Words marked with an asterisk will need to be memorized.

COMPREHENSION QUESTIONS

1. What happened during the rainstorm near Carthage?

2. How long did the happiness of Aeneas and Dido last?

3. What was the duty Aeneas had to fulfill?

4. What happened to Dido after Aeneas' departure?

LANGUAGE FACT I

IMPERFECT ACTIVE AND PASSIVE TENSE OF ALL CONJUGATIONS

In the story about Aeneas and Dido, you have noticed some new verb forms:

> *amābat, ārdēbat, cōnspiciēbantur, cupiēbat, vidēbātur.*
> These forms belong to the imperfect tense.

The imperfect is used for a narrative in the past. It represents the action as continuous, and the completion of the action is not the primary object of attention. In fact, "imperfect" means "not completed, not perfect." Usually the imperfect is translated with the auxiliary verb "was": for example, "I was walking." In some contexts the phrases "used to" or "kept on" translate the imperfect: for example, "I used to travel" or "I kept on traveling." Sometimes the simple past can be used: for example, "I felt."

The common element in the formation of the imperfect is the syllable **-bā-** toward the end of the word. The imperfect stem is formed from the present stem of the verb in the following way:

1. For first, second, and third conjugation verbs, the syllable **-bā-** is added to the present stem:

   > amā-bā-
   > tenē-bā-
   > petē-bā-

   The *-e-* of the third conjugation stem becomes long.

2. For fourth conjugation verbs, the two syllables **-ēbā-** are added to the present stem:

   > *audī-ēbā-*

   Third conjugation *-iō* verbs resemble verbs of the fourth conjugation:

   > *capi-ēbā-*

The endings are the same as in the present tense, except that the first person singular ending is **-m** instead of **-o**:

Active endings:		Passive endings:	
-m	-mus	-r	-mur
-s	-tis	-ris	-minī
-t	-nt	-tur	-ntur

First Conjugation: Imperfect Active

	Singular			Plural	
First person	parābam	I was preparing	parābāmus	we were preparing
Second person	parābās	you were preparing	parābātis	you were preparing
Third person	parābat	s/he/it was preparing	parābant	they were preparing

First Conjugation: Imperfect Passive

	Singular			Plural	
First person	parābar	I was being prepared	parābāmur	we were being prepared
Second person	parābāris	you were being prepared	parābāminī	you were being prepared
Third person	parābātur	s/he/it was being prepared	parābantur	they were being prepared

Second Conjugation: Imperfect Active

	Singular			Plural	
First person	tenēbam	I was holding	tenēbāmus	we were holding
Second person	tenēbās	you were holding	tenēbātis	you were holding
Third person	tenēbat	s/he/it was holding	tenēbant	they were holding

Second Conjugation: Imperfect Passive

	Singular			Plural	
First person	tenēbar	I was being held	tenēbāmur	we were being held
Second person	tenēbāris	you were being held	tenēbāminī	you were being held
Third person	tenēbātur	s/he/it was being held	tenēbantur	they were being held

Third Conjugation: Imperfect Active

	Singular			Plural	
First person	petēbam	I was seeking	petēbāmus	we were seeking
Second person	petēbās	you were seeking	petēbātis	you were seeking
Third person	petēbat	s/he/it was seeking	petēbant	they were seeking

Third Conjugation: Imperfect Passive

	Singular			Plural	
First person	petēbar	I was being sought	petēbāmur	we were being sought
Second person	petēbāris	you were being sought	petēbāminī	you were being sought
Third person	petēbātur	s/he/it was being sought	petēbantur	they were being sought

Fourth Conjugation: Imperfect Active

		Singular		Plural
First person	audiēbam	I was hearing	audiēbāmus	we were hearing
Second person	audiēbās	you were hearing	audiēbātis	you were hearing
Third person	audiēbat	s/he/it was hearing	audiēbant	they were hearing

Fourth Conjugation: Imperfect Passive

		Singular		Plural
First person	audiēbar	I was being heard	audiēbāmur	we were being heard
Second person	audiēbāris	you were being heard	audiēbāminī	you were being heard
Third person	audiēbātur	s/he/it was being heard	audiēbantur	they were being heard

Third Conjugation -*iō* verbs: Imperfect Active

		Singular		Plural
First person	cōnspiciēbam	I was observing	cōnspiciēbāmus	we were observing
Second person	cōnspiciēbās	you were observing	cōnspiciēbātis	you were observing
Third person	cōnspiciēbat	s/he/it was observing	cōnspiciēbant	they were observing

Third Conjugation -*iō* verbs: Imperfect Passive

		Singular		Plural
First person	cōnspiciēbar	I was being observed	cōnspiciēbāmur	we were being observed
Second person	cōnspiciēbāris	you were being observed	cōnspiciēbāminī	you were being observed
Third person	cōnspiciēbātur	s/he/it was being observed	cōnspiciēbantur	they were being observed

STUDY TIP

Remember: Those imperfect sheep always say "ba!"

▶ EXERCISE 1

Translate into English.

1. petēbātis
2. agēbāminī
3. relinquēbar
4. cōgitābāmus
5. servābat
6. intellegēbās
7. dolēbant
8. aestimābantur
9. līberābāmur
10. veniēbam

VOCABULARY TO LEARN

omit

NOUNS

dolor, dolōris, m. – grief, pain *dolful Dolores*

rēgīna, rēgīnae, f. – queen *Regina*

silva, silvae, f. – forest *Silven*

spēlunca, spēluncae, f. – cave *Spelunking*

tempestās, tempestātis, f. – storm *tempest*

ADJECTIVES

crūdēlis, crūdēle – cruel *crude*

novus, nova, novum – new *nova*
novice

VERBS

agō, agere, ēgī, āctum – to drive, lead, do, behave *act agent*

ārdeō, ārdēre, ārsī, —— – to burn, be on fire *arson / ardent*

cōnspiciō, cōnspicere, cōnspexī, cōnspectum – to look at, observe *conspicuous*

mittō, mittere, mīsī, missum – to send *intermitten*

relinquō, relinquere, relīquī, relictum – to leave behind, abandon *relinquish*

ADVERBS

ita – yes

minimē – no

quoque – also *(too)*

ūnā – together

ENCLITIC PARTICLES

-ne – added to the first word of a question

-que – and

▶ EXERCISE 2

Find the English derivatives based on the Vocabulary to Learn in the following sentences. Write the corresponding Latin word.

1. An active life will keep you alive longer.

2. After the regicide a republic was established.

3. I heard his ardent confession of love.

4. His embarrassment was conspicuous and everybody could see it.

5. After a tempestuous love affair they settled to quieter life.

6. He is an agent of a foreign state.

7. I advise you to relinquish these plans completely and move on.

8. Novelty is always exciting.

9. The decision was unanimous.

10. We haven't had any missive from him since he was deployed for the mission.

11. After the surgery she has had a perpetually dolorous expression.

12. Matches were found in his room and he was accused of arson.

13. They were walking in the mysterious woods and wondering whether they would meet any sylvan deities.

► EXERCISE 3

Change the following imperfect active verbs into the imperfect passive, keeping the same person and number. Translate the passive forms.

Example: cōnspiciēbant
cōnspiciēbantur   they were being observed

1. capiēbam
2. līberābāmus
3. audiēbātis
4. timēbant
5. aestimābat
6. firmābāmus
7. crēdēbās

► EXERCISE 4

Change the verbs in the following passage to the imperfect tense, keeping the same person, number, and voice. Translate the changed passage.

Example: Domī maneō.
Domī manēbam.   I stayed at home. *or* I was staying at home. *or* I used to stay at home.

Aenēās et Dīdō in silvā ambulant. Aenēās sē ā Dīdōne amārī et sē quoque Dīdōnem amāre intellegit. Sed tempestās ab Aeneā et Dīdōne timētur. In spēluncā manent. In spēluncā autem nōn timōrem sed gaudium sentiunt. Nam dē amōre cōgitant. Posteā saepe ūnā esse solent.

LANGUAGE FACT II

IMPERFECT TENSE OF *SUM* AND *POSSUM*

You have already met and learned the present indicative of the irregular and very often used verbs *sum* and *possum*. In the text at the beginning of the chapter, some new forms of these verbs appeared in following sentences.

> *Tunc propter amōrem Aenēās Dīdōque erant fēlīcēs.*
> Then because of <their> love Aeneas and Dido were happy.

> *. . . dolōrem vincere nōn poterat.*
> . . . <she> was not able to conquer <her> grief.

The new forms *erat* and *poterat*, from the verbs *sum* and *possum*, are in the imperfect tense. Remember that these verbs do **not** have a passive voice.

Imperfect Tense of *sum*					
		Singular		**Plural**	
First person	eram	I was	erāmus	we were
Second person	erās	you were	erātis	you were
Third person	erat	s/he/it was	erant	they were

Imperfect Tense of *possum*					
		Singular		**Plural**	
First person	poteram	I was able/could	poterāmus	we were able/could
Second person	poterās	you were able/could	poterātis	you were able/could
Third person	poterat	s/he/it was able/could	poterant	they were able/could

BY THE WAY

The forms of *possum* are almost the same as those of *sum*, with *pot-* added in front of the forms of *sum*. *Pot-* is a part of the adjective *potis*, which means "able, potent" (actually the English "potent" comes from the same root).

▶ EXERCISE 5

Translate into Latin.

1. (we) were able to
2. (he) was
3. (I) was able to
4. (they) were
5. (you [plural]) were
6. (you) were able
7. (s/he/it) was able
8. (we) were

LANGUAGE FACT III

ENCLITICS (-*QUE* AND -*NE*)

An enclitic is attached to the word preceding it. You have already noticed one enclitic used repeatedly in the passage adapted from Vergil at the beginning of this chapter:

> *Aenēās sē ā Dīdōne amārī intellegit dīcit***que** *sē quoque Dīdōnem amāre.*
> Aeneas realizes that he is loved by Dido, and he says that he also loves Dido.

> *Tunc propter amōrem Aenēās Dīdō***que** *erant fēlīcēs.*
> Then because of <their> love Aeneas and Dido were happy.

> *Vīta Dīdōnī mala esse vidēbātur mortem***que** *petere cupiēbat.*
> Life seemed to Dido to be bad, and she wished to seek death.

This is the enclitic -*que*, which means "and" (much like the conjunction *et*). Note that -*que* is always joined to the last of the two (or more) entities being joined.

You have also seen another enclitic in some exercises in previous chapters. This is *-ne*, which is added to the first word of any sentence to turn it into a question. Compare, for example, the two sentences below.

> *Mercurius Aenēam terram novam petere iubet.*
> Mercury orders Aeneas to seek a new land.

> *Mercurius**ne** Aenēam terram novam petere iubet?*
> Does Mercury order Aeneas to seek a new land?

The Latin word for "yes" is *ita*, and for "no" *minimē*.

Mercury (Hermes) wearing a traveler's hat (*petasus*) and carrying the caduceus.

Ruins of Carthage. When Aeneas left Carthage, Dido committed suicide. Many centuries later, the Romans destroyed the city of Carthage at the end of the Punic wars.

THE TRAVELS OF AENEAS

EURŌPA

ĪTALIA

CORSICA

SARDINIA

Rōma* Alba Longa
Lāvīnium
Cāiēta
Cūmae
Sibylla

Mare Tyrrhēnum

Tempestās ab
Iūnōne excitāta
Sepulcrum
Anchīsae
Scylla et
Charybdis
Carthāgō
SICILIA
Cȳclops

Mare Hādriāticum

GRAECIA
Būthrōtum
Actium
ITHACA

THRĀCIA
Aenos
Trōia
Pergamum

Mare Aegaeum

DĒLOS

Harpȳiārum
Īnsula

Mare Īonium

MELITA

CRĒTA

Mare Internum

Pontus
Euxīnus

A F R I C A

▶ EXERCISE 6

Read the following dialogue, which is written partly in English and partly in Latin. Translate the English parts into Latin, and the Latin parts into English. Use -ne for questions and -que for "and." Use the Reading Vocabulary; other words are explained below. The dialogue begins when Mercury, sent by Jupiter, appears before Aeneas.

Mercurius: Salvē! Esne Aenēās?

Aenēās: I am Aeneas. You seem to be very great! Are you a god?

Mercurius: Deus sum! Mercurius sum. Quid nunc parās?

Aenēās: Dido and I want to be king and queen in Carthage. I am building a cottage. Does the cottage seem beautiful?

Mercurius: Ita vērō! Sed cum Dīdōne manēre Carthāgineque habitāre nōn potēs.

Aenēās: Do you believe that love is bad? Do you understand that Dido and Aeneas must remain together?

Mercurius: Deī dē amōre hominum cōgitāre nōn solent. Amōrem Aenēae Dīdōnisque ūnīus assis aestimō! Aenēās Iovis verba audīre dēbet nec cum Dīdōne manēre!

Aenēās: Must I abandon Dido and sail to Italy?

Mercurius: Iuppiter tē iubet Dīdōnem relinquere Ītaliamque petere.

Aenēās: Jupiter is cruel! You are cruel! The gods are cruel!

Mercurius: Nōn deī, sed fāta sunt crūdēlia. Fāta dīcunt Aenēam Ītaliam petere dēbēre.

Aenēās: Must men be wretched?

Mercurius: Ita vērō. Posteā autem Aenēās erit celeber poētaque dīcet "Tantae mōlis erat Rōmānam condere gentem!"

condō, condere, condidī, conditum – to found	ita vērō – yes indeed
dīcet – will say (future tense)	mōlēs, mōlis, f. – weight, mass, trouble, effort
erit – will be (future tense)	nec – and not
fāta, fātōrum, n. pl. – the Fates	quid . . . ? – what . . . ?
gēns, gentis, f. – race, nation	salvē! – hello!
Iovis – of Jupiter (genitive case of Iuppiter)	tantus, tanta, tantum – so much, so great

TALKING

bene māne – early in the morning

excipiō, excipere, excēpī, exceptum – to pick up (someone in a vehicle)

iter faciō (facere, fēcī, factum) – I make a journey, travel

iter, itineris, n. – journey

pēs, pedis, m. – foot

prope (+ accusative) – near

raeda longa – bus

raeda, raedae, f. – car

birota, birotae, f. – bicycle

schola, scholae, f. – note that this word can mean both "school" and a particular "class." Later you will encounter some other words that mean just "school."

trāmen (trāminis, gen.*) subterrāneum* – subway train

TRAVELING TO SCHOOL

Mārcus: Diū pecūniam (*money*) servābam. Nam raedam habēre cupiēbam. Itaque raedam ēmī (*I bought*).

Christīna: Solēsne, Mārce, raedā tuā (*your*) ad scholam venīre?

Mārcus: Ita vērō. (*Yes indeed.*) Et in raedā mēcum (*with me*) venīre solet Helena. Quōmodo (*how*), Christīna, tū ad scholam venīre solēs?

Christīna: Raedā longā aut (*or*) trāmine subterrāneō ad scholam venīre soleō. Nam raedam nōn habeō, et ā scholā longē habitāmus. Cottīdiē (*every day*) iter longum facere dēbeō.

Mārcus: Quōmodo (*how*), Marīa, tū ad scholam venīre solēs?

Marīa: Birotā aut pedibus ad scholam venīre soleō. Nam prope scholam habitāmus. Itaque ad scholam aliquandō (*sometimes*) ambulāre possum. Cūr, Mārce, Helena tēcum (*with you*) semper ad scholam venit?

Mārcus: Ego et Helena iter ad scholam semper ūnā facere cupimus. Prīmum (*first*) iter ad casam Helenae faciō. Helena exspectat. Helenam excipiō. Deinde (*then*) iter ad scholam ūnā facimus.

CHAPTER 12

First, Second, and Third Person Personal Pronouns; First and Second Person Possessive Adjectives; Declension of *vīs*

Mucius Scaevola with his right hand in the fire. By Laurent Pecheux (1729–1821).

MEMORĀBILE DICTŪ

Fortēs fortūna adiuvat.
"Fortune helps the brave." (Terence, *Phormio*, 203)

This famous phrase, which features a pun on two similarly sounding words, comes from the Roman playwright Terence.

READING

The Roman historian Titus Līvius (59 BCE–17 CE), known to us as Livy, was born in Patavium, today called Padua, in northern Italy, and apparently moved to Rome as a young man. While he seems to have held no official political positions, he developed a good relationship with the emperor Augustus, whose great-nephew, the future emperor Claudius (10 BCE–54 CE), he encouraged to write history.

Livy's own history of Rome took its title—*Ab Urbe Conditā*, "From the Founding of the City"—from the phrase that Romans used to calculate dates. Comprised of 142 books, it begins with Rome's origins prior to its foundation in 753 BCE and concludes in 9 BCE. Only Books 1–10 and 21–45 survive, some of these with substantial gaps in the texts.

In the opening books of his history, Livy highlights the courage and virtues of the earliest Romans, qualities that he believes gave rise to Rome's later greatness. At various points, in fact, he contrasts these values with what he perceives as the decadence of his own era, by which time the Roman republic had become a vast, wealthy empire, with a government controlled by one man.

The following story from Book 2, chapter 12, of Livy's history is legendary, but describes events that were likely to have taken place around the end of the sixth century BCE. The Etruscans were besieging Rome. A young Roman man named Mucius volunteered to penetrate the enemy camp and assassinate the Etruscan king, Lars Porsenna. The plot failed, and Mucius was captured and dragged before the king. Although a helpless captive, Mucius displayed his defiance to Porsenna, through an act that explains why he was given the nickname "Scaevola," which means "left-handed."

DĒ MŪCIŌ SCAEVOLĀ

1   "Rōmānus sum" inquit Mūcius, "cīvis. Hominēs mē Mūcium vocant.
    Tē hostem occīdere cupiēbam. Mīlitēs tuōs nōn timēbam. Nunc
    mortem nōn timeō. Rōmānī vim hostium nōn timent. Multī sunt
    Rōmānī mihi similēs et parātī id facere, quod ego facere nōn poteram.

5   Semper igitur cīvēs nostrōs timēre dēbēs. Bellum contrā nōs geris nōn
    sōlum in castrīs, sed etiam domī, ubi hostēs occultī tē petunt." Rēx īrā
    movētur. Iubet mīlitēs Etrūscōs ignēs prope Mūcium pōnere. Deinde
    rēx, "Dīcisne mihi ex hostibus occultīs esse perīculum?" inquit. "Ego
    dīcō tibi ex ignibus esse nunc perīculum! Ignēs nunc timēre dēbēs,

10 nisi nōmina hostium occultōrum mihi statim dīcis!" Mūcius autem

subitō dextram in ignem pōnit. Ibi manēbat nec dolōrem ostendēbat. Attonitus rēx dextram Mūciī flammīs cōnsūmī videt. Tunc rēx Mūcium līberāre dēcernit: nam intellegit eum esse valdē fortem iūdicatque tantam fortitūdinem vincī nōn posse!

READING VOCABULARY

attonitus, attonita, attonitum – astounded

*cōnsūmō, cōnsūmere, cōnsūmpsī, cōnsūmptum – to consume

*dextra, dextrae, f. – right hand

Etrūscus, Etrūsca, Etrūscum – Etruscan

eum – him (masculine accusative singular)

*faciō, facere, fēcī, factum – to do, make

*gerere bellum – to wage war

*ibi (adv.) – there

*id – that (neuter accusative singular)

igitur (conj.) – therefore

*ignis, ignis, m. – fire

*inquit – says or said (note that in classical Latin this verb is only used with direct speech)

*īra, īrae, f. – anger

mē – me (accusative singular)

mihi – me (dative singular)

Mūcius (Mūciī) Scaevola (Scaevolae), m. – Mucius Scaevola

nisi (conj.) – if not, unless

*nōmen, nōminis, n. – name

*nōs – we (accusative singular)

*noster, nostra, nostrum – our

*occīdō, occīdere, occīdī, occīsum – to kill

occultus, occulta, occultum – hidden

*ostendō, ostendere, ostendī, ostentum – to show

parātus, parāta, parātum – prepared (often + infinitive)

*pōnō, pōnere, posuī, positum – to put, place

*prope + accusative – near

quod – which

*similis, simile + genitive or dative – like

*statim (adv.) – immediately

subitō (adv.) – suddenly

*tantus, tanta, tantum – so great

tē – you (accusative singular)

tibi – you (dative singular)

*tuus, tua, tuum – your, yours

ubi – where

*vim – accusative of *vīs*, meaning "force, strength"

*Words marked with an asterisk will need to be memorized.

COMPREHENSION QUESTIONS

1. How does Mucius threaten Porsenna? Fire

2. What is Mucius' reaction when Porsenna threatens him? he puts his hand in the fire

3. What does Porsenna do after Mucius' extraordinary action? lets him go

LANGUAGE FACT I

FIRST AND SECOND PERSON PERSONAL PRONOUNS

In the passage at the beginning of the chapter you notice a series of words in various cases meaning "me," "you," "us": *mē, tē, mihi, tibi, nōs*. The nominative singular *ego*, meaning "I," has already been introduced in the Vocabulary to Learn of Chapter 2, and the same is true of the nominative singular *tū*, which means "you."

Words of this type are pronouns; they take the place of nouns. In English, words like "she," "it," "they," "we," "you," and the like are pronouns. Here are the declensions of the first and second person personal pronouns, singular and plural.

First Person Pronoun

	Singular		Plural	
Nominative	ego	I	nōs	we
Genitive	meī	(to be discussed later)	nostrum/nostrī	(to be discussed later)
Dative	mihi	to/for me	nōbīs	to/for us
Accusative	mē	me	nōs	us
Ablative	mē	by/with me	nōbīs	by/with us

Second Person Pronoun

	Singular		Plural	
Nominative	tū	you	vōs	you *all*
Genitive	tuī	(to be discussed later)	vestrum/vestrī	(to be discussed later)
Dative	tibi	to/for you	vōbīs	to/for you *all*
Accusative	tē	you	vōs	you *all*
Ablative	tē	by/with you	vōbīs	by/with you *all*

BY THE WAY

In English, the second person pronoun "you" is the same in the singular and plural. In Latin, however, there is a separate form for the plural of the second person. Note that the gender distinction for "you" is apparent from the context.

▶ EXERCISE 1

Fill in the blanks with the correct form of the first or second person pronoun and translate both sentences. The verb in bold determines the person and number of the required personal pronoun.

Example: Dōnum _____ datur. Itaque dōnum mihi dare **dēbēs.**

Dōnum tibi datur.   A gift is being given to you.   Therefore you ought to give me a gift.

1. Dōna _____ datis. Itaque dōna vōbīs dare **dēbēmus.**
2. _____ valdē amāmus. Itaque nōs quoque amāre **dēbētis.**
3. _____ valdē amō. Itaque mē quoque amāre **dēbēs.**
4. Dē _____ semper cōgitās. Itaque dē tē semper cōgitāre **dēbēmus.**
5. Dē _____ semper cōgitātis. Itaque dē vōbīs semper cōgitāre **dēbeō.**
6. _____ **sumus** fēlīcēs. **Estisne** _____ fēlīcēs?
7. _____ **sum** fēlīx. **Esne** _____ fēlīx?

VOCABULARY TO LEARN

NOUNS

dextra, dextrae, f. – right hand

ignis, ignis, m. – fire

īra, īrae, f. – anger

nōmen, nōminis, n. – name

vīs, —, f.; pl. vīrēs, vīrium – force, strength

PRONOUNS

is, ea, id – s/he/it, this, that

nōs – we

vōs – you

ADJECTIVES

noster, nostra, nostrum – our

similis, simile + genitive or dative – like

tantus, tanta, tantum – so great

tuus, tua, tuum – your, yours

vester, vestra, vestrum – your, yours

VERBS

cōnsūmō, cōnsūmere, cōnsūmpsī, cōnsūmptum – to consume

faciō, facere, fēcī, factum – to do, make

inquit – s/he says or said (note that in classical Latin this verb is only used with direct speech)

occīdō, occīdere, occīdī, occīsum – to kill

ostendō, ostendere, ostendī, ostentum – to show

pōnō, pōnere, posuī, positum – to put, place

ADVERBS

ibi – there

statim – immediately

PREPOSITION

prope + accusative – near

PHRASES

bellum gerō – to wage war

prō vīribus – with all one's might

▶ EXERCISE 2

Find the English derivatives based on the Vocabulary to Learn in the following sentences. Write the corresponding Latin word.

1. Please state only the facts.

2. Be less ostentatious and more simple in your manner!

3. He was proud of his social position.

4. We all are consumers of various goods.

5. A simile is a figure of speech that involves comparison.

6. The gladiator handled the sword with great dexterity.

7. The ignition system of that car needs to be replaced.

▶ EXERCISE 3

Change the singular sentences into plural and the plural into singular and translate the changed sentence.

Example: Dextrās nōbīs datis.
Dextram mihi das.   You are giving me (your) right hand.

1. Nōs esse hostēs crēdunt.

2. Tē tempestatem cōnspicere cupiēbam.

3. Senex mihi similis nōn est.

4. Dē nōbīs mulierēs nōn cōgitant.

5. Dīcō tibi ē flammā esse perīculum.

6. Prope mē pōnitur ignis.

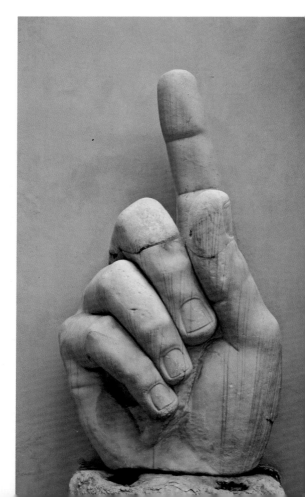

The right hand (*dextra*) from the colossal statue of the emperor Constantine.

LANGUAGE FACT II

THIRD PERSON PERSONAL PRONOUN *IS, EA, ID*

In the Latin reading passage you saw two other new pronoun forms in the following sentences.

> *Multī sunt Rōmānī mihi similēs et parātī **id** facere, quod ego facere nōn poteram.*
> There are many Romans like me and prepared to do **that** which I was not able to do (. . . prepared to do what I was not able to do).

> *Intellegit **eum** esse valdē fortem.*
> He understands that **he** (Mucius) is extremely brave.

The nominative singular forms of the third person pronoun in Latin are *is, ea, id*, in the masculine, feminine, and neuter respectively. These words are the equivalent of the English words "he," "she," "it." But sometimes the meaning of *is, ea, id* extends more widely and may be used as a kind of *demonstrative* to mean "this" or "that" (person or thing). Here are all the forms of this word:

Third Person Pronoun: *is, ea, id*

Singular

	Masculine	Feminine	Neuter
Nominative	is	ea	id
Genitive	ēius	ēius	ēius
Dative	eī	eī	eī
Accusative	eum	eam	id
Ablative	eō	eā	eō

Plural

	Masculine	Feminine	Neuter
Nominative	eī (iī)	eae	ea
Genitive	eōrum	eārum	eōrum
Dative	eīs (iīs)	eīs (iīs)	eīs (iīs)
Accusative	eōs	eās	ea
Ablative	eīs (iīs)	eīs (iīs)	eīs (eīs)

BY THE WAY

You may observe that *is, ea, id* follows mainly the first and the second declension, and in its dative singular has the ending of the third declension. However, the ending of the genitive singular matches none of the declensions we have seen so far. This is because *is, ea, id* belongs to a special declension shared by most pronouns. You will meet examples of this special pronominal declension again.

▶ EXERCISE 4

Change the nouns in parentheses to the correct corresponding form of *is, ea, id* and translate the changed sentence.

Example: Dextra (Mūciī) flammīs cōnsūmitur.
Dextra ēius flammīs cōnsūmitur.   His right hand is being consumed by flames.

1. Dolōrem (mulierum) vidēmus.

2. Māgna praemia (civibus) dantur.

3. Mūcius ē (rēgis) castrīs nōn fugit.

4. Mūcius (vītam) ā rēge nōn petēbat.

5. Mīles (bellum) nōn timēbat.

6. Lacrimīs (puellārum) movēbāmur.

7. Rēx (Mūciō) nōn crēdit.

8. Dē (patriā) saepe cōgitāmus.

9. Templum ā (duce) aedificātur.

The ancient Romans from early times to late imperial times built temples.
This temple (*templum*), was begun by the emperor Antoninus Pius in honor of his
deified wife, Faustina. After his death, the Romans dedicated the temple to both of them.

LANGUAGE FACT III

FIRST AND SECOND PERSON POSSESSIVE ADJECTIVES

Latin also has first and second person **possessive adjectives**. These words are like any other adjective, i.e., they agree in case, number, and gender case with the noun they refer to, but they also show personal possession ("my," "your," "our," etc.).

Here are the first and second person possessive adjectives, singular and plural:

Possessive adjectives: first and second person
meus, mea, meum – my (declines like *bonus, bona, bonum*)
tuus, tua, tuum – your (singular) (declines like *bonus, bona, bonum*)
noster, nostra, nostrum – our (declines like *pulcher, pulchra, pulchrum*)
vester, vestra, vestrum – your (plural) (declines like *pulcher, pulchra, pulchrum*)

Look closely at the following examples from the passage at the beginning of the chapter; you will see that these adjectives function just like other adjectives.

Mīlitēs tuōs nōn timēbam.
I was not afraid of your soldiers.

Semper igitur cīvēs nostrōs timēre dēbēs.
Therefore you must always fear our citizens.

Both possessive adjectives are in the accusative plural, because in each case the noun with which they agree is accusative plural.

▶ EXERCISE 5

Translate into Latin.

1. my son (nominative)

2. of my sons

3. to our daughter

4. our daughters (accusative)

5. by your word

6. your words (nominative)

7. with your (plural) horse

8. to your (plural) horses

▶ EXERCISE 6

Supply the correct form of the possessive adjective in parentheses and translate the completed sentence or phrase.

Example: īrae _____ (my)
īrae meae   to/for my anger   of my anger   my angers

1. nōminum _____ (your [plural])

2. Ā fīliō _____ equus dūcēbātur. (our)

3. Praemium _____ capis. (your)

4. Rēx _____ fīliās amābat. (my)

5. Hominēs terram _____ cōnspiciēbant. (our)

6. Nōn dēbēs dextram _____ in igne relinquere. (your)

LANGUAGE FACT IV

DECLENSION OF *VĪS*

You have already learned the third declension. There are, however, some irregular third declension nouns that must be learned individually because they have certain peculiarities. One of these nouns is *vīs*, which you have already met in the reading at the beginning of this chapter:

> Rōmānī **vim** hostium nōn timent.
> The Romans do not fear the force of enemies.

This common word means "force," or "violence," and sometimes (especially in the plural) "strength" or "energy." The plural can also denote "military forces." The phrase *prō vīribus* means "with all one's might" or "as best as one can."

Declension of *vīs*		
	Singular	**Plural**
Nominative	vīs	vīrēs
Genitive	-	vīrium
Dative	-	vīribus
Accusative	vim	vīrēs
Ablative	vī	vīribus

 STUDY TIP

Be very careful never to confuse the word *vīs* (especially its plural forms) with the second declension noun *vir* ("man").

▶ EXERCISE 7

Translate into Latin. The Reading Vocabulary may be consulted.

1. Now I understand, Mucius (*Mūcī*), that your courage cannot be conquered by flames.

2. You want to think about my death, but you see my bravery.

3. These things (use a form of *is, ea, id*) seem to be dangers to you, king, but not to our Roman soldiers.

4. "You must," said the king, "immediately tell me the names of my enemies."

5. "In my city," said Mucius, "there are many (people) similar to me."

6. "You cannot understand," said Mucius, "the courage of our soldiers."

Soldiers formed an integral part of the life of Romans from the time of Mucius Scaevola to the imperial era. This stone relief is from the Antonine column that was built by the emperor Marcus Aurelius in honor of his predecessor Antoninus Pius.

TALKING

aestās, aestātis, f. – summer

annī tempus (temporis, n.) – season

annus, annī, m. – year

arbor, arboris, f. – tree

autumnus, autumnī, m. – autumn

caelum, caelī, n. – sky, weather

calor, calōris, m. – heat (often used in the plural when referring to climate)

folium, foliī, n. – leaf

fulgur, fulguris, n. – lightning

gemma, gemmae, f. – bud

hiems, hiemis, f. – winter

ningit (impersonal) – it snows

nix, nivis, f. – snow

nūbēs, nūbis, f. – cloud

nūbilus, nūbila, nūbilum – cloudy

placeō, placēre, placuī – to please (+ dative)

serēnus, serēna, serēnum – clear, bright

sūdus, sūda, sūdum – clear, bright

tempestās, tempestātis, f. – storm

tonitruum, tonitruī, n. – thunder

vēr, vēris, n. – spring

Aestem relinquebantur.
Puella ad folios ambulat.

DISCUSSING THE WEATHER

Helena: Ningit hodiē (*today*). Nivēs nōn amō. Sī (*if*) ningit, domī manēre cupiō.

Marīa: Nivēs mihi placent. Bonum est in nivibus lūdere (*to play*). Quāle (*what sort of*) caelum tibi placet?

Helena: Caelum sūdum et serēnum mihi placet. Placet mihi aestās. Placent mihi calōrēs. Placet mihi mare. Nam aestāte (*during the summer*) prope mare lūdere possum. Placetne tibi, Mārce, aestās?

Mārcus: Aestās mihi placet. Omnia (*all*) annī tempora mihi placent. Quod (*what*) tempus tibi, Christīna, placet?

Christīna: Vēr mihi placet. Tunc caelum est serēnum, sed nūbilum. Nūbēs mihi pulchrae esse videntur. Gemmae quoque sunt vēre (*during the spring*) in arboribus.

Marīa: Vēr quoque mihi placet. Sed autumnum valdē amō. Tunc folia sunt pulchra: rubra (*red*) et flāva (*yellow*). Autumnō (*during the fall*) quoque sunt tempestātēs. Fēlīx sum, sī tonitrua audiō et fulgura videō.

REVIEW 4: CHAPTERS 10–12

VOCABULARY TO KNOW

NOUNS

deus, deī, m. – god

dextra, dextrae, f. – right hand

dolor, dolōris, m. – grief, pain

dōnum, dōnī, n. – gift

equus, equī, m. – horse

flamma, flammae, f. – flame

hostis, hostis, m. – enemy

ignis, ignis, m. – fire

īra, īrae, f. – anger

nōmen, nōminis, n. – name

nox, noctis, f. – night

perīculum, perīculī, n. – danger

rēgīna, rēgīnae, f. – queen

silva, silvae, f. – forest

spēlunca, spēluncae, f. – cave

tempestās, tempestātis, f. – storm

vīs, ——, f.; pl. vīrēs, vīrium – force, strength

PRONOUNS

is, ea, id – s/he/it, this, that

nōs – we

vōs – you

ADJECTIVES

ācer, ācris, ācre – keen, fierce

celeber, celebris, celebre – renowned, well-known, crowded

crūdēlis, crūdēle – cruel

fēlīx, fēlīcis – fortunate, happy

fortis, forte – brave, strong

noster, nostra, nostrum – our

novus, nova, novum – new

paucī, paucae, pauca (plural) – few

similis, simile + genitive or dative – like

tantus, tanta, tantum – so great

tuus, tua, tuum – your, yours

vester, vestra, vestrum – your, yours

VERBS

aedificō, aedificāre, aedificāvī, aedificātum – to build

agō, agere, ēgī, āctum – to drive, lead, do, behave

ārdeō, ārdēre, ārsī, —— – to burn, be on fire

capiō, capere, cēpī, captum – to take, adopt, capture: *cōnsilia capere* means "to make plans"

cōnspiciō, cōnspicere, cōnspexī, cōnspectum – to look at, observe

cōnsūmō, cōnsūmere, cōnsūmpsī, cōnsūmptum – to consume

cupiō, cupere, cupīvī, cupītum – to desire, want

dēleō, dēlēre, dēlēvī, dēlētum – to destroy

faciō, facere, fēcī, factum – to do, make

fugiō, fugere, fūgī, —— – to flee, run away

inquit – s/he says or said (note that in classical Latin this verb is only used with direct speech)

mittō, mittere, mīsī, missum – to send

moveō, movēre, mōvī, mōtum – to move

occīdō, occīdere, occīdī, occīsum – to kill

ostendō, ostendere, ostendī, ostentum – to show

pōnō, pōnere, posuī, positum – to put, place

pugnō, pugnāre, pugnāvī, pugnātum – to fight

relinquō, relinquere, relīquī, relictum – to leave behind, abandon

ADVERBS

ibi – there

ita – yes

minimē – no

quoque – also

statim – immediately

ūnā – together

PREPOSITION

prope + accusative – near

CONJUNCTION

nec – and not, nor

ENCLITIC PARTICLES

-ne – added to the first word of a question

-que – and

PHRASES

bellum gerō – to wage war

prō vīribus – with all one's might

▶ EXERCISE 1

Decline the following phrases.

1. *dōnum tuum* donī tui | dono tuo | donum tuum | dono tuo | dona tua | donorum tuorum | donis tuis | d

2. *hostis noster*

3. *rēgīna crūdēlis*

4. *equus celeber*

▶ EXERCISE 2

Conjugate the following verb in the present active and passive voice and give the present active and passive infinitives.

1. *cōnspiciō, cōnspicere, cōnspexī, cōnspectum*

▶ EXERCISE 3

Conjugate the following verbs in the imperfect active voice.

1. *pugnō, pugnāre, pugnāvī, pugnātum*

2. *fugiō, fugere, fūgī, ——*

3. *veniō, venīre, vēnī, ventum*

Conjugate the following verbs in the imperfect passive voice.

4. *moveō, movēre, mōvī, mōtum*

5. *ostendō, ostendere, ostendī, ostentum*

▶ EXERCISE 4

Make the adjective in parentheses agree with the noun. For some, more than one answer is possible.

Example: mīlitis miserī (fortis)
mīlitis fortis

1. poētā iūstō (celeber)
2. puellārum multārum (fortis)
3. lupae malae (fortis)
4. praemia māgna (celeber)
5. cōnsulēs bonī (ācer)
6. rēgum bonōrum (fēlīx)
7. viā longā (fēlīx)

▶ EXERCISE 5

Fill in the blanks with the correct form of the first or second person pronoun and translate the completed sentence. The verb in bold determines the person and number of the required personal pronoun.

Example: Nōmina hostium _____ dīcō. Itaque praemium mihi dare **dēbētis**.
Nōmina hostium vōbīs dīcō. Itaque praemium mihi dare dēbētis.
I am telling you (plural) the names of the enemies. Therefore you (plural) ought to give me a reward.

1. _____ esse sevērum dīcis. Sed animum **meum** tē nōn intellegere crēdō.
2. _____ vidēre possumus. Sed ā **vōbīs** nōn cōnspicimur.
3. Ā _____ valdē amāris. Sed **mē** nōn valdē amāre vidēris.
4. **Vidēris** mihi multōs habēre amīcōs. Itaque _____ esse fēlīcem putō.
5. Puella ā _____ amātur, sed _____ ūnīus assis aestimat. Itaque **doleō** et **sum** miser.
6. Intellegō, Mūcī, fortitūdinem **tuam** vincī nōn posse. Itaque _____ līberāre dēcernō.

▶ EXERCISE 6

Translate into Latin.

1. Must men fear the gods?
2. Do you say that these men are fortunate?
3. We must always love good and distinguished things (use -que for "and").
4. The cruel enemies were being killed.
5. We do not see that they are abandoning your camp.
6. Are the Greeks giving us gifts? I do not believe that they are good.
7. Bad things are not always observed by us.
8. We were fighting with all <our> might.
9. Were you leaving her behind?

▶ EXERCISE 7

Translate the following passage into English.

After Mucius Scaevola's exploits, the Etruscan king Porsenna decided to make peace with the Romans. It was stipulated as part of a peace agreement that the Romans would give hostages and the Etruscans would keep them. However, one of the hostages, a young woman named Cloelia, defiantly escaped from the prison camp with a group of young Roman women.

Cloelia et aliquot mulierēs ex castrīs Etrūscōrum fugiunt Rōmamque petunt. Tunc Porsenna magnā īrā capitur et lēgātōs ad Rōmānōs mittit: "Nēmō vestrum dēbet foedus nostrum unīus assis aestimāre. Itaque Cloelia dēbet ad castra Etrūscōrum revenīre. Sī Cloelia ad castra nostra revenit, eam līberābō." Cloelia id facit et rēx Etrūscōrum eam līberat. Is intellegit nōn sōlum virōs Rōmānōs, sed etiam mulierēs Rōmānās esse valdē fortēs.

aliquot – some, a certain number
Cloelia, Cloeliae, f. – Cloelia
Etrūscus, Etrūscī, m. – Etruscan
foedus, foederis, n. – treaty
lēgātus, lēgātī, m. – ambassador

līberābō – future of līberō, first person singular
nēmō – nobody, none
Porsenna, Porsennae, m. – Porsenna
reveniō, revenīre, revēnī, reventum – to return
sī (conj.) – if

The Romans set up a female equestrian statue in honor of Cloelia, which was unheard of at that time. Some believe that the statue, later destroyed, was to a goddess, and associated with Cloelia only because of the legend.

MERCURY

Mercury, known to the Greeks as Hermes, belonged to the younger generation of Olympian gods. Son of Zeus and the nymph Maia, he displayed signs of extreme intelligence and cunning from the day after his birth. He invented the lyre by carving the shell of a tortoise and stretching strings over it. He then stole the cattle of his older brother, the god Apollo, and quickly returned home. When Apollo finally found him there, he was innocently lying in his cradle and pretended to have nothing to do with the theft. Eventually Apollo and Hermes were reconciled when Hermes gave his brother the newly invented lyre.

Hermes gives Apollo the cithara in exchange for a herd of cattle. By Francesco Albani (1578–1660).

After Hermes grew up, he become the official herald of the gods and was often represented with winged shoes, a traveler's hat, and a staff with two entwined snakes, called a caduceus. In addition to being the patron of merchants, thieves, and travelers, he was regarded as the trickster among the gods. He was also viewed as the god of boundaries, and the violation of boundaries, because he moved easily and often from one place to another; he even accompanied the souls of dead people to the underworld. Statues of the god Hermes, called herms, were placed on roads, in public locales, and on house doors in order to bring good luck.

A second-century CE Roman copy of an original bronze statue of Hermes from the school of Praxiteles.

READ THE FOLLOWING PASSAGE

Mercurius erat deōrum nūntius. Ad hominēs saepe mittēbātur. Iuppiter Mercurium ad Aenēam mittit: nam Iuppiter nōn cupit Aenēam cum Dīdōne manēre. Itaque Aenēās Ītaliam petere ab eō iubētur, et ēius iussa ē Mercuriō audit. Mercurius nōn sōlum deōrum iussa hominibus dīcēbat, sed etiam umbrās mortuōrum ad īnferōs dūcēbat. Itaque hominēs Mercurium nōn semper amābant: saepe eum timēbant!

Aenēās, Aenēae, m. – Aeneas
Dīdō, Dīdōnis, f. – Dido
dūcō, dūcere, dūxī, ductum – to lead
īnferī, īnferōrum, m. – the underworld,
   the inhabitants of the underworld
Ītalia, Ītaliae, f. – Italy

iussum, iussī, n. – command
Mercurius, Mercuriī, m. – Mercury
mortuī, mortuōrum, m – the dead
nūntius, nūntiī, m. – messenger, message
umbra, umbrae, f. – shadow, ghost

CONNECTING WITH THE ANCIENT WORLD

ROMAN FOOD

In Chapter 10 you saw some Latin words relating to food and meals. The ancient Romans usually ate three meals a day: *ientāculum*, breakfast; *prandium*, lunch; *cēna*, dinner. They sometimes omitted the first two, however, or only ate very light fare, such as water in the morning, or a piece of bread with cheese. Lunch usually consisted of bread, cold meat, fruit, and vegetables, all washed down with a bottle of wine. The main meal for the Romans was dinner, which they ate after their bath, before nightfall.

Yet in imperial times, when excessive eating became more customary, dinner could begin as early as noon and last until midnight. It was served

Flagon with a straw covering and a glass goblet on a mosaic from a *triclīnium*.

in a special room called the *triclīnium*, which is also the name of the couch on which people reclined to eat. The *triclīnium* consisted of three sections, arranged around three sides of the table. Reclining was not only more comfortable physically for those dining but was also considered a mark of elegance. Dinner guests washed their hands before dinner and frequently during dinner, since they used their fingers for handling their food, though knives with iron blades or handles of bone were used to cut up food, and spoons of bronze, silver, or bone were also available. Guests brought their own napkins.

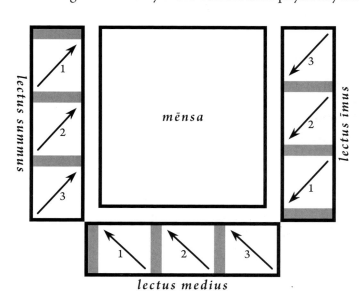

Diagram of a typical Roman dining room (*triclīnium*) with a table (*mēnsa*) in the center surrounded on three sides by couches for the guests to recline upon while eating.

A Roman dinner could be comprised of as many as seven courses, and feature elaborate dishes of meat, fowl, and fish, artfully presented. The main meal consisted of three courses: the appetizer (*gustātiō*); the main course (*prīma mēnsa*); and the dessert course called the *mēnsa secunda*, "second table." Since eggs were eaten at the beginning of the meal and apples at the end, the expression *ab ōvō ūsque ad māla* (literally translated "from the egg to apples," our "from soup to nuts") characterizes the meal. During dinner itself, there were dances, recitations, and games, and, especially at relatively frugal meals, philosophical conversations. In the imperial period dining was sometimes marked by immoderation and excess: dinner guests might visit the so-called vomiting room after stuffing themselves with food so that they could continue their feasting.

From different periods of the Roman occupation near the Ljubljanica River in Slovenia come these artifacts: mortar, helmet, ladle, saucepan, oil lamps, and axe.

Wooden plates with spoons of bronze used by the Roman soldiers during the time of Caracalla.

Wine was also consumed, at times excessively, over the course of Roman banquets. The thickly textured wine from southern Italy was usually mixed with water, a custom the Romans shared with the Greeks. Romans also liked *mulsum*, a mixture of wine and honey. In his *Satyricon*, a novel in prose and verse, the first-century CE Roman author Petronius offers a picturesque description of a banquet hosted by a newly wealthy man of questionable taste named Trimalchio whose feast is characterized by both culinary and behavioral excesses.

EXPLORING THE MYTH OF THE TROJAN HORSE

NEVER LOOK A GIFT HORSE IN THE MOUTH

The story of the Trojan horse resonates throughout literature and art. It is first found in three separate accounts in Homer's *Odyssey* (4.266–89; 8.499–520; 11.523–38), written probably in the eighth century BCE. In Homer's account the crafty Odysseus conceived the idea of building a giant horse in which to conceal armed Greeks. Epeius was the craftsman of the horse. Homer does not tell us how many warriors the horse held, but he specifically mentions the heroes Odysseus, his usual companion Diomedes, the Spartan king Menelaus, the rather insignificant Antiklos, and Neoptolemus, Achilles' son. The Trojans debated what to do with the strange horse: to destroy it with axes, throw it over a cliff, or take it into their city. There is no mention in Homer of the Greek agent Sinon who, in later accounts such as Vergil's

Marble bust of Homer from the first or second century CE, discovered in Baiae, Italy.

(*Aeneid* 2.13–267), treacherously convinced the Trojans that the horse was a sort of symbolic offering to replace the Palladium, a sacred statue of Minerva (the Greek Athena) that had been stolen from her Trojan temple by Odysseus and Diomedes. Sinon pretended that the Greeks had returned home, since the gods were angry with them. In fact, they had concealed their fleet behind the island of Tenedos, just offshore from Troy. Sinon falsely claimed that, if the Trojans took the horse into the city, it would protect them. The opposite, of course, was true. The horse was so large that, in order to bring it into the city, the Trojans had to dismantle part of the walls and gates that had protected them so well for nearly ten years.

In Homer's account there is also no mention of the priest Laocoön who warned against bringing the horse into Troy. Laocoön first appears in a fragment of a Sophoclean play (fifth century BCE). His story is very familiar today primarily because of Vergil's vivid description but also because of a dramatic large sculpture of Laocoön and his sons being strangled by sea-serpents. This ancient sculpture was unearthed on the outskirts of Rome in 1506 CE and was assumed to be the statue that Pliny the Elder (first century CE) reports was in the palace of the emperor Vespasian (69–79 CE). The intriguing question is whether the sculpture predates Vergil's account (written prior to 19 BCE) or is a depiction of it. The sculpture is still a major attraction in the Vatican Museum in Rome.

As the story of the horse developed over time, new details were given. Vergil added the names of Thessandrus, Sthenelus, Thoas, Acamas, Machaon, and Epeius himself to those warriors hidden in the horse. He omitted Diomedes and Antiklos and, of course, called Odysseus by his Roman name, Ulysses. Quintus Smyrnaeus (fourth century CE) in his continuation of Homer's story, *The Fall of Troy* (Book 12.243 ff.) names thirty warriors but adds that there were also many others. Smyrnaeus also depicts the prophetess Cassandra warning the Trojans about the danger hidden in the horse. In his version it is not Laocoön's gruesome death that undermines his warning but a madness sent by Athena.

Trojan Horse used during the filming of the movie *Troy*.

One wonders about the origin of the story of the Trojan horse. Was it really an implement of war filled with armed men? Or was it symbolic? A wooden object would make sense as a replacement for the wooden Palladium. But why a horse? Horses, as the animals of the cavalry, are associated with war. The area of Troy itself was also famous for horses, such as the fabulous horses of the Trojan ally King Rhesus and the chariot-driving warriors of the Hyksos. Homer describes Ilium (Troy) as "rich in horses" and the Trojan hero Hektor as "breaker of horses." Neptune was the god who created horses and horses were sacrificed to him. He and Apollo were said to have built the great walls of Troy. It was because they were denied payment for their labor that Neptune then sided against the Trojans. Neptune was also called "earth-shaker" because of his association with earthquakes. Could the Trojan horse refer symbolically to the enmity of Neptune in causing an earthquake that destroyed Troy?

In later literature the story of the Trojan horse has come to epitomize treachery. In his *Inferno, Canto* 26.52–63, Dante (1265–1321) includes Odysseus and Diomedes in the Eighth Circle of hell that houses fraudulent counselors. They burn together wrapped in a shared flame. Sinon is also in the Eighth Circle housed with the falsifiers (*Canto* 30.91–129). He is unable to move for all eternity and a burning smoke rises from him as if from wet hands in wintertime. Chaucer (c.1343–1400) in his *Hous of Fame* follows Vergil's version and speaks of Sinon and his "false forswerynge [forswearing]" (153) as the cause of Troy's fall.

The first surviving artistic depiction of the Trojan horse is found on a Cycladic storage jar from about 670 BCE, not long after the apparent composition of the *Odyssey*. A wall painting from the Roman city of Pompeii (before 79 CE) shows several Trojans pulling the horse into the city with ropes. In a manuscript illustration, "The Trojan Horse Disgorges Its Burden," from a late fifteenth-century French version by LeFevre, three soldiers climb out of a hatch in the side of the horse. One of the more famous later depictions of the horse is a painting by Giovanni Tiepolo (1727–1804), *The Building of the Trojan Horse.*

In more recent times the story of the Trojan horse has been a popular theme in cartoons and movies. *The New Yorker* over the years has included numerous cartoons by artists such as Bender, Bliss, Larson, Fradon, Kliban, Ziegler, and others. They reinvent the theme by fashioning a Trojan cat, a Trojan dog, and many humorous variants. Other cartoonists have offered similarly witty takes on the theme. Hollywood has also embraced the image of the horse in a variety of films. One of the more extensive scenes in *Helen of Troy* (1956) reenacts the night that the festive Trojans brought the horse into the doomed city. The horse was enormous, but was made of balsa wood so that the actors could easily pull it! In *The Trojan Horse* (1961) a very large wooden horse is escorted into the city through elaborate gates. Wolfgang Petersen's recent film *Troy* (2004) includes the Trojan horse looming in the background as the Greeks run back to their ships.

A very different approach to the Trojan horse was taken by the comedy troupe Monty Python in *Monty Python and the Holy Grail* (1975). They parody the horse by creating a rabbit on wheels! King Arthur and his Knights of the Round Table have created it to fool the French, who indeed draw the animal into their castle. Unfortunately, the Knights had forgotten to climb inside! Much more recently the Trojan horse was featured in an episode of *The Simpsons* where Homer (Simpson) is Odysseus. Homer, Lenny, Carl, and Moe climb out of the horse and kill the Trojans who are "sleeping like babies."

The story of the Trojan horse has also entered the modern realm of computers and advertising. A particularly nasty computer virus that can cause a computer or whole system to crash is called a Trojan Horse. An advertising campaign for network security features a Trojan horse in the midst of a city. The horse is trapped in a cage fashioned from zeroes and ones.

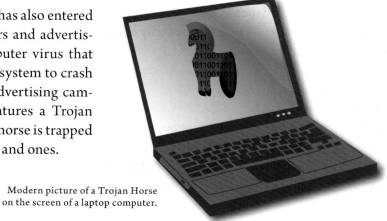

Modern picture of a Trojan Horse on the screen of a laptop computer.

At Troy today there is a large wooden horse with cut-out windows so that tourists can pretend to be invading Greeks. There is also a model (life-size or larger) in the Wisconsin Dells, Wisconsin as part of a theme park named Mt. Olympus. The go-carts race on a pathway that goes underneath the wooden horse's belly.

The Trojan horse is a symbol that seems to thrive and gives testimony to the endurance of the Classics in every age. It is intriguing to speculate how the symbol will continue to develop in the future.

BONNIE A. CATTO
Professor of Classics
Assumption College
Worcester, Massachusetts

MĪRĀBILE AUDĪTŪ

PHRASES AND QUOTATIONS RELATING TO WAR AND PEACE

PHRASES AND QUOTATIONS

- Arma cēdant togae. "The war should yield to peace," literally "Weapons should yield to the toga." (Cicero, *On Duties* 1.77) quotes these words from his own lost poem about his consulship.

- Cāsus bellī. "A case for war." A modern Latin expression that applies to a situation provoking or justifying a war.

- Dīvide et imperā! "Divide and rule!" A motto of any imperialist policy. The source is unclear, though the phrase is repeated in many authors.

- Dulce et decōrum est prō patriā morī! "It is sweet and decorous to die for the fatherland." (Horace, *Odes*, 3.2.13)

- Sī vīs pācem, parā bellum! "If you want peace, prepare for war!" A common Roman proverbial expression based on the Roman military historian Vegetius.

- Ubi sōlitūdinem faciunt, pācem appellant. "Where they make a desert, they call it peace." (Tacitus, *Agricola*, 30.6) Words of a British leader about a Roman policy of expansion.

- Vae victīs! "Woe to the conquered!" (Based on Livy, *From the Founding of the City* 5) This phrase tells the story of the capture of Rome by the Gauls in fourth century BCE, when it becomes clear that no rights existed for the defeated.

Sculpture of a Roman soldier. Villa Borghese.

CHAPTER 13

Present Tense Positive and Negative Imperatives; First and Second Person Personal Pronouns, Genitive Case; Third Person Possessive Pronoun and Adjective

A view of the Roman Forum showing the Via Sacra as well as the remains of the Temple of Vesta and the Temple of Antoninus and Faustina.

MEMORĀBILE DICTŪ

Carpe diem!

"Seize the day!" (Horace, *Odes*, 1.11.8.)

This phrase has become the byword for those who want to savor and treasure every moment in life, which is what Horace recommends in this poem, after stressing the uncertainty of the future.

READING

After the defeat of Antony and Cleopatra at Actium in 31 BCE, which brought an end to Rome's civil wars, Octavian assumed total control of the Roman state and adopted the name Augustus. Claiming, however, to be restoring the Roman republic, he merely referred to himself as Rome's *prīnceps*, "first citizen." Historians thus refer to his reign, which lasted until his death in 14 CE, as the "Augustan principate." Although he continued to wage wars outside of Rome's boundaries during most of his principate, Augustus took credit for establishing an era of "Roman peace," the *pāx Rōmāna*.

Much of the literature produced during Augustus' principate, such as Vergil's *Aeneid*, treated topics of major political significance. Yet many of the authors who flourished during this period wrote of individual human concerns and emotions. Among them was Quīntus Horātius Flaccus (65–8 BCE), known to us as Horace, another poet who benefited from the patronage of Augustus' friend Maecenas.

Horace wrote poetry in various genres, most of Greek origin. His poems often voice a concern with the issue of human happiness, and assert that it can be achieved through the pursuit of equilibrium and moderation, as well as by fully appreciating every moment in life. Two phrases from his lyric verses called the *Odes* succinctly capture his philosophy of living, and abide with us today: *aurea mediocritās*, "the golden mean," and *carpe diem*, "seize the day."

The following passage is adapted from Horace, *Satire* 1.9, and describes an annoying encounter he experienced in the Roman Forum.

DĒ HOMINE IMPORTŪNŌ

1   Ambulābam in viā Sacrā et dē nūgīs meīs cōgitābam. Accurrit homō
tantum nōmine mihi nōtus. Is bracchium meum capit atque dīcit:
"Quid agis, dulcissime rērum?" "Bene," dīcō, "et cupiō omnia quae tū
cupis." Tum discēdō. Is tamen mēcum ambulat. Eum rogō: "Quid prō

5   tē facere possum?" "Nōlī fugere," dīcit importūnus, "sed mēcum manē!"
"Nōn mihi licet;" respondeō, "dēbeō enim amīcum trāns Tiberim
invīsere. Valē!" "Audī mē!" dīcit importūnus, "Nihil aliud facere dēbeō
et nōn sum piger. Tē relinquere nōlō. Tēcum venīre possum." Miser
ambulābam; nam eum ā mē discēdere cupiēbam. Importūnus

10   autem dē Maecēnāte ēiusque amīcīs rogābat. "Ūnusquisque nostrum,"

respondēbam, "apud Maecēnātem locum suum habet: nōn tantum
dīvitēs et doctī." Erāmus iam prope templum Vestae. Valdē cupiēbam
ab importūnō relinquī, sed is mē nōn relinquēbat. Tunc homō ad nōs
subitō venit et importūnum vocat: "Quō ambulās? Mēcum ad iūdicem
15 venīre dēbēs." Deinde importūnum ad iūdicem dūcit et mē servat.

READING VOCABULARY

accurrō, accurrere, accurrī, accursum – to run up

*alius, alia, aliud – another, other

*apud + accusative – at the house of

*atque (conj.) – and

audī! (second person singular) – hear!

bracchium, bracchiī, n. – arm

*discēdō, discēdere, discessī, discessum – to leave,
  withdraw, go away

*dīves, dīvitis – rich

*doctus, docta, doctum – learned

*dūcō, dūcere, dūxī, ductum – to lead

dulcissime rērum – dear fellow, literally "the sweetest
  of all things"

ēius – his

*enim (adv.) – for, in fact

importūnus, importūna, importūnum – boorish

invīsō, invīsere, invīsī, invīsum – to visit

*iūdex, iūdicis, m. – judge

*licet + dative + infinitive – it is allowed, it is permit-
  ted (for someone) (to do something)

locus, locī, m. – place

Maecēnās, Maecēnātis, m. – Maecenas

*mēcum = cum mē

*nihil – nothing

nōlī fugere! (second person singular) – do not run!

*nōlō (irregular verb) – not to want, to be unwilling

nōtus, nōta, nōtum – known

nūgae, nūgārum, f. pl. – trifles

*omnis, omne – each, every, all

piger, pigra, pigrum – lazy

*prō + ablative – for, on behalf of

quae (neuter plural accusative) – what, which

*quid? – what

quid agis – how are you?

quō? – to what place?

*respondeō, respondēre, respondī, respōnsum – to
  answer

*rogō, rogāre, rogāvī, rogātum – to ask

sacer, sacra, sacrum – holy, sacred

*suus, sua, suum – his, her, its, their

*tantum (adv.) – only

*tēcum = cum tē

trāns Tiberim – on the other side of the Tiber river

*tum (adv.) – then

ūnusquisque nostrum – each one of us

*valē! (second person singular) – goodbye! (literally
  "be well!")

Vesta, Vestae, f. – Vesta

Via Sacra – a street in the Roman Forum

* The words with an asterisk will need to be
  memorized.

COMPREHENSION QUESTIONS

1. Where was Horace when the described events happened?

2. What happened to Horace? What is he complaining about?

3. What did Horace say about Maecenas and his circle?

4. How did Horace get rid of his troubles?

LANGUAGE FACT I

PRESENT TENSE POSITIVE AND NEGATIVE IMPERATIVES

In the chapter reading passage you have noticed some new verb forms: *manē, valē, audī*. These are commands.

The command is a mood of the verb called the **imperative**. The mood you have been concerned with so far has been the **indicative**—it states the simple fact of an action.

The indicative mood represents the action as actually happening: *manēs*, "you remain."

The imperative mood represents the action as commanded to happen: *manē!* "remain!"

There are only two forms for the present active imperative: the second person singular (for commanding one person) and the second person plural (for commanding more than one person).

Here is how you form the present active imperative:

> **Singular active command**
> For verbs of all four conjugations, the singular form is identical to the stem (ending *-ā, -ē, -e*, and *-ī*, respectively). The imperative of the *-io* verbs looks like that of third conjugation verbs.

> **Plural active command**
> The plural imperative form of all conjugations ends in *-te*.

For verbs of the first, second, and fourth conjugations, *-te* is added directly to the stem. In the third conjugation (including *-iō* verbs), *-e-* changes to *-i-* before *-te*.

For a **negative** command, use *nōlī* (singular) and *nōlīte* (plural) followed by an infinitive. Do not use *nōn*.

> *Nōlī discēdere!* "Do not go away!"
> *Nōlīte discēdere!* "Do not go away (plural)!"

BY THE WAY

The forms *nōlī* and *nōlīte* are present active imperatives of the irregular verb *nōlō*, "not to want."

Present Tense Positive and Negative Imperatives

	First Conjugation	Second Conjugation	Third Conjugation	Fourth Conjugation	Third Conjugation -iō Verbs
Singular Positive	parā! (prepare!)	tenē! (hold!)	pete! (seek!)	audī! (hear!)	cape! (seize!)
Plural Positive	parāte! (prepare!)	tenēte! (hold!)	petite! (seek!)	audīte (hear!)	capite! (seize!)
Singular Negative	nōlī parāre! (do not prepare!)	nōlī tenēre! (do not hold!)	nōlī petere! (do not seek!)	nōlī audīre! (do not hear!)	nōlī capere! (do not seize!)
Plural Negative	nōlīte parāre! (do not prepare!)	nōlīte tenēre! (do not hold!)	nōlīte petere! (do not seek!)	nōlīte audīre! (do not hear!)	nōlīte capere! (do not seize!)

BY THE WAY

In an English translation, there is no difference between singular and the plural commands.

STUDY TIP

Remember the Latin greetings *salvē* and *salvēte* from Chapter 1; these are second conjugation active imperative forms. Use **salvē** when greeting one person, and **salvēte** for two or more people. When bidding goodbye, use **valē** and **valēte**. Both *salvēre* and *valēre* mean "to be well."

▶ EXERCISE 1

Change the following present active infinitives into the imperative form indicated in parentheses. Translate each form.

Example: cōnspicere (plural)
cōnspicite!   observe (plural)!

1. pugnāre (plural)
2. ostendere (singular)
3. mittere (plural)
4. sentīre (singular)
5. invidēre (singular)
6. timēre (singular)
7. aestimāre (singular)
8. fugere (singular)

VOCABULARY TO LEARN

NOUN

iūdex, iūdicis, m. – judge

PRONOUNS

mēcum = cum mē – with me
nihil – nothing
quid? – what
tēcum = cum tē – with you

ADJECTIVES

alius, alia, aliud – another, other
dīves, dīvitis – rich
doctus, docta, doctum – learned
omnis, omne – each, every, all
suus, sua, suum – his, her, its, their

VERBS

discēdō, discēdere, discessī, discessum – to leave, to go away

dūcō, dūcere, dūxī, ductum – to lead
licet + dative + infinitive – it is allowed, it is permitted (for someone) (to do something)
nōlō (irregular verb) – not to want, to be unwilling
respondeō, respondēre, respondī, respōnsum – to answer
rogō, rogāre, rogāvī, rogātum – to ask
valē! – goodbye!

ADVERBS

tantum – only
tum – then

PREPOSITIONS

apud + accusative – at the house of
prō + ablative – for, on behalf of

CONJUNCTIONS

atque – and
enim – for, in fact

▶ EXERCISE 2

Find the English derivatives based on the Vocabulary to Learn in the following sentences. Write the corresponding Latin word.

1. The judicial power is separated from the executive one. *iudex*

2. Nihilism is a frequently encountered attitude among young people. *Nihil*

3. There is alienation in big cities.

4. He was awarded a doctorate in law.

5. What would be your response to this accusation?

6. I gave a valedictory speech in my high school.

7. Do you have a driver's license?

8. The interrogation did not provide a lot of answers.

9. Who is omnipotent and omniscient?

10. An aqueduct is a structure through which water is transported.

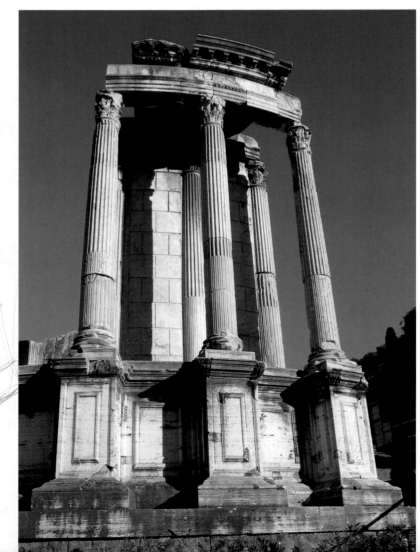

The remains of the Temple
of Vesta, once a round structure.

▶ EXERCISE 3

Change the following positive imperatives into the negative and translate each negative form.

Example: respondē!
nōlī respondēre!   do not answer!

1. pugnāte!
2. discēde!
3. dolēte!
4. mittite!
5. vince!

6. putāte!
7. pete!
8. cape!
9. venīte!

▶ EXERCISE 4

Translate the following imperatives that Horace might have said to the boor and the boor to Horace.

Horace:
1. Free me!
2. Leave!
3. Flee!
4. Do not tell!
5. Leave me!

Boor:
1. Hear!
2. Believe me!
3. Wait!
4. Stay!
5. Answer!

LANGUAGE FACT II

FIRST AND SECOND PERSON PERSONAL PRONOUNS, GENITIVE CASE

When the personal pronouns *ego, tū, nōs,* and *vōs* were introduced in Chapter 12, you noticed that more was to be said about the genitives of these words. This is because the genitive of these pronouns is used quite differently from all the other declined forms.

Genitive of the First and Second Person Personal Pronouns			
First Person Singular	**Second Person Singular**	**First Person Plural**	**Second Person Plural**
meī	tuī	nostrī/nostrum	vestrī/vestrum

STUDY TIP

The genitive personal pronouns *meī, tuī, nostrī,* and *vestrī* are identical to the genitive singular masculine/neuter forms of the possessive adjectives, *meus, tuus, noster, vester.*

It may seem surprising, but in classical Latin these genitives are **not** used to indicate possession. Possession is indicated by possessive adjectives: *liber vester,* "your book," *amor meus,* "my love," etc.

The genitives of the personal pronouns are used in two situations:

- When the genitive of the personal pronoun is **partitive**.

    Horace says to the boor in the chapter reading:

    > *Ūnusquisque **nostrum** locum suum habet.* "Each one of us has his place."

    The genitive *nostrum* expresses the totality, a part of which is indicated (*ūnusquisque*).

- When the genitive of the personal pronoun is joined to a noun that is closely related to a verb. This genitive is called **objective**.

    Look at the following example:

    > *Tē amō.* "I love you."

    > *Meus amor tuī est māgnus.* "My love for (of) you is great."

Tuī in the second sentence is an objective genitive. *Tuī* provides an object for the noun *amor* much in the same way as *tē* provides an object for the verb *amō*.

A verb simply has its accusative direct object. A noun, however, cannot take a direct object, and instead takes an objective genitive.

BY THE WAY

The forms *nostrum* and *vestrum* are used only when the genitive is partitive, and the forms *nostrī* and *vestrī* are used when the genitive is objective.

Examples:

> *multī vestrum*, "many of you (plural)" – **partitive**

> *amor vestrī*, "love of you (plural)" – **objective**

▶ EXERCISE 5

Translate into English. Identify the type of genitive (modifying/partitive/objective) in each sentence. The Reading Vocabulary may be consulted.

1. Paucī nostrum verba hominis importūnī audīre cupiunt.

2. Omnēs vestrum hominēs importūnōs fugere vidēminī.

3. Importūnus timōre meī nōn capiēbātur, sed mēcum ambulābat.

4. Da mihi auxilium propter tuum meī amōrem!

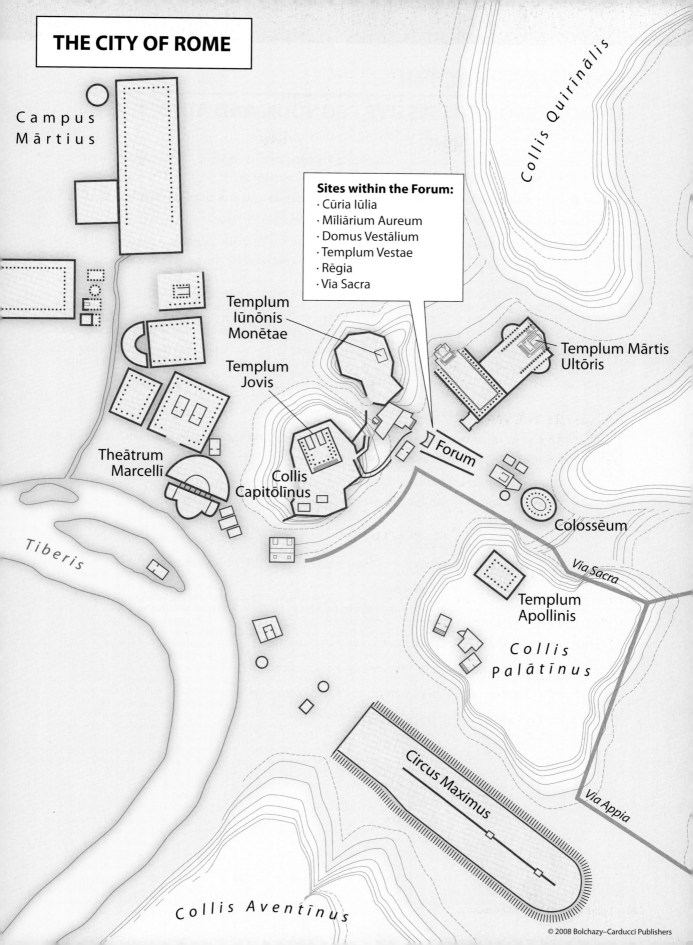

THE CITY OF ROME

Campus
Mārtius

Collis Quirīnālis

Sites within the Forum:
· Cūria Iūlia
· Mīliārium Aureum
· Domus Vestālium
· Templum Vestae
· Rēgia
· Via Sacra

Templum
Iūnōnis
Monētae

Templum Mārtis
Ultōris

Templum
Jovis

Forum

Theātrum
Marcellī

Collis
Capitōlīnus

Colossēum

Tiberis

Via Sacra

Templum
Apollinis

Collis
Palātīnus

Via Appia

Circus Maximus

Collis Aventīnus

© 2008 Bolchazy–Carducci Publishers

LANGUAGE FACT III
THIRD PERSON POSSESSIVE PRONOUN AND ADJECTIVE

In the chapter reading you saw the following sentences:

> *Importūnus autem dē Maecēnāte **ēiusque** amīcīs rogābat. "Ūnusquisque nostrum,"*
> *respondēbam, "apud Maecēnātem locum **suum** habet."*
>
> The boor, however, asked about Maecenas and **his** friends. "Each one of us," I
> answered, "has **his** place at the house of Maecenas."

In the first of these sentences the possessive pronoun for the third person is expressed by the genitive of *is, ea, id*, while in the second sentence it is expressed by the possessive adjective *suus, sua, suum*.

Why is there this difference?

The possessive adjective *suus, sua, suum* is used when it refers to the subject of the sentence. This possessive adjective is called reflexive, because it is "bent back" to the subject (the verb *reflectō* in Latin means to "bend back").

> *Importūnus verba **sua** amat.*
> The boor likes his words (i.e., his own words).

The genitive of *is, ea, id* (singular *ēius*, and plural *eōrum, eārum, eōrum*) is used when it refers to someone/something other than the subject.

> *Horātius verba **ēius** nōn amat.*
> Horace does not like his words (i.e., the words of the boor).

More examples:

> *Rōmānī mīlitēs **suōs** cūrant.*
> The Romans take care of their soldiers (i.e., their own soldiers).
>
> *Hostēs mīlitēs **eōrum** timent.*
> The enemies are afraid of their soldiers (i.e., the Roman soldiers).

▶ EXERCISE 6

Fill in the blanks with the correct third person possessive pronoun (her, his, its, their) and translate each sentence.

Example: Audiō puellam et _____ verba amō.
Audiō puellam et ēius verba amō.   I hear the girl and I love her words.

1. Iūdicem timeō atque ___ēius___ verba exspectō. →*reffering to object*
   I expect
2. Rōma est mīlitum patria. Mīlitēs prō patriā ___suā___ pugnant. →*reffering to soldiers*
   Rome homeland of soldier
3. Poētārum verba audīre cupimus. Verba enim ___eiorum___ amāmus.
   we desire to hear the words of the poets
4. Puella passerem amat atque passerem in gremiō ___suō___ tenet. →*reffering to*

▶ EXERCISE 7

Translate into Latin. The Reading Vocabulary may be consulted.

1. Come with me!

2. Should I come with you?

3. Come with me (plural)!

4. Should we come with you?

5. Do not go away!

6. Do not go away (plural)!

7. Do not lead (plural) us to the judge!

8. The athlete was taking care of his body.

9. The boorish man was asking and the poet was answering nothing. The poet was not listening to his words.

10. All of us were asking you (plural). All of you (plural) had to answer.

11. The poet was saying to the boorish man: "Leave me because of love for me!"

propter amorem

TALKING

Quota hōra est? "What time is it?"

Est hōra prīma. "It's one o'clock."

. . . *secunda.* "It's two o'clock."

. . . *tertia.* "It's three o'clock."

. . . *quārta.* "It's four o'clock."

. . . *quīnta.* "It's five o'clock."

. . . *sexta.* "It's six o'clock."

. . . *septima.* "It's seven o'clock."

. . . *octāva.* "It's eight o'clock."

. . . *nōna.* "It's nine o'clock."

. . . *decima.* "It's ten o'clock."

. . . *ūndecima.* "It's eleven o'clock."

. . . *duodecima.* "It's twelve o'clock."

Est hōra prīma (secunda etc.) et quādrāns. "It's a quarter past one (two etc.)."

Est hōra prīma (secunda etc.) et dīmidia. "It's half past one (two etc.)."

Est hōra prīma (secunda etc.) et dōdrāns. "It's three quarters past one (two etc.)."

Est merīdiēs. "It's midday."

Est media nox. "It's midnight."

The Romans used sundials to determine the hour of the day.

Here is a table of the first ten cardinal and ordinal numerals in Latin.

	Cardinal numerals	**Ordinal numerals**
1-I	ūnus, ūna, ūnum	prīmus, prīma, prīmum
2-II	duo, duae, duo	secundus, secunda, secundum
3-III	trēs (m./f.), tria (n.)	tertius, tertia, tertium
4-IV	quattuor	quārtus, quārta, quārtum
5-V	quīnque	quīntus, quīnta, quīntum
6-VI	sex	sextus, sexta, sextum
7-VII	septem	septimus, septima, septimum
8-VIII	octō	octāvus, octāva, octāvum
9-IX	novem	nōnus, nōna, nōnum
10-X	decem	decimus, decima, decimum

Roman numerals are still used today, as seen engraved on this set of books.

BY THE WAY

The Romans used to count the daytime hours from the first hour, *hōra prīma* (about 6 AM), to the twelfth hour, *hōra duodecima* (about 6 PM). For example, our 11 AM is, according to the Romans, the fifth hour, *hōra quīnta*. The length of the Roman hour varied according to the time of year, since they told time by the sun.

They divided the night into watches: first watch, *vigilia prīma* (about 6 PM–9 PM), second watch, *vigilia secunda* (about 9 PM–midnight), third watch, *vigilia tertia* (about midnight–3 AM), fourth watch, *vigilia quārta* (about 3 AM–6 AM).

LATE FOR SCHOOL

Helena: Properā (*hurry*), Mārce! Sumus in morā (*delay*).

Mārcus: Dēbēmusne properāre?

Helena: Ita (*yes*), properāre dēbēmus.

Mārcus: Quota hōra est?

Helena: Est hōra octāva et quādrāns.

Mārcus: Tum properāre nōn dēbēmus. Nam schola (*school*) incipit (*starts*) hōrā octāvā et dīmidiā (*at 8:30*).

Helena: In scholam tamen hōrā octāvā et quādrante (*at 8:15*) intrāre dēbēmus. Nam librōs parāre dēbēmus.

Mārcus: Ego autem hōram prīmam exspectō.

Helena: Cūr? (*Why?*)

Mārcus: Nam hōrā prīmā est fīnis (*end*) scholārum.

Helena: Nōlī dē fīne scholārum nunc cōgitāre, sed mēcum venī!

CHAPTER 14

First and Second Conjugation Verbs: Future Active and Passive Tense; Future Tense of *Sum* and *Possum*; Relative Pronouns; Relative Clauses

Pyramus and Thisbe. By Lucas Cranach, the Elder (1472–1553).

MEMORĀBILE DICTŪ

Omnia vincit amor.

"Love conquers all things." (Vergil, *Eclogue* 10.69)

This sentence became proverbial for the power of love.

READING

One of the most brilliant and productive poets who lived during the reign of Augustus was Publius Ovidius Nāso (43 BCE–17 CE), whom English speakers call Ovid. He began his career as a writer of love poems, but expanded his literary repertoire to include more ambitious forms of poetry, most notably the mythological epic *Metamorphōsēs*, "Transformations." After his exile to the shores of *Pontus* on the Black Sea in 8 CE, to a place in what is now Romania, he turned his pen to a series of sorrowful reflections and laments, poems he called *Trīstia* ("Sad Songs") and "Letters from Pontus" (*Epistulae ex Pontō*). He was exiled by order of Augustus, but the reasons for his banishment remain unclear.

Below is an excerpt from the *Metamorphōsēs*: perhaps his most widely read work, it is a broadly ranging collection of mythological tales, and one of our best sources for earlier Greek mythology. Its title relates to the fact that every myth depicts the transformation of a human into an animal, vegetable, or mineral. In the text that follows, adapted from Book 4.55–166, you will be transported to the exotic oriental atmosphere of ancient Babylon.

The story explains why the mulberry tree produces dark-colored berries.

DĒ PȲRAMŌ ET THISBĒ

1   Pȳramus prope Thisbēn habitābat. Is eam amābat et ab eā amābātur.
       Propter odium tamen, quod erat inter eōrum parentēs, Pȳramus et
       Thisbē ūnā esse nōn poterant. Parietī, quī eōs sēparābat, verba saepe
       dīcēbant. "Semper, male pariēs, amantēs sēparās!" Sed quoque
5   parietem rogābant: "Licetne, bone pariēs, per tē verba mittere?"
       Pȳramus et Thisbē tandem clam convenīre dēcernunt. "Tē in agrīs
       prope arborem, in quā sunt pōma alba, hāc nocte vidēbō," inquit
       Pȳramus. Thisbē prīma venit et exspectat. Leaena subitō ad Thisbēn
       appropinquat. Leaena sanguinem in ōre habet. Nam leaena animal
10   comēdēbat. Thisbē timet et in spēluncam fugit, sed vēlāmen puellae
       in terram cadit. Leaena vēlāmen ōre suō tangit et sanguis in vēlāmine
       manet.
       Pȳramus venit et videt vēlāmen, in quō sanguis cōnspicitur. Thisbē
       iam nōn vīvere vidētur. Pȳramus valdē dolet et sē gladiō occīdit. Intereā
15   Thisbē ex spēluncā ambulat et videt Pȳramum in terrā mortuum iacēre.
       Thisbē gladium ex pectore Pȳramī eximit et sē quoque occīdit. Pȳramī
       et Thisbēs sanguis in terram fluit. Pōma arboris mox erunt rubra.

READING VOCABULARY

*albus, alba, album – white

amāns, amantis, m./f. – lover

appropinquō, appropinquāre, appropinquāvī, appropinquātum + *ad* + accusative – to approach

*arbor, arboris, f. – tree

*cadō, cadere, cecidī, cāsum – to fall

clam (adv.) – secretly

*comedō, comedere, comēdī, comēsum – to eat

*conveniō, convenīre, convēnī, conventum – to meet

erunt – will be

eximō, eximere, exēmī, exēmptum – to take out

*fluō, fluere, flūxī, fluxum – to flow

*gladius, gladiī, m. – sword

hāc nocte – tonight

*iam (adv.) – already, yet

in quā (feminine) – on which

in quō (neuter) – in which

inter + accusative – between

intereā (adv.) – meanwhile

leaena, leaenae, f. – lioness

mortuus, mortua, mortuum – dead

*mox (adv.) – soon

*odium, odiī, n. – hatred

*ōs, ōris, n. – mouth

*parēns, parentis, m./f. – parent

pariēs, parietis, m. – wall

*pectus, pectoris, n. – chest

*per + accusative – through

pōmum, pōmī, n. – fruit, berry

*prīmus, prīma, prīmum – first

Pȳramus, Pȳramī, m. – Pyramus

*quī – which

quod – which

*ruber, rubra, rubrum – red

*sanguis, sanguinis, m. – blood

*sēparō, sēparāre, sēparāvī, sēparātum – to separate, to divide

*tangō, tangere, tetigī, tāctum – to touch

Thisbē, Thisbēs (gen.), Thisbē (dat.), Thisbēn (acc.), Thisbē (voc.) f. – Thisbe

vēlāmen, vēlāminis, n. – veil

vidēbō – I will see

*Words with an asterisk will need to be memorized later in the chapter.

COMPREHENSION QUESTIONS

1. What was Pyramus and Thisbe's problem?

2. What resolution did they come to at last?

3. Why did Pyramus kill himself upon his arrival?

4. What happened to Thisbe at the end of the story?

LANGUAGE FACT I

FIRST AND SECOND CONJUGATION VERBS: FUTURE ACTIVE AND PASSIVE TENSE

In the Latin reading passage, Pyramus, when talking to Thisbe about the time they have arranged for a meeting, says: *Tē . . . hāc nocte vidēbō*, "I will see you tonight." The form *vidēbō* belongs to the future tense of the verb *video*.

First and second conjugation verbs have similar future forms: add to the stem of the verb **-bō, -bis, -bit, -bimus, -bitis, -bunt** (active voice) and **-bor, -beris, -bitur, -bimur, -biminī, -buntur** (passive voice).

First Conjugation: Future Active

		Singular		Plural
First person	parābō	I will/shall prepare	parābimus	we will/shall prepare
Second person	parābis	you will prepare	parābitis	you will prepare
Third person	parābit	s/he/it will prepare	parābunt	they will prepare

First Conjugation: Future Passive

		Singular		Plural
First person	parābor	I will/shall be prepared	parābimur	we will/shall be prepared
Second person	parāberis	you will be prepared	parābiminī	you will be prepared
Third person	parābitur	s/he/it will be prepared	parābuntur	they will be prepared

Second Conjugation: Future Active

		Singular		Plural
First person	tenēbō	I will/shall hold	tenēbimus	we will/shall hold
Second person	tenēbis	you will hold	tenēbitis	you will hold
Third person	tenēbit	s/he/it will hold	tenēbunt	they will hold

Second Conjugation: Future Passive

		Singular		Plural
First person	tenēbor	I will/shall be held	tenēbimur	we will/shall be held
Second person	tenēberis	you will be held	tenēbiminī	you will be held
Third person	tenēbitur	s/he/it will be held	tenēbuntur	they will be held

STUDY TIP

In an old fairy tale two princes had changed themselves into storks so that they could hear what people thought about them. One of them explained to the other how they could get back to their human form. "You have to remember and say a very difficult ancient word," said the prince, "MUTABOR."

For you, however, who have just learned the future tense, there will be no difficulty in the form *mūtābor*. It is simply the future passive indicative first person singular of the verb *mūtō*: "I will be transformed." Remember the form *mūtābor*, if you do not want to remain a stork!

BY THE WAY

The future tense of *amō* is *amābō*. It means not only "I will love," but also "please." For example: *Amābō tē, da mihi librum.* "Please, give me the book."

The logic is as follows: "I will love you, and I will be pleased with you, if you do such and such."

▶ EXERCISE 1

Change the following verbs into future active, in the person and number indicated. Translate the new form.

Example: sēparō (first person singular)
sēparābō   I will separate

1. iūdicō (first person singular)

2. aedificō (third person plural)

3. doceō (second person singular)

4. doleō (first person plural)

5. servō (third person singular)

6. iubeō (second person plural)

7. parō (third person plural)

8. iaceō (first person singular)

9. soleō (second person plural)

10. pugnō (third person singular)

VOCABULARY TO LEARN

NOUNS

arbor, arboris, f. – tree

gladius, gladiī, m. – sword

odium, odiī, n. – hatred

ōs, ōris, n. – mouth

parēns, parentis, m./f. – parent

pectus, pectoris, n. – chest

sanguis, sanguinis, m. - blood

PRONOUN

quī, quae, quod – which, who, that

ADJECTIVES

albus, alba, album – white

prīmus, prīma, prīmum – first

ruber, rubra, rubrum – red

VERBS

cadō, cadere, cecidī, cāsum – to fall

comedō, comedere, comēdī, comēsum – to eat

conveniō, convenīre, convēnī, conventum – to meet

fluō, fluere, flūxī, fluxum – to flow

sēparō, sēparāre, sēparāvī, sēparātum – to separate

tangō, tangere, tetigī, tāctum – to touch

ADVERBS

mox – soon

iam – already

PREPOSITION

per + accusative – through

▶ EXERCISE 2

Find the English derivatives based on the Vocabulary to Learn in the following sentences. Write the corresponding Latin word.

1. I will need to buy an expectorant for my cough.

2. Children need attentive parental care.

3. Please, approach this delicate problem with a lot of tact.

4. I am fluent in Spanish.

5. In our country there is separation of state and church.

6. Representatives from all over the world came to this convention.

7. Because of her sanguine character she bore the difficulties cheerfully.

8. Please, show me the album with the wedding pictures!

9. Under this rubric the issue of property is dealt with.

10. For this class you will need to prepare several oral presentations.

11. The gladiators came into the arena.

12. Doing so much homework is odious to me.

13. He was elected the prime minister of England.

14. Do you want to come for a walk in the arboretum?

15. As she spoke, there was a lovely cadence in her voice.

▶ EXERCISE 3

Change the present or imperfect tense verbs into the future, keeping the same person, number, and voice. Translate both forms.

Example: amābām   I loved/used to love/was loving
amābō   I will love

1. respondēbās
2. līberātur
3. sēparāris
4. nāvigat
5. cōgitābāmus
6. dēleō   *I destroy*
7. dēbēbātis   *yall ought*
8. docēbant
9. firmāminī
10. invidēmur
11. iūdicābantur
12. moveor   *I was moved*

LANGUAGE FACT II

FUTURE TENSE OF *SUM* AND *POSSUM*

You have already learned the present and the imperfect tense of the irregular verbs *sum* and *possum*. In the story about Pyramus and Thisbe you read the following: *Pōma arboris mox erunt rubra,* "The berries of the tree will soon be red." In this sentence you see the future tense form of the verb *sum*.

Note the red color of the mulberry resulting from the spilling of blood according to myth.

Here is the future indicative of *sum* and *possum*.

Future Tense of *sum*				
		Singular		**Plural**
First person	erō	I will/shall be	erimus	we will/shall be
Second person	eris	you will be	eritis	you will be
Third person	erit	s/he/it will be	erunt	they will be

Future Tense of *possum*				
		Singular		**Plural**
First person	poterō	I will/shall be able	poterimus	we will/shall be able
Second person	poteris	you will be able	poteritis	you will be able
Third person	poterit	s/he/it will be able	poterunt	they will be able

BY THE WAY

In the same way as in the imperfect tense, also the future forms of *possum* are almost identical with those of *sum*, the prefix *pot-* being added in front of the forms of *sum*.

▶ EXERCISE 4

Change the present or imperfect tense verbs into the future, keeping the same person and number. Translate both forms.

Example: es
eris   you are   you will be *[handwritten: you were able]*

1. poterātis *[handwritten: poteritis y'all were able]*
2. erant *[handwritten: erunt]*
3. potest
4. sumus
5. possunt
6. erās
7. erātis
8. poterat
9. poteram
10. erat

▶ EXERCISE 5

Translate into Latin. The Reading Vocabulary may be consulted for names.

1. I am able to hear a story. I was able to hear a story. I will be able to hear a story. *[handwritten: audire fabulam]*

2. Pyramus is not happy. He was not happy. He will not be happy.

3. You, Pyramus, are not happy. You, Pyramus, were not happy. You, Pyramus, will not be happy.

4. Are they able to meet? They were not able to meet. They will be able to meet.

5. You, Pyramus and Thisbe, are not able to be together. You, Pyramus and Thisbe, were able to be together, but will not be able to be together.

6. We were able to tell about love, we are able and we will be able.

LANGUAGE FACT III

RELATIVE PRONOUNS; RELATIVE CLAUSES

In the story at the beginning of the chapter Pyramus says:

> *Tē in agrīs prope arborem, in **quā** sunt pōma alba, hāc nocte vidēbō.*
> Tonight I will see you in the fields near the tree in **which** there are white berries.

This sentence contains a relative clause. A relative clause begins with a **relative pronoun** (in English "that," "who/whose/whom," or "which"). The relative pronoun stands in for a word in the main clause; this word is called the relative pronoun's **antecedent**, because it usually precedes the relative clause.

A relative pronoun has the same number and gender as its antecedent. In the example given above, the relative pronoun *quā* has the same number and gender as its antecedent *arborem*, i.e., singular and feminine.

A relative pronoun has its own case, independent of its antecedent. This is because a relative pronoun belongs to a separate part of a sentence, the relative clause. A relative clause has its own grammatical structure. In the example above, *quā* is ablative because it follows the preposition *in*. The relative pronoun may perform any case function.

Here is the declension of the relative pronoun.

Relative Pronoun

Singular

	Masculine		Feminine		Neuter	
Nominative	quī	who, which, that	quae	who, which, that	quod	which, that
Genitive	cūius	whose, of whom, of which	cūius	whose, of whom, of which	cūius	of which
Dative	cui	to/for whom, to/for which	cui	to/for whom, to/for which	cui	to/for which
Accusative	quem	whom, which, that	quam	whom, which, that	quod	which, that
Ablative	quō	by/with whom, by/with which	quā	by/with whom, by/with which	quō	by/with which

Plural

	Masculine		Feminine		Neuter	
Nominative	quī	who, which, that	quae	who, which, that	quae	which, that
Genitive	quōrum	whose, of whom, of which	quārum	whose, of whom, of which	quōrum	of which
Dative	quibus	to/for whom, to/for which	quibus	to/for whom, to/for which	quibus	to/for which
Accusative	quōs	whom, which, that	quās	whom, which, that	quae	which, that
Ablative	quibus	by/with whom, by/with which	quibus	by/with whom, by/with which	quibus	by/with which

BY THE WAY

Some of the endings of the relative pronoun are similar to those of the first and second declension, while others resemble endings of the third declension. Some, e.g., genitive singular, resemble no noun declension.

Here are more examples of relative clauses. Note that a relative clause conveys information about a noun in the clause on which it depends, and in this way the whole relative clause functions like an adjective.

> *Puella quam Pȳramus amat est bona.*
> The girl that (whom) Pyramus loves is good.

Quam is feminine singular, since it refers to a feminine singular antecedent, *puella*; *quam* is accusative, since it is a direct object of *amat*.

> *Pariēs cui Pȳramus verba dīcit respondēre nōn potest.*
> The wall to which Pyramus says words cannot answer.

Cui is masculine singular, since it refers to *pariēs*; it is dative, since it is an indirect object of *verba dīcit*.

▶ EXERCISE 6

Find three more relative clauses in the Latin Reading passage and translate. Give the reason for the case, number, and gender of the relative pronoun. The Reading Vocabulary may be consulted.

▶ EXERCISE 7

Translate the following Latin sentences into English, and English sentences into Latin.

1. My parents, whom I am asking about many things, know many things.
2. Pugnābitis cum mīlitibus quī timōrem in pectoribus suīs nōn habēbunt.
3. The citizens to whom swords are being given are strong.
4. Poēta, ex cūius ōre verba nunc audīmus, est celeber.
5. The sparrow seeks the finger of the mistress who is holding him.
6. The animal that she fears leaves.
7. Lacrimae fluēbant ex oculīs hominis cui fābula nārrābātur.
8. You ought not to have the hatred that is in your heart.
9. Puella dē cūius vītā is dolēbat vīvēbat.

A lion such as the one in this mosaic scared Thisbe.

TALKING

(īnstrūmentum, īnstrūmentī, n.) computātōrium – computer

computātōrium gestābile – laptop

interrēte, interrētis, n. – internet

īnscrīptiō (īnscrīptiōnis, f.) ēlectronica – e-mail address

epistula ēlectronica – email

nūntiī subitāneī – instant messaging

Nāvigō in interrētī. "I surf the internet"

Per interrēte garriō. "I have an internet chat"

Quae est tua īnscrīptiō ēlectronica? "What is your e-mail address?"

Mitte ad mē epistulam ēlectronicam! "Send me an e-mail!"

Quaeram in interrētī. "I will check on the internet."

CHATTING ON THE INTERNET

Helena: Poterāsne, Mārce, herī (*yesterday*) pēnsum (*homework*) tuum facere?

Mārcus: Nōn poteram. Nam multa alia facere dēbēbam.

Helena: Nāvigābāsne in interrētī?

Mārcus: Aaa . . .

Marīa: (*INTRAT*) Salvēte, Mārce et Helena! Pulchrōs nūntiōs subitāneōs ad mē, Mārce, herī mittēbās.

Helena: Nūntiōs subitāneōs?!

Marīa: Ego et Mārcus herī diū in interrētī nāvigābāmus, et per interrēte garriēbāmus. Hodiē quoque nāvigābimus. Nōnne (*won't we*), Mārce?

Helena: Itaque nōn poterās, Mārce, pēnsum parāre propter nūntiōs quōs ad Marīam mittēbās. (*DISCĒDIT*) Valēte!

Mārcus: Manē, Helena! Nōlī mihi īrāscī (*get angry*)! Hodiē (*Today*) in interrētī nōn nāvigābō. Pēnsum meum parābō. Poterimus quoque ūnā ambulāre. Ambulābimusne hodiē ūnā?

Helena: Vidēbimus . . . Tē cōmpellābō (*will call*).

CHAPTER 15

Third and Fourth Conjugation Verbs: Future Active and Passive Tense; Interrogative Pronouns and Adjectives

The death of Seneca, who was ordered to commit suicide by the emperor Nero. By Luca Giordano (1634–1705).

MEMORĀBILE DICTŪ

Dūcunt volentem fāta, nōlentem trahunt.

"Destiny guides the the individual who is willing, drags the unwilling." (Seneca, *Moral Letters* 107.11)

Originally written by the Greek philosopher Cleanthes, and translated into Latin by Seneca, this motto encapsulates the willingness of the Stoics to comply with destiny.

READING

Lūcius Annaeus Seneca (ca. 4 BCE–65 CE) is known as Seneca the Younger to distinguish him from his father, Seneca the Elder, an acclaimed teacher of Roman oratory. Born in Spain, he came to Rome as a child, and was attracted in his early years by philosophy, particularly Stoicism. A skilled orator who attained the political office of *quaestor*, he was exiled to Corsica in 41 CE by the emperor Claudius, but recalled in 49 CE through the influence of Claudius' wife Agrippina, and named tutor to her son, the future emperor Nero. Upon Nero's accession in 54 CE, Seneca became his political advisor and minister. Yet his authority with his former student waned, and he was forced to commit suicide—which he did with memorable Stoic fortitude—in 65 CE.

Seneca wrote dramas, which survive as the major ancient examples of tragedy in Latin, as well as philosophical essays and treatises, a work on natural phenomena, and a satire on Claudius' death. However, he is best known for his collection of writings addressed to his friend Lucilius. Called *Epistulae Morālēs*, "Moral Letters," they take the form of letters, but are better described as short essays addressing various philosophical issues from a personal perspective and in a conversational tone. In the letter below, an adapted version of *Epistulae Morālēs* 12, Seneca discusses old age, presenting it as a personal encounter.

SENECA SENECTŪTEM SUAM CONVENIT

1   Seneca Lūcīliō salūtem dīcit.

Ubīque argūmenta senectūtis meae videō. Est mihi vīlla rūstica. Veniō in vīllam meam et vīlicus mihi dīcit sē dēbēre multa in vīllā reparāre. Dīcit sē omnia facere, sē nihil neglegere, sed vīllam esse

5   vetustam. Sed ego vīllam aedificāveram! Quid mihi erit? Corpusne meum cadet sīcut vīllae meae saxa?

"Tū," inquam, "arborēs neglegis: nōn habent folia. Tūne aquam arboribus das?"

"Arborēs," inquit, "semper cūrābam et cūrābō nec umquam ā mē

10   neglegentur. Sed sunt vetustae."

Id tibi dīcam, Lūcīlī, quod fortasse nōn crēdēs esse vērum: mē arborēs posuisse!

Tunc iānuam cōnspiciō. Ibi stat senex, quī mē spectat.

"Quis est senex?" inquam. "Cūr mē spectat?"

15   "Nōnne cōgnōscis mē?" inquit senex. "Ego sum Fēlīciō, quōcum solēbās puer lūdere. Eram quondam parvus amīcus tuus."

Difficile mihi est cōgnōscere amīcum meum! Nam senex, quī ante
mē stat, quī dentēs nōn habet, nōn vidētur similis puerī parvī, quōcum
lūdere solēbam!

20   Vīlla mea mihi vidēbātur dīcere: "Ecce senectūs tua!" Senectūs ad nōs
omnēs veniet etiam imparātōs. Itaque eam exspectāre dēbēmus. Parātī
esse dēbēmus.

READING VOCABULARY

aedificāveram – had built

*ante + accusative – in front of

*argūmentum, argūmentī, n. – proof, indication, argument

cadet – will fall

cōgnōscō, cōgnōscere, cōgnōvī, cōgnitum – to recognize, get to know

crēdēs – you will believe

*cūr (adv.) – why?

dēns, dentis, m. – tooth

dīcam – I will say

*difficilis, difficile – difficult

*ecce (interjection) – look here!

*etiam (adv.) – even, also

Fēlīciō, ——, m. – Felicio, a servant's name

folium, foliī, n. – leaf

*fortasse (adv.) – perhaps

iānua, iānuae, f. – door

imparātus, imparāta, imparātum – unprepared

*inquam – I say/I said (only introducing direct speech)

Lūcīlius, Lūcīliī, m. – Lucilius was a friend of Seneca's to whom he addressed his philosophical essays in the form of letters

lūdō, lūdere, lūsī, lūsum – to play

neglegentur – they will be neglected

*neglegō, neglegere, neglēxī, neglēctum – to neglect

nōnne? – don't you?

parātus, parāta, parātum – prepared

*parvus, parva, parvum – small

posuisse – have placed, have planted

*quis – who?

quōcum – with whom = cum quō (the preposition cum is attached to the end of the relative pronoun)

quondam (adv.) – once

reparō, reparāre, reparāvī, reparātum – to repair

*rūsticus, rūstica, rūsticum – rural, rustic

salūtem – health, greeting: this is the accusative singular of the noun salūs, salūtis, f.; it appears at the beginning of a letter with the name of the sender in the nominative, the addressee in the dative, and the verb dīcit.

*saxum, saxī, n. – stone, rock

Seneca, Senecae, m. – Seneca

*senectūs, senectūtis, f. – old age

*sīcut (adv.) – just as

spectō, spectāre, spectāvī, spectātum – to gaze, to stare at

*stō, stāre, stetī, statum – to stand

*ubīque (adv.) – everywhere

*umquam (adv.) – ever

veniet – will come

*vērus, vēra, vērum – true

*vetustus, vetusta, vetustum – old

vīlicus, vīlicī, m. – bailiff, steward

*vīlla, vīllae, f. – country house, villa

*Words marked with an asterisk will need to be memorized later in the chapter.

COMPREHENSION QUESTIONS

rustic

1. What were Seneca's first impressions when he visited his country house?

2. Who was Felicio and why did Seneca not recognize him?

3. What did Seneca learn from his visit to the country house?

LANGUAGE FACT I

THIRD AND FOURTH CONJUGATION VERBS: FUTURE ACTIVE AND PASSIVE TENSE

In the previous chapter you met the future tense of first and second conjugation verbs. In this chapter you meet the future tense of the third and fourth conjugations. Notice the verb forms in these sentences from the chapter reading passage.

> *Corpusne meum* **cadet** *sīcut vīllae meae saxa?*
> Will my body collapse, just like the stones of my villa?

> *"Arborēs," inquit, "semper cūrābam et cūrābō nec umquam ā mē* **neglegentur . . ."**
> "I always took care of the trees," he said, "and will take care of them and they will never be neglected by me . . ."

> *Id tibi* **dīcam**, *Lucīlī, quod fortasse nōn* **crēdēs** *esse vērum . . .*
> I shall tell you something, Lucilius, which you will perhaps not believe is true . . .

> *Senectūs ad nōs omnēs* **veniet** *etiam imparātōs.*
> Old age will come to all of us even <when we are> unprepared.

Boldface letters indicate the future forms belonging to the third and the fourth conjugations.

Instead of the consonant **-b-** that is characteristic of the future of the first and second conjugations, you see the vowels **-a-** and **-e-** in the future forms of the third and fourth conjugations.

 STUDY TIP

In the future,
First and second conjugation,
You will see a "b,"
But in the third and fourth
It's an "a" or an "e."

Third conjugation verbs form their future by adding to the stem the personal endings: **-m, -s, -t, -mus, -tis, -nt** (active), and **-r, -ris, -tur, -mur, -minī, -ntur** (passive). The **-e-** of the stem changes to **-a-** in the first person active and passive.

Fourth conjugation verbs form their future by adding **-a-** to the stem in the first person active and passive, and **-e-** in the second and third persons, followed by the personal endings.

The future of third conjugation **-iō** verbs is identical to the future of fourth conjugation verbs.

Third Conjugation: Future Active

	Singular		Plural	
First person	petam	I will/shall seek	petēmus	we will/shall seek
Second person	petēs	you will seek	petētis	you will seek
Third person	petet	s/he/it will seek	petent	they will seek

Third Conjugation: Future Passive

	Singular		Plural	
First person	petar	I will/shall be sought	petēmur	we will/shall be sought
Second person	petēris	you will be sought	petēminī	you will be sought
Third person	petētur	s/he/it will be sought	petentur	they will be sought

Fourth Conjugation: Future Active

	Singular		Plural	
First person	audiam	I will/shall hear	audiēmus	we will/shall hear
Second person	audiēs	you will hear	audiētis	you will hear
Third person	audiet	s/he/it will hear	audient	they will hear

Fourth Conjugation: Future Passive

	Singular		Plural	
First person	audiar	I will/shall be heard	audiēmur	we will/shall be heard
Second person	audiēris	you will be heard	audiēminī	you will be heard
Third person	audiētur	s/he/it will be heard	audientur	they will be heard

Third Conjugation -iō verbs: Future Active

	Singular		Plural	
First person	capiam	I will/shall take	capiēmus	we will/shall take
Second person	capiēs	you will take	capiētis	you will take
Third person	capiet	s/he/it will take	capient	they will take

Third Conjugation -iō verbs: Future Passive

	Singular		Plural	
First person	capiar	I will/shall be taken	capiēmur	we will/shall be taken
Second person	capiēris	you will be taken	capiēminī	you will be taken
Third person	capiētur	s/he/it will be taken	capientur	they will be taken

STUDY TIP

Note that in the third conjugation the future and present passive indicative second person singular are identical, aside from the length of the vowel *-e-*:

relinqueris – you are being abandoned

relinquēris – you will be abandoned

▶ EXERCISE 1

Change the present or imperfect tense verbs into the future, keeping the same person, number, and voice. Translate both forms.

Example: cadēbās   you were falling
cadēs   you will fall

1. mittitur
2. sciunt
3. comedēbāmus
4. dūcēbāminī
5. relinquitis
6. ostendēbar
7. occīdēbāmur
8. faciēbat

VOCABULARY TO LEARN

NOUNS

argūmentum, argūmentī, n. – proof, indication, argument

saxum, saxī, n. – stone, rock

senectūs, senectūtis, f. – old age

vīlla, vīllae, f. – country house, villa

PRONOUN

quis, quid? – who? what? (interrogative pronoun)

ADJECTIVES

difficilis, difficile – difficult

parvus, parva, parvum – small

quī, quae, quod? – what? which? (interrogative adjective)

rūsticus, rūstica, rūsticum – rural, rustic

vērus, vēra, vērum – true

vetustus, vetusta, vetustum – old

VERBS

inquam – I say/I said (only introducing direct speech)

neglegō, neglegere, neglēxī, neglēctum – to neglect

stō, stāre, stetī, statum – to stand

ADVERBS

cūr – why?

etiam – even, also

fortasse – perhaps

sīcut – just as

ubīque – everywhere

umquam – ever

PREPOSITION

ante + accusative – in front of

INTERJECTION

ecce – look here!

▶ EXERCISE 2

Find the English derivatives based on the Vocabulary to Learn in the following sentences. Write the corresponding Latin word.

1. Where is the source of the difficulty?

2. Do not neglect your duties!

3. I usually get up at 6 AM.

4. This is a rather unrefined, rustic recipe.

5. Senile debility may come with old age.

6. Nothing moves here; everything is static.

7. These documents need to be verified.

8. The argumentation needs to be internally coherent and valid.

9. You can see advertisements everywhere: they are ubiquitous.

10. We may buy a house in a small village.

LANGUAGE FACT II

INTERROGATIVE PRONOUNS AND ADJECTIVES

In the reading passage adapted from Seneca at the beginning of this chapter you meet two new interrogative words. These are the equivalents of the English interrogative pronouns "who?" and "what?"

> ***Quid** mihi erit?*
> What will be <in store> for me?

> ***Quis** est senex?*
> Who is the old man?

In Latin there is an interrogative pronoun and an interrogative adjective. The interrogative pronoun stands alone, without modifying another noun. The interrogative adjective modifies a noun, and agrees with it in case, number, and gender (like any adjective).

The nominative singular interrogative pronoun is *quis* (masculine and feminine) and *quid* (neuter); it is *quī, quae, quae* in the plural. **Note that in the plural all forms of the interrogative pronoun are identical to those of the relative pronoun.**

A terracotta bust of the pseudo-Seneca was found in Herculaneum and closely resembles the actual bust of Seneca now in the Archaeological Museum in Naples.

BY THE WAY

The reason for the lack of separate feminine forms in the singular is that an unspecified question beginning with *quis* is actually asking about a human person in general without reference to its gender.

Study these uses of the interrogative pronoun:

> *Quis veniet?* – "Who (m./f.) will come?"
>
> *Quem amās?* – "Whom (m./f.) do you love?"
>
> *Cūius est liber?* – "Whose (m./f.) book is it?"
>
> *Quī vōbīs auxilium dabunt?* – "Who will give you help?"

Sometimes a question is asked using an interrogative adjective. **The interrogative adjective is identical to the relative pronoun in all its forms.**

Study these uses of the interrogative adjective:

> *Quī ager est tuus?* – "Which field is yours?"
>
> *Quam fēminam amās?* – "Which woman do you love?"
>
> *Cūius magistrī verba audīs?* – "Which teacher's words do you hear?"
>
> *Quās terrās capiunt Rōmānī?* – "Which lands do the Romans seize?"

Here are the declensions of the interrogative pronoun and the interrogative adjective.

Interrogative Pronoun
Singular

	Masculine and Feminine		Neuter	
Nominative	quis	who	quid	what
Genitive	cūius	whose	cūius	of what
Dative	cui	to/for whom	cui	to/for what
Accusative	quem	whom	quid	what
Ablative	quō	by/with whom	quō	by/with what

Plural

	Masculine		Feminine		Neuter	
Nominative	quī	who	quae	who	quae	what
Genitive	quōrum	whose	quārum	whose	quōrum	of which
Dative	quibus	to/for whom	quibus	to/for whom	quibus	to/for which
Accusative	quōs	whom	quās	whom	quae	which
Ablative	quibus	by/with whom	quibus	by/with whom	quibus	by/with which

Interrogative Adjective
Singular

	Masculine		Feminine		Neuter	
Nominative	quī	which	quae	which	quod	which
Genitive	cūius	of which	cūius	of which	cūius	of which
Dative	cui	to/for which	cui	to/for which	cui	to/for which
Accustive	quem	which	quam	which	quod	which
Ablative	quō	by/with which	quā	by/with which	quō	by/with which

Plural

	Masculine		Feminine		Neuter	
Nominative	quī	which	quae	which	quae	which
Genitive	quōrum	of which	quārum	of which	quōrum	of which
Dative	quibus	to/for which	quibus	to/for which	quibus	to/for which
Accusative	quōs	which	quās	which	quae	which
Ablative	quibus	by/with which	quibus	by/with which	quibus	by/with which

STUDY TIP

The interrogative adjective is identical to the relative pronoun *quī, quae, quod* in all its forms. So, the interrogative adjective does not require knowing any new forms—you learned them when you learned the relative pronoun in Chapter 14.

The interrogative pronoun is identical in form to the relative pronoun only in the plural.

BY THE WAY

When the preposition *cum* ("with") is used with a relative or an interrogative pronoun or interrogative adjective, it is attached to the end of the word: *quōcum, quācum, quibuscum.* Compare *mēcum* and *tēcum.*

Ancient Roman villas, also known as country houses, were large and often elaborately decorated as the frescoes on the walls of the Villa of the Mysteries in Pompeii show.

▶ EXERCISE 3

Translate into Latin.

1. Whose villa is old?

2. Whose (plural) villas are old?

3. What villa is old?

4. Which villas are old?

5. Whom is the old man observing?

6. Which friends is the old man observing?

7. Which old man is observing me?

8. To which farmer will you give the field?

9. To which farmers will you give the fields?

10. Which farmers will give me the fields?

11. With whom will you walk to the villa?

12. With whom (plural) will you stay in the villa?

▶ EXERCISE 4

Translate the following questions. Then choose the best answer for each and translate. The Reading Vocabulary may be consulted.

1. Cui vīlicus dīcit sē dēbēre multa in vīllā reparāre?

    Vīlicus puerō dīcit sē omnia facere.

    Senecae vīlicus dīcit sē dēbēre multa in vīllā reparāre.

    Vīlicus dīcit vīllam Senecae esse vetustam.

2. Quid vīlicus sē neglegere dīcit?

    Vīlicus dīcit sē arborēs neglegere.

    Vīlicus dīcit Senecam nihil neglegere.

    Vīlicus dīcit sē nihil neglegere.

3. Quid dē sē cōgitat Seneca?

    Seneca cōgitat sē esse vetustum sīcut vīllam.

    Seneca cōgitat vīlicum dēbēre multa in vīllā reparāre.

    Seneca cōgitat vīllam ā vīlicō nōn cūrārī.

A Roman coin with a portrait of Nero's head.

4. Quae folia sunt in arboribus?

    Folia ā vīlicō negleguntur.

    Arborēs nōn habent folia.

    Folia pulchra in arboribus cōnspiciuntur.

5. Ā quō arborēs semper cūrābantur nec umquam neglegentur?

    Vīlicus arborēs semper cūrābat nec eās negleget.

    Arborēs negleguntur: itaque nōn habent folia.

    Ā Senecā arborēs semper cūrābantur nec umquam neglegentur.

6. Quae arborēs vetustae esse dīcuntur?

    Arborēs nōn sunt vetustae.

    Fēlīciō arborēs vetustās habet.

    Arborēs Senecae dīcuntur esse vetustae.

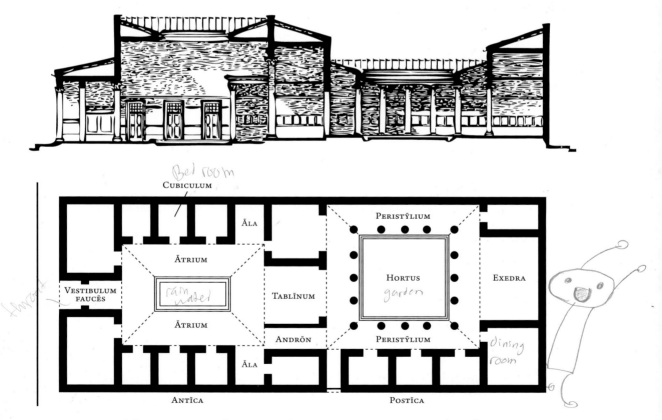

While ancient Roman villas were complex structures, a Roman city house (*domus*), as the diagram shows, was much more compact.

7. Quem cōnspicit senex, quī in iānuā stat?

> Senex, quī in iānuā stat, dentēs nōn habet.

> Senecam cōnspicit senex, quī in iānuā stat.

> Ā Senecā cōnspicitur senex, quī in iānuā stat.

8. Ad quōs hominēs veniet senectūs?

> Ad imparātōs hominēs veniet senectūs.

> Ad Senecam veniet senectūs.

> Ad omnēs hominēs veniet senectūs.

▶ EXERCISE 5

Read the following dialogue, which is written partly in English and partly in Latin. Translate the English parts into Latin, and the Latin parts into English. The Reading Vocabulary may be consulted.

Fēlīciō: Who is coming to the villa now? Whom do I observe?

Seneca: Seneca sum. Vīlla est mea.

Fēlīciō: What are you saying? You can't be Seneca!

Seneca: Senecane esse nōn possum? Seneca sum!

Fēlīciō: You don't seem to me to be Seneca: You seem to me to be an old man!

Seneca: Senex sum et Seneca.

Fēlīciō: What man do you think I am?

Seneca: Putō tē esse senem, quī dentēs nōn habet.

Fēlīciō: What boy was accustomed to play with you as a boy?

Seneca: Fēlīciō, amīcus parvus, mēcum puerō lūdere solēbat.

Fēlīciō: Who do I seem to be to you? I was Fēlīciō. I am Fēlīciō. I will be Fēlīciō.

Seneca: Tū es Fēlīciō! Ego sum fēlīx! Difficile mihi erat, Fēlīciō, tē cōgnōscere. Nam, sīcut Seneca, tū quoque es senex. Sed amīcum meum tandem videō!

TALKING

rūrī – in the country

rūre – from the country

rūs – to the country

sēmita, sēmitae, f. – path

birota, birotae, f. – bicycle

birotā vehor, veheris, vehitur, vehimur, vehiminī, vehuntur – I, you, s/he, etc. ride a bicycle(s) (literally "I, you, s/he, etc. am, are, is carried on a bicycle")

deambulō, deambulāre – to take a walk (for sightseeing or pleasure)

mantica (f.) dorsuālis – backpack

sub dīvō – in the open, under the sky

tentōrium (n.) plicātile – foldable or roll-up tent

A TRIP TO THE COUNTRY

Marīa: Crās (*tomorrow*) ūnā cum parentibus rūs ībō (*I will go*).

Helena: Amāsne terram rūsticam?

Marīa: Terram rūsticam valdē amō. Parentēs quoque eam amant. Sī (*if*) ōtium (*leisure*) habēmus, terram rūsticam petimus.

Mārcus: Quid, Marīa, rūrī faciēs?

Marīa: Agrī sunt pulchrī, arborēs sunt pulchrae. In silvīs et ego et parentēs sēmitās petimus. Placet (*it pleases*) parentibus ibi deambulāre.

Christīna: Tibine, Marīa, in silvīs deambulāre placet?

Marīa: Ita vērō. (*Yes indeed.*) Sed parentēs nōn diū in silvīs manent. Post aliquot hōrās (*after a few hours*) fatīgantur (*they get tired*) et vīllam petere cupiunt. Sunt seniōrēs (*older*).

Christīna: Quid tunc facis? Tūne cum eīs vīllam petis?

Marīa: Interdum (*sometimes*). Sed interdum sōla (*alone*) agrōs et silvās petō. Ibi diū birotā vehor. Interdum mēcum manticam dorsuālem et tentōrium plicātile habeō. Tunc vīllam nōn petō, sed sub dīvō dormiō (*I sleep*).

REVIEW 5: CHAPTERS 13–15

VOCABULARY TO KNOW

NOUNS

arbor, arboris, f. – tree

argūmentum, argūmentī, n. – proof, indication, argument

gladius, gladiī, m. – sword

iūdex, iūdicis, m. – judge

odium, odiī, n. – hatred

ōs, ōris, n. – mouth

parēns, parentis, m./f. – parent

pectus, pectoris, n. – chest

sanguis, sanguinis, m. – blood

saxum, saxī, n. – stone, rock

senectūs, senectūtis, f. – old age

vīlla, vīllae, f. – country house, villa

PRONOUNS

mēcum = cum mē – with me

nihil – nothing

quī, quae, quod – who, which, that (relative pronoun)

quis, quid – who? what? (interrogative pronoun)

tēcum = cum tē – with you

ADJECTIVES

albus, alba, album – white

alius, alia, aliud – another, other

difficilis, difficile – difficult

dīves, dīvitis – rich

doctus, docta, doctum – learned

omnis, omne – each, every, all

parvus, parva, parvum – small

prīmus, prīma, prīmum – first

quī, quae, quod – what? which? (interrogative adjective)

ruber, rubra, rubrum – red

rūsticus, rūstica, rūsticum – rural, rustic

suus, sua, suum – his, her, its, their

vērus, vēra, vērum – true

vetustus, vetusta, vetustum – old

VERBS

cadō, cadere, cecidī, cāsum – to fall

comedō, comedere, comēdī, comēsum – to eat

conveniō, convenīre, convēnī, conventum – to meet

discēdō, discēdere, discessī, discessum – to leave, go away

dūcō, dūcere, dūxī, ductum – to lead

fluō, fluere, flūxī, fluxum – to flow

inquam – I say/I said (only introducing direct speech)

licet + dative + infinitive – it is allowed, it is permitted for someone to do something

neglegō, neglegere, neglēxī, neglēctum – to neglect

nōlō (irregular verb) – not to want, to be unwilling

respondeō, respondēre, respondī, respōnsum – to answer

rogō, rogāre, rogāvī, rogātum – to ask

sēparō, sēparāre, sēparāvī, sēparātum – to separate

stō, stāre, stetī, statum – to stand

tangō, tangere, tetigī, tāctum – to touch

valē! – goodbye!

ADVERBS

cūr – why?

etiam – even, also

fortasse – perhaps

iam – already

mox – soon

sīcut – just as

tantum – only

tum – then

ubīque – everywhere

umquam – ever

PREPOSITIONS

ante + accusative – in front of

apud + accusative – at the house of

per + accusative – through

prō + ablative – for, on behalf of

CONJUNCTIONS

atque – and

enim – for, in fact

INTERJECTION

ecce – look here!

▶ EXERCISE 1

Conjugate the following verbs in the future active voice.

1. *respondeō, respondēre, respondī, respōnsum*

2. *cadō, cadere, cecidī, cāsum*

3. *conveniō, convenīre, convēnī, conventum*

Conjugate the following verbs in the future passive voice.

1. *rogō, rogāre, rogāvī, rogātum*

2. *cōnspiciō, cōnspicere, cōnspexī, cōnspectum*

▶ EXERCISE 2

Give the imperative singular and plural of the following verbs and then change these forms into negative imperatives.

Example: cadō

cade   cadite   nōlī cadere   nōlīte cadere

1. comedō
2. discēdō
3. conveniō
4. neglegō
5. respondeō
6. rogō
7. sēparō
8. tangō
9. fugiō

▶ EXERCISE 3

Fill in the blanks with the missing relative pronoun, interrogative pronoun, or interrogative adjective. Translate the sentences.

Example: _____ vestrum respondēbit?
Quis vestrum respondēbit?   Which of you will answer?

1. Prope _____ arborem tē vidēbō?

2. Senectūs, _____ multī timent, nōn semper est mala.

3. Respondē hominī _____ tē rogat!

4. Vīlla rūstica, in _____ diū nōn vīvēbam, vetusta mihi vidēbātur.

5. _____ argumentīs ostendēs senectūtem esse bonam?

▶ EXERCISE 4

Fill in the blanks with the correct third person possessive form of *suus, sua, suum* or *ēius, eōrum, eārum*. Translate the sentences.

Example: Vir ā poētā nōn discēdēbat, sed poēta nōn cupiēbat _____ verba audīre.
Vir ā poētā nōn discēdēbat, sed poēta nōn cupiēbat ēius verba audīre.
The man was not leaving the poet, but the poet did not want to hear his words.

1. Hominēs saepe verba _____ amant, verba tamen aliōrum nōn amant.

2. Puer et puella amōrem _____ servāre cupiēbant, sed propter odium parentum difficile erat id facere.

3. Puer putābat puellam iam nōn vīvere et dē _____ morte dolēbat.

4. Omnēs senectūtem _____ timent.

5. Doctī _____ que verba multa dē senectūte docent.

▶ EXERCISE 5

Fill in the blanks with the correct genitive form of the first or second person, singular or plural pronoun. Identify the type of genitive. Translate the sentences.

Example: Vōs potestis mihi auxilium dare. Quis _____ mihi auxilium dabit?
Vōs potestis mihi auxilium dare. Quis vestrum mihi auxilium dabit?
You can give me help. Which of you will give me help?   Partitive genitive.

1. Propter amōrem _____ tēcum semper manēbō.

2. Hostēs gladium meum cōnspiciunt et propter timōrem _____ stant nec moventur.

3. Vōs estis mīlitēs crūdēlēs. Timor _____ nōs movet.

4. Nōs difficilia nōn timēmus. Multī enim _____ difficilia petunt.

5. Multīs hominibus licet in vīllam nostram convenīre, sed propter odium _____ nōn veniunt.

Statue of the Roman emperor
Augustus, who asked Vergil to write the *Aeneid*.

▶ EXERCISE 6

Translate into English.

The following text is adapted from Vergil's *Aeneid*, excerpts of which you read in Chapters 10 and 11. You remember how Aeneas abandoned Queen Dido, and how Dido, overwhelmed with grief, committed suicide. Later Aeneas met Dido's ghost in the underworld, but she turned her face away from her former lover, and refused to talk to him. The main reason for Aeneas' descent to the world of the dead, however, was to meet his father Anchises and to learn from him both his own fate and that of his people. Here Aeneas and Anchises converse in the land of the shadows.

"Nunc tē tua fāta docēbō. Diū nāvigābis, diū pugnābis et tandem domum veniēs. Nam novam urbem condēs. Nōmen urbis erit Rōma. Hominibus subiectīs Rōmānī parcent et hominēs superbōs vincent. Tandem imperātor omnibus populīs pācem dabit," inquit Anchīsēs.

"Quī imperātor pācem dabit, pater?" rogat Aenēās.

"Pāx omnibus populīs ab imperātōre Augustō dabitur, cūius nōmen ubīque audiētur," respondet Anchīsēs.

Aenēās, m. – Aeneas	imperātor, imperātōris, m. – emperor
Anchīsēs, m. – Anchises	parcō, parcere, pepercī, parsum + dative – to spare
condō, condere, condidī, conditum – to found	populus, populī, m. – people
domum – homeward, home	subiectus, subiecta, subiectum – subdued
fātum, fātī, n. – fate, destiny	superbus, superba, superbum – proud

CONSIDERING THE CLASSICAL GODS

Statue of Minerva wearing her helmet, from Austria.

MINERVA

Three more female goddesses belong to the family of the Olympians. Athene, or Athena, whose Latin name is Minerva, is a daughter of Jupiter and Metis, the goddess of wisdom. Because Jupiter feared that the offspring of Metis would overthrow him, he swallowed the pregnant Metis and delivered the baby Minerva from his own body: his concerns were confirmed when she emerged from her father's head already helmeted and shining in her armor. Minerva is the goddess not only of war but also of wisdom and practical intelligence. Skillful in weaving as well, she serves as a protectress of Athens, the city whose own name is related to her Greek name. According to Greek myth, however, the god Neptune at one time challenged Minerva's position, and the Athenians characteristically decided to choose their patron divinity by democratic election. In return for the people's support, Neptune offered a spring of salt water, Minerva an olive tree. She was victorious, and her gift of major importance—the olive oil produced by the tree— is of great significance in the Mediterranean world.

Minerva wears her war helmet on this cameo.

DIANA

We have already encountered Artemis, Apollo's twin sister, and the daughter of Zeus and Leto: known in Latin as Diana. She dwells in the woods, where a retinue of nymphs follow her. She is associated with virginity and hunting, and with the moon and magic. There are self-contradictory elements to the image of this goddess. Mistress of animals, she is also a huntress; a virgin, she also protects childbirth; although the possessor of youthful beauty and charm, she has a cold heart. When the hunter Actaeon saw her bathing, she turned him into a stag as punishment for having gazed at her naked body, and his own dogs devoured him. When Niobe, mother of seven sons and seven daughters, boasted that her children were greater than those of Leto, the goddess' own offspring Diana and Apollo took offense, and cruelly slaughtered all fourteen of her sons and daughters. Unable to endure her grief, Niobe turned into a stone.

Statue of Diana, the huntress.

VENUS

Aphrodite, called Venus in Latin, is the most beautiful goddess. Often referred to by the adjective "golden," she is said to possess a magic girdle that excites the power of love. Among her other symbols are the apple and pomegranate (since its seeds symbolize fertility), the goat (since it is associated with lust), the swan, the dove, and the sparrow (the love object in Catullus' Poem 2).

The famous statue called the Venus of Milo.

Paradoxically, Venus is married to Vulcan, the crippled blacksmith of the Olympians. She often has other lovers, most notably Mars, the god of war. A skillful metal worker and craftsman, Vulcan is portrayed as having prepared a trap of chains for Venus and Mars, which caught them in the midst of their embraces. The boy Cupid, called Eros in Greek, who pierces human hearts with love arrows, is Venus' son. So is Aeneas, the result of her union with a mortal, the Trojan shepherd Anchises.

READ AND TRANSLATE THE FOLLOWING PASSAGES

Arachnē valdē bene texere poterat. Putābat sē posse Minervam vincere. Arachnē dīcēbat: "Minerva est dea, sed cum eā certābō eamque vincam. Ēius ars nōn est valdē māgna." Minerva verba Arachnēs audiēbat et māgnā īrā movēbātur. "Nunc in arāneam mūtāberis;" inquit Minerva, "semper texēs, sed verba dīcere nōn poteris." Propter īram deae misera Arachnē corpus arāneae iam habēbit.

Arachnē (nom.), Arachnēs (gen.) – Arachne (this name means "spider" in Greek)	dea, deae, f. – goddess
arānea, arāneae, f. – spider	Minerva, Minervae, f. – Minerva
ars, artis, f. – art, skill	mūtō, mūtāre, mūtāvī, mūtātum – to change
certō, certāre, certāvī, certātum – to compete	texō, texere, texuī, textum – to weave

Venus amōre Adōnidis ardēbat. Nam Adōnis erat valdē pulcher. Mārs odiō movēbātur. "Quis est Adōnis?" inquit Mārs, "Homō quī ā deā amātur." Mārs aprum ad Adōnidem mittit, quī eum occīdit. Sanguis ex pectore Adōnidis fluit. Venus sanguinem videt et Adōnidem vocat: "Nōlī ā mē sēparārī! Amōre tuī teneor." Adōnis tamen iam nōn vīvere vidētur. Tum Venus Adōnidem in flōrem rubrum mūtat.

Adōnis, Adōnidis, m. – Adonis	Mārs, Mārtis, m. – Mars
aper, aprī, m. – boar	mūtō, mūtāre, mūtāvī, mūtātum – to change
flōs, flōris, m. – flower	Venus, Veneris, f. – Venus

CONNECTING WITH THE ANCIENT WORLD

ROMAN CITIES AND ROADS

CITIES IN THE ROMAN EMPIRE

In the reading for Chapter 13 we saw the poet Horace strolling in the Roman Forum. During the first two centuries CE, many new cities were founded in the Roman Empire, and other, older settlements were totally rebuilt. These Roman cities were ordinarily planned as a unit, usually on a grid pattern. In this respect they differed from Rome itself, which had grown up slowly and in a haphazard fashion. Except for a few isolated areas, such as the great *fora* designed and built by various emperors, Rome was a maze of poorly lit and badly drained alleys surrounded by wooden tenements (*īnsulae*).

By way of contrast, the newer provincial cities had excellent and well-drained roads; public latrines at carefully placed intervals, a good supply of water, public baths, mosaics and other artistic adornments, council buildings, and *basilicae*, buildings used for judicial proceedings or commercial exchanges. In some provincial cities one might find public libraries, and the market-places were decorated with inscriptions, in Greek or Latin, recording honors to citizens, decrees of emperors pertaining to the city, and other public and religious events.

The ruins of these provincial cities are still visible, especially in places such as Ephesus in Turkey and Djemila in North Africa. Wealthy local aristocrats often assumed the costs of the adornment and amenities for these cities, in accordance with a civic tradition started in classical Greece, which obligated those with substantial financial resources to sustain a greater share of enhancing the *polis*, or city-state.

Ruins of the ancient Roman city of Sabratha in Libya.

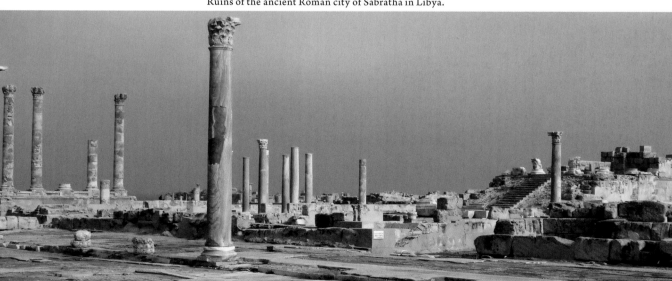

In the largest of the Roman provincial cities, there might be public distributions of grain, which allowed the very poorest inhabitants to obtain a certain basic subsistence, at little or no cost. Likewise in the cities with more substantial populations, the inhabitants might be entertained by gruesome gladiatorial contests—even in the Greek world under the Roman Empire—and chariot races. Nevertheless, most people in urban areas lived in cramped squalor, and the concept of privacy as we know it hardly existed.

A stretch of the old Appian Way, known as the *Via Appia*.

ROADS IN THE ROMAN EMPIRE

Roman cities were connected by an extensive road-system with excellent paved roads. The Romans were determined to be masters of the landscape. Furthermore, the roads were indispensable for their military operations, but they also facilitated commerce and travel to all parts of the empire. One of the most famous roads is the *Via Appia* (312 BCE), which connected Rome with southern Italy, called the "queen" of the roads, many parts of which still survive. This road was named after Appius Claudius, the magistrate responsible for its construction. The *Via Flaminia,* which went northwards from Rome and the *Via Aemilia*, an extension of this road later paved by Augustus, were likewise named after the magistrates who built them.

Milestones gave the name of the builder, the date of construction, and also indicated which emperors had a part in road-building. The actual work was done by soldiers between campaigns under the supervision of Roman field engineers. Construction depended on what material was available locally and and the nature of the terrain. Thus, the surfacing material varied. Vitruvius, who worked for both Julius Caesar and Augustus as an architect, discusses the process of road construction. The field engineer mapped out as straight a line as possible. Trenches (*fossae*) were dug to the bedrock and dirt carried away in baskets. A foundation of lime mortar or sand was laid to form the level base (*pavīmentum*). The next layer consisted of more concrete mixed with stones, gravel, or sand and lime poured in layers. The top surface (*summum dorsum*) consisted of polygonal blocks of stone (which you see in pictures) that were six inches or more thick and carefully fitted on top of the still moist cement. When worn out and in need of repair, the stones were turned over and replaced in the top layer. Roads were higher in the middle than on the sides and had side gutters or ditches to help with drainage. For pedestrians a footpath was available on either side, sometimes paved. The width of the road was supposed to allow two vehicles to meet and pass each other. Not all roads met this criterion, depending on their importance.

Since "all roads lead to Rome," Augustus in 20 BCE erected near the center of the Roman Forum the Golden Milestone (*Mīliārium Aureum*), a bronze monument that listed the distances to various cities in the empire via the large system of roads that the Romans had constructed. This inspired the Zero Milestone (1929) in Washington, D.C., which is meant to be the point from which road distances in the United States can be calculated.

This fragment of a Roman milestone shows the distance to the next Roman town along the road, *Colonia Agrippina*, known today as Cologne, Germany.

EXPLORING ROMAN LAW

THE JUSTICE SYSTEM IN ANCIENT ROME

Horace is out for a relaxing, solitary stroll in downtown Rome when someone rushes up to him and insists on joining in—the Bore, the Boor, the Pest. Midway through the original text of this poem (words from which are quoted below), when the two have reached the Temple of Vesta at the Forum's east end, the reader learns that the Bore is a defendant in a lawsuit and that he has given guarantees to meet the plaintiff for their date in court. If he doesn't, he'll lose the case (*perdere lītem*). He asks Horace for legal counsel, but Horace begs off, claiming he knows nothing about Roman civil law (*cīvīlia iūra*). He nevertheless follows the Bore, apparently into the Forum proper where, as described at the end of the poem, the Bore's legal opponent (*adversārius*), the plaintiff, suddenly comes upon them. He asks Horace to witness, or testify to (*antestārī*), what he is going to do. Horace agrees. The plaintiff then seizes the Bore and hauls him off to court (*rapit in iūs*), both of them shouting. A crowd gathers to see what's going on. The long-suffering poet escapes—or does he? Despite the usual view (Horace flees the scene), it has been suggested that the satire's closing words are ironic: Horace has evaded further direct communication with the Bore, but now finds himself embroiled as witness in an obviously contentious lawsuit (T. Mazurek, *Classical Journal* 93 [1997–98] 1–17).

Statue of Justice holding the scales.

The two parts of *Satire* 1.9 just summarized are very interesting for Roman legal procedure and its social environment. We don't know the exact nature of the case against the Bore, but he was certainly a defendant in what we would call a "civil suit"; this was not a criminal case. The satire's technical language indicates that the procedures being followed dated back at least to the codification of Roman law known as the Twelve Tables (451–450 BCE). The original bronze tablets of this code have not survived—it's a hypothesis that they were destroyed during the Gallic invasion of the 390s BCE—but there are enough quotations from the Tables in later Roman authors to illustrate the local, the agrarian, and—most strikingly—the archaic nature of the code's provisions. Take for example Table 8.1: "If a person has sung against another person or composed a song (*carmen*) so as to cause loss of reputation (*infāmia*) or insult (*flāgitium*), let him be clubbed to death"; or the more sophisticated Table 8.2: "If a person has maimed another's limb, unless he makes an informal agreement to settle with him, let there be retaliation in kind (*tāliō*)."

Despite their antiquity, most of the Twelve Tables' provisions remained "the law of the land" four centuries later in Horace's lifetime (65–8 BCE). They would not be formally supplanted until the emperor Justinian's great codification (*Code, Digest, Institutes*) of the sixth century CE. It was this later codification, an extensive compilation of Roman laws and legal writings, that would have such a profound impact on later European law, perhaps most famously in France's Napoleonic Civil Code of 1804. England, on the contrary, had in the Middle Ages developed its own native Common Law system, largely resistant to outside influences. English Common Law in turn provided the basis for the American legal system. The lone exception is the state of Louisiana, a Spanish, then a French possession, which even today operates under a Civil Code dating to 1870 (earlier Louisiana codes date to 1808 and 1825).

Noteworthy for Horace's satire is that from the time of the Twelve Tables, and no doubt even earlier, it was the plaintiff's responsibility to see to the defendant's appearance in court: he had to do it himself. If the defendant did not cooperate, the plaintiff could seize the defendant by force (*per manum*), but for this to be legal he had to have a competent witness. Horace evidently felt it his duty as a Roman citizen to comply with the plaintiff's request. A less compliant person could have refused, since neither plaintiff nor defendant had any power to "subpoena" witnesses.

Note also that earlier the Bore had asked Horace for legal assistance. Horace was not a lawyer, but like many elite Romans, and despite his denial, he is known to have had an extensive grasp of the law. In the late republic and early empire, the practice of Roman law was becoming more professionalized, but lawyers (even Cicero) and judges were not specifically trained; they had no degrees, there were no bar exams. Lawyers or advocates were therefore mostly educated amateurs. Romans eligible on the basis of their social status to serve as judges (*iūdicēs*) had their names listed in an album. Their names would be selected for individual cases in a preliminary hearing before the *praetor* (the chief judicial magistrate in Rome, elected annually) with the cooperation of the parties concerned. Some Romans did come to be recognized for their expertise in law, as evidenced in their legal opinions and extensive writings (later excerpted in Justinian's *Digest*). These specialists are usually referred to not as lawyers but as jurists.

Romans giving legal advice or acting as advocates, unlike American lawyers today (unless these are offering their services "prō bonō"), did not charge fees—this was thought to be unworthy of their elite social status—though they could accept honoraria. They were expected to provide assistance from a sense of social obligation or friendship. Notice therefore the audacity of the Bore in assuming Horace's friendship (Horace claimed he just knew the Bore's name, nothing more). Notice also the Bore's shamelessness, especially in the final scene as described above. No self-respecting Roman would want to have been at the center of such a public ruckus, thereby suffering loss of that essential Roman quality known as *dignitās*!

JAMES G. KEENAN
Professor of Classics
Loyola University Chicago
Chicago, Illinois

MĪRĀBILE AUDĪTŪ

PHRASES AND QUOTATIONS RELATING TO LEGAL MATTERS

PHRASES AND QUOTATIONS

- Alibi. Literally, "elsewhere." It is formed from the same verbal elements found in *alius*, "another," and *ibi*, "there." If individuals have an alibi, it means that they can show that they were somewhere else at the time when a crime took place.

- Cui prōdest? "Whom does <the crime> benefit?" A question posed when determining who has committed a crime by considering the motive.

- Dē iūre. "According to the law."

- Flagrante dēlictō. "While the crime is blazing," "red-handed." A legal term indicating that a criminal has been caught in the very act of committing an offense.

- Habeās corpus. "You should have the body!" A legal principle, which originated in ancient times, and according to which a person cannot be unlawfully detained.

- Prō bonō. "For the public good." An expression used for legal work undertaken voluntarily and without payment as a public service.

- Sub poenā. "Under <the threat of> penalty." Witnesses are summoned by a judicial authority to appear in court, and give or produce evidence, under the threat of punishment or penalty, an English word that is derived from Latin *poena*, punishment.

CHAPTER 16

Perfect Tense Verbs; Perfect Stem, Perfect Active Tense of All Conjugations; Perfect Tense of *Sum* and *Possum*; Dative of Possession

Oil painting of the eruption of Mt. Vesuvius. By Jean Baptiste Genillon (1750–1829).

MEMORĀBILE DICTŪ

Quid sī nunc caelum ruat?

"What if the sky should fall now?" (Terence, *The Self-Tormentor*, 719)

A proverbial saying for anything regarded as improbable and beyond our power.

READING

Born into a wealthy northern Italian family in about 61 CE, Gāius Plīnius Caecilius Secundus is known to us as Pliny, and specifically as Pliny the Younger, to distinguish him from his uncle and adopted father Pliny the Elder (ca. 23/24–79 CE). His career in public administration culminated in his governorship of Bithynia, a province in what is today Turkey. He appears to have died in around 112–113 CE.

An individual of immense learning and oratorical talent, Pliny has left us ten books of letters that offer a vivid picture of upper-class life during the Roman Empire at the height of its prosperity and power.

The following passage is an adapted and abbreviated version of the sixteenth letter in his sixth book of letters. Here he describes the eruption of Mount Vesuvius, which destroyed the towns of Pompeii, Herculaneum, and Stabiae on the Bay of Naples in 79 CE. In this letter he also relates the death of his uncle, author of the *Historia Natūrālis*, "Natural History," a multi-volume encyclopedia of lore about the human as well as natural world.

DĒ MONTIS VESUVIĪ INCENDIŌ

1　Avunculus meus Mīsēnī erat classis praefectus. Eō diē, quō tantae
　　clādis initium fuit, avunculus forīs iacēbat librīsque studēbat. Māter
　　mea eī nūbem subitō ostendit novam et inūsitātam, quae in caelō prope
　　montem Vesuvium vidēbātur esse. Nūbēs fōrmam habuit similem
5　fōrmae, quam in arboribus saepe vidēmus. Nam summa nūbēs in
　　multās partēs sīcut in rāmōs sēparābātur. Avunculus, homō rērum
　　nātūrae valdē studiōsus, causam nūbis intellegere cupīvit. Iussit igitur
　　nāvēs parārī: nam ad lītus nāvigāre cupīvit, quod est prope montem
　　Vesuvium. Deinde nauta epistulam avunculō dedit. "Fēmina," inquit
10　nauta, "quae prope montem Vesuvium habitat, epistulam ad tē mīsit."
　　Avunculus epistulam lēgit et statim intellēxit in monte Vesuviō esse
　　incendium māgnum: fēminam perīculum timēre nāvibusque fugere
　　cupere. Animus fortis avunculō erat. Cōnsilium igitur novum cēpit. Ad
　　hominēs nāvigāre dēcrēvit, quī prope montem Vesuvium habitābant, et
15　eōs perīculō māgnō līberāre. Nam saxa et cinerēs calidī ē caelō in eōs
　　cadēbant. Illūc igitur nāvigāvit, sed numquam revēnit. Ibi enim fūmus
　　fūnestus et cinerēs eum cum multīs aliīs oppressērunt.

READING VOCABULARY

*avunculus, avunculī, m. – uncle

*caelum, caelī, n. – sky, heaven, weather

calidus, calida, calidum – hot

*causa, causae, f. – cause, reason

cēpit cōnsilium– he made a plan

*cinis, cineris, m. – ash

*clādēs, clādis, f. – disaster

*classis, classis, f. – fleet

cupīvit – wanted, desired

dēcrēvit – he decided

dedit – gave

eō diē – on that day

*fēmina, fēminae, f. – woman

forīs (adv.) – outside

fuit – was

*fūmus, fūmī, m. – smoke

*fūnestus, fūnesta, fūnestum – deadly

habuit – had

*igitur (conj.) – therefore (usually the second word in its clause)

illūc (adv.) – to that place, thither

*incendium, incendiī, n. – conflagration, eruption

initium, initiī, n. – beginning

intellēxit – understood

inūsitātus, inūsitāta, inūsitātum – strange, unusual

iussit – he ordered

*lēgit – read

*lītus, lītoris, n. – shore

*māter, mātris, f. – mother

Mīsēnī – at Misenum (*Mīsēnum, ī, n.* – a base for the imperial Roman navy in the Bay of Naples)

mīsit – sent

*mōns, montis, m. – mountain

*nāvis, nāvis, f. – ship

nāvigāvit – he sailed

*nūbēs, nūbis, f. – cloud

*numquam (adv.) – never

*oppressērunt – overwhelmed, suppressed

ostendit – pointed out

*pars, partis, f. – part

praefectus, praefectī, m. – prefect, commander, chief

rāmus, rāmī, m. – branch

rērum nātūra, nātūrae, f. – nature

revēnit – he returned

*studeō, studēre, studuī, —— + dative – to study, to be eager for, to be interested in

studiōsus, studiōsa, studiōsum + genitive – interested in, a student of

summus, summa, summum – the top of

Vesuvius, Vesuviī, m. – (Mount) Vesuvius

*Words marked with an asterisk will need to be memorized later in the chapter.

COMPREHENSION QUESTIONS

1. What event interrupted the studies of Pliny's uncle?

2. What did Pliny's uncle decide to do?

3. What changed his mind?

4. What happened to Pliny's uncle at the end of the story?

LANGUAGE FACT I

PERFECT TENSE VERBS

In the Latin reading passage there are some new forms of verbs already treated in earlier chapters. These are forms of the perfect tense, a tense that refers primarily to past time:

cēpit "s/he/it took" (perfect tense of *capiō*)

dedit "s/he/it gave" (perfect tense of *dō*)

fuit "s/he/it was" (perfect tense of *sum*)

habuit "s/he/it had" (perfect tense of *habeō*)

In the same passage there are also perfect tense forms of verbs that have not appeared in previous chapters.

lēgit "s/he read" (perfect tense of *legō*)

The meaning of the perfect differs in subtle ways from the imperfect—the past tense introduced in Chapter 11. While the imperfect tense refers to a **continuing** action or state in the past, the perfect indicates either a single act in the past or a **completed** action.

For example, *dīcēbat*, means "s/he was saying" (i.e., a continuing action), but *dīxit* (the same verb in the perfect tense) usually means "s/he said" or "s/he did say" (once and for all).

But the perfect has yet another distinctive meaning. It can refer to an action completed just before the present time. In English the auxiliary verb "have" or "has" indicates this distinction. In Latin this nuance is clear from the context (e.g., adverbs may indicate that an action has just been completed). In the following sentences the verb *legere* ("to read") is used in the imperfect tense and in both meanings of the perfect tense.

Librum legēbat. "S/he was reading the book."

Librum legēbat. Deinde dīxit: "Librum tandem lēgī." "S/he was reading the book. Then s/he said: "At last I have read the book."

Librum lēgit. "S/he read the book."

When the past action is negative, or is to be emphasized, "did" is used in the translation.

Librum nōn lēgī. "I did not read the book."

Librum lēgī. "I did read the book."

▶ EXERCISE 1

Find and translate nine more perfect tense forms from the Latin reading passage.

VOCABULARY TO LEARN

NOUNS

avunculus, avunculī, m. – uncle

caelum, caelī, n. – sky, heaven, weather

causa, causae, f. – cause, reason

cinis, cineris, m. – ash

clādēs, clādis, f. – disaster

classis, classis, f. – fleet, class (of people)

fēmina, fēminae, f. – woman

fūmus, fūmī, m. – smoke

incendium, incendiī, n. – conflagration, eruption

lītus, lītoris, n. – shore

māter, mātris, f. – mother

mōns, montis, m. – mountain

nāvis, nāvis, f. – ship

nūbēs, nūbis, f. – cloud

pars, partis, f. – part

ADJECTIVE

fūnestus, fūnesta, fūnestum – deadly

VERBS

legō, legere, lēgī, lēctum – to read, to choose

opprimō, opprimere, oppressī, oppressum – to overwhelm, suppress

studeō, studēre, studuī, —— + dative – to study, to be eager for, to be interested in

ADVERB

numquam – never

CONJUNCTION

igitur – therefore (usually the second word in its clause)

▶ EXERCISE 2

Find the English derivatives based on the Vocabulary to Learn in the following sentences. Write the corresponding Latin word.

1. Celestial phenomena greatly interest me.

2. Archaeologists found several cinerary urns at that site.

3. These people are introducing a totally subjective mode of thinking in which causality plays no role.

4. Terrible destruction was caused in the city by incendiary bombs.

5. Naval architecture is a very exacting science.

6. Karl Marx advocated an entire philosophy of history based on class conflict.

7. Your teacher has a very avuncular manner.

8. The littoral region here sustains a wide variety of plant and animal life.

9. This part of the hospital is the maternity ward.

10. Underprivileged people in the Roman world were cruelly oppressed.

11. The gender of this noun is feminine.

12. The carpet in the apartment was so dirty it had to be fumigated.

13. Why were you not present at the lecture?

14. I agree with you only partially.

15. I will be a lifelong student.

▶ EXERCISE 3

Translate each sentence with special attention to the previously discussed meanings of the perfect tense verb in parentheses.

Example: "Perīculum nōn intellēxī (first person singular), sed nunc intellegō," inquit avunculus. "Iam igitur dēcrēvī (first person singular) ad hominēs, quī prope montem habitant, nāvigāre."
"I did not understand the danger, but now I understand <it>," said uncle. "Therefore I have already decided to sail to the people who live near the mountain."

1. Nautae prope lītus manēbant. Caelum semper cōnspiciēbant. Deinde cōnsilium cēpērunt (third person plural). Nāvem parāre dēcrēvērunt (third person plural).

2. Epistulam ad hominēs, quī in viā exspectābant, statim mīsimus (first person plural), et eōs ad nōs venīre iussimus (first person plural).

3. Nautās exspectābāmus. Nunc eōrum nāvēs vidēre possumus. "Nautae," inquit amīcus meus, "vēnērunt (third person plural)!"

LANGUAGE FACT II

PERFECT STEM, PERFECT ACTIVE TENSE OF ALL CONJUGATIONS

The perfect is not only distinctive in its meaning; it has a series of forms that are very distinctive too.

You have already learned that **the principal parts** of a verb are used to make different verb forms. Most verbs have four principal parts. The first and second principal parts are important for the present, imperfect, and future tenses discussed in previous chapters. But the forms of the perfect active tense are derived from the **third** principal part of any verb.

Below are the principal parts of a verb from each conjugation. Note carefully the third principal part: this principal part is the form of the first person singular of the perfect active indicative.

First conjugation:	parō, parāre, **parāvī**, parātum – I prepare
Second conjugation:	teneō, tenēre, **tenuī**, tentum – I hold
Third conjugation:	dīcō, dīcere, **dīxī**, dictum – I say
Fourth conjugation:	audiō, audīre, **audīvī**, audītum – I hear
Third conjugation (-iō):	capiō, capere, **cēpī**, captum – I take

Learning the perfect forms is much easier than it might at first appear, because the perfect active endings are the same for **all** four conjugations. These endings are added to the perfect stem, which is found by dropping the **-ī** found in the third principal part.

Here are some general patterns for forming the perfect stem:

- Many first conjugation verbs form their perfect stem by adding *-v-* after the *-ā-* in the present stem (*parāvī*).
- Many fourth conjugation verbs form their perfect stem by adding *-v-* to the *-ī-* in the present stem (*audīvī*).
- Many second conjugation verbs have a perfect stem that ends in *-u-* before the *-ī* of the perfect ending (as in *tenuī* above).

None of these patterns is absolutely consistent.

Remember: add the same endings to the perfect stem of any verb, regardless of conjugation. Here is the perfect active of *parō* and *capiō*. Since the endings are the same, you do not need to learn different paradigms for all conjugations.

Perfect Active: *parō*

Singular

First Person	parāv-ī	parāvī	I prepared, did prepare (or) I have prepared
Second Person	parāv-istī	parāvistī	you prepared, did prepare (or) you have prepared
Third Person	parāv-it	parāvit	s/he/it prepared, did prepare (or) s/he/it has prepared

Plural

First Person	parāv-imus	parāvimus	we prepared, did prepare (or) we have prepared
Second Person	parāv-istis	parāvistis	you prepared, did prepare (or) you have prepared
Third Person	parāv-ērunt	parāvērunt	they prepared, did prepare (or) they have prepared

Perfect Active: *capiō*

Singular

First Person	cēp-ī	cēpī	I took, did take (or) I have taken
Second Person	cēp-istī	cēpistī	you took, did take (or) you have taken
Third Person	cēp-it	cēpit	s/he/it took, did take (or) s/he/it has taken

Plural

First Person	cēp-imus	cēpimus	we took, did take (or) we have taken
Second Person	cēp-istis	cēpistis	you took, did take (or) you have taken
Third Person	cēp-ērunt	cēpērunt	they took, did take (or) they have taken

STUDY TIP

When you learn a new verb, learn all four principal parts. The endings of the perfect active are themselves very simple, and the same for all the conjugations.

▶ EXERCISE 4

Change each infinitive into the perfect active form indicated in parentheses. Translate the changed form.

Example: iubēre (perfect active second person singular)
iussisti   you ordered/did order/have ordered

1. sēparāre (perfect active third person plural)

2. legere (perfect active first person plural)

3. discēdere (perfect active third person singular)

4. tangere (perfect active second person singular)

5. ārdēre (perfect active third person plural)

6. respondēre (perfect active second person plural)

7. cadere (perfect active second person singular)

8. dēlēre (perfect active third person plural)

9. opprimere (perfect active third person singular)

10. neglegere (perfect active first person plural)

11. stāre (perfect active third person plural)

Daylight view of the excavated ruins of Pompeii with Mt. Vesuvius in the background.

► EXERCISE 5

Change the following present tense verbs into the perfect, keeping the same person and number. Translate the changed sentence. The Reading Vocabulary may be consulted.

Example: Ad hominēs nāvigāre dēcernō.
Ad hominēs nāvigāre dēcrēvī.   I decided to sail to the people.

1. Ego et avunculus librōs legimus.
2. Nūbem novam in caelō cōnspicimus.
3. Hominēs rērum nātūrae studiōsī causam nūbis novae intellegunt.
4. Dīcit nauta: "Mē iubēs nāvēs statim parāre."
5. Perīculum valdē timētis. Novum igitur cōnsilium capere dēbētis.
6. Saxa et cinerēs calidī ē caelō subitō cadunt.
7. Eōrum epistulam iam legō.

LANGUAGE FACT III

PERFECT TENSE OF *SUM* AND *POSSUM*

You have already learned the principal parts of the irregular verbs *sum* and *possum*. You will remember that they lack a fourth principal part, but each has a third principal part, which is the first person singular of the perfect tense.

> sum, esse, fuī, —— – to be
>
> possum, posse, potuī, —— – to be able

BY THE WAY

Sum and *possum* have no passive forms.

Now it is easy to supply all the forms of the perfect active for each verb.

Perfect Tense of *sum*

Singular

First Person	fu-ī	fuī	I was (or) I have been
Second Person	fu-istī	fuistī	you were (or) you have been
Third Person	fu-it	fuit	s/he/it was (or) s/he/it has been

Plural

First Person	fu-imus	fuimus	we were (or) we have been
Second Person	fu-istis	fuistis	you were (or) you have been
Third Person	fu-ērunt	fuērunt	they were (or) they have been

Perfect Tense of *possum*

Singular

First Person	potu-ī	potuī	I was able, could (or) I have been able
Second Person	potu-istī	potuistī	you were able, could (or) you have been able
Third Person	potu-it	potuit	s/he/it was able, could (or) s/he/it has been able

Plural

First Person	potu-imus	potuimus	we were able, could (or) we have been able
Second Person	potu-istis	potuistis	you were able, could (or) you have been able
Third Person	potu-ērunt	potuērunt	they were able, could (or) they have been able

Statue of a dancing faun in the *impluvium* of the atrium in the House of the Faun in Pompeii.

▶ EXERCISE 6

Translate into Latin. The Reading Vocabulary may be consulted.

1. Were you (plural) able to see the stones and hot ashes in the sky?

2. At that time you were able to send a man to the people who lived near Mount Vesuvius.

3. We were not able to read the woman's words.

4. Then there was suddenly a conflagration in the mountain.

5. I have already been able to read the letter of the woman. Now I am preparing the ships.
    (handwritten: iam, potui, legere feminae)

6. You were able to free the people from great danger.
    (handwritten: Potuit liberare homines ab magno periculo.)

LANGUAGE FACT IV

DATIVE OF POSSESSION

In the passage at the beginning of this chapter you might have thought the following sentence was distinctive. Here you see a usage of the dative case that has not been discussed so far.

> *Animus fortis avunculō erat.*
> My uncle had a brave spirit.

This sentence has been translated with the verb "have," even though the Latin verb "to have" is not present. The person who owns or has something may be expressed in the dative case with some form of the verb *esse* ("to be"). Here the Latin literally says "For/to my uncle there was a brave spirit." The dative of possession emphasizes the fact of possession.

Another example:

> *Mihi sunt multī librī.*
> I have many books.

BY THE WAY

You can, of course, express possession using the verb *habeō*. In this case, the dative of possession is not used:

> *Multōs librōs habeō.*

(handwritten:)
6. Homines ab magno periculo liberare potuit.
5. Iam Epistulam feminae legere potui. Numc naves paro

▶ EXERCISE 7

Translate into Latin in two ways, using both the verb *habeō* and the dative of possession.

Example: I have many friends.
Multōs amīcōs habeō.   Mihi sunt multī amīcī.

1. Do you have an uncle?

2. He has a small mouth.

3. We have cruel enemies.

4. What names do you (plural) have?

5. They have rustic villas.

A street in excavated Pompeii. Note the narrow road, the sidewalk, and
in the middle of the street are raised stones that allowed people to cross
the road, which might be filled with water or garbage.

▶ EXERCISE 8

Translate the following passage into English. Refer both to the Reading Vocabulary and the words explained below.

Plīnius: Nūbem māgnam, quae est in caelō prope montem Vesuvium, iam cōnspexit māter. Nūbemne, avuncule, vidēre potes?

Avunculus: Nūbem vidēre possum. Sum senex, sed mihi sunt oculī bonī atque validī.

Plīnius: Quae est haec nūbēs? Ēius fōrma mihi vidētur esse nova. Tālis forma arboribus, nōn nūbibus esse solet.

Avunculus: Ubi prīmum māter tua nūbem mihi ostendit, eam esse inūsitātam intellēxī. Ad montem igitur nāvigāre causamque nūbis investīgāre cupīvī. Sed cōnsilium mūtāvī.

Plīnius: Cūr cōnsilium mūtāvistī?

Avunculus: Fēmina, cūius vīlla ā monte Vesuviō nōn longē est, epistulam ad mē mīsit, in quā dīxit flammās ē monte venīre: saxa cinerēsque calidōs in hominēs cadere: ibi esse perīculum māgnum.

Plīnius: Tūne igitur dē hominibus, quī ibi habitant, cōgitāvistī?

Avunculus: Ita vērō.

Plīnius: Quid faciēs?

Avunculus: Illūc nāvigābō hominēsque perīculō māgnō līberābō.

Plīnius: Animus tibi est fortis!

haec (feminine demonstrative) – this
investīgō, investīgāre, investīgāvī, investīgātum – to trace out, investigate
ita vērō – yes indeed

mūtō, mūtāre, mūtāvī, mūtātum – to change
tālis, tāle – such a
ubi prīmum – as soon as
validus, valida, validum – healthy, strong

TALKING

fēriae, fēriārum, f. pl. – vacation

fēriās agere – have a holiday

acta, actae, f. – the (sandy) seashore

aprīcor, aprīcārī – to sunbathe

assāre in crāticulā (assō, assāre, assāvī) – to barbecue

folle volātilī lūdō (lūdere, lūsī, lūsum) – to play volleyball

harēna, harēnae, f. – sand

natō, natāre, natāvī, ——— – to swim

sōl, sōlis, m. – the sun

sōle adustus, adusta, adustum – suntanned

sub dīvō – in the open, under the sky

umbella, umbellae, f. – sunshade, umbrella

unguentum, unguentī, n. – sunscreen

natātōrium, natātōriī, n. – swimming pool

RELAXING AT THE BEACH

Helena: Quandō (*when*), Christīna, ē lītore in urbem revēnistī (*returned*)?

Christīna: Et ego et parentēs herī (*yesterday*) revēnimus. Fēriās (*holidays*) bonās ēgimus. Lītus enim valdē amāmus.

Marīa: Adusta sōle mihi nōn vidēris. Nōnne (*surely*) tū et parentēs in actā aprīcārī solētis?

Christīna: Numquam forīs (*outside*) iacuimus, nisi (*unless*) unguentō oblitī (*smeared*). Medicī dīcunt hominēs nōn dēbēre diū in sōle manēre nisi unguentīs oblitōs.

Helena: Quid aliud cum parentibus in lītore fēcistī?

Christīna: Parva castella (*castles*) ex harēnā aedificāvimus. Folle volātilī lūsimus. Vespere (*in the evening*) cibum (*food*) in crāticulā assāre sub dīvō semper solēbāmus.

Mārcus: Ea omnia in terrā fēcistī. Aquamne timuistī? Nōnne natāre solēbātis?

Christīna: Māne (*in the morning*) in natātōriō natāre solēbam. Hōrīs postmerīdiānīs (*in the afternoon hours*) autem saepe in actā sub (*under*) umbellā iacēbam prope mare librīsque studēbam.

Mārcus: Etiam in lītore, etiam in fēriīs librōs cūrābās! Quī homō sīc (*so*) umquam fuit dīligēns (*diligent*) ut (*as*) tū?!

Christīna: In scholā Latīnā (*in the Latin class*) ante fēriās dē montis Vesuviī incendiō lēgimus. Eō tempore, quō incendium in monte fuit, Plīnius et ēius avunculus forīs iacēbant librīsque studēbant!

CHAPTER 17

Pluperfect Active Tense of All Conjugations; Pluperfect Tense of *Sum* and *Possum*; Fourth Declension Masculine, Feminine, and Neuter Nouns

The 64 CE fire in Rome as painted by Henryk Siemiradzki (1843–1902).

MEMORĀBILE DICTŪ

Sine īrā et studiō.

"Without anger and partisanship." (Tacitus, *Annals* 1.1)

This is the promise made by the Roman historian Tacitus in the beginning of his *Annals*. The phrase has become proverbial for claims of impartiality in historical writing.

READING

Pliny the Younger addresses the letter about the death of his uncle to his good friend, the historian Cornēlius Tacitus (ca. 56–116/120 CE). Tacitus' major writings include the *Historiae*, "Histories," covering the period between 69 and 96 CE, and the *Annālēs*, covering from 14 to 68 CE; in both works he exposes abuses of power by the Roman imperial government in those years. He also wrote three briefer works: the *Germānia*, the only surviving ethnographical and geographic treatise in Latin; the *Agricola*, a biography of his wife's father of that name, a one-time governor of Britain; and the *Dialogus dē Ōrātōribus*, "Dialogue about Orators," which seeks to explain the decline of political eloquence characteristic of the Roman republic in his own time.

The following text, Chapters 38–39 of *Annālēs*, Book 16, tells about the fire that destroyed Rome in 64 CE. It does not omit the persistent rumor that the emperor Nero himself had started the conflagration, supposedly in pursuit of inspiration for his own artistic efforts about the fall of Troy! After having failed to dissipate the rumor despite offers of financial compensation to the fire's victims, Nero found a scapegoat, by accusing the Christians, a fairly new religious sect then making its presence visible in Rome, of having started the fire.

DĒ INCENDIŌ RŌMĀNŌ

1 Initium māgnī incendiī Rōmānī fuit in tabernīs, in quibus flammae
   mercimōniīs facile alēbantur. Quae fuit ēius incendiī causa? Fortasse
   Nerō imperātor dolō id fēcit; fortasse alia erat causa. Māiōrem tamen
   clādem Rōmānī numquam vīderant. Ignis impetū ventōrum vectus
5 circum corripuit nec ēius vīs opprimī potuit. Domibus nōn erant
   mūnimenta, templīs nōn erant mūrī. Viae erant angustae et flexae.
   Itaque sine impedimentīs flammae omnia dēvastābant. Flammae iam
   ubīque ārdēbant antequam hominēs eās exstinguere temptāvērunt.
   Propter lacrimās et timōrēs fēminārum et propter eōs quī hūc atque
10 illūc currēbant omnia erant in tumultū. Omnia loca ex omnibus
   partibus ignī corripiēbantur. Virī mulierēsque in viīs et agrīs fugiēbant
   et multī eōrum in terram cadēbant. Nam eīs, quī omnia sua omnēsque
   suōs āmīserant, propter dolōrem iam nōn erant vīrēs. Itaque eōs ignis
   cōnsūmpsit. Aliī autem hominēs fācēs in ignem iaciēbant, quod fortasse
15 iussū imperātōris faciēbant.

READING VOCABULARY

*alō, alere, aluī, altum/alitum – to feed, nourish

*āmīserant – had lost

angustus, angusta, angustum – narrow

antequam (conj.) – before

circus, circī, m. – circus, Circus Maximus

*corripiō, corripere, corripuī, correptum – to seize, occupy, engulf

*currō, currere, cucurrī, cursum – to run

*dēvastō, dēvastāre, dēvastāvī, dēvastātum – to devastate

*domibus – to the houses

*exstinguō, exstinguere, exstīnxī, exstīnctum – to extinguish

*facile (adv.) – easily

fax, fācis, f. – torch

flexus, flexa, flexum – curved

hūc atque illūc – hither and thither, to and fro

*iaciō, iacere, iēcī, iactum – to throw

impedimentum, impedimentī, n. – impediment

*imperātor, imperātōris, m. – general, emperor

*initium, initiī, n. – beginning

*impetū – by force of

*iussū – by the order

*locus, locī, m. – place; locī, locōrum, m. pl. – passages of a book; loca, locōrum, n. pl. – geographical places

māiōrem (accusative singular feminine) – bigger, greater

mercimōnium, mercimōniī, n. – merchandise

mūnimentum, mūnimentī, n. – protection, fortification

*mūrus, mūrī, m. – wall

Nerō, Nerōnis, m. – Nero

*sine + ablative – without

taberna, tabernae, f. – shop

*temptō, temptāre, temptāvī, temptātum – to try

*in tumultū – in uproar, in confusion

vectus, vecta, vectum – carried, driven

*ventus, ventī, m. – wind

vīderant – had seen

*Words marked with an asterisk will need to be memorized later in the chapter.

STUDY TIP

Remember to distinguish between:

ignis – a general word for fire; fire as an element;

flamma – a flame, a part of *ignis*;

incendium – a conflagration, fire as a disastrous event.

COMPREHENSION QUESTIONS

1. How did the fire at Rome start? *Nero*

2. Why did the fire spread so quickly?

3. Why did some people have no strength to flee?

4. Why were some people throwing torches into the fire?

LANGUAGE FACT I

PLUPERFECT ACTIVE TENSE OF ALL CONJUGATIONS

In the chapter reading about the fire of Rome, you meet several new verb forms:

>*vīderant*, "they had seen"

>*āmīserant*, "they had lost."

These are forms of the pluperfect active tense.

The pluperfect (literally "more than perfect") indicates an action already completed prior to another action in the past. In English the pluperfect is typically indicated by the auxiliary verb "had."

In the text above:

>*Māiōrem tamen clādem Rōmānī numquam vīderant.*
>However, the Romans had never seen a greater disaster.

The Romans had not seen a greater disaster *before* the great fire: this action of not seeing had **already** taken place before the great fire.

>*Nam eīs, quī omnia sua omnēsque suōs āmīserant, propter dolōrem iam nōn erant vīrēs.*
>In fact, those who had lost all their things and all their people did not have strength any more because of pain.

Some had lost all their things and all their people *before* they did not have any strength: this action of having lost everything had **already** taken place before their loss of strength.

The formation of the pluperfect active is simple, and is the same for all conjugations. Use the perfect tense stem, i.e., a verb's third principal part minus the ending *-ī*. To this stem add the pluperfect endings:

Pluperfect Active: *parō*

	Singular		Plural	
First person	parā**veram**	I had prepared	parā**verāmus**	we had prepared
Second person	parā**verās**	you had prepared	parā**verātis**	you had prepared
Third person	parā**verat**	s/he/it had prepared	parā**verant**	they had prepared

Pluperfect Active: *capiō*

	Singular		Plural	
First person	cēp**eram**	I had taken	cēp**erāmus**	we had taken
Second person	cēp**erās**	you had taken	cēp**erātis**	you had taken
Third person	cēp**erat**	s/he/it had taken	cēp**erant**	they had taken

STUDY TIP

You already know the pluperfect endings, because they are identical to the imperfect active forms of *sum* ("I am"), which you have studied in Chapter 11. To know the pluperfect endings, it is not necessary to learn any new forms at all!

▶ EXERCISE 1

Change the perfect tense verbs into the pluperfect, keeping the same person and number. Translate the changed form.

Example: aluī

alueram   I had nourished

1. corripuī *corripueram I had engulfed*
2. temptāvī *temptaveram I had tried*
3. exstīnxī *exstinxeram I had extinguished.*
4. āmīsī *amiseram I had lost*
5. cucurrī *cucurram I had run*
6. lēgī *legeram I had read*

VOCABULARY TO LEARN

NOUNS

cornū, cornūs, n. – horn

domus, domūs, f. – house, home

imperātor, imperātōris, m. – general, emperor

impetus, impetūs, m. – impetus, force, attack

initium, initiī, n. – beginning

iussus, iussūs, m. – order (this word typically occurs only in the ablative singular)

locus, locī, m. – place; locī, locōrum, m. pl. – passages of a book; loca, locōrum, n. pl. – geographical places *(group-o-ppls)*

manus, manūs, f. – hand

mūrus, mūrī, m. – wall

tumultus, tumultūs, m. – uproar, confusion

ventus, ventī, m. – wind

VERBS

alō, alere, aluī, altum/alitum – to feed, nourish

āmittō, āmittere, āmīsī, āmissum – to lose

corripiō, corripere, corripuī, correptum – to seize, engulf

currō, currere, cucurrī, cursum – to run

dēvastō, dēvastāre, dēvastāvī, dēvastātum – to devastate

exstinguō, exstinguere, exstīnxī, exstīnctum – to extinguish

iaciō, iacere, iēcī, iactum – to throw

temptō, temptāre, temptāvī, temptātum – to try *Attempt*

ADVERB

facile – easily

PREPOSITION

sine + ablative – without

The Latin words *cornū* (horn) and *cōpia* (supply) are the two roots of the English word cornucopia, known as a horn of plenty.

▶ EXERCISE 2

Find the English derivatives based on the Vocabulary to Learn in the following sentences. Write the corresponding Latin word.

1. An attempt was made to rescue the lost mountaineers.
2. It is now time for your local weather forecast.
3. The dinosaurs are an extinct species.
4. The divorce decree determined which spouse had to pay alimony to the other.
5. I cannot breathe well; the ventilation in the building is not good.
6. Government officials assessed the areas devastated by the hurricane.
7. "Sit down!" is a jussive sentence.
8. After the initial shock, everyone is trying to cope with the bad news.
9. Could you describe to me the curriculum of your program?
10. In imperial times Rome expanded throughout the Mediterranean world.
11. We admired the murals in the old church.
12. These are problems of a domestic nature.
13. Would you agree to be a facilitator for our discussion?
14. I feel rejected by you.
15. Those were tumultuous times for the Roman republic.
16. Nowadays fewer and fewer people do manual work.
17. Impetuous people often regret their actions when it is too late!

▶ EXERCISE 3

Change the present tense verbs into the pluperfect, keeping the same person and number. Translate the changed form.

Example: agimus
ēgerāmus   we had driven/behaved/done

1. rogātis
2. discēdunt
3. alitis
4. studet
5. fugis
6. stās
7. habēmus
8. legō
9. invidētis
10. tangis
11. sciō

LANGUAGE FACT II

PLUPERFECT TENSE OF *SUM* AND *POSSUM*

Once you know the perfect stem of *sum* and *possum*, you can easily supply the perfect and pluperfect forms, since the endings are identical to those of other verbs.

You have already met the perfect forms of *esse* and *posse* in the previous chapter. Here are their pluperfect forms.

	Pluperfect Tense of *sum*				
	Singular			**Plural**	
First person	fu**eram**	I had been		fu**erāmus**	we had been
Second person	fu**erās**	you had been		fu**erātis**	you had been
Third person	fu**erat**	s/he/it had been		fu**erant**	they had been

	Pluperfect Tense of *possum*				
	Singular			**Plural**	
First person	potu**eram**	I had been able		potu**erāmus**	we had been able
Second person	potu**erās**	you had been able		potu**erātis**	you had been able
Third person	potu**erat**	s/he/it had been able		potu**erant**	they had been able

▶ EXERCISE 4

Translate into Latin. Personal pronouns can be omitted.

1. We had not been able to run.
2. I had already been in the villa.
3. I had not been able to leave my mother.
4. Had you (plural) already been in a disaster?
5. Had you been able to walk to the shore?
6. Many women had already been in the ship.
7. Had you (plural) been able to flee?
8. Men had not been able to extinguish the conflagration.
9. The judge had not been able to stand.
10. The smoke had already been everywhere.
11. Had you often been there?
12. We had already been in a storm.

LANGUAGE FACT III
FOURTH DECLENSION NOUNS

In the chapter reading you saw some words with unfamiliar endings:

> *impetū ventōrum*
> by the force of the winds

> *Omnia erant in tumultū.*
> Everything was in confusion.

> *iussū imperātōris*
> by the order of the emperor

The forms *impetū*, *tumultū*, and *iussū* belong to the fourth declension. This declension has the characteristic vowel **u**, which appears in almost all its cases.

bruhhh

A bust of a young Nero.

Nouns of this declension are mostly masculine, with a few feminines and neuters.

Feminine and masculine nouns of the fourth declension have identical endings.

Neuter nouns have the ending *-ū* in the nominative singular, and follow their own sub-type.

Here are the declensions of the two sub-types of the fourth declension: masculine/feminine nouns and neuter nouns.

Fourth Declension Masculine, Feminine, and Neuter Nouns

Singular

	Masculine		Feminine		Neuter	
Nominative	tumult**us**	the confusion	man**us**	the hand	corn**ū**	the horn
Genitive	tumult**ūs**	of the confusion	man**ūs**	of the hand	corn**ūs**	of the horn
Dative	tumlt**uī**	to/for the confusion	man**uī**	to/for the hand	corn**ū** (*i*)	to/for the horn
Accusative	tumlt**um**	the confusion	man**um**	the hand	corn**ū**	the horn
Ablative	tumlt**ū**	by/with the confusion	man**ū**	by/with the hand	corn**ū**	by/with the horn
Vocative	tumlt**us**	o, confusion	man**us**	o, hand	corn**ū**	o, horn

Handwritten annotations: impetus, impetūs, impetuī, impetum, impetū, impetus

Plural

	Masculine		Feminine		Neuter	
Nominative	tumlt**ūs**	the confusions	man**ūs**	the hands	corn**ua**	the horns
Genitive	tumlt**uum**	of the confusions	man**uum**	of the hands	corn**uum**	of the horns
Dative	tumlt**ibus**	to/for the confusions	man**ibus**	to/for the hands	corn**ibus**	to/for the horns
Accusative	tumlt**ūs**	the confusions	man**ūs**	the hands	corn**ua**	the horns
Ablative	tumlt**ibus**	by/with the confusions	man**ibus**	by/with the hands	corn**ibus**	by/with the horns
Vocative	tumlt**ūs**	o, confusions	man**ūs**	o, hands	corn**ua**	o, horns

BY THE WAY

Fourth declension masculine/feminine nouns look identical to second declension masculine nouns in their nominative singular forms. The genitive singular form of the noun will indicate whether it is from the fourth or second declension.

STUDY TIP

The neuter rule applies in the fourth declension: the neuter nominative, accusative, and vocative have identical forms.

Note also that the dative of *cornū* does not have the ending *-uī*: the dative ending *-uī* only occurs in masculine and feminine nouns.

There is one more fourth declension noun in the text at the beginning of the chapter: *domus*.

> *Domibus nōn erant mūnimenta.*
> The houses did not have protections.

Domus has a few irregular forms (variable between the fourth and the second declensions), and it will be worthwhile to learn them, because this word is so common.

domi = at home

Declension of *domus*

	Singular	Plural
Nominative	dom**us**	dom**ūs**
Genitive	dom**ūs** *domi.* (*locative*)	dom**uum** (dom**ōrum**)
Dative	dom**uī** (dom**ō**)	dom**ibus**
Accusative	dom**um**	dom**ōs** (dom**ūs**)
Ablative	dom**ō** (dom**ū**)	dom**ibus**
Vocative	dom**us**	dom**ūs**

BY THE WAY

You already know a very important form of *domus* that does not appear on the list above, because it does not fit in the usual paradigm of cases. This form is *domī*, which is only used to mean "at home." *Domī* is called the locative, because it refers to a "location."

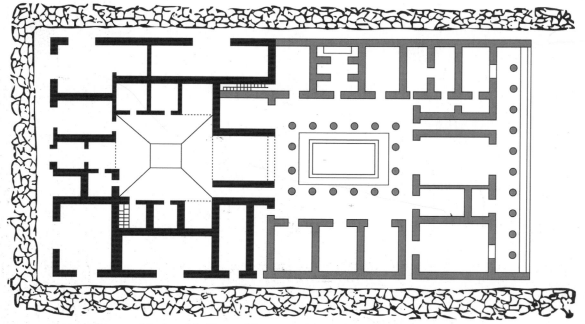

Compare this plan of the House of the Faun in Pompeii with the Roman *domus* on p. 255.

▶ EXERCISE 5

Decline the following nouns.

1. *impetus, impetūs,* m. – attack

2. *genū, genūs,* n. – knee

▶ EXERCISE 6

Make the adjective in parentheses agree with the noun. For some, more than one answer is possible.

Example: manuī (meus)
manuī meae

1. cornibus (longus)
2. tumultuum (māgnus)
3. impetuī (fūnestus)
4. domūs (noster)
5. cornū (pulcher)
6. manum (armātus)
7. domibus (vester)
8. cornua (omnis)
9. manibus (multus)

The ruins of the Roman Forum may begin to give you an idea of what this busy place looked like during the fire in Rome in 64 CE.

▶ EXERCISE 7

The following imaginary dialogue is between two Romans in the Roman Forum during the fire of 64 CE. Translate the parts that are in English into Latin, and the parts that are in Latin into English. The Reading Vocabulary may be consulted.

Rōmānus 1: Fūmum et flammās cōnspiciō. Ex quā parte urbis vēnērunt? Quae est causa tumultūs?

Rōmānus 2: Therefore you do not know that Rome is on fire.

Rōmānus 1: Vērumne dīcis? Quod incendium? Quis id fēcit?

Rōmānus 2: The emperor ordered people to make the fire. For (he) had always desired to see the city in flames.

Rōmānus 1: Nōn possum id crēdere. Ārdetne Rōma iussū imperātōris?

Rōmānus 2: It is true, however. I saw people who had prepared torches and were throwing them with their hands in the houses and the temples.

Rōmānus 1: Nunc dē domō meā cōgitō. Familia enim mea domī est. Corripiturne domus mea quoque flammīs? Manetne familia domī?

Rōmānus 2: (I) do not know. I saw many men and women who were fleeing. They had abandoned their houses and all their things.

Rōmānus 1: Cōnspice! Perīculum iam est prope nōs. Quis hās flammās exstinguet?

Rōmānus 2: The force of the fire is too great and cannot be suppressed. The disaster will destroy Rome.

TALKING

valētūdō, valētūdinis, f. – health

Quālis est valētūdō tua? "How is your health?"

Quōmodo tē habēs? "How are you?"

Valētūdō mea est bona/prōspera. "My health is good."

Valētūdō mea est mala/adversa. "My health is bad."

Bene valeō. "I am feeling well."

Haud bene valeō. "I am not feeling well."

Aegrōtō. "I am ill."

Remedium quaerō. "I am looking for a remedy/cure."

Dēbēs adīre medicum. "You have to go to the doctor."

medicus, medicī, m.; *medica, medicae,* f. – doctor

nosocoma, nosocomae, f. – nurse

nosocomium, nosocomiī, n. – hospital

medicāmentum, medicāmentī, n. – medicine, drug

assicūrātiō, assicūrātiōnis, f. *medica* – insurance

febrīcitō, febrīcitāre, febrīcitāvī, —— – to have a fever

Gravēdine (gravēdō, gravēdinis, f.) *labōrō (labōrāre, labōrāvī, labōrātum).* "I have a cold."

Caput <mihi> dolet. "I have a headache."

Sūme aspirīnum. "Take aspirin."

RECOVERING FROM AN ACCIDENT

Magistra: (*teacher*) Salvēte, omnēs! Nōn videō Marīam. Vōsne Marīam vīdistis?

Christīna: Marīa mē herī (*yesterday*), magistra, telephonicē compellāvit (*called me on the phone*). Manum suam frēgerat (*had broken*). Vōs scītis Marīam amāre agrōs. Dum ambulat in agrīs, ceciderat.

Magistra: Ēheu (*alas*), dē eā clāde doleō. Quid nunc Marīa facit?

Christīna: Herī, eō tempore quō mēcum verba faciēbat, iam petīverat nosocomium et vīderat medicum. Medicus in manū gypsum (*cast*) posuerat. Propter dolōrem Marīa medicāmenta capere dēbēbat. Fortasse nunc quoque valētūdinem cūrat.

Helena: (AD CHRISTĪNAM ET MĀRCUM) Poterimusne post scholam (*after school*) domum Marīae petere? Nam cupiō eam vidēre et cum eā manēre. Fortasse Marīa quoque cupit amīcōs vidēre.

Magistra: Bonum cōnsilium.

MARĪA INTRAT, QUAE GYPSUM IN MANŪ GERIT

Marīa: Salvēte, amīcī amīcaeque (*male and female friends*)!

Omnēs: Salvē, Marīa! Gaudēmus (*we are glad*) tē esse in scholā! Quōmodo sē habet manus tua?

Marīa: Manus valdē dolet. Itaque scrībere (*to write*) nōn possum.

Magistra: Manus tua sinistra (*left*) aegrōtat nec eā manū scrībere potes. Sed dextra tua bene valēre vidētur. Itaque dextrā scrībere poteris.

CHAPTER 18

Future Perfect Active Tense of All Conjugations; Future Perfect Tense of *Sum* and *Possum*; Fifth Declension Nouns

Sculpture of Cupid and Psyche. By Antonio Canova (1757–1822).

MEMORĀBILE DICTŪ

Quod nēmō nōvit paene nōn fit.

"What no one knows almost does not happen." (Apuleius, *Transformations* 10.3)

This saying exemplifies the logic "Not known, not done" aimed at alleviating the remorse of the human conscience over bad deeds.

READING

In the middle of the second century CE, which coincided with a relatively stable period for Roman society under a series of "good" emperors—Hadrian, Antoninus Pius, and Marcus Aurelius (117–180 CE)—Latin literature developed an increasingly pronounced taste for "archaism": the use of rare or obsolete words and expressions from early Latin. A major work that represents this archaizing trend is the "Golden Ass," or *Metamorphōsēs,* "Transformations," by the North African writer Āpulēius. Along with the *Satyricon* of Petronius, which was likely written in the time of Nero, it is one of the two examples that have survived of the ancient novel in Latin.

In it, Apuleius relates the story of Lucius, a Greek whose excessive curiosity and interest in magic result in his transformation into a donkey. Apuleius' love of archaic and rare words adds to the color and vividness of his narration about the adventures and misfortunes experienced by Lucius, in the form of a beast of burden. The same stylistic traits figure in the excerpt from the novel that you will read here, the love story of Cupid and Psyche.

DĒ CUPĪDINE ET PSYCHĒ

1   Rēx trēs fīliās habēbat. Duae eārum erant pulchrae, sed tertia
soror erat pulchritūdine praeclāra. Nōmen eī erat Psychē. Propter
pulchritūdinem Psychē ā multīs virīs colēbātur. Tandem Venus putāvit
Psychēn, quae nōn erat dea, nōn dēbēre ab aliīs tam multum colī.

5   Itaque Venus Cupīdinem, fīlium suum, vocāvit eīque dīxit: "Mitte, fīlī,
sagittam in cor Psychēs! Puella malī virī amōre corripī dēbēbit." Cupīdō
puellam petīvit, eam cōnspexit et ipse amōre statim ārsit. Puella
quoque iam nōn poterat alium virum amāre. Sorōrēs marītōs habēbant,
sed Psychē marītum nōn habēbat. Pater dē fīliae fātō valdē dolēbat

10   et cōnsilia deōrum dē eā rē petīvit. Deī rēgī ita respondērunt: "Sī
cōnsilium nostrum petis, audī! Dūc fīliam tuam in summum montem
et discēde! Cum discēsseris, belua ad eam veniet." Rēx dolēbat, sed
fīliam ad montem dūxit. Ibi somnus Psychēn cēpit. Post somnum
Psychē vīdit sē esse in domō pulchrā et intellēxit sē iam habēre

15   marītum valdē bonum, quī eam amābat atque cūrābat. Is tamen faciem
suam uxōrī numquam ostendēbat. Psychē ēius faciem vidēre cupīvit et,
dum marītus dormiēbat, lūmen ad faciem mōvit. Gutta oleī in faciem
marītī cecidit eumque ex somnō excitāvit. Marītus erat ipse Cupīdō!
"Cūr id fēcistī?!" exclāmāvit Cupīdō et statim ēvanuit. Psychē eum

20   per omnēs terrās diū quaesīvit. Nam Venus fīlium suum occultāverat.
Cupīdō quoque cum Psȳchē esse cupiēbat. Tandem Venus auxilium iīs
dare dēcrēvit. Itaque Cupīdō et Psȳchē semper ūnā manēre poterunt.
Māgna est vīs amōris.

READING VOCABULARY

belua, beluae, f. – beast

*colō, colere, coluī, cultum – to worship, cultivate

cor, cordis, n. – heart

*cum (conj.) – when, after

cum discesseris – when you leave

Cupīdō, Cupīdinis, m. – Cupid (in Greek Eros)

*dea, deae, f. – goddess

*dormiō, dormīre, dormīvī, dormītum – to sleep

duae (feminine) – two

*dūc! – present imperative of *dūcō, dūcere, dūxī, ductum*, to lead, take

ēvanēscō, ēvanēscere, ēvanuī, ——— – to disappear

*excitō, excitāre, excitāvī, excitātum – to awaken, wake up, rouse, stir up

*exclāmō, exclāmāre, exclāmāvī, exclāmātum – to exclaim

*faciem – face

*fātum, fātī, n. – fate, destiny

gutta, guttae, f. – drop

ipse (masculine nominative singular) – himself

*ita (adv.) – so, in such a way

lūmen, lūminis, n. – light

*marītus, marītī, m. – husband

*multum (adv.) – much

*occultō, occultāre, occultāvī, occultātum – to hide

oleum, oleī, n. – oil

*pater, patris, m. – father

*post + accusative – after

Psȳchē (genitive Psȳchēs, dative Psȳchē, accusative Psȳchēn, ablative Psȳchē) – Psyche

pulchritūdō, pulchritūdinis, f. – beauty

*quaerō, quaerere, quaesīvī, quaesītum – to look for, search

sagitta, sagittae, f. – arrow

*dē rē –about the thing

*sī (conj.) – if

*somnus, somnī, m. – sleep

summus, summa, summum – the top of

*tam (adv.) – so

tertius, tertia, tertium – third

trēs (nominative and accusative) – three

*uxor, uxōris, f. – wife

Venus, Veneris, f. – Venus (Greek Aphrodite)

*Words marked with an asterisk will need to be memorized later in the chapter.

COMPREHENSION QUESTIONS

1. Why did Venus decide to punish Psyche?   *She was beautiful (2)*

2. What happened when Cupid was sent to Psyche?

3. Why did Psyche stay unmarried for a long time?

4. Who was the secret husband to whom Psyche was taken?

5. Why were Cupid and Psyche separated?

6. What happened at the end of the story?

LANGUAGE FACT I
FUTURE PERFECT ACTIVE TENSE OF ALL CONJUGATIONS

In the Latin reading passage you noticed a verb form whose tense you do not yet know: *discesseris*.

Discesseris is an active form of the **future perfect** tense.

The future perfect active is formed by adding the endings *-erō, -eris, -erit, -erimus, -eritis, -erint* to the perfect stem.

Once again (as in the perfect and pluperfect active) there is no difference in endings among the four conjugations: simply add the new endings to the perfect stem.

Future Perfect Active: *parō*

Singular

First Person	parāv**erō**	I will/shall have prepared
Second Person	parāv**eris**	you will have prepared
Third Person	parāv**erit**	s/he/it will have prepared

Plural

First Person	parāv**erimus**	we will/shall have prepared
Second Person	parāv**eritis**	you will have prepared
Third Person	parāv**erint**	they will have prepared

Future Perfect Active: *capiō*

Singular

First Person	cēp**erō**	I will/shall have seized
Second Person	cēp**eris**	you will have seized
Third Person	cēp**erit**	s/he/it will have seized

Plural

First Person	cēp**erimus**	we will/shall have seized
Second Person	cēp**eritis**	you will have seized
Third Person	cēp**erint**	they will have seized

STUDY TIP

The endings of the future perfect closely resemble the future forms of *sum: erō, eris, erit, erimus, eritis, erunt*. The only difference is in the third person plural ending, *-erint*.

STUDY TIP

Do not confuse the following third person plural forms!

> **erunt** – they will be (future active)
>
> amāv**ērunt** – they loved (perfect active)
>
> amāv**erint** – they will have loved (future perfect active)

The future perfect tense indicates an action that will have been completed before a future action occurs. It is translated in English in the following way: "I will (shall) have done something (before something else happens)."

The future perfect tense is rarely used by itself in a sentence. It is commonly used in a subordinate clause to indicate an action prior to a simple future tense that appears in the main clause.

> Cum **discesserit**, belua ad eam veniet.
> When she will have left (you leave), a beast will come to her.
>
> Sī **exspectāveris**, ad tē veniam.
> If you will have waited (you wait), I will come to you.

STUDY TIP

Note that in "when" and "if" clauses English uses the simple present tense where Latin uses the future perfect tense, along with the simple future tense in the main clause (where Latin also uses the simple future). In fact, the Latin construction represents real time much more exactly than English, since the event in the "when" or "if" clause will have to happen before the conclusion. This will help you remember how these sentences are constructed in Latin.

Apuleius, author of *Metamorphōsēs*, lived during the reign of Marcus Aurelius, the emperor seated on this bronze equestrian statue. Michelangelo placed this statue on the Capitoline Hill but during the 1980s it was moved inside the Capitoline Museum to protect it from pollution. A replica stands in its place outside the museum today.

▶ EXERCISE 1

Change the future tense verbs into the future perfect, keeping the same person and number. Translate the changed form.

Example: ambulābis
ambulāveris   you will have walked

1. legēmus
2. studēbit
3. veniētis
4. quaerent
5. occultābunt
6. respondēbitis
7. excitābō
8. dūcēs
9. exstinguēmus
10. iaciam
11. corripient
12. exclāmābō
13. negleget
14. dēvastābitis

VOCABULARY TO LEARN

NOUNS

dea, deae, f. – goddess

diēs, diēī, m./f. – day

faciēs, faciēī, f. – face

fātum, fātī, n. – fate, destiny

marītus, marītī, m. – husband

merīdiēs, merīdiēī, m. – midday

pater, patris, m. – father

rēs, reī, f. – thing, matter

somnus, somnī, m. – sleep

uxor, uxōris, f. – wife

VERBS

colō, colere, coluī, cultum – to worship, cultivate

dormiō, dormīre, dormīvī, dormītum – to sleep

excitō, excitāre, excitāvī, excitātum – to awaken, wake up, to rouse, to stir up

exclāmō, exclāmāre, exclāmāvī, exclāmātum – to exclaim

occultō, occultāre, occultāvī, occultātum – to hide

quaerō, quaerere, quaesīvī, quaesītum – to look for, search

ADVERBS

ita – so, in such a way

multum – much

tam – so

PREPOSITION

post + accusative – after

CONJUNCTIONS

cum – when, after

sī – if

▶ EXERCISE 2

Find which of the words below are English derivatives based on the Vocabulary to Learn in the following list. Write the corresponding word. For some, more than one English word can be related to the same Latin word.

excitement   duchess
extinction   duke
extortion   facial
question   fatal
querulous   factitious
occultism   marital
occident   maroon
exclamation   dormitory
excavation   dormant
cumin   doorway
cult   paternal
culture   pottery
ductile

▶ EXERCISE 3

Change the present tense verbs into the perfect, the imperfect tense verbs into the pluperfect, and the future tense verbs into the future perfect. Translate the changed form.

Example: amābās
amāverās   you had loved

1. cadunt
2. iaciētis
3. occultābās
4. temptābit
5. legēbāmus
6. quaeris
7. iubēbō
8. stābant
9. occīdēmus
10. respondēbunt
11. veniam

LANGUAGE FACT II
FUTURE PERFECT TENSE OF *SUM* AND *POSSUM*

The future perfect of *esse* and *posse* is not so irregular as one might expect. Once you know the perfect stems of these verbs (*fu-* and *potu-*), you simply add the future perfect active endings.

Future Perfect Tense of *sum*

Singular

First Person	fu**erō**	I will/shall have been
Second Person	fu**eris**	you will have been
Third Person	fu**erit**	s/he/it will have been

Plural

First Person	fu**erimus**	we will/shall have been
Second Person	fu**eritis**	you will have been
Third Person	fu**erint**	they will have been

Future Perfect Tense of *possum*

Singular

First Person	potu**erō**	I will/shall have been able
Second Person	potu**eris**	you will have been able
Third Person	potu**erit**	s/he/it will have been able

Plural

First Person	potu**erimus**	we will/shall have been able
Second Person	potu**eritis**	you will have been able
Third Person	potu**erint**	they will have been able

▶ EXERCISE 4

Change the following verbs to the future perfect tense, keeping the same person and number, and translate both forms.

Example: potuistis
potueritis   you (plural) were able   you (plural) will have been able

1. potuērunt
2. es
3. eram
4. eritis
5. poterāmus

6. potueram
7. fuit
8. poterās
9. fueram

LANGUAGE FACT III

FIFTH DECLENSION NOUNS

In the story about Cupid and Psyche, you encountered two nouns that belong to the fifth declension (the last declension in Latin!). You probably did not notice any peculiarity in these forms, since they resemble the third declension: *dē eā rē*, "about this thing"; *faciem*, "face," *ad faciem*, "to the face"; *in faciem*, "onto the face."

There are not many words in the fifth declension (just as there are not too many words belonging to the fourth declension). The characteristic vowel throughout the fifth declension is -*e*-.

Here are the paradigms of two words of the fifth declension. The first one is the very common Latin word *rēs, reī*, f., "thing," and the second one is *diēs, diēī*, m./f., "day."

Fifth Declension

Singular

Nominative	rēs	the thing	diēs	the day
Genitive	reī	of the thing	diēī	of the day
Dative	reī	to/for the thing	diēī	to/for the day
Accusative	rem	the thing	diem	the day
Ablative	rē	by/with the thing	diē	by/with the day
Vocative	rēs	o, thing	diēs	o, day

Plural

Nominative	rēs	the things	diēs	the days
Genitive	rērum	of the things	diērum	of the days
Dative	rēbus	to/for the things	diēbus	to/for the days
Accusative	rēs	the things	diēs	the days
Ablative	rēbus	by/with the things	diēbus	by/with the days
Vocative	rēs	o, things	diēs	o, days

STUDY TIP

Here is a tip to remember the dative and ablative plural of *rēs*. The word "rebus," with the meaning of "crosswords" or "puzzle," is derived from a medieval game monks played that involved the names of different things. Literally, it is the ablative plural of *rēs*, "<to play> with things."

BY THE WAY

Note that words like *diēs*, which have a vowel before the nominative singular ending -*ēs* (e.g., *diēs* and *faciēs*), have a long -*ē*- in the genitive and dative singular endings -*ēī*. This is an exception to the general rule that vowels in front of vowels are short—but there is no rule without exceptions.

Fifth declension nouns are mostly feminine, with a couple of masculine exceptions: *diēs, diēī* can be both masculine and feminine: it is masculine, unless it indicates a day decided upon (like a deadline or an appointment); and *merīdiēs, merīdiēī* (derived from *diēs*), which is masculine. The latter means literally "midday," and sometimes "south" (since the sun points south at midday).

BY THE WAY

The abbreviations AM and PM are from the Latin *ante merīdiem*, "before midday," and *post merīdiem*, "after midday."

STUDY TIP

This gender/declension bell curve illustrates the most frequent genders in each of the five declensions.

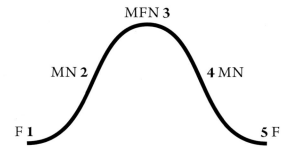

BY THE WAY

You have probably heard the Spanish greeting *Buenos días*. It means literally "Good day." *Buenos* comes from *bonus* and *días* from the fifth declension noun *diēs*.

▶ EXERCISE 5

Make the noun in parentheses agree with the adjective. Translate the phrase.

Example: bonīs (rēs)
rēbus   to/for good things *or* by/with/good things

1. fēlīcī (diēs)
2. longārum (diēs)
3. miserō (merīdiēs)
4. pulchrae (faciēs)
5. omnibus (diēs)

6. multōrum (diēs)
7. vetustam (faciēs)
8. iūstās (rēs)
9. fūnestā (rēs)

The look of love on these sculptured faces is a reminder of Cupid and Psyche's feelings.

▶ EXERCISE 6

Translate into English.

1. Sī bene salūtāveris, bene salūtāberis.
2. Cum faciem marītī cōnspexerit, intelleget eum esse Cupīdinem.
3. Sī cupīveris mē amāre, tē quoque amābō.
4. Sī ante merīdiem mē excitāveris, multās rēs faciam.
5. Sī ēius fāta occultāverimus, nōn timēbit.
6. Cum locum diū quaesīveritis, tandem eum cōnspiciētis.

▶ EXERCISE 7

Translate into Latin. Use a future perfect in the subordinate clause.

1. If we do not fear the fates, we will win.
2. If the wife desires to look at the face of the husband, she will wake him up.
3. When a happy day comes, all things will be good.
4. When the father leads her to the mountain, he will have to leave her there.
5. When you sleep for a long time, it will already be midday.
6. If the goddess gives help, we will soon be husband and wife.

TALKING

dēns, dentis, m. – tooth

gingīva, gingīvae, f. – gum

gena, genae, f. – cheek

obtūrāmentum, obtūrāmentī, n. – filling

Dēns <mihi> dolet. "I have a toothache."

Not always known as a chubby cherub, this statue shows a youthful Eros or Cupid.

woah bah

Dēbeō īre ad medicum dentārium. "I have to go to the dentist."

Dentēs mundō (mundāre, mundāvī, mundātum). "I clean my teeth."

Medicus dentārius dentēs radiīs dēpinget (dēpingō, dēpingere, dēpīnxī, dēpictum). "The dentist will take X-rays of the teeth."

Medicus dentārius terebram adhibēbit. (adhibeō, adhibēre, adhibuī, adhibitum) "The dentist will use the drill."

Dolōrem timeō. "I am afraid of the pain."

Medicus dentārius tibi medicāmen anaestheticum ministrābit. (ministrō, ministrāre, ministrāvī, ministrātum) "The dentist will give you anesthesia."

Nihil in genā meā sentiō. "I have no feeling in my cheek."

Dentēs bis in annō mundārī dēbent. "<One's> teeth have to be cleaned twice a year."

GOING TO THE DENTIST

Christīna: Salvē, Marīa! Quōmodo nunc valēs? (*How are you now?*) Quōmodo manus tua valet?

Marīa: Iam manus mea bene valet. Quōmodo vōs valētis, Helena et Christīna?

Christīna: Ego bene valeō.

Helena: Ego autem male (*badly*) valeō.

Christīna et Marīa: Cūr?

Helena: Hodiē (*today*) ad medicum dentārium īre dēbeō. Medicum dentārium timeō.

Marīa: Omnēs ad medicum dentārium bis in annō īre dēbēmus. Nam dentēs mundārī debent. Nōlī timēre!

Helena: Sed dēns meus dolet. Propter eam causam medicum dentārium petō.

Christīna: Tū, Helena, nimis (*too*) multa crūstula (*cookies*) comedere solēs. Itaque medicus in dentem tuum obtūrāmentum pōnet. Prīmum (*first*) fortasse dentem radiīs dēpinget.

Helena: Dolōrem timeō.

Christīna: Medicus medicāmen anaestheticum tibi ministrābit. Cum medicāmen tibi ministrāverit, tunc terebram adhibēbit. Nōlī timēre! Quandō (*when*) īre dēbēbis?

Helena: Merīdiē. Prīmum prandium (*lunch*) comedam et crūstula.

REVIEW 6: CHAPTERS 16–18

VOCABULARY TO KNOW

NOUNS

avunculus, avunculī, m. – uncle

caelum, caelī, n. – sky, heaven, weather

causa, causae, f. – cause, reason

cinis, cineris, m. – ash

clādēs, clādis, f. – disaster

classis, classis, f. – fleet, class (of people)

cornū, cornūs, n. – horn

dea, deae, f. – goddess

diēs, diēī, m./f. – day

domus, domūs, f. – house, home

faciēs, faciēī, f. – face

fātum, fātī, n. – fate, destiny

fēmina, fēminae, f. – woman

fūmus, fūmī, m. – smoke

imperātor, imperātōris, m. – general, emperor

impetus, impetūs, m. – impetus, force, attack

incendium, incendiī, n. – conflagration, eruption

initium, initiī, n. – beginning

iussus, iussūs, m. – order (this word typically occurs only in the ablative singular)

lītus, lītoris, n. – shore

locus, locī, m. – place; locī, locōrum, m. pl. – passages of a book; loca, locōrum, n. pl. – geographical places

manus, manūs, f. – hand

marītus, marītī, m. – husband

māter, mātris, f. – mother

merīdiēs, merīdiēī, m. – midday

mōns, montis, m. – mountain

mūrus, mūrī, m. – wall

nāvis, nāvis, f. – ship

nūbēs, nūbis, f. – cloud

pars, partis, f. – part

pater, patris, m. – father

rēs, reī, f. – thing, matter

somnus, somnī, m. – sleep

tumultus, tumultūs, m. – uproar, confusion

uxor, uxōris, f. – wife

ventus, ventī, m. – wind

ADJECTIVE

fūnestus, fūnesta, fūnestum – deadly

VERBS

alō, alere, aluī, altum/alitum – to feed, nourish

āmittō, āmittere, āmīsī, āmissum – to lose

colō, colere, coluī, cultum – to worship, cultivate

corripiō, corripere, corripuī, correptum – to seize, engulf

currō, currere, cucurrī, cursum – to run

dēvastō, dēvastāre, dēvastāvī, dēvastātum – to devastate

dormiō, dormīre, dormīvī, dormītum – to sleep

dūcō, dūcere, dūxī, ductum – to lead, take

excitō, excitāre, excitāvī, excitātum – to awaken, wake up, rouse, stir up

exclāmō, exclāmāre, exclāmāvī, exclāmātum – to exclaim

exstinguō, exstinguere, exstīnxī, exstīnctum – to extinguish

iaciō, iacere, iēcī, iactum – to throw

legō, legere, lēgī, lēctum – to read, choose

occultō, occultāre, occultāvī, occultātum – to hide

opprimō, opprimere, oppressī, oppressum – to overwhelm, suppress

quaerō, quaerere, quaesīvī, quaesītum – to look for, search

studeō, studēre, studuī, —— + dative – to study, be eager for, be interested in

temptō, temptāre, temptāvī, temptātum – to try

ADVERBS

facile – easily

ita – so, in such a way

multum – much

numquam – never

tam – so

PREPOSITIONS

post + accusative – after

sine + ablative – without

CONJUNCTIONS

cum – when, after

igitur – therefore (usually the second word in its clause)

sī – if

▶ EXERCISE 1

Conjugate the following verbs in the perfect active and give the translation for each form.

1. *occultō, occultāre, occultāvī, occultātum*

2. *studeō, studēre, studuī, ——*

3. *opprimō, opprimere, oppressī, oppressum*

4. *dormiō, dormīre, dormīvī, dormītum*

5. *iaciō, iacere, iēcī, iactum*

▶ EXERCISE 2

Conjugate the following verb in the pluperfect active and give the translation of each form.

1. *temptō, temptāre, temptāvī, temptātum*

▶ EXERCISE 3

Conjugate the following verb in the future perfect active and give the translation of each form.

1. *alō, alere, aluī, altum*

Pliny's uncle, Pliny the Elder, sailed across the Bay of Naples (seen in this panoramic view) in an attempt to rescue people being threatened by the eruption of Mt. Vesuvius, looming in the background.

▶ EXERCISE 4

Give the perfect, pluperfect, and future perfect active first person singular for each of the following verbs.

Example: āmittō

āmīsī   āmīseram   āmīserō

1. corripiō
2. currō
3. dūcō
4. dēvastō
5. excitō
6. exclāmō
7. exstinguō
8. legō
9. quaerō

▶ EXERCISE 5

Decline the following phrases.

1. *manus longa*

2. *spēs fēlīx (spēs, speī, f. – hope)*

▶ EXERCISE 6

Translate into Latin.

1. If you see fire, flee! (use the future perfect tense in the subordinate clause)

2. The conflagration had seized all the houses.

3. If you are able to flee, you will be saved. (use the future perfect tense in the subordinate clause)

4. Do you have strength? Will you be able to run? (use dative of possession in this sentence)

5. Fire, smoke, ashes came from the mountain and devastated the shore.

6. Many people did not have houses any more. They had lost everything. (use the dative of possession in this sentence)

7. "Fates are cruel!" exclaimed people.

▶ EXERCISE 7

For each question, choose the best answer and translate. The Reading Vocabulary for Chapters 16–18 may be consulted.

1. Cūr avunculus Plīniī, quī studēbat, librōs suōs relīquit?

    Avunculus ambulāre cupiēbat.

    Avunculus librōrum iam nōn erat studiōsus.

    Avunculus causam nūbis inūsitātae intellegere cupīvit.

2. Cūius epistulam tunc nauta avunculō dedit?

    Nauta epistulam mātris Plīniī avunculō dedit.

    Nauta epistulam suam avunculō dedit.

    Nauta epistulam fēminae, quae prope montem Vesuvium habitābat, avunculō dedit.

3. Cūr fēmina epistulam ad avunculum mīserat?

    Fēmina perīculum timēbat et auxilium petēbat.

    Fēmina cum avunculō nāvigāre cupiēbat.

    Fēmina cum avunculō librōs legere cupiēbat.

4. Potuitne avunculus fēminam servāre?

    Avunculus fēminam servāre nōn potuit; nam fūmus cinerēsque eam ūnā cum aliīs oppressērunt.

    Avunculus omnēs servāvit.

    Avunculus ūnā cum multīs aliīs revēnit.

5. Ex quō locō incendium Rōmānum initium cēpit?

    Incendium ex tabernīs, in quibus erant mercimōnia, initium cēpit.

    Incendium ex templīs et ex domibus initium cēpit.

    Incendium ex agrīs initium cēpit.

6. Fuitne Nerō causa incendiī?

      Omnēs putant Nerōnem esse causam incendiī.

      Nerō fortasse fuit causa incendiī.

      Omnēs dīcunt Nerōnem nōn esse causam incendiī.

7. Quid Cupīdō dē Psȳchē sentiēbat?

      Cupīdō amōre Psȳchēs ārsit.

      Cupīdō volēbat Psȳchen beluae dare.

      Cupīdō Psȳchen numquam vīdit.

8. Potuitne tandem Psȳchē esse uxor Cupīdinis?

      Psȳche diū Cupīdinem quaesīvit, sed eum nōn vīdit.

      Venus Cupīdinem ā Psȳchē semper occultāvit.

      Tandem Cupīdō et Psȳchē ūnā fēlīcēs esse poterant.

CONSIDERING THE CLASSICAL GODS

BACCHUS

Bacchus, the ancient Greco-Roman god of wine, was also called Dionysus in Greek and Liber in Latin. He was a relatively late addition to the pantheon of the twelve Olympian gods. His father is Jupiter; his mother, Semele, a mortal woman. Consequently he is the only deity on Olympus of partially human descent. The circumstances of his birth are extraordinary. Ever-vengeful and eternally jealous, Juno paid a visit to the young princess Semele, who had been rejoicing in Jupiter's attentions, and convinced Semele to ask her divine lover to manifest himself to her with a display of his true divine power. Jupiter thus appeared with his thunderbolt

A floor mosaic from Corinth, Greece, showing the head of Bacchus.

and lightning, which no human was able to see at a close distance, and consumed Semele by fire. Since Semele had conceived a child by Jupiter, he removed the infant from her womb and implanted him in his thigh, delivering the baby several months later. This story of how Jupiter gave birth to Bacchus has much in common with the account, which you read in an earlier chapter, of how Jupiter swallowed Minerva's mother and delivered her daughter from his head.

A brooch portraying the head of a youthful Bacchus.

Bacchus is conceptualized as the complete opposite of Apollo. Whereas Apollo represents all that is rational, moderate, and harmonious, Bacchus is irrational, immoderate, and excessive. Not only is he god of wine and uncontrolled emotion, but also of vegetation and the uncontrolled power of nature. A diverse group of followers composes his retinue: female worshippers called bacchants, or maenads (a word literally meaning "crazy women") who run wild in the forest, dancing, singing, and producing wine by scratching the earth while in an inspired state; satyrs, little men with horns on their head and the tail of a horse or a goat, also representing the uncontrollable forces of nature; sileni, older satyrs; and finally Pan, god of the woods, shepherds, and fertility, represented as a man with the horns, hindquarters and feet of a goat, who would surprise humans in the forests and inspire terror in them (our word "panic" is derived from his name).

An oil painting called "The Feast of Bacchus." By Velázquez (1599–1660).

Mosaic from Roman Britain showing Bacchus riding a tiger.

READ AND TRANSLATE THE FOLLOWING PASSAGE

This story tells about the origin of the flute.

Pān erat deus agrōrum et silvārum. Pān semper nympham Sȳringem quaerēbat. Nam ex tempore quō Sȳringem cōnspexerat, is amōre ārsit, sed Sȳrinx Pāna nōn amābat. Pān Sȳringī dīcēbat: "Sī mea fueris, dōna pulchra tibi dabō." Nympha tamen nōn cupiēbat dōna habēre et ā deō amārī, et fūgit. Pān post eam quoque cucurrit et eam capere temptāvit. Tandem nympha ad rīvum pervēnit et in rīvum intrāvit. Deī Sȳringem servāvērunt eamque in harundinem mūtāvērunt. Tum Pān ex harundine organum mūsicum parāvit, quō organō mūsicō posteā lūdēbat.

harundō, harundinis, f. – reed
lūdō, lūdere, lūsī, lūsum – to play
mūsicus, mūsica, mūsicum – musical
mūtō, mūtāre, mūtāvī, mūtātum – to transform
nympha, nymphae, f. – nymph
organum, organī, m. – instrument

Pān, genitive Pānos, accusative Pāna – Pan
perveniō, pervenīre, pervēnī, perventum – to arrive
Sȳrinx, Sȳringis, f. – a name of the nymph turned into is a reed, which was used for creation of the musical instrument syrinx or flute (compare "syringe," so called because of its shape)

GLADIATORIAL GAMES

The Romans were said to desire only *pānem et circēnsēs* (Juvenal, *Satires*, 10.81), "bread and entertainment." This statement may not apply to the Romans of the early Republic, who are said to have been industrious and self-disciplined. But by imperial times most of those who lived in the Roman world did not have much of a stake or share in Rome's wealth and power, and even the affluent and advantaged seem to have craved immediate pleasures that suggest an interior emptiness: such, at least, is the implication of the overeating and vomiting at banquets, and the bloody spectacles often seen in the amphitheatres.

A view of the outside of the famous Colosseum in Rome.

Rome's amphitheatre, the Colosseum, was the most famous of Roman amphitheatres but most cities, like Pompeii, also had their own amphitheatre.

The gladiatorial games rank among the most famous of these spectacles. They were staged in the great Roman amphitheatres; while the Greeks built semi-circular performance spaces accommodated to natural slopes, the Romans never complied with nature, preferring instead to erect fully circular amphitheatres regardless of the physical surroundings. The most celebrated amphitheatre was, of course, the Roman Colosseum, a multi-storied building with complicated layers of seats, reflecting the organization of Roman society as a whole. People from all classes attended the gladiatorial competitions, and the emperor played a leading role in the event as well.

Mosaic from the House of the Gladiator in Cyprus showing two gladiators and their Greek names, Margareites and Hellenikos.

The name gladiator comes from *gladius*, "sword," the weapon with which the gladiators fought. Gladiators were slaves, prisoners of war, convicted criminals, and occasionally people of free birth who chose this occupation for the lack of anything better. In fact, the gladiatorial profession had a certain appeal and prestige, although the owners or trainers of gladiatorial troops, called *lanistae*, ranked at the bottom of the social scale, despite the wealth that many acquired.

Combats between gladiators did not necessarily end with the death of the loser. After one of the combatants acknowledged that he had been defeated, it was possible for him to be spared; the public only needed to shout *mitte*, "set him free," and the emperor would signify with a gesture of his thumb whether the loser should live or die. A thumb directed upward seems to have meant "kill him," while a thumb pointed downward signaled "let him go." The pride and savage joy with which large audiences watched these spectacles probably is connected with the military enthusiasms of the ancient Romans, which had brought their city to world supremacy.

In addition to single combats with swords, there were fights between men and animals; this practice survives in the modern bullfights that still take place in Spain and Latin America. There were also fights between animals themselves. The exhibition of exotic animals from different parts of the Roman Empire had a political purpose, reminding the spectators how far the boundaries of the Roman world extended, and of all the living creatures that it had subdued and now contained. Other forms of entertainment included the ever-popular chariot races and a small-scale naval battle between gladiators called a *naumachia*, for which the emperors would flood an entire square with water from the river Tiber.

A poster showing the armor of gladiators and the Latin phrase *Avē Caesar, Imperātor, Moritūrī Tē Salūtant.* ("Hail Caesar, emperor, those about to die, salute you.")

The seats, the arena, and the sub-structures under the arena are seen in this view of the inside of the Colosseum.

EXPLORING ROMAN DISASTERS

EARTH, AIR, FIRE, AND WATER

In modern times we witness untold suffering and loss of life from disasters such as floods, earthquakes, fire, violent winds, and volcanoes. The ancient Romans also suffered from the ravages of such occurrences.

For tens of thousands of years, a dozen volcanoes or more have menaced the Italian peninsula, from Lardarello (between Italy's western coast and Sienna) to Pantelleria (between Sicily and Tunisia). Lake Albano, just southeast of Rome, is located in the crater of a volcano. The Aeolian islands, just north of Sicily and off the toe of Italy, contain four volcanoes, one of which, Vulcano, contains the source for our word "volcano." Not surprisingly, popular leg-

View of an active volcano.

end in ancient times said that the fire-god Vulcan had his forges in this part of the world. Mount Etna, near Sicily's eastern coast, is Europe's tallest active volcano: almost 3,000 feet taller than Washington State's Mount St. Helens, whose eruption on May 18, 1980, killed 57 people. At almost 11,000 feet tall, Etna is more than twice as tall as Vesuvius (c. 4,200 feet), whose eruption caused the most famous natural disaster to strike the Roman world.

Fresh lava from a volcano.

In 63/62 CE, Herculaneum and Pompeii had suffered damage from an earthquake, but on August 24, 79 CE, the two-day long eruption of Mount Vesuvius, which had been the site of the rebel slave Spartacus' camp in 71 BCE, devastated the western coast of Italy near the Bay of Naples, especially the towns of Herculaneum and Pompeii. Although we do not know how many people survived Vesuvius' eruption, the loss of life was 500 times greater than that of St. Helens and is probably equal to that caused by the eruptions of Mount Pelée on the Caribbean island of Martinique from April to August, 1902, in which approximately 30,000 people died. Whereas the Pompeians were buried beneath about 13 feet of volcanic pumice and ash, flows of lava and mud over sixty feet deep covered Herculaneum. Thanks to the innovative techniques of Italian archaeology, Giuseppe Fiorelli (1823–1896) poured plaster into cavities made in the ash and when the plaster hardened he removed the surrounding ash. In a few cases, we are able to see the exact position in which both humans and animals died.

Letters (6.16 and 6.20) from Pliny the Younger, who was in the region during Vesuvius' eruption, describe in detail the appearance of the volcano's cloud (shaped like the umbrella pine trees that grow in Italy), and tell about the heroic efforts of his uncle, Pliny the Elder, who lost his life while investigating the eruption and trying to rescue people by ship from the affected area. Just

A plaster cast of one of many victims who died during the eruption of Mt. Vesuvius.

as in modern times we see political leaders touring disaster sites and attempting to offer some measure of support and comfort to the victims, Titus, the Roman emperor at the time of Vesuvius' eruption, is reported to have shown a fatherly care and concern with respect to relief efforts needed to help the people affected by the eruption (Suetonius, *Titus* 8.3). Archaeologists continue to excavate sites in the Naples region, which have provided a massive amount of information about life in these ancient Roman towns. Not only did the eruption of Vesuvius bury persons, their possessions, and homes, but now multi-spectral imaging with infrared and ultra-violet light is allowing scholars to begin to read some of the almost 1800 papyrus scrolls that were found charred in Herculaneum's so-called Villa of the Papyri.

In contrast to the disaster caused by Vesuvius in 79 CE, probably the second most famous disaster to strike the Romans was caused by fire. Unlike the horrific fire that ravaged Chicago in October of 1871, which was rumored to have started when a cow kicked over a lantern, Rome's worst fire was rumored to have been started upon the orders of its emperor, Nero (Suetonius, *Nero* 38.1; Dio Cassius 62.16.1–2). Nero is even reported to have sung a poem about the fiery destruction of Troy (Suetonius, *Nero* 38.1; Tacitus, *Annals* 15.39; Dio Cassius 62.18.1) while watching the blaze from the roof of his palace, and later to have built a new palace, the *Domus Aurea* ("Golden House"), on ground leveled by the fire.

Although we tend to think of Rome as being a city of fired brick, limestone, and marble, most of the city's inhabitants lived in cheaply constructed apartment buildings (*īnsulae*), whose wooden framing was highly susceptible to fires. Thus, it is not surprising that fire caused a disaster that Dio Cassius (62.17.3) would describe as the worst disaster to befall Rome since the Gauls had sacked the city around 386 BCE. As is the case in many fires, such as those that frequently ravage California, high winds contributed to the week-long fire that destroyed Rome. On 19 July, 64 CE, this fire started near the Circus Maximus, southwest of the Palatine Hill, and swept northward. It completely destroyed over twenty percent of the city and left only about a quarter of the city unscathed. Comparable to the situation after Hurricane Katrina in New Orleans, in which even some police officers were found looting, in Dio Cassius we read of Roman soldiers, with a view toward looting, helping to spread the fire. Despite rumors that Nero was responsible for the fire, Tacitus does report that the emperor did provide emergency housing (some space even in his own gardens) for those displaced by the blaze and made grain available at a reduced price. Still, Tacitus (*Annals* 15.44) also says that Nero tried to shift blame for the fire from himself to the city's Christians, whom Tacitus says were generally disliked. Nero had many Christians arrested and tortured, either by crucifixion, setting fire to them, or feeding them to dogs.

Although not as well-known as the eruption of Vesuvius or Nero's fire, the Romans, like the inhabitants of New Orleans during Hurricane Katrina in August 2005, were vexed by floods. As with the Hebrew story of Noah in Genesis, the Romans preserved in their mythical tradition the story of a great flood. A detailed account of this appears in Ovid's *Metamorphōsēs* (1.163–415). According to Ovid, Jove decided to destroy the human race by flood because of their wicked nature. Just as the Hebrew God did for Noah, Jove decided to save Deucalion and his wife Pyrrha because of their virtuous behavior. After nine days of rain (compare forty in Genesis), the boat carrying Deucalion and his wife came to rest on the slopes of Mount Parnassus in central

Greece. In contrast, the second-century CE mythographer Hyginus (*Fables* 153) has their boat land on Italian soil, namely the slopes of Mount Etna in Sicily. After landing on the mountain, Deucalion and Pyrrha created a new human race by throwing stones behind their backs. The stones Deucalion threw turned into men, while Pyrrha's stones became women. Pliny the Elder (*Natural Histories* 3.112), writing in the first century CE, relates that the Umbrians, the oldest of Italy's tribes (living in the region northeast of Rome), also survived the flood.

For Rome herself, the threat of flood was a frequent possibility because of the city's location on the Tiber River. Interestingly enough, the flooding of the Tiber traditionally contributed to the survival of Rome's founders, Romulus and Remus. When the evil king Amulius ordered his henchmen to drown these twin sons of his fraternal niece, the men were unable to approach the Tiber because it had flooded. Therefore, the men left the infants in a gentle pool of shallow water from which they were later rescued (see Livy, *Ab Urbe Conditā* 1.4.5–7). According to tradition, Romulus founded Rome on April 21, 753 BCE. While one natural disaster helped save the infant Romulus, another natural phenomenon marked him as a divine. According to the Roman historian Livy (1.16.2), Romulus' mortal life on earth ended when a whirlwind (*procella*) swept him up into heaven.

Although the Tiber's flooding contributed to the salvation of Romulus, floods were more often regarded as a sign of the divine displeasure. During the middle of the fourth century BCE, a plague led the Romans to try to appease the wrath of the gods by holding Rome's first theatrical productions in the Circus Maximus. When, at this time, the Tiber flooded the Circus, the Romans were even more convinced that the gods were displeased with them. Four centuries later, the Tiber's floods were still wreaking havoc upon Rome and contributed to the city not appearing as majestic as might be expected for the capital of a vast empire. Whereas in modern times people put up sandbags to protect their homes from flooding, during Augustus' rule he had the Tiber cleared of trash and widened in an effort to diminish the threat of the flooding.

Although the forces of nature that affected the ancient Romans are removed from us by some two thousand years, the toll upon both people and property was as real then as it is today. With the eruption of Vesuvius, this disaster sealed a moment in time that allows us an astonishing glimpse into the lives of an ancient culture. Ancient reports of such disasters also reveal that government officials, both then and now, struggle to prevent or to cope with the suffering of their people; and, both in the past and present, government officials are sometimes blamed for contributing to or not alleviating suffering. Most ancient Romans, of course, would attribute such disasters to divine anger. Although most Americans would discount this cause for natural disasters, even in our own times we can find some well-known religious leaders who will attribute events such as Hurricane Katrina to God's wrath.

John E. Thorburn
Associate Professor of Classics
Baylor University
Waco, Texas

MĪRĀBILE AUDĪTŪ

QUOTATIONS RELATING TO ATTITUDES TOWARD AND COPING WITH MISFORTUNES

QUOTATIONS

- Animus meminisse horret. "My mind shudders to remember." (Vergil, *Aeneid*, 2.12) The words of Aeneas when he starts telling the tragic story of the fall of Troy.

- Citō ārēscit lacrima, praesertim in aliēnīs malīs. "The tear dries out quickly, especially <shed> for the misfortunes of others." (Cicero, *The Divisions of Oratory*, 57)

- Commūne naufragium omnibus est cōnsōlātiō. "A common shipwreck is a comfort to everyone." Anonymous saying about the paradoxical human way of accepting misfortune when someone else is involved.

- Nē cēde malīs. "Do not yield to misfortunes!" (Vergil, *Aeneid*, 6.95) The Cumaean Sibyl, a prophetess, encourages Aeneas on the difficult path in front of him.

Pompeii was not the only city destroyed by the eruption of Mt. Vesuvius. This excavated
street scene comes from the ruins of Herculaneum, also destroyed by the volcano's eruption in 79 CE.
To the right behind the columns, one can see the petrified mud of the mudslide caused by Mount Vesuvius' eruption.

CHAPTER 19

P erfect Passive Participle; Perfect Passive Tense of All Conjugations; Review of Principal Parts of Verbs; Demonstrative Pronoun and Adjective *Hic*

Anonymous picture of Attila the Hun
called the "scourge of God."

MEMORĀBILE DICTŪ

Imperium sine fīne.

"Empire without end." (Vergil, *Aeneid*, Book 1.279)

Jupiter promises Aeneas' mother Venus that he will bestow this gift upon the future Roman race. The idea of Rome as unending in time as well as space survives in the description of Rome as "the eternal city."

READING

A historian with a vivid and intense literary Latin style, Ammiānus Marcellīnus was born in the city of Antioch in Syria in around 330 CE, where he received a Greek literary education. His *Rēs gestae ā fīne Cornēlī Tacitī* ("Deeds accomplished from the end of Cornelius Tacitus' [history]") was designed as a continuation of Tacitus' *Annālēs* and *Historiae*. While the first thirteen books of his narrative have been lost, Books 14 through 31 survive. They contain a compelling account of events from 353 to 378 CE, some of which Ammianus—a Roman army officer stationed in both the western and eastern parts of the empire and a participant in the emperor Julian's campaigns against the Persians—witnessed at first hand. Of special interest are his digressions on noteworthy aspects of culture, society, and politics.

In this passage, adapted from Book 31.2.1–11, Ammianus describes the customs of the fearsome Huns, a nomadic people who originally came from central Asia. Their movements in the third and fourth centuries CE pushed other peoples westward into the Roman Empire, especially the Germanic Ostrogoths and Visigoths, well before the Huns themselves began invading the Roman empire in the mid-fifth century CE.

DĒ HŪNĪS

1 Dē Hūnīs in librīs patrum nostrōrum nōn multa sunt dicta. Hī sunt
   ferī et ferōcēs. Terribilēs vidērī cupiunt timōremque in aliīs hominibus
   excitāre. Itaque faciēs eōrum cōnsultō vulnerantur. Postquam vulnera
   sānāta sunt, cicātrīcēs manent, propter quās barba crēscere nōn potest.

5 Hōrum fōrma nōn est pulchra, sed terribilis!

   Rādīcēs herbārum, quae correptae sunt ex agrīs, comedunt et
   animālium carnem, quae nōn cocta est sed paulisper trīta. Nam carō,
   antequam ab eīs comeditur, posita est inter equum et femora ēius quī in
   equō sedet et ibi paulisper manet.

10 Casās nōn habent, sed forīs habitant et vīvunt. Vestīmenta gerunt ex
   animālium pellibus facta.

   Semper in equīs manent: in equīs comedunt, in equīs dormiunt, in
   equīs pugnant. In hostēs impetūs celeriter faciunt, quōs in proeliō saepe
   laqueīs capiunt et captōs gladiīs occīdunt.

READING VOCABULARY

antequam (conj.) – before

*barba, barbae, f. – beard

captōs – seized

*carō, carnis, f. – meat, flesh

*celeriter (adv.) – swiftly

cicātrīx, cicātrīcis, f. – scar

*cocta est – has been cooked

cōnsultō (adv.) – on purpose

correptae sunt – have been snatched

*crēscō, crēscere, crēvī, ——— – to grow

facta – made

femur, femoris, n. – the upper leg, the thigh

*ferōx, ferōcis (genitive) – fierce, ferocious

ferus, fera, ferum – wild, savage

*forīs (adv.) – outside, in the open

gerō – with clothing or articles of clothing as its object, this verb means "to wear"

*herba, herbae, f. – plant, vegetation

*hī – these <people>

hōrum – of these <people>

Hūnī, Hūnōrum, m. pl. – the Huns

*inter + accusative – between, among

laqueus, laqueī, m. – noose, lasso

paulisper (adv.) – for a little while

*pellis, pellis, f. – skin, hide

posita est – has been placed

*postquam (conj.) – after

*proelium, proeliī, n. – battle, combat

rādīx, rādīcis, f. – root

*sānāta sunt – have been healed

*sedeō, sedēre, sēdī, sessum – to sit

sunt dicta – have been said

*terribilis, terribile – terrifying

*trīta <est> – has been rubbed

*vestīmentum, vestīmentī, n. – garment, (pl.) clothes

*vīvō, vīvere, vīxī, vīctum – to live

*vulnerō, vulnerāre, vulnerāvī, vulnerātum – to wound

*vulnus, vulneris, n. – wound

*Words marked with an asterisk will need to be memorized later in the chapter.

COMPREHENSION QUESTIONS

1. Why did the Huns wound their own faces?

2. What was the Huns' diet?

3. Where did the Huns live?

4. What was used for the Huns' attire?

LANGUAGE FACT I

PERFECT PASSIVE PARTICIPLE

In the passage above there are some words that function like adjectives, yet they are related to verbs. In fact, their forms are familiar too, because you have already learned these forms as the **fourth** principal part of the verb.

> *Vestīmenta gerunt ex animālium pellibus **facta**.*
> They wear clothes <having been> **made** from the skins of animals.

Note that "having been" is inserted in angle brackets before the perfect passive participle, where English idiom does not usually express it.

> *Hostēs in proeliō saepe laqueīs capiunt et **captōs** gladiīs occīdunt.*
> They often catch enemies in battle with lassos, and with swords they slay the enemies <having been> caught.

These words are **participles,** which are verbal adjectives. Like verbs, participles have tense and voice. Like adjectives, participles modify and agree with a noun or pronoun in case, number, and gender.

In the sentences above, you see the **perfect passive participle**. This participle is perfect, since it refers to something that has already been done, and its voice is passive. Thus, in the first sentence *facta* (modifying *vestīmenta*) means "having been made" or, as commonly shortened in English, simply "made"; in the second sentence *captōs* (modifying *hostēs*) means "having been caught" or "caught."

For most Latin verbs there are three other participles: these will be introduced in later chapters.

Below are the principal parts of verbs from each conjugation. Note carefully the neuter **fourth** principal part, which reveals the form of the perfect passive participle of each verb.

First conjugation:	occultō, occultāre, occultāvī, **occultātum** ("concealed"/"having been concealed")
Second conjugation:	videō, vidēre, vīdī, **vīsum** ("seen"/"having been seen")
Third conjugation:	dīcō, dīcere, dīxī, **dictum** ("said"/"having been said")
Fourth conjugation:	audiō, audīre, audīvī, **audītum** ("heard"/"having been heard")
Third conjugation (*-iō*)	capiō, capere, cēpī, **captum** ("caught"/"having been caught")

By taking the **-um** ending off the fourth principal part, you have found the stem of the perfect passive participle. This is one more reason why it is important to **learn all principal parts with each verb.**

The first and second declension adjective endings *-us, -a, -um* are added to the stem of the perfect passive participle. Participles, because they are adjectives, have case endings. Since the perfect passive participle is an adjective of the first and second declensions, you already know its endings. As a reminder, look at all the forms of *captus, capta, captum* ("caught").

Declension of the Perfect Passive Participle

Singular

	Masculine	Feminine	Neuter
Nominative	captus	capta	captum
Genitive	captī	captae	captī
Dative	captō	captae	captō
Accusative	captum	captam	captum
Ablative	captō	captā	captō
Vocative	capte	capta	captum

Plural

	Masculine	Feminine	Neuter
Nominative	captī	captae	capta
Genitive	captōrum	captārum	captōrum
Dative	captīs	captīs	captīs
Accustive	captōs	captās	capta
Ablative	captīs	captīs	captīs
Vocative	captī	captae	capta

The perfect passive participle can be represented in various ways in English. The most literal way to represent the meaning is to include "having been" before the English past participle. So, for example, *vīsus, vīsa, vīsum* is translated "having been seen" or simply "seen." It is also possible to represent the meaning of the perfect passive participle with a clause or a phrase. You will see how this can be done in future chapters.

Here are some perfect passive participles:

> *vocātus, vocāta, vocātum* – having been called, called
>
> *aedificātus, aedificāta, aedificātum* – having been built, built
>
> *quaesītus, quaesīta, quaesītum* – having been sought, sought
>
> *vīsus, vīsa, vīsum* – having been seen, seen
>
> *neglēctus, neglēcta, neglēctum* – having been neglected, neglected

Note that the perfect passive participle refers to a time before that of the main verb. This is always true no matter the tense of the main verb. The tense of the participle is relative to the tense of the main verb, **not** to the present tense of the person narrating. Notice the examples that follow.

> *Vocātus ab imperātōre vēnit.*
> Having been called by the general, he came. (or) Called by the general, he came.

Here the main verb is in the perfect tense. The participle *vocātus* ("having been called") refers to a time even before the action described by *vēnit*, i.e., first the man was called by the general, then (obeying the call) he came.

> *Mīlitibus vocātīs praemia māgna imperātor dabit.*
> To the soldiers having been called/summoned the general will give large rewards. (or) To the called/summoned soldiers the general will give large rewards.

Here the main verb *dabit* ("will give") is in the future. The perfect participle *vocātīs* ("having been called") refers to some time before the action of this future verb. First the soldiers will be called, then the general will give them the rewards.

STUDY TIP

There are also principal parts in English verbs: for example; "see," "saw," "seen." The past participle in English "seen" corresponds roughly to the fourth principal part, or perfect passive participle in Latin. Another way to find a past participle of any verb in English is to start a phrase with the words "having been . . ." and then think of the form that would appropriately follow these words. In the case of the verb "to see," for example, the correct form after "having been . . ." is "seen."

BY THE WAY

Note that, with the exception of some verbs that you will study later, there is no perfect participle in Latin with an active meaning. So while you have *vocātus* meaning "having been called," there is no Latin participle that means "having called." In Latin, however, the idea equivalent to the perfect active participle (i.e., a phrase like "having called") can easily be expressed in other ways: these various equivalents to the meaning of a perfect active participle will be studied later.

▶ EXERCISE 1

Translate into English.

1. Hūnōs ā nōbīs vīsōs timēbāmus.

2. Hūnī urbem ā cīvibus relictam dēvastāvērunt.

3. Animālia ad nōs ducta cūrāre dēbēmus.

4. Hostēs victōs capere potuimus.

5. Dē rēbus ā Rōmānīs gestīs multa nunc legimus.

6. Praemium tibi dēbitum habēs.

VOCABULARY TO LEARN

NOUNS

barba, barbae, f. – beard

carō, carnis, f. – meat, flesh

herba, herbae, f. – plant, vegetation

pellis, pellis, f. – skin, hide

proelium, proeliī, n. – battle, combat

vestīmentum, vestīmentī, n. – garment, (pl.) clothes

vulnus, vulneris, n. – wound

DEMONSTRATIVE PRONOUN/ ADJECTIVE

hic, haec, hoc – this

ADJECTIVES

ferōx, ferōcis – fierce, ferocious

terribilis, terribile – terrifying

VERBS

coquō, coquere, coxī, coctum – to cook

crēscō, crēscere, crēvī, —— – to grow

sānō, sānāre, sānāvī, sānātum – to heal

sedeō, sedēre, sēdī, sessum – to sit

terō, terere, trīvī, trītum – to wear out, to rub

vīvō, vīvere, vīxī, vīctum – to live

vulnerō, vulnerāre, vulnerāvī, vulnerātum – to wound

ADVERBS

celeriter – swiftly

forīs – outside, in the open

PREPOSITION

inter + accusative – between, among

CONJUNCTION

postquam – after

▶ EXERCISE 2

Find the English derivatives based on the Vocabulary to Learn in the following sentences. Write the corresponding Latin word.

1. You should go to the barber and get a haircut!

2. The clergy were conspicuous in the ceremony with their splendid vestments.

3. A crescendo of sound came from the orchestra as the symphony began.

4. All restaurants and public eating places must be sanitary.

5. I like herbal dressing on my salad.

6. The warehouse was filled with victuals for the army.

7. The general decided to retreat, knowing his troops would be too vulnerable in such an exposed position.

8. The celerity of the cheetah, the fastest of all land animals, is amazing.

9. That old saying is too trite for me to use it again.

10. That is an interesting concoction you have prepared. Does it taste good?

LANGUAGE FACT II

PERFECT PASSIVE TENSE OF ALL CONJUGATIONS

In some sentences of the passage at the beginning of the chapter the perfect passive participle is used together with forms of the verb *sum* ("to be").

> *Dē Hūnīs in librīs patrum nostrōrum nōn multa **sunt dicta**.*
> Not many things **have been said** about the Huns in the books of our fathers.

> *Postquam vulnera **sānāta sunt**, cicātrīcēs manent . . .*
> After the wounds **have been healed**, scars remain . . .

> *Rādīcēs herbārum, quae **correptae sunt** ex agrīs, comedunt et animālium carnem, quae nōn **cocta est**, sed paulisper **trīta <est>**.*
> They eat the roots of plants, which **have been snatched** from fields and the meat of animals, which **has not been cooked**, but **rubbed** for a little while.

> *Carō, antequam ab eīs comeditur, **posita est** inter equum et femora ēius quī in equō sedet . . .*
> The meat, before it is eaten by them, **has been placed** between the horse and the thighs of the person who sits on the horse . . .

Sometimes the perfect passive participle means "was . . ." rather than "has/have been . . ." as in the following sentence.

> *Urbs ā Hūnīs **est dēvastāta**.*
> The city **was devastated** by the Huns.

In these sentences you see the **perfect passive indicative** whose forms are made up of the perfect passive participle in combination with the present indicative of the verb *sum*. This is true of all conjugations. So, once you know the perfect passive participle of a verb, it is easy to form the perfect passive indicative. For example, here are the forms of the perfect passive indicative of *exspectāre* and *audīre*.

Horses had various uses for both the Huns and the Romans not only in war but also in other aspects of their lives.

Perfect Passive: *exspectō*

Singular

First Person	exspectātus, exspectāta, (exspectātum) sum	I was awaited, have been awaited
Second Person	exspectātus, exspectāta, (exspectātum) es	you were awaited, have been awaited
Third Person	exspectātus, exspectāta, exspectātum est	s/he/it was awaited, has been awaited

Plural

First Person	exspectātī, exspectātae, (exspectāta) sumus	we were awaited, have been awaited
Second Person	exspectātī, exspectātae, (exspectāta) estis	you were awaited, have been awaited
Third Person	exspectātī, exspectātae, exspectāta sunt	they were awaited, have been awaited

Perfect Passive: *audiō*

Singular

First Person	audītus, audīta, (audītum) sum	I was heard, have been heard
Second Person	audītus, audīta, (audītum) es	you were heard, have been heard
Third Person	audītus, audīta, audītum est	s/he/it was heard, has been heard

Plural

First Person	audītī, audītae, (audīta) sumus	we were heard, have been heard
Second Person	audītī, audītae, (audīta) estis	you were heard, have been heard
Third Person	audītī, audītae, audīta sunt	they were heard, have been heard

Note that parentheses have been placed around some of the neuter forms of the participial elements in these verbs. This is because people, not things, are usually the subjects of first and second person passive verbs.

There are two important things to remember about the use of the perfect passive tense:

First, the participial element of the verb will agree in case, number, and gender, with the subject of the verb. If the subject is singular, the participial element of the verb will be nominative singular agreeing with that subject. Its gender will, of course, be the same as the subject's, e.g., *Puella exspectāta est* ("The girl has been expected/awaited"). Similarly, if the verb is plural, the participial element of the verb will be in the nominative plural and agree with the subject in gender, e.g., *Nōs cīvēs nōn sumus audītī* ("We citizens have not been heard").

Second, the word order of the perfect passive verb is flexible. The auxiliary verb may either follow or precede the participial element, and it may even be separated from it by a few intervening words, especially adverbs, e.g., *Sum quoque in urbe relictus* ("I too have been left in the city").

BY THE WAY

The participial element of a perfect passive verb will always be nominative (singular or plural) in direct speech, since it will agree with the nominative subject.

> *Puella est exspectāta.*
> The girl has been awaited.

The perfect passive participle by itself can appear in any case, since it is simply an adjective agreeing with a noun.

> *Puellae exspectātae praemium dedimus.*
> We gave the reward to the girl having been awaited.

STUDY TIP

Be careful **never** to translate the perfect passive tense auxiliary verb (*sum, es, est,* etc.) as the equivalent of the present tense. *Puella est exspectāta* means "the girl **has been** awaited," **NOT** "the girl **is** awaited." The phrase "is awaited" is *exspectātur,* a present passive tense in Latin.

▶ EXERCISE 3

Fill in the blanks in the following sentences with the correct form of the perfect passive tense of the verb using the infinitive in parentheses. Then translate each sentence. The Reading Vocabulary may be consulted.

Example: Casae ā Hūnīs nōn _____ . (aedificāre)
Casae ā Hūnīs nōn sunt aedificātae.   The dwellings were not/have not been built by the Huns.

1. Agrīne vestrī ā Hūnīs _____ ? (dēvastāre)

2. Timorne in Rōmānīs ā Hūnīs _____ ? (excitāre)

3. Faciēsne Hūnōrum cōnsultō _____ ? (vulnerāre)

4. Urbēs Rōmānōrum tandem _____ . (līberāre)

5. Vestīmenta eōrum ex animālium pellibus _____ . (facere)

6. Sumus fēlīcēs: nōs laqueīs Hūnōrum nōn _____ . (capere)

7. Dīcō vōs esse fēlīcēs, quī ā Hūnīs nōn _____ . (capere).

► EXERCISE 4

Translate into English. Some of these sentences contain a perfect passive verb, while others have a perfect passive participle. Identify which of the two is used in each sentence. The Reading Vocabulary may be consulted.

Example: Nōn multa dē Hūnīs sunt dicta.
Not many things have been/were said about the Huns.   perfect passive tense

1. Verba dicta audīvimus.

2. Faciēs Hūnōrum vulnerātās vidēmus.

3. Faciēs Hūnōrum cōnsultō sunt vulnerātae.

4. Rādīcēs herbārum ex agrīs correptae sunt.

5. Rādīcēs herbārum ex agrīs correptās comedere nōn possumus.

6. Carnem coctam comedere solēmus.

7. Carō nōn est cocta.

8. Hostēs in proeliō sunt captī.

9. Hostēs in proeliō captōs vidēre nōn potuimus.

LANGUAGE FACT III

REVIEW OF PRINCIPAL PARTS OF VERBS

This is a good time to review some basic points about the four principal parts of a typical verb of any conjugation.

In chart form:

First principal part	**Second principal part**
a. Supplies 1st person singular, present active tense.	a. Supplies present active infinitive.
b. Distinguishes -io verbs from other third conjugation verbs.	b. Indicates verb's present stem, used in present, future, and imperfect tenses (active and passive).
c. Clarifies distinction between second conjugation verbs (-ēre) and third conjugation verbs (-ere).	c. Indicates verb's conjugation.
Third principal part	**Fourth principal part**
a. Supplies 1st person singular, perfect active tense.	a. Supplies supine (to be learned later).
b. Indicates verb's perfect active stem, used in perfect, pluperfect, and future perfect (active).	b. Indicates perfect passive participle stem.
	c. Indicates verb's perfect passive stem, used in perfect, pluperfect, and future perfect (passive).

In summary form:

1. From the **second principal part** (**present active infinitive**), you learn the present stem of the verb, and therefore the conjugation to which it belongs.

2. From the **first principal part** (**first person singular, present active indicative**), you can detect third conjugation -*io* verbs and easily distinguish verbs belonging to the second conjugation (with a few exceptions).

3. From the **first and second principal parts** you can form the present, future, and imperfect tenses, active and passive.

4. From the **third principal part** (**first person singular perfect active indicative**) you can form the perfect, future perfect, and pluperfect tenses of the verb in the active voice.

5. From the **fourth principal part** (**nominative neuter singular perfect passive participle**—sometimes called the supine, about which you will learn later) you can form the perfect, future perfect, and pluperfect tenses of the verb in the passive voice.

▶ EXERCISE 5

Change the following verbs below into the form indicated in parentheses and translate the changed form.

Example: timeō (first person plural imperfect passive)
timēbāmur   we were being feared

1. sānō (third person plural perfect passive)
2. doceō (third person singular future passive)
3. vīvō (first person singular pluperfect active)
4. vulnerō (second person plural perfect passive)
5. iaciō (second person singular future passive)
6. āmittō (second person singular imperfect passive)
7. colō (first person plural perfect active)
8. crēscō (third person plural future active)
9. sedeō (second person singular future perfect active)
10. ārdeō (second person singular pluperfect active)
11. terō (third person singular pluperfect active)

LANGUAGE FACT IV

DEMONSTRATIVE PRONOUN AND ADJECTIVE *HIC*

You have already learned the first and second person personal pronouns, as well as the pronoun *is, ea, id*, which is both a third person personal pronoun, as well as a demonstrative adjective ("this," "that").

In the reading at the beginning of this chapter you have met another demonstrative word that means "this."

> **Hī** *sunt ferī et ferōcēs.*
> **These** <people> are ferocious and wild.

> **Hōrum** *fōrma nōn est pulchra, sed terribilis!*
> The appearance of **these** <people> is not handsome, but terrifying!

Here is the declension of *hic, haec, hoc.*

Demonstrative Pronoun/Adjective *hic*

Singular

	Masculine	Feminine	Neuter
Nominative	hic	haec	hoc
Genitive	hūius	hūius	hūius
Dative	huic	huic	huic
Accusative	hunc	hanc	hoc
Ablative	hōc	hāc	hōc

Plural

	Masculine	Feminine	Neuter
Nominative	hī	hae	haec
Genitive	hōrum	hārum	hōrum
Dative	hīs	hīs	hīs
Accusative	hōs	hās	haec
Ablative	hīs	hīs	hīs

▶ EXERCISE 6

Translate into Latin.

1. They often remain on these horses.
2. This is the sword of this general.
3. They eat only these plants.
4. These are the names of brave men.
5. Wounds remain in/on the face of this soldier.
6. Many things have been said about the bravery of these women.
7. Do not (plural) give these great rewards to these ferocious people!

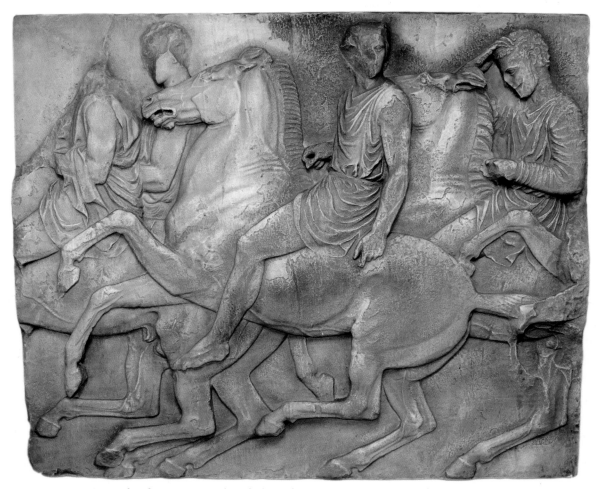

Horses played an important role in the lives of ancient people, whether Greek, Roman, or Huns.

▶ EXERCISE 7

Translate the following dialogue into English. Refer both to Reading Vocabulary and the words explained below.

A Roman ambassador around the year 440 CE has come to the camp of the Huns to negotiate with Attila, their king, about the tribute that the Romans will pay the Huns to stop them from attacking Roman territory.

Rōmānus: Cūr Hūnī terribilēs vidērī cupiunt?

Attila: Nōn est nōbīs difficile hostēs vincere, quī nōs timent.

Rōmānus: Multī dīcunt propter hanc causam faciēs Hūnōrum cōnsultō vulnerārī. Estne hoc vērum?

Attila: Vērum est! Mīlitēsne meī tibi videntur esse ferōcēs?

Rōmānus: Ita! Hōs hominēs timeō.

Attila: Itaque nōn erit difficile Hūnīs Rōmānōs in proeliō vincere.

Rōmānus: Ita crēdimus. Iam ā Rōmānīs sum ad tē missus, quī cupiunt Hūnīs multa dōna dare. Sī Hūnī Rōmānōs in pāce relīquerint, Rōmānī Hūnīs dōna, praemia, multās rēs bonās dabunt.

Attila: Cōnsilium praeclārum! Amō hoc cōnsilium. Sed dē dōnīs et praemiīs, quae Rōmānī Hūnīs dabunt, posteā dīcēmus. Nunc cēnābimus.

Rōmānus: Cōnsilium praeclārum! Mēne ad casam tuam dūcēs? Ubi cēna habēbitur?

Attila: Nōs Hūnī sumus fortēs, ferī, ferōcēs, nōn miserī, sīcut vōs Rōmānī. Casās nōn habēmus, sed forīs habitāmus et vīvimus. Forīs igitur cēnābimus. Cibum bonum nōbīscum habēbis.

Rōmānus: Cēnāre sum parātus. Sed quid videō? Estne haec carō cocta? Et quae sunt hae herbae? Herbae nōn videntur esse, sed herbārum rādīcēs!

Attila: Hoc est vērum, quod dē herbīs dīxistī. Carō autem cocta nōn est, sed paulisper trīta. Carō enim, antequam ā nōbīs comeditur, posita est inter equum et femora ēius quī in equō sedet et ibi paulisper manet. Carō igitur est ad cēnam bene parāta. Quid dicīs? Cēnābisne nōbīscum?

Rōmānus: Iūlius Caesar quondam dīxit: "Vēnī, vīdī, vīcī!" Hic Rōmānus, quī cum Hūnīs cēnāre dēbet, haec verba dīcit: "Vēnī, vīdī, victus sum."

cēna, cēnae, f. – dinner
cēnō, cēnāre, cēnāvī, —— – to dine
cibus, cibī, m. – food

nōbīscum = cum nōbīs
quondam (adv.) – once
ubi? – where?

TALKING

abstergeō, abstergēre, abstersī, abstersum – to wipe away

armārium, armāriī, n. – cupboard, closet

excutiō, excutere, excussī, excussum – to shake out

exsūgō, exsūgere, exsūxī, exsūctum – to suck out

<pulveris> haurītōrium, haurītōriī, n. – vacuum cleaner

lavō, lavāre, lāvī, lautum – to wash

lectum sternō, sternere, strāvī, strātum – to make a bed

lectus, lectī, m. – bed

lintea, linteōrum, n. pl. – linens

māchina (māchinae, f.) *lavātōria* – washing machine

mundus, munda, mundum – neat and clean

ōrdinō, ōrdināre, ōrdināvī, ōrdinātum – to arrange, put in order

pavīmentum, pavīmentī, n. – floor

pulvis, pulveris, m. – dust

(domum) pūrgō, pūrgāre, pūrgāvī, pūrgātum – to clean (the house)

scōpae, scōpārum, f. pl. – broom

tapēte, tapētis, n. – carpet

vēlum, vēlī, n. – curtain

verrō, verrere, verrī, versum – to sweep

CLEANING THE HOUSE

Christīna: Ubi (*where*) herī (*yesterday*) erās? Birotīs (*on bicycles*) vectī sumus (*we rode*). Pulchrum erat caelum!

Marīa: Auxilium mātrī dare dēbēbam. Māter enim domum pūrgāre herī dēcrēvit.

Mārcus: Quid fēcit pater tuus?

Marīa: Pater quoque auxilium mātrī dedit. Māter eum iussit pavīmentum scōpīs verrere.

Mārcus: Paterne hoc fēcit?

Marīa: Pater nōn solum hoc fēcit, sed etiam multās aliās rēs.

Mārcus: Quae aliae rēs ā patre sunt factae?

Marīa: Pater lintea lectōrum omniaque tapētia excutere dēbēbat.

Helena: Pater tuus dīligenter (*with care*) labōrāvit (*worked*). Quid tū, Marīa, faciēbās?

Marīa: Māter mē iussit rēs in armāriīs positās ōrdināre. Dēbēbam quoque pulverem abstergēre, quī in armāriīs anteā (*earlier*) crēverat. Etiam iussū mātris pulverem ē vēlīs et ē pavīmentō celeriter haurītōriō exsūxī.

Helena: Quam (*how*) dīligenter labōrāvistis! Sine dubiō (*doubt*) nihil aliud facere dēbēbātis!

Marīa: Etiam aliās rēs fēcimus. Et ego et pater omnēs lectōs strāvimus. Deinde multa lintea in māchinā lavātōriā lāvimus. Domus nostra nunc est munda!

Mārcus: Quid fēcit māter tua?

Marīa: Māter nōs haec omnia facere iussit.

CHAPTER 20

Pluperfect Passive Tense of All Conjugations; Perfect Active and Passive Infinitives; Demonstrative Pronoun and Adjective *Ille*

A young Augustine with his mother Monica. By Ary Scheffer (1795–1858).

MEMORĀBILE DICTŪ

Cor ad cor loquitur.

"Heart to heart," literally "A heart speaks to a heart."

A Latin saying that originated in the autobiographical *Confessions* of the influential early Christian writer Augustine, and is echoed in our English expression "heart to heart talk." This phrase was also the motto of Cardinal J. H. Newman in the nineteenth century.

READING

Aurēlius Augustine (354–430 CE), perhaps the most important early Christian thinker, was born in Tagaste in northern Africa, a part of the Roman Empire that is today Algeria. Although his mother, Monica, was a devout Christian, he rejected her beliefs as a young man. He moved to Rome, where he taught rhetoric and benefited from the patronage of the pagan orator Symmachus. In 386, however, while serving as public orator of Milan, Augustine was converted to Christianity by Ambrose, bishop of Milan. He himself later became bishop of Hippo in North Africa.

Among his most famous works are the *Cōnfessiōnēs*, "Confessions," and the *Dē Cīvitāte Deī*, "About the City of God." The latter work, imbued with a Christian vision, represents human history as part of a divine plan.

In the following passage, *Cōnfessiōnēs* 2.4.9, Augustine recalls an episode of his youth.

DĒ FŪRTŌ PIRŌRUM

1   Cum lēgēs hūmānae tum dīvīnae fūrtum pūnīre solent. Etiam fūr
    alium fūrem aequō animō nōn tolerat. Nec fūr dīves fūrem pauperem
    tolerat. Ego quoque fūrtum facere cupīvī et fēcī. Hoc tamen nōn
    propter egestātem fēcī, sed propter amōrem inīquitātis. Petīvī enim

5   rēs quibus abundābam, nōn quibus egēbam. Nam ipsō fūrtō dēlectārī
    cupiēbam, nōn rēbus quās petēbam. Prope domum meam erat pirus
    pōmōrum plēna, quae valdē pulchra vidēbantur. Ego et paucī aliī
    adulēscentēs improbī domōs nostrās noctū (per tōtum enim diem
    lūserāmus) relīquimus et illam arborem petīvimus. Omnia pōma ex

10 eā excussimus et nōbīscum asportāvimus. Pauca eōrum comēdimus,
    paene omnia porcīs ēiēcimus. Nam nōn cupiēbāmus comedere pōma,
    quae ā nōbīs erant capta. Omnēs enim in domibus nostrīs bonīs
    cibīs abundābāmus. Cupiēbāmus contrā lēgēs rēs facere et inīquitāte
    dēlectārī. Hūius malitiae causa erat ipsa malitia. Rēs malās, rēs inīquās

15 amāvī, amāvī rēs malās et inīquās facere.

        Nunc adolēvī et cor meum iam intellegit mē rēs malās amāvisse, iam
    intellegit rēs malās ā mē esse factās.

READING VOCABULARY

*abundō, abundāre, abundāvī, abundātum + ablative – to abound with

adolēscō, adolēscere, adolēvī, adultum – to grow up

*adulēscēns, adulēscentis, m./f. – young man, young lady

*aequus, aequa, aequum – even; aequō animō – indifferently (with even spirit)

amāvisse – have loved

asportō, asportāre, asportāvī, asportātum – to carry away

cibus, cibī, m. – food

*cor, cordis, n. – heart

cum ... tum ... – both ... and ...

*dēlectō, dēlectāre, dēlectāvī, dēlectātum – to delight, please

*dīvīnus, dīvīna, dīvīnum – divine

*egeō, egēre, eguī, —— + ablative – to lack something

egestās, egestātis, f. – lack, poverty

ēiciō, ēicere, ēiēcī, eiectum – to throw away

erant capta – had been taken

esse factās – have been done

excutiō, excutere, excussī, excussum – to shake off

*fūr, fūris, m. – thief

*fūrtum, fūrtī, n. – theft

*hūmānus, hūmāna, hūmānum – human

*illam – that

improbus, improba, improbum – bad, wicked

*inīquitās, inīquitātis, f. – injustice

inīquus, inīqua, inīquum – unjust

ipsa – itself

ipsō – by itself

*lēx, lēgis, f. – law

*lūdō, lūdere, lūsī, lūsum – to play

malitia, malitiae, f. – badness, wickedness

nōbīscum = cum nōbīs

*noctū (adv.) – during the night

*paene (adv.) – almost

*pauper, pauperis (genitive) – poor

pirum, pirī, n. – pear (fruit)

pirus, pirī, f. – pear tree

*plēnus + genitive or + ablative – full of

*pōmum, pōmī, n. – fruit

porcus, porcī, m. – pig

*pūniō, pūnīre, pūnīvī, pūnītum – to punish

tolerō, tolerāre, tolerāvī, tolerātum – to tolerate, to bear

tōtus, tōta, tōtum – whole

*Words marked with an asterisk will need to be memorized later in the chapter.

COMPREHENSION QUESTIONS

1. What did Augustine steal, and what did he do with the things he stole?

2. What was Augustine's motivation to steal?

3. When did the theft happen, and when does Augustine write about it?

LANGUAGE FACT I

PLUPERFECT PASSIVE TENSE OF ALL CONJUGATIONS

Take a close look at one of the sentences from Augustine's autobiography:

> *Nōn cupiēbāmus comedere pōma, quae ā nōbīs **erant capta.***
> We did not want to eat the fruits that **had been taken** by us.

In Chapter 17 you learned the **pluperfect active** of verbs of all conjugations. Now you meet the **pluperfect passive**.

The pluperfect passive is formed much like the perfect passive you learned in the last chapter, using a nominative perfect passive participle with a form of *sum* as an auxiliary verb for all conjugations.

Yet, the pluperfect passive is easily distinguished from the perfect passive—while the perfect passive has as its auxiliary verb the **present** forms of *sum*, the pluperfect passive has as its auxiliary verb the **imperfect** forms of *sum*. The pluperfect passive of the verb *parō* will serve as an example for all conjugations.

Pluperfect Passive: *parō*		
Singular		
First Person	parātus, parāta, (parātum) eram	I had been prepared
Second Person	parātus, parāta, (parātum) erās	you had been prepared
Third Person	parātus, parāta, parātum erat	s/he/it had been prepared
Plural		
First Person	parātī, parātae, (parāta) erāmus	we had been prepared
Second Person	parātī, parātae, (parāta) erātis	you had been prepared
Third Person	parātī, parātae, parāta erant	they had been prepared

STUDY TIP

Note that in the plural not only the verb *sum*, but also the participle needs to be plural.

▶ EXERCISE 1

Change the pluperfect active verbs into the pluperfect passive, keeping the same person and number. Translate the passive form.

Example: nārrāverāt

nārrātus, nārrāta, nārrātum erat   s/he/it had been told

1. dēlectāverāmus
2. lēgerant
3. oppresserātis
4. rogāverat
5. līberāverāmus
6. relīquerās
7. pūnīveram
8. quaesīverant
9. excitāverātis

VOCABULARY TO LEARN

NOUNS

adulēscēns, adulēscentis, m./f. – young man, young lady

cor, cordis, n. – heart

fūr, fūris, m. – thief

fūrtum, fūrtī, n. – theft

inīquitās, inīquitātis, f. – injustice, mischief

lēx, lēgis, f. – law

pōmum, pōmī, n. – fruit

DEMONSTRATIVE PRONOUN/ ADJECTIVE

ille, illa, illud – that

ADJECTIVES

aequus, aequa, aequum – even; aequō animō – indifferently

dīvīnus, dīvīna, dīvīnum – divine

hūmānus, hūmāna, hūmānum – human

pauper, pauperis – poor

plēnus + genitive or + ablative – full of

VERBS

abundō, abundāre, abundāvī, abundātum + ablative – to abound with

dēlectō, dēlectāre, dēlectāvī, dēlectātum – to delight, please

egeō, egēre, eguī, —— + ablative – to lack something

lūdō, lūdere, lūsī, lūsum – to play

pūniō, pūnīre, pūnīvī, pūnītum – to punish

ADVERBS

noctū – during the night

paene – almost

▶ EXERCISE 2

Find the English derivatives based on the Vocabulary to Learn in the following sentences. Write the corresponding Latin word.

1. They were very cordial to me and welcomed me at their home.

2. That spy was making furtive telephone calls.

3. Do you need legal advice?

4. The dinner was delicious.

5. We need to take punitive action.

6. Why do you have this adolescent attitude?

7. All people must have equal rights.

8. I will be going to Divinity School next fall.

9. The whole summer we have been working in Habitat for Humanity.

10. His best trait is that he has patience in abundance.

LANGUAGE FACT II

PERFECT ACTIVE AND PASSIVE INFINITIVES

Now return to Augustine's autobiography and take a close look at this sentence.

> *Cor meum iam intellegit mē rēs malās **amāvisse**, iam intellegit rēs malās ā mē **esse factās**.*
> My heart already understands that I loved bad things; it already understands that bad things were done by me.

So far you have only learned the present active and passive infinitives. In the sentences above there are two new infinitives—the perfect active and perfect passive infinitives. *Amāvisse* is a perfect active infinitive, and *esse factās* is a perfect passive infinitive.

Unlike the present active and passive infinitives, the perfect active infinitive has the same endings for all conjugations, and the perfect passive infinitive is formed the same way for all conjugations.

Augustine as bishop of Hippo.

The perfect **active** infinitive is made up of the perfect active stem (from the verb's **third** principal part) with the ending *-isse*.

The perfect **passive** infinitive is made up of the perfect passive participle (the verb's **fourth** principal part), which must agree in case, number, and gender with the expressed or implied noun or pronoun that is its subject, along with *esse*, the infinitive of the verb "to be."

Perfect Active Infinitive	
parāv-isse	to have prepared

Perfect Passive Infinitive	
parātus, parāta, parātum esse	to have been prepared

BY THE WAY

The perfect infinitive of *sum* is *fuisse*, and of *possum* is *potuisse*. Both forms are formed regularly by adding the suffix *-isse* to the perfect stems *fu-* and *potu-*. Remember that *sum* and *possum* do not have passive forms and thus do not have perfect passive infinitives.

Present and Perfect Infinitives			
Present Active Infinitive	**Present Passive Infinitive**	**Perfect Active Infinitive**	**Perfect Passive Infinitive**
parāre to prepare	parārī to be prepared	parāvisse to have prepared	parātus, parāta, parātum esse to have been prepared

When are the perfect infinitives used?

Perfect infinitives are used in the accusative and infinitive construction (the indirect statement) in a way similiar to the present infinitives with one major difference—while the **present** infinitive indicates **the same time as** the main verb, the **perfect** infinitive always indicates **a time before** the main verb. The tense of the infinitive is relative to that of the main verb. By studying these two sentences, you will understand this concept better.

Perfect infinitive (time before the main verb).

> *Augustīnus intellēxit sē rēs malās iam fēcisse.*
> Augustine understood that he had already done bad things.

Present infinitive (same time as the main verb).

> *Augustīnus nōn intellegēbat sē rēs malās tunc facere.*
> Augustine did not understand that he was doing bad things at that time.

Note that in the accusative and infinitive construction the participle (which is a part of the perfect passive infinitive) is always in the accusative, and that it agrees in number and gender with the accusative subject of the indirect statement.

*Dīcō **virum** esse **cōnspectum.*** "I say that the man has been looked at."

*Dīcō **virōs** esse **cōnspectōs.*** "I say that the men have been looked at."

*Dīcō **fēminam** esse **cōnspectam.*** "I say that the woman has been looked at."

*Dīcō **fēminās** esse **cōnspectās.*** "I say that the women have been looked at."

BY THE WAY

The word "to," which usually translates the infinitive, is rarely used in the English translation of the accusative and infinitive construction.

▶ EXERCISE 3

Translate the following sentences and then change all the present infinitives into perfect infinitives. Translate the changed sentence. The Reading Vocabulary may be consulted.

Example: Dīcō mē librum legere.

I say that I am reading a book.   Dīcō mē librum lēgisse.   I say that I have read a book.

1. Augustīnus dīcit prope domum suam arborem esse et eam arborem multa pōma pulchra habēre.

2. Augustīnus nārrat sē rēs malās cupere et fūrtō dēlectārī.

3. Augustīnus dīcit omnia pōma ab adulēscentibus ex arbore excutī atque asportārī.

4. Augustīnus dīcit sē pauca pōma comedere et paene omnia ēicere.

Augustine must have stolen
a pear as tempting as this one.

▶ EXERCISE 4

Fill in the blanks with the correct form of the pluperfect passive indicative, or the perfect infinitive and translate the sentences. The Reading Vocabulary may be consulted.

Example: Dīxī mē haec omnia iam _____. (audiō)
Dīxī mē haec omnia iam audīvisse.   I said that I had already heard all these things.

1. Omnia pōma ab Augustīnō et ab ēius amīcīs iam ex arbore _____. Tunc pauca pōma eī comēdērunt. (excutiō)

2. Adulēscentēs paucīs tantum pōmīs _____. Alia pōma porcīs eiēcērunt. (dēlectō)

3. Improbī adulēscentēs putābant fūrtum bene _____. (faciō)

4. Augustīnus tandem intellēxit sē nōn bene _____. (faciō)

LANGUAGE FACT III

DEMONSTRATIVE PRONOUN AND ADJECTIVE *ILLE*

In Chapter 19 you learned the demonstrative *hic, haec, hoc* ("this"). In this chapter reading you encountered another demonstrative word that means "that."

> ***Illam** arborem petīvimus.*
> We went to **that** tree.

Here is the declension of the demonstrative pronoun and adjective *ille.*

Demonstrative Pronoun/Adjective *ille*		
Singular		
	Masculine	**Feminine**	**Neuter**
Nominative	ille	illa	illud
Genitive	illīus	illīus	illīus
Dative	illī	illī	illī
Accusative	illum	illam	illud
Ablative	illō	illā	illō
Plural		
	Masculine	**Feminine**	**Neuter**
Nominative	illī	illae	illa
Genitive	illōrum	illārum	illōrum
Dative	illīs	illīs	illīs
Accusative	illōs	illās	illa
Ablative	illīs	illīs	illīs

STUDY TIP

Note that the declension of *ille, illa, illud* is quite similar to the declension of *is, ea, id* (which you learned in Chapter 12). The genitive and dative singular are irregular, while the rest resemble first and second declension endings.

BY THE WAY

The demonstrative *hic, haec, hoc* means "this" and indicates a person or thing that is close; the demonstrative *ille, illa, illud* means "that" and indicates a person or thing that is far. When a series of things or persons has been mentioned, *hic* often refers to the last in the series and means "the latter," while *ille* refers to a previously mentioned person or thing and means "the former."

Just as is true with *is, ea, id*, both *hic, haec, hoc* and *ille, illa, illud* can be used either as demonstrative pronouns or demonstrative adjectives.

Demonstrative Pronoun	*Hic mox respondēbit.* "He (this <man>) will reply soon."
Demonstrative Adjective	*Hic vir mox respondēbit.* "This man will reply soon."
Demonstrative Pronoun	*Illae dōna exspectant.* "They (these <women>) expect gifts."
Demonstrative Adjective	*Illae mulierēs dōna exspectant.* "Those women expect gifts."

▶ EXERCISE 5

Substitute *ille* for *hic* in the following phrases. Give the case and number of each phrase and translate.

Example: hoc fūrtum
illud fūrtum   nominative *or* accusative singular   that theft

1. hās inīquitātēs
2. hī fūrēs
3. hūius cordis
4. hīs adulēscentibus
5. hārum lēgum
6. hōrum pōmōrum
7. hāc causā
8. hīs lītoribus
9. haec odia
10. hōc saxō
11. huic carnī

▶ EXERCISE 6

Fill in the blanks with the correct pluperfect passive form of the verb in the parentheses and translate both sentences.

Example: Domum vīdimus. Iam _____. (aedificō)
Domum vīdimus. Iam erat aedificāta.   We saw the house. It had already been built.

1. Hostēs fūgērunt. Iam ā nōbis _____. (vincō)
2. Flammās vīdimus. Incendium nōn _____. (exstinguō)
3. Diū tē quaesīvī. Nam bene _____. (occultō)
4. Puer nōn gaudēbat. Nam ā mātre _____. (pūniō)
5. Ad nōs vēnistis. Nam ā nōbīs _____. (vocō)

TALKING

argentāria, argentāriae, f. – bank

computus, computī, m. – account

fiscus, fiscī, m. – safe, account

nummī, nummōrum, m. pl. – coins

monēta (monētae, f.) *chartācea* – paper money

pecūlium, pecūliī, n. – savings

syngrapha, syngraphae, f. or *assignātiō (assignātiōnis,* f.) *argentāria* – a check

chartula, (chartulae, f.) *creditōria* – credit card

talērus, talērī, m./*dollarium, dollariī,* n. – dollar

centēsima, centēsimae, f. – cent, penny

pecūnia numerāta – cash

emō, emere, ēmī, ēmptum – to buy

solvō, solvere, solvī, solūtum – to pay

Quantī cōnstat? "How much does it cost?"

Cōnstat decem talēris (dollariīs). "It costs ten dollars."

The Romans minted various types of coins such as the *as, dēnārius,* and *aureus*. This coin is a *dēnārius*. Coins in general were called *nummī,* which word is related to the English word "numismatics," the study of coins.

Pecūniam dēpōnō (dēpōnere, dēposuī, dēpositum). "I deposit money."

Pecūniam collocō (collocāre, collocāvī, collocātum). "I invest money."

Pecūniam eximō (eximere, exēmī, exēmptum). "I take out money."

Commodō (commodāre, commodāvī, commodātum) pecūniam. "I lend money."

Mūtuor pecūniam. "I borrow money."

Pecūniae (dative) parcō. "I save money."

GOING SHOPPING

Marīa: Salvēte, amīcī! Vultisne (*do you all want*) mēcum venīre?

Helena: Quō (*where, to which place*) venīre dēbēmus?

Marīa: Ad vīcum tabernārum (*mall*). Vestīmentum enim ibi vīdī, quod emere (*buy*) cupiō.

Helena: Quāle (*what kind*) est illud vestīmentum?

Marīa: Est vestīmentum aestīvum (*summer*) valdē pulchrum. Vestīmentum aestīvum diū ā mē erat quaesītum et tandem praeteritā hebdomade (*last week*) rem pulchram cōnspexī.

Christīna: Cūr statim nōn ēmistī?

Marīa: Pecūniā egēbam.

Helena: Quid nunc? Estne tibi nunc pecūnia?

Marīa: Pater chartulam creditōriam mihi dedit.

Helena: Vērumne dīcis? Quantī cōnstat vestīmentum quod habēre cupis?

Marīa: Centum (*one hundred*) talērīs.

Christīna: Ego pecūniae parcō et pecūlium in argentāriā habeō. Sī vestīmentum emere cupiō, pecūniam ex fiscō eximō. Rēs chartulā creditōriā nōn emō et pecūniam nōn dēbeō.

Marīa: Tū es fēlīx. Ex manibus meīs pecūnia fluere vidētur.

Fourteenth century illuminated manuscript of the writings of Boethius,
illustrating the wheel of fortune.

MEMORĀBILE DICTŪ

Tempora mūtantur et nōs mūtāmur in illīs.

"Times are changing and we are changing in them."

This well-known line of verse probably dates from some time in the Middle Ages, and concisely
expresses the recognition that human life and human beings change and are changeable.

READING

Anicius Manlius Sevērīnus Boēthius (ca. 480–ca. 524 CE) lived after the dissolution of the Roman Empire in the West, at a time when the Ostrogoths under Theodoric the Great had established a kingdom in Italy. Scion of a noble Roman family, Boethius served in the king's administration; eventually, for reasons that are unclear, the king turned against Boethius, accused him of sedition, and sentenced him to death.

Boethius knew Greek well, and translated Plato and Aristotle into Latin. He also wrote important treatises on music and Christian theology. But his literary masterpiece, written in prose alternating with verse, is the *Cōnsōlātiō Philosophiae*, the "Consolation of Philosophy." It takes the form of a dialogue between Philosophy, allegorically represented as a mystical female figure, and the imprisoned Boethius himself.

In the selection below, adapted from the second book of the *Cōnsōlātiō Philosophiae*, Fortune is personified, and speaks in her own defense against those who blame "bad fortune" for the loss of power and prosperity. Her nature, it seems, is "to come and go." Here the action of Fortune is compared to that of an endlessly turning wheel that raises people up for a time, but always sends them back down to a lowly condition. This image of the "wheel of fortune" was very popular during the Middle Ages and early modern era; it is frequently depicted in drawings or paintings in medieval manuscripts.

DĒ ROTĀ FORTŪNAE

1   Tū multās rēs ā mē accēpistī. Tē diū alēbam. Dīvitiās habēbās et
    honōrēs. Errāvistī. Putābās tē illās rēs tibi ad tempus datās semper
    habitūrum esse. Sed cōnstantia est ā mē aliēna. Semper discessūra nihil
    tibi dedī. Tandem ā mē relictus es. Dīvitiae et honōrēs mēcum
5   discessērunt. Cūr mē reprehendis? Nihil, quod erat tuum, ex tē ēripuī.
    Fūrtī mē accūsāre nōn poteris!

    Hominēs multās rēs habent, sed nihil possident. Ego Fortūna omnia
    possideō. Sī rēs hominibus ā mē datae erunt, illās rēs posteā recipiam.
    Nam omnēs rēs illae sunt meae, nōn hominum. Sī homō ā mē relictus
10 erit, omnēs rēs eī datae mēcum discēdent. Omnium dīvitiārum
    rērumque quās hominēs habent externās sum domina. Numquam cum
    ūllō homine semper maneō, sed omnēs dīvitiae rēsque externae semper
    mēcum manent.

15   Omnia in vītā hominum semper mūtantur. Hominēs vīvunt sīcut in māgnā rotā, quae circum axem semper versātur. Haec rota est mea! Homō, quī in rotā meā sublātus erit, posteā prō certō dēscendet et cadet. Homō igitur, quī dīvitiās et honōrēs habet, prō certō scīre dēbet sē tandem illās rēs relictūrum esse.

READING VOCABULARY

*accipiō, accipere, accēpī, acceptum – to accept, receive

*accūsō, accūsāre, accūsāvī, accūsātum + accusative + genitive – to accuse someone of something

ad tempus – for the time being, for a while

*aliēnus, aliēna, aliēnum + ā/ab + ablative – foreign to, inconsistent with

*axis, axis, m. – axle, axis

*circum + accusative – around

*cōnstantia, cōnstantiae, f. – constancy

datae erunt – will have been given/are given

*dēscendō, dēscendere, dēscendī, dēscēnsum – to descend

discessūra – about to depart/go away

*dīvitiae, dīvitiārum, f. pl. – wealth, riches

*ēripiō, ēripere, ēripuī, ēreptum – to snatch away

*errō, errāre, errāvī, errātum – to wander, make a mistake

*externus, externa, externum – outward, external

*fortūna, fortūnae, f. – fortune, the goddess Fortune

habitūrum esse – going to have/would have

*honor, honōris, m. – honor, public office or distinction

*mūtō, mūtāre, mūtāvī, mūtātum – to change

*possideō, possidēre, possēdī, possessum – to possess

*prō certō – for certain, for sure

*recipiō, recipere, recēpī, receptum – to take back

relictūrum esse – will leave behind

relictus erit – will have been left/abandoned/is left/ abandoned

*reprehendō, reprehendere, reprehendī, reprehēnsum – to blame, rebuke

*rota, rotae, f. – wheel

sublātus erit – will have been raised up/is raised up

*tollō, tollere, sustulī, sublātum – to lift up, raise; to destroy

*ūllus, ūlla, ūllum – any

*versō, versāre, versāvī, versātum – to turn

*Words marked with an asterisk will need to be memorized later in the chapter.

COMPREHENSION QUESTIONS

1. Of what does Boethius accuse Fortune?

2. Why does Fortune reject Boethius' accusations?

3. What does Fortune say about her relationship with men?

4. What does Fortune want to say with the image of the wheel?

LANGUAGE FACT I

FUTURE PERFECT PASSIVE TENSE OF ALL CONJUGATIONS

In the chapter reading you see some verb forms that consist of the perfect passive participle together with the future forms of *sum*.

> *Sī rēs hominibus ā mē **datae erunt**, illās rēs posteā recipiam.*
> If things will have been given to people by me, I will take those things back afterwards.
> Or, in more colloquial English: If things are given to people by me,
> I will take those things back afterwards.

> *Sī homō ā mē **relictus erit**, omnēs rēs eī datae mēcum discēdent.*
> If a person will have been abandoned by me, all things given to him will go away <from him> with me.
> Or, in more colloquial English: If a person is abandoned by me, all things given to him will go away <from him> with me.

> *Homō, quī in rotā meā **sublātus erit**, posteā prō certō dēscendet et cadet.*
> A person who will have been lifted up in my wheel will afterwards descend and fall for certain.
> Or, in more colloquial English: A person who is lifted up on my wheel will afterwards descend and fall for certain.

These are forms of the future perfect passive tense; they are formed with the perfect passive participle along with forms of *erō*, the future tense of *sum*.

You now know all the tenses in the active and the passive voice.

BY THE WAY

When you studied the future perfect active in Chapter 18, it was used to indicate **a time before a future time**. This is equally true of the future perfect passive. So keep in mind what you already know about the meaning of the future perfect—where Latin (more accurately) uses the future perfect, English typically uses the simple present. Colloquial English (as the above sentences demonstrate) rarely or never says "will have."

As in the perfect and pluperfect passive, you do not need separate paradigms for the future perfect passive of all four conjugations. Once you know the perfect passive participle (from the fourth principal part of most verbs), simply combine it with the future tense of the verb *sum*.

STUDY TIP

Note that in the third person plural of the future perfect the active ending is *-erint* but the passive participle accompanies *erunt*, e.g., *audīverint*, but *audītī erunt*.

Future Perfect Passive: *exspectō*

Singular

First Person	exspectātus, exspectāta, (exspectātum) erō	I will/shall have been awaited
Second Person	exspectātus, exspectāta, (exspectātum) eris	you will have been awaited
Third Person	exspectātus, exspectāta, exspectātum erit	s/he/it will have been awaited

Plural

First Person	exspectātī, exspectātae, (exspectāta) erimus	we will/shall have been awaited
Second Person	exspectātī, exspectātae, (exspectāta) eritis	you will have been awaited
Third Person	exspectātī, exspectātae, exspectāta erunt	they will have been awaited

Future Perfect Passive: *audiō*

Singular

First Person	audītus, audīta, (audītum) erō	I will/shall have been heard
Second Person	audītus, audīta, (audītum) eris	you will have been heard
Third Person	audītus, audīta, audītum erit	s/he/it will have been heard

Plural

First Person	audītī, audītae, (audīta) erimus	we will/shall have been heard
Second Person	audītī, audītae, (audīta) eritis	you will have been heard
Third Person	audītī, audītae, audīta erunt	they will have been heard

Note that parentheses have been placed around some of the neuter forms of the participial elements in these verbs. This is because people, not things, are usually the subjects of first and second person passive verbs.

STUDY TIP

Keep in mind that the entire perfect system in the passive voice (i.e., the perfect, pluperfect, and future perfect passive) is formed by combining the perfect passive participle with the appropriate tense of *sum*:

- the perfect passive is formed with the perfect passive participle and the present tense of *sum*;
- the pluperfect passive is formed with the perfect passive participle and with the imperfect tense of *sum*;
- the future perfect passive is formed with the perfect passive participle and with the future tense of *sum*.

▶ EXERCISE 1

Translate the following perfect or pluperfect passive forms and then change them into the future perfect passive, keeping the same person and number. Translate the changed form.

Example: dictum est
it was/has been said   dictum erit   it will have been said

1. mūtāta sum
2. acceptus erās
3. reprehēnsae estis
4. accūsātī sunt
5. versātī sumus
6. neglēctus eram
7. sublātum est

VOCABULARY TO LEARN

NOUNS

axis, axis, m. – axle, axis

cōnstantia, cōnstantiae, f. – constancy

dīvitiae, dīvitiārum, f. pl. – wealth, riches

fortūna, fortūnae, f. – fortune, the goddess Fortune

honor, honōris, m. – honor, public office or distinction

rota, rotae, f. – wheel

ADJECTIVES

aliēnus, aliēna, aliēnum + ā/ab + ablative – foreign to, inconsistent with

externus, externa, externum – outward, external

futūrus, futūra, futūrum – about to be (the future active participle of *sum, esse, fuī*)

ūllus, ūlla, ūllum – any

VERBS

accipiō, accipere, accēpī, acceptum – to accept, to receive

accūsō, accūsāre, accūsāvī, accūsātum + accusative + genitive – to accuse someone of something

dēscendō, dēscendere, dēscendī, dēscēnsum – to descend

ēripiō, ēripere, ēripuī, ēreptum – to snatch away

errō, errāre, errāvī, errātum – to wander, make a mistake

mūtō, mūtāre, mūtāvī, mūtātum – to change

possideō, possidēre, possēdī, possessum – to possess

recipiō, recipere, recēpī, receptum – to take back

reprehendō, reprehendere, reprehendī, reprehēnsum – to blame, rebuke

tollō, tollere, sustulī, sublātum – to lift up, raise; destroy

versō, versāre, versāvī, versātum – to turn

PREPOSITION

circum + accusative – around

PREPOSITIONAL PHRASE USED ADVERBIALLY

prō certō – for certain, for sure

▶ EXERCISE 2

Find the English derivatives based on the Vocabulary to Learn in the following sentences. Write the corresponding Latin word.

1. The rotary motion of a cyclone is said to add force to its violent winds.

2. We should not reject things simply because they seem alien to us.

3. Our descendants must inherit a safer and cleaner world.

4. You do not need to speak in such an accusatory tone.

5. The motion of the hummingbird often appears to be quite erratic.

6. Sometimes distinguished citizens are given honorary degrees, even when they have never completed the academic curriculum leading to the degree.

7. When you buy dinner for these visitors, please be sure to ask the waiter to give you a receipt.

8. Scientists are steadily learning more about genetic mutations.

9. I often think my parents are too possessive.

10. Unethical behavior in anyone, but especially in a public official, is reprehensible.

LANGUAGE FACT II

FUTURE ACTIVE PARTICIPLE

In the passage at the beginning of the chapter, you saw a new form of participle. This is the future active participle. It occurs in this sentence:

> Semper **discessūra** nihil tibi dedī.
> Always **about to go away** I gave you nothing.

The future active participle has the meaning "(being) about to . . . ," or "(being) ready to . . . ," or "(being) on the point of . . . ," or "going to . . . ." The future active participle, especially in the works of writers who lived after Cicero, also may indicate the intention or purpose of the subject.

The stem of the future participle is the same as that of the perfect passive participle, so it is found in a verb's fourth principal part. The endings of the future participle are the same for all conjugations. The future participle of any verb is formed by taking away the **-um** of the fourth principal part and substituting in its place the endings **-ūrus, -ūra, -ūrum**. Here are the future participles of a few verbs already familiar to you.

> *audītūrus, audītūra, audītūrum* – about to hear/going to hear
>
> *cōnspectūrus, cōnspectūra, cōnspectūrum* – about to observe/going to observe
>
> *cūrātūrus, cūrātūra, cūrātūrum* – about to care for/going to care for
>
> *missūrus, missūra, missūrum* – about to send/going to send
>
> *receptūrus, receptūra, receptūrum* – about to take back/going to take back

▶ EXERCISE 3

Write the three nominative singular forms of the future active participle for each of the following verbs. Translate each participle.

Example: curō

curātūrus, -a, -um   about to care *or* going to care

1. legō	6. cadō	11. stō
2. mūtō	7. dormiō	12. possideō
3. respondeō	8. pugnō	13. agō
4. temptō	9. cupiō	14. dēleō
5. currō	10. gerō	

LANGUAGE FACT III

FUTURE ACTIVE INFINITIVE

Now that you know how to form the future active participle, you also know how to form the future active infinitive. There are a few examples of the future active infinitive in the passage at the beginning of this chapter.

> *Putābās tē illās rēs tibi ad tempus datās semper **habitūrum esse**.*
> You thought you would always have those things given to you for the time being.

> *Homō igitur, quī dīvitiās et honōrēs habet, prō certō scīre dēbet sē tandem illās rēs **relictūrum esse**.*
> Therefore a person who has wealth and honors ought to know for certain that he will finally leave those things behind.

The future active infinitive consists of the future active participle and *esse* (the infinitive of *sum*). The participle, of course, agrees in case, number, and gender with its subject. In the accusative and infinitive construction after a verb of speaking or thinking, the participle will agree with the accusative subject. If the future active infinitive is used after the verb *videor*, "I seem," the participle is in the nominative.

> *Hic homō **errātūrus esse** vidētur.*
> This man seems to be going to/about to make a mistake.

You can now make indirect statements (after a verb of saying or thinking) expressing different time relations to the main verb: before, same time, and after. To illustrate this, consider these sentences.

(1) *Putās tē verba Fortūnae audīre.* (**same time in the present**)
You think you are hearing the words of Fortune.

Putābās tē verba Fortūnae audīre. (**same time in the past**)
You thought you were hearing the words of Fortune.

(2) *Putās tē verba Fortūnae audīvisse.* (**time before present time**)
You think you have heard the words of Fortune.

Putābās tē verba Fortūnae audīvisse. (**time before past time**)
You thought you had heard the words of Fortune.

(3) *Putās tē verba Fortūnae audītūrum esse.* (Note that if *tē* referred to a female person, then the infinitive would be *audītūram esse*.) (**time after present time**)
You think you are going to hear/will hear the words of Fortune.

Putābās tē verba Fortūnae audītūrum esse. (**time after past time**)
You thought you were going to hear/would hear the words of Fortune.

These sentences clearly illustrate the following principles:

(1) In an indirect statement, the present infinitive refers to time contemporary with the main verb (regardless of the tense of the main verb).

Natural Science and Philosophy are personified in this reproduction of a woodcut from a German edition of Boethius.

(2) In an indirect statement, the future infinitive refers to time after that of the main verb (regardless of the tense of the main verb).

(3) In an indirect statement, the perfect infinitive refers to time prior to that of the main verb (regardless of the tense of the main verb).

In general, the tense of the infinitive in the indirect discourse does not indicate time on its own, but a time relation to the verb of the main clause.

BY THE WAY

Latin has no future passive infinitive that is commonly used. The ideas and relationships that would be expressed by a future passive infinitive can be expressed in Latin, but by other constructions that you will learn later.

▶ EXERCISE 4

Identify whether a future active participle or a future active infinitive is used in the following sentences and then translate each sentence.

Example: Fortūna dīvitiās et honōrēs semper ēreptūra timētur ā mē.
(future active participle)   Fortune, always about to snatch away riches and honors, is feared by me.

1.   Fortūnam dīvitiās et honōrēs ēreptūram esse crēdō.

2.   Fortūna dīvitiās et honōrēs ēreptūra esse vidētur.

3.   Dōna et praemia datūra Fortūna ab hominibus amātur.

4.   Fortūna dōna et praemia datūra esse vidētur.

5.   Fortūnam dōna et praemia datūram esse nōn crēdimus.

▶ EXERCISE 5

Translate into Latin.

1.   Fortune seems to be about to give me nothing.

2.   We believe that Fortune will never leave.

3.   I am going to abandon my riches.

4.   You (plural) believe that Fortune will always possess all external things.

5.   Do I seem to you to be going to descend soon on Fortune's wheel?

▶ EXERCISE 6

Translate the following questions. Then choose the best answer for each and translate. The Reading Vocabulary may be consulted.

1. Cūr Boēthius sē errāvisse dīcit?

   Tandem ā Fortūnā relictus est.

   Fortūna omnia possidēbat.

   Putābat sē dīvitiās et honōrēs semper habitūrum esse.

2. Cūr dīcit Fortūna sē fūrtī accūsārī nōn posse?

   Dīvitiae et honōrēs cum Fortūnā discessērunt.

   Fortūna nihil, quod erat Boēthiī, ex eō ēripuit.

   Fortūna erat semper discessūra et tandem Boēthium relīquit.

3. Cūr cōnstantia ā Fortūnā aliēna esse dīcitur?

   Fortūna numquam cum ūllō homine semper manet.

   Sī rēs hominibus ā Fortūnā datae erunt, Fortūna illās rēs posteā recipiet.

   Fortūna omnia possidet.

4. Cūr omnēs dīvitiae rēsque externae dīcuntur esse Fortūnae, nōn hominum?

   Hominēs multās rēs habent, sed nihil possident.

   Hominēs putant sē rēs sibi ad tempus datās semper habitūrōs esse.

   Dīvitiae rēsque externae cum homine manent dum Fortūna cum eō manet, sed semper cum Fortūnā manent.

5. Cūr hominēs dīcuntur vīvere sīcut in māgnā rotā?

   Haec rota circum axem semper versātur.

   Fortūna hanc rotam possidet.

   Omnia in vītā hominum semper mūtantur.

6. Cūr prō certō scīre dēbet homō, quī dīvitiās et honōrēs habet, sē tandem illās rēs relictūrum esse?

   Fortūna omnia possidet.

   Homō, quī in rotā Fortūnae sublātus erit, posteā prō certō dēscendet et cadet.

   Hominēs putant sē rēs sibi ad tempus datās semper habitūrōs esse.

TALKING

accendō, accendere, accendī, accēnsum – to light

aperiō, aperīre, aperuī, apertum – to open

candēla, candēlae, f. – candle

celebrō, celebrāre, celebrāvī, celebrātum – to celebrate

diēs nātālis fēlīcissimus – an extremely happy birthday

diēs nātālis fēlīx – a happy birthday

diēs nātālis, m. – birthday

fasciculus, fasciculī, m. – package, parcel

Grātissimī vēnistis. "Welcome to you all ([literally] very pleasing you have come)."

lībum, lībī, n. – cake

nātālicia, nātāliciae, f. – a birthday party

nātāliciam agitāre – to put on/celebrate a birthday party

nātālicium (dōnum), n. – birthday gift

Quot annōs nāta/us es? "How old are you?"

Septendecim annōs nāta/us sum "I am seventeen years old."

Diēs nātālis tibi fēlīx sit! "Happy birthday!"

Sit tibi Fortūna propitia! "May Fortune be kind to you!"

A BIRTHDAY PARTY

HELEN OPENS THE DOOR OF HER PARENTS' HOUSE TO ADMIT MARK, CHRISTY, AND MARY, WHO BRING BRIGHTLY WRAPPED PACKAGES.

Marīa, Mārcus, Christīna: (*IN UNISON*) Salvē (*greetings*), Helena! Sit tibi Fortūna propitia nōn sōlum hōc diē nātālī sed etiam per tōtam (*whole*) vītam!

Helena: Grātissimī vēnistis! Diēs nātālis meus erit fēlīcissimus, quia (*because*) vēnistis! Bonum est nātālem diem cum amīcīs celebrāre.

Mārcus: Nātāliciam apud tē agitāre cupimus. Dōna nātālicia habēmus multa.

Helena: Sī mihi dōna erunt data tot (*so many*) et tanta, dīvitiās māgnās habēbō.

Christīna: Lībum etiam habēmus.

Helena: Mox comedēmus. Prīmum (*first*) autem fasciculōs illōs pulchrōs aperīre cupiō.

Christīna: Quot annōs, Helena, hodiē (*today*) nāta es?

Helena: Hodiē septendecim annōs nāta sum.

Christīna: Itaque septendecim candēlās in lībō pōnere dēbēbimus.

Mārcus: Quis candēlās accendet?

Helena: Ego!

Mārcus: Bene. (*Fine.*) Deinde vehementer (*strongly*) efflāre (*blow out*) dēbēbis omnēsque candēlās simul (*simultaneously*) exstinguere. Tunc lībum—sed nōn candēlās—comedēmus!

Helena: Exspectāte! Prīmum fasciculōs illōs aperiam, deinde candēlās accendēmus lībumque comedēmus!

VOCABULARY TO KNOW

NOUNS

adulēscēns, adulēscentis, m./f. – young man, young lady

axis, axis, m. – axle, axis

barba, barbae, f. – beard

carō, carnis, f. – meat, flesh

cōnstantia, cōnstantiae, f. – constancy

cor, cordis, n. – heart

dīvitiae, dīvitiārum, f. pl. – wealth, riches

fortūna, fortūnae, f. – fortune, the goddess Fortune

fūr, fūris, m. – thief

fūrtum, fūrtī, n. – theft

herba, herbae, f. – plant, vegetation

honor, honōris, m. – honor, public office or distinction

inīquitās, inīquitātis, f. – injustice, mischief

lēx, lēgis, f. – law

pellis, pellis, f. – skin, hide

pōmum, pōmī, n. – fruit

proelium, proeliī, n. – battle, combat

rota, rotae, f. – wheel

vestīmentum, vestīmentī, n. – a garment, (pl.) clothes

vulnus, vulneris, n. – wound

DEMONSTRATIVE PRONOUNS/ADJECTIVES

hic, haec, hoc – this, latter

ille, illa, illud – that, former

ADJECTIVES

aequus, aequa, aequum – even; aequō animō – indifferently

aliēnus, aliēna, aliēnum + ā/ab + ablative – foreign to, inconsistent with

dīvīnus, dīvīna, dīvīnum – divine

externus, externa, externum – outward, external

ferōx, ferōcis (genitive) – fierce, ferocious

futūrus, futūra, futūrum – about to be (the future active participle of *sum, esse, fuī*)

hūmānus, hūmāna, hūmānum – human

pauper, pauperis (genitive) – poor

plēnus + genitive or + ablative – full of

terribilis, terribile – terrifying

ūllus, ūlla, ūllum – any

VERBS

abundō, abundāre, abundāvī, abundātum + ablative – to abound with

accipiō, accipere, accēpī, acceptum – to accept, receive

accūsō, accūsāre, accūsāvī, accūsātum + accusative + genitive – to accuse someone of something

colō, colere, coluī, cultum – to worship, cultivate

coquō, coquere, coxī, coctum – to cook

crēscō, crēscere, crēvī, —— – to grow

dēlectō, dēlectāre, dēlectāvī, dēlectātum – to delight, please

dēscendō, dēscendere, dēscendī, dēscēnsum – to descend

egeō, egēre, eguī, —— (+ ablative) – to lack something

ēripiō, ēripere, ēripuī, ēreptum – to snatch away

errō, errāre, errāvī, errātum – to wander, make a mistake

lūdō, lūdere, lūsī, lūsum – to play

mūtō, mūtāre, mūtāvī, mūtātum – to change

possideō, possidēre, possēdī, possessum – to possess

pūniō, pūnīre, pūnīvī, pūnītum – to punish

recipiō, recipere, recēpī, receptum – to take back

reprehendō, reprehendere, reprehendī, reprehēnsum – to blame, rebuke

sānō, sānāre, sānāvī, sānātum – to heal

sedeō, sedēre, sēdī, sessum – to sit

terō, terere, trīvī, trītum – to wear out, rub

tollō, tollere, sustulī, sublātum – to lift up, raise; to destroy

versō, versāre, versāvī, versātum – to turn

vīvō, vīvere, vīxī, vīctum – to live

vulnerō, vulnerāre, vulnerāvī, vulnerātum – to wound

ADVERBS

celeriter – swiftly

forīs – outside, in the open

noctū – during the night

paene – almost

PREPOSITIONS

circum + accusative – around

inter + accusative – between, among

CONJUNCTION

postquam – after

PREPOSITIONAL PHRASE USED ADVERBIALLY

prō certō – for certain, for sure

▶ EXERCISE 1

Conjugate the following verb in the perfect passive voice.

1. *vulnerō, vulnerāre, vulnerāvī, vulnerātum*

Conjugate the following verb in the pluperfect passive voice.

1. *mūtō, mūtāre, mūtāvī, mūtātum*

Conjugate the following verb in the future perfect passive voice.

1. *ēripiō, ēripere, ēripuī, ēreptum*

▶ EXERCISE 2

Write the perfect passive and future active participles of the following verbs and translate both forms.

Example: accūsō.

accūsātus, accūsāta, accūsātum   accused *or* having been accused

accūsātūrus, accūsātūra, accūsātūrum   about to accuse *or* going to accuse *or* intending to accuse

1. coquō
2. dēlectō
3. sānō
4. terō
5. versō

▶ EXERCISE 3

Decline the following phrases.

1. *hoc pōmum*
2. *illa inīquitās*

▶ EXERCISE 4

Change the direct statement into an indirect statement using the accusative and infinitive construction. Make the tense and voice of the infinitive fit the context. Then translate the sentence.

Example: Fortūna poētae dīcit: "Multa dedī et nihil aliud iam dabō."
Fortūna poētae dīcit sē multa dedisse et nihil aliud sē esse datūram.
Fortune says to the poet that she has given many things and that she will give nothing else (other).

1. Poēta dīcit: "Sum ā fortūnā relictus et omnia bona sunt ab eā ērepta."
2. Poēta dīcit: "Fortūnam fūrtī accūsābō."
3. Nam poēta dīcit: "Omnēs rēs prō certō possidēbam."
4. Fortūna dīcit: "Omnia in vītā hominum semper mūtantur."
5. Fortūna quoque dīcit: "Hominēs vīvunt sīcut in māgnā rotā."

▶ EXERCISE 5

Fill in the blanks with the correct perfect passive or future active participle of the verbs in parentheses. Make the participle agree with the noun in case, number, and gender. Translate the sentences.

Example: Faciēs _____ Hūnnōrum sunt terribilēs. (vulnerō)
    Hūnnī, Hūnnōrum, m. pl. – Huns
Faciēs vulnerātae Hūnnōrum sunt terribilēs.   The wounded faces of the Huns are terrible.

1. Hūnī _____ terribilēs vidērī cupiunt. (pugnō)
2. Hūnī vestīmenta ex animālium pellibus _____ gerunt. (faciō)
3. Hūnī carnem nōn _____, sed _____ comedere solent. (coquō, terō)
4. Eī nōn sōlum carnem, sed etiam herbās ex terrā _____ capiunt. (ēripiō)
5. Hūnī _____ in equīs suīs sedent. (dormiō)

▶ EXERCISE 6

Translate into Latin.

1. Augustine was blamed. For many bad things had been done by him.

    Augustīnus, Augustīnī, m. – Augustine

2. The tree was sought by Augustine and by his friends. Plans had been made by them about a theft.

3. All the fruits had been taken from the tree. Not many of them, however, were eaten by the thieves.

4. After Augustine is accused of theft, he will be suffering. (use the future perfect in the subordinate clause)

5. If the injustice is understood by Augustine, he will want to be punished. (use future perfect in the subordinate clause)

Augustine wearing the headdress (miter), the cape (cope),
the ring, and holding the staff (crozier) of his bishopry.

VULCAN

The last god in the Olympian pantheon is Vulcan, known in Greek as Hephaestus. He is the son of Jupiter and Juno, although according to one myth Juno produced Vulcan without a male partner, owing to her jealousy of Jupiter for giving birth to Minerva from his head. However, Vulcan had the unfortunate physical imperfection of being lame in both feet. Upon seeing her newborn offspring, Juno, ashamed at his deformity, cast him out of heaven. Vulcan later took revenge on his mean-spirited mother by fashioning for her a special golden chair from which she could not move when she sat in it. Then he departed from Olympus, refusing to release Juno until Bacchus, god of wine, made him drunk, which caused Vulcan to return. In another ancient source, Vulcan's lameness is explained as the result of his interference in a quarrel between Jupiter and Juno. Jupiter, in a fit of rage, is said to have grasped Vulcan by the ankle and flung him down to earth.

Vulcan is also a blacksmith, and in that capacity was portrayed as making Jupiter's thunderbolts. He is the god of fire as well, and of the arts in which fire is employed. He is a highly skilled craftsman in spite of his physical handicap, and is noted for creating legendary

A modern statue of Vulcan overlooking Birmingham, Alabama.

works of art, such as the shields of the Greek hero Achilles and the Roman hero Aeneas. Special honor was paid to Vulcan on the Greek island of Lemnos, where he was supposed to have landed after being tossed out of heaven; the words "volcano" and "volcanic" are derived from Vulcan's Latin name.

You have now completed all the mythology readings about the pantheon of the gods and goddesses. In ancient Rome, there was a temple built to all the gods, called the Pantheon.

The Doric-style Temple of Hephaestus, once known as the Theseion, was constructed in the fifth century BCE and overlooks the agora in Athens.

The original Pantheon, a temple to all the gods, was built by Agrippa in 27 BCE after the victory at the battle of Actium in 31 BCE. Burned in the great fire of Rome, the Pantheon was rebuilt in 125 CE during the reign of the emperor Hadrian.

The Romans were known for their use of domes in architecture. The interior dome of the Pantheon features a hole in the roof, called the *oculus* or "eye."

READ AND TRANSLATE THE FOLLOWING PASSAGE

You have read about Aeneas in Chapter 11.

Aēnēās diū per multās terrās māgnā cōnstantiā errāverat et per multa maria nāvigāverat. Multae rēs ab eō erant vīsae atque factae. Terrae aliēnae perīculōrum plēnae ab eō erant petītae. Dīdō rēgīna ab eō erat amāta et posteā relicta. Tandem Aēnēās in Ītaliā prope patriam futūram erat. Ibi hostēs terribilēs eum exspectābant. Cum iīs pugnātūrus Aēnēās armīs egēbat. Ēius māter Venus Vulcānum petīvit et rogāvit: "Poterisne scūtum prō fīliō meō parāre?" Venus dīxit Aēnēam esse hostēs victūrum et post Aēnēam Rōmānōs māgnam glōriam habitūrōs esse. Dīxit Vulcānum haec omnia in scūtō caelāre dēbēre. Vulcānus novum scūtum excūdit, quō armātus Aēnēās in proelium intrāvit et hostēs vīcit.

Aēnēās, Aēnēae, m. – Aeneas
caelō, caelāre, caelāvī, caelātum – to engrave
Dīdō, Dīdōnis, f. – Dido
excūdō, excūdere, excūdī, excūsum – to forge
glōria, glōriae, f. – glory

Ītalia, Ītaliae, f. – Italy
scūtum, scūtī, n. – shield
Venus, Veneris, f. – Venus
Vulcānus, Vulcānī, m. – Vulcan

CONNECTING WITH THE ANCIENT WORLD

ROMAN EDUCATION

During the early republic, Roman fathers taught their sons to read and write, while the education of girls was limited to spinning and weaving. But in later periods Roman parents of means entrusted the education of their children to slaves of Greek origin, known as *paedagōgoi,* "leaders of the children," and private tutors with special expertise in literature and rhetoric, usually slaves or freed slaves. While girls did not attend school outside the home, they often benefited from the presence of learned tutors in their households, and there is much evidence that Roman women were readers and writers.

A Roman primary school was called the *lūdus litterārius.* Children from elite backgrounds (sons of equestrians and senators) attended school. However, Horace's father, a freedman, had his son educated at Rome rather than at a local school. Pupils usually wrote on wax tablets, using the back of the pen to smooth the wax when they made an error they wished to erase. From this practice came the proverb *Saepe stilum vertās,* "Turn the pen often," an admonition to revise one's writings frequently. Only capital letters were used. The pace of learning was fairly slow. Teachers were allowed to inflict corporal punishment if pupils misbehaved. The first century CE Roman poet Martial complained about the classroom noise that resulted from shouting and beatings.

Boys attended Roman middle schools, or *schola grammaticī,* from the age of twelve on, where the program of study focused on Latin and Greek grammar and literature. At this level students read aloud and recited passages previously learned by heart, and also listened to the meticulous explanations of the text they were reading by the teacher, called a *grammaticus.* Enunciation was stressed because of the importance of oratory in Roman public life.

From the second to third century CE, this relief on a stele shows a teacher with a student.

The upper school was known as a *schola rhētoris*, and there, from age fifteen on, students concentrated on studying rhetoric from skilled experts, the rhetors. They were instructed in how to compose and arrange the six parts of a public speech: the *exordium*, beginning; *nārrātiō*, the statement of facts; *partītiō*, the outline; *cōnfirmātiō*, the proof; *refūtātiō*, the refutation; and the *perōrātiō*, summing up, or conclusion. Teachers in schools of rhetoric also gave the students exercises in writing *chrīae*, sentences proposed for grammatical and logical development in different ways. Students often were assigned to present imaginary cases, and write speeches defending both sides of a given case.

For further education especially talented and ambitious Roman males, such as Cicero, traveled to Greece, listened to the illustrious rhetoricians there, and visited the libraries, *bibliothēcae*. The most famous library in the classical world was that of Alexandria in Egypt. Built in the third century BCE, it was burned during the later part of classical antiquity. There were several libraries in Athens, as well as one on the island of Rhodes, located at the school attended by Cicero. Libraries at Rome were at first private collections, but in the latter part of the first century BCE the first public library was established on the Aventine Hill.

The façade of the library of Tiberius Julius Celsus in Ephesus.

EXPLORING ROMAN LIBRARIES

PUBLIC LIBRARIES AND THEIR BOOKS

Formal education in the Roman world had three stages: a teacher called a *magister* or *litterātor* taught the basics of reading, writing, and mathematics; the *grammaticus* taught language and literature, especially poetry; and in the final stage (the most important for those destined for or aspiring to a public career in the courts and politics) a *rhētor* supervised training in public speaking.

Before the late first century BCE, those at Rome who desired "further education" through reading had two resources available to them: booksellers' shops (which seem to have offered mostly "school books," that is, those texts most used by schoolmasters, like Vergil's *Aeneid*, and "best sellers," like elegiac poetry) and friends with book collections. Some wealthy aristocrats owned huge libraries: Sulla took "the library of Aristotle" from the conquered city of Athens in 84 BCE, and Lucullus, who became notorious for a life of luxurious retirement from political activity, used his library to attract Greek scholars to his household. The orator and author Cicero mentions a library in at least three of his residences: the *domus* on the Palatine in Rome, the country villa at Tusculum, and the seaside house at Antium. As in other areas of life, the Romans adopted the Greek name for an institution associated with Greek culture: the Greek word *bibliotheke* became the Latin *bibliothēca*.

Julius Caesar planned many improvements for the city of Rome, including "making public the largest possible Greek and Latin libraries," according to his biographer Suetonius (who was himself in charge of Rome's public libraries). Caesar may have hoped that his library would surpass the famous library at Alexandria in Egypt, established by the Macedonian dynasty of the Ptolemies in an effort to preserve all of Greek literature; at the least, Caesar's library would have put Latin literature on an equal basis with Greek literature.

Julius Caesar did not live to see the fulfillment of his plans for a "public library," but Asinius Pollio, one of Caesar's closest lieutenants, established a library between 39 and 28 BCE in the Ātrium Libertātis, a public building on the slopes of the Capitoline hill that had previously housed a shrine of the goddess Liberty and the records of the censors. Rome soon had two more libraries, both associated with the building program of the emperor Augustus: one in the porticoes attached to the temple of Apollo, next to the emperor's house on the Palatine hill, and another in the Porticus of Octavia in the Campus Martius. Subsequent emperors built more public libraries, including the library in the Temple of Peace built by Vespasian and the library in the Forum of Trajan.

The builders of Rome's public libraries, and the authors whose works would be in them, expected at least some members of the public to enter them. Horace and Ovid anticipated readers of their poetry in Rome's first public libraries. When an ancient author mentions by name specific users of Rome's libraries, however, they are either writers or scholars, or connected to the emperor's family, or both. Readers seem to have treated Rome's public libraries during the Empire just as readers had treated private libraries in aristocrats' homes during the Republic, as private spaces where scholars and friends gathered to discuss literature and philosophy.

The Forum of Trajan provides the best evidence available for the appearance of Rome's public libraries. Two rooms, one to either side of the courtyard around the Column of Trajan, show the plan considered characteristic of Roman libraries: wall-niches into which book cabinets were set, columns separating the niches, a low platform running around the base of the wall giving access to the book cabinets, unobstructed floor space where readers might sit, marble and other colored stone covering walls and floors, and separate rooms for the Latin and Greek collections. Libraries were decorated with large numbers of statues, portrait busts, or both, especially of authors.

Perhaps inspired by the example of the emperors in Rome, some aristocrats donated magnificent libraries to their home towns: the orator and administrator Pliny the Younger dedicated a library in Comum in northern Italy, and the consul Tiberius Julius Aquila dedicated a library to his father, the consul Tiberius Julius Celsus, in Ephesus in the province of Asia. In the interior of the library of Celsus, at the middle of the back wall, was an apse; beneath the apse lay a chamber, accessible from a passage that separated the

Near Trajan's column was the library of Trajan.

A close-up view of the façade of the library of Tiberius Julius Celsus in Ephesus.

inner and outer walls of the library building. This chamber held a marble sarcophagus containing a lead coffin, apparently that of Celsus. He seems to have achieved the rare privilege of burial within a city; and the library named after him served also as his tomb monument.

Some believe that the great imperial bath buildings or *thermae* of Rome included libraries, which we might take as evidence for a wide reading audience in Rome. The baths of Trajan, Caracalla, and Diocletian all contain rooms identified as libraries on the basis of their architectural form, particularly the presence of wall-niches in paired rooms. The presence of libraries fits with the general idea that the *thermae* provided facilities not only for bathing but for a wide range of athletic, social, and cultural activities. The evidence for libraries in bathing complexes, however, is weak. No literary evidence or inscription clearly proves that there were ever libraries in baths; and no archaeological remains of rooms in baths can be shown definitely to have been libraries.

The standard form of "book" for the Romans was the roll; a reader needed both hands to handle a roll, one to unroll a new section for reading, the other hand to roll up the section already read. A roll might be made up of sheets either of papyrus or animal skin. For papyrus paper, two layers of strips from the plant's soft interior, at right angles to one another, were pressed together, releasing a natural gummy substance, which bonded together the strips and layers. Animal skins (of sheep, goats, or cattle) might be tanned to produce leather, or a more complicated process of washing, depilating, soaking in lime, and stretching and drying on a frame might be used to produce parchment. Dried sheets of paper were glued together, sheets of skin were sewn together, to form a roll. Rolls were written on only one side; but once a roll was no longer in use, pages might be cut from the roll to be reused: preserved papyrus sheets from Greco-Roman Egypt often have literary texts on one side (the original side used, or "rectō") and private documents—letters, receipts, accounts—on the other (the reused or "versō"). The usual writing implement was a reed pen with a split nib, like a modern fountain pen; black ink was made from soot or lampblack mixed with gum.

One set of "library rules" survives from the Roman Empire, on an inscription from the library of Pantainos (named after the man who donated it), which sat beside a very busy corner of the Agora in Athens: it specifies the hours of operation ("from the first hour to the sixth hour") and that no book is to be removed from the library. The inscription does not say who can enter and use the library. In a world where no more than ten percent of the population may have been literate, perhaps it was unnecessary to specify who could use the library: those with the necessary education, leisure time, and desire to visit a public library were probably few in number. Roman public libraries were monuments to literature and culture, and they demonstrated that the Romans were worthy successors to the cultural heritage and achievements of the Greeks.

T. Keith Dix
Associate Professor of Classics
University of Georgia
Athens, Georgia

PHRASES, QUOTATIONS, AND ABBREVIATIONS RELATING TO SCHOOLS, LIBRARIES, AND BOOKS

PHRASES AND QUOTATIONS

- Alma māter. "Nurturing mother." Common name for a university that a person has attended.

- Alumnus/Alumna. "A nurtured <son/daughter>." Graduate of a college or a university.

- Ex librīs. "From the books," words often found on special plates inside the cover of books indicating the owner, whose name should be in the genitive case.

- Floruit. (abbreviated *fl.*) "Flourished." An indication of the time when a certain person was most active.

- Vādemēcum. "Go with me!" A small manual or reference work.

- Verbātim. "Word by word," precisely and accurately.

ABBREVIATIONS

- AD. An abbreviation for *Annō Dominī*, "in the year of the Lord," an older expression for CE, "Common Era."

- e.g. An abbreviation for *exemplī grātiā*, "for the sake of an example or illustration."

Ex Librīs, a Latin phrase meaning "From the books," is sometimes found on a bookplate pasted on the inside cover of a book, followed by the name of the person who owns the book.

APPENDIX A

CHRONOLOGICAL LIST OF THE AUTHORS AND WORKS STUDIED

Titus Maccius Plautus (b. Sarsina, Umbria; 254 BCE–184 BCE), *Menaechmī*, "The Menaechmi."

Publius Terentius Afer (b. Libya; between 195 and 185 BCE–ca. 159 BCE), *Adelphī*, "The Brothers."

Mārcus Tullius Cicero (b. Arpinum, southeast of Rome; 106 BCE–43 BCE), *Dē officiīs*, "On Duties"; *Epistulae*, "Letters."

Gāius Iūlius Caesar (b. Rome; 100 BCE–44 BCE), *Dē bellō Gallicō*, "On the Gallic War."

Gāius Valerius Catullus (b. Verona; 84 BCE–54 BCE), *Carmina*, "Poems."

Cornēlius Nepos (b. northern Italy; ca. 100 BCE–ca. 25 BCE), *Dē virīs illustribus*, "On Famous Men."

Gāius Sallustius Crispus (b. Aminternum, near Rome; 86 BCE–35/34 BCE), *Dē coniūrātiōne Catilīnae*, "About the Plot of Catiline."

Publius Vergilius Maro (b. Mantua; 70 BCE–19 BCE), *Aeneīs*, "Aeneid."

Titus Līvius (b. Padua; 59 BCE–17 CE), *Ab Urbe Conditā*, "From the Founding of the City."

Quintus Horātius Flaccus (b. Venusia, southern Italy; 65 BCE–8 BCE), *Saturae*, "Satires."

Publius Ovidius Nāso (b. Sulmo, Italian Apennines; 43 BCE–17 CE), *Metamorphōsēs*, "Transformations."

Lūcius Annaeus Seneca (b. Corduba, Spain; ca. 4 BCE–65 CE), *Epistulae*, "Letters."

Gāius Plīnius Caecilius Secundus (b. Como, northern Italy; ca. 61 CE–ca. 112/113 CE), *Epistulae*, "Letters."

Cornēlius Tacitus (b. probably northern Italy; ca. 56 CE–116/120 CE), *Annālēs*, "Annals."

Āpulēius (b. Madaurus, North Africa; second century CE), *Metamorphōsēs*, "Transformations."

Ammiānus Marcellīnus (b. probably Antiochia, Syria; ca. 330/395 CE), *Rēs gestae ā fīne Cornēliī Tacitī*, "Deeds Accomplished from the End of Cornelius Tacitus' History."

Aurēlius Augustīnus (b. Tagaste, North Africa; 354 CE–430 CE), *Cōnfessiōnēs*, "Confessions."

Anicius Manlius Severīnus Boēthius (b. Rome; ca. 480 CE–ca. 524 CE), *Cōnsōlātiō Philosophiae*, "Consolation of Philosophy."

APPENDIX B

ADDITIONAL STATE MOTTOES

Ad astra per aspera. "To the stars through difficulties!" Motto of Kansas

Alīs volat propriīs. "Flies with own wings." Motto of Oregon

Cēdant arma togae. "Let arms yield to the toga." Motto of Wyoming

Crēscit eundō. "It grows by going." Motto of New Mexico

Deō grātiās habeāmus. "Let us be grateful to God." Motto of Kentucky

Dīrigō. "I direct." Motto of Maine

Dītat Deus. "God enriches." Motto of Arizona

Dum spīrō spērō. "As long as I breathe, I hope." Motto of South Carolina

Esse quam vidērī. "To be rather than to seem." Motto of North Carolina

Estō perpetua! "Be eternal!" Motto of Idaho

Excelsior. "Ever upward." Motto of New York

Labor omnia vincit. "Work overcomes all things." Motto of Oklahoma

Nīl sine nūmine. "Nothing without divine will." Motto of Colorado

Quae sūrsum volō vidēre. "I want to see the things that are above." Motto of Minnesota

Quī transtulit sustinet. "He who has transplanted sustains." Motto of Connecticut

Sī quaeris paenīnsulam amoenam, circumspice! "If you are seeking a lovely peninsula, look around!" Motto of Michigan

Virtūte et armīs. "With courage and with weapons." Motto of Mississippi

State seal of Arizona with the Latin words *Dītat Deus.*

APPENDIX C

GRAMMATICAL FORMS AND PARADIGMS

Only forms taught in the book are listed in this appendix.

DECLENSIONS OF NOUNS

First Declension

	Singular	Plural
Nominative	lupa	lupae
Genitive	lupae	lupārum
Dative	lupae	lupīs
Accusative	lupam	lupās
Ablative	lupā	lupīs
Vocative	lupa	lupae

Second Declension: *amīcus*

	Singular	Plural
Nominative	amīcus	amīcī
Genitive	amīcī	amīcōrum
Dative	amīcō	amīcīs
Accusative	amīcum	amīcōs
Ablative	amīcō	amīcīs
Vocative	amīce	amīcī

Second Declension: *puer*

	Singular	Plural
Nominative	puer	puerī
Genitive	puerī	puerōrum
Dative	puerō	puerīs
Accusative	puerum	puerōs
Ablative	puerō	puerīs
Vocative	puer	puerī

Second Declension: *ager*

	Singular	Plural
Nominative	ager	agrī
Genitive	agrī	agrōrum
Dative	agrō	agrīs
Accusative	agrum	agrōs
Ablative	agrō	agrīs
Vocative	ager	agrī

Second Declension: *vir*

	Singular	Plural
Nominative	vir	virī
Genitive	virī	virōrum
Dative	virō	virīs
Accusative	virum	virōs
Ablative	virō	virīs
Vocative	vir	virī

Second Declension: *bellum*

	Singular	Plural
Nominative	bellum	bella
Genitive	bellī	bellōrum
Dative	bellō	bellīs
Accusative	bellum	bella
Ablative	bellō	bellīs
Vocative	bellum	bella

Third Declension: Masculine and Feminine Nouns

	Singular	Plural
Nominative	passer	passerēs
Genitive	passeris	passerum
Dative	passerī	passeribus
Accusative	passerem	passerēs
Ablative	passere	passeribus
Vocative	passer	passerēs

Third Declension: Neuter Nouns

	Singular	Plural
Nominative	tempus	tempora
Genitive	temporis	temporum
Dative	temporī	temporibus
Accusative	tempus	tempora
Ablative	tempore	temporibus
Vocative	tempus	tempora

Third Declension: *i*-stem Nouns
Same Number of Syllables (Masculine and Feminine)

	Singular	Plural
Nominative	cīvis	cīvēs
Genitive	cīvis	cīvium
Dative	cīvī	cīvibus
Accusative	cīvem	cīvēs
Ablative	cīve	cīvibus
Vocative	cīvis	cīvēs

Third Declension: *i*-stem Nouns
Different Number of Syllables (Masculine and Feminine)

	Singular	Plural
Nominative	urbs	urbēs
Genitive	urbis	urbium
Dative	urbī	urbibus
Accusative	urbem	urbēs
Ablative	urbe	urbibus
Vocative	urbs	urbēs

Third Declension: *i*-stem Nouns
(Neuters in -*al*, -*ar*, -*e*)

	Singular	Plural
Nominative	mare	maria
Genitive	maris	marium
Dative	marī	maribus
Accusative	mare	maria
Ablative	marī	maribus
Vocative	mare	maria

Third Declension: *vīs*

	Singular	Plural
Nominative	vīs	vīrēs
Genitive	—	vīrium
Dative	—	vīribus
Accusative	vim	vīrēs
Ablative	vī	vīribus
Vocative	vīs	vīrēs

Fourth Declension: Masculine and Feminine Nouns

	Singular	Plural
Nominative	tumultus	tumultūs
Genitive	tumultūs	tumultuum
Dative	tumultuī	tumultibus
Accusative	tumultum	tumultūs
Ablative	tumultū	tumultibus
Vocative	tumultus	tumultūs

Fourth Declension: Neuter Nouns

	Singular	Plural
Nominative	cornū	cornua
Genitive	cornūs	cornuum
Dative	cornū	cornibus
Accusative	cornū	cornua
Ablative	cornū	cornibus
Vocative	cornū	cornua

Fourth Declension: *domus*

	Singular	Plural
Nominative	domus	domūs
Genitive	domūs	domuum (domōrum)
Dative	domuī (domō)	domibus
Accusative	domum	domōs (domūs)
Ablative	domō (domū)	domibus
Vocative	domus	domūs

Fifth Declension: *rēs*

	Singular	Plural
Nominative	rēs	rēs
Genitive	reī	rērum
Dative	reī	rēbus
Accusative	rem	rēs
Ablative	rē	rēbus
Vocative	rēs	rēs

Fifth Declension: *diēs*

	Singular	Plural
Nominative	diēs	diēs
Genitive	diēī	diērum
Dative	diēī	diēbus
Accusative	diem	diēs
Ablative	diē	diēbus
Vocative	diēs	diēs

DECLENSIONS OF ADJECTIVES

Adjectives of the First and Second Declension: *iūstus*

	Singular			Plural		
	Masculine	**Feminine**	**Neuter**	**Masculine**	**Feminine**	**Neuter**
Nominative	iūstus	iūsta	iūstum	iūstī	iūstae	iūsta
Genitive	iūstī	iūstae	iūstī	iūstōrum	iūstārum	iūstōrum
Dative	iūstō	iūstae	iūstō	iūstīs	iūstīs	iūstīs
Accusative	iūstum	iūstam	iūstum	iūstōs	iūstās	iūsta
Ablative	iūstō	iūstā	iūstō	iūstīs	iūstīs	iūstīs
Vocative	iūste	iūsta	iūstum	iūstī	iūstae	iūsta

Adjectives of the First and Second Declension: *pulcher*

	Singular			Plural		
	Masculine	**Feminine**	**Neuter**	**Masculine**	**Feminine**	**Neuter**
Nominative	pulcher	pulchra	pulchrum	pulchrī	pulchrae	pulchra
Genitive	pulchrī	pulchrae	pulchrī	pulchrōrum	pulchrārum	pulchrōrum
Dative	pulchrō	pulchrae	pulchrō	pulchrīs	pulchrīs	pulchrīs
Accusative	pulchrum	pulchram	pulchrum	pulchrōs	pulchrās	pulchra
Ablative	pulchrō	pulchrā	pulchrō	pulchrīs	pulchrīs	pulchrīs
Vocative	pulcher	pulchra	pulchrum	pulchrī	pulchrae	pulchra

Adjectives of the First and Second Declension: *miser*

	Singular			Plural		
	Masculine	**Feminine**	**Neuter**	**Masculine**	**Feminine**	**Neuter**
Nominative	miser	misera	miserum	miserī	miserae	misera
Genitive	miserī	miserae	miserī	miserōrum	miserārum	miserōrum
Dative	miserō	miserae	miserō	miserīs	miserīs	miserīs
Accusative	miserum	miseram	miserum	miserōs	miserās	misera
Ablative	miserō	miserā	miserō	miserīs	miserīs	miserīs
Vocative	miser	misera	miserum	miserī	miserae	misera

Adjectives of the Third Declension: Three Nominative Endings

	Singular			Plural		
	Masculine	**Feminine**	**Neuter**	**Masculine**	**Feminine**	**Neuter**
Nominative	ācer	ācris	ācre	ācrēs	ācrēs	ācria
Genitive	ācris	ācris	ācris	ācrium	ācrium	ācrium
Dative	ācrī	ācrī	ācrī	ācribus	ācribus	ācribus
Accusative	ācrem	ācrem	ācre	ācrēs	ācrēs	ācria
Ablative	ācrī	ācrī	ācrī	ācribus	ācribus	ācribus
Vocative	ācer	ācris	ācre	ācrēs	ācrēs	ācria

Adjectives of the Third Declension: Two Nominative Endings

	Singular		Plural	
	Masculine / Feminine	**Neuter**	**Masculine / Feminine**	**Neuter**
Nominative	fortis	forte	fortēs	fortia
Genitive	fortis	fortis	fortium	fortium
Dative	fortī	fortī	fortibus	fortibus
Accusative	fortem	forte	fortēs	fortia
Ablative	fortī	fortī	fortibus	fortibus
Vocative	fortis	forte	fortēs	fortia

Adjectives of the Third Declension: One Nominative Ending

	Singular			Plural		
	Masculine	**Feminine**	**Neuter**	**Masculine**	**Feminine**	**Neuter**
Nominative	fēlīx	fēlīx	fēlīx	fēlīcēs	fēlīcēs	fēlīcia
Genitive	fēlīcis	fēlīcis	fēlīcis	fēlīcium	fēlīcium	fēlīcium
Dative	fēlīcī	fēlīcī	fēlīcī	fēlīcibus	fēlīcibus	fēlīcibus
Accusative	fēlīcem	fēlīcem	fēlīx	fēlīcēs	fēlīcēs	fēlīcia
Ablative	fēlīcī	fēlīcī	fēlīcī	fēlīcibus	fēlīcibus	fēlīcibus
Vocative	fēlīx	fēlīx	fēlīx	fēlīcēs	fēlīcēs	fēlīcia

DECLENSIONS OF PRONOUNS

Personal Pronouns: First and Second Person

	First singular	Second singular	First plural	Second plural
Nominative	ego	tū	nōs	vōs
Genitive	meī	tuī	nostrī/nostrum	vestrī/vestrum
Dative	mihi	tibi	nōbīs	vōbīs
Accusative	mē	tē	nōs	vōs
Ablative	mē	tē	nōbīs	vōbīs

Personal Pronoun: Third Person; Demonstrative Pronoun/Adjective: *is, ea, id*

	Singular			Plural		
	Masculine	**Feminine**	**Neuter**	**Masculine**	**Feminine**	**Neuter**
Nominative	is	ea	id	eī (iī)	eae	ea
Genitive	ēius	ēius	ēius	eōrum	eārum	eōrum
Dative	eī	eī	eī	eīs (iīs)	eīs (iīs)	eīs (iīs)
Accusative	eum	eam	id	eōs	eās	ea
Ablative	eō	eā	eō	eīs (iīs)	eīs (iīs)	eīs (iīs)

Possessive Adjectives

First Person Singular	meus, mea, meum
Second Person Singular	tuus, tua, tuum
Third Person Singular	suus, sua, suum / ēius
First Person Plural	noster, nostra, nostrum
Second Person Plural	vester, vestra, vestrum
Third Person Plural	suus, sua, suum / eōrum, eārum, eōrum

Relative Pronoun and Interrogative Adjective: *quī, quae, quod*

	Singular			Plural		
	Masculine	**Feminine**	**Neuter**	**Masculine**	**Feminine**	**Neuter**
Nominative	quī	quae	quod	quī	quae	quae
Genitive	cūius	cūius	cūius	quōrum	quārum	quōrum
Dative	cui	cui	cui	quibus	quibus	quibus
Accusative	quem	quam	quod	quōs	quās	quae
Ablative	quō	quā	quō	quibus	quibus	quibus

Interrogative Pronoun: *quis, quid?*

	Singular		Plural		
	Masculine / Feminine	Neuter	Masculine	Feminine	Neuter
Nominative	quis	quid	quī	quae	quae
Genitive	cūius	cūius	quōrum	quārum	quōrum
Dative	cui	cui	quibus	quibus	quibus
Accusative	quem	quid	quōs	quās	quae
Ablative	quō	quō	quibus	quibus	quibus

Interrogative Adjective: *quī, quae, quod?*

	Singular			Plural		
	Masculine	Feminine	Neuter	Masculine	Feminine	Neuter
Nominative	quī	quae	quod	quī	quae	quae
Genitive	cūius	cūius	cūius	quōrum	quārum	quōrum
Dative	cui	cui	cui	quibus	quibus	quibus
Accusative	quem	quam	quod	quōs	quās	quae
Ablative	quō	quā	quō	quibus	quibus	quibus

Demonstrative Pronoun/Adjective: *hic, haec, hoc*

	Singular			Plural		
	Masculine	Feminine	Neuter	Masculine	Feminine	Neuter
Nominative	hic	haec	hoc	hī	hae	haec
Genitive	hūius	hūius	hūius	hōrum	hārum	hōrum
Dative	huic	huic	huic	hīs	hīs	hīs
Accusative	hunc	hanc	hoc	hōs	hās	haec
Ablative	hōc	hāc	hōc	hīs	hīs	hīs

Demonstrative Pronoun/Adjective: *ille, illa, illud*

	Singular			Plural		
	Masculine	Feminine	Neuter	Masculine	Feminine	Neuter
Nominative	ille	illa	illud	illī	illae	illa
Genitive	illīus	illīus	illīus	illōrum	illārum	illōrum
Dative	illī	illī	illī	illīs	illīs	illīs
Accusative	illum	illam	illud	illōs	illās	illa
Ablative	illō	illā	illō	illīs	illīs	illīs

CONJUGATIONS OF VERBS

Present Active

	First conjugation	Second conjugation	Third conjugation	Fourth conjugation	Third conjugation -iō
First person singular	parō	teneō	petō	audiō	capiō
Second person singular	parās	tenēs	petis	audīs	capis
Third person singular	parat	tenet	petit	audit	capit
First person plural	parāmus	tenēmus	petimus	audīmus	capimus
Second person plural	parātis	tenētis	petitis	audītis	capitis
Third person plural	parant	tenent	petunt	audiunt	capiunt

Present Passive

	First conjugation	Second conjugation	Third conjugation	Fourth conjugation	Third conjugation -iō
First person singular	paror	teneor	petor	audior	capior
Second person singular	parāris	tenēris	peteris	audīris	caperis
Third person singular	parātur	tenētur	petitur	audītur	capitur
First person plural	parāmur	tenēmur	petimur	audīmur	capimur
Second person plural	parāminī	tenēminī	petiminī	audīminī	capiminī
Third person plural	parantur	tenentur	petuntur	audiuntur	capiuntur

Imperfect Active

	First conjugation	Second conjugation	Third conjugation	Fourth conjugation	Third conjugation -iō
First person singular	parābam	tenēbam	petēbam	audiēbam	capiēbam
Second person singular	parābās	tenēbās	petēbās	audiēbās	capiēbās
Third person singular	parābat	tenēbat	petēbat	audiēbat	capiēbat
First person plural	parābāmus	tenēbāmus	petēbāmus	audiēbāmus	capiēbāmus
Second person plural	parābātis	tenēbātis	petēbātis	audiēbātis	capiēbātis
Third person plural	parābant	tenēbant	petēbant	audiēbant	capiēbant

Imperfect Passive

	First conjugation	Second conjugation	Third conjugation	Fourth conjugation	Third conjugation -iō
First person singular	parābar	tenēbar	petēbar	audiēbar	capiēbar
Second person singular	parābāris	tenēbāris	petēbāris	audiēbāris	capiēbāris
Third person singular	parābātur	tenēbātur	petēbātur	audiēbātur	capiēbātur
First person plural	parābāmur	tenēbāmur	petēbāmur	audiēbāmur	capiēbāmur
Second person plural	parābāminī	tenēbāminī	petēbāminī	audiēbāminī	capiēbāminī
Third person plural	parābantur	tenēbantur	petēbantur	audiēbantur	capiēbantur

Future Active

	First conjugation	Second conjugation	Third conjugation	Fourth conjugation	Third conjugation -iō
First person singular	parābō	tenēbō	petam	audiam	capiam
Second person singular	parābis	tenēbis	petēs	audiēs	capiēs
Third person singular	parābit	tenēbit	petet	audiet	capiet
First person plural	parābimus	tenēbimus	petēmus	audiēmus	capiēmus
Second person plural	parābitis	tenēbitis	petētis	audiētis	capiētis
Third person plural	parābunt	tenēbunt	petent	audient	capient

Future Passive

	First conjugation	Second conjugation	Third conjugation	Fourth conjugation	Third conjugation -iō
First person singular	parābor	tenēbor	petar	audiar	capiar
Second person singular	parāberis	tenēberis	petēris	audiēris	capiēris
Third person singular	parābitur	tenēbitur	petētur	audiētur	capiētur
First person plural	parābimur	tenēbimur	petēmur	audiēmur	capiēmur
Second person plural	parābiminī	tenēbiminī	petēminī	audiēminī	capiēminī
Third person plural	parābuntur	tenēbuntur	petentur	audientur	capientur

Perfect Active

First person singular	parāvī
Second person singular	parāvistī
Third person singular	parāvit
First person plural	parāvimus
Second person plural	parāvistis
Third person plural	parāvērunt

Perfect Passive

First person singular	parātus, parāta, (parātum) sum
Second person singular	parātus, parāta, (parātum) es
Third person singular	parātus, parāta, parātum est
First person plural	parātī, parātae, (parāta) sumus
Second person plural	parātī, parātae, (parāta) estis
Third person plural	parātī, parātae, parāta sunt

Pluperfect Active

First person singular	parāveram
Second person singular	parāverās
Third person singular	parāverat
First person plural	parāverāmus
Second person plural	parāverātis
Third person plural	parāverant

Pluperfect Passive

First person singular	parātus, parāta, (parātum) eram
Second person singular	parātus, parāta, (parātum) erās
Third person singular	parātus, parāta, parātum erat
First person plural	parātī, parātae, (parāta) erāmus
Second person plural	parātī, parātae, (parāta) erātis
Third person plural	parātī, parātae, parāta erant

Future Perfect Active

First person singular	parāverō
Second person singular	parāveris
Third person singular	parāverit
First person plural	parāverimus
Second person plural	parāveritis
Third person plural	parāverint

Future Perfect Passive

First person singular	parātus, parāta, (parātum) erō
Second person singular	parātus, parāta, (parātum) eris
Third person singular	parātus, parāta, parātum erit
First person plural	parātī, parātae, (parāta) erimus
Second person plural	parātī, parātae, (parāta) eritis
Third person plural	parātī, parātae, parāta erunt

Present Imperative

	First conjugation	Second conjugation	Third conjugation	Fourth conjugation	Third conjugation -iō
Second person singular positive	parā	tenē	pete	audī	cape
Second person plural positive	parāte	tenēte	petite	audīte	capite
Second person singular negative	nōlī parāre	nōlī tenēre	nōlī petere	nōlī audīre	nōlī capere
Second person plural negative	nōlīte parāre	nōlīte tenēre	nōlīte petere	nōlīte audīre	nōlīte capere

Participles

Perfect passive	parātus, parāta, parātum
Future active	parātūrus, parātūra, parātūrum

Infinitives

	Active	Passive
Present	parāre	parārī
Perfect	parāvisse	parātus, parāta, parātum esse
Future	parātūrus, parātūra, parātūrum esse	—

The Irregular Verb *sum*

	Present	Imperfect	Future	Perfect	Pluperfect	Future perfect
First person singular	sum	eram	erō	fuī	fueram	fuerō
Second person singular	es	erās	eris	fuistī	fuerās	fueris
Third person singular	est	erat	erit	fuit	fuerat	fuerit
First person plural	sumus	erāmus	erimus	fuimus	fuerāmus	fuerimus
Second person plural	estis	erātis	eritis	fuistis	fuerātis	fueritis
Third person plural	sunt	erant	erunt	fuērunt	fuerant	fuerint
Infinitive	esse	—	futūrus, -a, -um esse	fuisse	—	—

The Irregular Verb *possum*

	Present	Imperfect	Future	Perfect	Pluperfect	Future perfect
First person singular	possum	poteram	poterō	potuī	potueram	potuerō
Second person singular	potes	poterās	poteris	potuistī	potuerās	potueris
Third person singular	potest	poterat	poterit	potuit	potuerat	potuerit
First person plural	possumus	poterāmus	poterimus	potuimus	potuerāmus	potuerimus
Second person plural	potestis	poterātis	poteritis	potuistis	potuerātis	potueritis
Third person plural	possunt	poterant	poterunt	potuērunt	potuerant	potuerint
Infinitive	posse	—	—	potuisse	—	—

APPENDIX D

LATIN SYNTAX

Only syntax taught in the book is listed in this appendix.

USE OF CASES

Case	Function
Nominative	Subject. Predicate nominative (noun or adjective).
Genitive	Modifier (often possession). Partitive genitive. Objective genitive.
Dative	Indirect object. Possession.
Accusative	Direct object. Place to which. Accusative subject of indirect statement.
Ablative	Agent (with passive voice). Manner. Instrument (means). Separation. Place from which. Place where.
Vocative	Direct address.

PREPOSITIONS

Preposition	Case	Meaning
ā, ab	ablative	by, from, away from
ad	accusative	towards, to, into
ante	accusative	in front of
apud	accusative	at the house of
circum	accusative	around
contrā	accusative	against
cum	ablative	with
dē	ablative	about, concerning, down from, from
ē, ex	ablative	from, out of
in	ablative	in, on
in	accusative	into, to
inter	accusative	between, among
per	accusative	through
post	accusative	after
prō	ablative	for, on behalf of
prope	accusative	near
propter	accusative	because of
sine	ablative	without

CONJUNCTIONS

Conjuction	Meaning
atque	and
autem	however
cum	when, after
dum	while
enim	for, in fact
et	and
igitur	therefore
itaque	and so
nam	for, in fact
nec	and not, nor
nōn sōlum . . . , sed etiam . . .	not only . . . , but also . . .
postquam	after
-que	and
sed	but
sī	if
tamen	however

INTERROGATIVE WORDS

Interrogative Word	Meaning
cūr?	why?
-ne?	interrogative particle
quī? quae? quod?	which? what?
quis? quid?	who? what?

SUBJECT-VERB AGREEMENT

The subject agrees with the verb in number.

Puer currit.   The boy is running.

The predicate nominative agrees with the subject in case and number. Predicate adjectives also agree with the subject in gender.

Vīta est gaudium.   Life is joy.

Praemium est māgnum.   The prize is great.

NOUN-ADJECTIVE AGREEMENT

The adjective agrees with the noun in case, number, and gender.

Ōrātiōnem longam audīvī.   I heard a long speech.

Librum celebrem legō.   I am reading a renowned book.

FUNCTIONS OF THE INFINITIVE

1. Complementary with *dēbeō, possum, soleō*.

   The infinitive can complete the meaning of these verbs. Example: in the sentence *legere dēbeō*, which means "I ought to read," the infinitive completes the meaning of "I ought."

2. Indirect statement after verbs of saying and thinking.

   In English, a subordinate statement after a verb of saying or thinking begins with the conjunction "that." In classical Latin no such conjunction is used; instead the subordinate statement expresses its subject as an accusative and its verb as an infinitive, making the subordinate indirect statement a kind of object for the verb of saying or thinking. Consider the English sentence, "I think that the book is good." In Latin the same sentence, *Putō librum esse bonum*, expresses the subject of the indirect statement in the accusative case (*librum*) and the verb of the indirect statement as an infinitive (*esse*).

3. Nominative and infinitive.

   In Latin the accusative and infinitive construction noted above is typically not used with a passive verb of saying or thinking. Instead, the subject of the indirect statement is also the subject of the verb of saying or thinking, and so appears in the nominative case (along with any predicate nouns or adjectives). The verb of the indirect statement is still expressed as an infinitive. In this case, Latin is much closer to English. Consider the English sentence, "The book is thought to be good." In Latin the same sentence, *Liber bonus esse putātur*, expresses the subject and its predicate in the nominative case (*Liber bonus*) while the verb of the indirect statement is expressed as an infinitive (*esse*).

TENSES OF THE INFINITIVE IN THE INDIRECT STATEMENT

In Latin, when the verb of an indirect statement is represented by an infinitive, the tense of that infinitive expresses time **relative to the main verb**. This is not the same as in English, where the tense of the verb within an indirect statement is not always relative to its main verb.

Infinitive	Time in relation to main verb	Example
Present Infinitive	SAME	***Putō** multōs hominēs librum **legere.** = I **think** that many people **are reading** the book.* *Putābam multōs hominēs librum **legere.** = I **used to think** that many people **were reading** the book.*
Perfect Infinitive	BEFORE	***Putō** multōs hominēs librum **lēgisse.** = I **think** that many people **have read** the book.* ***Putābam** multōs hominēs librum **lēgisse.** = I **used to think** that many people **had read** the book.*
Future Infinitive	AFTER	***Putō** multōs hominēs librum **lectūrōs esse.** = I **think** that many people **will read** the book.* ***Putābam** multōs hominēs librum **lectūrōs esse.** = I **used to think** that many people **would read** the book.*

EXPRESSION OF POSSESSION WITH PERSONAL PRONOUNS AND DEMONSTRATIVES

Possession is **not** indicated by the genitive of first and second person pronouns (*ego, tū, nōs, vōs*) or by the genitive of the reflexive pronoun of the third person (*suī, sibi, sē, sē*). These pronouns have corresponding possessive adjectives (*meus, tuus, noster, vester, suus*) to indicate possession.

Examples:

Librum meum habeō.	I have my book.
Librum tuum habeō.	I have your book.
Librum vestrum habeō.	I have your (plural) book.
Librum nostrum habētis.	You (plural) have our book.
Librum suum habent.	They have their (own) book.
Librum suum habet.	S/he has her/his (own) book.

However, possession **is** indicated by the genitive of the *non-reflexive* third person pronouns (*is, ea, id*).

Examples:

Librum ēius habet.	S/he has her/his (someone else's) book.
Librum eōrum habent.	They have their (other people's) book.

In general, the genitive case often shows possession.

liber puellae	the book of the girl

Possession can also be expressed by a dative of possession.

Mihi sunt multī librī.	I have many books.

TRANSITIVE AND INTRANSITIVE VERBS

A transitive verb can take an accusative direct object when the subject performs an action on someone or something.

Example:

Librum teneō.	I hold a book.

Intransitive verbs **do not** take an accusative direct object, because they merely express the state or condition of the subject.

Examples:

Liber est meus.	The book is mine.
In casā meā maneō.	I am staying in my house.

SUBSTANTIVE ADJECTIVES, ESPECIALLY NEUTER PLURAL

Sometimes adjectives without an expressed noun are used to indicate generic persons or things. Gender and context make the frame of reference clear.

Examples:

Fortēs *fugere nōn solent.*	Brave people are not accustomed to flee.
Bonī mala *nōn laudant.*	Good people do not praise bad things.

CONSTRUCTION OF THE RELATIVE PRONOUN

A relative pronoun refers to a logically preceding word (called an antecedent) that is usually expressed, but sometimes only implied. A relative pronoun logically reflects its antecedent's gender and number, but the pronoun's case (again logically) is determined by its use in its own clause.

Example:

Hī sunt librī **quōs** *habēmus.*	These are the books that we have.

PARTICIPLES AS VERBS AND ADJECTIVES

A participle is both an adjective and a verb. Like an adjective, it agrees with a noun (expressed or implied). Like a verb, it relates an action and is modified by adverbial constructions.

Examples:

Librum ab amīcō datum habeō.
I have the book (having been) given by a/my friend.

Fortūna semper discessūra nihil dat.
Fortune, always being about to go away, gives nothing.

APPENDIX E

HISTORICAL TIMELINE

Authors and Literary Periods		Roman History and Legend
	ca. 1183 BCE	Fall of Troy
	753 BCE	Founding of Rome by Romulus and Remus
	753–509 BCE	**Monarchy**
Earliest Latin inscriptions	ca. 600 BCE	
Early Latin Literature	late sixth century–84 BCE	Mucius Scaevola attempted assassination of Porsenna
	509–31 BCE	**Roman Republic**
	480 BCE	Battle of Thermopylae
Laws of the Twelve Tables	451–450 BCE	Creation of the Twelve Tables law code
	390s–380s BCE	Gallic invasions of Rome [throughout the 4th century]
	312 BCE	Construction of the Via Appia by Appius Claudius Caecus
Livius Andronicus	284–204 BCE	
	280–279 BCE	Pyrrhus of Epirus invades Italy
	264–241 BCE	First Punic War
Plautus	254–184 BCE	
Ennius	239–169 BCE	
Cato the Elder	234–149 BCE	
	218–202 BCE	Hannibal invades Italy; Second Punic War
Terence	195 or 185–ca. 159 BCE	
	149–146 BCE	Third Punic War; destruction of Carthage
	133, 123–122 BCE	Tribunates of Tiberius and Gaius Gracchi
Cicero	106–43 BCE	
Caesar	100–44 BCE	
Cornelius Nepos	ca. 100–ca. 25 BCE	
	89 BCE	Conflict between Marius and Sulla: First Civil War

Sallust	86–35/34 BCE	
Catullus	84–54 BCE	
Golden Age Literature	83 BCE–17 CE	
	82–80 BCE	Sulla's dictatorship
	73–71 BCE	Spartacus and Slave Revolt
Vergil	70–19 BCE	
Maecenas	70–8 BCE	
Horace	65–8 BCE	
	63 BCE	Catiline conspiracy
	63/62 BCE	Pompeii earthquake
	59 BCE	First Triumvirate formed: Caesar, Crassus, Pompey
Livy	ca. 59 BCE–17 CE	
	58–51 BCE	Caesar's conquest of Gaul
Tibullus	ca. 54–19 BCE	
Propertius	ca. 50–15 BCE	
	49 BCE	Caesar crosses the Rubicon: Second Civil War
	44 BCE (March 15)	Caesar's assassination
	43 BCE	Second Triumvirate formed: Antony, Lepidus, Octavian
Ovid	43 BCE–17 CE	
	42 BCE	Defeat of Brutus and Cassius at Philippi: Third Civil War
	39–28 BCE	Asinius Pollio builds a library on slopes of Capitoline
	31 BCE	Defeat of Antony and Cleopatra at the Battle of Actium
	31 BCE–180 CE	**Early Roman Empire**
	27 BCE–14 CE	Augustus
	27 BCE	Octavian assumes the name Augustus
	27 BCE	Agrippa builds Pantheon
	14–37 CE	Tiberius
Silver Age Literature	17–150 CE	
Petronius	first century CE	
Seneca	ca. 4 BCE–65 CE	
Pliny the Elder	ca. 23/24–79 CE	
Frontinus	ca. 30–104 CE	
	37–41 CE	Caligula
Martial	ca. 40–102 CE	

	41–54 CE	Claudius
	54–68 CE	Nero
Tacitus	ca. 56–116/120 CE	
Juvenal	ca. 60–ca. 140 CE	
Pliny the Younger	ca. 61–ca. 112 CE	
	63 CE	Earthquake in Pompeii
	64 CE (July 19)	Great Fire in Rome
	69–79 CE	Vespasian
Suetonius	ca. 69–ca. 140 CE	
	79–81 CE	Titus
	79 CE (August 24)	Eruption of Vesuvius
	80 CE	Colosseum is dedicated in Rome
	81–96 CE	Domitian
	96–109 CE	Nerva
	98–117 CE	Trajan
	112 CE	Forum of Trajan, column dedicated
	117–138 CE	Hadrian
Hyginus	second century CE	
	125 CE	Hadrian rebuilds Pantheon
Apuleius	second century CE	
	135 CE	Library of Celsus is completed in Ephesus
	138–161 CE	Antoninus Pius
Late Latin Literature	150–400 CE	
	161–180 CE	Marcus Aurelius
	180–476 CE	**Late Roman Empire**
	180–192 CE	Commodus
	193–211 CE	Septimius Severus
	211 CE	Geta
	211–217 CE	Caracalla
	222–235 CE	Severus Alexander
	235–284 CE	The "Military" emperors
Dio Cassius	early second century CE, late third century CE	
	284–305 CE	Diocletian
	293 CE	Instituting the Tetrarchy
	312–337 CE	Constantine
	313 CE	Edict of Milan, toleration of Christianity

	330 CE	Establishment of Constantinople as Capital of the Empire
Ammianus Marcellinus	ca. 330–395 CE	
Augustine	354–430 CE	
	361–363 CE	Julian
	386 CE	Augustine's conversion
	395 CE	Division of the Empire upon death of Theodosius I
Quintus Smyrnaeus	fourth century CE	
Medieval Latin Literature	400–ca. 1400 CE	
	410 CE	Alaric and Visigoths sack Rome
	434–451 CE	Attila the Hun's rule
	455 CE	Vandals sack Rome
	476–ca. 1400 CE	**Medieval Era**
	476 CE	Traditional date of the fall of the Roman Empire
	476 CE	Romulus Augustus, last Roman emperor, is deposed by Odoacer
Boethius	ca. 480–ca. 524 CE	
	493 CE	Theodoric (the Ostrogoth) assumes control over Italy
	527–565 CE	Justinian
	528–534 CE	Law Code of Justinian
	1453 CE	Fall of Constantinople and the Eastern Roman Empire to the Ottoman Turks

This glossary contains the **Vocabulary to Learn** from all the chapters.

LIST OF ABBREVIATIONS:

(1) = first conjugation
abl. = ablative
acc. = accusative
adj. = adjective
adv. = adverb
conj. = conjunction
dat. = dative
f. = feminine

gen. = genitive
inf. = infinitive
m. = masculine
n. = neuter
pl. = plural
prep. = preposition
sg. = singular

NOTE:

The genitive of second declension words ending in **-ius** or **-ium** is indicated with a single **-ī**, which is the genitive ending itself. Note that in the full form of the genitive there is normally a double **i**: *fīlius, -ī (= fīliī); gaudium, -ī (= gaudiī).*

A

abandon, relinquō, -ere, relīquī, relictum

abound with, abundō (1) + *abl.*

about, dē, *prep. + abl.*

about to be, futūrus, -a, -um, *participle*

accept, accipiō, -ere, -cēpī, -ceptum

accuse someone of something, accūsō (1) + *acc. + gen.*

adopt, capiō, -ere, cēpī, captum

after, cum, *conj.;* postquam, *conj.*

after, post, *prep. + acc.*

afterwards, posteā, *adv.*

against, contrā, *prep. + acc.*

all, omnis, -e, *adj.*

almost, paene, *adv.*

already, iam, *adv.*

also, etiam, *adv.;* quoque, *adv.*

always, semper, *adv.*

among, inter, *prep. + acc.*

and, et, *conj.;* atque, *conj.;* -que, *conj.*

and not, nec, *conj.*

and so, itaque, *conj.*

anger, īra, -ae, *f.*

animal, animal, -ālis, *n.*

another, alius, alia, aliud, *adj.*

answer, respondeō, -ēre, -spondī, -spōnsum

any, ūllus, -a, -um, *adj.*

appearance, fōrma, -ae, *f.*

argument, argūmentum, -ī, *n.*

armed, armātus, -a, -um, *adj.*

around, circum, *prep. + acc.*

ash, cinis, -eris, *m.*

ask, rogō (1)

at home, domī

at last, tandem, *adv.*

at the house of, apud, *prep. + acc.*

athlete, āthlēta, -ae, *m.*

attack, impetus, -ūs, *m.*

await, exspectō (1)

awaken, excitō (1)

away from, ā *or* ab, *prep. + abl.*

axis, axle, axis, -is, *m.*

B

bad, malus, -a, -um, *adj.*

battle, proelium, -ī, *n.*

be, sum, esse, fuī, ——

be able, possum, posse, potuī, ——

be accustomed, soleō, -ēre, solitus sum + *inf.*

be afraid, timeō, -ēre, timuī, ——

be eager for, studeō, -ēre, studuī, —— + *dat.*

be inert, iaceō, -ēre, iacuī, ——

be interested in, studeō, -ēre, studuī, —— + *dat.*

be on fire, ārdeō, -ēre, ārsī, ——

be unwilling, nōlō, *irregular verb*

beard, barba, -ae, *f.*

beautiful, pulcher, pulchra, pulchrum, *adj.*

because of, propter, *prep. + acc.*

beginning, initium, -ī, *n.*

behave, agō, -ere, ēgī, āctum; **(s/he) behaves,** sē gerit

believe somebody, crēdō, -ere, crēdidī, crēditum + *dat.*

between, inter, *prep. + acc.*

blame, reprehendō, -ere, -prehendī, -prehēnsum

blood, sanguis, sanguinis, *m.*

body, corpus, -oris, *n.*

book, liber, librī, *m.*

bosom, gremium, -ī, *n.*

boy, puer, puerī, *m.*

brave, fortis, -e, *adj.*

brook, rīvus, -ī, *m.*

build, aedificō (1)

burn, ārdeō, -ēre, ārsī, ——

but, sed, *conj.*

by, ā or ab, *prep. + abl.*

C

call, vocō (1)

camp, castra, -ōrum, *n. pl.*

can, possum, posse, potuī, ——

capture, capiō, -ere, cēpī, captum

care for, cūrō (1)

carry, gerō, -ere, gessī, gestum

cause, causa, -ae, *f.*

cave, spēlunca, -ae, *f.*

chain, vinculum, -ī, *n.*

change, mūtō (1)

chest, pectus, -oris, *n.*

choose, legō, -ere, lēgī, lēctum

citizen, cīvis, -is, *m./f.*

city (city of Rome), urbs, urbis, *f.*

clothes, vestīmenta, -ōrum, *n. pl.*

cloud, nūbēs, -is, *f.*

combat, proelium, -ī, *n.*

come, veniō, -īre, vēnī, ventum

concerning, dē, *prep. + abl.*

conflagration, incendium, -ī, *n.*

confusion, tumultus, -ūs, *m.*

consider, putō (1)

constancy, cōnstantia, -ae, *f.*

consul, cōnsul, -ulis, *m.*

consume, cōnsūmō, -ere, -sūmpsī, -sūmptum

cook, coquō, -ere, coxī, coctum

cottage, casa, -ae, *f.*

country house, vīlla, -ae, *f.*

courage, fortitūdō, -inis, *f.*

crowded, celeber, -bris, -bre, *adj.*

cruel, crūdēlis, -e, *adj.*

cultivate, colō, -ere, coluī, cultum

D

danger, perīculum, -ī, *n.*

darkness, tenebrae, -ārum, *f. pl.*

daughter, fīlia, -ae, *f.*

day, diēs, diēī, *m./f.*

deadly, fūnestus, -a, -um, *adj.*

death, mors, mortis, *f.*

deception, dolus, -ī, *m.*

decide, dēcernō, -ere, -crēvī, -crētum + *inf.*

defeat, vincō, -ere, vīcī, victum

delight, dēliciae, -ārum, *f. pl. (noun)*

delight, dēlectō (1) *(verb)*

descend, dēscendō, -ere, -scendī, -scēnsum

design, parō (1)

desire, cupiō, -ere, -īvī, -ītum

destiny, fātum, -ī, *n.*

destroy, dēleō, -ēre, dēlēvī, dēlētum; tollō, -ere, sustulī, sublātum

devastate, dēvastō (1)

difficult, difficilis, -e, *adj.*

disaster, clādēs, -is, *f.*

distinguished, praeclārus, -a, -um, *adj.*

divine, dīvīnus, -a, -um, *adj.*

do, agō, -ere, ēgī, āctum; faciō, -ere, fēcī, factum

down from, dē, *prep. + abl.*

drive, agō, -ere, ēgī, āctum

during the night, noctū, *adv.*

dwell, habitō (1)

E

each, omnis, -e, *adj.*

easily, facile, *adv.*

eat, comedō, -ere, -ēdī, -ēsum

emperor, imperātor, -ōris, *m.*

enemy, hostis, -is, *m.*

enter, intrō (1)

envy someone, invideō, -ēre, invīdī, invīsum + *dat.*

eruption, incendium, -ī, *n.*

esteem, aestimō (1)

even, aequus, -a, -um, *adj.*

even, etiam, *adv.*

ever, umquam, *adv.*

every, omnis, -e, *adj.*

everywhere, ubīque, *adv.*

example, exemplar, -āris, *n.;* exemplum, -ī, *n.*

exceedingly, valdē, *adv.*

exclaim, exclāmō (1)

expect, exspectō (1)

external, externus, -a, -um, *adj.*

extinguish, exstinguō, -ere, exstīnxī, exstīnctum

eye, oculus, -ī, *m.*

F

face, faciēs, -ēī, *f.*

fall, cadō, -ere, cecidī, cāsum

family, familia, -ae, *f.*

famous, praeclārus, -a, -um, *adj.*

far, longē, *adv.*

farmer, agricola, -ae, *m.*

fate, fātum, -ī, *n.*

fatherland, patria, -ae, *f.*

fear, timor, -ōris, *m. (noun)*

fear, timeō, -ēre, timuī, —— *(verb)*

feed, alō, -ere, aluī, altum/alitum

feel, sentiō, -īre, sēnsī, sēnsum

feel pain, doleō, -ēre, doluī, ——

ferocious, ferōx, -ōcis, *adj.*

fetter, vinculum, -ī, *n.*

few, paucī, -ae, -a, *pl. adj.*

field, ager, agrī, *m.*

fierce, ācer, ācris, ācre, *adj.;* ferōx, -ōcis, *adj.*

fight, pugnō (1)

finger, digitus, -ī, *m.*

fire, ignis, -is, *m.*

first, prīmus, -a, -um, *adj.*

flame, flamma, -ae, *f.*

flee, fugiō, -ere, fūgī, ——

fleet, classis, -is, *f.*

flesh, carō, carnis, *f.*

flow, fluō, -ere, flūxī, fluxum

for (conj.), enim, *conj.;* nam, *conj.*

for (prep.), prō, *prep. + abl.*

for a long time, diū, *adv.*

for certain, for sure, prō certō, *adverbial phrase*

force, vīs, —— *f.; pl.* vīrēs, vīrium; impetus, -ūs, *m.*

foreign to, aliēnus, -a, -um, *adj. + prep.* ā/ab *+ abl.*

forest, silva, -ae, *f.*

form, fōrma, -ae, *f.*

former, ille, illa, illud

fortunate, fēlīx, -īcis, *adj.*

fortune, fortitūdō, -inis, *f.*

Fortune, the goddess Fortūna, -ae, *f.*

free someone from something, līberō (1) *+ acc. + abl.*

friend, amīcus, -ī, *m.*

from, ā *or* ab, *prep. + abl.;* ē *or* ex, *prep. + abl.*

fruit, pōmum, -ī, *n.*

full of, plēnus, -a, -um, *adj. + gen.* or *+ abl.*

G

garment, vestīmentum, -ī, *n.*

general, dux, ducis, *m.*

geographical places, loca, locōrum, *n. pl.*

get ready, parō (1)

gift, dōnum, -ī, *n.*

girl, puella, -ae, *f.*

give, dō, dăre, dedī, dătum

go to, petō, -ere, petīvī, petītum

god, deus, -ī, *m.*

goddess, dea, -ae, *f.*

good, bonus, -a, -um, *adj.*

goodbye!, valē!

great, māgnus, -a, -um, *adj.*

grief, dolor, -ōris, *m.*

grow, crēscō, -ere, crēvī, ——

H

hand, manus, -ūs, *f.*

happy, fēlīx, -īcis, *adj.*

hatred, odium, -ī, *n.*

have, habeō, -ēre, habuī, habitum

head, caput, -itis, *n.*

head for, petō, -ere, petīvī, petītum

heal, sānō (1)

hear, audiō, -īre, audīvī, audītum

heart, cor, cordis, *n.*

heaven, caelum, -ī, *n.*

help, auxilium, -ī, *n.*

her, suus, -a, -um, *possessive adj.;* ēius

herself, sē, *acc. of the reflexive pronoun*

hide, pellis, -is, *f. (noun)*

hide, occultō (1) *(verb)*

himself, sē, *acc. of the reflexive pronoun*

his, suus, -a, -um, *possessive adj.,* ēius

hold, teneō, -ēre, tenuī, tentum

home, domus, -ūs, *f.*

honor, honor, -ōris, *m.*

horn, cornū, -ūs, *n.*

horse, equus, -ī, *m.*

house, domus, -ūs, *f.*

household, familia, -ae, *f.*

however, autem, *conj.;* tamen, *conj.*

human, hūmānus, -a, -um, *adj.*

hurt, doleō, -ēre, doluī, ——, *(intransitive)*

husband, marītus, -ī, *m.*

I

I, ego, *personal pronoun*

I do not care a bit, aestimō ūnīus assis

if, sī, *conj.*

immediately, statim, *adv.*

impetus, impetus, -ūs, *m.*

important, māgnus, -a, -um, *adj.*

in, in, *prep. + abl.*

in fact, enim, *conj.;* nam, *conj.*

in front of, ante, *prep. + acc.*

in such a way, ita, *adv.*

in the open, forīs, *adv.*

inconsistent with, aliēnus, -a, -um, *adj. + prep.* ā/ab *+ abl.*

indication, argūmentum, -ī, *n.*

indifferently, aequō animō

injustice, inīquitās, -ātis, *f.*

into, ad, *prep. + acc.;* in, *prep. + acc.*

it is allowed to, it is permitted (for someone to do something) licet *+ dat. + inf.*

its, suus, -a, -um, *possessive adj.;* ēius

itself, sē, *acc. of the reflexive pronoun*

J

joy, gaudium, -ī, *n.*

judge, iudex, -icis, *m. (noun)*

judge, iūdicō (1) *(verb)*

just, iūstus, -a, -um, *adj.*

just as, sīcut, *adv.*

K

keen, ācer, ācris, ācre, *adj.*

kill, occīdō, -ere, occīdī, occīsum

king, rēx, rēgis, *m.*

know, sciō, scīre, scīvī, scītum

L

lack something, egeō, -ēre, eguī, —— + *abl.*

land, terra, -ae, *f.*

lap, gremium, -ī, *n.*

large, māgnus, -a, -um, *adj.*

latter, hic, haec, hoc

law, lēx, lēgis, *f.*

lead, agō, -ere, ēgī, āctum; dūcō, -ere, dūxī, ductum

leader, dux, ducis, *m.*

learned, doctus, -a, -um, *adj.*

leave, discēdō, -ere, -cessī, -cessum

leave behind, relinquō, -ere, relīquī, relictum

legitimate, iūstus, -a, -um, *adj.*

letter (epistle), litterae, -ārum, *f. pl.*; epistula, -ae, *f.*

letter (of the alphabet), littera, -ae, *f.*

lie down, iaceō, -ēre, iacuī, ——

life, vīta, -ae, *f.*

lift up, tollō, -ere, sustulī, sublātum

like, similis, -e, *adj.* + *gen.* or + *dat.*

listen, audiō, -īre, -īvī, -ītum

literature, litterae, -ārum, *f. pl.*

little house, casa, -ae, *f.*

live (be alive), vīvō, -ere, vīxī, vīctum

live (dwell), habitō (1)

long, longus, -a, -um, *adj.*

look at, cōnspiciō, -ere, -spexī, -spectum

look for, quaerō, -ere, quaesīvī, quaesītum

look here!, ecce, *interj.*

lose, āmittō, -ere, -mīsī, -missum

love, amor, -ōris, *m.* (*noun*)

love, amō (1) (*verb*)

M

make, faciō, -ere, fēcī, factum

make a mistake, errō (1)

make a speech, ōrātiōnem habeō

make plans, cōnsilia capiō

man, vir, virī, *m.*

man (i.e., human being), homō, -inis, *m.*

many, multus, -a, -um, *adj.*

matter, rēs, reī, *f.*

meat, carō, carnis, *f.*

meet, conveniō, -īre, -vēnī, -ventum

memory, memoria, -ae, *f.*

midday, merīdiēs, -ēī, *m.*

mind, animus, -ī, *m.*

mistress, domina, -ae, *f.*

mother, māter, mātris, *f.*

mountain, mōns, montis, *m.*

mouth, ōs, ōris, *n.*

move, moveō, -ēre, mōvī, mōtum

much, multus, -a, -um, *adj.*

much, multum, *adv.*

must, dēbeō, -ēre, dēbuī, dēbitum + *inf.*

my, meus, -a, -um, *possessive adj.*

N

name, nōmen, -inis, *n.*

near, prope, *prep.* + *acc.*

neglect, neglegō, -ere, neglēxī, neglēctum

never, numquam, *adv.*

new, novus, -a, -um, *adj.*

nice, pulcher, pulchra, pulchrum, *adj.*

night, nox, noctis, *f.*

no, minimē, *adv.*

nor, nec, *conj.*

not, nōn, *negative adv.*

not only . . . , but also . . . , nōn sōlum . . . , sed etiam . . .

not want, nōlō, *irregular verb*

nothing, nihil, *negative pronoun*

nourish, alō, -ere, aluī, altum/alitum

now, nunc, *adv.*

O

observe, cōnspiciō, -ere, -spexī, -spectum

often, saepe, *adv.*

old, vetustus, -a, -um, *adj.*

old age, senectūs, -ūtis, *f.*

old man, senex, -is, *m.*

on, in, *prep.* + *abl.*

on account of, propter, *prep.* + *acc.*

on behalf of, prō, *prep.* + *abl.*

only, tantum, *adv.*

oracle, ōrāculum, -ī, *n.*

order somebody to do something, iubeō, -ēre, iussī, iussum + *acc.* + *inf.*

order, iussus, -ūs, *m.*

other, alius, alia, aliud, *adj.*

ought to, dēbeō, -ēre, dēbuī, dēbitum + *inf.*

our, noster, nostra, nostrum, *possessive adj.*

out of, ē *or* ex, *prep.* + *abl.*

outside, forīs, *adv.*

outward, externus, -a, -um, *adj.*

overcome, vincō, -ere, vīcī, victum

overwhelm, opprimō, -ere, oppressī, oppressum

owe, dēbeō, -ēre, dēbuī, dēbitum

P

pain, dolor, -ōris, *m.*

parent, parēns, parentis, *m./f.*

part, pars, partis, *f.*

particle added to the first word of an interrogative sentence, -ne

passages of a book, locī, locōrum, *m. pl.*

peace, pāx, pācis, *f.*

people, hominēs, hominum, *m. pl.*

perhaps, fortasse, *adv.*

pet, dēliciae, -ārum, *f. pl.*

place, locus, locī, *m.* (*noun*)

place, pōnō, -ere, posuī, positum (*verb*)

plan, cōnsilium, -ī, *n.*

plant, herba, -ae, *f.*

play, lūdō, -ere, lūsī, lūsum

please, dēlectō (1)

poet, poēta, -ae, *m.*

poison, venēnum, -ī, *n.*

poor, pauper, pauperis, *adj.*

possess, possideō, -ēre, possēdī, possessum

prepare, parō (1)

preserve, servō (1)

proof, argūmentum, -ī, *n.*

public office or distinction, honor, -ōris, *m.*

punish, pūniō, -īre, pūnīvī, pūnītum

put, pōnō, -ere, posuī, positum

Q

queen, rēgīna, -ae, *f.*

R

raise, tollō, -ere, sustulī, sublātum

read, legō, -ere, lēgī, lēctum

reason, causa, -ae, *f.*

rebuke, reprehendō, -ere, -prehendī, -prehēnsum

receive, accipiō, -ere, -cēpī, -ceptum

red, ruber, rubra, rubrum, *adj.*

regard, aestimō (1)

remain, maneō, -ēre, mānsī, mānsum

renowned, celeber, -bris, -bre, *adj.*

reward, praemium, -ī, *n.*

rich, dīves, dīvitis, *adj.*

riches, dīvitiae, -ārum, *f. pl.*

right hand, dextra, -ae, *f.*

road, via, -ae, *f.*

rock, saxum, -ī, *n.*

Roman, Rōmānus, -a, -um, *adj.*

Rome, Rōma, -ae, *f.*

rouse, excitō (1)

rub, terō, -ere, trīvī, trītum

run, currō, -ere, cucurrī, cursum

run away, fugiō, -ere, fūgī, ——

rural, rūsticus, -a, -um, *adj.*

rustic, rūsticus, -a, -um, *adj.*

S

s/he/it, is, ea, id, *personal pronoun*

sail, nāvigō (1)

sailor, nauta, -ae, *m.*

save, servō (1)

say, dīcō, -ere, dīxī, dictum

say/said, inquam, (*only introducing direct speech*); **s/he says/said,** inquit (*only introducing direct speech*)

sea, mare, maris, *n.*

search, quaerō, -ere, quaesīvī, quaesītum

see, videō, -ēre, vīdī, vīsum

seek, petō, -ere, petīvī, petītum

seem, videor

seize, corripiō, -ere, -ripuī, -reptum

send, mittō, -ere, mīsī, missum

separate, sēparō (1)

serious, sevērus, -a, -um, *adj.*

severe, sevērus, -a, -um, *adj.*

shadows, tenebrae, -ārum, *f. pl.*

she-wolf, lupa, -ae, *f.*

ship, nāvis, -is, *f.*

shore, lītus, -oris, *n.*

should, dēbeō, -ēre, dēbuī, dēbitum + *inf.*

show, ostendō, -ere, ostendī, ostentum

similar, similis, -e, *adj.* + *gen.* or + *dat.*

sister, soror, -ōris, *f.*

sit, sedeō, -ēre, sēdī, sessum

skin, pellis, -is, *f.*

sky, caelum, -ī, *n.*

sleep, dormiō, -īre, dormīvī, dormītum

sleep, somnus, -ī, *m.*

small, parvus, -a, -um, *adj.*

smoke, fūmus, -ī, *m.*

snatch away, ēripiō, -ere, -ripuī, -reptum

so great, tantus, -a, -um, *adj.*

so, tam, *adv.*

soldier, mīles, -itis, *m.*

son, fīlius, -ī, *m.*

soon, mox, *adv.*

soul, animus, -ī, *m.*

sparrow, passer, -eris, *m.*

speech, ōrātiō, -ōnis, *f.*

spirit, animus, -ī, *m.*

stand, stō, -āre, stetī, statum

stir up, excitō (1)

stone, saxum, -ī, *n.*

storm, tempestās, -ātis, *f.*

story, fābula, -ae, *f.*

stream, rīvus, -ī, *m.*

strength, vīs, ——; *f., pl.* vīrēs, vīrium

strengthen, firmō (1)

strict, sevērus, -a, -um, *adj.*

strong, fortis, -e, *adj.*

study, studeō, -ēre, studuī, —— + *dat.*

suddenly, subitō, *adv.*

suppress, opprimō, -ere, oppressī, oppressum

swiftly, celeriter, *adv.*

sword, gladius, -ī, *m.*

T

take, capiō, -ere, cēpī, captum; dūcō, -ere, dūxī, ductum

take back, recipiō, -ere, -cēpī, -ceptum

take care of, cūrō (1)

teach, doceō, -ēre, docuī, doctum

tear, lacrima, -ae, *f.*

tell, nārrō (1)

temple, templum, -ī, *n.*

terrifying, terribilis, -e, *adj.*

that, ille, illa, illud, *demonstrative pronoun and adj.;* is, ea, id, *demonstrative pronoun and adj.*

that, quī, quae, quod, *relative pronoun*

theft, fūrtum, -ī, *n.*

their, suus, -a, -um, *possessive adj.,* ēius

themselves, sē, *acc. of the reflexive pronoun*

then, deinde, *adv.;* tum, *adv.;* tunc, *adv.*

there, ibi, *adv.*

therefore, igitur, *conj.*

thief, fūr, fūris, *m.*

thing, rēs, reī, *f.*

think, cōgitō (1); putō (1)

this, hic, haec, hoc, *demonstrative pronoun and adj.;* is, ea, id, *demonstrative pronoun and adj.*

through, per, *prep. + acc.*

throw, iaciō, -ere, iēcī, iactum

time, tempus, -oris, *n.*

to, ad, *prep. + acc.;* in, *prep. + acc.*

together, ūnā, *adv.*

touch, tangō, -ere, tetigī, tāctum

towards, ad, *prep. + acc.*

tree, arbor, -oris, *f.*

trickery, dolus, -ī, *m.*

true, vērus, -a, -um, *adj.*

try, temptō (1)

turn, versō (1)

U

uncle, avunculus, -ī, *m.*

understand, intellegō, -ere, intellēxī, intellēctum

uproar, tumultus, -ūs, *m.*

V

vegetation, herba, -ae, *f.*

very, valdē, *adv.*

villa, vīlla, -ae, *f.*

voyage, nāvigō (1)

W

wage war, bellum gerō

wait for, exspectō (1)

wake up, excitō (1)

walk, ambulō (1)

wall, wall-fence, mūrus, -ī, *m.*

wander, errō (1)

want, cupiō, -ere, -īvī, -ītum

war, bellum, -ī, *n.*

water, aqua, -ae, *f.*

we, nōs, *personal pronoun*

wealth, dīvitiae, -ārum, *f. pl.*

weapons, arma, -ōrum, *n. pl.*

wear out, terō, -ere, trīvī, trītum

weather, caelum, -ī, *n.*

well, bene, *adv.*

well-known, celeber, -bris, -bre, *adj.*

what?, quid?, *interrogative pronoun,* quod?, *interrogative adj.*

wheel, rota, -ae, *f.*

when, cum, *conj.*

which? quī, quae, quod?, *interrogative adjective*

which, quī, quae, quod, *relative pronoun*

while, dum, *conj.*

white, albus, -a, -um, *adj.*

who, quī, quae, quod, *relative pronoun*

who?, quis?, *interrogative pronoun*

why, cūr, *adj.*

wife, uxor, -ōris, *f.*

wind, ventus, -ī, *m.*

with, cum, *prep. + abl.*

with all one's might, prō vīribus

with me, mēcum

with you, tēcum

without, sine, *prep. + abl.*

wolf, *see she-wolf*

woman, fēmina, -ae, *f.;* mulier, -ieris, *f.*

word, verbum, -ī, *n.*

worship, colō, -ere, coluī, cultum

wound (noun) vulnus, -eris, *n.*

wound (verb) vulnerō (1)

wretched, miser, -a, -um, *adj.*

Y

yes, ita, *adv.*

you (pl.), vōs, *personal pronoun*

you (sg.), tū, *personal pronoun*

young lady, young man, adulēscēns, -entis, *m./f.*

your, yours (pl.), vester, vestra, vestrum, *possessive adj.*

your, yours (sg.), tuus, -a, -um, *possessive adj.*

This glossary contains the **Vocabulary to Learn** * as well as the **Reading Vocabulary** from all the chapters.

*All words from the **Vocabulary to Learn** are starred and coded, e.g., C12 means the word first appeared as **Vocabulary to Learn** in Chapter 12. In a very few instances, an additional meaning for the word is given in a later part of the text. Such additional meanings appear in the Glossary and when the additional meaning is part of the **Vocabulary to Learn**, the chapter introducing that additional meaning is also noted.

LIST OF ABBREVIATIONS:

(1) = first conjugation
abl. = ablative
acc. = accusative
adj. = adjective
adv. = adverb
conj. = conjunction
dat. = dative
f. = feminine

gen. = genitive
inf. = infinitive
m. = masculine
n. = neuter
pl. = plural
prep. = preposition
sg. = singular

NOTE:

The genitive of second declension words ending in *-ius* or *-ium* is indicated with a single *-ī*, which is the genitive ending itself. Note that in the full form of the genitive there is normally a double *i*: *fīlius, -ī (= filiī); gaudium, -ī (= gaudiī)*.

A

ā *or* **ab,** *prep. + abl.,* by, from, away from* C5

absum, abesse, āfuī , ——, to be absent, away

abundō (1) *+ abl.,* to abound with* C20

accipiō, -ere, -cēpī, -ceptum, to accept, receive* C21

accurrō, -ere, -currī, -cursum, to run up

accūsō (1) *+ acc. + gen.,* to accuse someone of something* C21

ācer, ācris, ācre, *adj.,* keen, fierce* C10

ad tempus, for the time being, for a while

ad, *prep. + acc.,* towards, to, into* C4

adolēscō, -ere, adolēvī, adultum, to grow up

adulēscēns, -entis, *m./f.,* young man, young lady* C20

aedificō (1), to build* C10

Aenēās, Aenēae (gen.), Aenēae (dat.), Aenēam/ān (acc.), Aenēā (abl.), Aeneas, Trojan refugee, legendary founder of Roman race

aequus, -a, -um, *adj.,* even; **aequō animō,** indifferently* C20

Aeschinus , -ī, *m.,* Aeschinus

aestimō (1), to regard, esteem; **aestimō ūnīus assis,** I do not care a bit* C7

ager, agrī, *m.,* field* C3

agō, -ere, ēgī, āctum, to drive, lead, do, behave* C11

agricola, -ae, *m.,* farmer* C1

albus, -a, -um, *adj.,* white* C14

aliēnus, -a, -um, *adj. + prep.* ā/ab + *abl.,* foreign to, inconsistent with* C21

alius, alia, aliud, *adj.,* another, other* C13

alō, -ere, aluī, altum/alitum, to feed, nourish* C17

amāns, amantis, *m./f.,* lover

ambulō (1), to walk* C2

amīcus, -ī, *m.,* friend* C3

āmittō, -ere, -mīsī, -missum, to lose* C17

amō (1), to love* C2

amor, -ōris, *m.,* love* C7

Amūlius, -ī, *m.,* Amulius

angustus, -a, -um, *adj.,* narrow

animal, -ālis, *n.,* animal* C9

animus, -ī, *m.,* spirit, soul, mind* C3

ante, *prep. + acc.,* in front of* C15

antequam, *conj.,* before

Apollō, Apollinis, *m.,* Apollo, god of the sun, poetry, light, music

appropinquō (1), to approach

apud, *prep. + acc.,* at the house of* C13

aqua, -ae, *f.,* water* C1

arbor, -oris, *f.,* tree C14

ārdeō, -ēre, ārsī, ——, to burn, be on fire* C11

argūmentum, -ī, *n.,* proof, indication, argument* C15

arma, -ōrum, *n. pl.,* weapons* C9

armātus, -a, -um, *adj.,* armed* C4

asportō (1), to carry away

at, *conj.,* but

Athēniēnsēs, Athēniēnsium, *m. pl.,* the Athenians

āthlēta, -ae, *m.,* athlete* C1

atque, *conj.,* and* C13

attonitus, -a, -um, *adj.,* astounded

auctōritās, -ātis, *f.,* authority

audiō, -īre, audīvī, audītum, to hear, listen* C9

autem, *conj.,* however* C4

auxilium, -ī, *n.,* help* C5

avunculus, -ī, *m.,* uncle* C16

axis, -is, *m.,* axle, axis* C21

B

barba, -ae, *f.,* beard* C19

bellum, -ī, *n.,* war* C4; **bellō iūstō,** through open warfare

belua, -ae, *f.,* beast

bene, *adv.,* well* C1

bonus, -a, -um, *adj.,* good* C4

bracchium, -ī, *n.,* arm

C

cadō, -ere, cecidī, cāsum, to fall* C14

caelum, -ī, *n.,* sky, heaven, weather* C16

calidus, -a, -um, *adj.,* hot

callidus, -a, -um, *adj.,* clever, cunning

capiō, -ere, cēpī, captum, to take, adopt, capture; **cōnsilia capere,** to make plans* C10

caput, -itis, *n.,* head* C9

carō, carnis, *f.,* meat, flesh* C19

Carthāgine, at Carthage, in Carthage

Carthāgō, -inis, *f.* Carthage

casa, -ae, *f.,* little house, cottage* C3

castra, -ōrum, *n. pl.,* camp* C4

Catilīna, -ae, *m.,* Catiline, a bankrupt revolutionary whose plot to overthrow the republic was exposed by Cicero

Catullus, -ī, *m.,* Catullus, Roman poet

causa, -ae, *f.,* cause, reason* C16

celeber, -bris, -bre, *adj.,* renowned, well-known, crowded* C10

celeriter, *adv.,* swiftly* C19

cibus, -ī, *m.,* food

cicātrīx, cicātrīcis, *f.,* scar

cinis, -eris, *m.,* ash* C16

circum, *prep. + acc.,* around* C21

circus, -ī, *m.,* circus, often referring to the Circus Maximus in particular

cīvis, -is, *m./f.,* citizen* C9

clādēs, -is, *f.,* disaster* C16

clam, *adv.,* secretly

clāmor, -ōris, *m.,* shout, cry

classis, -is, *f.,* fleet* C16

claudō, -ere, clausī, clausum, to lock up

clīvus, -ī, *m.,* hill

cōgitō (1), to think* C5

cōgnōscō, -ere, -nōvī, -nitum, to recognize, get to know

colō, -ere, coluī, cultum, to worship, cultivate* C18

comedō, -ere, -ēdī, -ēsum, to eat* C14

coniūrātiō, -ōnis, *f.,* plot

cōnsilium, -ī, *n.,* plan* C5

cōnspiciō, -ere, -spexī, -spectum, to look at, observe* C11

cōnstantia, -ae, *f.,* constancy* C21

cōnsul, -ulis, *m.,* consul* C9

cōnsultō, *adv.,* on purpose

cōnsūmō, -ere, -sūmpsī, sūmptum, to consume* C12

contrā, *prep. + acc.,* against* C8

conveniō, -īre, -vēnī, -ventum, to meet* C14

coquō, -ere, coxī, coctum, to cook* C19

cor, cordis, *n.,* heart* C20

cornū, -ūs, *n.,* horn* C17

corpus, -oris, *n.,* body* C9

corripiō, -ere, -ripuī, -reptum, to seize* C17

crēdō, -ere, crēdidī, crēditum + *dat.,* to believe somebody* C9

crēscō, -ere, crēvī, ——, to grow* C19

crūdēlis, -e, *adj.,* cruel* C11

Ctēsiphō, -ōnis, *m.,* Ctesipho

cum ... tum ... , both ... and ...

cum, *conj.,* when, after* C18

cum, *prep. + abl.,* with* C3

Cupīdō, Cupīdinis, *m.,* Cupid (in Greek, Eros)

cupiō, -ere, -īvī, -ītum, to desire, want* C10

cūr, *adv.,* why? * C15

cūria, -ae, *f.,* senate (building)

cūrō (1), to care for, take care of* C2

currō, -ere, cucurrī, cursum, to run* C17

D

dē, *prep. + abl.*, about, concerning, down from* C5

dea, -ae, *f.*, goddess* C18

dēbeō, -ēre, dēbuī, dēbitum + *inf.*, ought, must, should; to owe* C2

dēcernō, -ere, -crēvī, -crētum + *inf.*, to decide, determine* C8

deinde, *adv.*, then* C3

dēlectō (1), to delight, please* C20

dēleō, -ēre, dēlēvī, dēlētum, to destroy* C10

dēliciae, -ārum, *f. pl.*, delight, pet

dēliciae, -ārum, *f. pl.*, delight, pet* C7

Delphicus, -a, -um, *adj.*, belonging to Delphi, Delphic

Delphīs, at Delphi

Dēmea, -ae, *m.*, Demea

dēns, dentis, *m.*, tooth

dēscendō, -ere, -scendī, -scēnsum, to descend* C21

deus, -ī, *m.*, god* C10

dēvastō (1), to devastate* C17

dextra, -ae, *f.*, right hand* C12

dīcō, -ere, dīxī, dictum, to say* C8

Dīdō, Dīdōnis, *f.*, Dido, exile from Phoenician Tyre, founding queen of Carthage

diēs, diēī, *m./f.*, day* C18

difficilis, -e, *adj.*, difficult* C15

digitus, -ī, *m.*, finger* C7

discēdō, -ere, -cessī, -cessum, to leave* C13

discō, -ere, didicī, ——, to learn

diū, *adv.*, for a long time* C2

dīves, dīvitis, *adj.*, rich* C13

dīvīnus, -a, -um, *adj.*, divine* C20

dīvitiae, -ārum, *f. pl.*, wealth, riches* C21

dō, dāre, dedī, dătum, to give* C4

doceō, -ēre, docuī, doctum, to teach* C5

doctus, -a, -um, *adj.*, learned* C13

doleō, -ēre, doluī, ——, to feel pain, hurt* C5

dolor, -ōris, *m.*, grief, pain* C11

dolus, -ī, *m.*, trickery, deception* C4

domī, at home* C3

domina, -ae, *f.*, mistress* C7

domus, -ūs, *f.*, house, home* C17

dōnum, -ī, *n.*, gift* C10

dormiō, -īre, dormīvī, dormītum, to sleep* C18

Druidēs, -um, *m. pl.*, the Druids

dūcō, -ere, dūxī, ductum, to lead, take* C13

dulcissime rērum, dear fellow, literally "the sweetest of all things"

dum, *conj.*, while* C6

duo, duae, dua, *numeral*, two

dux, ducis, *m.*, leader, general* C8

E

ē *or* **ex**, *prep. + abl.*, from, out of* C4

ecce, *interj.*, look here! * C15

egeō, -ēre, eguī, —— + *abl.*, to lack something* C20

egestās, -ātis, *f.*, lack, poverty

ego, *personal pronoun*, I* C3

ēiciō, -ere, eiēcī, eiectum, to throw away

enim, *conj.*, for, in fact* C13

eō diē, on that day

epistula, -ae, *f.*, letter* C5

equus, -ī, *m.*, horse* C10

ēripiō, -ere, -ripuī, -reptum, to snatch away* C21

errō (1), to wander, make a mistake* C21

et, *conj.*, and* C1

etiam, *adv.*, even, also* C15

Etrūscus, -a, -um, *adj.*, Etruscan

ēvanēscō, -ere, ēvanuī, ——, to disappear

excitō (1), to awaken, wake up, rouse, stir up* C18

exclāmō (1), to exclaim* C18

excutiō, -ere, -cussī, -cussum, to shake off

exemplar, -āris, *n.*, example* C9

exemplum, -ī, *n.*, example* C6

exeunt, they exit, go out

eximō, -ere, -ēmī, -ēmptum, to take out

exspectō (1), to wait for, await, expect* C2

exstinguō, -ere, exstīnxī, exstīnctum, to extinguish* C17

externus, -a, -um, *adj.*, outward, external* C21

F

Fābricius, -ī, *m.*, Fabricius

fābula, -ae, *f.*, story* C2

faciēs, -ēī, *f.*, face* C18

facile, *adv.*, easily* C17

faciō, -ere, fēcī, factum, to do, make* C12

familia, -ae, *f.*, family, household

familia, -ae, *f.*, family, household* C5

fātum, -ī, *n.*, fate, destiny

fātum, -ī, *n.*, fate, destiny* C18

fax, fācis, *f.*, torch

Fēlīciō, ——, *m.*, Felicio, a servant's name

fēlīx, -īcis, *adj.*, fortunate, happy* C10

fēmina, -ae, *f.*, woman* C16

femur, femoris, *n.*, the upper leg, the thigh

ferōx, -ōcis, *adj.*, fierce, ferocious* C19

ferus, -a, -um, *adj.*, wild, savage

fīlia, -ae, *f.*, daughter* C1

fīlius, -ī, *m.*, son C3

firmō (1), to strengthen* C6

flamma, -ae, *f.*, flame* C10

flexus, -a, -um, *adj.*, curved

fluō, -ere, flūxī, fluxum, to flow* C14

folium, -ī, *n.,* leaf

forīs, *adv.,* outside, in the open* C19

fōrma, -ae, *f.,* form, appearance* C2

fortasse, *adv.,* perhaps* C15

fortis, -e, *adj.,* brave, strong* C10

fortitūdō, -inis, *f.,* courage* C8

fortūna, -ae, *f.,* fortune, the goddess Fortune* C21

frāter, frātris, *m.,* brother

fugiō, -ere, fūgī, ——, to flee, run away* C10

fūmus, -ī, *m.,* smoke* C16

fūnestus, -a, -um, *adj.,* deadly* C16

fūr, fūris, *m.,* thief* C20

fūrtum, -ī, *n.,* theft* C20

futūrus, -a, -um, *participle,* about to be* C21

G

Gallī, -ōrum, *m. pl.,* the Gauls, the inhabitants of France

gaudium, -ī, *n.,* joy

gaudium, -ī, *n.,* joy* C5

gerō, -ere, gessī, gestum, to carry; **sē gerit,** s/he behaves C9; *with clothing or articles of clothing as its object,* to wear; **bellum gerere,** to wage war* C12

gladius, -ī, *m.,* sword* C14

Graecia, -ae, *f.,* Greece

Graecus, -a, -um, *adj.,* Greek; **Graecī, -ōrum,** *m. pl.,* the Greeks

gremium, -ī, *n.,* bosom, lap* C7

gutta, -ae, *f.,* drop

H

habeō, -ēre, habuī, habitum, to have* C2

habitō (1), to live, dwell* C2

hāc nocte, tonight

herba, -ae, *f.,* plant, vegetation* C19

heus!, hey!

hic, haec, hoc, *demonstrative pronoun and adj.,* this, latter* C19

homō, -inis, *m.,* man (i.e., human being); *pl.* people* C8

honor, -ōris, *m.,* honor, public office or distinction* C21

hostis, -is, *m.,* enemy* C10

hūc atque illūc, hither and thither, to and fro

hūmānus, -a, -um, *adj.,* human* C20

Hūnī, -ōrum, *m. pl.,* the Huns

I

iaceō, -ēre, iacuī, ——, to lie down, be inert* C6

iaciō, -ere, iēcī, iactum, to throw* C17

iam, *adv.,* already* C14

iānua, -ae, *f.,* door

ibi, *adv.,* there* C12

igitur, *conj.,* therefore* C16

ignis, -is, *m.,* fire* C12

ille, illa, illud, *demonstrative pronoun and adj.,* that, former* C20

illūc, *adv.,* to that place, thither

imparātus, -a, -um, *adj.,* unprepared

impedimentum, -ī, *n.,* impediment

imperātor, -ōris, *m.,* emperor* C17

impetus, -ūs, *m.,* impetus, force, attack* C17

importūnus, -a, -um, *adj.,* boorish

improbus, -a, -um, *adj.,* bad, wicked

in, *prep. + abl.,* in, on* C3

in, *prep. + acc.,* into, to* C4

incendium, -ī, *n.,* conflagration, eruption* C16

industria, -ae, *f.,* industry, care

inīquitās, -ātis, *f.,* injustice* C20

inīquus, -a, -um, *adj.,* unjust

initium, -ī, *n.,* beginning* C17

inquam, I say/I said (*only introducing direct speech*)* C15

inquit, s/he says or said (*only introducing direct speech*)* C12

intellegō, -ere, intellēxī, intellēctum, to understand* C8

inter, *prep. + acc.,* between, among* C19

intereā, *adv.,* meanwhile

intrō (1), to enter* C4

inūsitātus, -a, -um, *adj.,* strange, unusual

invideō, -ēre, invīdī, invīsum + *dat.,* to envy someone* C7

invīsō, -ere, invīsī, invīsum, to visit

ipse, ipsa, ipsum, *demonstrative pronoun and adj.,* -self

īra, -ae, *f.,* anger* C12

is, ea, id, *personal and demonstrative pronoun and adj.,* s/he/it, this, that* C12

ita, *adv.,* so, in such a way C18; yes* C11

Ītalia, -ae, *f.,* Italy

itaque, *conj.,* and so* C1

iubeō, -ēre, iussī, iussum + *acc. + inf.,* to order somebody to do something* C4

iudex, -icis, *m.,* judge* C13

iūdicō (1), to judge* C6

Iuppiter, Iovis, *m.,* Jupiter, king of gods (in Greek, Zeus)

iussus, -ūs, *m.,* order (*usually employed in the ablative singular only*)* C17

iūstus, -a, -um, *adj.,* legitimate, just* C4

L

lacrima, -ae, *f.,* tear* C5

laqueus, -ī, *m.,* noose, lasso

leaena, -ae, *f.,* lioness

legō, -ere, lēgī, lēctum, to read, choose* C16

lēx, lēgis, *f.,* law* C20

liber, librī, *m.,* book* C6

līberō (1) + *acc.* + *abl.,* to free someone from something* C8

licet + *dat.* + *inf.,* it is allowed, it is permitted for someone to do something* C13

ligneus, -a, -um, *adj.,* wooden

littera, -ae, *f.,* letter of the alphabet; **litterae, -ārum,** *f. pl.,* literature, letter (epistle)* C6

lītus, -oris, *n.,* shore* C16

locus, -ī, *m.,* place; **locī, -ōrum,** *m. pl.,* passages of a book; **loca, -ōrum,** *n. pl.,* geographical places* C17

longē, *adv.,* far* C5

longus, -a, -um, *adj.,* long* C5

Lūcīlius, -ī, *m.,* Lucilius, a friend of Seneca's to whom he addressed his philosophical essays in the form of letters

lūculentus, -a, -um, *adj.,* splendid

lūdō, -ere, lūsī, lūsum, to play* C20

lūmen, -inis, *n.,* light

lupa, -ae, *f.,* she-wolf* C1

M

Maecēnās, Maecēnātis, *m.,* Maecenas, friend of Augustus, patron of the arts

māgnus, -a, -um, *adj.,* large, great, important* C4

māiōrem, *adj.* (*accusative singular feminine*), bigger, greater

male, *adv.,* badly

malitia, -ae, *f.,* badness, wickedness

malus, -a, -um, *adj.,* bad* C4

maneō, -ēre, mānsī, mānsum, to remain* C6

manus, -ūs, *f.,* hand* C17

Mārcus Tullius Cicerō, -ōnis, *m.,* Marcus Tullius Cicero

mare, maris, *n.,* sea* C9

marītus, -ī, *m.,* husband* C18

Mārs, -tis, Mars, the god of war (in Greek, Ares)

māter, mātris, *f.,* mother* C16

mēcum = cum mē, with me* C13

mellītus, -a, -um, *adj.,* sweet as honey

memoria, -ae, *f.,* memory* C6

mercimōnium, -ī, *n.,* merchandise

Mercurius, -ī, *m.,* Mercury, messenger god, patron of merchants, travelers, thieves (in Greek, Hermes)

merīdiēs, -ēī, *m.,* midday* C18

meus, -a, -um, *possessive adj.,* my* C7

mīles, -itis, *m.,* soldier* C8

minimē, *adv.,* no* C11

Mīsēnum, -ī, *n.,* a base for the imperial Roman navy in the Bay of Naples; **Mīsēnī,** at Misenum

miser, misera, miserum, *adj.,* wretched* C5

mittō, -ere, mīsī, missum, to send* C11

mōns, montis, *m.,* mountain* C16

mordeō, -ēre, momordī, morsum, to bite

mors, mortis, *f.,* death* C9

mortuus, -a, -um, *adj.,* dead

moveō, -ēre, mōvī, mōtum, to move* C10

mox, *adv.,* soon* C14

Mūcius (-ī) Scaevola (-ae), *m.,* Mucius Scaevola

mulier, -ieris, *f.,* woman* C9

multum, *adv.,* much* C18

multus, -a, -um, *adj.,* much, many* C6

mūnimentum, -ī, *n.,* protection, fortification

mūrus, -ī, *m.,* wall, wall-fence* C17

mūtō (1), to change* C21

N

nam, *conj.,* for, in fact* C5

nārrō (1), to tell* C2

nauta, -ae, *m.,* sailor* C1

nāvigō (1), to sail, voyage* C8

nāvis, -is, *f.,* ship* C16

-ne, a particle added to the first word of an interrogative sentence* C11

nec, *conj.,* and not, nor* C10

necō (1), to kill

neglegō, -ere, neglēxī, neglēctum, to neglect* C15

nēminī, to nobody

Nerō, Nerōnis, *m.,* Nero, Julio-Claudian emperor

nihil, *negative pronoun,* nothing* C13

nisi, *conj.,* if not, unless

nōbīscum = cum nōbīs

noctū, *adv.,* during the night* C20

nōlō, *irregular verb,* not to want, be unwilling

nōlō, *irregular verb,* not to want, be unwilling* C13

nōmen, -inis, *n.,* name* C12

nōn sōlum . . . , sed etiam . . . , not only . . . , but also . . .*C5

nōn, *negative adv.,* not* C2

nōnne?, don't you?

nōs, personal pronoun, we* C12

noster, nostra, nostrum, *possessive adj.,* our* C12

nōtus, -a, -um, *adj.,* known

novus, -a, -um, *adj.,* new* C11

nox, noctis, *f.,* night* C10

nūbēs, -is, *f.,* cloud* C16

nūgae, -ārum, *f. pl.,* trifles

num?, do I? (negative answer implied)

numquam, *adv.,* never* C16

nunc, *adv.,* now* C2

O

ō, *interjection*, oh!

occīdō, -ere, occīdī, occīsum, to kill

occīdō, -ere, occīdī, occīsum, to kill* C12

occultātus, -a, -um, *adj.*, hidden

occultō (1), to hide* C18

occultus, -a, -um, *adj.*, hidden

oculus, -ī, *m.*, eye* C7

odium, -ī, *n.*, hatred* C14

oleum, -ī, *n.*, oil

omnis, -e, *adj.*, each, every, all* C13

opprimō, -ere, oppressī, oppressum, to overwhelm, suppress* C16

oppugnō (1), to attack

ōrāculum, -ī, *n.*, oracle* C8

ōrātiō, -ōnis, *f.*, speech; **ōrātiōnem habēre**, to make a speech* C9

ōs, ōris, *n.*, mouth* C14

ostendō, -ere, ostendī, ostentum, to show* C12

P

paene, *adv.*, almost* C20

papae!, wow!

parātus, -a, -um, *adj.*, prepared (often + *inf.*)

parēns, -rentis, *m./f.*, parent* C14

pariēs, parietis, *m.*, wall

parō (1), to prepare, get ready C2, design* C5

pars, partis, *f.*, part* C16

parvus, -a, -um, *adj.*, small* C15

passer, -eris, *m.*, sparrow* C7

pater, -tris, *m.*, father* C18

patria, -ae, *f.*, fatherland* C2

paucī, -ae, -a, *adj.*, few* C10

paulisper, *adv.*, for a little while

pauper, pauperis, *adj.*, poor* C20

pāx, pācis, *f.*, peace* C7

pectus, -oris, *n.*, chest* C14

pellis, -is, *f.*, skin, hide* C19

per, *prep. + acc.*, through* C14

perīculum, -ī, *n.*, danger* C10

permoveō, -ēre, -mōvī, -mōtum, to perturb

Persae, -ārum, *m. pl.*, the Persians

petō, -ere, petīvī, petītum, to seek, head for, go to* C8

piger, pigra, pigrum, *adj.*, lazy

pīpiō, -āre, ——, ——, to chirp

pirum, -ī, *n.*, pear (fruit)

pirus, -ī, *f.*, pear tree

plēnus, -a, -um, *adj. + gen. or + abl.*, full of* C20

pluit, -ere, pluit, ——, *an impersonal verb (used only in 3rd sg.)*, to rain

plūs quam, more than

poena, -ae, *f.*, punishment

poēta, -ae, *m.*, poet* C1

pōmum, -ī, *n.*, fruit* C20

pōnō, -ere, posuī, positum, to put, place* C12

porcus, -ī, *m.*, pig

porta, -ae, *f.*, gate

possideō, -ēre, possēdī, possessum, to possess* C21

possum, posse, potuī, ——, to be able, can* C6

post, *prep. + acc.*, after* C18

posteā, *adv.*, afterwards

posteā, *adv.*, afterwards* C1

postquam, *conj.*, after* C19

praeclārus, -a, -um, *adj.*, famous, distinguished* C4

praefectus, -ī, *m.*, prefect, commander, chief

praemium, -ī, *n.*, reward* C4

prīmum, *adv.*, first

prīmus, -a, -um, *adj.*, first* C14

prō certō, *adverbial phrase*, for certain, for sure* C21

prō Iuppiter!, by Jove!

prō, *prep. + abl.*, for, on behalf of* C13

proelium, -ī, *n.*, battle, combat* C19

profuga, -ae, *m.*, deserter

prope, *prep. + acc.*, near* C12

propter, *prep. + acc.*, because of, on account of* C6

Psȳchē (gen. Psȳchēs, dat. Psȳchē, acc. Psȳchēn, abl. Psȳchē), Psyche

puella, -ae, *f.*, girl* C1

puer, puerī, *m.*, boy* C3

pugnō (1), to fight* C10

pulcher, pulchra, pulchrum, *adj.*, beautiful, nice* C5

pulchritūdō, pulchritūdinis, *f.*, beauty

pūniō, -īre, pūnīvī, pūnītum, to punish* C20

putō (1), to think, consider* C7

Pȳramus, -ī, *m.*, Pyramus

Pyrrhus, -ī, *m.*, Pyrrhus, king of Epirus

Pȳthia, -ae, *f.*, the Pythian priestess, responsible for uttering the ambiguous oracles at the shrine of Apollo at Delphi, Greece

Q

quaerō, -ere, quaesīvī, quaesītum, to look for, search* C18

-que, *conj.*, and* C11

quī, quae, quod, *relative pronoun*, which, who, that* C14

quī, quae, quod?, *interrogative adjective*, which? what? * C15

quid agis, how are you?

quis, quid?, *interrogative pronoun*, who? what? * C13

quō?, to what place?

quōcum = cum quō, with whom

quōmodo, how?

quondam, *adv.*, once

quoque, *adv.*, also* C11

R

rādīx, rādīcis, *f.*, root

rāmus, -ī, *m.*, branch

recipiō, -ere, -cēpī, -ceptum, to take back* C21

rēgīna, -ae, *f.,* queen* C11

relinquō, -ere, relīquī, relictum, to leave behind, abandon* C11

Remus, -ī, *m.,* Remus, brother of Romulus

reparō (1), to repair

reprehendō, -ere, -prehendī, -prehēnsum, to blame, rebuke* C21

rēs, reī, *f.,* thing, matter* C18

respondeō, -ēre, -spondī, -spōnsum, to answer* C13

revēniō, -īre, -vēnī, -ventum, to return

rēx, rēgis, *m.,* king

rēx, rēgis, *m.,* king* C8

Rhēa Silvia, Rhēae Silviae, *f.,* Rhea Silvia, vestal virgins

rīvus, -ī, *m.,* brook, stream* C3

rogō (1), to ask* C13

Rōma, -ae, *f.,* Rome* C1

Rōmānus, -a, -um, *adj.,* Roman

Rōmānus, -a, -um, *adj.,* Roman* C4

Rōmulus, -ī, *m.,* Romulus, legendary founder of Rome

rota, -ae, *f.,* wheel* C21

ruber, rubra, rubrum, *adj.,* red* C14

rūsticus, -a, -um, *adj.,* rural, rustic* C15

S

sacer, sacra, sacrum, *adj.,* holy, sacred

sacra, -ōrum, *n. pl.,* religious rites

saepe, *adv.,* often* C6

sagitta, -ae, *f.,* arrow

salūtem plūrimam dīcit + *dat.,* s/he greets (someone) (a standard formula for beginning a letter). Literally it means "(s/he) says (i.e., wishes) very much health (the best of health) to …"

salvē!, hello!

sanguis, sanguinis, *m.,* blood* C14

sānō (1), to heal* C19

saxum, -ī, *n.,* stone, rock* C15

scientia, -ae, *f.,* knowledge

sciō, scīre, scīvī, scītum, to know* C9

sē, *acc. of the reflexive pronoun,* herself, himself, itself, themselves* C7

sed, *conj.,* but* C4

sedeō, -ēre, sēdī, sessum, to sit* C19

sella, -ae, *f.,* seat, chair

sēmoveō, -ēre, sēmōvī, sēmōtum, to remove

semper, *adv.,* always* C5

Seneca, -ae, *m.,* Seneca, Roman author

senectūs, -ūtis, *f.,* old age* C15

senex, -is, *m.,* old man* C7

sentiō, -īre, sēnsī, sēnsum, to feel* C9

sēparō (1), to separate* C14

servō (1), to save, preserve*

sevērus, -a, -um, *adj.,* serious, strict, severe C7*

sī, *conj.,* if* C18

sīcut, *adv.,* as

sīcut, *adv.,* just as* C15

silva, -ae, *f.,* forest* C11

similis, -e, *adj.* + *gen.* or + *dat.,* like, similar* C12

sine, *prep.* + *abl.,* without* C17

soleō, -ēre, solitus sum + *inf.,* to be accustomed* C6

sōlus, -a, -um, *adj.,* sole, only

somnus, -ī, *m.,* sleep* C18

soror, -ōris, *f.,* sister* C7

spectō (1), to look at, gaze, stare at

spēlunca, -ae, *f.,* cave* C11

statim, *adv.,* immediately* C12

stō, -āre, stetī, statum, to stand* C15

studeō, -ēre, studuī, —— + *dat.,* to study, be eager for, be interested in* C16

studiōsus, -a, -um, *adj.* + *gen.,* interested in, a student of

subitō, *adv.,* suddenly*

sum, esse, fuī, ——, to be* C6

summus, -a, -um, *adj.,* the top of

suus, -a, -um, *possessive adj.,* his, her, its, their* C13

Syrācūsānus, -a, -um, *adj.,* from Syracuse

T

taberna, -ae, *f.,* shop

tam, *adv.,* so* C18

tamen, *conj.,* however* C5

tandem, *adv.,* at last* C8

tangō, -ere, tetigī, tāctum, to touch* C14

tantum, *adv.,* only* C13

tantus, -a, -um, *adj.,* so great* C12

tēcum = cum tē, with you* C13

tempestās, -ātis, *f.,* storm* C11

templum, -ī, *n.,* temple* C8

temptō (1), to try* C17

tempus, -oris, *n.,* time* C9

tenebrae, -ārum, *f. pl.,* shadows, darkness* C6

teneō, -ēre, tenuī, tentum, to hold* C2

Terentia, -ae, *f.,* Terentia, wife of Cicero

terō, -ere, trīvī, trītum, to wear out, rub* C19

terra, -ae, *f.,* land* C1

terribilis, -e, *adj.,* terrifying* C19

tertius, -a, -um, *adj.,* third

Themistoclēs, Themistoclis, *m.,* Themistocles, Athenian general

Thisbē, Thisbēs (gen.), Thisbē (dat.), Thisbēn (acc.), Thisbē (voc.), *f.,* Thisbe

timeō, -ēre, timuī, ——, to fear, be afraid* C3

timor, -ōris, *m.,* fear* C8

tolerō (1), to tolerate, bear

tollō, -ere, sustulī, sublātum, to lift up, raise, destroy* C21

tonō, -āre, -uī, ——, to thunder

tōtus, -a, -um, *adj.,* whole

trāns Tiberim, on the other side of the Tiber river

trēs, tria, *numeral,* three

trīstitia, -ae, *f.,* sadness

Trōia, -ae, *f.,* Troy

Trōiānus, -a, -um, *adj.,* Trojan

tū, *personal pronoun,* you (sg.) * C3

tum, *adv.,* then* C13

tumultus, -ūs, *m.,* uproar, confusion* C17

tunc, *adv.,* then* C8

tuus, -a, -um, *possessive adj.,* yours, your (sg.) * C12

U

ubi, *adv.,* where

ubīque, *adv.,* everywhere* C15

Ulixes, Ulixis, *m.,* Odysseus, Ulysses (Latin)

ūllus, -a, -um, *adj.,* any* C21

umquam, *adv.,* ever* C15

ūnā, *adv.,* together* C11

ūnusquisque nostrum, each one of us

urbs, urbis, *f.,* city (usually the city of Rome) * C9

uxor, -ōris, *f.,* wife* C18

V

valdē, *adv.,* very, exceedingly* C3

valē!, goodbye!* C13

vectus, -a, -um, *adj.,* carried, driven

vēlāmen, vēlāminis, *n.,* veil

venēnum, -ī, *n.,* poison* C4

veniō, -īre, vēnī, ventum, to come* C9

ventus, -ī, *m.,* wind* C17

Venus, Veneris, *f.,* Venus, goddess of beauty and love (in Greek, Aphrodite)

verbum, -ī, *n.,* word* C7

versō (1), to turn* C21

vērus, -a, -um, *adj.,* true* C15

Vesta, -ae, *f.,* Vesta, goddess of the hearth (in Greek, Hestia)

vester, vestra, vestrum, *possessive adj.,* yours (pl.), your* C12

vestīmentum, -ī, *n.,* garment, (pl.) clothes* C19

Vesuvius, -ī, *m.,* (Mount) Vesuvius

vetustus, -a, -um, *adj.,* old* C15

Via Sacra, a street in the Roman Forum

via, -ae, *f.,* road* C3

victōria, -ae, *f.,* victory

videō, -ēre, vīdī, vīsum, to see, (passive) seem* C2

vīlicus, -ī, *m.,* bailiff, steward

vīlla, -ae, *f.,* country house, villa* C15

vincō, -ere, vīcī, victum, to conquer, defeat* C8

vīnctus, -a, -um, *adj.,* bound, chained

vinculum, -ī, *n.,* chain, fetter* C4

vir, virī, *m.,* man* C3

vīs, ——, *f., pl.* **vīrēs, vīrium,** force, strength; **prō vīribus,** with all one's might* C12

vīta, -ae, *f.,* life* C6

vīvō, -ere, vīxī, victum, to live* C19

vocō (1), to call* C2

vōs, *personal pronoun,* you (pl.) * C12

vulnerō (1), to wound* C19

vulnus, -eris, *n.,* wound* C19

vult, he wishes

Xerxēs, Xerxis, *m.,* Xerxes, the great king of the Persians (who invaded Greece in 480 BCE)

BIBLIOGRAPHY

LATIN GRAMMAR

Allen, J. H., and J. B. Greenough. *Allen and Greenough's New Latin Grammar.* Edited by Anne Mahoney. Newburyport, MA: Focus Publishing/R. Pullins, 2001.

Gildersleeve, Basil L., and Gonzalez Lodge. *Gildersleeve's Latin Grammar.* 3rd ed. 1895. Reprint, Wauconda, IL: Bolchazy-Carducci Publishers, 2003.

LATIN COMPOSITION

Minkova, Milena. *Introduction to Latin Prose Composition.* Wauconda, IL: Bolchazy-Carducci Publishers, 2007. First published 2002 by Wimbledon Publishing Co.

Minkova, Milena, and Terence Tunberg. *Readings and Exercises in Latin Prose Composition: From Antiquity to the Renaissance.* Newburyport, MA: Focus Publishing/ R. Pullins, 2004.

Mountford, James F., ed. *Bradley's Arnold Latin Prose Composition.* Rev. ed. Wauconda, IL: Bolchazy-Carducci Publishers, 2006.

LATIN DICTIONARIES

Lewis, Charlton T., and Charles Short. *A Latin Dictionary.* Oxford: Clarendon Press, 1879.

Oxford Latin Dictionary. Edited by P. G. W. Glare. Oxford: Clarendon Press, 1982.

Smith, William, and Theophilus D. Hall. *Smith's English-Latin Dictionary.* Reprinted from the 1871 American Book Company edition, *A Copious and Critical English-Latin Dictionary,* with a new foreword by Dirk Sacré. Wauconda, IL: Bolchazy-Carducci Publishers, 2000.

CONVERSATIONAL LATIN

Traupman, John. *Conversational Latin for Oral Proficiency.* 4th ed.: *Audio Conversations.* Performed by Mark Robert Miner et al. Compact disks. Wauconda, IL: Bolchazy-Carducci Publishers, 2006.

LATIN LITERATURE

Albrecht, Michael von. *A History of Roman Literature: From Livius Andronicus to Boethius.* Leiden: Brill Academic Publishers, 1997.

IJsewijn, Jozef. *Companion to Neo-Latin Studies, Part I: History and Diffusion of Neo-Latin Literature.* 2nd ed. Supplementa Humanistica Lovaniensia, 5. Leuven: University Press, 1990.

IJsewijn, Jozef, and Dirk Sacré. *Companion to Neo-Latin Studies, II: Literary, Linguistic, Philological and Editorial Questions.* 2nd. ed. Supplementa Humanistic Lovaniensia, 14. Leuven: Leuven University Press, 1998.

Mantello, Frank, and Arthur G. Rigg. *Medieval Latin. An Introduction and Bibliographical Guide.* Washington, D.C.: The Catholic University of America Press, 1996.

HISTORY OF THE LATIN SPEAKING WORLD

Boatwright, Mary T., Daniel J. Gargola, and Richard J. A. Talbert. *A Brief History of the Romans.* New York: Oxford University Press, 2006.

Holmes, George. *The Oxford History of Medieval Europe.* Oxford: Oxford University Press, 2001.

Thompson, Bard. *Humanists and Reformers: A History of the Renaissance and Reformation.* Grand Rapids and Cambridge: William B. Eerdmans Publishers, 1996.

MYTHOLOGY

Colakis, Marianthe, and Mary Joan Masello. *Classical Mythology and More: A Reader Workbook.* Wauconda, IL: Bolchazy-Carducci Publishers, 2007.

Morford, Mark P. O., and Robert J. Lenardon. *Classical Mythology.* 8th ed. New York: Oxford University Press, 2006.

DAILY LIFE

Brucia, Margaret A., and Gregory Daugherty. *To Be a Roman: Topics in Roman Culture.* Wauconda, IL: Bolchazy-Carducci Publishers, 2007.

Carcopino, Jérôme. *Daily Life in Ancient Rome.* New Haven and London:Yale University Press, 1968.

Newman, Paul B. *Daily Life in the Middle Ages.* Jefferson, NC: McFarland & Company, 2001.

ENGLISH ETYMOLOGY

Oxford Dictionary of English Etymology. Edited by C. T. Onions et al. New York: Oxford University Press, 1966.

PHOTOGRAPHY CREDITS

INTRODUCTION
Etruscan Sarcophagus (© 2008 Jupiter Images Corp.)
Engraved stone 1 (© 2008 Shutterstock Images LLC)
Engraved stone 2 (© 2008 Shutterstock Images LLC)
Roman Baths (© 2008 Shutterstock Images LLC)
Tiber River (© 2008 Jupiter Images Corp.)
Ruins in Carthage (© 2008 Shutterstock Images LLC)

CHAPTER 1
Romulus and Remus (Scala/Art Resource, NY)
Capitoline Wolf (© 2008 Shutterstock Images LLC)
Pont du Gard (© 2008 Shutterstock Images LLC)
SPQR (© 2008 Shutterstock Images LLC)
Greek Wrestlers (© 2008 Shutterstock Images LLC)
Farmer with Sheep (© 2008 Jupiter Images Corp.)

CHAPTER 2
Three Actors (Erich Lessing/Art Resource, NY)
Mask of Comedy (© 2008 Shutterstock Images LLC)
Theatre in Ephesus (© 2008 Shutterstock Images LLC)
Sabratha Relief (© 2008 Shutterstock Images LLC)

CHAPTER 3
Choreographer (Erich Lessing/Art Resource, NY)
Bosra Theatre (© 2008 Shutterstock Images LLC)
Masks (© 2008 Jupiter Images Corp.)
Theatre of Marcellus (© 2008 Shutterstock Images LLC)
Roman Road (© 2008 Shutterstock Images LLC)

REVIEW 1
Writing Utensils (Erich Lessing/Art Resource, NY)

CLASSICAL GODS 1
Mars and Venus (© 2008 Jupiter Images Corp.)
Zeus coin (© 2008 Shutterstock Images LLC)
Jupiter and Juno (Scala/Art Resource, NY)

Temple of Hera II (© 2008 Jupiter Images Corp.)
Mt. Olympus (© 2008 Shutterstock Images LLC)

ANCIENT WORLD 1
Butchershop (Alinari/Art Resource, NY)
Building a Wall (© 2008 Jupiter Images Corp.)
Mosaic of Slaves (© 2008 Jupiter Images Corp.)

EXPLORATION 1
Comedy Mask (© 2008 Jupiter Images Corp.)
Caesarea Theatre (© 2008 Shutterstock Images LLC)

MĪRĀBILE AUDĪTŪ 1
Jerash Theatre (© 2008 Jupiter Images Corp.)

CHAPTER 4
Pyrrhus (SEF/Art Resource, NY)
Roman Legionary (© 2008 Jupiter Images Corp.)
Legionary Actors (© 2008 Shutterstock Images LLC)
Centurion (© 2008 Shutterstock Images LLC)

CHAPTER 5
Porculo and Wife (Alinari/Art Resource, NY)
Bust of Cicero (© 2008 Jupiter Images Corp.)
Cicero Sign (© 2008 Shutterstock Images LLC)

CHAPTER 6
Norma and the Druids (Bildarchiv Preussischer Kulturbesitz/Art Resource, NY)
Letters on Stone (© 2008 Shutterstock Images LLC)
Julius Caesar Stamp (© 2008 Shutterstock Images LLC)
Caesar and Commentaries (Scala/Art Resource, NY)
Women during Gallic Invasion (© 2008 Jupiter Images Corp.)

REVIEW 2
Roman Weapons (National Museum of Slovenia, by Tomaz Lauko)

Basilica of Maxentius (© 2008 Shutterstock Images LLC)

CLASSICAL GODS 2

Trevi Fountain (© 2008 Shutterstock Images LLC)

Neptune Fountain (© 2008 Shutterstock Images LLC)

Charon (© 2008 Jupiter Images Corp.)

House of the Vestals (© 2008 Shutterstock Images LLC)

Demeter and Triptolemus (© 2008 Jupiter Images Corp.)

ANCIENT WORLD 2

Toilette of the Bride (Alinari/Art Resource, NY)

Sabine Women (© 2008 Shutterstock Images LLC)

EXPLORATION 2

Funerary Bust (© British Museum/Art Resource, NY)

Young Roman Boy (© 2008 Shutterstock Images LLC)

Child with Amphora (© 2008 Shutterstock Images LLC)

MĪRĀBILE AUDĪTŪ 2

Annuit coeptīs (© 2008 Shutterstock Images LLC)

Caveat ēmptor (© 2008 Shutterstock Images LLC)

Three Dimension @ (© 2008 Shutterstock Images LLC)

CHAPTER 7

Pompeian Couple Fresco (Scala/Art Resource, NY)

Coin of an *As* (© 2008 Shutterstock Images LLC)

Dove Mosaic (© 2008 Shutterstock Images LLC)

Sparrow (© 2008 Shutterstock Images LLC)

Thermopolium (© 2008 Shutterstock Images LLC)

CHAPTER 8

Themistocles (Scala/Art Resource, NY)

Greek Warship (© 2008 Shutterstock Images LLC)

Leonidas (© 2008 Jupiter Images Corp.)

Delphic Sibyl (© 2008 Shutterstock Images LLC)

Sanctuary of Athena (© 2008 Shutterstock Images LLC)

CHAPTER 9

Cicero Denounces Catiline (Scala/Art Resource, NY)

Roman Body Armor (© 2008 Jupiter Images Corp.)

Side of the Senate House (© 2008 Shutterstock Images LLC)

Mediterranean Sea (© 2008 Shutterstock Images LLC)

REVIEW 3

CLASSICAL GODS 3

Pompeiian Statue of Apollo (© 2008 Shutterstock Images LLC)

Ruins at Delos (© 2008 Shutterstock Images LLC)

Daphne (© 2008 Shutterstock Images LLC)

Temple of Apollo, Corinth (© 2008 Shutterstock Images LLC)

ANCIENT WORLD 3

Man Wearing a Toga (© 2008 Shutterstock Images LLC)

Bust of Roman Men and Women (© 2008 Shutterstock Images LLC)

MĪRĀBILE AUDĪTŪ 3

Ē plūribus ūnum on coin (© 2008 Shutterstock Images LLC)

Ē plūribus ūnum on stamp (© 2008 Jupiter Images Corp.)

Dollar Bill (© 2008 Shutterstock Images LLC)

CHAPTER 10

Reconstructed Wooden Horse (© 2008 Jupiter Images Corp.)

Odysseus Vase (© 2008 Jupiter Images Corp.)

Vergil Mosaic (© 2008 Jupiter Images Corp.)

CHAPTER 11

Dido and Aeneas Hunting (Bridgeman-Giraudon/Art Resource, NY)

Mercury with Caduceus (© 2008 Jupiter Images Corp.)

Ruins of Carthage (© 2008 Shutterstock Images LLC)

CHAPTER 12

Mucius' Hand in the Fire (Alinari/Art Resource, NY)

Constantine's Hand (© 2008 Shutterstock Images LLC)

Temple of Antoninus (© 2008 Shutterstock Images LLC)

Antonine Column (© 2008 Jupiter Images Corp.)

REVIEW 4
CLASSICAL GODS 4
Hermes and Apollo (Erich Lessing/Art Resource, NY)

Statue of Hermes (© 2008 Jupiter Images Corp.)

ANCIENT WORLD 4
Mosaic of Flagon and Goblet (© 2008 Shutterstock Images LLC)

Triclinium Diagram (© 2008 Jupiter Images Corp.)

Wooden Plates (© 2008 Shutterstock Images LLC)

Slovenian Artifacts (National Museum of Slovenia, by Tomaz Lauko)

EXPLORATION 4
Bust of Homer (© 2008 Jupiter Images Corp.)

Wooden Horse (© 2008 Shutterstock Images LLC)

Computer Screen (© 2008 Shutterstock Images LLC)

MĪRĀBILE AUDĪTŪ 4
Roman Soldier (© 2008 Shutterstock Images LLC)

CHAPTER 13
Via Sacra in Forum (Scala/Art Resource, NY)

Temple of Vesta (© 2008 Shutterstock Images LLC)

Sundial (© 2008 Shutterstock Images LLC)

Bookends (© 2008 Jupiter Images Corp.)

CHAPTER 14
Suicide of Thisbe (Bridgeman-Giraudon/Art Resource, NY)

Mulberry Branch (© 2008 Shutterstock Images LLC)

Lion Mosaic (© 2008 Jupiter Images Corp.)

CHAPTER 15
Suicide of Seneca (Erich Lessing/Art Resource, NY)

Bust of Pseudo-Seneca (© 2008 Jupiter Images Corp.)

Interior of Villa of Mysteries (© 2008 Jupiter Images Corp.)

Nero Coin (© 2008 Shutterstock Images LLC)

Villa Diagram (© 2008 Jupiter Images Corp.)

REVIEW 5
Sculpture of Augustus (© 2008 Shutterstock Images LLC)

CLASSICAL GODS 5
Athena Statue in Austria (© 2008 Shutterstock Images LLC)

Minerva Cameo (© 2008 Jupiter Images Corp.)

Statue of Diana (© 2008 Shutterstock Images LLC)

Venus of Milo (© 2008 Shutterstock Images LLC)

ANCIENT WORLD 5
Sabratha, Libya (© 2008 Jupiter Images Corp.)

Via Appia (© 2008 Shutterstock Images LLC)

Roman Milestone (© 2008 Shutterstock Images LLC)

EXPLORATION 5
Justice with Scales (© 2008 Shutterstock Images LLC)

CHAPTER 16
Eruption of Vesuvius (Réunion des Musées Nationaux/Art Resource, NY)

Vesuvius and Ruins (© 2008 Shutterstock Images LLC)

Statue of Faun (© 2008 Shutterstock Images LLC)

Pompeian Street Scene (© 2008 Shutterstock Images LLC)

CHAPTER 17
Torches of Nero (Erich Lessing/Art Resource, NY)

Cornucopia (© 2008 Jupiter Images Corp.)

Bust of Nero (© 2008 Jupiter Images Corp.)

Plan of the House of the Faun (© 2008 Jupiter Images Corp.)

Ruins in the Forum (© 2008 Shutterstock Images LLC)

CHAPTER 18
Cupid and Psyche (© 2008 Shutterstock Images LLC)

Marcus Aurelius (© 2008 Shutterstock Images LLC)

Faces with Loving Looks (© 2008 Shutterstock Images LLC)

Roman Eros (© 2008 Shutterstock Images LLC)

INDEX

Note: A reference to xxvii or 192 indicates the main text, while xxviip or 192p indicates a picture or its caption.

A

ab urbe conditā, AUC (method of dating), 192

Ab Urbe Conditā (work of Livy), 192, 329

Abbreviations, 109, 310, 388

Ablative case
   of agent, 76
   of instrument (means), 129
   of manner, 128–129
   of place from which, 129
   of place where, 131–132
   with prepositions, 405
   of separation, 129

Accent, xxviii

Accusative case, 7
   and infinitive (indirect statement), 116–118, 407
   of place to which, 131
   with prepositions, 405

Acheron, 99

Achilles, 380

Actaeon, 265

Actium, 220, 380p

Active and passive voices, 72–73

AD and CE, 388

Adjectives, 4. *See also* Participles
   1st and 2nd declension in *-us, -a, -um*, 64, 397
   1st and 2nd declension in *-er*, 77–78, 397–398
   3rd declension in one, two, and three endings, 169–171, 398
   demonstrative
      hic, 343, 358, 400
      ille, 357–358, 400

interrogative, 251–253, 399–400

possessive
   1st and 2nd person, 199, 399, 408
   3rd person, 228, 399, 408

reflexive, 228

as substantives, 172–173, 409

Adonis, 266

Adverbs, 4

Aeneas, 177–178, 177p, 186p, 263, 266, 380, 381
   travels of, mapped, 187p

Aesculapius (Asclepius), 153

Aetna, Mount. *See* Etna, Mount

Agent, ablative of, 76

Agreement
   noun-adjective, 64–65, 77, 406
   in perfect passive system, 339–340
   predicate noun in indirect statement, 117
   subject-verb, 23, 406

Agricola (Tacitus), 217, 288

Agrippina, 246

Alaric, xxxi

Alba Longa, 2

Alexander the Great, 58

Alexandria, 383

Alphabet, Latin, xxiii–xxv, 382
   in inscriptions, xxvp, 8p, 85p
   names of letters in, xxivp
   vs. English alphabet, xxiv

AM and PM, 310

amābō, "please," 236

Ammiānus Marcellīnus, 332, 389
   Rēs gestae, reading from, 332

Amphitheatres, 323p, 324

Amphitrite, 98

Amulius, 2, 329

Anchises, 263, 266

Ancus Martius, xxx

Angles and Saxons, xxxi

Annālēs, Annals (Tacitus), 287–288, 328, 332

annō Dominī (AD), 388

ante merīdiem (AM), 310

antecedent, 240–242

Antoninus Pius, 198p, 201p, 251p, 302

Antony, Mark, 158, 160, 220

Apollo, 153–154, 153p, 155, 214, 265, 321, 384

Appian Way, 268, 268p

Āpulēius, 302, 305p, 389
   Metamorphōsēs
   quoted, 301
   reading from, 302–303

Aqueducts, 5p

Arachne, 266

Archias, 96

Ares. *See* Mars

Aristotle, 160, 384

Armor, military, 139p

Artemis. *See* Diana

as (coin), 115p

Asclepius (Aesculapius), 153

Athena. *See* Minerva

Athens, 264

Athens, politics of, 158–160

Atlantis, 98

Attila the Hun, 331*p*

Attire, 156–157

Auctions, slave, 51

Augustan age, poets of, 112

Augustine (Aurēlius Augustīnus),
349*p*, 350, 378*p*, 389

 Cōnfessiōnēs, 389

  quoted, 349

  reading from, 350

Augustō auguriō, xxx

Augustus Caesar, xxx, 54*p*, 160,
164, 177, 220, 262*p*, 329

Aurelius, Marcus, 201*p*, 302, 305*p*

B

-*BĀ*-, sign of the imperfect tense,
180

Babies, 104–105

Babylon, 234

Bacchants (Maenads), 321

Bacchus (Dionysus, Liber),
320–322, 320*p*, 321*p*, 322*p*,
379

Base of noun, shown by genitive, 11

Basilicae, 267

 of Maxentius, 97*p*

Bathhouses, xxix*p*

 libraries in, 386

 Seneca on, xxix

Bay of Naples, 316–317*p*

Beast fights, 325

Bishop, symbols of, 378*p*

Boēthius, Anicius Manlius
Severinus, 362, 369*p*, 389

 Cōnsōlātiō Philosophiae, reading
from, 362–363

Bookrolls, 387

Books, 384–387

The Bore (in Horace's *Satires*),
270–271

Boys, education of, 106–107,
382–383

"Bread and circuses" (Juvenal), 323

bulla, 105, 107

Burgundians, xxxi

Busts, portrait, 74*p*, 104*p*, 157*p*,
251*p*, 294*p*

Byzantium, xxxi

C

Caduceus, 186*p*, 210

Caesar, Gāius Jūlius, xxx, 38*p*,
82, 86*p*, 89*p*, 91*p*, 160, 384,
389

 Dē bellō Gallicō, reading from, 82

 quoted, 81

Callimachus, 112

Campus Martius, 47

Cardinal numbers, 230

carpe diem, 219–220

Carthage, xxxiv, 178, 186*p*

Cartoons, Trojan Horse in, 215

Cases of nouns and adjectives, 6–7,
405. *See also under* specific
cases

Cassandra, 155, 214

Catiline, 135*p*, 136

Cato the Censor (Cato the Elder),
quoted, xxxiv

Catullus, Gāius Valerius, 265, 389

 quoted, 111

 reading from, 112

CE, and AD, 388

Celsus, Tiberius Julius, 385–386

 library of, 383*p*

cēna, dinner, 211–212

Centurion, 66*p*

Ceres (Demeter), 96, 98, 100–101,
101*p*

Chariot races, 47, 325

Charon, 99, 99*p*

Chaucer, Geoffrey, 215

Children, 104–107, 105*p*

chrīae, 383

Christians, 288

Cicero, Marcus Tullius, 58, 74*p*,
383–384, 389

Dē Officiīs, reading from, 58

 letters, reading from, 70

 Philippics, 158

 quoted, 135, 217, 330

 and Terentia, 102

Circus Maximus, 328

Cities, 267–268

Citizenship, Athenian and Roman,
158–159

Claudius, 246

Clauses, relative, 240–242, 409

Cleanthes, 246

Cleito, 98

Cleopatra, 54, 220

Clio, 174*p*

Clodia, 112

Cloelia, 208

Clothing, 156–157

Coins

 as, 115*p*

 dēnārius, 359*p*

Colosseum, 323*p*, 324, 325*p*

Comedy. *See also* Plautus; Terence

 actors, 15*p*

 masks, 23*p*, 37*p*, 53*p*

 stage-decorations, 25*p*

 theatre, 32*p*, 38*p*, 54*p*

Coming of age ceremonies, 107

Comitia Centuriāta, 159

Comitia Tribūta, 159

Commands (positive and
negative), 222–223, 403

'Common Era' (CE), *vs.* AD, 388

Complementary infinitive, 88, 407

cōnfirmātiō, 383

Conjugations, 18

 first and second, 18

 third, 126

 third -*iō*-, 166

 fourth, 138–139

Conjunctions, 4

 listed, 406

Consonants, pronunciation of, xxvii

LATIN FOR THE NEW MILLENNIUM
ELECTRONIC RESOURCES FOR STUDENTS

VISIT LNM.BOLCHAZY.COM

Latin for the New Millennium provides a variety of online materials that complement your Latin lessons and encourage **active use of Latin** within **fun learning environments**. Audio, games, and more await with new content added frequently.

QUIZ YOURSELF ONLINE

REINFORCE YOUR UNDERSTANDING OF LATIN GRAMMAR

Check out *lookingatlatin.com*—with over 5,000 exercises—covering all points of Latin grammar. These online exercises build your Latin skills because they are self-correcting. Just ten to thirty-five questions per part of speech or point of grammar make these questions very manageable for students.

Spend some time doing Latin online and watch your understanding of Latin grow!

PRACTICE YOUR LATIN ONLINE AS YOU MEET LATIN STUDENTS FROM AROUND THE WORLD!

Visit Bolchazy-Carducci's Roman villa in Teen Second Life™ where Latin is the *lingua franca*. Students over 18 may visit Bolchazy-Carducci's Latin site in the Main Grid of Second Life™.

Practice writing and speaking Latin as you apply what you are learning through the readings and dialogues presented in each chapter of *Latin for the New Millennium*.

Go solo from home or join your class in the computer lab for speaking Latin aloud.

iPODIUS

For Latin audio, video, vocabulary flashcards, and other software downloads, visit *ipodius.bolchazy.com*, Bolchazy-Carducci's online multimedia store.

SO, YOURS IS A MORE ADVENTUROUS BENT . . .

COMPUTER GAMES EXCITE YOUR IMAGINATION . . .

Bolchazy-Carducci Publishers sponsors a Latin-language guild, *Carpe Praedam* within the enormously popular on-line game, World of Warcraft™. Guild members currently include both teachers and students who use the game to **practice their conversational Latin skills while questing for treasure and honor.**

YOU'D LIKE TO SHARE YOUR INSIGHTS ABOUT STUDYING LATIN?

eClassics

You're invited to join hundreds of Latinists on eClassics. Similar to Facebook, but especially designed for classics, eClassics is easy to use and provides the contemporary learning tools you like. Just click on *eClassics*.

With online exercises, games, and virtual worlds, *Latin for the New Millennium* provides the contemporary learning tools you like.

EXCITED ABOUT A PROJECT YOU DID IN CLASS?

Talk to your teacher about sharing it through the LNM Teachers' Lounge. That would be pretty cool!

ROMAN TOWN:
THE PREMIER ARCHAEOLOGY VIDEO GAME FOR KIDS

CREATED BY: DIG-IT! GAMES
UNEARTH THE ROMAN TOWN OF FOSSURA, DESTROYED IN 79 AD BY THE ERUPTION OF MOUNT VESUVIUS

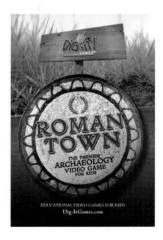

Who were the Romans? Here's your chance to find out. Discover buildings, ancient artifacts and priceless treasures. You may even uncover the remains of former residents.

Immerse yourself in ancient Roman history with 3D-rendered graphics allowing you to explore as if you were actually there. The dig is just the beginning. Reconstruct artifacts, solve the mysterious secrets about the past and discover what life was like for kids like you centuries ago. Sound like fun? It's real archaeology on your computer. The premier archaeology game—*Roman Town*—is an amazingly entertaining way to learn.

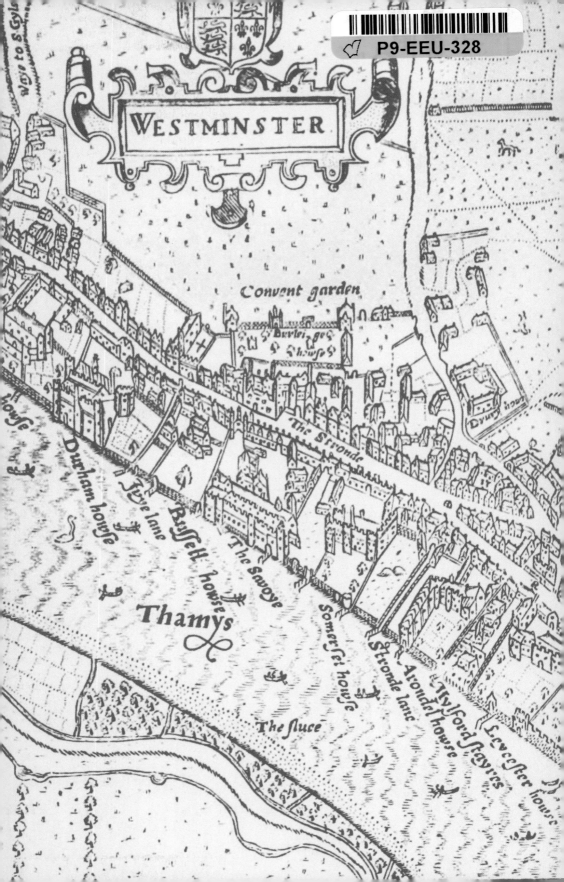

DARK AEMILIA

DARK AEMILIA

A Novel of
Shakespeare's Dark Lady

Sally O'Reilly

Picador

———

New York

DARK AEMILIA. Copyright © 2014 by Sally O'Reilly. All rights reserved. Printed in the United States of America. For information, address Picador, 175 Fifth Avenue, New York, N.Y. 10010.

www.picadorusa.com
www.twitter.com/picadorusa
www.facebook.com/picadorusa
picadorbookroom.tumblr.com

Picador® is a U.S. registered trademark and is used by St. Martin's Press under license from Pan Books Limited.

For book club information, please visit www.facebook.com/ picadorbookclub or e-mail marketing@picadorusa.com.

Endpaper maps by John Norden, 1593

Library of Congress Cataloging-in-Publication Data is available upon request.

ISBN 978-1-250-04813-4 (hardcover)
ISBN 978-1-250-04814-1 (e-book)

Picador books may be purchased for educational, business, or promotional use. For information on bulk purchases, please contact Macmillan Corporate and Premium Sales Department at 1-800-221-7945, extension 5442, or write specialmarkets@macmillan.com.

Originally published in Great Britain by Myriad Editions

First U.S. Edition: June 2014

10 9 8 7 6 5 4 3 2 1

To Georgia, with love

Past cure I am, now reason is past care,
And frantic-mad with evermore unrest;
My thoughts and my discourse as madman's are
At random from the truth, vainly expressed;
For I have sworn thee fair, and thought thee bright
Who art as black as hell, as dark as night.

William Shakespeare
Sonnet 147

DRAMATIS PERSONAE

AEMILIA BASSANO, later LANYER, a Lady, Poet and Whore
WILLIAM SHAKESPEARE, a Poet
ALFONSO LANYER, a Recorder Player, Husband to Aemilia
HENRY CAREY, Lord Hunsdon, a Lord Chamberlain
HENRY LANYER, a Schoolboy, Son to Aemilia
JOAN DAUNT, an Apothecary and Serving Woman
ANTHONY INCHBALD, a Dwarf and Landlord
SIMON FORMAN, a Cunning-man and Lecher
TOM FLOOD, a Player
ANNE FLOOD, a Widow, Mother to Tom
MOLL CUTPURSE, a Cutpurse and Cross-dresser
ELIZABETH TUDOR, a Queen
RICHARD BURBAGE, a Player and Sharer
FATHER DUNSTAN, a Priest
PARSON JOHN, a Parson
LETTICE COOPER, a Lady-in-Waiting to the Queen
CUTHBERT TOTTLE, a Bookseller and Printer
THOMAS DEKKER, a Poet and Pamphlet-writer
MARIE VERRE, a Servant
LILITH, a Demon
ANN SHAKESPEARE, Wife to William Shakespeare

Various courtiers, players, musicians, street vendors, wives, servants, wherrymen, citizens, browsers, cozeners, plague-victims, prentice-boys, witches and wraiths

Prologue

I am a witch for the modern age. I keep my spells small, and price them high. What they ask for is the same as always. The common spells deal in love, or what love is meant to make, or else hate, and what that might accomplish. I mean the getting of lovers or babies (or the getting rid of them) or a handy hex for business or revenge. When a spell works, they keep you secret, and take the credit. When it fails, of course, the fault is yours. So a witch is wise to be cautious, quiet, and hard to find.

That was true even before they started the burnings. Across the sea in Saxony and such places, whole market squares are set alight; the thatch roars up into the night; five score witches burn at once. Most would not even know how to charm a worm out of a hole. Old, and stupid, and too visible, that was their mistake. In England too, blood is let to put a stop to magic. I saw a witch hanged in Thieving Lane. They sliced off her hands and tongue, and split her down from neck to crotch, so all her guts spilled out before her eyes. They were like werewolves, mad for gore. I can still hear the voice she made with her wound-mouth: a call to Evil and a plague on all the lot of them. (This was a true witch, five hundred years old.)

But now I want to tell you my story. About Aemilia, the girl who wanted too much. Not seamed and scragged as I am now, but quick and shimmering and short of patience. About my dear son, whom I love too well. About my two husbands, and my one true love. And Dr Forman, that most lustful of physicians. The

1

silk dress I wore, the first time I went to ask for his predictions. Yellow and gold, with a fine stiff ruff that crumpled in a breath of rain. How my skin was set dark against it; how the people stared when I rushed by.

Act I

Passion

Scene I

Whitehall, March 1592

'The Queen!'

'The Queen comes! Lights, ho!'

It is night, and a Thames mist has crept over Whitehall, so the great sprawl of the palace is almost hid from sight.

'Bring lights!' come the voices again, and the doors of the great hall are flung open, and a hundred shining lanterns blaze into the foggy night, and serving men rush out, torches aflame, to show the way.

And here she is, great Gloriana, and a light comes off her too, as she progresses towards the wide entrance and its gaggle of waiting gentlemen, and the Master of the Revels puffing on the steps. There never was a mortal such as she. Behind her is the moving tableau of her ladies, silver and white like the nymphs of Nysa. Beyond them, the spluttering torches and the night sky. She is set among the fire-illuminated faces like a great jewel, so that as I look at her I blink to save my sight. Her face is white as bone, her lips the colour of new-spilt blood. Her eyes, dark and darting, take in all before her and give nothing back. And her hair, the copper hue of turning leaves, is dressed high in plaits and curlicues and riddled with pearls.

'Is Mr Burbage with us?' she demands, as she sets her small foot on the bottom step. 'Is he within? We've heard this is a comedy – we want his promise we shall be forced to laugh.'

I look down at the skirts of her farthingale, which is of Genoa velvet, glittering with a multitude of ant-sized gems.

The Master of the Revels makes his lowest bow. 'He is waiting, Your Majesty. He and the playwright are inside.'

'Is it witty?' she demands of him. 'We are in peevish spirits. This cloaked-up night disquiets us.'

'I laughed until I thought I had the palsy,' says the Master of the Revels. 'I trust it will divert Your Majesty.'

'Trust! Hmm. You are amusing us already. What did you say it was called?'

'It is *The Taming of the Shrew*, Your Majesty.'

'Ha!' says the Queen. Which could mean anything. I follow her whispering, simpering retinue and we go inside.

At one end of the long banqueting hall is a grand archway, built after the manner of the theatre at Venice. The archway shows a magnificent Roman street lined with gold and marble columns. Above the street is a plaster firmament. King Henry built the banqueting hall in the years of his great glory, and the ceiling, which swirls with choirs of angels, seems nearly high enough to reach to heaven itself, while the walls are hung with cloth-of-gold and tissue like the hazy outskirts of a dream. The most powerful lords and ladies in England are perched upon the stools and benches which are ranged before the stage, and above them all, upon a raised dais, stands the throne. It glitters as the pages bear their lanterns into the hall, dividing into twin processions of golden light. Even this seat itself has its own air of expectancy, as if it shares the Queen's fine discernment and knows what makes the difference between what is merely diverting, and what is worthy of royal acclaim.

The Queen processes to her throne and sits upon it with great exactness, and her ladies arrange themselves around her. When all are assembled, and after much bowing and flummery, the play begins. After a few moments, I see that this is a work of the direst cruelty. And I form the opinion that the playwright

– whoever he might be – is nothing better than a rat-souled scoundrel who thinks that belittling a woman will make him twice the man. He is not content that a woman has no more freedom than a house-dog. Nor that she does not even own the chair she sits upon, nor go to school, nor follow a profession (unless she is a widow who must work in her dead husband's place). No. He must make a mock of her, and push her down still further, till her face is squashed into the street-mud. And what grates such fellows most of all is one like me: a woman with a fiery spirit, and a quick tongue.

He makes his Katherine bold, only to call her 'Kate' and starve her of both food and her right name. '*What, did he marry me to famish me?*' she asks, and I see that it is so. A beggar is better treated than a scolding wife. If a woman is wise, she knows when to speak out and when she must be silent. Even the Queen herself plays a careful game, hiding behind paint and posture. Me? I am never quiet enough.

There is a rustling all around me as courtiers shift and make way. The consort divides like the Red Sea, and one of their number, my pretty cousin Alfonso Lanyer, drops his recorder. He catches my eye and winks at me, and I pretend not to see him. Alfonso is distinguished not by his playing but by two bad habits: womanising and losing money at dice.

The cause of the commotion is the arrival of my lover, Henry Carey, Lord Hunsdon, a man whose very tread makes all around take notice. Upright and soldierly, as this was his profession for many years. He does not suffer fools; he does not suffer anyone. Excepting only the Queen (who is his cousin) and me. He is forty years older than I am, so some may think we are like May and December in the old stories. Yet we were lovemaking this afternoon. Afterwards, he washed and clothed me with his own hands in the fine new dress I am wearing now. The farthingale is even wider than I am used to, so it seems I have a whole chamber swinging round my hips. The skirts are Bruges satin,

of popinjay blue, and the sleeves are tinselled silk, stitched with narrow snakes of silver. As a final gift, he coiled my hair into a caul of sapphires. When I looked in the mirror, my reflection was so perfect that it made me afraid. I, who am not afraid of anything.

I kiss him when he sits beside me.

'God's blood, this is a rum play, by the looks of it,' he whispers. 'What's it all about? Can't he find a better jade to please him?'

I put my fingers to my lips. 'She won't obey him, sir,' I mutter into his ear. 'He is hooked in by her haughty ways, and then sets out to punish her.'

'What nonsense,' says Hunsdon, rather loudly. 'A man must choose a woman that suits his fancy, not seek to change some baggage that does not. Fellow must be a barking fool.'

'Hush, my lord,' I say. There is laughter and I cuff him lightly on the shoulder. He seizes my hand and holds it in both his own.

But then I am caught by Katherine's voice.

'Such duty as the subject owes the prince,
Even such a woman oweth to her husband,
And when she is forward, peevish, sullen, sour . . .'

She speaks the words of a woman beaten, or pretending to be beaten, which is much the same.

'And not obedient to his honest will,
What is she but a foul contending rebel,
And graceless traitor to a loving lord?'

'I have another gift for you,' whispers Hunsdon, pulling me closer. 'A waistcoat of quilted silver sarsanet.' For a soldier, he has a cunning eye for fashion.

'My lord! Another present?'

'I will give it to you when you come to my rooms. Tonight?'

'If you like.'

He squeezes my hand.

After the play is finished and Kate is crushed and made the most obedient of wives, there is much clapping and cheering. The Queen raises her hand. She is smiling, but her eyes are cold.

'We want to see the playwright!' she commands. 'Where is he? Let him step forward!'

He comes from behind a pillar, slightly hesitant. 'Your Majesty,' he says, with an actor's bow. He is tall, lean and watchful, with deep-set eyes. And artful in his dress, with gold earrings and fine gloves.

She regards him for a moment, her smile in place. 'A bawdy tale, more fit for a country inn than for a monarch and her great Court, would you not say?'

He bows again. He looks pale. 'I would say there is low life in it, and high-flown characters too, such as the person of Bianca.'

The Queen's smile disappears. 'A lesson, if anyone is listening, that might teach a lady to beware of being fenced in for a wife. First they trap you, then they seek to change you. And those of us with a handsome dowry must be wariest of all.'

Her ladies giggle at this, shimmering in their silver robes.

'It is a fable, Your Majesty, not taken from the life.'

This is in the nature of a contradiction. The room gasps, silently. All eyes are on the Queen's face. Her expression is blank, her vermilion mouth a flat line. 'We do not need a lesson from you in the antecedents of your little drama. There is nothing new under the sun, least of all your plot.'

Then, with a sudden smile, her mood seems to change.

'We are grateful to you for showing us what we already know. Sometimes, in our experience, this is desirable in a drama. Sometimes we want fairyland, and wild diversion spread before

us, and sometimes we wish to be confirmed in our most sensible opinion. Our opinion being, in this case, that marriage favours men.'

The playwright, looking ill at ease, bows again.

'Was it not your intention? To show women the dangers of the married state? To have us run from such enslavement, in which our husband will be our lord and master in the eyes of God?'

The playwright clears his throat. 'I intended, Your Majesty, to tell a good tale of an unruly woman, who found her true vocation in the – '

The Queen interrupts him. 'Do you have such a wife?'

He blinks. 'Such a . . . ?'

'Such a one as this. One "peevish, sullen, sour" who does not know her place.'

'Her place, Your Majesty, is in Stratford, and mine is in London.'

There is a silence for a moment, then the Queen begins to laugh, and all around her laugh too. The grinning players look sideways at the poet. The Queen flips her hands, dismissing him, and the audience breaks apart in a clamour of excited talk. It is a gay scene. The new play is a success.

Hunsdon sweeps off to consult with Her Majesty on some urgent matter, and I find myself alone in the great hall, sitting stiffly on a stool. All I can think of is this Katherine and her plight, and the cruel way that she was brought to heel.

I feel a presence, shadow-like, and turn my head. It is the playwright. He bows, even more deeply than he had done before the Queen. I stand up, my bright skirts whirl, and the stool falls over.

'I know you,' he says, which is hardly courtly.

I nod.

'Aemilia Bassano.'

I nod again.

'I've seen you . . . talking . . .'

I curtsey, mockingly. Wonders will never cease – a comely woman who can speak.

He takes a step nearer. 'So . . . brightly. So . . . full of erudition. I've heard you quoting Ovid. Like a scholar!'

I will tell him nothing. I will not say they brought me up at Court. I will not say I am a musician's orphan. I look at him, his dark-rimmed eyes. What is he after? Most men leave me alone, fearing the wrath of Hunsdon. But this one has a reckless look to him.

'Why are you so silent?' he asks.

'I'm silent when I need to be. If it were otherwise, I'd be a fool.'

'Silent with Lord Hunsdon?'

'That's no business of yours.'

'But you speak with him?'

'Of course I do! I'm not the Sphinx.'

He looks me up and down. 'The words you choose must be poetical indeed. To earn such splendour.'

'I am the Lord Chamberlain's mistress.'

'And for that great rank you sold your virtue?'

'How dare you speak like that to me?'

He waits, as if expecting me to say more, but I do not oblige him.

'Silent again?'

'I have nothing to say to you.'

'And yet, I can see you thinking.'

'Oh, surely! My thoughts are there for all to look upon, because my head is made of glass.'

'I believe that you say very little, compared to what is in your mind.'

'You have no idea how much I talk, or what I say. You don't know who I am, or what I know. But, as your play showed us, if she is to prosper, a woman sometimes needs to act the mouse.

Wasn't that your message? Better a pliant mouse than a wicked shrew?'

'Are you such a one? A secret, wicked shrew?'

I breathe deeply, wondering that my heart is beating so loudly, my face burns and yet I shiver with rage. And then the words pour out.

'I wish that you had killed poor Katherine! I'd rather you had abused her in the Roman style, and made her eat her own children baked inside a pie! Why give her fine and dazzling speeches, only to gag her and make her drab?'

He boggles at me in disbelief. 'I . . . *what* do you say?'

'There's not a scene in your bloody *Titus* that made my heart weep as did this dreadful tale! Shame on you, for humbling that brave soul!'

'*What*?'

'Shame on you. Your play is cruel, and beast-like, sir.'

He smiles slowly. Then he turns and strides away. When he reaches the door, he calls out over his shoulder, 'You are the most beautiful woman at Court. But I expect you know that. There's no one else comes near you.'

My head reels, my guts are water, but I gather myself, right the stool and say, 'That poisonous play is what passes for poetry, is it? If you are in the company of Men and strut in hose?'

He stops, one hand on the door handle and turns to look at me.

I know I have said too much already, but it seems I can only carry on. 'Some lame tale of witless, vile humiliation? A woman-hater's boorish jape? I could do better myself, I swear.'

He forces a sort of laugh. It is a strange noise, almost like a sob. Then he comes back and stands in front of me. He is slightly too close. His eyes are angry, but for a moment he says nothing. Then he says, 'I wish you joy of Hunsdon and your perfumed palace bed.'

'Thank you, sir. In that, I shall oblige you.'

He hesitates once more, then says, 'You're his mouse, but I would that I could make you my shrew.'

Before I can find the words to answer, he has gone.

Scene II

Hunsdon is out of sorts, complaining of cramps in his calves and pains in his belly. As I lie tossing and turning and trying to find a cool place on the bolster, I roll over to see him lying still, looking up into the darkness.

'I am growing old, Aemilia,' he says. 'I shan't live much longer.'

I curl myself around him, suddenly overwhelmed with tenderness and fear. 'Henry! What are you saying?'

'It is only the truth. You will outlive me. You will be out in the world, walking in the streets, lusted for by all who see you, and I will be dead and buried, and who knows what will happen? I was selfish to take you for my mistress.'

'No! How can it be selfish to protect and cherish me, for all these years? You are the kindest man at Court, I swear.'

'But I have ruined you.'

I swallow hard. 'My dear Henry! No one could have loved me better.'

'Another man could have married you,' says Hunsdon. 'I was greedy.' He pulls the counterpane around him and twists his old body away from me, and after a moment he begins to snore, and it is my turn to lie there, staring at the dark.

I think of the first days of our courtship, after my mother died. In the depths of my slumber, I left my chamber, close to the servants' quarters, and, dressed in nothing but my white gown, walked unknowing into the middle of a feast given in Hunsdon's honour. He led me by the hand to his own bed, returned to the

celebrations, and then spent the night in his dressing room, leaving me undisturbed. Most honourable. And yet also canny, for from that day on, quite alone and sorely frightened by the constant lechery of the courtiers who wanted to have me for a night or so, I felt that here was one man I could trust.

After that, he wooed me with kind words, small gifts and imported books from the Low Countries, and the next time I found myself in his fine bed he lay with me. He was surprised to find me still a virgin and yet eager in my pleasure, and we did not sleep a wink that night. That was the first night – there have been many since. I have been his sole mistress for six years. No other man dares trespass on his territory.

Next morning, I wake late. Hunsdon has gone, but I see that he has bought me yet more gifts: a pair of new sleeves embroidered with gold angel wings, silk gloves as pale as hoar-frost, and a dainty silver knife in a leather sheath. I draw this out and look at it. Surely it is bad luck to give such a weapon to your love? I turn it this way and that, looking at the sunlight glinting on the silver blade. I touch its sharp tip with the end of my finger, and it draws a tiny drop of blood, no bigger than a ladybird. I lick the blood, wondering why God made it taste so sweet.

I go over to the window-seat and look down into the park through the small panes that make neat squares of my view. It is a clear, bright day, and the leafless branches of the oak trees are stark against the sky. When I push the window open the air is sharp, and I can smell woodsmoke and hear the hoarse cry of a stag somewhere in the forest. Yet I must not be distracted. I take up a sheet of foolscap that lies beside me and the quill that I have newly sharpened. I dip in my silver inkpot and pause, the shining nib suspended over the white sheet. I am writing a poem for Hunsdon, in the courtly style. Perhaps some fine lines might pin my passion to my lord. Besides which, words have the effect

of calming me, like a long drink of ale. I love to read poetry, and yearn to write it, but what is in my head and what comes out upon the paper are never even near the same.

I have two lines so far:

My lord is like a damask rose
He smiles at me where'er he goes . . .

Could a lord be like a rose? In truth, Hunsdon is more like a handsome thistle. But 'rose' is easier to rhyme. For 'thistle' I have only 'gristle', which will not do. I try to think of some more martial flower. A plant with dignity and strength – and a straight back. No name comes to me. My mind is restless and distracted. Each poet, they say, must suffer for love before he finds his Muse. And I am suffering now.

A harvest mouse is climbing in the ivy growing outside. It is twisting its long tail around the stalks, and looks so dainty and moves so quick that it seems fairy-like, and as though a breath of wind might send it flying through the air. I think of my conversation with the playwright. The memory itches in my head. A secret shrew, am I? Or like this creature, a little mouse? I wonder what it would be like, to be its size and scurry into the wainscot, hidden from public sight. But if I went from here, what is there? The City streets are full of fire and noise and pestilence, and beyond them lie the brutal fields. So where is *my* place? I would rather be a female Colossus, naked to the waist, bestriding all of London with a foot on each side of the Thames. I would look down upon the sprawl of Whitehall and its chequer-board of courts and gardens, then wade across the sea to France and stroll to floating Venice and its brighter sun.

Oh, Lord. It is no use. This is not a day to stay dutifully indoors. What will become of me? I want to know. Why did Hunsdon tell me so suddenly that I was ruined? Could it be true? I have never seen myself in such a way, being given to bold

thoughts about my future. Am I not admired and respected at the Court? Have I not shifted well for myself, though a bastard and an orphan, so that I am now ensconced in splendour at the heart of England? Great men push and shove and spend their whole fortunes to be part of the Queen's circle, and here I am: at its centre. Even she has told me that I am mightily well read, and sometimes speaks to me in Greek. Yet have I thrown away all hope of making my own stamp upon the world? Could this be possible?

There are ways, of course, to throw light upon such questions. If that learned Dr Dee were still at the palace I might have asked him to give me a reading, since his charts are by far the best in London, and he has always been kind to me. But he is back at Mortlake now, and not so often at the Court. The Queen believes, I think, that she has magical qualities of her own, since she was chosen by Almighty God himself. Thus her royal touch can cure diseases, and her powers of perception exceed those of any low-born man.

What to do? What to *do*? I cannot be still. All the while, I seem to see that playwright looking at me as if he were examining all my thoughts and secrets. What a vile, impertinent and damnable fellow! It is all too much. I call my servant Alice, and make her lend me her oldest cloak and most unbecoming coif, an ugly linen hood with strange ear-pieces. Tying it under my chin, I pay her a silver sixpence to keep silent, and take up a nosegay of sweet herbs. Then I creep down the back staircase of my apartments, which lead to the stable-yard, and head for the river and Whitehall Stairs.

Dr Dee is not the only famous necromancer in London. There are plenty of charlatans – like the notorious Edward Kelley – but also some whose fame recommends them. And there is one particular man I know of, a most extraordinary character. He lives at Stone

House, in the revestry of St Botolph's church on Thames Street, and his name is Simon Forman.

I make my way in haste along the narrow streets with my vizard down, picking my way around the spewed filth and avoiding the stinking kennel that gushes along beside my feet. The bright sky seems further from me now, high and pure and unreachable. I look up, and see the clouds banked into linen piles, a pattern of swallows turning first this way, then that. Between us is a veil of hidden spirits, waiting, watching, depending on mortal frailty.

Dr Forman's door is opened by an odd-looking little man, shorter than I am, with red hair, freckled skin and a yellow beard. He reminds me of a scrawny tabby-cat. Yet he is dressed to some effect, in a long purple robe with fur-trimmed sleeves, and has a confident and sprightly manner. There is no doubt that I have come to the right place.

'You are late,' he says.

'No, sir, there must be some confusion. I am not expected.'

He beckons me inside. 'I am not sure yet of your name, but you are entirely the person whose arrival I anticipated.'

'I do not see how you can "expect" a person who is unknown to you,' I say.

'Yes, yes, yes,' says Dr Forman. 'I saw that yellow dress. Though I don't believe the cap is yours, nor yet your dag-tailed cloak.'

I sit down on the chair he offers, too anxious and confused to argue further, and look around me. It is a lofty, ecclesiastic room, with a chill coming off the walls in spite of the log fire in the hearth. There are strange charts and pictures on the walls, and I notice a globe set upon a cedarwood stand, a quadrant, used to measure the altitude of the stars and a watch clock, with seconds marked around its rim.

'Now, let me see . . .' Dr Forman sits down beside me and looks at me intently. 'You say you know who I am?'

'You are Simon Forman. A necromancer. And you cured yourself of the plague.'

'Correct, insofar as that is of course my name; correct in that I have a physick for the pestilence, incorrect in this: "necromancer" is not my occupation. I am a physician.'

'There are as many degrees of *that* profession as there are lice upon a doxy's head.'

He smiles at me. I notice that his eyes seem paler at the centre, around his pupil. Then he rummages around in a wickerwork basket, humming to himself. Taking out a leather-bound volume and some papers, he clears his throat, picks up his quill, dips it in his ink-pot and says, 'Name?'

'I thought you knew me.'

'No, my dear, I merely said I was expecting you. Your name?'

'Aemilia Bassano.'

He looks at me over his spectacles, his ginger eyebrows raised. 'Indeed! Most interesting.' He scribbles, smiling. 'This is fortunate, a most auspicious turn . . .'

After a moment, he puts his quill down and clears his throat again. 'Now, what do you know about magic?'

'That it exists. That there are wise men who have spent years learning it, and wise women, who know what they are about through instinct and old tales.'

'Aha! Yes. I knew that you were clever.'

I flush in spite of myself. 'By looking at me?'

'From your reputation. And your *extra-ordinary* manner. Has the Lord created a separate degree for you? I cannot for the life of me see where you fit.'

'I don't need to "fit", sir. I will find my own place.'

'You are a scholar, so I have heard?'

'I believe I know as much as any lord, and more than all ladies, excepting only our great Queen.'

'A bold claim! There are great ladies whose knowledge of the ancients is far in excess of mine.'

19

'I speak of knowledge, sir, which is not the bed-equal of learning. A fool may learn, but what will he know? Teach a jackanapes his Latin and he can cant out Cicero. I speak of what comes from learning. I speak of understanding.'

'I see. And where has this "understanding" taken you?'

'To the brink of what can be borne. To a certainty that what contains me will always be too small. To a fear that I shall not be happy. To the quest for a twin soul.'

He sits back in his chair, settles himself more comfortably in his robes, and says, 'I can tell you a little of your future if you will tell me a little of your past. I see rich widows and Court ladies and all manner of womenfolk in their various degrees, but I have never seen one quite like you.'

So I tell him. I tell him that I do not think of myself as clever, or unusual, or in any manner different from any other girl whose father had been murdered before her eyes, or for whom music and poetry are a daily joy.

He strokes his beard. 'Who killed your father?'

'I don't know. Some years before his death, there was a first attempt, and the conspirators were tortured and banished. But we don't know who murdered him. No one knows.'

He nods. 'What did your mother say about this?'

'It was never spoken of.'

'Not even after he was murdered?'

'Not even then. We talked about his life, not his death. How his father made instruments for the Doge of Venice, and how Baptiste – my father – sailed all the way to London with his five brothers, and was the greatest player in the King's consort – '

'And after he died?'

'Mother kept his recorder hidden in a secret place, but I knew where it was. And sometimes, when I was alone, I would get it out and play some notes upon it, and it seemed to me . . .' I hesitate, not sure if I want to say more.

'What?'

It had seemed that the recorder held its own music, and there were notes waiting for me, and the sound flowed upwards; so beautiful. This was the reason that I began to play the virginals, and would practise and practise. I was seeking those sweet notes.

'You are gifted,' says Forman, decisively. 'You are your father's daughter. And yet you didn't ask your mother why he was killed? Or who did this terrible thing?'

I shrug. 'Murder is common enough.' I do not say that I know it was bound up with the extraordinary beauty of his music, and with his being a Jew. I know that great gifts come at a price, and that not all talent inspires admiration. His was too much; it set him apart.

I know that I was happy, those first seven years. So much of what I remember is like a giant's eye view of people far below, and this is because my father was in the habit of walking with me on his shoulders. I remember tangling my fingers in his black, curling hair, and seeing the panorama of the streets and fields stretching out around me, and the sudden knowledge that this was a busy and various world, and that behind one thing lay another, and then another, and this roof-muddle and chimney-forest and mêlée of men and carts and horses was all around, on every side. The Jesuits say a child is theirs for life if they have him for seven years. I have often wondered if being carried on his shoulders in this manner made me see the world through his eyes. And perhaps it was his tenderness that gave me my reverence for love.

My memories have distracted me. Forman is writing in his book.

'And this great learning of yours,' he says, scratching away. 'How did you come to acquire it?'

'Through application, sir,' I say, stiffly.

'Someone must have helped you. Someone must have given you books, and their time, and the benefit of their knowledge.'

'When I was a little girl I used to play for the Queen, because she liked me. And this continued after my father died. One day, Lady Susan Bertie heard me playing, and talked to me, and asked my mother if I could join her household, down in Kent. My mother agreed, as long as she could come to see me. So from that time – two years after my father's death – I lived between the Berties' house and Court.'

'And who taught you?'

'Lady Susan. I would say she formed my mind, being of the unusual opinion that girls can learn as fast and as well as boys.'

'You are fortunate.'

'A fortunate freak.'

He is still writing, looking well pleased with our conversation.

'So can you advise me?' I ask.

'What I am dealing with is the higher magic,' says he, without looking up. He stops writing and looks at the nib of his pen. 'Which is the study of such sciences as astrology – the prediction of men's fate by making a study of the stars – and alchemy, in which base metal is turned into gold. Your wise woman, on the other hand, deals in what I like to call "household magic" – the stuff of life.'

'Of love and sickness and herbal remedies and the like. Simple enough. Any fool might understand the difference.'

'Of course, of course, it is very simple indeed, yet not all of my clients are as *knowledgeable* as you are. Let us say, to put it crudely, that the wise woman deals with magic pertaining to the body, whereas high magic is the magic of the mind.' He taps his forehead. 'In short, it is a wondrous thing. It is *science*.'

'Which leaves aside the simple fact that our enquiring mind is contained within our earthly body. Like all distinctions made within your "science", this is merely conjecture, a chosen supposition.'

'Dear lady, I could indulge my taste for dialectic with you all day, but we must get on.'

The doctor measures and reckons and mutters and writes, and takes books down from this bookshelf and puts them back again, and considers me from between half-closed eyes and writes down some further observations.

Finally, he looks up and smiles, showing exceptionally black and fetid teeth, and says, 'It's done.'

'So . . . what is my future?' I ask. 'What will become of me?'

'Too vague. Ask me a proper question.'

'Shall I be married?'

'Yes.'

'To one I love?'

'No.'

'Then I am doomed.'

'But you will truly love. Your love will be . . .' He looks down at his notebook. 'Your love will be the better part of you.'

I stand up. 'You have sat there, looking at me as if you could read every fragment of my existence like one of your queer old books, and you can't tell me anything that's any use at all!'

'No use? I thought I was being most informative.'

I toss a crooked florin at him. 'There's your fee – I'm not parting with a penny more.'

He picks it up. 'I wouldn't want more. It is a pleasure doing business with a lady of such passion. But you, on the other hand, should want a great deal more than this.'

'Of course I want more! Did I not just say so? I want to know . . . what will become of me.'

'But what of art? What of that clever mind of yours – all the Plato and the Seneca that furnishes it? There is something trapped behind that siren's face. You've as good as said so.'

'Could learning be my destiny?'

'Do you want it to be?'

I frown, uncertain. 'Could *poetry*?'

He beams, and dips his quill once more into the pot. 'How your eyes shone when you said that word!'

I feel a pang of hope and recognition. 'Then . . . what is your prediction?'

'You will be remembered.'

The room is getting dark. He lights a candle.

'There is one more thing you want to ask me.'

My mind says, *Ask him! Ask him, you fool!* But I do not know how to begin. 'I don't have any other questions,' I say.

'Then why did you come?'

'I could not settle.'

He leans forward and, to my horror, kisses me gently on the mouth. His breath is hot and sour. 'I'd ask you to stay with me . . . longer. But I fear you'd break my heart.'

I push him away. 'I'd break your head, sir, before I broke anything.'

He stands up, frowning, and fetches my cloak. As he puts it about my shoulders, he says, 'His name is Shakespeare. William Shakespeare.'

'Whose name?' But I know. Of course I know.

'The playwright you want so badly.'

'What . . . ?'

'He will be your lover. At least I hope so, for if you won't have him he'll run as mad as Legion.'

'Possessed by evil spirits?'

'Driven insane by wild desire. Judging from *his* chart, that would be a national deprivation.'

I stare at him, finally astonished by his science. Forman fixes me with his weird gaze.

'Intense sort of fellow. It doesn't take an astrologer to see that.'

'You know him?'

'He was here this morning.'

'What?'

He opens the door. 'Be careful how you go. Those stairs are slippery.'

Scene III

My servant Alice rushes into my chamber all fly-brained and affected. She is a silly girl and I can see she has recently been conversing with some man she thinks important, or handsome at the very least.

'I have a letter, mistress,' she says, pink in the face.

I flinch. There is not a hair's breadth between what I most fear and what I want more than anything. Anyone who has loved two men at once knows that it's not an abundant feeling, but mean and sweaty and undignified.

'Give it to me,' I say. It is a long slip of foolscap, the colour of buttercream, folded and sealed with red wax. Alice stands, smiling, at the foot of the bed, as if she is expecting to watch me break the seal. 'Get out, you brainless creature!' I say. 'And . . .'

'Yes, mistress?'

'You are free for the rest of the day. Go to see your mother at Islington. The country air will do you good.'

'But . . . mistress!'

'Go on!' I throw the letter on to the table as if I were not interested in its contents. 'My lord is coming soon, and wants to see me alone.'

'But I thought – '

'Alice! Go!'

As soon as I hear the door to my apartment close I grab the letter and tear it open. It has to be from *him*. It has to be.

It is from Petruchio.

Madam,

I am writing to you on behalf of Mr W.S. on the matter of his play The Taming of the Shrew, *which sadly failed to please you. His thoughts are these:*

First, is he the only man to write a tale about the taming of a Shrew? (He is not: the tale is as ancient as old Ovid.) Second, is this the cruellest tale of woman-taming, or the crudest? (It is not: this Katherine keeps her dignity more than most of her fair sex, and speaks most ably, too.)

Further, if you recall the exact words of this tamed Shrew, you will know that she agrees to her husband's will and rule on the understanding that he is 'loving' – a fair bargain, would you not say? Therefore, she is making a truce. She is no scold, dumbed by a bridle.

And lastly, as this is an entertainment, laid on for the drunkard Sly, Mr W.S. had hoped that his audience would see this for a tale enlivened by his Wit. In short, a comedy of levity as well as form. So his wish is that it might amuse a Lady, learned as you are, rather than cause Rage.

I ask you humbly, as Mr Shakespeare's prattler, the voicer of his words, please do not judge the Poet by his Puppet.

With great respect,
Petruchio

What had I expected of this poet? Too much, it seems. He has sent this to me not out of admiration, or even lust, but only to convince me of the greatness of his Art. He does not see in me someone of fellow mind, as I had almost hoped, but as an audience member lacking in the proper perceptions, the fit response. The squibbling, shifty knave cannot even lower himself to put his right name on this letter, but must pretend his 'puppet' is writing in his stead! God's blood.

I confess, though I should respond with silence, I must reply. I can't let this letter, this preening, false-writ scrawl, be the last word in our discourse. I cannot let this 'playwright', some provincial chance-man, swelled with pride, put *his* words over mine. No. Katherine will speak. I write thus, with my left hand:

Petruchio,

I speak on behalf of one who was enraged to see a play so violent and ill-tempered, fuelled by cruelty and bile. If this is comedy, then take yourself to Tyburn and laugh with the mob who like jigs danced by corpses.

It would be easier to laugh at your foul 'jokes' if Women were not caged, and tethered, and made small. If they owned property, or goods, or their own skin. If they had gold, or land, or the respect of Men. If, unchaperoned, they could walk the streets and smell the bakemeats and the brew-shops. Or ride astride a horse, or put their plays upon the stage, or speak in Court, or choose their mate, or go abroad, upon a ship (in search of the Americas, or Oriental spice).

As for Wit, if you steal this from a woman, and make her call the moon the sun or darkness light, then she is done for. Because Wit is all she has. It's Wit that gives us life, or we have nothing left to nourish us. It is our sole possession.

Make a joke of all this if you will, put a play within a play, and say 'all's false'. You still make the bully smile to see himself reflected in your person. Greedy, preening, bed-smug Petruchio.

Katherine (and never Kate)

I dispatch this letter and time goes on its way, and I live my life as I must. I dissemble. I read my Bible. I eat my milksops and

apricocks and drink my Madeira wine. I seem to have bewitched myself: this letter should never have been sent. I wonder if it found its mark. Was it lost in the Globe, where it was sent? Was it found by some other knave, and laughed around the theatre? Will it threaten my future (though nameless, and disguised)? If he read it, the Poet, did he frown or smile, or throw it on the fire? Did he turn from it without a thought, or brood on it, and go back to his pages, not so sure of them? Did he? I look inside my head, as if a picture of the world beyond these rooms was hidden there. And my life is just as it has always been: the life of a kept whore, the highest in the land. Dressed like a princess, a taffeta angel, a fairy in cloth-of-gold. But all I am is Queen of cunts.

And then. Then it comes, the answer, from the Pen. It is a different sort of letter altogether.

> *Katherine,*
> *You truly own your wit, and no one can take it from you. Not this Petruchio, for certain. I would not seek to curb your headstrong humour, not in life.*
> *Not if you were my Wife.*
> *I do not believe there is a man in Christendom who could own you. You would put God Himself on his mettle.*
> *Petruchio*

I read this several times.

This, then, is the way he wants to play it. He will lure me with his silken little lies, to tie me up with my particularity. There is no one like me, no, therefore I need not think of my gender, nor of any woman as my equal or my sister. I can be Chosen, and set above all others. Still the false princess, decked out in Sin.

I use my right hand this time, for speed, but none who knew me would recognise my furious scrawl.

Petruchio,

You deserve no more than a blank page, a blank stare for your blank verse. Husbands abuse their wives, and tyrannise them, and they are less than their equals. In spirit, virtue, soul, and body, Man is the weakling. The woman brings forth men, so SHE is the source of all life. And the Man, with his dangling, clownish wren-cock, puffs himself up to twice his natural size. (Twice, do I say? No, tenfold!) He makes the Woman small so he can spit in her eye.

Man must sing a weak, cruel song to comfort his cold nights. You don't fool me by saying I am different from the others of my sex. I am not different, I am the same but more so.

> *Katherine*

There. It's gone, and this wild feeling is all spent. I have turned longing to gall, my dusk-dreams to white rage. I can read, I can dance, I can lie with a skilful lover. I can wear my new sleeves and my embroidered gloves and I can sip from a silver cup. I can watch the sun rise and see it setting, a blaze of Heaven. I am young, and I can savour all the daily miracles of life. Something happened, nothing happened; it is the same. It is all the same. Days pass. Weeks go by. I am forgotten. He is forgotten. His eyes watch me from the glass but they are my eyes; they are a trick of the light. The years will make sense of me again; it is not possible to fall so hard for nothing, for words and a hungry look, a moment in time.

Then, just as I am beginning to believe that I might be myself again, this letter comes.

Dark Aemilia,

I will not say 'Katherine'; but I do not know how to address you, meaning, with what form of embellishment, so

let there be none. You find me churlish and insulting, even when my wish is only to entertain.

What do I want to say? I want to be honest with you. As you know, I have a wife, and, as you may not realise, also children. So.

I have walked the streets of London these past weeks till the very cobblestones cried out for me to stop. I have seen necromancers in search of the antidote to these violent, obsessive and lunatic cravings, a cure for foolish and forbidden love. I have been drunker than I had thought possible (I am generally given to sober industry and good fellowship). I have made myself so ill with this that I felt it must be a form of penance for a sin that I have committed only in my heart.

What do I wish to ask you? Not to exist? Never to have existed? To return to my mind and stay there? For I fear I may have conjured you from my febrile imaginings. I thought that you were locked up safely in my mind. I thought that in this actual, tangible world, women were just as women are. Which is to say, loud strumpets in foul taverns; dull ladies in fine houses; vain damsels waiting on the Queen. Or serving-wenches, or dairy-maids, or worldly widows . . . the common run of women in their place, with the qualities that place prescribes. But what are you? A scholar or a mistress? A temptress or a wife? An angel or a witch? I cannot say. And, as I cannot, I don't know what I want to ask.

But I do. I do know what I want to ask. But I cannot and will not ask it.

There is a fine play on at the Bel Savage Inn, off Ludgate Hill, written by my friend Kit Marlowe. The title is Dr Faustus. *I will be there tomorrow afternoon. I expect you are engaged in some palatial busyness already. I am certain that this will be the case. If you come, come alone, and dress plainly. It's not Whitehall Palace. It is not even as*

respectable as the Rose. I will be outside at half-past one. To take the air, you understand. It will be of no matter to me if you are not there, and I do not, indeed, expect you. Nor can I quite believe that I am writing these words at all, nor that I shall seal this note and entrust it to some messenger. No, I will take the thing myself.

I am your most unworthy servant,
Will Shakespeare

I read this delirious missive in a state of trembling disbelief. Twice. Then a third time, hardly breathing. He writes to me, in my name, and he signs himself as . . . himself. No dissembling here, none at all. He has lost his reason. I have heard that this is sometimes the way with poets. Of course I cannot go. A royal mistress has a position to maintain, and her reputation to consider. And he is treating me like a common street-drab, truly. But my eyes keep wandering back to the looping words . . . *I fear I may have conjured you from my febrile imaginings . . . temptress . . . angel . . . witch . . .*

There is no question of accepting such a preposterous invitation. (To an inn, no less! To see a play! And 'alone' – what can he be thinking of?) If he isn't mad he is determined to insult me. There is a class of man who would as soon humiliate a woman as lie with her, and, again, those of a poetic disposition are often afflicted with this vice. And more – he is asking me to lower myself to this station, of tavern-doxy, behind the back of my protector, the great Lord Chamberlain himself. The words blur in front of me when I think of this. The affront to Hunsdon is even greater than the insult to me. All I have to do is show this little love-note to my lord and Will Shakespeare will be shut out of London's play-world and doubtless locked up in the Clink as well. The risk he is taking is out of all proportion to the pleasure he might gain.

I have seen necromancers in search of the antidote to these violent, obsessive and lunatic cravings, a cure for foolish and forbidden love.

Oh! He has felt it. He has felt the same. The same . . . There will be no other.

I sit down upon the rush-strewn floor, and command my body not to lust for something so ridiculous, command my skin to harden and my loins to . . . well. My mind not to summon up that profane word: 'loins'. Am I myself? Am I? What is this 'self', this pretty thing I have become? Was there another way? Another Aemilia that I could have been, could still be? I still care for Lord Hunsdon, and he has treated me with respect and sweetness for six long years. He is like a father to me, as well as a loving spouse. This longed-for letter is a vile temptation and a deceiver's snare.

And yet . . . I close my eyes, and see Will's face again. So I open them, blinking. Some speak of love as fever – if this is a sort of love, it is a vicious malady indeed. (*'And yet, who are you, to think about adultery?'* says the Devil standing behind me. *'You are no one's wife. Hunsdon's marriage bed is cold because of you. There is no virtue in your nature. You are just a whore – what's to stop you now?'*) If this is love, then it should be accorded some respect. There is not much love at Court, only place-men, and place-women, and place-fucking. If this is love, I need it. I must have it.

Will Shakespeare's letter has infected me with his insanity. My life depends on my destroying this unworthy note and forgetting that I ever saw it. I tear it into a hundred tiny pieces, go to the fireplace and toss the fragments on to the flames. One tiny piece of paper flutters down and falls among the ashes. On it is written 'Faustus'.

I try to distract myself with finery. I put on a yellow silk dress, and the new sleeves, and a wonderful ruff that makes me

look like the Faerie Queene. I make a mouth at myself in the glass. Then I lean forward and kiss my reflection, blurring my own image with my hot breath. Lord, what is this yearning? Am I going mad? There must be sanity in Latin. In Plato, surely, so I call on him to help me. But another plain and lumpen English phrase comes to mock me, some words from Gower: '*It hath and shall be evermore, that love is master where he will.*' My mind is a mess of twisted things, like a squiggling heap of worms.

I reason thus. I may lose everything. I may gain everything. Life is a fleeting shadow. Death is eternal, and there is no fervid fornication in the charnel house. I have not known this thing before. I do not know what this thing is. I am not afraid.

I am not afraid.

Spring has forgotten us this year. Eddies of snow flurry from the cold grey clouds. My cloak is too thin, and my horse's hooves slip and slither on the hard ground. I am pretending to be more respectable than I am. I am used to that, at least. As he trots along Fleet Street, I shiver in the icy chill. Yet as the wind numbs my body I am grateful – for this distracts my mind. All I can think is how much I wish to sit before a roaring fire. If there is a poet there, so be it. If he is William Shakespeare, what of it? Or so I nearly think, as I crosss the bridge over Fleet River. The Bel Savage is, I know, close by. I have been there to see a new play with my lord. When I came before, I was borne upon a barge along the river, then taken in a private carriage from Blackfriars Stairs. This time I have only Frey to carry me, and, when I see the squat shape of the Inn and the clustering stables around it, I falter, and pull him to a walk. Even from this distance I can hear shouts and laughter, and the sound of an old ballad being belted out in chorus.

I am minded to turn Frey's head and ride back to Whitehall when I see a man, walking towards me along the road. Broad-

shouldered, and with a countryman's gait, easy and long-limbed. It is strange to see the playwright in the open air. In my mind's eye he is always cooped up with his pages, or cheek-by-jowl with others of his sort, in some crowded City tavern.

He stops, and holds the bridle, and we look at each other for a moment, then swiftly look away.

'Is it really you, Aemilia?' he says.

'So it would seem.'

'The fevered champion of shrews and vixens? I can scarce believe it.'

'I am still their champion,' say I, 'fevered or otherwise.' But then realise I am addressing myself to my horse's yellowed mane. I wriggle my feet free of the stirrups and Will helps me down, and I feel the hardness of his arms through his thick sleeves. I dare not look at him, and sense that he dares not look at me. We must seem like two gaping fools, staring this way and that, as if the white sky and the cold street fill us with astonished wonder. My skin burns and my heart is pounding and I want to turn and run.

'I didn't think you'd come,' says he, patting Frey's nose. 'You seemed so angry with me.'

'Nor did I,' I say. 'Nor should I have.'

'Your letters were – '

'They were from Katherine. I have never written to you.'

He laughs. 'Katherine writes well.'

'I wish I could say the same for Petruchio.'

'He is a lost soul, my lady.'

'Lost?'

He shakes his head. 'Look, madam . . . I have a room . . .'

'Indeed! What do you take me for?' I turn away, ready to mount Frey again. 'I've made a terrible mistake, I'm not myself.'

Will turns me to face him. 'Aemilia – madam – please. It's my mistake . . . it's me who is not . . . myself. Please. I meant to say – a room where we can see the play. In private. Away from the crowd.'

I collect myself. 'Thank you,' I say. 'This meeting must indeed be private. That is thoughtful of you.'

We stand in silence for a moment. I have had dreams less dreamlike.

'I have a mask,' I say. I pull my vizard down, foolishly, so that my blushing face is hidden. In some mad part of my mind I wish I were Katherine, the True Shrew.

Will takes my hand most formally, and kisses the tips of my gloved fingers as if I were the Queen herself. I see that his own hands are ungloved. They are long, fine-boned and marked with lamp-black. Our eyes jolt together, and I feel something swoop and fall inside me.

'Come. Come inside . . . out of the cold.' A groom takes my horse, and Will leads me to the inn, my hand held firm in his. But he makes no other move to touch me, at which I feel a strange ache, the like of which I have not known before. It is the infection again, that disease that was carried in his letter.

Inside, the blistering March cold is soon forgotten. There is a warm buzz of talk and the glass windows twinkle in the firelight. The press of people gives off its own heat. There are young and old, men and women, drunk and sober, sitting in snug wooden booths, or gathered round the fire, house-dogs snoring at their feet. Will leads me up a narrow staircase, till we come to a small, oak-panelled room.

He closes the door and leads me to a table. Next to it is a curtained window. Drawing back the curtain, he nods to me and I see that it looks out into the inn-yard. Two hay carts have been backed together at one end, to form a makeshift stage. This is shrouded all in black, with a carved wooden chair and oak table at one end. A group of men are hammering nails into a trapdoor that has been constructed in the floor of one of the carts, and which seems not be to working as it should. Another man stands apart, dressed in black like the stage hangings, with a giant cross around his neck.

'Ned Alleyn,' says Will, opening the window.

'He is Faustus?'

'He is, and most excellent in the part.' He beckons me over, and I stand a few inches from him, not daring to go nearer. '*Too* excellent, one might almost say. Some of the players believe he wears that cross for good reason.'

I see that Alleyn's face is drawn and pale in the afternoon light. He looks anxious, and bends down to look at the trapdoor and consult with the carpenters. A cold draught comes from the open window, and the sound of hammering echoes in the frosty air.

'What do you mean?'

'When he summons Mephastophilis, the agent of Satan, he uses true magic. He uses words that good Christians would never utter, for fear of losing their immortal souls. The trap-door in the cart looks like a simple piece of stage-work now, but when the play begins it seems to have a different function, as if it can truly link the men upon the stage with the hidden fires of Hell.'

'Why draw upon such evil?'

'To make a wonder of it. To shock and amaze the crowd, so that they will speak of nothing else. To go beyond where tame and tedious playmaking has gone before.'

'Plays like yours?'

He laughs, his eyes hard. 'It's true. He has gone beyond what passed as "good enough" before. Romance, comedy, low-brow tragedy – only one step beyond a mystery play – each written with a paucity of pain and passion. We've settled for too little.'

'Or you have.'

He stares at me. 'Or I have, yes. But I am quick to learn.'

Ned Alleyn's posturing Faustus is a fool, but his descent is terrifying enough to grip me. He prowls and leers upon the boards like a staked bear at the pit, growling and griping against

his mortal prison, and who but an idiot could not see where that would end? Mephastophilis, summoned by real magic or no, is just a tall player with a head slightly too large for his frame. Will is close beside me as I lean out into the cold air to get a better view. Then, suddenly, his breath is soft in my ear. 'Are you surprised that I set out to charm you with Marlowe's evil play?'

I turn and my lips accidentally brush his cheek. His skin is cold beneath the stubble. Something is sticking in my throat, and I have to press my legs close together beneath my skirts to halt their quivering.

'To charm me? Or tempt me?'

He steps backwards, raising his arms as if in innocence. 'Tempt you, Katherine? I wouldn't dare.'

'Perhaps you want to quell me. Scare me, with this diabolic stuff. Then I will fall . . .'

'Fall where?'

'To Hell, perhaps, or Limbo . . .'

'There is no Limbo now, my lady; it is forbidden.'

'Oh, this is Limbo, Petruchio, do not doubt it. I am caught between reality and poetry – and between . . .' I hesitate, not able to go on.

'Between what?'

He is closer now. How did he come closer? I am vapour, liquid, longing. I want to say, *Between two men*. Or even, *Between two lovers*. But they would have to crush me beneath a stone-piled door before I'd spit the words out.

'Why are you so cautious?' he asks.

'Why would I be otherwise?'

He pulls me round and looks into my eyes. 'I wanted you to see this. I knew you would understand it.'

'What do you mean?' The voice that comes from my stopped throat sounds sane enough, not strange. And this is most peculiar, for I could not say what's stage and what's sky, or my whole name, or any part of Plato.

The Seven Deadly Sins are on the stage, each a conjured demon brought forth by Faustus. One by one he names and dismisses them. First comes Pride, then Covetousness, then Wrath, Envy, Gluttony and Sloth. Then:

'What are you, Mistress Minx, the seventh and last?'
'Who, I, sir? I am one that loves an inch of raw mutton
better than an ell of fried stockfish, and the first letter of
my name begins with lechery.'

Lechery is the last sin, so why is there another demon, as yet uncounted? I stare hard, but I cannot see it clearly: the other devils are in the way, their bodies shift and shuffle around it so. I can make out a hooded figure, taller than the others, and motionless. Its face is shadow but from its outline rises up the faintest pall of vapour. The players around it falter. The demon lifts its head, and the cowl falls back.

I strain to look, yet cannot see it.

I hear a woman scream. 'God's death, the Devil himself is on the stage!'

Cries and shouting spread across the courtyard. 'Heaven help us, Judgement Day has come!' There is a terrible roaring and shrieking, and the next thing I see is a prentice-boy run on to the stage wielding a flaming torch, bellowing more horribly than a bowelled man, and the stage is alight and the players are running this way and that way, and the crowd has erupted and people are banging on the closed doors of the courtyard to get out. Through the smoke I think I can see the still figure of the demon, but the shadows flicker and I cannot be certain.

'What's this?' gasps Will. The shouts of terror grow louder, the flames higher . . . I cannot see . . . I crane forward. The courtyard is in shadow, the stage obscured by smoke. I blink, sure that my eyes are tricking me, and, when I look again, sure enough the figure has gone. But the awful screams and wails continue, and I

see the prentice-boy convulsing on the ground before the stage, his legs kicking and his arms flailing. He has gone stark mad.

Will grabs my arm. 'Aemilia, let's go, let's find a place to – '

I pull away from him, and run.

I am halfway back down Fleet Street before I stop, remembering my horse, and then I double up, my chest heaving. I cannot think; I cannot breathe. The dreadful sound of the prentice-boy is trapped inside my head, and I can still see the weird jerking of his limbs. The gloomy, freezing afternoon seems haunted with floating spectres. Even my steaming breath is ghost-like.

A hand falls on my shoulder and I scream.

'Aemilia! Aemilia, it's me.' Will pulls me towards him and holds me tightly, trembling almost as much as I am.

'What *was* that?' I ask. 'Did Marlowe summon Satan? Is he *mad*?'

Will's head is buried in my shoulder. 'I don't know. I don't know what he is about. Something has possessed him, some desire he hardly seems to understand. But that is his weird fancy, not ours.' He straightens up and looks down at me. 'Come with me,' he says. 'There is somewhere we can speak, alone.'

My body still shakes with cold and terror. He wraps his cloak around my shoulders. We make our way off the road and along a muddy track. At the end of it, I see a ruined abbey, surrounded by a coppice of naked winter trees. Some of the buildings are half-dismantled, the stone doubtless purloined to build new homes for wealthy men. But the abbey house is intact. We follow an overgrown pathway that leads to a side door. Will opens it with a key hanging upon a hook. Inside, he lights a torch, and locks the door behind us. The house reeks of damp, and I can hear water dripping. He takes me up a flight of creaking wooden stairs till we come to a solar on the upper floor. It is still furnished, and someone has prepared it for us. I see that Will

has been bold enough to hope that he might bring me here, and has laid it out accordingly. There is a bed in one corner, made up freshly with black silk bolsters and a white counterpane. And even logs in the fireplace. Will lights these, and his hands steady as he holds them to the flames.

'It was a stage trick,' he says, as he watches the fire grow higher. He seems to be returning to himself, making a pattern of what seemed unfathomable. 'Kit is ambitious. What better way to make his name?'

'What about that poor prentice-boy? What about the fire?'

'The boy could have conspired with him. What you see is not always the truth.'

'What else can you depend on?'

'It's not Satan that frightens me,' he says. 'It's Kit.'

He comes towards me, and helps me out of the cloak. 'I don't want to talk about this any longer,' he says, softly. 'One day, I will write a greater play than that. I wanted you to see it.'

'Why? If you are going to be greater?'

'Because I want you to know me.'

'Why?'

'Because I want *you*.'

I hold him at arm's length. I feel as if I have stepped into another world, as if this secret room is an enchanted place. What I do here is separate and different from every other part of my life. Time, too, seems twisted out of shape. And as for virtue . . . well.

'I want you,' he repeats. 'If you can forgive me for abusing Katherine.'

He has small white teeth. There is a blue vein snaking from his left eye to his hairline. His eyelashes are thick and black and make his eye-whites seem paler. There is a scar at the base of his neck, like a dagger-nick, in the same place that I have a black mole. If we lay together, they would fit quite neat together. He looks more Spanish than English. He looks more Jewish than Gentile. He looks like me.

'Aemilia,' he says. 'Are you listening?'

'Yes. You want me for your whore.'

'I want you for everything.'

'I am whored already. Shall I be doubly sinful? And what about your sin, your soul, your wife?'

'I can't help it. I can't . . . stop. This is not some fuck-led dalliance.'

'Not very poetical, is it? And if not fuck-led, what is it led by? You don't deny that you want me to be your little strumpet, and then – if you're minded – I must soothe you with some poesy when we are done? Is that the "everything" you have in mind?'

He holds my wrist. His long fingers easily encircle its narrow bones. 'I want *you*, Aemilia,' he says again. 'I want to know you. Because there is no one like you.'

'That's true enough. And I fear that there is nobody like *you*, or else I might be in some warmer chamber, with a man who's free.'

'Hunsdon isn't free.'

'But he is powerful. He does what he likes.'

He grips my wrist more tightly, staring at me till I feel the room recede and cannot think. 'My wife is far away from London, and I have had mistresses enough since we've lived apart. It's an itch, a thrill, a need.'

'Enough? How many?'

'Several. Plenty.'

'More than three?'

'I haven't counted.'

'More than seven?'

'I don't know!'

I yank my hand away. 'So, I'm the new diversion, am I?'

He takes both my hands. 'Please. Aemilia Bassano. My lady. I don't want you to be my mistress. I want you for my love.'

'Love! What about Hunsdon, and your poor neglected wife?'

41

'He has abandoned his own lady, so I shall not grieve for him. And my wife, as I've confessed, has been deceived already.'

He is clearly untaught in the art of disputation; his arguments are useless. But at least he can speak. I can't say anything.

Will stares at me. 'You came,' he says. He smiles at me, a pure, sweet smile. 'In spite of everything, you came.'

'I did.' A feeling of pure happiness begins to take possession of me. There are arguments; there are things I should say to him. But what are they? 'I had to.'

'You have risked your place – your station.'

'I have.' I begin to laugh, half-drunk with the madness of it. 'Such as it is. Do whores have a place in this Manworld? Have we been allocated a tier of Being?'

He leans down and kisses me for the first time, and I won't describe it because I can't. The world has shifted now; madness is closer.

'This room is ours, and secret,' says Will.

We kiss again. Madness, madness, it's at my feet.

'Will you come to bed with me, Aemilia?'

I stare at him, unblinking. I should say something. I should make him wait. This is what I have instead of virtue: the power to make one man wait. Only it seems I don't even have that false virtue; I can't play the Anne Boleyn game. Withhold and promise, promise and withhold. I can't do either. I am lost.

He draws me closer and unpins one of my sleeves. It is one of Hunsdon's gifts, patterned with angels. My naked arm gleams pale in the firelight.

'Are you an angel, too?' asks Will, eyes shining. 'Or a witch?'

I look at him, solemn as a virgin bride.

He lays the sleeve down on a chair by the bed and begins to unpin its fellow. I watch his fingers, my breath coming faster.

Scene IV

From that day on, we meet in that secret room as often as we dare, and our shuttered love flourishes. I was happy with the lovemaking of Hunsdon, but this is of a different order. Sometimes gentle, slow and almost sacred in its intensity. Sometimes raw and ugly, raging, screaming and obscene. I find that Will loves most what he hates strongly; that what I do to give him the greatest pleasure revolts him even as he comes, jerking and crying out my name. I, who have been fucking a man I saw as father-like since I was sixteen, have no shame. I see bed as a place to try every version of delight that a body might endure, and in Will I find a lover who does everything to please me. The more we do, the greater his desire, and the greater his desire, the closer I feel to a sort of ecstatic disappearance. I want that. I want to reach a height of passion of such a degree that I might never return to myself, but remain there, locked inside him, and he in me.

I like it best at the brightest hour of morning, with the shutters open and the sunlight streaming down upon us as we go at it, open-eyed. 'See this?' I say. 'See this?' He buys a heavy mirror at the Royal Exchange and carries it to our room one night, and it reflects all we do. I hardly sleep when I am apart from him, and cannot eat. My ribs stick out and my poor dugs have nearly vanished and my lord worries for me, fearing I have a tumour or some other malady. If it is madness, it is also the most precious and bright-hued time in my life.

* * *

I am lying on a riverbank, looking up into a cloudless May sky. Skylarks are singing and the Thames is lapping at my feet. I close my eyes. The sun warms my cheek. My chemise tickles my skin. A fly lands on my arm and waves its foremost legs at me. I sit up and look around me. Will is sitting beside me, clutching a wad of foolscap and reading intently. His shirt is unbuttoned, so that I can see the pale skin of his chest. I want to lean across and touch it.

He looks over at me, frowning. 'You haven't answered me,' he says.

I look at him, distracted. 'What was the question?' I say, smoothing down the sun-warmed folds of my chemise.

'The question I just asked you.'

'Ask it again.'

'You say you want to be a poet. But what sort of stuff is this? A bosom-brained Court lady could pen something like it. Where is your learning? Where is your wit?'

He throws the pages down. I remember what Simon Forman said, and pick them up. I can do better. I know I can do better.

'If I worked on them . . . so they were improved. What then?'

'I don't know. You could find a patron, and a publisher.' He leans over and begins to kiss my neck.

'A bastard concubine could be a published poet?'

'Why not?' He has lifted my hair and is kissing the hidden skin beneath it.

I push him away. 'You're making a mockery of me.'

'As you wish. Leave this Art to those who understand it.' He is laughing openly at me now. 'You are such a wondrous pretty thing – no need to strive for a life of the mind.'

I slap his face, slightly harder than I intended. 'A woman can do anything, if she has a mind to it. The Queen writes verse.'

He clutches his cheek in mock pain. 'The Queen, good lady, is a prince. No, no, you are quite right. Stick to your love ditties; true Art is quite beyond you.'

'What about you, the palace playwright? Everything you know, you learned at a country grammar school.'

'Whereas *your* learning . . .'

'Is of the Ancients, as you would expect.'

'Oh, indeed. A little of Athens, and much of Rome.'

'Much of both, sir. The trivium, of grammar, logic and rhetoric.'

'Ay, like a learned blade at Oxford.'

'Like the learned fellows everywhere. And also the quadrivium . . .'

'Of arithmetic, geometry, astronomy . . .' He hesitates, unsure.

'And music.'

'Of course – you are the lady of the virginals.' He seems to think this is a joke of some kind, so I keep silent. 'And this has fitted you for . . . rutting with an aged soldier, has it?'

I get to my feet and walk to the river's edge, hating him suddenly. He comes up behind me.

'It has fitted me for discontent,' I say.

'You see?' He pulls me close. 'We are two of a kind. Would I have written plays if I had known my station? Or would I have stayed in Stratford, making gloves for the gentry?'

I let him kiss me, but am still preoccupied. 'I know enough to be a poet, I have read enough to know how it should be done, but I don't know how to make my lines sing better!' I say. 'I can't turn thoughts to written words! There is some magician's trick to it.'

Will leads me back to the grassy knoll and spreads out his cloak so that we can lie down again. 'There is no magic,' he says. 'Treat words as if they were rubies.' He unhooks the beaded hood from my hair, so that it falls around me, curled by its enclosure. 'Choose the right one for each part of every line.' He undoes my stomacher and lifts it away. 'Write every line as though your life depended on it.' He opens the front of my chemise and regards my dugs quizzically, as if deciding whether or not to buy them. 'As if the executioner was standing by your shoulder, and this

45

was the last chance to speak that you would ever know.' With that, he pushes my chemise back, so my white shoulders are naked in the sun.

I do not smile, nor assist him in his task. 'That sounds like a kind of madness, I say. 'I fear I am too sane.'

He laughs again. The sun has browned his face. His eyes are full of sky. His lips are swollen red from reckless kissing.

'Do you want me?' he asks, very serious.

Oh, I do. I do.

And so we make love in the sunshine. Till at last Will calls my name, over and over. 'Aemilia! Aemilia! Aemilia!'

I need the skills of a player myself, in my dealings with Lord Hunsdon. It tears at me to lie to him, who was all in all to me for so many years. But I do so just the same, the whole summer long. And it scares me to think that, if he knew how I betrayed him, his anger would know no bounds. I once saw him kill a dog that turned. He beat the creature till it could not stand, and the ground was running with its blood. And that dog loved him, and had sighed at his feet with its great head upon its paws, watchful of his safety. If he knew how I lay with Shakespeare, and what we did, and how we cried out together in the boundless repetition of our lust, what would he do to me? I do not know.

But what I fear is not his power to hurt me, although I know that he could wield it, but that discovery would put an end to my deception. My true life is lived in those secret times with Will, which make the fakery of my Court life fade to nothing. Each time we meet, he gives me a letter, and I give him one in return. He says my words are his comfort when we are apart; his missives to me are more beautiful than I can say. These are not just letters which talk of love, but which talk of everything. (And if you think me a fool as well as a wanton, then let me say these letters are written in a sort of code.)

Today I am trying to put such thoughts from my mind, and I am reading St Paul's letters to the Corinthians in my chamber, disliking his view of women. But Hunsdon comes in, and says, 'Aemilia, are you tired of your life here?'

I put St Paul down, taking my time about it. 'Tired in what way, sir?'

He sits beside me. 'You know what I have spoken of. I am growing older.'

'Not to me,' I smile and touch his cheek, trying to read his expression. 'You are my lord in all things, dear Henry.'

He takes my hand and places it in my lap. 'What do you say to this – we go away from here?'

'Go? Where?'

'To Titchfield, where Wriothesley has his seat.'

The fear rises in me – is this a trick? A ruse to get me away from Will? I smile, and lean across to kiss him. 'Why, what shall we do there, my love?'

'The Queen is going on a progress.'

'But is this newly thought of?'

'Her Majesty has been out of sorts, and blames the parched and putrid drains. She wants fresh air, clean rooms, and some diversion. The players have a new piece, and they're to stage it there for her.'

The fear remains. 'Which piece is this?'

'*Love's Labour's Lost*. Wriothesley has commissioned it, Shakespeare has wrote it, and he assures me it is good. Some comedy or other. He claims it's better than the *Shrew*.'

'Mr Shakespeare?' I feel the room swimming around me. 'And . . . Mr Burbage? Will they be there too?'

'Most decidedly they will! Why would they not be? It will be an entertainment for us all. And much needed, before the nights draw in, and the autumn creeps upon us. Place House is handsome, and the country all around is green and pleasant. And it's not too far – no more than three days' ride.'

'But . . . are you sure you want me with you?' Hunsdon usually leaves me behind if he goes on a progress with the Queen. It is unspoken but understood between us that it pleases his wife better if I stay in my Whitehall rooms when he is gone from London, as if my body was a chance adornment of the palace and not a chosen pleasure. Travelling with his lordship is too spouse-like. So is this suggestion a sign of his growing fondness for me, or his burgeoning mistrust?

He kisses my obedient little breasts, pushed up tight and high by whalebone and fashion. 'But me no buts, my dearest chuck. We shall have the players to please us by day, and by night we shall have our sport together.'

Scene V

There is little sign of the countryside being green and pleasant during our journey, which seems to take three weeks, not three days. A great storm rages for the whole duration, so fiercely that I cannot ride, which I prefer, but instead must leave poor Frey to be ridden by a servant, while I am piled into a coach with a heap of scented, smirking ladies, all of whom seem party to some private joke. This conveyance bumps and trundles along, giving us all great discomfort, and the rain is so heavy that it trickles through the leaking roof, and soaks our cloaks, and the ladies declare that they will all die of the sweats, which sets them off again in the most hysterical and unpleasant-sounding laughter. I stare out of the window, watching the dark clouds flying and wondering at the amount of mud that churns along our way. We should have been better off in an Ark than a wobbling coach, for the wrath of God seems to be upon us and the heavens turned to perpetual water, as if the ocean has risen to the sky and must now fall down upon us, returning to its rightful place beneath the moon.

At last, the coach shudders to a halt, and I look outside. Through the falling rain I can make out a huge edifice, long and many-windowed, its lights blurred by the downpour. Stout towers reach up into the stormy sky, and it is neatly turreted, like a child's picture of a castle. Herded inside with my giggling companions, I am dazzled by the brilliant splendour of the great hall, so high and spacious as to rival that at Nonsuch, if not Whitehall. There are chandeliers and torches everywhere, casting their flaming light on many-coloured tapestries and

golden panelling, so that I feel as if I am walking into a giant's treasure casket. The gallery above our heads is filled with musicians, who sing sweet and unfamiliar melodies as we come in – though of course these newly written tunes are not for us but for Her Majesty, whose entrance follows ours and we must push ourselves against the walls as she sweeps past, smiling with marble impregnability.

As I make my way up the great staircase, with Hunsdon close behind me, I see that Will is standing at the top. I never saw him look so handsome. He is dressed in black. He stares at me solemnly as he bows before the ascending procession of courtiers and I feel a sudden urge to weep. I have never wanted him so much, nor feared so painfully that I may not have him.

Hunsdon catches my arm. 'Aemilia, have you met our great scribe?'

I turn to look at him, chiefly so I can avoid looking at Will. 'What scribe is this, my lord?'

'Young Will Shakespeare.' Reaching Will's side, he grasps him by the shoulder. 'This is my sweet mistress, sir. As clever as she is beautiful, and quite as skilful in . . . every art as any man could wish.'

Will bows, unsmiling.

'Aemilia fancies herself a poet, don't you, my dear?'

I can only incline my head, scarlet with discomfort.

'I am sure that no poetry she could ever write would match the perfect symmetry of her face,' says Will. His voice is cold.

'Symmetry, sir! It's not the length of a lady's nose that keeps an old man happy. You poets! What a strange set of fellows you are! Do you slake your lust with symmetry, or with sport?'

Will bows again, as if to acknowledge Hunsdon's superior wisdom. 'Poets are poor lovers, my lord. We save our deepest passions for the page.'

Hunsdon laughs and takes my arm. 'Come now, Melia, forgive us for our idle talk. Let's go to our chamber and read some

verse!' He makes a final bow to Will, the faintest inclination of his head. 'She prefers Sidney's *Astrophil and Stella* to your *Venus and Adonis* – what d'you say to that?'

Tonight, as luck would have it, my lord is in an amorous mood. Despite the fact that he has been a lusty lover for many years, in recent months he has been too tired or ill to fornicate with me, but this night he is keen to get to bed early, and undoes my bodice breathing heavily, showing every sign of wanting to have me as he used to. I confess, with Will nearby I can't bear the thought of this, and come up with the stratagem of reading my poetry to my lord, as a supposed preliminary to our love-making. In fact, as I had hoped, Hunsdon is snoring peacefully after three stanzas.

For a while I lie next to him, singing a lullaby and stroking his white hair back from his brow. And then I stop singing, and watch him breathing, steady as a rivertide. I pull the counterpane over him to keep the night chill from waking him, slip a shawl over my nightgown, and pick up a candle from our bed-table. I am an assiduous adulteress, and I noted where the players are sleeping. Will was given a small chamber to himself, while the other players were given a large room in the eaves. Will claimed he needed a quiet room to finish some writing. I don't know if this is true, or if he is hoping that I might find a way to go to him, at dead of night. Whether this was the case or no, I will do it. The thought of his look as I climbed the stairs with Hunsdon drives me on.

I close the door of my bedchamber behind me, and tiptoe across the dark landing. The house spreads all around me, like a village in the sky, with corridors and staircases leading in every direction. Shielding the flame with my hand, I make my way silently along, counting the doors and noting my way. I hardly dare breathe, and hate my own heart for its fulsome beating. Yet I swear to God I have never felt more alive than I do at this

moment, fearing discovery, astonished at my own foolishness and longing to lie once more with my lover, skin to skin.

Just as I pass a grand, carved door to one of the great bedchambers at the front of the house, I hear a noise and stop still, a dribble of sweat trickling down my neck. I can hear voices shouting, and dare not take another step lest they burst out of the door. I can see nowhere to hide, so I stay, motionless, like a vole sensing the descending hawk. As I stand there, the voices rise higher and higher, and I recognise one of them: it is that of our boyish host, Henry Wriothesley, the Earl of Southampton. The other – a deeper man's voice – I do not know.

'Oh my lord,' says this voice. 'Oh my lord! Oh my lord! Oh my lord! Oh my lord!' Each cry is followed by a bang, like a board being struck in steady rhythm. I stand, terrified, willing myself to move, but unable to take a step.

There is a pause on the other side of the door, yet not silence. The two voices mingle to make the strangest noise, part scream, part groan. Then the deeper voice makes a peculiarly terrible sound, a wolfish howl.

Now comes Wriothesley's light and laughing tone, as if he had had no part in what had gone before. 'Say, "Oh my Lord God."'

'My lord?'

'Say "Oh my Lord God" each time I go up you.'

Then they were off again.

'Oh my Lord God!'

Bang.

'Oh my Lord God!'

Bang.

'Oh my Lord God!'

This time it builds and builds till the final scream is so loud that I am sure the whole household will come running. A drop of candle-wax spills on my wrist, and wakes me from my trance. I hasten along the passage until I come to a narrow flight of stairs

I had noted earlier. I climb them, breathless, and there, at the top, is a door, no bigger than the way into a priest hole. I pray to God that I have remembered right, and tap at it, three times.

The door opens immediately, as if the occupant had been waiting for me.

Will is wearing a nightshirt, but his bed, which I can see over his shoulder, has not been slept in. Close by is a table, on which a candle burns, cluttered with papers – he has indeed been writing. This is his habit at night: he is the only person I have ever met who sleeps as restlessly as I do. For a moment, we look at each other.

'What's this about *Astrophil and Stella*?' he says. 'Disloyal minx.' Then he smiles and pulls me inside.

Scene VI

Having deceived Hunsdon and borne silent witness to Wriothesley's peculiar sodomy, I am trembling with shock and fear. Yet once I am in Will's bed I forget all my terror, and what we do now is like no other love-making that I have ever known, such is its silence and its slow tenderness. As we twist and rock together, I feel my mind fill with a profound sweetness, and I smile as I kiss him, locked closer, closer till we finish as one creature, still soundless, deeply bound. There is such joy in me that I am shocked to find that we are soaked with tears. And when we both lie tangled in my loose black hair, Will whispers, 'We are married now, my love. I have no wife but you.'

We lie silent for a long time. Will strokes the round mole at my throat.

'What's this, my little sorceress,' he says, 'if not your third dug, where you give suck to your familiar?'

'Shall you be my familiar, then?'

'I would be nothing else, if it were possible.'

'Do you ever wonder if the creatures of the night are those that God did not get quite right?' I ask, dreamily.

He is busy kissing the mole upon my neck, but begins to shake with silent laughter. 'Such as what, my strange one? Such as yourself?'

'Well, both of us are wide awake when others sleep. So you are night-odd too . . .' I laugh myself, and twist my neck away. 'But I meant – badgers, hedgehogs, moles. Or bats. All the odd things that are queer to look at.'

'What of the owls, though?' says Will. 'An owl is perfect.'

'Perhaps he is the king of all nocturnal beasts,' I say. 'Unrivalled beneath the moon. He rules us too.'

His lifts his shadowed face to stare into my eyes with mock puzzlement. 'What *are* you, Bassano?' he asks. 'Where did they find you?'

'I found a bat once, fallen from the roof beams,' I whisper.

'Foolish bat, if it could not fly better!' says Will, kissing his way from my neck to my breasts.

'It was a baby, hardly bigger than two farthings,' say I, gasping as he begins to suck. 'I kept it in a little box and fed it with cow's milk in a thimble, and it grew to full size, though I never would have thought it possible.'

'Your witch's magic, I have no doubt of it.' His hands are creeping down, over the skin of my belly.

'Afterwards, it made its home in the eaves of my apartment, and I would see it at dusk, spinning around the roof beams with sightless ease. And it would still come down and drink milk from a saucer, like a tiny flying cat.'

'Fortunate bat, to sip from your saucer!' His fingers have found their place, and he begins to jerk them in a rhythm that I know and love, and for some time neither of us speaks, but go at it bat-like, knowing our way.

'I cannot bear to be without you,' I say at last. 'I cannot live like this, divided, like Judas.'

'What else can we do?' says Will. 'Where else can we go?'

'I don't know,' I say. I think of Hunsdon, pumping away with his old man's wiry passion, and feel the bile rise in my throat. 'I cannot bear to lie with Hunsdon! I am no better than a tavern whore, turning tricks for trinkets.'

'This is our world,' he says, with his arms around me. 'There is no escape, except when we are lost together, and it's those times that we must think of, and seek out, and keep safe.'

I kiss his ink-black, cunt-wet fingers.

'Why can't your words save us? Why can't we set up in some fine house, Lord and Lady Letters? Why must it be so squalid and profane?'

'Aemilia.' He strokes my hair. 'Before I knew this, I knew nothing. Nothing of love, and what I knew of life was book-learned, or filched from other poets, or sketched to please the crowd. My plays were martial, my poetry a forged confection, like a sugar-swan. No more. No more.'

'What – and you were married? And had little children? And this taught you nothing?'

'Nothing of this,' he whispers into my hair. 'Of *eros* and its wondrous madness. I love you, and, if that is wrong, so be it.'

Then sleep comes. I wake and hear the sweet song of the nightingale and see a faint light round the shuttered window. Sitting upright, I notice that the candle has burned right down. Will is fast asleep, curled into his pillow. I kiss his sleeping mouth, slip from the bed, pull on my nightgown and shawl and leave with anxious haste. I retrace my steps as quickly as I dare but, as I pass Wriothesley's door, it opens. A figure steps out and stands in my path. I am filled with horror. It is the young earl, in a splendid purple robe, like some Roman pontiff. In the half-light, I can only see his outline, slim and flimsy as a girl, and the pale aureole of his curling hair, which hangs loose about him.

'What's this?' he says, in a loud voice, more suited to the daytime.

I stare at him, in an agony of horror.

'It's Hunsdon's pretty mistress, if I'm not mistaken? Pert Aemilia, the bed-wise scholar.'

'It is, my lord.' He may speak as loudly as he wishes; I will whisper.

'What are you about, my swarthy little puss? Why are you not with his lordship, in his chamber?'

'I was restless, my lord.'

'Restless! Oh, my sweet lady. You should have come to me –
and with me – sweet and stealthy restlessness of woman! I would
have given you no rest at all.'

'I have been . . . walking in the garden,' I say. 'My mind was
disturbed. I sometimes walk at night.'

Wriothesley comes towards me and kneels down. I see that
the grey light is casting day-shapes on the dark landing – here
a carved chair, there a great urn. Hunsdon might be waking
up, and wondering where I am. He picks up the hem of my
nightgown and scrutinises it carefully. He looks up at me, his
blue eyes suddenly illuminated in a ray of morning light.

'No dew on your gown, I see.' He stands up and comes
close, so I can smell the semen on him. 'But I daresay you are
drenched . . . in some other place.'

I smile at him, desperate. 'When I came to myself I was
standing upon the pathway, looking up at the moon,' I say,
twisting my hands together. 'Sometimes my night-walks bring
forth new ideas for poems.'

'Indeed!' He smirks, and kisses me lightly on the cheek.
'Perhaps one day you will write a poem for me.'

The performance is the cause of much excitement. The beauteous
Rosaline has made a great impression on our host. Yet I find
myself distracted all the way through. Will is playing Berowne,
and his words make me ache. I cannot look at him. After it is over,
the Queen announces that she must see the gardens and out we
spill, out of the dark Play-Room, down the handsome staircase
and out into the square of summer light. A storm has soaked the
fields and gardens and disappeared without a trace, so that the
dripping trees and heavy flowers have the brightness of spring,
and yet are deep-coloured with summer's heavier hues.

The Queen and her ladies process along the wide garden
paths, surveying the knot garden and fanning themselves as they

talk and laugh. I fall behind them, so tired that black shards of night faze in and out of my sight. I feel sick and strange, wishing in one part of myself that I could leave all this spoiled and rotten life behind me, and enter some cool nunnery and pray my way slowly back to God. I am sick of Greeks, and Romans, and learning; sick of fine clothes and smart words and the ways of Court, in which everything is permissible if the Queen wishes or approves it, or does not deign to notice it.

Indeed, I am so worn out that I do not at first notice that Will has fallen into step beside me.

'How are you today, my love?' he asks.

I turn to look behind me, but no one is walking within earshot. 'I am well, sir,' I say.

'What do you think of all this?' he asks, indicating the wide garden which has subjugated Nature with such ruthless symmetry.

'It is very fine.'

'Could you see yourself in such a place? A country lady?'

'Certainly not! The life of a country lady consists mostly of praying, walking, Bible-reading and being unwell.'

Will throws his head back and laughs delightedly. 'God's teeth, you have a way with words, Aemilia! What a summary!'

'Ssh, do not laugh so loudly. Hunsdon will hear you.' I look across the knot garden to the far window. Hunsdon and his advisors are in an important huddle, discussing affairs of state. The Queen and her ladies have settled down in a leafy bower. A lute-player is hurrying towards them, as if anxious to stave off the spectre of boredom with his sweet songs.

Will is abruptly serious. 'At least a country lady has a place. A position.'

'Oh, surely. She is planted in her lord's estate, like an oak tree, and she must manage servants and clink with keys to all that must be locked and tidy. For variety, she may admire her fine linen or fish for trout.'

'A pleasant enough existence.'

'While her lord parades himself at Court, perhaps gaming, perhaps fornicating, and probably amusing himself around the town or at the theatre. Did I miss my vocation, in being too much the bastard whore to make a proper match? I think not.'

'You are a woman, Aemilia. You cannot rise above that.'

'Why not? If Our Lord rules over all the magnificence and violence of Creation, then why must his women be so timid and obedient?'

'Aemilia – '

'All of it is His – the wolves and roaring bears, the wild boar, the proud lion, the swift claws of the eagle and the kite.'

'Madam, if I may only speak – '

But I will have my say. 'Think of it all – the secret vastness of the great Leviathan that slides, lightless and unclassified, beneath the mighty ocean. And we placid little Marthas may have the hearth.'

'You are too clever for this old game. You should rule kingdoms, not that dotard Hunsdon.'

'Ay, that would be a fine thing. Except that our Prince is also the keeper of her own prison. She rules her own spirit quite as harshly as she rules any of us.'

We walk on in silence for a while, with a cautious space between us. Only my skirt touches him as it swishes along the path.

'What riles me is the littleness of learning,' I say, suddenly.

'The what? Is this more of your philosophy?'

'The facts and factions, the scholars in their ponderousness of robes and competition and self-display and mutual vilification.'

'Ha! Yes. Now this, I like.'

'How can any man know a little and not crave to know much more – the "all" that is the sum of what we have? To go beyond the walls of this fine college or that one, and be Godlike in his wisdom, so that the map of all learning is stretched before his gaze?'

'They are gentlemen. They have nothing more to prove.'

'I cannot credit it, the narrow, self-regarding focus of the scholar on his portion of Cicero and Seneca, his puffed-upness with it, his satisfaction with the verse he's stuffed whole into his empty head. For every Bacon there are a thousand lettered dolts.'

'Lady, what fuels this rage? You speak like no one else I know.'

'Oh, yes, I should calm myself. I am just a woman, accidentally and freakishly deformed by teaching which took no regard of my station, nor of my sex.'

Will stops and turns to face me. 'God above, you're like a maze, with every twist and turn taking me further from the sober world! Such anger and . . .' here he swallows '. . . such ardour. I never knew anything like the earthly joy you spun with me last night. I keep thinking of your soft tears in the darkness, and how they mixed with mine.'

'My love,' I whisper. 'We must be cool in daylight.'

'And of . . . Jesu. I am sick with love for you, Aemilia. I am ill with it.'

'Will, be quiet, don't speak of these things in this place! Be cautious!'

'I cannot be cautious and love you. I must be reckless, or give you up.'

'No, sir, you must be cautious and not give me up!'

'How does Rosaline compare to Katherine?' he asks, abruptly.

'How . . . what?'

'It is the man who is quelled in this tale, don't you see it? Who must cool his ardour and his arrogance to win his love. She is as far removed from that poor Shrew as I could make her. And she is darkly beautiful, like another lady that I know.'

I can't help laughing in spite of myself. 'There is a message in that play for me, is there?'

'It's a love letter to my own fine, clever Rosaline, who makes me think and makes me weep and will not let me have my way.'

'Oh, sir! Now you are playing with me! How have you been thwarted? Why, there is not a man alive who has got his way with me as you have, or for whom I've taken greater risks!'

A drop of rain falls heavily on my hand. I look up, and see the storm clouds have returned. The knot garden is empty, and we are standing at a stone gate, at the furthest side from the house.

He is standing closer now, and as the new rain falls he pushes me into the gateway and I see there is a tiny room within it, with a stone slit for a window and a cracked oak door.

'Will, I . . .'

But I move first, kissing him so hard I bite his lip and taste his blood, and as the storm breaks with a clattering roar of thunder we fall together in the garden room, and he kicks the door shut and somehow my skirts are undone and I am in my under-shift wedged halfway up the wall, and Will is tight inside me pushing higher with each shuddering breath, and I am shouting with each thunderclap, as nearly mad as I have ever been, and as close to Heaven as I'll ever come. Unless God is more forgiving than I dare to hope.

Scene VII

This is a fervent time, and I must remember it. I must keep it with me. I am writing notes on what we do, and how we love, all of them in Hebrew, which I know Hunsdon can never read. It is a sad fact of our lives that it is easier to convey pain and sorrow than pleasure and happiness – I trust that in the afterlife we shall find perfection more to our liking. This is a passion that transforms me, and a love that makes the world glitter. It is nothing like drunkenness, nor like witchcraft neither: it is like being reborn in Eden. And I have him: he is mine and no one else's. And I am his: no other man comes close. What happened to us before, and whatever sadness may come after – they cannot touch this period of our glorious rapture. Will belongs to me, and I rejoice in my dominion, and he is at once my equal and my lord.

We snatch at time together when we can, not just lustful but curious, and hungry to know each other's minds. We read together and write together, and laugh and weep and whisper in that secret room. And yet it's true, our wildest rapture is to *occupy* each other, in that modern phrase, and each time we lie together we count it a miracle, and wonder if a greater ecstasy could be reached than that which we knew in our last coupling; and each time it turns out that it can. Such is the way with new lovers when their bodies match.

The greatest miracle, I must say, is that for many months no child comes of all this exultant fornication. But Nature will have its way in the end, as Nature must. And there is no question: keeping two lovers makes me careless and distracted, for I

have been a watchful, canny mistress for many years. I used to keep myself away from Hunsdon at my fertile times, and if my curse was late I would take a vile cure made from mandrake root. Which did its work, though each draught nearly killed me. I proceeded with these treatments with such success that I have come to think I must be barren, or that Hunsdon's seed is spent.

It turns out that, rather than being barren, I am like a mossy bank in springtime, ready to burst forth with new life. One day, soon after Michaelmas, I realise that my curse-blood is late. I cannot remember when it last flowed. Quite unconcerned, and confident that I can soon put this to rights, I say nothing. I take my usual draught of poison, pinching my nose to get it down. Then I wait for the blood to come, calmly enough to start with. But this time nothing happens, excepting only that my belly seems tighter than a drum. I take another draught, a heftier dose this time, which gives me fearful cramps. This time I am certain the brew has done its work, and wait once again. Again, nothing. Now, with mounting fear, I begin to pray for my deliverance, though it is of course against the teachings of Our Lord to ask for an unborn child to die. Night after night, I lie awake, dry-eyed. I know only too well what happens to a kept mistress who finds herself in this predicament. She is cast off, and sent away. I must free myself. I must get rid of it.

But who will help me? There is no one I can trust, no one I can turn to. Dr Forman might have a tincture he can give me, but I am not certain he would keep the secret. My dugs – so recently the size of winter apples – have swelled up so they seem ready to burst out of my bodice, and are painful to the touch. And I seem to have gained a layer of fat, even though everything I eat tastes like pewter. If I were a pig, I would soon be ready for the pot. I am nauseous and dizzy and can barely think. The pregnancy itself seems like a spell. I sleep in dream snatches, and see Will and Hunsdon fuck together, and wake twisted in the bed-sheets, crying out.

At last my head clears. Hunsdon has gone away, to execute some Catholics at York. And I hold Will off, writing a coded note to say I am too ill to meet him in our little room. Which is no more than the truth. If I am to do something to save myself, the time to act is now.

Alice, as luck would have it, is a stupid, unobservant girl, who lives most vividly in the looking glass. Thus, she sees nothing strange in my repeated bouts of puking.

'Dear me, mistress, what have you eaten?' says she, fetching me a cup of small beer as I empty my guts into the close stool. 'You've been ill for days! And yet you're no thinner – there's a marvel!'

'A marvel indeed,' I say, sipping from the cup. My mind is sharper after this last horrid spewing-up, as if I have rid myself of some internal confusion along with my breakfast. 'We must go out.'

'Are you sure you're well enough, mistress? You're very pale.'

'I am well enough to visit an apothecary,' I say. 'To seek a cure for this unpleasant malady.'

'Oh, but I could go for you,' says the girl, all eager. I know why: she will have the chance to prance past the law students at Middle Temple, showing off her pretty clothes, though they are like as not more interested in Aristotle's 'Refutations' than in her Spanish ruff. 'Oh – please let me!'

'No, Alice, we shall both go. Hurry up, and don't start messing with your cap. I'm well enough now, but may soon be worse again.'

Most of the apothecaries' shops are found in Bucklersbury, a narrow street which winds away from Cheapside. In the swirling City stenches this is a place which offers a rare delight to Londoners, for you can smell it half a mile away, such is the sweet

scent of its herbs and spices. But, of the hundred apothecaries who trade in the City, I have heard that half are useless and the rest are cozeners. On most occasions I send a servant to see Ned Hollybushe, whose father has wrote an excellent book upon this subject. But today . . .

'Why here, mistress? Off the beaten way?' asks Alice. 'This is not our usual man!' We have arrived in a cramped courtyard, which reeks even more strongly than the busy street. The jutting storeys of the ancient houses make it dusk at midday. An open shop front stands before us, the counter folded out so that – in theory – we can see within. But all that is visible is the shop sign, which is a hanging tortoise. Behind this I can see nothing.

'Wait here,' I say.

'Oh, but, mistress . . .'

'Do what I tell you.'

And, with that, I push open the door of the shop and go inside. What strikes me first is its exotic scent, something between the smell of cumin and sweet basil. But as I look around me I see that the shop is very different from what I have been expecting. Though it is ill lit, there is a shaft of sunlight coming from a window set high in the wall, and I see that it is a larger space than had seemed possible from the street. The walls are dull red and lined with shelves, upon which are ranged pots and pitchers and drug-jars made of blue and white porcelain, painted with red and blue flowers and symbols and marked with the name of the herb or spice which they contain. On the floor beside the counter is a giant pestle and mortar, as big as a bucket. Everything is polished and clean, so that the falling rays of sunlight are reflected in the shining surfaces. So much precision and order, such neatness – I confess I am surprised.

Behind the counter stands the apothecary, Widow Daunt. She wears a white bonnet, and her face is sallow and deeply lined. Her expression is somewhat sour, as if a shop like hers might do very well if only she didn't have the bother of serving customers.

But there is no shortage of these. Joan Daunt is well known for her foul but cunning remedies.

Indeed, there are two people at the counter. A tall woman and her old manservant. The woman is wearing a fine wool cloak and her golden hair is arranged with great care. She turns to look as I come in, and I see that she has an old, shrivelled face, which is out of keeping with her good clothes and upright carriage. Her pretty hair must be a wig.

'Is that all you have to say?' she asks, turning back to look at Widow Daunt.

'All what?' asks the Widow. She has a surly manner, for a shopkeeper.

'That you can do nothing else for me?'

'What I have to say, madam, is that you came to me for an elixir to make you beautiful. Sparing your feelings as best I may, I told you no such thing exists, and gave you what I could, instead. And that was a potion to make a young man *think* you comely, at least for the space of one night.'

'Wine can accomplish that much,' says the woman.

'Indeed it can, and I told you at the time that there was wine in that mixture and by all accounts it did its work.'

'He loved for one night, that is true.'

'So our deal is sound.'

The woman draws breath deeply, and I realise that she is on the brink of tears.

'It is not enough, Mistress Daunt! I demand more! I want more from you!'

Joan Daunt leans forward across the counter. 'What more would that be, mistress?'

'I want him to love me!' wails the woman. 'I had him! I had him for one night – and what joy it was! And, when day broke, he looked down on me and fled the chamber. Make him love me! I demand you make him love me!'

'How shall I do such a thing?'

'Give me another potion! A stronger one this time.' She nods, and the manservant produces a money bag.

'Something to make him love you for longer?' asks Widow Daunt.

'I want you to make me young again. And beautiful. Forever. I have money. I don't care what pain I suffer, or how vile the treatment.'

Widow Daunt seems to find this a very good joke. 'Madam, I am an apothecary, not Almighty God. Take your business elsewhere. Or you could always pray.'

The woman nods to the servant and he takes the Widow by the shoulders. 'Do as my mistress says, or take the consequences,' he says. 'Do it, old woman, or you will suffer for it.'

'Get away with you, you buffoon!' says the Widow. 'I will not be spoken to like that in my own shop! Get out, the pair of you!'

Then the woman leans forward and slaps her hard, across the face.

This is quite enough. I throw the hood from my head and approach them. 'Kindly do the Widow's bidding and leave this shop, if you have no further business,' I say. 'I have waited long enough to be served, and you are wasting my time as well as insulting her. You can't bully your way to beauty, madam, nor bribe your looks back from Time. They've gone, and there's an end to it.'

The woman turns her tear-stained face to me. 'It is all very well for *you*,' she says. 'Old age comes to all of us, but *you* are still young.'

'Get out, the pair of you,' I say. 'Leave the Widow be, and go about your business.'

The servant keeps his grasp. I draw out Hunsdon's paper-knife and point it at his neck. 'This knife was given me by the great John Dee himself. There is venom in this blade. One prick from this and you'll fall stone dead, right on the spot. The last

person to feel its point lived for just two minutes. It's not a sight I'd wish to see again.'

The servant lets go of the widow and leans away from me, his veined eyes full of terror.

'Who on *earth* are you?' shrieks the woman. 'Who is John Dee to you?'

'I am Queen Mab,' I say, 'for all it's got to do with you.'

The strange pair leave. Joan Daunt waits until the door bangs shut, and then turns to look at me. She seems neither alarmed nor grateful for my help.

'How can I help you?' she asks, looking me over. 'I see you have plenty of need for cures.'

'Do you, indeed?' A wave of sickness comes over me.

'You'll end up keeping it,' she says.

'Keeping what?'

'The child.'

'I never said . . .'

'You didn't have to.'

'Well, you are quite wrong. I do want rid of it.'

'Yes, but I just told you – '

'I need something strong. And I don't mind what you put in it. A hanged man's sperm is fine with me. It can burn my womb out, for all I care.'

'So that you could never have a child?'

'Why should I want one? All they do is bind you, and I am bound enough already.'

The Widow stares at me, and I see something unexpected: kindness. 'Sit down,' she says. 'I'll do you something. But you won't drink it.'

She collects together some jars and bottles, takes out a pestle and mortar – of larger than usual size – and fills it with leaves and fragments, which she begins to grind. Then she scoops a hideous little fish from a jar and scrapes the scales from its wriggling form. These she places into a clay burner and a most obnoxious

perfume fills the air. What she has made – a sickly, semi-liquid paste, the colour of a dog turd – she squeezes into a tiny vial and stops with wax.

'Your remedy,' she says, handing it to me. 'Swallow it in one draught. The babe will come out in three spasms, whole and pulsing, but too small for you to see its face. It will be dead in five minutes.'

I open my mouth to speak, but she holds up her finger.

'Be careful. You are in a bad way. And your old life is over, have no doubt of that. And . . . when you need me, send word.'

'I have servants, Mistress Daunt. I am well cared for.'

'Nonetheless, I wait upon your word. And, when I hear from you, then I will come. Remember that.'

I look at the vial and its horrid contents, puzzled. The potion is not still, but heaves and oozes, as if in some low kind of pain. And the stench is such that I can smell it through its coat of glass.

Scene VIII

I will wait one more day, to see if my curse might start. Another night of prayer might see the unborn child bleed harmlessly away. The potion looks so horrible, and the thought of swallowing it is disgusting to me. But it is hard to wait for anything. I sit at my virginals in my parlour, and try to play a tune. It is a pretty piece called 'Giles Farnaby's Dream', which can usually calm my nerves but today it only vexes me: its brightness seems too far removed from the world I know. I look at the painted wainscot, the Turkey carpet which takes pride of place over the fireplace, the half-finished skirt that lies in a ripple of azure satin across my bed. Nothing seems real. I am like a child's toy, which is now broken and must be mended. My head aches. My eyes are sore. My velvet bodice digs into my flesh. I slam the lid down on the virginals, so that the strings let out a plaintive note. Snatching up my cloak, I rush down the stairwell and into the courtyard. I feel as if there must be a way out of all this trouble, if only I could clear my head and think. The gateway to St James's Park is open. I slip through it, and hurry into the darkening trees.

I put my face in my hands and moan. What to do? What to do? It is Will's child, I am sure of it – the fruit of all our hidden passion. I am not certain where the souls of unborn, unbaptised children are supposed to go, now that the Queen of England is our Pope, but in the old days they dwelt in Limbo. It does not sound like a good place for my unborn babe to be. Yet what else can I do but kill it? There is no way out. I should have kept away from Will. But I did not, I could not. Now what will become of me?

Just as I am racked with another bout of sobs, I find that I am not alone. Someone is by me. Someone's arms are around me.

'Aemilia – my love! What's wrong? You're cold – you're trembling!' Will's voice is soft and tender.

'Will!' I cry. I am almost afraid to look him in the eye, in case he can see what I am thinking. But I can't look anywhere else. How can he not know? How can I hide my knowledge from him? 'What are you doing here? What is the matter?'

'My love,' he says. His face is shining, as if he has found some new wonder in the world. 'I had to see you.'

'But . . . You know we must be . . .' I catch my breath. When were we ever 'careful'?

'Listen – listen . . .' He stares down at me. 'I came because there is something I must say.'

It is so sweet to see him, and look at his face, and hear him speaking so tenderly to me that I cannot help but weaken. Silently, I weep against his shoulder.

'What is it?' He looks down at me, eyes shadowed in the moonlight.

I struggle with myself, not knowing what to say. 'Oh . . . I am so unhappy that I can't be with you, and must live with Hunsdon, in the palace . . .' This is almost the truth. And yet, of course, I want to say, *Will, I am pregnant, and I cannot say for sure if it is yours, and yet I believe it is, and I've got a draught to get rid of it, and I thought that I could do this, and go on as before, but now I find I'd rather die. Please help me.* Even with his arms around me, I feel alone, and as if I have betrayed him.

He kisses me, and holds me tight against him. I can smell the leather of his doublet and the tavern stench of old ale and tobacco. 'Come, come, we can't stay here,' he says. (And how this sweet 'we' tears at me.) 'We must find somewhere warmer . . . there is an inn on the other side of the park where we can go. Here – look . . .' He pulls a stage mask from his sleeve, made of

black velvet stiffened with bombast. 'You can be the mysterious lady and I will be your humble squire.'

When we are settled by the fire in an upstairs room, he takes my hands and holds them. 'Still cold, so cold, my love.'

'I am better now.' I stare at him, lulled by the fire and by a mute happiness that he is here.

'Aemilia, come and live with me.'

'Oh, Will! But what of Hunsdon?'

'I will care for you. You don't need him.'

'Don't be such a fool.'

'Leave him, and be *my* mistress.'

'Living how, exactly?'

'I'll be your protector.'

'And where shall we live?' I ask.

'I . . . have expectations.'

'Expectations?'

'My plays will make me rich. I am certain of it. How can it be otherwise?' He kisses my hand, and then reaches across and touches my icy cheek. 'You know that this is what should happen. You know that we can only be happy if we are joined together – think of it: to have each other in the daytime, in the open, instead of these furtive fornications and sneakings round at dead of night! To eat together, or stroll in the Exchange!'

He speaks as if he was offering me a chance to live with him in Heaven.

'I never heard such foolishness . . . how can this be possible?'

But he is determined. 'Listen, my love. There is a logic in the universe that goes beyond mere common sense – and this is the logic of our two lives, intermingling.'

'Will, I – '

'Our two selves, undivided. Don't you agree?'

'Of course, but – '

'Come with me! Come away with me, and who knows what will happen to us? Let's take our chance.'

'If only it were possible!'

'It is possible, my sweet Aemilia! It is possible. Just think of it . . .'

I close my eyes and see it.

He leans closer. 'Aemilia. You cannot deny me. You cannot deny yourself.'

Scene IX

Could I un-lord myself, and live with Will? I suppose I could. If there were no baby, and I had money, and I was sure I wouldn't starve. If there were no censure; if poets' mistresses were not seen as tavern whores. Should I drink Joan's brew, and end the baby, and live with my love – *be* that whore? At least my life will be a sort of whole; I'll be a common doxy, but I'll have the right man in my bed.

I pray for forgiveness, open that dread casket once again and take out the vial. The shifting, surging potion has expanded and mounted up the sides of the glass, like a semi-liquid fungus. My guts heave. I take the stopper out, and am assaulted by its appalling stench.

But what's that? I hear a sound and whirl around to see what it could be. It is – I could have sworn – the sound of a newborn crying. Plaintive, urgent, relentless. I turn full circle, startled. Outside the sky is grey and heavy rain is falling: a ceaseless rhythm is beating at the window panes. Of course, the noise must be a seagull's cry, echoing down the chimney. I raise the vial and tip it slowly towards my lips.

There it is again, even clearer than before. I lower the glass, trembling with nausea. I have never heard a seagull make such a sound. I replace the cork, open the window casement and the rainstorm rips into the room, drenching my dress and hair. Hardly noticing the sudden cold, I peer out into the storm, half-expecting to see an abandoned infant lying by the palace wall. It is not unknown for women to leave their newborn babies there,

in the mistaken belief that royal largesse will ensure that they are well looked after. On this day, though, there is no baby. There is nothing.

I feel so sad about the empty, lonely gardens, and the fact that there is no crying child that I begin to weep. I think of those poor girls who bring their babes and leave them in this place, open to the elements: tiny, weak, milk-smelling creatures, unshriven, unbegun. And this in a city which pities no one, in which wealth is everything and penury the norm. Those poor children! Those wretched, abandoned souls! I weep silent, penitent tears. I cannot do it. I cannot kill this child. I hurl the vial out of the window. I hear a soft crack as it hits the ground and – in spite of the rain – I smell something sourly burning. I lean out and let the rain mix with my tears. And I know that, if I can't kill this unborn infant, then I can't leave my rich protector, furious and betrayed. Because if I am going to have this child I need him. No, let me be honest: I need his money. I do not know who has fathered this child, but I know who the mother is well enough. A penniless, bastard whore, half-Jewish, long orphaned. Nobody. I think of Will, expectant and full of love. If I could unmake everything so that I could be with him . . . but no. My thoughts fly to the four corners of the world, and then return, defeated.

The rain pelts harder and seems to wash some sense into me, and in the end I reach the conclusion that I like least and which pains me most. But I cannot see another way.

This next morning I wake early and lie still. I open my eyes and stare at the canopy above me. I have the whole bed to stretch out in, and I do so, pushing my warm feet into its coldest corners. The new day brings no hope, but in its light I know that I have made a wise decision. I have come up with a stratagem that will save my child, and keep us from the streets. It is not a design of

any great cleverness or cunning. It is simply this: if Hunsdon thinks the child is his, he will provide for me. If he thinks I have betrayed him, he will cast me out with nothing. Therefore, my affair with Will must end, and never be discovered. As a loyal but careless mistress I might be married off to some lowly courtier – one happy to take the dowry Hunsdon settles on me as his bribe for taking on spoiled goods.

Hunsdon is due back from York at any time. Better to do nothing, and let my failure to appear convey its own message to Will. I curl myself into a ball, and pull the eiderdown around me, and wait for the time to pass. My head aches with grief, and I am filled with bitter anger that this must be my lot. If I am such a faithless whore, why am I disabled by scruples I can't afford? A depraved and desperate woman should be ruthless in the execution of her desires. There is no place for me in the hierarchy of mankind, and, to make things worse, my own character is wrongly put together. I have the mind of a philosopher, the education of a prince and the morality of a nun. The agony of my condition forces me to puke into a bucket with more violence than usual.

Spent and white-faced, I get up and dress and read the Bible with such fierce attention that I fear my eyeballs will drop out. Then I think again of the letter that I have not written, and this reminds me of those Will has sent to me, so I pull them out from beneath the mattress and throw them on the fire. I do not cry. I do not think of all those lost times, crumpling and burning to black ash. And yet, in spite of all this, and of all my determination to do nothing, when I look at the clock I find that just forty minutes have passed. I think that Hell must not only be a place of fire and punishment, but of clocks that tick and tock in an eternal present, where nothing ever happens.

I stand up, and pace up and down the chamber saying, 'It's Hunsdon's child. It's Hunsdon's child.' As if I were casting a spell. I can't be still. I can't stop my ceaseless walking, so I

continue in this manner until at last, exhausted, I fall down senseless on the bed.

When I wake, Hunsdon himself is sitting beside me, his clothes still mud-splattered from his journey. He is looking down at me and stroking my hair, but he is not smiling.

He says, 'I have a gift for you.'

I struggle up on to my elbows and we kiss each other softly. I try to read his expression.

'A gift! You are so kind!'

'Not kind, my dear. It is only just that you should have it. I have loved you very well.'

A chill comes on me. 'Why do you say "have loved"?' I ask. 'I'm not dead.'

'No, my dear,' says he. 'Too full of life.' He pats my tight belly. His face is heavy.

I feel the world lurch, and look down at my body. 'You know,' I say. But I pray he only guesses the half of it.

'I shall build you a house, at Long Ditch. At Westminster, quite close by.'

Hunsdon is a soldier, not a politician. When there are decisions to be made, he makes them quickly.

'I . . . I'm sorry for it,' say I. 'So many years without falling pregnant, and then . . . it was my carelessness. My fault.'

He sighs and begins to pull off his boots. 'You can't blame yourself, my poor child,' he says. 'I put it there.'

I say nothing, at once relieved and quite bereft of hope.

'What shall I do there, all alone?' I ask, trying to keep my voice from rising to a wail. 'Like some dowager, pensioned off?' My mind says, *Do not question your salvation, Aemilia; take the house and keep silent.*

He leans across and kisses me gently. 'You are to marry,' says he. 'You won't be alone.'

My mouth is dry. 'Who shall I marry, my lord?'

'Alfonso Lanyer.'

'Lanyer! Oh, Henry! Whose thought was this?'

'He's always had his eye on you.'

'But sir – '

'Enough, Aemilia! He is one of your own.'

One of my own! This is a cruel blow indeed. Alfonso Lanyer is a prize fool, a womaniser and a gambler at the tables. Handsome enough, for sure. But as a husband! I want to cry out, to explain that this can never be, yet of course I cannot, in case my reluctance to marry one man suggests I might have a preference for another.

The wedding is all agreed. I stay in my room, reading and praying and seeking peace of mind. When Alice brings me letters, I make her put them on the fire. I know who they are from. I walk through my life like my own spectre, my heart and soul torn out of me, sustained only by the love-child that grows inside.

I do have one remaining hope. Which is that I might take with me, out into the cold world beyond the life of Court, a little of my learning. And that I might be allowed to write my poetry and to improve it, sustained by a patron willing to support me. This is a man's business, but I am as well educated as any man, and so, if any woman could succeed in such a project, it might be me. If the Countess of Pembroke is celebrated for her verse, is it so extraordinary an ambition to hope that I might be celebrated for mine? She has made her country home a supposed 'paradise for poets' – could I not make my own small house a place of industry and reflection?

The day before I am to leave Whitehall, I give Hunsdon some of my poems, which I have copied in my best script.

'They are pretty, my dear, thank you,' says Hunsdon. He sits apart from me, on a cedar wood chair, and seems preoccupied.

'You know me: I do like a play, and a good ballad that tells a tale, but . . . I'm not a man for sonnets and such fancification.'

'I wrote them all for you.'

'Indeed, I know it. And I am touched, very touched indeed. Now, tell me, do you like the house?'

'I like it very much. Thank you my lord. I am grateful – beyond grateful.'

'I think you will be very well accommodated. The solar, in particular, I have appointed to the highest specification.'

'The specification is quite perfect.'

'You will be married soon, as you know.'

'Yes, sir.'

'Good. Very good.'

I look down, so he can't see the expression on my face.

'He is a bloody fool, Alfonso, but they say the ladies like him,' says Hunsdon.

'They do indeed,' I say.

'He's always admired you.'

'Yes, sir. You said so.'

'So he'll be . . . good to you. You know. Shame for it all to go to waste.' He nods to me in a general way, which hints at our gaudy nights.

'Yes, sir.' I take a breath. 'Henry, I should like to have a patron.'

'A what, my dear?'

'A patron.'

He stares at me, speechless with astonishment.

'I know it is unusual,' say I.

'Unusual . . . ? What are you talking about?'

'I mean . . . someone who has position, who might be interested in my . . . verse.'

'Christ's blood! These lines you've scrawled, you mean?' He waves my poems in the air. 'These funny little ditties?'

'They are poems, my lord. I know they need more work.'

'Good God,' he says. 'I fear that your condition has affected your faculties, poor child. You're barking mad.'

'No, indeed, my lord.'

'Whoever would have thought it? You always seemed so sharp.'

'I don't believe I am going mad at all, sir. I have always wanted to make more of my poetry, to learn how to improve it, and how to . . . apprentice myself to it.'

He shakes his head. 'I will tell you this, Aemilia, you're a strange one. The night-walking is just the half of it.'

This makes me want to weep. I think of the night-walking that had first made Hunsdon notice me, soon after my mother died. But there is no time to mourn the passing of his gentle but insistent courtship.

'Would it be possible to find someone, now that I'm no longer your mistress?' I say. 'I mean, there would be no disgrace attached to you, would there?'

He stares at me with his calm grey eyes, that only see what is solid and tangible. 'I never heard of such a thing.'

I let my words spout out, madly, in case I hesitate and never get them out at all. 'I don't want to vanish quite away. I'll cause no trouble, keep from the Court, not bother you or speak out of turn, or do anything that might displease you . . . but if I had some support, some patronage . . . as a man would . . .' I look at him beseechingly. 'Might anyone consider it?'

He seems dumbfounded, then begins to chuckle. 'My dear girl, how will I do without you? You are quite as entertaining out of bed as in it. Why not? Why not, indeed?' He laughs so merrily that I have to fight to hide my irritation.

'What would you suggest, sir? For someone in my situation? I have some verses – I could send them, if you are happy for me to do this.'

'To whom?'

'Whomever you suggest.'

'Lord above! I've no idea. Did you like the inlaid stools I gave you? Did you like the Aldersgate tiles, and the silver tankards? I have thought of everything, have I not?'

'Everything is there. It is perfect.'

He smiles, very pleased with himself. 'Of course, I did ask Lady Anne for her advice. I thought you wouldn't mind.'

I smile so hard my cheeks ache. It was logical for him to ask his wife's opinion, though hardly kind to either of us. 'Her ladyship has exquisite taste.'

He gets up and warms his back before the fire for a moment. 'I shall not see you again, after this conversation. I am sorry for it, and I shall miss you sorely. But a break has to be made, and I am afraid the time has come.'

I nod silently. My hands are very still. My heart beats slowly, slowly. I can control myself, no matter how the world might heave and lurch around me.

Scene X

God still being in his Heaven, though mightily indifferent to me, the morning before my wedding day I take myself off to the quiet of the abbey. I sit down on the rush-strewn flags and pray.

'When the wicked man turneth away from his wickedness that he hath committed, and doeth that which is lawful and right, he shall save his soul . . . I acknowledge my transgressions and my sins . . .'

'Aemilia!'

I open my eyes. My pregnant state makes my mind slow, my view of the world outside my body more hazy with each passing day. Is God speaking to me? But no, it is a white-faced Will. His eyes are set in dark rings; he is hatless and his hair is pushed behind his ears as if had just risen from bed.

'We must speak – come!'

He drags me down the damp passage to the high-walled abbey garden. At the far side of the quadrangle, an old servant is sweeping up dead leaves.

I stare at Will, shocked and yet for all my woe relieved to have him near.

'Is it true?' he asks. 'They say you're pregnant!'

I cover my face with my hands and turn away.

He pulls me round and prises my hands away. I am forced to look at him, and see that his eyes are wet with tears.

'Are you having a child?'

I can't reply.

'And are you marrying . . . Alfonso Lanyer?' He seems barely able to speak the name.

I look down at the muddy ground, licking the salt tears from my lips. Last night was stormy, and a fat worm is slithering in a puddle. Avoiding his gaze, I say, 'I don't expect you to understand.'

'Oh, Aemilia! Look at me!' He seizes hold of me and shakes me, gently. I don't want to look at him, but I am forced to. His gaze seems blacker and darker than it has ever been, as if it were a reflection of my own eyes. 'Have pity! I've never loved, never known what it was to love, never known such pain and wonder as I have known since I met you.'

I can't help myself. 'My love,' I say. 'My heart will break!' I take his face between my hands and kiss his eyes, his cheeks, his lips. We embrace as tenderly as we had on that strange and silent night at Titchfield. It seems as though a thousand years have passed since that sweet time.

He draws back and tucks a strand of my hair inside my bonnet. 'Answer me one question.'

I smile up at him, full of sorrow. 'I will answer it, I promise.'

'Are you having a child?'

I swallow bile. 'Yes.'

'Then – come with me! Be my mistress, be mine . . .'

'It isn't yours.'

His face hardens and his arms drop to his sides. We stare at each other.

'How do you know?'

It is all I can do to remain standing. I put my arm out and steady myself against the cold stone wall. 'I lay with Hunsdon, just as I lay with you.'

He winces and turns his back. For a moment I think he will walk away, but then he says, 'As you did for years before you met me, and nothing came of it.' There is no tenderness now; each word is hard and separate.

I go over to him, and turn him around to face me. I see, with a wrench of grief, that his face is contorted with pain. I want to embrace him, hold him close, and pretend that things could be as they were before. But I can do nothing. 'You can't protect me,' I whisper.

'He's marrying you off!' says Will, with a great sob. 'To a brainless knave who cheats at dice! A fine way to "protect" you! Are you grateful to him for that? Are you really such a whore as to be bought so cheap?'

'He has given me a dowry, and a house. He has bought me a place in the world. I will be respectable. With you, I would have nothing. Don't you see? We had a room, nowhere else. We were like conspirators, not man and wife.'

Now he weeps openly, shuddering sobs that seems to tear out of him. 'You would have everything. Everything! What is there, that is greater than our love? What in this whole world? Tell me! Tell me!'

My tears flow too, but all this weeping makes me angry. 'A lord may have a wife and keep a mistress,' I cry. The old man has stopped sweeping and is staring over at us. I lower my voice, but speak with desperate fury. 'A playwright can barely keep himself! Half of your noble profession are in the debtors' prison! I'm not living with my child, as a poet's whore, in some filthy ale-house! Or a back-street alley, like a pauper – how can you even ask me to think of such a thing?'

Will breathes deeply and closes his eyes, as if searching for the incantation that will change my mind and make me his. 'I can ask you because I love you. I can ask you because, without you, my life is a just a shabby, ceaseless repetition, and I don't believe there are two other people, in this whole great City, who have loved as we have loved. I can ask you because you are the woman I will always need, and look for, and revere. That is why I can ask you. And you, you speak of money! My God, has the Court so corrupted you? Is that all you can conceive of: the bald, material world?'

84

I shake my head. 'You cannot keep me, Will. You are being a fool.'

'I have my work to keep us.'

'Oh, yes! Play-making, and poetry! You're one step up from vagrancy.'

There is silence again. I think, *I cannot go on with this. I cannot keep pretending that I am strong enough to live without you.*

Will pulls his cloak around him, as if in preparation for departure. 'I thought you wanted to be a poet yourself? How can you speak of what I do with such contempt?'

'It's all words. Words, words, words. What are they? Flimsy, floating, fancy things, not real. You make it sound as if I expect a suite of rooms at Whitehall – that's not fair! But I do need a house, and bowls, and spoons, and chattels. And food and clothing and a safe haven from the streets. I've traded in my virtue, and now I'm trading in my love, so I can look after my child. If Hunsdon is marrying me off – so be it.'

He stares down at me, breathing hard. 'You'll bed that worm Alfonso, instead of lying with me? You'll let him have you, night after night? You'll do with him all those sublime and secret things that you have done with me?'

'You are not free! Will you keep the baby in a box of feathered hats? Shall it crawl across the stage-boards before it speaks? Will you feed this babe before you feed the ones that are already born, at Stratford? In wedlock? Leave me be! Stop torturing me with what you call love, and which is a sort of twisted lust!'

He stares at me as if I were at the bottom of an abyss. His face is as white as a winding sheet. Even his lips are pale. 'How can you say that? You know I love you.'

I close my eyes. 'I know it.'

'And you love me.'

He comes back and holds me in his arms and I hide my face in his neck. After a moment, I look up at him and say, 'I do love you. Will. If love alone could keep us, we would never part.'

'Then . . .' He hardens his grip around me, but I pull away.

'But love never kept anyone,' I cry. 'Did it? And we are joined to others. And we must survive and so must they. I am to marry Lanyer, and he will be my lord, and I will be his wife and his word will be my law. I will be tamed, like poor Kate in your play. See – how wise and prescient you were!'

'It's not possible. My darling, darling Aemilia. It cannot be.'

'It is the only way.'

And then, not able to bear another word of this, I turn and run across the garden. Will yells after me, 'It is not finished! I will not let you go! Hear me, Aemilia! We are not done!'

I look over my shoulder, my hands pressed to my mouth. Will has disappeared. The old man is staring after me, his broom suspended in mid-air.

Scene XI

For the first few weeks of my union with Alfonso, I try to pretend
that he does not exist, and he pleases me by keeping away. I spend
my days writing, sitting in the solar and looking down at the
street, watching my belly grow. I soon look like a plum pudding.

A letter arrives for me one day. To my surprise, it is from
Hunsdon. I tear it open, wondering if he might have changed
his mind. Perhaps he wants me to be his mistress again. Perhaps
Lady Anne has driven him mad with boredom. But no. It is a
short note.

> *My dear Aemilia,*
>
> *I trust you are well. How do you like the set of Antwerp
> porringers?*
>
> *I had a thought, in answer to that odd question of
> yours. William Cecil is your man. Old Burghley takes a
> somewhat utilitarian view of the printed word, but the
> fellow has more influence with publishers than anyone at
> Court. He will know who – if such a fellow exists – might
> back a woman. (Though I warn you, my sweet lady, your
> ambition is quite absurd.) Good luck with him, dear girl.*
>
> *Your loyal servant,*
> *Henry*

Burghley House is on the north side of the Strand. It is a
handsome brick building, three storeys high, built around two

courtyards. I am shown into the library, which looks out over the gardens and the fields of Covent Garden which lie beyond. I can see two youths playing tennis on a paved court, and a servant working in the orchard. As I watch the young men, I reflect that I have about as much power as the leather ball that bounces back and forth between them.

It surprises me that Burghley has agreed to see me: he is known to be uxorious and upstanding, and has never approved of me. 'Utilitarian', Hunsdon said; could it be that Burghley has some use for me? I turn away from the window and look around me. The panelling is carved and painted, the floors newly strewn with sweet-smelling rushes and the air is hushed, as if in mute respect for all the learning in the room. It seems to me that Burghley owns quite as many books as his monarch.

'I see you are one who appreciates the beauty of learning.' The voice is silk-smooth, like the pages of a book. I look up, and my heart lurches. Standing in the doorway is not the austere, white-bearded Burghley but Henry Wriothesley, fair hair curled, dressed in peacock blue. He is regarding me with a knowing half-smile. He is one of Burghley's circle, but even so the sight of him is an unpleasant shock.

'Mistress Lanyer, how you have blossomed! Really . . . there is so much more of you as a Lanyer than there was when you were a mere Bassano!'

'I am here to see Lord Burghley, your lordship,' I say, coldly. 'Is he here?'

'Nooo, sadly. No. He told me to inform you that he has been called away on urgent business. But I bethought me . . .' He comes closer, smiling at his own affected speech. 'I bethought me – why waste this lovely visitor? Given that we have already met, and the lovely visitor is so . . . lovely.'

He walks around me, daintily, first this way and then that, and I smell the rich scent of his clothes. He smiles at my fattened face and sprouting breasts, seeming well pleased. He picks a

book up from the table beside me. It is *The Rape of Lucrece*, by a Mr W.S.

'Dear Will,' he says, flipping it open. 'I've commissioned him to write a new comedy. Did you know?'

'No, sir, I did not. I am not . . . closely acquainted with Mr Shakespeare.'

He raises his fine brows. 'Really? You surprise me.'

'I have come to speak of my own work, sir.'

But he doesn't seem to hear me. '*A Comedy of Errors* – a noble title, don't you think? He is writing it at this very moment.'

'If I were to have a patron, sir, I might work upon my poems and make them . . . more than they are now.'

'Quill scratching fast across the page,' says the earl, apparently talking to himself. He looks up and smirks. 'Very well, you pretty pregnant thing, let's hear this verse of yours.'

'I was going to talk about my verses with Burghley. Your lordship.'

'So he told me. But I am a greater patron of the arts than he! You see – how fortuitous it is that I am here, instead of him! The stars are smiling on you.'

'I am not sure that I share your favourable opinion. Can you tell Lord Burghley that I would be happy to see him on another occasion?'

He smiles, shaking his head. 'He will not do it, my bloated chuck. It's not like you to be obtuse. Look at you! Hunsdon has cast you off, and you're the size of a cow-shed.'

'Then I must go.'

'Then you won't have a patron, will you? You will go back into the . . . outer darkness, whence you came. I hear he built a pretty house for you, which would fit into this library ten times over.'

He comes closer to me, smiling more sweetly than before. 'Forgive me. Forgive me. I would like to hear your verse. I see no reason why a lady like yourself – one well-known for her

intelligence and learning – should not be a writer as good as any man!'

'You surprise me, sir!'

'I am young, mistress. I am part of the modern age. You are ill-served, and misunderstood.'

'That's true enough!'

'You see? I understand you. I know my reputation may be off-putting, but lay your prejudice aside. Let me hear your verses. Please.' He takes my hand, still smiling. 'Come and sit with me, and read your verse and I will see . . . what I can do.'

He leads me to the corner of the library and gestures towards a low bed heaped with velvet cushions. I pull my hand away.

'Isn't there somewhere else . . . more public?'

'Come, you're not afraid of me? A woman of your bearing? It is I who should be afraid! Look at you! God's blood. Almost too beautiful.' He pours out two glasses of wine and hands one to me. 'Almost. But not quite.'

I can hear two voices. But which is the angel, and which the devil? *'Run! Flee! Escape!'* says one. *'Stay! This could be your salvation! Prove yourself!'* says the other. He is smiling, smiling. I can feel the baby moving inside me. I wonder if, like me, it is afraid.

When I realise that I am scared of him, I force myself to step forward and take the glass, and sip it. For I am afraid of no one, and nothing, except Death itself. I will take this chance, and see where it leads. While I read, Wriothesley at first contents himself with listening 'raptly', which is to say, he acts out the role of one who listens with exaggerated astonishment and delight. His mock entrancement has the effect of making the shortcomings of my verse more obvious to me, and I vow that, if nothing else, I will make my poems better in future, even if I die in the attempt. And I also notice, as I read the stumbling, bumbling words, that his lordship is edging ever closer to me on the divan, so that, when I come to the end of the third stanza of the third poem, his

breath is on my neck. When I finish, there is silence for a moment, and then he takes my face between his hands and twists it round so he can scrutinise it. Then he says abruptly, 'Your eyes are black, aren't they? Truly black. I have never seen such a thing.'

I stand up.

'The Bassanos are Venetian,' I say. 'My father was a Marrano, some say from Africa.'

He stretches out on the bed, with his head propped on his elbows. 'You know, I have had my eye on you since the night we met,' says he.

'Have you?'

'Do you want to know what I think?' he asks.

I say nothing.

'You are *greedy*. Greedy for pleasure, my glorious hussy. Greedy for men.'

'No!'

'Or should I say – for *poets*?'

I stare, and he gets up and winds his arm around my waist. 'Standing by Will Shakespeare's stairway, in a dry nightgown with a wet cunt. Oh, don't look at me like that, sweet lady. I could smell it from where I stood.' He bends down, as he did that night, but this time his hand creeps underneath my skirts and I feel his silky fingers stroke the inside of my leg. 'He had you good and plenty, didn't he? Am I not right? I'll never forget the look upon your face. He fucked you all the way to Heaven, that gentle poet. Pumping like Beelzebub, I'll wager.' Now his hand is creeping up the soft skin of my thigh. 'Luckiest of poets.'

With a sudden motion Wriothesley forces me down, and I am lying on my back upon the low bed. I feel his weight upon me. He is heavier than he looks, and I scream out. 'My lord! My baby – be careful with my baby!'

'Ah, the poet's bastard, is it, lodged inside you?' He begins to laugh – a boy's laugh, hysterical and shrill. With a sudden force of effort I push him away and he falls to the ground, still laughing.

He stands up and shakes out his sleeves. 'Listen. I know you have been lying with William. I am a witness to it. If you want me to keep this information private – which I suspect you do – then I am determined to extract a fair price from you. If you wish to keep yourself from me – and that is entirely your decision – then I will let Lord Hunsdon know that his dowry missed its mark, and that he may as well have gone down to the Liberties and paid for any shilling strumpet to live like a merchant's wife.'

'No!' I see myself, clear and sharp. A street-walker, a doxy, a common whore. I see my baby, a harlot's brat, shrivelling in my arms.

He whispers, 'But if you want to keep your little house – with your little monkey in it – then I suggest that you sin a little and let me lie beside you.'

'I would rather die, sir. Look upon me! Have pity on my state.' The room is shifting; sweat is rolling down my neck into my gown. What can I do? What can I say?

'Think carefully, Aemilia. They say you are a woman possessed of a fine mind. Well, use it.'

Before I can speak, he has pulled me down so that I sprawl on top of him. 'No, sir!' I scream. 'No, I will not do it . . .'

He rips my skirts out of the way and, despite the swollen mound of my belly, he forces himself into me. His cock is a fire-poker and he is sucking at my sore dugs and then my senses are black.

When I look up, damp and trembling, Will is standing at the doorway, holding a book in his hand. His eyes are fixed on me with such an expression of disbelieving horror that I cannot speak, nor even think, but only stare back at him, my thighs spread and my soiled shift clutched between my fingers.

Wriothesley has his eyes closed. 'Oh, foul Jezebel,' he says. 'There is not a whore in London who is a better fuck. Come, I demand you kiss me.' He puckers up and points to his full red lips.

I look at Will. His face is pale and thinner than when last I saw him, with shadows beneath his cheekbones, and his eyes are black-rimmed from stage-paint that has not been properly wiped off, and his beard is new-trimmed and his razor must have nipped his skin, for there is a stab of scarlet on his left cheek. He is speechless; he is stone.

Wriothesley opens his eyes and looks at Will calmly. 'Forgive us, dear Will,' he says. 'Such scenes as this are hardly to be expected in a library. Patrons should be more sedate than this. I have my . . . position to consider.' He smirks up at me.

I pull myself up, and his lordship's limp cock flops down on to his white stomach. Will is gone. Liquid trickles down my leg. I pull down my skirts, pick up my slippers and run after him, tripping over my dress and sobbing without tears.

The library opens on to a wide landing. Everything gleams and glitters. I can't tell what is what, nor recall the names for things. Where is Will? Which way did he go? There is a stairway, sweeping downwards. He is not there. I run the other way, down a long gallery with sunlight sparkling through leaded windows. There is bright colour – Turkey carpet colour; there are high paintings of men with cruel faces. All are Wriothesley, sneering down. There is a doorway, between two carved chairs. There is Will, framed inside it, with his back to me, still as a statue.

I go through the door and close it behind me. We are standing in a small chamber, stark and plain. There is a table and a chair, and a riot of paper. A window looks out across a stableyard.

'Sit,' he says, without turning to face me.

'I'd rather stand,' I say, but then sink down on to the chair. My sight is wraithed with black vapour, like smithy-smoke. Will stares out of the window.

'Will . . .' I begin. 'This . . . thing. The thing you saw . . .'

He turns at last, but remains silent. His eyes are cast down.

'My love,' I say. 'My dearest . . .'

He will not look at me.

'I implore you, sir!' I hold out my hand. 'Truly, I implore you . . . Listen to me!'

At last, he looks at me, arms rigid by his sides. 'Listen to you?' he says. His voice is hoarse. 'Listen to you? What can you *say*?'

'That I was . . . I was tricked . . .'

'How did he trick you? Did he shape-shift, so he looked like me? Did he wizard himself inside you, with the magic of his mighty phallus?' He stares at me. 'Well? Did he?'

This time I am the one who is silent. I hang my head.

'I have seen Hell. I have seen a Beast with two backs. I have seen everything I loved and honoured made vile and evil. That is the thing that I have seen.'

'Listen, I – '

'There are no words, Aemilia. There is no "listen", and then some sentences that you can conjure which I will take into my mind, so we can be as we were. This is Death. This is the end of what I loved, and what I thought I knew, and what made my life bearable, for all its pain and sorrow. This fine woman, this great spirit, this mind beyond compare – a rutting strumpet!'

'I was reading him my poems and – '

'Oh, Christ Jesu!' He turns and throws open the window, as if the room is suffocating him. 'Your wretched poems! They are no good, my sweet. They are just doggerel, my lovely one. You may be the equal of all comers in the areas of algebra and astronomy and what you will, but let me tell you, a poet is not a learned man who pens out his learned thoughts in comfort and complacency! A poet is a madman, who knows nothing, and makes a world of his insanity. And you, my lady, may be a scholar and you are certainly a whore, but you will never be a poet.'

I can't weep. I can't think. I try to say, *He blackmailed me, he was going to tell Hunsdon all about you* – but I cannot see how to say this without making him even angrier, if that is possible. All I can think of is that I must go, away, and escape his burning eyes, and the hatred and contempt in his voice. I stand up.

'Goodbye, Will.'

'Goodbye? Jesu, is that it?'

'You said there are no words. And you are right, there is none. I have sinned and we are done.'

'Ay, we are done alright, for you have killed my soul!'

'I love you, Will.'

This seems to goad him more than anything I have said or done, for suddenly he is wild with rage and tears the pages on his desk and throws them round the room. 'Love me! Love me! God's blood, what do you do to men you hate? You are a witch – a witch; you have ensnared me and you are trying to destroy me!' He runs towards me, brandishing the torn paper. 'What can I say? What can I do?'

'If you think I do not love you, this is false, and what I did today was – '

'Oh – you say this is false?' He is so close now that his spittle wets my face and I see the blue veins jumping in his forehead. 'Look – I have a new phrase . . .' He runs to the table, takes up a quill and scribbles fiercely on one of the torn pages. 'Praise God – I am still a writer! Praise him, praise him, the poet lives! Look . . .' He runs back to me. 'See? See here? What I have wrote – you are still my Muse, Mistress Busycunt . . . see – "the bay where all men ride"! You see? I have made you into Art. That, that is poetry. Poetry is pain. Poetry is blood and hatred. D'you see?'

As he gets angrier, I grow colder. I am a prisoner in this place, and can only stare, round-eyed, at what I have made him. 'Will . . .' say I. 'Please, I beg you – '

'What, will you contradict me? How dare you contradict me? You came into my bed straight from Hunsdon's . . .'

'How could I do otherwise, when – '

'I saw the look upon his face when he arrived with you! Jesu, you whipped that old goat to a frenzy even as he edged towards the grave! As for Wriothesley – well, forgive me for my boldness! I just saw you, straddling the fellow, with your great-belly in

your mother's hands as he shafted up inside you! God's balls, I'd sooner spit my own arse on Satan's cock than witness such a thing again!'

'I am no Jezebel. If you would only hear me!'

'Jezebel! What did she do to deserve comparison with you? I need new words for sin, for you have torn up decency and thrown it to the four winds.'

I stand at last, though I don't know how my shuddering legs can carry me. The babe is kicking, and I fear all this torment might force it early into the world.

'Farewell, Will,' I say. I go to the doorway, and turn to look at him. 'If you will not let me speak, if you will not understand . . .' But he is sitting at his desk, writing, his body racked with sobs.

Scene XII

Sometimes I read so hard and so long that when I close my eyes I see a million dancing letters, formed of white light against my own darkness. Sometimes, when I examine my face in the looking glass, my eyes are sore and bloodshot. Sometimes I think I see words falling down my cheeks, mixed with my tears.

My little house is made from seasoned Kentish oak, its heartwood turned outward to withstand the wind and weather. Thirty trees were felled to make it, sky-shifting branches fallen among wet fern. I first saw it when it was no more than a wooden skeleton, bare timbers sticking out of the mud, each one marked with a Roman numeral. It looked squashed and small, stuck between two older buildings. I could scarce believe that I was supposed to mark out my new life on so little ground. But within a week the carpenters added walls and floors and windows, like the lungs and belly of a man, and strangely it seemed to grow in size. Even so, my courage falters when I think of all the trammelled years I am doomed to spend inside it, a placid little Jill-in-a-box.

My space is this: six rooms in all, with the main door opening into a hallway, which is like a little version of the great hall in a great house, and is two storeys in height. A wooden staircase ascends from its centre. At the back of the hall is a door which leads to the kitchen, with its open hearth and cupboards, which Hunsdon has filled with the finest pewter. Around the fire is a fine array of pots, grid-irons, coal rakes and toasting irons, and from the ceiling hang pots, saucepans and frying pans. On one

side of the kitchen is a low door, leading to the garden, such as it is, and the privy. At the top of the hall stairs is a handsome solar, an oak-panelled sitting room with a grander fireplace than the kitchen hearth, some heavy carved chairs and a long oak dining table. And on the floor above are two bedchambers, also brightly painted and well furnished with curtained beds and solid old chests. All are gifts from Hunsdon.

The gift I value most is the pair of Flemish virginals which have been placed in the hall. The elegant instrument takes up the most part of one wall. Most beautiful, its soundboards painted with flowers, birds and moths, all within blue scalloped borders. The natural keys are covered in bone, and the sharps are chestnut. The inside of the lid is embellished with a Latin motto: *Sic transit gloria mundi.* The notes it makes are soft and plangent and take me far away, back into a world of long galleries echoing with music and private laughter, of lush gardens overlooked by mullioned windows, of feasts and opulence and the giddy knowledge that the furled papers on my lord's table will govern the lives of earls and paupers, scribes and burghers, pimps and haberdashers, all across the realm.

At the very top of the house is a little garret, with straw-stuffed eaves coming down almost to the wooden floor. This is the servant's room, and has in it just a truckle bed and a three-legged stool. If I stand on this – though it wobbles badly – I can put my head through the window in the thatch, and see as far as the City with its Roman walls and mess of roofs and smoking chimneys, and above these the pointing fingers of a dozen churches, and the mighty Ark which is blasted, spireless St Paul's.

Act II

Prophecy

Scene I

Smithfield, Avgvft 1602

My hectic son is hardly able to breathe with the wonder and wickedness of it all. His eyes are everywhere: Bartholomew Fair, the greatest Fair in England. Such a press of people that you can barely work out where you stand. And what people – half the underworld is here: cutpurses from Damnation Alley, tricksters from Devil's Gap, vagrants from Snide Street. Everything muddled: stalls and sideshows, fops and ladies, apes and peacocks. As big a hotchpotch as the filthy warren of London itself. You can buy anything – oysters, mousetraps, gingerbread men; a hobbyhorse, a songbird or a bale of cloth. Pay to see a cockfight or a puppet show or join a game of dice and thimble. Everywhere is bother, jostle and noise. High fashion and foul breath, all pressed together: children and dotards, dogs and chancers, pigs and prostitutes. And the two of us – Henry leaping at my side, desperate to be off to buy a cheese-cake from Holloway or a Pimlico pie. Rattles, drums and fiddles rip into the air. The smell of roasting pork rises up from the eating-houses. One step too quick and you will fall upon a sweetmeat-seller or topple on the side-rope of a dancing tent. Here – a great, pockmarked head, ducking out of the crowd and leering at my chest. There – a glimpse of putrefying tumour, sprouting from a beggar's shoulder, tattered shirt turned down so the passers-by can get an eyeful and toss a halfpenny his way. 'Show! Show! Show' calls the crowd, all about us, pushing and shoving, careless of a small boy and a slight woman.

We are smack-bang in the middle of it all: besieged by every kind of mountebank and con-man, bawdy and punk. I try to side-step one way, thinking I see some open ground to my left, in front of the fish-scale virgin's stand, but a giantess blocks my path, stinking like Hound's Ditch and with a back as wide as a cart. So I twist another way, Henry's hand gripped in mine, but up loom three pissed prentice-boys, arm in arm, faces running sweat, eyes rolled back in their heads.

Henry is nearly ten. A boy who likes to throw himself to the ground, run, yell, eat. Hell-bent on everything. Big-boned, but pretty, with his flushed cheeks and fuzz of gold hair. Nothing like Alfonso, but we don't speak of that.

'Mother! Over there – can we see the baby with two heads?'

'No.'

'Why?

'I'll be sick.'

'The bearded mermaid?'

'No.'

'The pig-trotter man?'

'No.'

'The midget unicorn?'

'No.'

'Why? Why? All the boys at my school have seen the midget unicorn! Why can't I?'

I don't know why the thought of standing in a cramped booth, face to face with some freak – man-made or a slip of nature – makes me feel so weak and dizzy. I've seen it all before, and worse. So has Henry, come to that. He likes a good execution, that child; nothing lily-livered about him. Perhaps I'm pregnant again. My pregnancies ebb and flow in my body like the river tide. Few last more than six weeks. A good thing, as we live on next to nothing, and Alfonso is an idle dolt, barely able to put his doublet on the right way around.

'Buy my fat chickens!'

'Fresh asparagus!'

'Any baking pears?'

Now Henry's face is winding up into a baby-scowl. His curiosity amounts to a disease.

'You *said* I could come to the Fair, and now we can't *do* anything!'

'Henry!'

'Termagant!'

'Wherever did you – ?'

'Whore!'

'Obnoxious brat! How dare you!'

He slips his hand from mine and he's off.

'Henry!'

I look this way, and that. No idea which way to chase him. He has no money, will not go far. But I'm wrenched with fear. All I can see are the lurid banners: 'Giant Blackamoor' . . . 'Child Leprechaun' . . . 'Neptune from the Deep'.

'Henry!'

How will he hear me? My loud cries are lost in a multitude of voices.

'Posset for you, lady?' A skinny lad with a tray hanging from his neck.

'See the man who swallows fire!'

A blind girl thrusts her pouch at me. 'Sugar-pane fancies! Sweetest in Smithfield!'

'Henry!'

Then, the crowd pushes me forward till I am jammed hard against a wooden palisade. I can barely see through the spaces between the planks, but can just make out the back view of a fairground caller, dressed in scarlet like an alderman.

'Upwards of ten feet high!' he cries. 'His consumption of hay, corn, straw, carrots, water is that of twenty men! The Oliphant, the human race excepted, is the most respectable of animals! He has ivory tusks, four feet long, as sharp as swords! His trunk

serves him instead of hands and arms! He can lift a man with it, or a mouse!'

The crowd surges forward behind me. Where is Henry? If the mob pushes at him as violently as this, he will suffocate in the crush.

'He remembers favours as long as injuries: in short, if you aid him, he will repay you. If you harm him, he will never forget . . .'

I have never seen an Oliphant, though I have read of them and seen a drawing. And at Whitehall Palace there was a monstrous tusk, among the Queen's objects and treasures, which were brought from all the corners of the world. It was heavier than any sword or musket. I don't believe this mountebank has an Oliphant in his tent – a great bull, perhaps, with an adder for its trunk, and dark hangings to keep the creature in the shadow. This is the Devil's marketplace, after all.

But Henry? Where is Henry? I turn, and begin to force my way out through the mass of people. And then a woman stands in front of me. Bars my way. Her face is almost touching mine. She is motionless; her face a mask. Looking into her cold eyes, I could not say her age, or type.

'Tell your fortune?'

'No. Go away. I'm looking for my little boy.'

'Oh, *he's* safe enough. For now, at least.'

'Where is he?'

'Tell your fortune?'

'Where's my son?' I try to push past her.

She sidesteps so she still blocks my way. 'Cost you nothing.'

'Where can I find him?'

'Not a penny.'

'I don't want my fortune told! But I'd give you five shillings gladly if you told me where to find him.'

'For nothing, I'll tell you this. You've a whore's past, and a poet's future.'

'Get out of my way!'

I turn, but now face a much older creature, shrivelled and black.

'Beware of slip-shod words,' she says. She looks into me with unseeing eyes. 'Words will make you, and undo you. You will aim too high, and fall too low.'

'What are you – lunatics? Or purse-thieves?' I look behind me. 'Are there three of you, a third to pick my pocket?'

'Beware of your own wit,' says the first woman, her voice whispering in my ear. 'Your human pride.'

'As for your son . . .' The crone's flesh reeks of piss and sweet decay.

'What?'

'The plague is coming.'

'The plague is always coming. No wonder your predictions cost nothing.'

'Not like this.'

And then – they are gone.

I spin round, full circle, hemmed in by the throng of fair-goers, the tricksters and the tricked. Then, stop. Another face. Smiling at me, all rouged and painted. A face out of place and time.

'Well, how delightful!' it says. 'Aemilia Bassano! I would not have known you.' A dramatic and unnecessary curtsey, and I have time to work out who this is.

'Lettice Cooper.' We were Court ladies together, ten years ago. She is flanked by two servants.

'*Lady* Lettice,' she says, 'to you.' She raises her eyebrows in disdain so that her manservant smirks to oblige her (odious palace arse-licker). If I have changed, then so has she. Always careful of her looks, she has plucked and powdered herself out of existence. She has taken Her Majesty for a model, and to no good effect, having made herself a doll-face of false surprise.

She hands her purse to her serving woman, and holds out her hand. I take it. Her fingers are silky, slippery.

'You!' she says. 'Who was once so beautiful! I would never have thought it!'

'Thought what? That I would turn out such a hag?'

'Oh! My dear, have you quite lost your mind? Why would I say such a thing? They say the natural look will be in next year. In France, the ladies are letting their hair grow quite low on the forehead. You will be all the rage.'

'Lettice . . .'

'*Lady* Lettice . . .'

'I have lost my son . . .'

'He is dead?'

'Only lost – mislaid . . .'

'It comes as no surprise. I've heard you spoil that bastard boy and he runs wild.'

'I had forgot the ways of Court.'

'Indeed.'

'Common people have better manners.'

A neat, malicious smile. 'I see Alfonso, from time to time, of course. In the distance. Quite the merry thing, those tunes from Mr Tallis. *Dear* Alfonso. With his little pipe . . .'

As she moves away, she seems to remember something. 'Oh – Aemilia. Oddly enough, I met a man the other day who was asking after you. That jumped-up fellow who used to be with the Lord Chamberlain's Men. With the awful *accent*, you know?'

'No, I don't.'

'Face of a clerk, but wears an earring. Arrogant, for a provincial.'

Arrogant is clue enough. And she would know his name in any case. He has been doing very well for himself of late.

'What did he say?'

'Mmm . . . can't quite think. Oh, well – it can't have been important . . .'

'If you see him again, tell him I hope he burns in hell.'

'What, the author of those pretty sonnets? He pleases everyone, they say.'

'Not all his sonnets are pretty, your ladyship, and he certainly does not please me.'

She bows her head, seeming delighted with our exchange. 'Do you know, I believe that his star may continue to ascend, even without your blessing?' She walks on.

Then, through a gap in the crowd, I see Henry, staring up at a sugar-plum stall. I catch up my dress and struggle through the mob, taking no notice of the shouts of annoyance as I elbow my way forward.

'Henry, for God's sake! I have been so worried! What were you thinking of, running off like that?'

He is crying. 'I'm sorry, Mother. I said bad words to you. The Devil tempted me.'

I hug him tight. His body is burly, already hard-muscled. He is growing up a manly man, the equal of anyone, if not their better.

'I don't deserve a sugar-plum, do I?' he says. 'Though they are so round and sweet to look at.'

'No, you don't.'

'Not even one. You must punish me, so that my character will be built up strong.'

'Not even one.' I squeeze him tighter.

'I'm a bad, rude, evil creature.'

'Bad and rude, Henry.' I bend down and kiss his hair. 'But never evil.'

The stall is heaped with sweets and fancies made from sugar and marzipan. There are animals, birds and tiny baskets. Wine glasses, dishes, playing cards and little flutes, all made as dainty and perfect as God's creation. I've seen such craftsmanship at Court, painstakingly fashioned for royal banquets. But never outside the palace. Even there, they were not as beautiful as this luscious, lustrous fruit. The sugar-plums are piled head high, a

rampart of dark pinks and soft purples, frosted with sugar like a fairy shroud. I look at the stall-holder. She is as lovely as her dainty wares, fair-skinned, with yellow hair plaited tightly back from her brow.

'How many do we get for a halfpenny?' I ask.

She smiles. 'Two pocketfuls, mistress.'

'Go on, then, Henry,' I say, pushing him forward.

She fills his pockets and I give her the coin.

'One for you?' says Henry, turning to me with his best smile.

'One for me.' I choose a fat, mauve fruit. The sugar tingles on my lips as I bite into it. But my attention is distracted – I see the two witch-women, sitting on the ground just by the stall . . . I bite down, and my tooth cracks on the plum-stone. There is a sudden pain, a knife-jab in my gums.

I grab my jaw. 'See – there!' I shout.

Henry turns to look, mouth full. 'What? Where?'

They have disappeared. A trumpet band starts up. A troupe of acrobats is turning cartwheels. A bear begins to dance, its moaning growl like human words.

I peer distractedly. 'Nothing. Just . . . nothing.'

'Did you hurt your mouth?' says Henry.

'I think so.' I take the mush of plum, sugar and gore out of my mouth and look at it in my palm. There is a shard of tooth there. More than that. Half a molar.

'So much blood, Mother!' says Henry. He seems well satisfied. 'Would you like another one?'

Scene II

At first the pain is a hot, tender spot in my mouth, nothing more. My tongue keeps searching for it, poking into the fiery hole which had once been filled with tooth. All about it, my gum is raw and swollen. At breakfast time, I soak my bread in weak ale and suck down the brownish porridge like an infant. In the evenings, even though it is summertime, I sit on a stool near the fire, warming my naked feet as if soothing one part of my body would bring relief to another. It does nothing of the kind, of course. I force myself to think about something else. There is no shortage of subjects to think about, after all. Money, motherhood, the uncertain future, and the business of being married to a flimsy and improvident musician. And that isn't all. As well as the throbbing hole in my mouth, my day at the Fair has left me with a feeling of unease and dread, like a drunk's dawn gloom.

So I try to distract myself with reading. I once knew the great libraries of England: it is from these places that I have furnished the small library in my own head. And I have a few books still. I love to smell them and feel their pages beneath my fingers. They are kept in different parts of the house, so they come easily to hand when I have a moment to myself. I read with so much intensity that my head reels, for learning is there, and facts and a treasure chest of oddments of the world, trapped in ink. In the solar there is Foxe's *Book of Martyrs,* of course, and in the kitchen I keep Job Hortop's *Travels* next to the simples cupboard, being the tale of an old man who was press-ganged and sent on the Guinea voyage of 1567 and saw two of his company slain and eaten by sea-horses.

And his ship captured a most monstrous Alligator, which had a hog's head and a serpent's body but was scaled in every part, each scale the size of a saucer, and with a long and knotted tail and they baited it with a dog and caught it with their ropes.

As I stir the pot in the kitchen I feast my mind upon Hortop's wild tales, of how he and his companions fell among the Indians and were cruelly treated, but then discovered good Christian Indians (for such a thing is possible, it seems), and later found a sea creature who was half-man, half-fish, and his upper body brown as a mulatto. Then he went from there to Spain, where he was put to torture by the Inquisition (for good Christian Spaniards conduct themselves like savages) and two of his shipmates were burned, but he was sent to the galleys, which he rowed for ten years.

What I believe is that such a rollicking life of colour and calamity is the only kind a man should have, this life being a brief slit between two measureless eternities, and by 'man' I mean man and woman, for there would be no man alive today without the fairer sex and men are not half as clever as they think themselves and we are more than twice as strong as we let on.

Oh, and in my bedroom, to distract me from Alfonso's curtain-lectures about his great importance at Court, I keep Harington's translation of *Orlando Furioso*. Which tells the story of a man who – his wife being false – ranges over the whole of Europe looking for a good woman yet finds not one. This story so annoyed the Queen that she called Harington – who was her godson – to her Presence Chamber and gave him her harsh opinion. Of course, I agreed with Her Majesty that such stories are vile bawdy and not for Court ladies, yet, being no longer one of their number, I can both laugh at these naughty women and share a little of their forbidden lust, remembering my own misdoings and those little secret come-cries that we fist-muffle when we must. Such memories I will take as close to the graveside as I dare, and offer them up in exchange for Eternal Redemption at the moment of my last breath.

Some of my books have been wrote by women, too. I wish I could say these are the best of them, but this is not so. Compared to Hortop's terrifying journeys, reading the Countess of Pembroke's *Ivychurch* and *Emanuel* (translations from Mr Tasso) is like walking with a prelate in a country garden. Though her hexameters are handsome and there is no such thing as a book which is worthless. I have read her works with close attention, schoolboylike, and they are all excellently rhymed.

I pick up the *Martyrs*, and then Hortop, but cannot lose myself in them as is my usual custom. I am on the outside, and the worlds inside their covers are locked in. And I can't evict the memory of Lettice Cooper from my mind. Her talk of the poet and his sonnets disturbs me. My old lover has remade the form. He sent me a bundle of verses, written out in his own hand, full of bile and hatred for me and everything that we'd done. My only comfort is that they have not been printed. I have never thanked him for his poisoned gift, and prefer to think him dead. I should have burned them, but could not. In any case, each one has lodged itself in my mind, which keeps them stored neatly and for all time. I am the victim of my fine memory. All of them retain the power to hurt me, but there is one which is stuck fast, and goes round and round my head, day after day.

Stuck it is, stuck as a pig in dung. I sit in my room, and my head is full of it. The casement window has a high view of Long Ditch, and Camm Row beyond.

Th'expense of spirit in a waste of shame
Is lust in action, and till action lust
Is perjured, murdr'ous, bloody, full of blame . . .

This is the present moment, respectable. Actual. To the east, I can see the towers of Whitehall Palace; beyond that is Charing Cross, where Cockspur meets the Strand.

Savage, extreme, rude, cruel, not to trust,
Enjoyed no sooner, but despised straight,
Past reason hunted and no sooner had . . .

'No sooner had'! Oh, you had me, sir, right enough; you had me for a harlot and a fool. To the north are the fields of Haymarket and St Martin's, to the west, open country.

Mad in pursuit, and in possession so,
Had, having, and in quest to have, extreme,
A bliss in proof, and, proved, a very woe,
Before a joy proposed, behind, a dream . . .

'And, proved, a very woe'. That's me, the proven woe, the peerless whore, only enticing when unfucked; once fucked, I'm beastly, loathsome, ugly. A sly witch in a tale. You cannot see the river from this chamber, but if you stick your head out of the window you can hear the shouts of the wherrymen touting for business at the water's edge.

All this the world well knows, yet none knows well
To shun the Heav'n that leads men to this Hell.

You had me, Will, and you had no pity for me, and you have me still.

It is two days since my accident with the sugar-plum. Alfonso is standing in the downstairs hall, practising his monotonous tunes. His lips are pursed and his childish pipe trills out its familiar fluting patterns. The highest notes bore inside my jawbone.

'Alfonso?' Against my cheek I hold a linen bag, filled with burned and powdered rosemary wood. It has been prepared with great care by Joan, our old serving woman.

My husband lowers the recorder, a patient expression on his face. 'What, dear Aemilia?'

'When are you going to give me some money?'

'Quite soon, my love.' Off he goes again.

'How soon?'

An even more forgiving expression, worthy of St Peter. 'I'm a musician, not an alchemist, sweet chuck . . .'

'I don't expect you to make gold from base metal; I expect you to earn it.'

'When the concert is over.'

'Which concert?'

'The concert for the Queen's birthday. We get five shillings extra, apiece.'

'So till then we starve.'

He starts again, the notes in beautiful order, his life a mess of debt and deceit.

Joan is making her slow way down the staircase with a pail of rainwater. She is a narrow scrawn of a woman, and as she grows older it seems the years are scraping the flesh from her bones. Now Joan is a common name in London, but this is the very same Joan Daunt who owned the apothecary's shop in Bucklersbury. It was burned down by a mob the night that I summoned her to help at Henry's birth. And all its precious contents went up with it: the jars and vials and herbs and potions, the tinctures and the spices and rare ingredients from Turkey, China and beyond. Henry was a breech-baby. Born backwards, and would have died if it had not been for Joan.

'It's a bad do,' she says, throwing the water out of the door and into the street. The cat, Graymalkin, who has been sunning himself on the threshold, yowls and runs away. 'You can see blue sky through two holes now, each as big as a man's fist. We'll soon have the floor rotten, and that'll be the next expense.'

Alfonso has the recorder to his lips. He closes his eyes and blows, but no sound comes. He blows again. Nothing. He lowers

his instrument once more, flushed with anger. 'I am the head of this household, and I demand silence!' he shouts. 'I must have . . . your wifely respect, Aemilia! And Joan's – servantly obedience.'

Pain's hot-poker twists in my gum. 'There is silence, husband,' I tell him. (A London silence, at least, which is to say that through the open front door swoop the city sounds of dogs barking, hammers beating, babies crying, couples fornicating, pigs snorting, cartwheels clattering and all the other Babel noise of people and creatures and buildings and shops and stews all piled together pell-mell.) 'At least, the only noise I hear is you. As for obedience . . .'

Joan lowers her eyes and coughs as she makes her way back up the stairs with the empty pail.

Alfonso looks at me, as if he is still trying, after almost ten years, to work out what he has taken on and whether he can survive it. He is a pretty man, I'll say that for him, with his dark skin and black coiled hair. The Lanyers have French blood, and this shows in the way he has of dressing himself. Even in his plain cambric shirt he cuts an elegant figure, and his dainty fingers hold the pipe as if it was a living thing.

'Why do you stare, Alfonso?'

'Why do you question me, wife?'

In bed, it is easy to feel lust for Alfonso, with his hard, lean body and his soft kisses. But in this house it is my word that carries weight, not his. This is in part because he spent all my dowry in a twelvemonth, gaming and dicing and showing off. Also because his musician's 'duties' – piping, gossiping and the wearing of a short mandilion – keep him at Court for long hours, overnight if there is a feast or a celebration. He comes and goes at odd times, like Graymalkin.

Yet there is more to it than that. Each time Joan reads my Tarot cards, a different pattern tells the same story – we are out of balance, my husband and I. If Henry is spoiled it is all my doing, because I decide when he is praised and when he is punished. Joan, too, listens to me, and not her master.

'Your face is swelling up still,' Alfonso says, as if deciding to withdraw from battle. 'You need to see the barber surgeon and have that tooth pulled, what's left of it. He should bleed you, too. There may be poison.'

Without replying, I go out into the bright morning bustle of Long Ditch, with its clustered wooden buildings. It is a street that does not know its place. Although it is close to the rambling sprawl of Whitehall, it is itself of no account. The dwellings were thrown up hastily, without forethought or symmetry. Some are no wider than their own front door, with four storeys piled above, seeming likely to overbalance and tumble down into the street. Others are hovel-high and no bigger than a cow-barn. And yet we are overlooked by Camm Row, and the calm and solid homes of great men like Sir Edward Hoby and the Earls of Hertford, Derby and Lincoln. Such great, commanding houses! Their casement windows glow bright with candles long after dark, and every house has a walled garden behind. Our mean dwellings are like birds' nests in comparison. All of us cheek-by-jowl, breathing the same smoke-filled air. The red kites, wheeling above, must see us coming in and out like little dolls, shaking our linen or stepping out in our fine gowns.

I look around me, thinking how much easier it would be to know my place if my position in the world had a little more sense to it. We know that God presides at the top, followed by the Angels, with Man below. And then Woman lower yet – above the animals, but a lesser mortal than her bed-fellow. By Our Lord's ordinance we are the weaker, lesser sex. It is a system, certainly. But where is my place in this ordered universe? I was first a bastard, then a lady (educated in Greek and Latin if you please), then a courtesan – on account of being a comely orphan. And now, a drudge. What few skills are called for to fill this station, I do not possess. Where is the divine plan there?

If I had less learning it might be easier to bear, but I am sure that few Court ladies know their Ovid as I do, could recite the Psalms in Latin or have the tales of Holinshed off by heart. In

short, I have been tutored like a young lord, which is worse than useless to me now. If the aim of learning is a fitting-out to modern purpose, I say it falls far short, both for the young lords and for me. What has modern man learned from the Greeks – I mean in relation to his behaviour? Not enough, in my opinion. He is not the master of his passions. He is not wise. Men fight and tyrannise each other, and are given to extremes in blood and anguish, revelry and ribaldry. Great learning should lead to great lives – ha! Like the learned counsel at the Inns of Law, I rest my case.

So I am ill suited to being a City house-wife, married to a pile of wood and wattle-and-daub. Which pile, I must tell you, is not even my own. Within one year of our union, my dear spouse had spent my dowry, and within eighteen months he had borrowed money against my little house to pay his debts at table. So this place, fitted out with such care by my Lord Hunsdon (and in consultation with his lady wife) is no longer mine. It belongs to one Anthony Inchbald, an avaricious Dwarf and quite the greediest of landlords. I am surely married to the greatest fool in Christendom, yet I am his to ruin if he so wishes. I'm his possession: my whole mind and all its furnishings. Sometimes, I think of my mother and father. There was no ceremony to mark their union, saving only a handfasting, and yet they loved each other well. My own case is the opposite: it is a paper wedding, and all that joins me to Alfonso is expedience and the odd bout of merry fucking. (Forgive me, but I am only mortal, and the poor monkey has no other purpose I can think of.)

My mind rages, but here I stand in my drab dress, a creature half-mad with the tooth-ache. Wood smoke drifts upwards from the close-crowded chimneys of the houses opposite. The cat is still shaking his tail in angry jerks, ears flat to his head. He lifts one paw and shakes it singly, and little shining droplets of water catch the sunlight as they fall.

Widow Flood, my neighbour, comes out of her door with a full pot, and pours the foul-nosed contents into the reeking

kennel that runs down the centre of the street. She is a plump woman, with a pleasant, open face, but she has an irksome weakness: knowingness. On all subjects she believes herself the expert. And she is an over-dresser, too, in keeping with this good opinion of her status. Even in the house she wears a white lawn ruff. Her face pokes out from the wired cloth like a pig's head on a platter, and she takes care to hold the pot well away from the wide bulk of her farthingale. So grand, and yet the ferryman of her own filth. You could not tell a baronet from a bee-keeper in the streets of London.

'Tooth still bad, Aemilia?' She puts the pot on the ground next to her and stands back, hands on her padded hips, as if ready to enjoy the sun. Noticing a dead rat lying near, she kicks it on to the dung-pile that banks against her house. Beneath her fine skirt she is wearing wooden pattens.

'Still bad.'

'The barber surgeon should pull it for you.'

'Indeed.'

'Should bleed you, too, for safety's sake.'

'You should join my husband's recorder band, since you pipe the same tune.'

She laughs. 'Pain can make you surly, Aemilia. It's good advice.'

Anne Flood was well-named. Good advice flows from her, and good fortune to her. Even her husband's death has been a sort of blessing, since he was a wintry old skinflint, a haberdasher by trade, who was more than twice her age when they married. Her son Tom has just been apprenticed to the Lord Chamberlain's Men, and will soon be prancing on the boards at the Globe.

But here is Joan with a bolster to shake out. 'There is devilment behind this, Mistress Flood,' she says, flapping it fiercely. 'I don't like it. The air is full of spirits and the streets are full of demons, preying on the unwary.' She folds the bedding against her chest and holds it tight against her.

'Spell-making?' Anne Flood's eyes glint. She is curious about my clever servant, whose knowledge of witchcraft far outstrips that of the other women in the street.

'Something wicked. And no village art, neither. Devil's magic. It was not by chance they met her. They were waiting.'

'Shush, Joan, don't speak of it,' I say. But the witches' words have stuck in my head. *'The plague is coming.'* And not as I have known it. *'Not like this.'* I feel the wisdom of Joan's words – there was some design behind our meeting, something I don't yet understand.

Anne nods. 'Speak of the Devil and he will appear. We should praise the good Lord, and pray for our immortal souls.'

'Amen to that,' says Joan, crossing herself. 'God have mercy. Let each of us know our place. That magic which can ease our suffering and help us along our way is well enough. That which seeks to harness Evil will always do us harm.'

I put my arm about her shoulders. 'It is a tooth-ache, my good Joan, that's all. I broke my tooth on a plum-stone; there was no fiendishness.' I push her gently towards the house. 'It's nearly twelve – go and prepare something for us to eat. Something soft that will swallow down easy. I could eat rabbit stew, on the left side. Or a little scraped cheese, with sage and sugar . . .'

She goes muttering into the house.

Anne is still pressing her case. 'All that is needed is a trip to the barber. I know of a man in the Shambles who is most excellent,' she says. 'Pulls teeth like eels from mud – you hardly feel a thing. See?' She grins, showing off her graveyard gaps with pride. 'He broke my jaw once, trying to gouge out a buried wisdom tooth. Almost too much even for him. But it soon mended.'

That night, my face swells fit to fill the bedchamber. Sleep twists pain into trumpets, drum beats, the drone of an afternoon recorder. The dreams I have are dense and dazzling; my head aches with

the colour and busyness of them. I see the Queen again, not as she must be now, but as I used to know her, ten years ago. She is herself, and yet not herself: a tapestry in gold and green thread, a painted face on a wood panel, a straight-backed monarch sitting on a jewelled throne. Satan might send us pain; God soothes us with insanity to make a picture of it.

The rose garden at Whitehall, enclosed on four sides by high, crenellated walls. The heads of traitors all around, dripping fat-rot on to the pathways. Rose-heads rising ever higher. The Queen appears from the privet maze, fanning herself in the summer heat, face white in spite of the sun.

'Ay,' *she says.* 'Dark Aemilia, inspirer of our cousin's lust. We two – freakish black, and freakish red, would you not say?'

'Your Majesty?'

'Both of us midnight-weird.'

I curtsey as low as I can, as if my legs were liquid.

'For God's sake! Is this how you behave in the presence of other mortal beings? Stand up!'

She pulls me to my feet. She is shorter than me, face withered under the layer of white powder. Her fierce blue eyes are hungry for information, but flat, with nothing behind. Like a kite, looking sideways as it scoffs its offal. She takes my arm and sweeps me along the path beside her.

'You,' *she says.* 'Plaything of my Lord Hunsdon, yes?'

'Yes, Your Majesty.'

I look down and my child Henry is curled inside me, unborn, though a hefty boy of almost ten.

'Plaything, or his tormenter?'

'I – his tormenter, madam. Or both, by turns, madam.'

'He in charge? Or you, by any chance?' *She waves a courtier away. He is carrying a galleon in full sail, ocean waves drenching the padded sleeves of his doublet.*

'He is always in charge, madam. I am but a weak and feeble woman.'

The Queen's face is rigid with amusement. Her ladies come tittering towards us, carrying baskets filled with fiery sugar-plums, hitching their skirts so their beaded hems sweep clear of the wet grass.

Scene III

Have I woken? Or is this still sleep? Night-time, or day? I can see only darkness, but fancy there is sunlight too, coming at me from around Alfonso's head.

'Aemilia! You are awake! What a fever you have run – we have barely slept.'

Joan's face looms in front of me. She is holding a great wooden spoon, fit for a giant, which she forces into my mouth. There is some heavy, treacly substance on it, tasting of wine and hartshorn. Splinters of pain send more sunlight into my head; the morning rays seem to be breaking my skull apart. The scream which echoes from the walls might be my own noise, I suppose, listening to the sound with mild surprise. What tooth-ache is this?

'She must see the physician,' says Alfonso.

'Physician! What skill will he have, to cure such a condition?' asks Joan. 'This is more than tooth-ache. I said so before. More like the dropsy or the sweats.'

'The sweats! Don't say it! Unless we do something, she will die! I never saw such a thing – all from an ailing tooth.' His voice is breaking. 'I shall send for him now . . .'

'There is no physician on this earth that can give her the help she needs, master.' Joan speaks so firmly to her 'master' that if I weren't so ill I would smile.

'Then the barber surgeon can pull it out. She would hear none of that, of course. If she only would have listened to me . . .'

'It's too far gone.'

If I could speak, I would tell them that some vileness is eating me from within, and the cracked tooth has been an entry point for some evil poison, just as a viper's bite looks like a pin-prick and yet may kill a calf. I try to speak – but my whole body is frozen, although my mind is clear. My body, my limbs, my aching head – all are rigid and inert. I am like living marble, fixed upon my bed.

'Why can't you cure her of this, woman?' shouts Alfonso, sounding close to tears. 'She swears by you and all your tricks. Much use your cures and treatments are to her now!'

'I told you, sir, there is something far beyond my remedies here. I have the skill to know that, and the wit to let another cure her who has more knowledge than I do. If you ask me, someone has put a spell on her.'

'A spell! God's blood, who would do such a thing? That's nothing more than fancy.'

I feel a wet cloth soothe my head. 'It could be belladonna,' says Joan, as cool liquid seeps into my hair. 'But . . . I can't be sure. The antidote to that is worse than the poison . . .' Thin hands smooth my cheek. 'I need advice, that's what I'm saying. You can see the state she's in – look, try to move her arm. It's like a rock.'

'Very well, go to the apothecary.'

'I *am* an apothecary. I need a cunning-man for this.'

'Jesu!' Alfonso's voice fades away, as if he had walked to the window. 'I'm not paying for some mountebank to come sliding in here, mutter some incantations and then go on his way.'

'Then she will die.'

'No!' I am surprised to hear the fear in his voice. Has the fool grown to love me? But men are simple, even the clever ones. He has me where he wants and, even now he's spent the dowry, he still has a roof over his head and a woman in his bed.

'Forman,' says Joan.

'Who?'

'Forman,' she repeats. 'The man we need is Simon Forman. I've heard her speak of him.'

'That turd-faced lecher! Most foul and Satan-bothering necromancer! Over my dead body will she see this man!'

'It's her dead body we'll have to worry about, not yours, unless we find some cure. Forman may be a lecher, and he may be a necromancer, but he is wise. They say he cured himself of plague – who else do you know who has done such a thing?'

'You speak out of turn.'

'Forgive me, but I am all on edge.' Joan's voice is soft, but furious.

I want to thrash my head about, or wave my hand as if to say, *Not that filthy little chance-man, with his tricky hands and his ready cock, God save us!* But I can't move, nor even blink my eye. And it occurs to me that if it is a choice between being entombed by my own flesh and bone, or being groped by a ginger goat, I had better choose the latter. And, with that wise thought, my mind slips into darkness.

'Now, my dear, you can open your eyes.'

I open them, expecting pain and calamity, but nothing happens. The ceiling above my head is a familiar criss-cross of wood panelling. If this is Heaven or Hell, it looks remarkably like my own house.

'See if you can get up,' says a quiet voice. 'It's all done now.'

I struggle up so that I am propped on my elbows. My mind feels clear and sharp, more so than it has for many months. A bearded, elderly man is sitting next to the bed. Dr Forman is smiling. There is something complacent in his attitude, as if he has won a wager. And behind his chair stands Joan, all twisted with anxiety.

'Oh, Aemilia, praise God!' she cries. 'You are better.'

I put my hand up to my cheek, aware of a mild soreness, but nothing like the agony and madness of the last few days. 'My tooth?'

Dr Forman holds up a glass vial. Inside it is something bloody and rotted, tiny as a baby's little finger. 'I don't know what magic these crones put on you, but really,' he says, 'I have never seen such vileness. I am afraid your poor husband has had to go to a tavern. He did not have the stomach for it.'

'And my son?'

'He is downstairs. He's asked for the tooth, but I'm not sure it's safe to give it to him.'

I rub my face, and stretch out my arms, which are stiff and painful. 'Never saw such vileness, you say? I find that hard to believe. A man with your wide experience of all things unspeakable and horrid.'

'I know you have a sharp tongue, Mistress Lanyer, but within a few days you would have been dead from this infection, and lying in your grave. I won't take the conventional remuneration from such an old friend as you, but a little gratitude would be an appropriate payment, I feel.'

Joan looks at him, quizzical. 'Gratitude? Isn't her money good enough for you?'

'Mistress Lanyer is well known to me,' says the doctor. 'I would rather have her friendship than her gold.'

Joan pulls a leather money-bag from her basket and holds it out to him. 'Take this, and let us keep it strictly business. Gratitude smacks of debts that stay unpaid.'

'Joan, let it be,' I tell her.

She looks at me, her green eyes cold. 'There is some magic which is better measured by a pile of coin. Or else the scent of it will linger, like a sick dog's stench.'

'Joan!'

'It was a simple request for thanks,' says Dr Forman, bowing stiffly. He stares at me. I had forgotten the strangeness of his gaze,

withdrawn and mesmerising at once. Last time I saw him, he was as ginger as a squirrel. Now his beard and hair are grey. He wears both long, as if styling himself a magus or a necromancer. And his robes are both mystical and splendid – his coat and breeches are purple velvet. Magic and medicine must have made him a rich man.

I sit up and swing my legs down to the floor. 'Thank you, Simon. I am sorry for my ill manners.'

'And so you should be, mistress,' says Joan. 'We'd given you up for dead.'

'You have skill in healing?' the doctor asks her.

Joan folds her arms across her chest. 'More than skill. It's in my blood.'

The doctor bows again, and smiles his sweetest smile. 'Then you have the better of me, most assuredly. What I know is merely the stuff of book-learning and weary application.'

'Will you like something to eat?' I ask.

'Thank you, you are kind. It is so many years since we have spoken. I have often thought of you, wondering how my predictions served you.'

Joan leaves to prepare some food.

Forman settles himself back in his chair. 'Well, well, Aemilia! If I were not a student of the constellations, I would call this a stroke of luck. As it is, I can see that the stars were in a most propitious alignment today. Which, if I may say so, marks a change where you are concerned.'

'I have not been blessed with great luck, except that I have my dear son Henry.'

He takes my hand and spreads out my palm. 'Dear, oh, dear. Hmm. What? You know full well the stars are not windows to the future, but perform a similar function to that which they fulfil on a dark night.'

'They shine, and they are mysterious.'

'Quite so, quite so.'

He looks at my palm again, frowning. 'Still scribbling at your verse, I see.'

'As often as I can. In the early morning, sometimes, or at the very dead of night.'

'Make time for those scrawled words. Make time for your mind.'

'I do, sir.'

He strokes his fingers across mine. 'I was hoping you might visit me for a friendly halek, dear lady, a little knee-trembler for old times' sake.'

I pull my hand away. 'Even though I have never fucked you in the past?' Forman is the only man I ever knew who had his own word for fornication: a clear sign of his dedication to that craft.

'Did you not? Ah, then, it is just that dreams and memories can entwine in the most confusing manner. In honour of many a merry skirmish, then, shall we say?'

'The answer is no.'

He sighs. 'You are cruel. But now . . .'

'Now, what?'

'Now, I feel that our time would be better spent looking, as far as we may with such feeble instruments as I possess, into the future. The possible, probable, potential future, as we astrologists like to say.'

He produces a pack of Tarot cards from a pocket inside his cloak. They are of ancient and arcane design. The pictures show men with the heads of eagles, and strange nymphs with gold faces and serpents for hair.

'Shuffle these,' he says, and I do so. He lays them out before me, face-down and with their edges overlapping. 'Choose three,' he says. 'Not in haste, but without too much thinking. Let your intuition lead you.'

I choose them, and he turns them over, one by one. In the centre is the glorious figure of an Empress, clothed in scarlet. On

her left side are two Lovers, arms and legs entwined. And on her right hand is the mounted figure of grim Death.

'What does this mean?' I ask.

But he is silent again. Then he picks up the card which shows the Lovers, and puts it down in front of me.

'This is a most auspicious card. When you came to see me . . . before . . . there was a certain poet in your stars.'

'That was a long time ago.'

'He loves you still.'

'Now I know there are limits to your magic. He does not love me in the least.'

'We are speaking of the same man, I take it?'

'We are speaking of one who wrote me the most vicious, evil lines I ever saw.'

'That cannot be!'

'Some poets write pretty sonnets to their lady-love. Not he. If there is such a thing as a hate sonnet, then I have been presented with that very thing.'

'A passing mood, perhaps? He feared he couldn't have you.'

'A very sheaf of loathing. I am, in his eyes, such a Muse as you might encounter in the fires of Hell.'

He stares at the cards, eyes half-closed.

'So you are wrong,' I say.

'No. There is no mistake.' He pats my shoulder. 'Oh, my dear Aemilia. What travails you have had. I wish that I could tell you that they are over.'

I look at the Death card and shiver. 'So, what does it mean?'

'You must be brave, and resourceful, and bold, to cope with what is yet to come. Yet I have faith in you. And there is brightness, too, if you will only see it. There is love.'

From the same pocket which had held the pack of cards he draws out a pamphlet. The title reads '*Malleus Maleficarum, Maleficas, & earum haeresim, ut phramea potentissima conterens.*'

'*The Hammer of Witches,*' I translate. '*Which destroyeth witches and their heresy as with a two-edged sword.* This has nothing to do with me! Why are you giving me this book, of all books?'

'Not a particularly romantic gift, I fear, but you may find it instructive. And . . . well. There is something that you must do – of an urgent and peculiar nature.'

I look at the pamphlet, puzzled.

'What is done cannot be undone, but what has come in consequence . . . Well. I can say no more. There is no time now to do a proper reading. Let me just say that there is much to know in this field, much you do not understand, and that there is something evil here. Something beyond ill-wishing. Come and talk to me again.'

'I am not a fool, Dr Forman. And I have had my fill of aged lovers.'

'My dear! You quite mistake my meaning. I would like to help you.'

'Very handsome of you.'

He bends closer, and I see a glint of something like fear in his eyes. And yet, what is there to be afraid of? 'Aemilia, you have a good mind, and more than enough curiosity. I asked you once what you knew of magic. Do you know more now?'

'A little.'

'From that servant of yours?'

'She's taught me a few remedies, and I can make a potion or a poultice for most of the common ailments.'

'Yes, yes. That is useful enough – but what you need is something which goes beyond the household skills of women. Something to help you in the most severe and terrible adversity.'

'What sort of something?'

'There is no time to tell you now. If I am not mistaken, I hear your serving-woman's footsteps on the stairs. But be sure of this: there are dark days ahead of you.'

Scene IV

Today I rise early, with the words of Dr Forman in my head. What are these 'dark days'? Can they be avoided? There is no doubt that the old lecher knows what he is about. Not only has he cured the infection, and not only is there barely a scar to show where the cursed tooth has been – all my other little aches and torments have gone. Those besetting symptoms that all of us in London must put up with: soot-wheeze, ale-runs, head-gripe, back-ache, lassitude and dread-belly – not to mention sundry scabs, carbuncles and lesions of the skin – all such ailments have vanished.

I get up and sit at the little table by the window, and look at the books and pages that are stacked in order there. I have little money for paper, so I have taken to scribbling in the margins of my books, adding my own thoughts to those of Hortop and Plato. What was Forman's advice? *'Make time for those scrawled words. Make time for your mind.'* Make time – now there's an exhortation! If only I could. I would spin it, the way that other housewives spin their wool, and I would fill the house with it, the product of my labours. I would weave sheets of genius and sheaves of golden poetry, the harvest of my hours. Standing up, I stretch my arms upward, letting my mind's attention dwell on every inch of my body. Every inch is free of pain. My body is well; my mind still rages in its skull. If I wish to be well in my mind, then I must write, and there is no cure for my ambition, and thank the Lord for that.

I cross to the mirror. Has Forman's art restored some of my lost beauty? I see that I am not, as Lettice claimed, a woman old

before her time. My hair is still black, without a single streak of white; my skin is unlined. My eyes, so much admired in the past, are dark, watchful, unblinking. When I look into them, I cannot tell what I am thinking. Perhaps I am still beautiful. Perhaps I might triumph over other matters. What is there to be afraid of? The plague? We have always lived with its comings and its goings. Fogs and dunghill odours bear contagion. Some say that Death is trapped in rugs and feather beds, and cover their faces when they pass a woollen draper's shop. Alfonso stuffs his dainty nose with herb-grace. Joan, with her store of soothing cures and potions, greets each new outbreak by hanging the house with rue. God will protect us, surely, until it is our time to meet Him. After all, there are ten thousand ways for Death to cut you down.

And so, in the days that follow I think, *Let God's will be done*. I can write my words, cross-hatched and cramped sideways in the margins of the works of great and famous men. I can gnaw at a chicken leg, delighting in the taste and texture of the meat, the greasiness of the bone. I am alive and well. The sun has forgotten us, the skies are dark and the streets and lanes are torrents of rainwater.

Yet what do I care if the sun shines, or the rain falls? I must go to the baker's, and the chandler's, to the cobbler and tailor, with my basket over my arm. And the mud and summer drizzle make me smile, even though my skirts are smeared with pavement mire, and I must barter for cheat-bread.

Do I think of Will? I will confess I do, for I see him every time I look at Henry, and even the touch of my own face reminds me of Will's skin. The Greeks knew far more of emotion than we do, and there is no English word for the feeling that I carry with me, shamed and rejected by the only man I ever loved. The Greek word is *pothos* – milder than wild *eros* but longer-lasting: a longing for someone unobtainable or far away. The nearest word we have is 'yearning'. I yearn for the Will I've lost, the Will who

loved me, and who will never come again. But I can make my mind blank, keep memory in a little box.

A fortnight after my meeting with the doctor, there is a loud knock on the door. Anne Flood is standing there, dressed in her usual absurd splendour, head trussed in a new style of starched ruff – French, I dare say – which seems fit to throttle her. I let her in and return to my task: I am marking out a pie crust, pressing my right thumb in a firm pattern round its edge.

'Aemilia!' she says. 'I have an invitation for you.'

'An invitation to what, Anne?' I have a feeling this will be an event I would rather not attend.

'Oh, it's Tom's first big performance! He is in a new play at the Globe. We are off tomorrow afternoon, and should be so delighted if you would come.'

My thumb jerks and rips the pastry, but I don't look up. 'Alfonso is at Court.'

'Come yourself! Bring Henry. And Joan, too. You should be there, not only because you are my good neighbour and have known Tom since he was an infant, but because of the very part he is playing.'

Graymalkin, as if curious to hear more, unfurls himself from his position next to the smouldering fire, and comes grandly over, blinking and stretching.

'The very part? He is the leading lady?'

'Oh, no, he is too green yet for that. Only fifteen, you know, for all he is so tall! No, he is a second-ranking character, but one essential to the plot. Or so he tells me. I have only seen the pages with his lines.'

'I fear I am – '

'But wait, wait till you hear! His character is you!'

A coldness in the air, a north breeze. I put the pie in the oven and slam the door. '*How* is it me?'

'Aemilia!' Anne looks triumphant. 'He is a serving lady called Aemilia! It must be you. A friend of Mr Shakespeare's as you were. And I doubt he knows many Venetians, and the play is set in Venice. It's about a Moor.'

'Anne, I'm not a Venetian, I was born at Bishopsgate . . .'

'Yes, but your father was. And he named you. And this "Aemilia" is cynical and worldly, and has a speech making little of men! You! To the very life!' She seems to think that I should share in her delight.

'I . . .' But, before I can think up my excuse, Henry is here, all bounce and frenzy. He falls over the cat, who runs away, furious, to lay waste to some rats.

'Mother! You are in a play! How good! Can we be at the front? Can we be groundlings? Please! I want to be a groundling. John Feather and John Dokes have both been groundlings, and they saw a whore suck a – '

'We are busy, Henry; we must – '

'We are *not* busy, Mother. You were going to make me swot my Latin.'

'It is most historical,' says Anne, seeing how to play it. 'Based on the *Decameron*, says Tom. Mr Shakespeare translated it himself, he's quite the linguist. Though not as handsome as Mr Burbage, I have to say.'

'Please, Mother!' Henry grips my arm and squeezes tight. 'One afternoon of Latin is not going to make me an Oxford man. And Tom is my very best friend. I shall be heartbroken if you say no.'

I count it a small victory that I have not set foot in the Globe for ten years. Nor have I been to the Rose, nor the Curtain, nor the Swan, nor the Fortune. All London might be in thrall to the theatre, but not me. And yet. I can't lie: as we come up to the great entrance gate to the play house, part of a dense London throng, I am as curious as Henry, who is leaping and dancing and

singing like a Bedlam boy. Joan has him by the arm, a grim set to her smile (she has no love for a play). I, meanwhile, am borne along by Anne, who is twenty times as giddy and talkative as my cavorting son.

'You see there?' She gestures at a portly nymph ahead of us in the line, with tight-curled hair and a tavern laugh. 'Breasts quite out – it's all the thing, they say, at Court. And yet, look, she's straight off to the pit, for all her gown is of silk taffeta.'

'A whore, Anne, as any fool can see.'

'Whore? Where, Mother?' comes from behind.

'Never mind that, Henry, you are here to see the play,' says Joan.

'What great big nipples has she, though! Half the size of her dugs! Mine are tiny beside hers.' Anne is frowning at the sight.

'Oh, yes, I see them now!' says Henry. 'Big as conkers!'

'Enough of this, in front of the child, Anne!'

'I quite forgot myself, forgive me.' But her expert eye has distracted her again. 'Is that Mr Burbage? Over there, with the gold and silver girdle? I am sure it must be him! Look at his actor's bearing – a true player, wouldn't you say?'

'That isn't Burbage. He will be in the tiring-house, waiting to go on.'

'It's him. Mr Burbage! Over here!'

'Not if he is the lead, which it says he is, on the playbill.' I flutter the bill before her face. 'Why would he be out here, gawping at the crowd?'

But Anne looks vague. She does not like me to draw attention to the fact that I can read.

Through the gate ahead of us, I can see the afternoon sun tilting down on to the pit, gilding the crowd that is gathering there. Eight-sided, the great Globe, like a Roman amphitheatre for our own day, the centre open to the air, the surrounding walls and galleries thatched. I have my pennies ready, to pay for a gallery bench, but Anne will have none of it: she pays for

each of us. We push our way along, past the doorkeeper and into the bright 'O' beyond. Henry bouncing up and down, no matter what Joan does to try and quiet him.

The crowd is an unruly mix, with only beggars and the drunkest fools kept out. While all of London, and of England, may be divided in rank and importance, with attention to each man's smallest difference in wealth or status or the opinion of his peers, here is a place where no one quite knows where he stands – excepting only that he should have a good view of the stage. Court folk and well-bred dandies might dance around each other, puffing pipes and opining on the latest works of Dekker, Middleton and the rest; but they are perilous close to all who seek to fleece them; the knaves and tricksters, cozeners and coney-catching foists. And there are also plenty of the middling folk among them: cheery shoemakers, solid burghers and prentice-boys, daft with youth. The finery of the rich is half-hidden in the crush of sallow kersey, dun coats and rough-sewn jerkins, so that here you might see a flash of bright velvet, there a yellow ruff, so big it blocks the view of those behind, and there again an azure ostrich feather, nodding prettily above the rollicking crowd.

We climb the stairs and reach our place, and I look around me. I had forgotten how grand the inside of a theatre can be. It is like entering a great cathedral before they stripped out the gold and daubed lime over the frescoes, but better, for there is no homily to endure. The main stage, set at the far end of the pit, has vast pillars on each side, painted in a swirling pattern to resemble marble. Above the stage is a canopy held up by two smaller pillars: the Heavens, decorated with the sun and moon and celestial bodies. Gold and scarlet hangings cover the back of the stage, hiding the tiring-house, and green rushes are strewn upon the stage itself. Running out into the pit is a long, narrow walkway, so the actors might dance among the groundlings.

The musicians are already assembling on the balcony, blowing and strumming raggedly. A few young blades are taking their

places on the edge of the stage, perched on three-legged stools, as eager to be part of the spectacle as they are to get a good view.

'Well,' says Anne, 'this *is* pleasant. I do so love a play.' She offers me a Seville orange, and I shake my head, nausea beginning to rise up in my throat. 'I don't for the life of me know what ails you,' she says. 'Why are you all on edge?'

'I am not well.'

She peels her orange with her squat white fingers. 'What is the matter?'

'I finished off a mutton pottage last night; perhaps it disagreed with me.'

Just then, something digs into my back. I turn, thinking it must be Henry. 'Keep still, child, can't you?'

But it is not Henry. It is a hunchback dwarf, bent over nearly double, so his head looks as if it is growing out of his chest. He is dressed well, like a prosperous guildsman. And yet this man does not belong to any guild. This is my landlord, Anthony Inchbald.

'Mr Inchbald,' I say. 'Good day to you, I am sure.'

'A pleasure to see you, as always, Mistress Lanyer. I suppose your husband told you I had called?'

'Sadly, no.'

'His mind seemed . . . occupied elsewhere.'

'I trust your visit was successful?'

He worms his way forward and settles himself next to me on the bench, legs dangling. He looks straight ahead, very calm.

'This will be a fine production,' he says. 'Love, and blood, and tragic death. What more can you ask for from a play?'

'What indeed?' say I.

'Though it's hard enough for a poet to keep pace with nature. I went to the bear garden yesterday. Saw the great beast Harry Hunks kill off four greyhounds, with a few claw-punches and much assurance!'

'Oh, sir!' says Henry, staring at Inchbald, wide-eyed. 'What joy!'

'One landed in the lap of the lady next to me, with two legs missing,' says Inchbald.

'By Our Lady! There could be nothing finer,' says Henry. 'I wish I could go. Mother keeps me from everything, I may as well live in a dog kennel for all the sport I see.'

'And there were rockets and fireworks, and hungry vagrants fighting for some bread and apples, and it all ended with an ape on horseback.'

'What are words compared to that?' I say, avoiding his gaze and staring into the crowd below, where I can see two cutpurses jostling their prey. One stuffs a purse into his doublet even as I watch.

Inchbald squints round at me. 'There was no success to be had.'

'At the bear pit?'

'At your house in Long Ditch.'

'I am sorry for that.'

He smiles. His two teeth are like twin pegs on a line. 'Nothing, in short, to be had at all. The cupboard, in a phrase, was bare. And yet you have the money for the Globe! I admire this, for I share your passion. A woman who would sooner be homeless than miss the latest offering from the Lord Chamberlain's Men. This I must applaud, even as I call the bailiffs to your door.'

'She is my guest, Mr Inchbald,' says Anne, leaning over me in a flurry of importance. Her house, too, belongs to him. 'We are all good friends here this afternoon. Your business can wait for another day.' She pats him playfully on the wrist. I am surprised she can bear to touch him.

'We have no business,' I say.

'Oh, I think we have,' says Inchbald. 'As long as I have your house, then we have business.'

'Ask my husband; he will pay you.'

'Your husband has air for brains. And his promises are worth less than a strumpet's virtue.'

'If he pays you, then who cares about his useless promises?'

'He has paid me nothing but promises all year.'

I look away, my face hot. What has my husband been up to now? Alfonso does not earn much, but it is enough to pay our rent. As long as he doesn't spend it first. But he can be trusted with nothing. I am like a widow with two sons, not a wife with one child. Lucky I keep a stash of Hunsdon's gold hid from him, to insure me against the debtors' clink.

'What can I give you? I have no money of my own. All I have is the idea for a pamphlet.'

'Words pay no debts. Give me deeds, Mistress Lanyer, give me money.'

'It's about the subjugation of Eve.'

'Hardly a subject to keep a roof over your head!'

'I also have a poem, a ballad, in the voice of Mary Magdalene.'

'Who will buy a ballad by a woman? I am as likely to purchase the tale of a tortoise, or the confessions of a crow.'

'Hush!' says Anne. 'The play is starting!'

Just as the trumpets and hautboys call us to order, there is a commotion in the pit. A fight seems to have broken out, somewhere near the stage.

I peer down, trying to get a better look. 'What's going on?'

'Some kind of disorder,' says Anne, standing up and shading her eyes with her hand.

'It's that freak Moll Cutpurse,' says Inchbald. 'They should lock her up for lewdness.'

There's a loud shriek, laughter, and then a figure seems to surge up out of the assembled mass, like a homunculus emerging from the mud. A young man is lifted on to the stage.

'Moll? A Molly-boy, from the stews?'

'A woman, if you can call it that,' says Inchbald. 'A blot on nature.'

137

The figure is sitting crookedly upon the boards, flat upon its arse with its legs splayed wide, face hidden by a wide-brimmed hat. Someone is calling from the crowd.

'A song, Moll Cutpurse! Give us one of your sweet songs!'

'An air, a dainty air to set the scene!' yells another voice. One of the law students on the stage gets up and gives her something. It is a lute. At the back of the stage I see a Fool, arms folded, laughing.

'Who's that?' I whisper to Anne.

'Robert Armin,' she says. 'Now, *he's* a saucy fellow!'

Moll Cutpurse sets the lute down with deliberation, then struggles, with great difficulty, to her feet. She throws down her hat and picks up the lute. She has a round, peasant face, and a huge red mouth, so that she is clown-like even without paint. Her hair is cut short like a boy's. In spite of this, and in spite of her doublet and breeches, there is something in the set of her shoulders and her way of strumming the lute which is pleasing. She bows, very low, as if she has already concluded a great performance. The audience claps and cheers. Some oranges are thrown on to the stage. She picks up two of these, and puts them in her shirt.

'You are most kindly, ladies, boys and men,' she shouts, bowing again. 'I shall repay this richness with some little ditty which I have made, adapted from thin air and the drunkish songs of bawds. If you are of a fribbling, foul-faced disposition, then close your ears. If not, kindly open them.'

'What else will you have us open, Moll?' shouts someone.

'Your purses, sir,' she calls back. 'Pull 'em back widely, at the lip.'

'Have you a sword, to entertain us?'

'No, sir, but poke me with yours and you'll get a shock.'

'I'll poke you any time!'

'Then you are in for fine sport. For I'm more wit-worm than wanton.'

Lots of screeching and guffawing at this.

'A wanton worm!'
'A worming wanton!'
'Wriggle-me-ree, Moll!'
'Wriggle with me!'

Then the shout goes up: 'A song, a song! Let's hear the bashful lady's song!' So she begins to sing, in a strong voice:

'There were three drunken maidens
Come from the Isle of Whyte
They drank from Sunday morning
Didn't stop till Saturday night.'

Another bow, and she begins to play her lute, not badly, though the notes do have a habit of sliddering around the tune. And then she goes on with her pretty ditty:

'When Saturday night did come, me boys,
They wouldn't then go out
These three drunken maidens
They pushed the jug about.'

Many people in the audience seem to know the words quite well, for there is much singing along and waving of caps. The song becomes a great roar:

'There's forty quarts of beer, me boys
They fairly drunk them out
These three drunken maidens
They fetched their sweet dugs out!'

Wild laughter and hooting follows, and coins shower on to the stage as well as oranges. Moll scoops these up quick: I see that she is not too drunk to forget her business, nor to sing while she gathers up her fee.

'O where are your feathered hats
Your mantles rich and fine?
They've all been swallowed up
In tankards of good wine.'

Now, the crowd goes quiet again, and Moll sings sweetly, seeming to have got her voice properly now, and she sounds like a perfect angel, sitting on a heavenly cloud:

'And where are your maidenheads
You maidens brisk and gay?
We left them in the ale house
We drank them clean away.'

Here is Armin, strutting his way along the walkway, smiling this way and that, his feet beating like drumsticks on the boards. He whirls Moll round, arm in arm, faster and faster, dancing around like a shittle-cock, till finally she flies off the stage and falls back into the crowd, roaring as she goes. (Though whether in sport or anger I can't tell.) So many arms are raised to catch her that she falls upon a feather bed of groundlings. She marches away, still singing. I watch her go, wondering if she is the first free woman I have seen in all my life.

The play begins. It is called *Othello, the Moor of Venice*. It is the worst and most lamentable tale, which makes you want to climb up on the stage and bang the players' heads together to set them straight. Othello, all talk and no sense, has the music of the language but no understanding of its hidden meanings. He chooses his wife wisely: she is a good and virtuous woman. (Though not sharp enough to keep her man in order.) His deputy, Iago, is recruited from the gates of Hell, being more or less a devil. Othello seems proud, but does not love himself well enough to trust his wife, and so he kills her. Murders her flat-out, in her nightgown. The thing he loves above all else, more than himself.

Well! There is no need. He is a Blackamoor, so it's a play to set the talk going, and he is mad in love with his fair wife. Could such a man exist? He is not half-beast, but demi-god. And his words have more tune in them than the oboes, lutes and viols that play between the acts. I know it is only Burbage who marches upon the stage, his face blacked, his voice mellifluous. But I believe he is the Moor. Then, my breath leaves me.

On to the stage comes bold Aemilia, serving maid to Desdemona, wife to Iago. Anne clutches my hand. 'Oh, Tom! The naughty baggage!' she says. Her boy is beautiful in his vivid scarlet dress (there is one of exactly that colour, hid away in my chamber in a cedar chest). His wig is black as a raven's wing, corkscrew-curled like Medusa's. (I touch my own black hair, as if to check it is not stolen.) He turns to Iago, hands on hips, saucy with indignation. I know enough of myself to know this is my own manner. He is an actor all right, this pretty boy! No wonder the company was so eager to take him on.

'He's good,' I hiss to Anne. But her hand is clutched over her mouth in disbelief.

Now Tom speaks, in his soft girl's voice.

'But jealous souls shall not be answered so;
They are not ever jealous for the cause,
But jealous for they art jealous; 'tis a monster
Begot upon itself, born on itself.'

My skin goes cold. Oh, Will, what treachery, that you would not believe me when I told you what was true! Your fine earl forced me; your jealousy was the making of your mind. *'Begot upon itself, born on itself.'* I had not put it quite so well, but the scene burns in my head. Wriothesley kissing me, seeking my screaming mouth and kissing me again, wet and slippy as a prentice-boy. How he grunted as he pushed his fat cock up inside me, and shrieked in ecstasy as he bounced and grafted.

The play holds us all; we are in its time and place, Othello is a grand fool, and his fear will be the finish of him. Aemilia, for all her spirit, will not save her mistress. And these words, too, are taken from the life.

> *'Why should he call her whore? Who keeps her company?*
> *What place? What time? What form? What likelihood?'*

In this play, it is the honour of the virtuous Desdemona that these lines defend. In reality, it was my own honour I sought to protect against the spite and jealousy of the poet himself, using, if not these very words, then something very like them. Will has retold another tale, it seems, as well as some old story by Cinthio.

The play is over. Desdemona, who was dead upon her bed, now parades before us in her white robes, hand in hand with Tom/Aemilia. We all stand to shout and cheer. Anne weeps. Joan grins – a rare sight, this. Inchbald dangles over the rail, waving his playbill, so fiercely that I think he'll fall and do us all a favour. And Henry whoops and yells, as if he were at the bear pit, dancing on the spot. Love, and blood, and tragic death. There is nothing like it.

'Oh, Mother,' he cries, 'what a miserable end! Can we see it again?'

'Once is enough,' I say. 'Wait till a new play comes; it won't be long.'

'And shall you bring me then?'

'I don't know. Perhaps Alfonso will come with you next time.'

'And shall we go to the tiring-house now, and see Tom?'

'It's no place for women,' says Anne.

'Or children,' says Joan. 'Unless they are players.'

'It's time to go,' say I, and, true to form, he's gone. 'Henry!' we cry, but off he runs, down the wooden stairs, nearly tripping an eel-man in his flight.

Inchbald, still leaning dangerously far over the balcony, says, 'There he goes, the young demon. Straight for the stage. Do you never think to beat him, Mistress Lanyer?'

I take no notice, but hurry down the stairs in pursuit and rush across the pit, weaving in and out of the boisterous crowd, till I come to the ladder at the foot of the stage.

'Henry!'

I hesitate. I should not, for form's sake, take another step. And yet, I cannot leave my silly son. I begin to climb, ignoring the cat-calls of the prentice-boys who stand behind me, and the shouts of disbelief from other, more respectable members of the crowd. At the top of the ladder, I look around. The people, down below, seem like one mass of watching faces. The pillars rise up on each side of me, like the gateway to Old Rome. In front of me, just a short distance across the stage, is the gold and crimson curtain of the tiring-house. A small foot – that of my son – disappears behind it.

'Henry, I shall whip you for this!'

More cheering. I can't go back; I must go on. I run across the stage, to escape those watching eyes as quick as I can. I hold my breath, screw up my courage, open the curtain and step inside.

Such a whirl of legs and arms and spinning bodies I never saw. All the cast are still in costume, and wearing the black masks of Court ladies. They are leaping and laughing, cloaks flying, skirts lifting, so I could not say how many there are, or who is who, except for Burbage, with his smudged and blackened face, and Desdemona, now wigless, in his gown. Stepping forward, hoping for a sight of Henry or Tom, I cast my eye around at the properties: there are banners and pikes propped against one wall;

before them, baskets and a coffin; beyond these, a table laden with books and platters and severed heads. But then my arm is caught and I am pulled into the middle of the spinning dance.

'Ho, mistress, step lively,' says one player, taking me by the waist.

'Fine ladies find themselves in strange places,' says another, spinning me round and passing me to his neighbour.

'No lady this – she's nearly as dark as the Moor,' says a third, turning me on my heels so I face yet another dancer. It's Burbage, the Moor himself.

'Aemilia, forgive us!' But he is laughing too, with an ale pottle in one hand. 'Nothing more sweetly comical than what's appalling, cruel and tragical. Oh, that poor, misbegotten Moor!'

'My son is here, hiding among – '

Then he is gone, too, so that I hardly have time to feel surprise that he recognised me after all these years. I am at the centre of a blurring circle, like the pole in May. I'm grasped once more, pulled through the crowd, the room dark and fast all round me, all men and boys, disguise and chaos. Then, suddenly, there is a voice in my ear. A breath on my neck.

'God's blood, I thought it must be you! Mistress Alfonso Lanyer, I can scarce believe it. What do you mean by coming here? I thought you loathed us players.'

I close my eyes. The sound of the players fades, seems to come from faraway. *He* is here. I knew he would be, but am still sick to hear his voice again.

I swallow, my eyes still shut. If I don't look at him, then perhaps I will be safe.

'I'm not here to see the players, sir.'

'Not the playwright, surely?'

Opening my eyes, I turn to face him. For an instant he is a stranger, and I see him as I would if I had never known him. A pale fellow, no longer young, but with an air of urgency about him. The instant passes, and I know him, as I know no one

except myself. Deep, shadowed eyes, searching my face with an expression that is caught between laughter and rage. A twist to his lips that makes me wonder who still kisses them. The years have broadened him and lined his face, but he is proud and handsome, more so than in his youth. I had hoped to find him shiny-bald and run to fat. But he is Will, the Will I have loved, and more himself than ever.

I gird myself. 'Mr Shakespeare.'

He bows.

'I'm – I have no wish to be here.'

'And I have no wish to see you here.' He smiles with stately cordiality.

'My boy is hiding here, with your Desdemona.'

His mouth tightens. 'Oh . . . *your* son, is he? I saw a silly knave with Tom.'

'He *is* a silly knave, but I love him dearly.'

'Your son,' he says. 'I often . . .'

'What?'

'My own boy is dead.' He looks away, frowning. 'Hamnet.'

'Oh – the poor child! I'm sorry for your loss.'

'Yes.' Now he is examining his wrist, as if he had some lines wrote on it. 'My wife . . . They sent a letter, but he was buried by the time I got to Stratford. There was heavy rain and . . . the way was hard.'

'I didn't know . . .' Will still smells of ink, I notice, as a butcher smells of blood. 'God bless his soul.'

'He was eleven.'

'Henry is nearly ten. I mean . . . I would die if anything . . .'

'Of course,' he says. Then, 'Henry. Ha!'

Our eyes meet, then jerk away.

Will reaches out, and touches my shoulder with his finger as if he's making sure I'm solid flesh. I feel a breath of longing, as if a ghost had stroked the skin between my thighs.

I brush his hand away.

'Do not dare to touch me. I am sorry for poor Hamnet, but don't imagine that I will ever forget your foul words and accusations.'

He withdraws his hand. 'Your kind words about my son don't absolve you of your guilt.'

'My *guilt*?'

'You are a faithless whore.'

'There's not enough gold in all of Cheapside to make me *your* whore for a single night.'

He laughs. 'Who said I'd pay a farthing? You're not such a tasty morsel now, mistress. I can feast nightly on a prettier dish.'

I think, *He loathes me. I am repulsive to him. So be it, so be it; I shall not set eyes on him again.* Standing straighter, I look him in the eye. 'Oh, surely. The anointed sovereign of sighs and groans. What fortunate young women, to be sweated over by a lewd old versifier like yourself.'

'Fortunate indeed. I see your mind is still sharp, even if your eyes are growing dull.'

Over his shoulder, I can see the actors parading about the tiring-room, doing a mock pavane. I must find Henry, and be gone.

'You are too arrogant, sir. Putting yourself above me with your cruel words. You think that honest folk are like players, running to and fro at the command of your invention? No. We are living beings, closer to angels than your shouting, painted shams.'

'Honest? A bawd like you is honest? Most entertaining! Now you are after Armin's job: you aim to be a clown . . .'

'Yes, sir. Honest now, and honest since you have known me. A woman may not be a jester, but a poet may be a fool.'

'I saw what I saw. You were false to me!'

'You *saw* me with Wriothesley. But you are all eyes and no sight. No matter – it's nothing to me now. And you have more than paid me back, sir, with your wicked, poisonous lines. You

turned your pain to wormwood poetry, and set every fibre of your genius to the task of breaking my heart!'

A shout goes up as John Heminge comes in with flagons of ale, followed by two boy players carrying trenchers loaded with fried collops, scented with frizzled fat, together with rabbit, humble pie, flat round manchets and other nunchions and snacks.

'Let us celebrate!' cries Burbage. He turns, and there's Tom, in his scarlet, and next to him I see my own son at last, who had slyly hid himself in the middle of the dancing men. Burbage waits till everyone has gathered round him, and quietened, and filled their cups. I stand quite still, hoping that, if I don't look at Will, he'll vanish into the crowd.

'This is a proud day for all of us, we merry Lord Chamberlain's Men, for we have two new triumphs to celebrate.' The whites of Burbage's eyes flash in his black face, which is streaked with dancing-sweat. 'We are, being players, part of one greater whole, with no leader, no prince to quell us, nor cunning-man to muddle us. We are brothers, and the success of one is the success of all.' I see that he is close to tears with the beauty of it.

Another speaker, smooth and cocksure. 'We are all as wise and foolish as each other, and in that lies our infinite wisdom. Till we reach the end of it.' It's Robert Armin. There is laughter, then silence. Everyone is waiting to hear what Burbage, the leader who would not be leader, will say next.

'First, we must celebrate our dear friend Will, and his new play, which is as sad and stately as we could wish. And which cannot fail.'

Hoots and laughter. 'Put money in thy purse!' calls someone.

'Most poetical and bloody,' cries Armin. 'The Blackamoor will get us gold.'

'And second – we have a new man among us, a beardless boy, but one who gave us a performance tonight that shows he is surely one of us. Tom Flood, you were a fine Aemilia!' There are more cheers, and someone makes Tom stand upon a stool. He

takes off his wig, and twists it in his hands, and bows in mock-ceremony. His face is pink, his dark curls fall into his eyes.

'Speech!' calls Will, beside me, and I catch his eye, and am stabbed right through. It is the strangest feeling. I know him from my own mirror. Each time my face has looked out, it was Will I saw there. And now I look at him and see my own face in the glass.

I have to leave. I turn and make my way through the laughter and shouting, and Tom beginning to say something, and being drowned out by his fellow players. I find Henry, and clench my hand firmly around his arm.

'We are off,' I tell him. 'And for once you will be beaten raw for this.'

But Will stands before me when we reach the door. His eyes flash from me, to Henry, then back again.

'An entrance is an entrance, and so a turn must follow,' he says. 'You have a part to play, now you have returned.' His shirt is undone beneath his doublet; the dark hairs of his chest are caught in a thick gold chain. He did not have this chain when last I touched that hidden skin. Who touches him now? The Stratford housewife? A pert mistress, peachier than me? I hear a voice: *You are mine, mine. You are me. We are joined, for good or ill.* Did someone speak? I am sick and giddy.

'Goodbye, Will. This is your world, your "stage". These are your people. Make your riddles, strut your words – none of this can interest me.' I have my arm round Henry, who is squirming to break free.

'It is not finished,' Will says. His eyes seem to deepen. 'You know that, just as I do.'

'What is not?' asks Henry.

'The ale,' I say. 'They've not yet drunk the ale.'

Scene V

When we get home, Alfonso is out. I wait till Henry is asleep, then I go to my chamber and lock the door. With a great effort, I push the bed aside, then scrabble back the rushes. There is a loose board beneath. I lift it up, and thrust my hand into the dusty floor-space. There it is. A bulging leather pouch. I pull it out. This is where I keep the gold coins left over from my dowry. Hidden from my spouse, of course, who cannot be trusted with three farthings.

Spreading my skirts, I tip the contents into my lap. Yet what is this? The flat shapes that tumble out lie heavy on my skirts. But they are grey stones, pebbles from the river shore. Where is my cherished hoard of gold and silver? Where is my money? I feel inside the bag again. Empty. I shake out my skirts, letting the stones roll among the rushes, and plunge my arm inside the hole once more. All I find is a dried-up spider, in a winding sheet of its own legs, and a tiny, shrivelled mouse.

Then I think – perhaps the coins have fallen out? Perhaps they are hidden in the dust and scrimmage. I go downstairs, and fetch a fish-hammer and a candle. I take up another floorboard, panting as I work at the rusty iron nails. Then another, ripping it with my hands, tearing my fingers on the splintered wood. Blood drips on to my clothes. I smear the sweat off my face, light the candle and lower it into the floor-space. The flickering light reveals only dirt and floor-beams. The space is empty. But no! There, in the far corner. A small shape . . . I extend my arm,

groping till I feel something with the tips of my fingers. I reach further, another inch, grasp it and pull it out.

It is a tiny pewter box, round and smooth. I prise open the lid and tip it up. Nine little dice fall into the palm of my hand. There must be a good reason why they have been hidden away so carefully. I examine them one by one. They are cheats' dice. Three are marked only with low numbers, three with high numbers, and three are weighted so they will fall the same way every time. They must belong to my husband. He has found my stash of money and gambled it away. But Alfonso is not just a fool, he is a trickster too. Not only has he lost my money, he has tried to swindle others out of theirs. Of course he is too stupid to succeed in such an enterprise. If he were any use as a cozener, he would have more than a bag of river stones to show for his dishonesty.

I sit hunched on the floor, not caring for my spoiled dress, thinking. I stare at the feeble candle-flame, the little light it throws on my little life. I see myself as I once was, listening as Lord Hunsdon talked, and, as the years went by, talking as he listened. He told me only the Queen had a better head for affairs of state than me. And that my Latin was a match for hers. He said I could have been an Oxford man, if I had been a man at all. And then he built me this boxed-in house and set me up with an addle-pate of a spouse.

It is true that Alfonso was pleased to have me, even though I was pregnant with another man's child. He saw that he was getting a handsome bargain. I would not have been kept so long by Hunsdon if I did not have a pretty face and a whore's skill in the bedchamber, and I came with a good dowry. He saw in me a lifetime of good fucking, and at least a year of good spending. And truth to tell, this is exactly what he got. To his credit, there is not an ounce of malice in the man, and he loves Henry as if he were his own child. In fact, such is his ability to see only what doesn't cause him pain, I believe he's come to feel that Henry is his natural son. So he is happy.

Only my poetry makes him angry. Property does not write poems. Property sits at home and puts her skill to churning butter. He seems to think my writing not only unwomanly, but also sacrilegious. 'What monstrous thing is this!' he cries, when he finds me scratching out a verse or scrawling down some passing thought. 'Play your virginals, if you want to show us how clever you are! Leave the words to the wits. God preserve us, get some food before me!' I hide my precious pages in the straw mattress, in case he throws them on the fire.

This is my lot. Wrong sex, wrong lovers, wrong place. The universe is neat as an egg, the layers held like white and yolk within its shell. I am neither white nor yolk, fish nor fowl. And now – what is my line of business now? If I could crawl into that hole, wrap myself in a death-caul like the shrunken spider and never be thought of again, I would do so.

But there is a cry from Henry's room. I put the dice-box in my pocket, unlock my door and hurry to his bedside.

He hugs me, as if he were still an infant. 'Mother!' he says. 'I dreamed that you were dead!'

I smooth his hair. He smells of smoke and sugar.

'My little one.' I kiss his cheek. 'Never fear. I'm not dead yet.'

'Nor me,' says Henry. He pulls away, wipes his eyes and looks at me. 'We shan't die for a while longer, either, shall we? God doesn't need us yet.'

'No, He doesn't.'

'And I am very sorry.'

'For what?' I have almost forgotten his flight to the tiring-room.

'For – all my bad ways.'

'You are just a boy, Henry.' I touch his cheek.

'I will stop all my running away.'

'Yes.'

'God would like that,' he says, sagely.

'Yes. You would make God very happy.'

I draw the counterpane tight around him before I close the curtains, making him a little tent, all snug.

By the time Alfonso comes home, it is midnight, and the trumpets have long since sounded the curfew at the City walls. I'm sitting outside the house, wrapped in a woollen cloak. It is a clear, chilly night and the crescent moon is an arc of silver, brighter than my missing coin. Alfonso is tottering and singing to himself, his recorder slung over his shoulders in its carrying case. I know the tune; it was composed by my uncle, Robert Johnson: 'The Witch's Dance', a favourite at Court. My husband comes slowly, slowly, weaving this way and that, whistling and humming and laughing, at one point almost falling in the town-ditch, at another sitting on the ground for several moments, tracing his own palm-lines in the moonlight.

When he sees me, he seems to be delighted, and not in the least surprised to find me waiting in the street.

'Aemilia!' he calls. 'Lady Aemilia! I am blessed in my work, yet even more so in my spouse.' He comes up and pulls me to my feet. 'Oh, wife! *Houses and riches are the inheritance of the fathers, but a prudent wife is from the Lord.*'

Alfonso is not devout by nature, and loves God most when he's in his cups. 'You have been at the Malmsey again, I see.'

'*May thy fountain be blessed, and rejoice with the wife of thy youth!*' he declaims, squeezing me tightly.

'Leave me be, husband.'

'*Let her breasts satisfy thee at all times and be thou ravished always with her love.*' He tries to land a kiss upon my lips, but I twist my head away and he slobbers on the doorpost instead. '*And why wilt thou, my son, be ravished with a strange woman, and embrace the bosom of a stranger.* Oh, woe is me!' He stares up adoringly at the door lintel.

'What have you done with it?' I ask, pushing him away.

'With what?' He turns, unsteadily, and puts one hand out to balance himself against the wall. 'Always questions, questions. Such a liveliness of mind. It doesn't augur well, my chuck. You should do more spinning.'

'My *money*, Alfonso. Where is my money? Did you lose it at the tables?'

'You have money?'

'Not any more.'

'Then how am I to blame for taking it?'

I grab him by the shoulders and shake him hard. 'Are you really so dull and brain-sickly? I *had* money, and now it is gone. Now all that remains is a pewter pot of tricksters' dice!'

'What are you saying?'

'That you are the cozener of your own wife and child, you worthless piece of scum!'

'Worthless . . . what? I know nothing of it.'

Disgusted, I begin pacing to and fro, too angry to keep still. 'What's more, I saw Inchbald today – or yesterday, I should rather say.'

'Oh! How is the dainty little fellow? Did you wish him well from me?'

'He told me we've paid no rent this year.'

'God's blood! The thieving scoundrel . . .'

'He'll be round tomorrow to collect what's his. Or else he'll take the house back.'

Alfonso closes his eyes as if making a difficult calculation. 'Hmm. Now, what *was* the problem with friend Inchbald . . . ? Perhaps there was a misunderstanding in our transaction. A tenacious fellow, we must give him that.'

I thrust my face close to his, ignoring his filthy tavern stench.

'Husband.'

'Yes?'

'Are you not ashamed?'

'Ashamed?'

'Are you not a *man*?'

'I do all a man can do! Who would do more is none!'

'More? Who could do *less*?' I tear at my hair. 'Lord God! Help me! I am like an anchorite, walled in to pray and meet my doom!'

'Mistress Lanyer, you are raving!'

'Raving? The madness is that I walk about quite calmly, knowing I am done for! I will be a pauper, thrust upon the parish! I will end my days in public view, a starving creature locked into a cage!'

Alfonso, pale already from strong drink, takes himself a shade whiter. 'Calm yourself, wife. Show some respect.'

'Respect! I may have to kill you.'

'You forget, I went off to the Azores with Ralegh and poor Essex.'

'And so did many others. You are meant to be a courtier, after all. The task was to make a name for yourself and seek preferment. Though, in your case, hope was set too high.'

'I almost drowned. Your vaunting ambition will be the death of me.'

'But you *lived.* More's the pity. When I think of all the honest, proper men who go to their graves each day, while you continue with your doltish prancing.'

'I was shot through the shirt – and scared out of my wits.'

'The Queen should never have agreed to send you with them, you brought such evil luck. When they went the first time, without you, their ships came back loaded down with gold. But what *your* great expedition brought back was half a chest of bullion. And the Spanish all but landed at Penzance.'

His shoulders sag.

'I tried. Strived.' He frowns at the word, seemingly drunk enough to wonder if this is French. 'I *strove.* Wanted to be made a knight, but only four were chosen.'

'You are a worm, Alfonso. A liar, a boil, a plague sore and a turd.'

'I am a *musician*. It's my vocation . . .' His eyes swivel. 'My art, my heart . . . A musician can't be called to order . . .'

'To order? What are you talking about? All you had to do was pay the rent.'

'Which is what I wanted. What they said they could do. They said I would win a crock of gold worth twenty times your little hoard . . .'

'Who said?'

'The women.'

'*Women*?'

'The three women with the magic dice.'

'Save us! You think those dice have magic in them? You can buy them anywhere. They surely took you for the stupidest gull they ever saw.'

'It seemed likely enough to me. They are from Persia. I thought, since I had lost some gold, I had better win it back for you.'

I roll my eyes. Then a thought strikes me. 'Three women? What manner of women?'

'Just – women. Of the common sort.'

'Old or young?'

'Both – a mixture.'

My heart beats harder. 'But one was young and fair. Was she not? With yellow hair and white skin?' I see her, clear as I see Alfonso, standing behind her rampart of evil sugar-plums.

He frowns again, pulls his recorder out, and is about to put it to his lips.

I snatch it from him. 'Alfonso! What did she look like?'

'I can't recall.'

'Where did you see them?'

His eyes are closing, and I shake his shoulder. 'Where did you see them?'

155

He thinks for a moment. 'Tyburn. Yes, most delightful spot. They told me they had business there.' He closes his eyes, and recites, '*Who can find a virtuous woman? For her price is far above rubies.*' Then he tips gently sideways and falls asleep at an angle, like the fallen stone of a Roman archway. I take the recorder inside for safe keeping and leave him there, locking the door behind me. If the Lord is willing, my sotted spouse will roll into the ditch and drown in piss and offal before dawn.

I sit at the kitchen table, still wrapped in my cloak. The night deepens, the shadows fill the house and my cheap candle gutters as the tallow trickles down the shaft. But my thoughts and fears grow wild in the darkness. There is witchcraft behind all this. Something wicked stalks me. I must face down this dark magic with magic of my own.

Some women in my sorry state might sell their bodies. There are those who'd say my life with Hunsdon was a whore's contract, so I have only a short distance to fall. But there is a world between having a royal protector and being humped by stinking tavern scum. I still have my wits, undimmed by time. I'm not done yet.

Scene VI

It is a bright September morning. Joan is mending an old smock of Henry's, head bent over her stitching. The needle flashes in and out of the dark fabric as she works, so fast that I can hardly see it.

She doesn't look up, but says, 'He lost it, didn't he?'

'Lost what?'

'Your money.'

I break off some bread. I am used to her strange way of knowing more than she should. Sometimes it annoys me, sometimes it alarms me. Today, I just feel tired.

'Is *all* my business your business?' I ask, sitting down next to her. 'Are *all* my affairs of your concern?'

'I live here, don't I, mistress? Those that have eyes to see know what is all around them.'

'Yes.' I chew in silence for a while. 'But some of us see more than others.'

'Sure enough,' says Joan, biting off the thread.

'Joan . . .'

'Mistress?'

'I need your help.'

'You've had my help these last nine years and more. And I don't begrudge it.'

'I know. I could not ask for a better servant.' I swallow the last bit of crust and shake the crumbs from my skirt. 'This art of yours . . . this knowledge. Of herbs and remedies and . . . spells. How did you come by it?'

She looks at me, her green eyes bright in her lined face. 'I learned it. From my mother, and she learned it from hers. It's a trade, of sorts, the business of an apothecary.'

'And yet you know more than most, don't you?'

'How can I tell what's in their minds? I only know what's in my own.' She returns to her stitching.

'Could you teach it to me?'

She continues sewing, smiling as she works. 'Teach! As if it were the cross-stitch?'

'Could I *learn* this skill?'

Her needle stops in mid-air.

'What for?'

'I am afraid. We have no money – as you guessed – and Inchbald owns this house. Alfonso wastes most of his wages at the tables – we are all but on the street. And . . .'

'And?' She looks at me again.

'The women at the Fair – there was something wrong. You said so yourself. Something evil in them.'

'And then they gave master the trickster's dice.'

I stare. 'Were you listening to us?'

She gazes back, unabashed. 'Only in my sleep.' Putting her sewing to one side, she shrugs. 'What I can teach you, mistress, is knowledge of herbs and simples and suchlike. Some cures and some small ways to help yourself, and others. So you can ward off harm.'

'What about a small hex, here and there?'

She smiles. 'Who would you hex?'

'I don't know. Someone who deserved it.'

'I'll try my best for you, mistress. But you know I would do all of this for you. There's no need to trouble yourself with it.'

'But I want to know myself. I want to understand.'

'I know you do, mistress.' She touches my arm. 'Be wary. And be patient. Do what I tell you, and no more. In this, I am the mistress, and you are my apprentice. You are asking a great deal

from me.' She gives me one of her narrow looks. 'That pamphlet Forman gave you – did you read it?'

'*The Hammer of Witches*?' There is no point asking how she knows of this, for she seems to have a better idea of my business than I do myself.

'You should read it. There are degrees in witchcraft, as in all things. First there is the wise woman, who knows of the lore that the Old Religion used to its own ends. Now that's all gone, and, as the new faith takes hold, more of us will suffer, I've no doubt of it. The next degree is occupied by Dr Forman and his like. They think experiments will help throw light on mystery, and who's to say – maybe they will? But the highest – and the lowest – form of witchcraft lies in wait for wise women and cunning-men alike. And that is the fatal knowledge that is possessed only by Satan and his familiars. This is a challenge to God, and will cost each man or woman who tries it their immortal soul. The spell those women put on you was of that order, in my opinion.'

I read this *Hammer* and think about this bolting-hutch of beastliness that is our world. Men hobble noble ladies with skirts and bind them with pearls. They snaffle scolds with bitch-bridles. They buy pretty maids for their bedchamber, from their fathers, or off the street. But those of us with nothing but our brains to keep us fare worst of all, as if the power to think was elvish-marked. Men will drown us and flay us; they will brand us and hang us; they will hound us from the light till we are the quintessence of dust. I read this book, and I think of this writer in his fine study, with the fire burning and his quill sharpened, his words scraping into the paper, into our souls. I think to myself, I am no man. But I can wield a pen. And I can learn to wield it well.

There are only four places in the whole of Europe that have become great cities. Venice, city of water and wonders. Constantinople, the gateway to the Orient. Paris, pride of France.

And London. In my own lifetime the City has grown, with tall new houses springing up, old ones split into different dwellings so that as many as a dozen families can live in a place designed for one. Outside the walls, and beyond the powers of City aldermen, builders and carpenters are free to do as they please. New buildings go up in unplanned confusion with no thought to how they fit in with what was there before. Haphazard houses block old thoroughfares, so there is no longer a way through. And side-streets shrink to rat-runs, too narrow for a full-grown man to pass. There are Roman ruins and pagan pillars; collapsed nunneries open to the sky; great mansions converted to spewing tenements; and newer, wooden houses, sprouting overnight. It is as if someone once planted the seed of a timber frame: a miller's son, let's say, in a fireside tale. The seed grew first to a house, and then a street, all neat and handsome, with windows well-set. But then, as trees sprout fungus, these streets gave forth their progeny. New rooms and chambers burgeoned forth. Little alleyways and cat-creeps were burrowed open, and dormer rooms grew upon the rooftops, like the sluttish baskets wove by nesting storks. (I knew a man who lived for six years in the belfry at St Margaret Lothbury. He was cast out only when they had to use the room for storing coal.) All is chaos, madness and clutter. Shouts and whistles, songs and ballads. French and Spanish, German, Russian. The accents of the Midlands, Wales, of Cornwall, York, the Norfolk flats. They are all here, filling the air. Babel is come to Albion.

How, then, shall a 'man' be heard? If the sound of words is drowned out, then let the people read them. Find a printing press, where each letter is placed with neat exactness in a frame, and your lines are blacked down on plain pages, like the Word of God. And if you want to see your thoughts made into books, and sold to Londoners, here, in the centre of the world, go to Paul's Churchyard. There, the dead lie close, in their eternal silence, freshly dug or grinning in the charnel house. And the quick shall make as much noise as we can before we go.

And so I make my way to this place of print and printshops. The sky is pale and piled with cloud. Kites are swooping and woodpigeons perch on the rooftops. I take a wherry as far as Paul's Wharf, holding a clove-stuffed orange to my nose to mask the stench of sewage and pitch. At the wharf, just by Burghley House, the scene of my undoing with Wriothesley, I pay the ferryman and go north between the Doctor's Commons and the College of Arms. It has rained heavily in the night, and the streets are muddy and foul. My pattens slither on the scree of shit from the overflowing ditch.

I cross Carter Lane, a yelling thoroughfare of rattling coaches, lowing cows and quarrelling prentice-boys, and finally reach the churchyard of the great cathedral, a towering Ark above the clustering streets. Our Lord may have thrown the moneylenders from the Temple, but he did not evict the ale-sellers, baker's boys, rooting pigs, pecking chickens, the football games, the beggars or the travelling players. On the left side is a row of houses: laundry flutters above the graves. And to the right, nestling close to the walls of St Paul's, are the open-fronted bookstalls, the object of my pilgrimage.

I am known to all the booksellers. They have all turned down my wares. Some call out as I pass.

'Good day to you, Mistress Lanyer. What is it this time, a pamphlet that says housework is a man's domain?'

'Mistress Lanyer, you are looking well. What do you have there, the secret of immortality?'

'Aemilia, over here! Let's see your fine words. I need a laugh this grey morning!'

'Get you gone!' I shout, over my shoulder. 'If men are so much to be admired and so high regarded in their dominion, how come crops fail, infants die, widows starve and the mad are shouting in the streets?' At that very moment, my eye falls on a Tom o'Bedlam, begging with his little kinchin-mort, a child of five or six years old. Her arms are withered like those of a sickly crone.

161

The very last stall belongs to Mr Cuthbert Tottle, who specialises in the rare and fancy. You might say he puts himself at the freak-show end of the market. The printing press itself is adapted from a wine press, among other such machines, and his folios and quartos are wine-soaked in their weird vagaries, written in the tradition of the ranting drunk. His religious tracts have the most gruesome woodcuts, such as a Jesuit hanging upside down, with two men sawing him in half between his buttocks. His polemical pamphlets have the rudest words about the Pope. And his pornography is the most salacious, with poses backwards, upside-down and sideways. His bestiaries tell tales of beasts I daresay never lived – the wild boar with a Cyclops head, the Tyger that suckled Dolphins, the mermaid that begat the Queen of Carthage and the Narwhal that swims the frozen oceans of the north, using its magic horn to cut a watery pathway through the ice. I like him for this, and he likes me (I think) for my sharp tongue, and the fact that I'm part-Venetian. His shop is always full of émigrés and refugees, and foreign words and noisy laughter.

Now I have something that I hope will appeal to Mr Tottle, with his love of the peculiar and extreme. It is the tale of Lilith, Adam's first wife. My father used to entertain me with this story when my mother was out of hearing. (She thought that Lilith was too wayward a creature to be the subject of a bedside tale.) Lilith was made from the same mud as Adam, according to old Hebrew lore. She thought herself his equal, so of course he threw her out and God gave him someone more amenable, made from his own rib. And this was Eve, the pliant mother of all mothers, born to take the blame for human sin. What my father did not tell me was that Adam and Lilith were estranged because, when they set to fornication, she refused to lie beneath him, but claimed her right to lie on top. For this, and this alone, she lost her place in Eden, and became a demon blamed for the deaths of newborn babes. (I found all this out many

years after, from the Queen's conjurer, John Dee.) So I feel for Lilith, though I fear her name. But will Tottle like this story? We shall see.

I take a breath and walk in. The shop is crowded, as ever, and as ever I am the only woman, save for his wife, who sits silent at the back of the shop, working on a gold-leaf illumination. Tottle himself is a big fellow, jovial and red-cheeked, fond of the ale-house. And yet he drives as hard a bargain as anyone. Even in the throes of boisterous laughter, his eyes are watchful.

A group of Frenchmen haggle with him over a barrel of new books. Two law students, one tall and dark, the other squat and ginger, peruse a squalid chap-book with great interest. Tottle is pouring wine for the students, while refusing to give the Frenchmen a better price for their book-barrel. But when he sees me he sets the bottle down and hurries over.

'Mistress Lanyer!' He glances at his wife. 'The lady poet! Is this good news? Do you have new words for me? Something I can sell this time?'

'I hope so,' I say, taking his offered hand. 'I need to keep a roof over my head.'

He laughs as though this were a very good joke. 'Oh, you ladies! All the same! If you can't get starch for the latest Parisian ruff, you think yourself paupers.'

'You mistake my station, Mr Tottle. I wish that you were right.'

'Let us see, then, what you have.'

He brings a seat for me, and pours out a glass of wine. I give him my pages, and he reads them, smiling all the while. Occasionally he gives a little chuckle, as if especially pleased by some particular word or phrase. When he has finished, he is still smiling. 'Well, well. You certainly have a way about you.' He looks down at my writing, and laughs again. 'Let us see what this assembly makes of this.'

'The Frenchmen?'

'They speak English as well as you or I when they are not affecting Gallic ignorance of Anglo-Saxon prices.' He calls his customers over. 'Gentlemen, pay attention, I have a pamphlet here that you might like to hear. Wife, put your work aside. Listen to this.'

They all turn to hear.

'The title is *The Song of Lilith, first among women.*' He looks up and every one nods. 'A fair title?'

The lawyers shrug. The Frenchmen raise their eyebrows. His wife's eyes are downcast.

'A fair title, then. We are curious, I think. Well, here is a little of the text.

'I am that Lilith which Man loves to hate
Night owl, screech-hag, black-eyed Fate.
Before poor Eve was blamed for human sin
I was Adam's wife, grown from mud like him
Commanded to lie beneath, I told him no
I cried the name of GOD, who made me go.
Eve did his will, being born of his own flesh
Till she bit the Fruit of Knowingness . . .'

Tottle lowers the pages and beams at me. 'Oh, most fine, most fine! You have an ear for the drama, a gift for polemic.'

'Is this a joke?' says one of the Frenchmen.

'Is it permitted?' asks one of the lawyers.

Tottle smiles, and continues.

'Are women evil? Do we walk at night?
A tribe of witches, addled by our spite?
I say we are not, and you do us wrong.
So hear this harlot tale, my siren song
Open your ears to hear the old spun new
Open your eyes to see another view.'

He looks up again, and the lawyers begin to laugh, and the Frenchmen, seeing it is an English joke, laugh too.

'There is more,' I say, snatching the pages from Tottle. 'This is not the best of it.'

Tottle takes me to one side. 'Indeed, it is not the best of anything. This is not what the public is looking for. Look around you, see what sells!'

'What sells is mostly pap and nonsense.'

'Maybe so, but it is pap and nonsense aptly done. This work . . . there is no audience for it. It's slip-shod, badly phrased and – I hate to say this, Aemilia, but I speak as an old friend – it's really little more than doggerel. You must find a better subject, and you must improve your mode of expression.'

I hate him then, with his round, soft smile. 'You are making a fool of me.'

'I'm trying to make you more than the author of the unpublishable.'

'I will try another seller, Mr Tottle. I don't need you.'

He bends towards me, confidential. 'You are a woman; we don't expect you to do this well. The wonder is that you do it at all.'

'Go and piss in a puddle.'

'No, look, madam, I am trying to help you. Consider the market. Religion is good, but don't go off on some mad rant. Remember that you need to *entertain* us. Readers like martyrs. Blood. Decapitation. A breaking of the body on the wheel, or a long-drawn-out crushing with stones. This can never fail – what we call a crowd-pleaser. Who dies in your story? Who is disembowelled? Or, if God is not your fancy, histories will always sell. But don't shilly-shally. Skewer the reader with your sword! Find me a gentil knight whose story is untold, a fierce dragon, a brave battle on a field of gore.'

'Boys' twaddle.'

'Oh, come now.'

'This is fine work. Only a man could fail to see it.'

'You have a fanciful nature. This can work in your favour. So give me a tale from far away. A minaret, a monster. A traveller's tale will always catch the eye.'

'A story for a merchant to relate, or some loquacious seaman.'

'Or fashion. Have you an eye for fashion?' He looks at me uncertainly. As usual, I am wearing my old grey dress, embellished only with a ruff that Anne has loaned me. My hair is scraped back under my bonnet, and my cheeks are ruddy from the sun.

I hesitate for a moment, thinking of Anne and her like, and some of the strange outfits that Alfonso insists on wearing when he goes off to play for the Queen. 'Cunning ways with cross-gartering?' I ask.

Tottle clasps my arm. 'Oh, most excellent notion! Can you do a thousand lines on this? New ideas, Venetian styles, the courtly colours? I could pay you two shillings. One shilling now, one shilling when you bring it in.'

On the one hand is poor Eve, downtrodden since the dawn of time. On the other is a month's security, which might be purchased for this sum.

'Done,' I say, holding out my hand.

The dwarf has spies, no doubt, or the gift of second sight. No matter: there he is. Sitting outside the charnel-house, scoffing an apple cake.

'Mistress Lanyer. You have my money?'

'One shilling,' I say. 'A down-payment.'

He chuckles. 'I like a lady with wit. But this is not the bargain.'

I glare at him.

'You are still a fine woman, Mistress Lanyer.'

'And this means – what?'

'It's common knowledge that once you used your face to your advantage. Not to mention your other parts, which I'm sure are quite as sweet. Of course, no courtier would look at you now. But a humble landlord, like myself, might take a sup.'

'What do you want?'

'Some time with you might settle half the debt.'

'Some *time*?'

'These are the terms I have agreed with Mistress Flood: I visit once a month, and she pays me in kind. And very kind she is too, if I may say so.'

He beckons me over. Reluctantly, I draw nearer. He clasps my hand in his dry little paw.

'Yet nobody would call her fair. Her breasts are like sacks of dough halfway down her belly. Yours, I can see through your shift, are still sweetly rounded. Just the shape for sucking.'

I pull my hand away, not sure whether to box his ears or smack his arse. 'You aren't even tall enough to reach them, you lecherous little toad.'

'Two fucks a month would do me nicely. I should look forward to it, which, between ourselves, is more than I do with some of my ladies. With some it's a case of skirts up, cock out, and let's go about our business. But with your good self . . .' The little turd is ogling me as if he thinks we might go to it right away.

I have to laugh, even though the thought of Anne Flood giving herself to this manikin sickens me. 'Oh, Mr Inchbald! Most lascivious of insects! I would rather die, sir.'

He brushes the crumbs from his beard. 'You take a foolish risk, in speaking to me so rudely. Remember who I am, and who you are. Your grand ways edge you ever closer to the gutter. You are nothing but an ageing whore.'

'A plague on you, Inchbald!' I call after him, as he goes hobbling on his way.

The plague. I wish I could unsay it. Like the Devil's name, it's better not to mention this curse upon our times. And down on

the harbour-side the busy ships are disgorging men and cargo from the furthest limits of the fevered globe. The wind picks up, the sky darkens. I feel the first sharp tang of autumn, and pull my cloak tighter around me. I look up, at the chasing clouds, knowing that what seems bleak now will soon look like Paradise.

'*The plague is coming*,' whispers a voice, and I look to see who speaks. But there is no one there. I stop: surely the voice was that of the old crone from the Fair? What do these creatures want, who stalk me with their foul predictions?

When I return home, I seek out *Malleus Maleficarum* and open it. I read till the candle has burned down and the words are scorched into my mind. We women, it seems, have a penchant for devilment, being so lascivious and lustful. A lecherous woman might lie with the Devil and become a witch in consequence. I remember my forced copulation with Wriothesley and Will's poisonous verse: this was how he saw me. '*All witchcraft comes from carnal lust*,' declaims the pamphlet, '*which in women is insatiable.*' And their device for recruiting new witches is to make something go amiss in the life of a respectable matron or young virgin, so that they consult a sorceress, and are tempted into witchcraft in their turn. I think about this for a long time, wondering if those fairground furies might have such a scheme in mind. But I am not like the other matrons, whose skill lies in the churning of butter and the fattening of geese. I am as clever as any man, and as cunning as any witch.

Scene VII

In my opinion, if we are made in God's image, it is God that we see dangling from the gibbet, and it is God's work to end a human life, not Man's. I know I am alone in this thought, as in so many others. But this scruple of mine about the executioner's craft has made any gallows-place a place of horror to me: I have no love for an execution. And there is no gallows-place more horrible than Tyburn Cross. It is a lonely, God-forsaken place, and the winds seem to sweep in from in all directions. The Triple Tree is a large triangular structure that stands upon the northwest road, in the way of passing traffic, so that the carters and horsemen can see what will befall those who break the English law. The ingenuity of its construction is that as many as twenty-four felons may be hanged at once, which is an expedient measure, as there is no shortage of murderers or cutpurses to keep the hangman busy. Beyond the Tree is an open field where soldiers are shot for their misdemeanours: I suppose this is of some benefit to them, as they die with their guts inside them, more or less.

When I was young, not long after I was married, I saw them execute poor Robert Southwell. He was a devout Jesuit, and tried to make the sign of the Cross with his pinioned arms, before quoting Romans: '*For Christ is the end of the law for righteousness to all that believeth.*' They wanted to bowel him alive, as they do all traitors, but Charles Blount and some of the other nobles jumped up and hugged Southwell's legs until his neck broke, to save him that final agony. He died so bravely that after his corpse was bowelled and quartered, and his blood flooded

169

across the highway, the assembled crowd was silent. There were no cheers or catcalls, and no one shouted 'Traitor!' in the customary way. And that silence filled me with a fragile hope for all of us, that we could recognise true goodness and respect it, even as the hangman acted out his ritual butchery in the name of Law.

I think of that day as I walk to Tyburn. It was fitting that Southwell was a Jesuit, for they are often accused of idolatry and witchcraft. Healing relics and icons are part of the Old Religion, but they have no place in the new one, and Catholic priests are sometimes accused of 'Devil-conjuring' among their many other crimes. Devil-conjuring is not a skill I'd take up lightly.

I watch the heavy carts clattering along the centre of the pitted roadway, while parties of horsemen overtake them, trotting briskly. Not many women to be seen today – just one or two ladies riding side-saddle. It's a position both ungainly and undignified, as if riding a horse sensibly is the proper business of a man. Did Diana the Huntress ride all skewed over in her lady's saddle? I think not. For the most part, men ride, while women have nothing better than their own legs to carry them.

It's a pale, sickly afternoon, with a foul wind. I walk slowly, unwilling to arrive. Tyburn is an evil place – they say that Satan walks there, and I can well believe it. As I come nearer, I see there is a row of corpses hanging from the Tree. I do not look close, but notice that one is a woman. The poor creature's breasts are showing through her torn dress. A kite is perched on the Tree, proud and puff-chested, as if displaying its wealth. When I am a few yards away, I stop, looking first one way down the high road and then the other. Black clouds loom overhead and rain begins to fall. I take shelter under an elm tree and watch the travellers passing by. I think of the ships landing at the quayside, and the rats scurrying behind the wainscot, and the stench of the dunghills piled against each common house, and the wrath of

God and a thousand things besides, and wonder which of these is to blame for the plague. God surely has a gift for punishment. We are accustomed to horror and fear, and so Hell is easier to summon in a fresco or imagination than Heaven, a place of obscure cloud and blurred inaction. Job has many brothers (and sisters) in his suffering and pain.

Time passes, and I have the strange sensation of watching it go on its way, in the guise of carriages and horsemen and herds of geese. At last, I see that the road has emptied, and night has snuffed out the feeble sun. All I can hear is the swish of the falling rain. There are no stars, but the moon shines bleakly through the clouds. The silvery light gives the world a shifting luminescence, and most objects are silhouettes. A solitary carriage clatters by me, pennants fluttering. It rounds the corner, heading for Oxford, and disappears from sight. Once more, the road is deserted except for a troop of muddy dogs, sniffing and snapping at each other. Then the leader of the pack – a barrel-bodied mastiff – raises its head, listening. It howls, and runs back along the London road. The other dogs follow, barking fiercely.

Swallowing, I turn my gaze back towards the Tyburn Tree. Five of the corpses still dangle against the wet sky. But the sixth – the woman – is lying on the ground, beneath a severed rope. Three figures are crouching over her. One of them is sawing at her neck with a long knife. I gather myself and begin to walk slowly towards them. As I approach, I feel the air thicken around me, and the sounds of voices come through the rain's hiss, as if conjured from its pattering repetition.

'Bassano.'

'Bassano.'

'Aemilia Bassano.'

'No, she's Lanyer now; they tied her to the fool.'

'But it's Bassano that we know, my dears.'

'Aemilia Bassano.'

'Bassano.'

The rain falls in sheets, half-blinding me, and I can't see my way clearly till I am right by the Tree. The three dark figures are standing around a black cauldron that bubbles and steams upon a fire of blue flame, which leaps and crackles despite the downpour. One of them is scraping the eyeballs out of the dead woman's head, and dropping the scarlet mess into the pot. Another holds a severed arm, and is busy prising out its fingernails. The third – an aged, decrepit crone – watches me with hooded eyes.

'She comes, see, sisters. Bassano comes.'

I feel a wind rise, which seems to come from the ground below me, so I am enveloped in a screaming cloud. My cloak is torn from me, and the bonnet ripped from my head, so my hair streams out behind me and I am staring at the three women.

'What do you want with me?' I shout. 'What do you mean by creeping round me and whispering of dread things, and the plague?'

They are silent, and I listen to the rain.

I gather my courage and try again. 'You have tricked my husband, and stolen my money. What is the meaning of this? Tell me! I demand to know.'

'She challenges us,' says one of them.

'You don't challenge us,' says another.

'But you may seek our counsel.'

'I don't want your counsel!' I cry. 'I want you to leave me be!'

The three figures separate and walk slowly around the Tree, so that their slow footsteps mark out a circle. A spume of dark flame flies up from the cauldron, and the earth around it heaves, like boiling porridge.

'Hail, Bassano, bastard of Bishopsgate!' cries the First Witch.

'Hail, Bassano, strumpet of Stratford!' says the Second.

'Hail, Aemilia, spawn of the Equivocator!' says the Third.

'What do you mean? What are you saying?' I am shaking, my hands twisted together. Sky and earth seemed to have merged into one.

'He tricked us.'

'He tried us, sorely.'

'We gave him what he asked for, and he gave us nothing back.'

I pushed my wet hair out of my eyes. 'Who did? Who tricked you?'

The air seeps sound again, all around me.

'Bassano!'

'Bassano!'

'Baptiste Bassano!'

A spectre starts to form in the dark flames spewing from the pot. I see with horror that the face of my father is forming in the vapour. He is bloody and screaming, as I saw him in his final moments.

'What do you want from my poor father? He is dead, let him rest!'

'He would'st be great.'

'Was not without ambition.'

'But too full o' the milk of human kindness to catch the nearest way.'

'What do you *mean*?'

'Ah, yes,' say three voices. 'He is dead, but his soul escaped us. We are owed a soul.'

'A soul was promised.'

'The plague is coming,' whispers the air around me.

'The plague is coming.'

Another image begins to take shape in the flames. I see a bed with the curtains closed. As I peer at it, the curtains are slowly drawn back by invisible fingers, and I see a figure lying there, in that final stillness that is waiting for us all. It is a child, a boy, his eyes staring upwards, Heavenwards, at nothing.

'Henry!' I scream. 'No – never! You shall not have him!'

And then I am lying beneath the gibbet, and there are five bodies staring down at me, and the witches have gone. I stand

up, shivering, my limbs stiff with cold. The rain has stopped and the clouds have blown away and the half-moon is reflected by the puddled ground.

Act III

Pestilence

Scene I

Weſtminſter, December 1602

The first sign is a giant comet which shoots across the sky soon after All Souls' Day. Like a wounded star, spewing its own brightness, it streaks across the heavens. The streets are full of staring citizens, squinting upwards. Children perch on windowsills. The boldest scramble up to the roof-thatch and cling there while the flaming star lights up the firmament, so that night is day and the City is ablaze with heavenly light. Then the rumours start. People have seen angels and coffins far above their heads. The graves at St Bride's Church crack open and the dead scream warnings from below. A phantom appears each night at Fetter Lane, bowing when the clocks strike twelve. The madmen at Bedlam break out and run into the streets, rending their hair and telling all who see them they must flee. 'Death is coming!' they shout. 'Death will come upon us!'

Winter sets in, and the sense of foreboding grows stronger, even though some say that cold weather dulls the power of plague vapour. Then one evening, as I am walking home at dusk, I see him. It is a clear, frosty night, with a full moon. There is a figure up ahead, a tall man in grey. At first, I do not mind him; there are others passing to and fro, and he does not strike me as strange or fearful. But as I walk I draw nearer to him; although I am proceeding at a normal pace, his steps are faltering, slow. Is it the slushy ground that holds him up? It rained heavily before the freeze set in, and the multitude of footprints have turned the

path to mush. As I come closer, I think that I know him, but could not say where from. He is broad-shouldered and well-dressed, and his fur-trimmed cloak trails behind him on the ground. Then he staggers and cries out, falling to his knees. There is a note of despair in that cry which chills my blood. I stand for a second, not knowing if I should flee, but something pulls me forward and I go to him.

'Sir?' I say. 'Can I . . .' And then he turns his head. It is my father, as I saw him last. His eye-sockets are sightless holes; his mouth is choking forth a torrent of blood. I reach out towards him, but my hands are those of a little child.

'What did you do, dear Father?' I call out. 'What did you promise? Tell me, sir, I beg you!'

Then I am alone. The shade has vanished. Above me, the moon shines, and all is silver, silent. When I get home, I pray till dawn.

It is a long, cold winter. The Thames freezes over but the ice is not strong enough to walk on. A group of children think to test this out, and dance merrily upon the frozen surface, downriver from the Bridge. They fall through into the black water, and all are drowned. A few days later, one of them is washed ashore at Deptford. A little girl, no more than three years old, in a transparent coffin of Thames ice. She still wears her little bonnet and leather shoes. Her eyes are wide open.

And then, in the darkest days of winter, comes the worst portent of all. The Queen is dying.

'What do you mean, *dying*?' I ask Alfonso, as he shakes out his snow-covered doublet and hangs it near the fire.

He holds out his hands to the flames. 'What I say. She took ill, with a fever, then kept to her rooms. Now she is removed to Richmond.'

'With the Court?'

'Her ladies, favourites, a few physicians. She has no need of music now.'

Snow is falling against the window-panes. Outside, it has settled on the sewer ditch, making dead dogs ecclesiastic marble.

'Dear Lord!'

'She is old, Aemilia. She is not as you remember her. She has been low in spirits since poor Essex was executed. She weeps all day, they say.'

'I can't believe she's dying.'

'You thought that she would live forever?'

'Perhaps I did.'

The thought of the Queen's death makes me feel giddy, as if her presence in the world is a talisman against the Evil Eye and the worst that could befall us. This is a foolish fancy, of course. The Queen is a just a woman, now fallen into the sour humour of the aged. What's more, her reign has had its share of adversity. We have suffered bad harvests, lean winters, persecution, defeats abroad and the fear of invasion. Even the plague itself has afflicted us many times. But although the sickness has been foul, and many have died, it has never compared to the old stories about the Black Death, when the quick became the dead without warning, the Reaper took the living as they sat at cards, whole villages died and the streets were piled with corpses. Worse could come than we have known. Before her time there was blood and madness. After she goes – who can tell?

Alfonso is at home, listless and charmless, not wanted by the dying monarch. Nor by me, the hale subject. He plays his neat tunes, or goes off curled and oiled to the gaming-house, to gamble with money he doesn't have. While he goes about his business, Joan teaches me her craft. She takes me out walking in the fields and among the hedgerows, and tells me tales of faeries and hobgoblins, of the ways of spirits and the living demons who inhabit the air around us, and who watch us as we go about our daily round. Though I say it myself, I am a ready pupil. It reminds

me of being a child again, when I was taken in hand by Susan Bertie and taught my Greek and Latin. Winter is not the best time to gather herbs and flowers, but we walk by the water meadows and Joan tells me all about them: how no two meadows are alike, how farmers will give each of them a name, just as they name their cows; and how pits and ponds have their own spirits. And how everything in nature has a name, a place and a purpose. She talks of beard grass, cat's tail and cock's foot, of crowflowers and salt marsh grass, which can grow underwater for many months. What I once saw as a barren place is full of life. And London, to me a place of wonders, is to Joan a brute invasion of the ancient land.

She teaches me about her apothecary's art: where each plant grows, the time to harvest it according to its governing planet, and when it can be pressed and stored. Nightshade grows under Mercury, and is an antidote to the power of witchcraft in men and beasts alike; cottonweed cures head-aches and infestations; while fleabane is the remedy for snake-bites and for gnats and fleas. Indeed, there is not a plant or simple growing in a single meadow in any corner of our land which is not a cure for some ailment, canker or distemper. I marvel that everything Joan knows is carried in her head, for she reads a little, but not easily, and prefers to store her knowledge in her memory.

I do not tell her about the witches: I fear to tell anyone what they said about my father. The meeting had the strange quality of nightmare, and the queer dreams I have when I walk in my sleep.

Joan's remedies mean that a trickle of money comes into the house, and we live frugally. Each morning, when the chores are done, I work on my cross-gartering pamphlet. This is proving an arduous task, as I have no interest in it. I have written some poetry too, but guiltily, knowing it will earn us nothing.

One night, long after curfew, when the streets are dark and only watchmen and spirits walk, there is a fearsome knocking. I sit up in bed, alert and listening. Was it our door, or the next one?

Could it be carousing players, come for Tom? Alfonso, at home for once, is whiffling next to me, too drunk to snore wholesomely. There is the knocking once again. I kick him in the balls.

'Husband, stir yourself!'

He yelps like a drowning pup and rolls away from me.

I kick his naked arse this time. 'See who wants us down below!'

Waking with a grunt, he looks around him, oiled hair perpendicular. 'Whassis?'

Bang, bang, bang. The whole house echoes with the sound. 'Who's within?' shouts a man's voice. 'I have a message from the Queen.'

Alfonso leaps up then, all right, lights a candle and goes running down the stairs half in his doublet, naked from the waist down. 'Yes, yes, yes! I come, I come.'

I follow him, shivering in my chemise, wondering who could want a drunken pipe-player at this hour. He pulls back the stiff locks and opens the door. A pale youth is standing there, thin-faced and blue-eyed with tiredness, wearing the Queen's livery and carrying a flaming torch.

'Her Majesty demands your presence,' says the youth, bowing. 'There is a boat on the river, ready to bring you to Richmond.' His rasping breath clouds the frosty night.

Alfonso stands erect, proud as a soldier. 'I will come now. Let me dress myself.' He turns to me in triumph. 'Aemilia, where is my best wool caster? And my mended doublet, and my . . .'

The messenger bows again, and begins to cough. Recovering himself, he says, 'Forgive me, sir, but it's *Mistress* Lanyer who is wanted by Her Majesty. Commanded to wait on her, this very night.'

Richmond! It was always the Queen's favourite palace. While it lacks nothing of Whitehall's grandeur, it is removed from

the hurly burly of the town, and its magnificence seems all the greater amid the surrounding woods and fields. It is the greatest palace in the kingdom, high-walled and turreted, with a thousand chimneys and dozens of Arabian minarets. There, the Queen would receive foreign guests, flirt and fool us all, and then sweep off to the hunt. I remember how I used to watch the cavalcade departing. Elizabeth was always controlled, always cunning. She laughed hard, rode fast, and would return blooded and wet. What memories. They seem more actual than the icy wind that freezes my face as I sit huddled in the cushioned barge; clearer than the sound of an ale-house brawl that comes drifting across the water. In the boat, all is darkness. The sky is black and starless beyond the torch that flickers on the prow. But in my mind it is bright day, and I am at Richmond in a fine silk gown, looking down from the battlements across a landscape that is like a vista of the afterlife. The pale heavens are infinite, and clouds trail and shift above the distant oak forests.

As the oars dip into the freezing water and the barge slips quietly along the Thames, I feel as if it is taking me back to my youth. I remember the first time I was summoned to play for the Queen. There was a long walk from room to room; the scent of ladies and candle-wax and lavender. There were faces, all twisted and polished for looking at. And then a door opened, and there she sat, a blur of red and gold. I climbed on to the seat beside the virginals, and the keys were my friends and gave me courage, so I began to play.

When I had finished, she said, 'You are too clever, for such a little scrap of person.' (I think I was eight, or perhaps nine.)

Not knowing what to reply, I looked over at Mother, and she nodded to me to say something. I got down from my seat and curtseyed as my mother had shown me.

'I am not clever, Your Majesty,' I said. 'I work hard and . . .' I broke off, not sure if I should go on.

'Yes?' The Queen's smile was slightly colder. She found my hesitation irksome.

'And I wish to know things.'

She seemed to like this.

'Ah, child,' she said. 'We are the cleverest of all, those of us who have a love of study. The curious mind seeks nourishment. Our curiosity will make us wise.'

The messenger is silent, snuffling into his handkerchief. In front of us, a boatman rows, impassive. They seem no more inclined to talk to each other than they do to speak to me.

'How does Her Majesty?' I ask, at last.

The messenger sneezes again. 'Badly,' he says, seeming to do badly enough himself, since I hardly think this is a fit way to discuss the sickness of the monarch. He blows his nose. His face is ghastly in the torchlight. 'She is like to die within the week. She has seen no one but Robert Carey, and a few favourites. She has asked for the Archbishop.'

'Does she fear that she is dying?'

'So it seems. Richmond is a house of rumour. Some said she died weeks ago, we had seen so little of her. She keeps to her chamber, and will do nothing but walk and walk, never sitting, as if she could outpace Death himself. She will not go to her bed, but rests on cushions, on the floor.'

'I cannot imagine it.'

'She cannot imagine it herself, I believe.'

There is silence for a moment. Then, in a sudden passionate rush, the messenger says, 'Just a few weeks ago, she gave an audience to the Venetian ambassador. She was dressed in a taffeta dress of silver and gold, and a thousand gemstones. She was witty, spry, easily a match for him. Everyone said so. He came out of the throne room saying she had kept her beauty yet.' He sneezes again. I look at his sickly face in the flickering torchlight. Then, he points. 'Look, there – you see? They are waiting for you.'

And there is Richmond, a beacon in the darkness. I can see the windows of the state rooms dazzling bright, an earthly copy of the stars. Even the doors stand open, and I can see light inside, a gilded stairway, and darkly silhouetted soldiers, standing guard.

Scene II

Inside, all is blazing light. Torches are racked on every wall, lamps flame, and glittering candelabra burn above my head. Once I took this moon-dimming brightness for granted, and the world beyond it seemed a place of shadow. Now I have returned, blinking and stumbling, from the outer darkness.

I am still blinking when we reach the Presence Chamber and Lettice Cooper sets down her sewing and comes over to me. She is done up in black velvet and seed pearls, hard-faced in the midst of this abundance.

'Her Majesty is not well,' she says, somewhat needlessly in my opinion.

I curtsey, in the Court style, to remind her I am not some common housewife.

'Which circumstance requires that we do her bidding, even whilst we fear that her requests may not reflect her wishes when in her right mind.'

I curtsey again. After all, I can't spit in her eye.

'So I would ask that you do not take up more of her time than is needed.' She hands me a little silver bell. 'And you ring this when you are done.' Then she points to its companion, a larger bell, of solid gold, it looks like. 'Likewise, we will ring this if we fear that you outstay your term. Is that understood?'

'Of course,' I say, tinkling the bell, to test it.

She frowns. 'Hush. All our nerves are a-jangle.'

Another lady looks up. It's young Lady Guildford, who was a girl last time I saw her. 'They are jangled indeed,' she

185

says. 'The world is upside-down. The dead speak, and the living haunt us.'

'Hush, my dear,' says Lettice. 'We will not speak of this.'

But Lady Guildford takes my arm. She is a wisp of a woman, with a child's high voice. 'Her Majesty has been lying in her withdrawing-room these ten days,' she says, staring intensely into my eyes as if to make sure I understand the full import of her words. 'She is much afraid. She will not get into her bed, not even at the dead of night. She said to me, "If you were in the habit of seeing such things in your bed that I do, you would not ask me to go there."'

'What does she see?'

'She did not say. But there is witchcraft afoot.'

'Why do you say so?'

'Yesterday, I sat with her so long, praying and thinking, that my legs were stiff and cramping, and I went out to take a little air. I came out, through this chamber, and the throne room, and the next room, and came out halfway down the Long Gallery. You know it?' Her eyes are full of terror.

'I remember it.'

'Well. I walked along there, all distracted, thinking of the poor Queen and all her sufferings, when I heard a noise behind me, in the passageway, and I turned to see if someone called me back . . .'

She hesitates.

'And – did they?'

'At first, I could not see clearly. The candles were guttering, and the place was half in darkness. Then, I saw it was Her Majesty. I thought she had risen, feeling more herself. I thought she must have followed me. You can imagine my joy to see her so much improved. I went towards her, but then she vanished.'

'What do you mean?'

'In terror, for I knew something was strange, I ran back to her room. The ladies were all as I had left them. And the Queen lay in

that same motionless slumber that I had seen before leaving her. I had seen an apparition, a spectre. Her spirit had left its place.'

Lettice frowns. 'That is more than sufficient,' she says. 'We are all sorely tired. There is likely nothing in it. These are heavy, dangerous times. Let's keep our wits about us.'

'My wits have not deserted me,' say I. 'Much else has been taken from me, but my common sense remains.'

Lettice frowns again, and proceeds towards the grand door to Elizabeth's withdrawing-room, the inner sanctum of her suite of private chambers, and beckons me to follow her. Her hand resting on the door, she speaks to me with quiet disdain.

'You are to enter her room alone, Aemilia.'

'Good.'

'You are to speak calmly to her, and take care that she does not become alarmed.'

'I shall do as you say.'

'You will find her changed.'

'Of course.'

'Remember, she is still the Queen, and in one thing she is as she always was. She will not submit. She will not die until she chooses to. She commands; she does not obey.'

The Queen is propped up with velvet cushions, half-upright like a wooden doll. Her eyes are cast down, and she sucks one finger. Her face is a mask of white ceruse, with a clown-mark of vermilion on each cheek. Below her chin hangs a great wattle of loose flesh, and this too is daubed with white. And she is wearing a splendid gown, a stiff and glistering carapace, encrusted with a multitude of gem-stones.

I stand just inside the door to her bedchamber – a room I have never entered before – not sure what to do next. It is hard to believe that we are quite alone. Every time that I saw her, in all my years at Whitehall, even when she had summoned me to speak Latin

to her or play my virginals to soothe her mind, there were others present. Hunsdon, Cecil, Dudley, a clutch of ladies, a couple of ambassadors. She moved around in a throng of obsequious advisors and hopeful acolytes. Now, there is no one. Breathless, I look around the cavernous room, lit by silver sconces. After my little house I feel I am truly in the land of giants. A fire – great enough to roast an ox – crackles in the stone fireplace. The high bed, carved and gilded and hung with cloth-of-gold and silver, looms high in the centre of the room. It is as big as a stage; its closely patterned curtains remind me of the heavy drapes before the Globe's tiring-room. The valance is cloth-of-silver, heavily fringed with gold, silver and silken threads, and decorated with the shapes of beasts. The canopy is set off with feathered plumes. Beyond it is a painted mural, showing Our Lord as a child talking to the elders, then as a grown man preaching to the crowd, and finally kneeling in the Garden of Gethsemane. And above all this is the carved ceiling, vari-coloured in the flame-light, embellished with the likenesses of deer and boar, pursued by leggy hounds among the twisting trees and leaves. It is as if all the Queen's old joys and pastimes are here to taunt her.

Only Christ is left to her. But she is not looking at Him. She is looking at the floor, as if she made a study of the finely patterned Turkey carpet on which she lies. I stand for so long that in the end I think I must withdraw. What if these are her final moments? Or if she is already dead? I am not the right person to be present.

But just as I am about to leave the room, she speaks, though hoarsely and not in her familiar voice. 'Is that really you, Aemilia Bassano?'

'It is, Your Majesty. Except . . .'

I was never good at speaking with enough care for the Court.

'Except?' She takes her finger from her mouth, and looks at me.

'I am Aemilia Lanyer now. Your Majesty.'

'Oh, indeed. Married off for colour, with your misbegot.' She coughs and shifts her body. 'Come close, come closer. I want to look at you properly.'

I approach her. Her eyes, once shrewd and mocking, are faded and tired. She has a rank, rotting smell about her. Her shimmering dress with its armour of jewels seems to imprison her where she sits, in her awkward position. She is quite still. Only her eyes move, studying me. 'Aemilia,' she says, finally. Her hand comes out, fingers swollen now, no longer elegant, the cracked nails vermilion like her cheeks. 'You are the most welcome sight, most welcome. And still beautiful, for all you are dressed like some village drab.'

I bow my head. 'Thank you, Your Majesty.'

She sighs, and pushes my arm away. 'Not "Majesty", please, not now. Be sparing in your language. My own words tire me, but so do those of other people. There is so little time.' She stretches out her left hand, and shows me her wedding finger. 'Look. I am bone-thin, but my hands are swelled! They had to cut my coronation ring right off me – see? My wedding band is gone. I am divorced from Albion. I am lost.'

I can't think what to say, so I kneel down beside her on the floor.

We sit in silence for a moment, staring at the fire.

'Are you wondering why I have asked to see you?' The Queen shifts slightly in her robe.

'I – hardly thought it my place to question anything, madam. I am grateful that you have called me here.'

'No, Aemilia, no. I don't believe that this is true. You are always seeking to know the reason for things, and I have rarely seen you grateful. You know your own worth; I always liked that in you.'

I smile in spite of myself. 'I thought, perhaps, you wanted to talk to me because I am better-read than your ladies, and their Latin is somewhat poor.'

She nods. 'You understand more than most, Aemilia, and I learned from Hunsdon's good opinion of you that you are true, and loyal, and a keeper of secrets.'

'Thank you,' say I, sounding unlike myself.

'I see myself in that fire,' she says. 'My little person, burned by flames, but never consumed. I see myself burning in Hell.'

'No! It cannot be so. They are waiting for you in Heaven. They will have prepared a throne right next to God Himself.'

'I shan't get into that great bed,' she says. 'Death is in there, you know. I saw him, staring round the drapes at me.'

'A trick of the light, madam.'

'Don't humour me. For you, a trick of the light. For me, no. My time is near. I should know. I chose it. I have a heat inside my breasts, Aemilia, which will not go. And around my throat an iron claw. I cannot swallow. The appetites of life are past.'

'But . . .'

'But? But what? Do you question your Prince?'

'We still need you.'

'Ha! Carey waits on my death so he can ride off to Scotland. Even though I have yet to let them know whether my studious Scottish cousin shall succeed me.'

'The people love you.'

Now she laughs, an odd sound, like tearing paper. 'They are tired of me, as I am tired of life.' Then she stops, very sudden, and stares at something past me. I look over my shoulder at the empty room, flickering and glimmering in the light of flames.

'Do you know why I am here?' she asks. 'At Richmond?'

'Because Whitehall is too cold?'

'No. This is my warm winter box, but I would have kept at Whitehall longer, had I dared. No. John Dee told me to come here. Or rather, he told me to go from there. So off we all came, all the boatloads of us, but much difference it made.' She glances towards the closed door as if to make sure that we aren't overheard. 'I want to die, you see. I want to be gone. Whether

Heaven or Hell will receive my soul, I know I am all but done with this life. But the journey out is full of pain.'

'I am sorry for that.'

'Don't spend your sorrow on me. Your turn will come, and I doubt you will be lying on a Turkey rug, as I am, with a blazing fire to warm you.'

'I doubt it too.'

'My mind is not still; it keeps flitting hither and thither, the past is before me. And, as it flitted, it saw *you*. For all your learning, a restless spirit. Is that not so?'

'It is.'

'Like me. I always saw it in you.'

'Like you! I would not presume to think so.'

'A bastard, like myself.'

'A bastard, yes.'

'And mother to a bastard child.'

'Better a bastard than the child of Captain Lanyer.'

She shakes her head, very slowly. 'Ah, we are more like each other than you know. And you are not mellowed with the years?'

'I am not mellowed.'

'Good. Hunsdon would be proud of you. And how does the boy?' I see that her eyes have filled with tears.

'He is well. I love him dearly, too much. He is his father's son.'

'And who would that be, Dark Aemilia?'

I look down.

'I always wondered if Hunsdon could really keep you to himself. And you were a wild one, mistress. Don't imagine that it went unnoticed.'

I say nothing.

'Nothing about *you* could go unnoticed,' she says, quietly. 'I used to watch you. Sometimes I thought you could be my obscure twin, a dark shadow of my own self. It has been hard enough for

me to use my mind – how must it be for poor Aemilia? If ever a woman was born out of her right place, it was you.'

I look away. In my mind's eye I see a child's hands spreading over ivory keys. They are ink-stained and the nails are bitten. I see a young woman in a yellow dress, glittering with jewels and borrowed pride.

'And there are more similarities between us than you know – more links between our two fates.' She pauses. 'And now . . . wife to a recorder player.'

'Yes, madam.'

'Is he a proper husband to you?'

'I couldn't say.'

'You hoped for more.'

'Wedlock is a narrow business.'

She laughs her tearing laugh again. 'Oh, Mistress Lanyer! You can still amuse me. Narrow, too narrow, you have it right. The bastards have the best of it.'

I hesitate again, not certain what to say. The Queen smiles, very thinly. 'It is an odd thing, but as I sit here, trapped in my own crock of bones, and as the world shrinks, as it must, something else happens. Do you know what that is?'

I nod. 'The world is far from you, so you see the pattern. I sometimes think of London the way a kite must see it. From above.'

'Sharp Aemilia. I should have made you Chancellor. If only I could have done. Yes. I see the world from far off, so though I am lodged here in my tiny room, propped next to my great bed of death, I see my life all clear, like the most wonderful tapestry of nonsense and pity.'

I watch her clown's face, lined with sadness.

'My esteemed brother-in-law, Philip, King of all Spain, of the Americas, the high seas, ended in a tiny room. No different, when he died in the Escorial, than the humblest of his servants. The world stretched from that palace, a great and grand dominion.

But in the end it was no longer his. He had to leave it.'

'And yet, it is a fine thing, to rule. You are not like other people.'

She flaps her hand, as if batting away the foolishness of this thought. She looks again into the corner of the room, and again I turn, wondering what she sees. As she speaks, her eyes are steady on this unseen presence. 'They cut her head off while she prayed. Did you know that?

'I did not know that.' I do not even know who she speaks of, but I dare to guess.

'The executioner, hot from Calais, got his man to catch my mother's eye, and slashed his blade right through her neck, in that moment. Cut right through the muscle and bone. He did his job well. Her lips were moving even as her head fell down into the straw.'

Now, I truly cannot speak. I cannot breathe.

The Queen presses on, remaining curiously still, as if all her living was in her head. 'Was that mercy? Do you think? To smite her before she knew, but also before she had finished her prayers? Did she die in grace?'

'I cannot tell. I pray to God she did.'

'They said she was a witch. Will God forgive a witch? Is it a mortal sin? There is a place for every creature, for every leaf and blossom of the Lord's creation. Even beggars. A wild rogue has his position, and an Abraham man, who rants and preaches in his rags. So witches, too, they must have a portion of their own.'

'That must be so, madam.'

'I thought to learn the craft, from Dr Dee, but it is harder than Greek or Latin.' She sucks her finger again, childish. 'I can read the Tarot. Such pretty cards.'

'Evil's in them, madam, if you ask me. I always draw the Devil.'

'One day, Dr Dee prepared a chart for me. In my privy chamber, just outside this door, I will never forget. And then he

refused to let me see. Later, I found out why. He saw it coming, this terrible duty. That I would be forced to kill my own kind. First Mary Stuart. God forgive me. I meted out to her what my father meted out to my poor mother.'

'No prince would have done otherwise.'

'And yet. That is not it . . . I killed my son. Robert Devereux, my dearest, bastard son. Not one clean blow for him, no! Three strikes of the axe. Mangled and bloodied, in an agony that *I* inflicted on him!'

'Madam, I – '

'Dreadful, most dreadful pain and suffering, that, but for me, he need never have endured! My little one, a traitor at my breast. Oh, I shall go straight to Hell! I am burning now!'

I fear she is out of her wits. 'Your Majesty – madam – you should rest now.'

She looks around her, as if she is unsure of her safety. 'They say I rule England like a king. But my duty is a prison. Would that I had the other power, that hideous, demonic gift!'

'What gift?'

'The greater one. That which makes castles into air, and air into castles. I would have done some mischief then. Sunk the Armada with the foul gale of my hag's breath. Torn down the Tower walls, and thrown the scaffold to the winds so he could go free, my naughty, upstart boy! Opened up the seven gates of London so he could gallop forth, go anywhere, in peace and freedom.'

'Oh, madam . . .'

'I dream it is so, I still dream it is so.' She starts. 'Are we alone? Is Hecate here? She is a greater Queen than I.'

'We are alone. But, madam – '

'And did I summon you, or did you come by chance?'

'You summoned me.'

'Ah, yes. You live at Long Ditch. You are married to that ape Alfonso.' She pauses, and squeezes my hand again. 'I have a

warning for you. That is why I have called you here. It concerns this thing, this matter of witchcraft. Dr Dee has told me something which concerns you . . .'

A bell tinkles. The Queen frowns. 'Tell them to go away. I am still their monarch, and I wish to speak to you for longer.'

I open the door a crack, and see Lettice Cooper's frowning face. 'Please leave us,' I say. 'Her Majesty wishes it.'

'Isn't Her Majesty done with you?' she asks.

'Done with me?'

'Address me as "my lady".'

'I have told you. My lady. She is not ready.'

'Would she not care for a drop of rose-water?' Her words are solicitous, but her tone is ice-cold. Before I can speak, there is an odd sound from the Queen behind me. I turn, and she is trying to rouse herself from her place, but is weighted down by the jewelled robe. One hand is raised, but, instead of words, all that comes this time is a strange cry, like the call of a gull. Lettice Cooper pushes past me, in a rustle of damask and velvet, and I stand back as she soothes the Queen, and offers her rose-water, which Elizabeth declines, turning her head away and pursing her lips tight shut. Then she points to me. Somewhat unwilling, Lettice nods to me. The Queen seems unable to summon her former strength, and stares at me for a moment, her eyes seeking mine as if I could explain a mystery that is puzzling her. She raises her hand again, beckoning me near. I stoop before her, obliged to lean over Lettice and her glistening skirts; she does not shift an inch.

'Wait . . .' The Queen stops.

I lean closer.

'Sa . . .'

'Your Majesty?'

She pulls me forward so that our cheeks touch. Her stench is overwhelming. Then she whispers, 'Save the boy. By fair means or foul. I could not save mine. Save yours. Guard him.'

Scene III

News of the Queen's illness has spread. London is silent, waiting. The ports are closed by government decree, and the dockyards stand empty. There is barely a sound along the alleyways and cat-creeps, or among the mean hovels in the east, or the grand courtiers' houses at the river's edge. The sound of hammering has ceased, the church bells have been muffled and even the dogs have stopped fighting. Only the sound of birds remains: the soft song of the woodpigeon, the peewit's cry, the seagulls calling and squawking, sometimes with the screams of dying babes, sometimes the chatter of Tower monkeys. The weather has changed, too. The snow has melted, and unseasonable sunlight floods the empty streets. Wild flowers have opened their petals, fooled by the early heat. The bluebell fields of Charing Cross are an azure wasteland.

It is a freakish spring, and these are strange days. I know we are willing Elizabeth to die. The golden time is over, and something else must follow. The old Queen seems as ancient as London Bridge itself, as relentless as the river tide, as long-lasting as a Sunday sermon. Now her life, like everything on earth, must end.

This is the subject of Father Dunstan's homily. He is a miserable, choleric old man, and he has taken the occasion of her illness, and the convenient deaths of several children of Long Ditch parish, as an excuse to ruminate upon the similarity of Flesh to Grass, and, by his religious logic, the need to obey the Word of God. He has chosen as his text, as is his usual habit, one of the *Homilies* most thoughtfully provided by poor Archbishop

Cranmer, who later plunged the very hand that wrote these words into the fire. The subject is 'Against Disobedience and Wilful Rebellion' and the method – again one our good priest is wont to use – the brute punishment of boring us to death. Father Dunstan's borrowed sermons, read out from his weighty book, are often two hours long.

So the droning progresses thus: *'. . . and as GOD would have man to be his obedient subject, so did he make all earthly creatures subject unto man, who kept their due obedience unto man, so long as man remained in his obedience unto GOD . . . in which obedience, if man had continued still, there had been no poverty, no diseases, no sickness, no death, nor other miseries wherewith mankind is now infinitely and most miserably afflicted . . .'*

He booms the words over the pulpit at us, daring us to daydream at the white-limed walls. I look down at Henry, who is scuffing his shoe round, making a circle in the strewing-herbs. I frown and pretend to cuff the top of his head, and he squints up at me, half-smiling.

'. . . He not only ordained that in families and households the wife should be obedient unto her husband, the children unto their parents, the servants unto their masters: but also . . .'

Alfonso, who was at the gaming tables last night, has his head bowed, his hands clasped before him, as if in prayerful thought.

'. . . the root of all vices, and mother of all mischiefs, was Lucifer, first GOD's most excellent creature, and most bounden subject, who by rebelling against the Majesty of GOD, of the brightest and most glorious Angel, is become the blackest and most foulest fiend and . . .'

Joan is standing a little apart from the three of us. She is staring at the priest, her green eyes giving nothing away. As I watch, I notice that she is rocking to and fro, to and fro, slowly, as if a gentle song were lulling her to sleep.

But then, as if he has observed that we are dozing through his tedious words, Father slams the book shut, and fixes the

congregation with a furious gaze. 'When Death comes for us, we must make our reckoning. We cannot tarry, we cannot bargain, we cannot name the day we are ready to meet our Maker. We must go when we are called, and there is no way back from the gates of Hell.' He seems to be staring at me, though I know this is how each person feels in a great crowd, confronted by a lone orator. The priest isn't addressing me, any more than Burbage aims his monologues at one particular groundling in the crowded Globe.

'Which of us will live to see Midsummer? Which of us will light a flame for Candlemas? Who will see another winter? Hmm? I ask you? Who can say this?'

Mouths gape. Eyes open. A lap-dog growls. 'Death is coming – for you, just as surely as for the Great and Good. Do not feel your Prince is nearer to the grave than Thee. There is not one of us that knows that we will live to see another dawn . . .'

Oh, Lord preserve us. I hate this worship of the dead.

'They say the plague ships are come from distant places, the Indies, and the Azores. They are docked now, at the quayside, by East India House. None can know what causes us to die when the sickness comes. The barrels are rolled into the taverns. The sailors are gone among us. It is God who sends the pestilence, and only God can save us. Fear him.'

I notice a man on Joan's left side, at the end of our pew. He is a brown-skinned, wrinkled peasant, a stranger in the parish. He regards the priest with an air of confusion and unease, blinking as if he can't quite see. He takes a dirty napkin from his leather doublet and mops his face, which dribbles sweat and is mottled purple. Joan catches my glance, and looks at him. Even as she turns, I see the bubo on his neck, yellow as a head of corn. He drops down on his knees. 'Lord have mercy!' he shouts. 'Lord have mercy on us!' It is the plague cry, the words the doomed daub upon their houses. And he vomits a bellyful of bile right out upon the herbs and rue. The old peasant might have the sweating sickness or the clap; he might have eaten a plate of mouldy mutton – it makes no

odds to me. I see that horrid image conjured by the witches: the dead child still in his bed. My skin goes cold. I take Henry's hand, push past Alfonso and run to the end of the pew.

'Do not run from Death!' shouts the priest.

'I run towards Life, Father,' I call over my shoulder. With Henry's hand clasped firm in mine, I run towards the back of the church.

'Jezebel!' he shouts. 'How dare you speak to your priest in this manner? Remember your place, and be silent.'

It's almost enough to make you laugh. What fools does God take us for? But I have no breath for laughing; I am turning the great iron catch on the church door, then pushing it open. Outside, it is a bright spring day. I look back and see all the rows of faces, turned towards me, and the priest, pale with anger, leaning over the pulpit.

I wake, suddenly. All is darkness: it is the dead of night. Aptly named. I know the Queen has gone. Did I hear a noise? A cry? A scream? A fired musket? Something has disturbed the blackest hour. I push back the eiderdown, and go to the window. Opening it quietly, I look both ways, up and down our street. The cold night air smokes my breath. There is nothing to be seen. All is silent beneath the stars. The only living creature is a house-cow, tethered opposite. She dozes by the water conduit, sleeping on her feet. Behind me, Alfonso rolls onto his back and sets to snoring louder. I crane my head to look westward, towards Richmond, but I am hemmed in with brick smoke-stacks and tight-sewn thatch.

The good news about the death of the Queen is that Alfonso is employed again. All the Court recorder players are summoned to Whitehall, to rehearse some new tunes for the funeral. They brought her corpse from Richmond in a lead coffin, and she is lying

in state at Westminster Hall to await the orders of King James of Scotland, soon to be King of England. The bad news is that we are still in a state of anxious waiting. The Queen is dead, but where is this new Prince? Alfonso says he is processing down from Scotland in grand style, meeting his northern subjects along the way. So we are suspended in a nowhere place between two monarchs. And, just as spirits walk between Christmas and Twelfth Night, so idle and malicious talk fills up this space. For evil is about us and among us, evil acts are more common than saintly deeds, wicked men prosper and the good starve; angels are frailer in our world than night's black agents, and in this dark and shifting place of nightmare we must seek protection where we may.

Rumours spring up and run along the streets. They say Elizabeth never saw her own face in her dotage, that her cheating courtiers gave her a magic mirror that reflected only what she had been in her youth. That when at last she saw her true self, aged, unadorned and ugly, she died of grief. (This was false, I knew. It was a twisted version of the truth, which was that John Dee gave her an obsidian mirror, and that she knew most precisely what its powers were, and valued it most highly.) And they say that her body was so racked with vile disease that it swelled monstrously and exploded, bursting forth from her coffin. I think this must be falsehood too, but then remember her swelling fingers and the missing coronation ring.

My husband has had plenty of time to learn his new tunes. But now, the day of her funeral has come.

'Wife, bring me my tasselled stockings!'

'They are on the bed, Alfonso.'

'Wife, my trunk hose! Be quick about it!'

'You are wearing your trunk hose. Arse-brain.'

'Wife . . .'

'Silence, husband! Put your clothes on, which are spread before you. You may be the master of your music, but you do not command your spouse.'

Off he flounces in a sulky humour. I watch him go, his pretty steps all dainty down the filthy street. I wonder, as I do so, what Will is wearing to bid his Queen farewell, and who has helped him with *his* trunk hose, and found his shirt, and watched him dress. Such thoughts can still confound me, so that time seems twisted and love and hate are twinned. But then Henry comes up behind me. 'Mother, shall we go and get a good place now? Tom says he will stand in King Street, to get a proper view.'

'I may go to King Street, young man, but you will stay inside the house with Joan.'

'But Mother – '

'But nothing. In this, for once, you will obey me. You know what I have said about the plague. Two dead in this street already. In the parish, seventeen. You must stay at home, and learn your lessons from your hornbook, and behave.'

'But – '

I raise my hand to him. 'Henry, if you do not do as I say, I will beat you. I will.'

'But you are going – '

I slap him hard across his cheek and his eyes are hard and angry.

'I hate you.'

'Good. I am your mother. This is as it should be.'

Outside, the streets are filled with a fairground throng of watchers and mourners. The way is blocked with every manner of person, old and young, men and women, ale-wives and aldermen, cozeners and cripples, all herded together, head to head and cheek to cheek. Had I not wished to see her one last time I would keep indoors myself, for I can see that, whatever miasma or mist brings the plague, we are all piling together in a manner most favourable to its passing on.

Anne Flood bustles up, done out like a Venetian courtesan.

'Come along, come quickly,' she says. 'We shall miss the best of it if we don't make haste.'

I have been avoiding her since Inchbald told me of their arrangement. Now I can no longer hold my peace. 'What's this I hear, about how you pay your rent? No wonder you can afford such dainty ruffs.'

She rolls her eyes. 'Will you judge me, for wishing to survive? Since Mr Flood passed on, I have lived on my wits, and what little he left me.'

'But lying with Inchbald! Anne! Does he not make you retch?'

'Certainly.' She gives me a piercing look. 'I consider you my good friend, Aemilia. And you told me once that you think of another man when Alfonso fucks you, though you are too close to tell me who it is. If you had to suck a dwarf's tiny cock to keep yourself respectable, you'd have my pity, not my contempt.'

I shrug, and we walk in silence for a while. This other man, this secret incubus of mine, is Will, of course. My demon lover. For a while, my skin prickles with the memory of lust. Hot lust, cold words. That's my great love. That's his legacy.

Then, overcome with curiosity, I ask, 'How tiny?'

She laughs. 'I've seen bigger on a newborn hedge-pig. Here, take this.' She passes me half an orange, which I press to my nose to mask the street-stink as we hurry along.

We come to the bottom of King Street and we can see the palace gates. The procession is upon us. First come the black-robed bell-ringers and marshall's men, calling, 'Make way, make way!' and clearing a passage through the crowds. They are followed by a procession of poor women – and just a few poor men – marching four abreast, all in black, eyes cast down. Then come artisans, messengers and servants from the Queen's woodland and stable. Then follow empty carts driven by stable boys, and two of her horses, riderless. One is covered in a black cloth, the other in black velvet. And this is but the start of it. Trumpeters blast their horns at the crowd, to keep us back, and sergeants-at-arms pace along the line.

Now come the standard-bearers, with the great symbols of the Tudor house: the Dragon, the Greyhound, the Lion and the Portcullis. Then the fifty-nine musicians – and there's my sweet husband, quite the prettiest of them all. Then the apothecaries, physicians and minstrels of the Court. Parliament, the Privy Seal, the gentlemen and children of the Chapel Royal, all singing a mournful tune. Here is Lord Zouche carrying the banner of Cheshire, Lord Herbert with the banner of Cornwall. Next came the Mayor and aldermen of London, and the gentlemen pensioners, with their axes carried downward. On and on they go. Here is the Welsh banner, there is Ireland, and there goes the French ambassador. His train is carried by a retinue of page-boys. It must be six yards long.

Anne is weeping at my shoulder. 'I shall never forget this!' she says. 'The poor Queen! God rest her!'

I see a weeping widow cut a purse, and pretend not to. I see a wet-nurse slap a baby to keep it quiet. I look for Will. I long to see him – and dread the sight of him.

At last we see the hearse itself, a chariot pulled by four horses in trappings of black velvet. As if this were one of her great triumphal processions, the Queen is there in person, a life-size waxwork, as magnificent in death as she ever was in life. The painted effigy reclines upon her coffin, dressed in Parliament robes, with a crown upon its head, and a sceptre in its hands. Above the hearse is a canopy, carried by six earls, with a dozen lesser nobles carrying six banners alongside.

'I never saw such a thing!' says Anne. 'I never did!'

'It's a shame her waxen self can't rule us,' I say, 'rather than some Scottish prince who knows as much of England as I do of France.'

'Oh, what will become of us?' Anne cries out. 'The pity of it! The pity of it!'

I watch the chief mourner pass, Lady Northampton, her black train carried by two countesses. It looks like a procession

from the Underworld itself. In my memory I see the Queen
laughing, striding, picking up her skirts to make more speed. I
see her drinking a glass of watered wine, accusing Blanche Parry
of making it too strong. I see her straighten the gold circlet upon
her curled red hair, when her beauty could still be faked for a
grand occasion. And I see her face, that last time, fallen into a
death-mask beneath the clown's paint.

As the hearse rumbles past, there is a general sighing,
groaning and weeping.

'God rest Your Majesty! God rest your soul!'

'Lord save you, for all eternity!'

'Lord Jesu, save us all!'

Suddenly, there is a terrible scream and the plague cry: 'Lord
have mercy on us!'

'Back, back,' shouts someone. 'See who comes – a plague-
mort! Mind yourselves . . .'

A young maiden is pushing to the front of the crowd. The
people fall back, more anxious to avoid her than to see the coffin
of our departed Queen. Once, this girl must have looked a little
like Elizabeth. She has the same bright red hair, crinkled and
shot with gold, and the same fair skin. But her beauty has been
blasted. Her eyes are sunken and bloodshot. Her face is swollen
and purple with plague-spots. The skin of her bare arms and
legs is covered in weeping lesions. She is half-naked, wearing
nothing but a linen undershift, torn and bloodied and hanging
from her shoulders. She cries out, and runs at the procession, but
a sergeant-at-arms pushes her back.

'Leave off – away!' he shouts, shoving her with his cere-
monial lance.

The distracted creature puts her head back and screams
again – such a soul-sick sound! She tears at her smock, grunting
and laughing, so it hangs down in front of her to show her white
breasts, covered in evil sores, putrid and stinking. There is barely
an inch of her that isn't riven and bleeding, as though she had

been flayed with a whip. She turns to face the crowd. 'You should kill me!' she calls out. Her voice is soft and childish. She catches the arm of an old man, standing next to me. He shakes her off, white with fear. 'Who will kill me? Who will cut my throat?'

No one speaks. The procession moves on. Now the Queen's ladies pass by, in orderly completeness, as if they can neither see us, nor hear us.

'You would slay me if I was a dog!'

'By Jesu, what are you all? Will no one help her?' Father Dunstan forces his way to the front. He pulls the maiden to her feet, and wraps her in his cloak. 'Shame on you!' he shouts.

The girl is chattering again. The cloak hides everything but her bright hair.

'Will you slay me, Father? Will you throw me to the dogs at Bankside? Or shall I poison them? Shall I poison them, Father?' But then she begins to convulse like a hanging man, and her mouth foams. Father Dunstan drags her away, through the parting crowd.

Scene IV

London is my home. A horde of bloody prentice-boys shouting
'Clubs!' can make me smile. I love the filthy bustle, and
would as soon hear the shout of the night watch as the song
of a nightingale. But we breathe yellow, corrupted air that
chars our throats. Even our snot is black with soot. The petty
pains of daily life are cruel enough. So it's not always plain
what is plague, and what is not. And the fear that every ague
and pustule is the harbinger of certain death can haunt the best
of us.

So. There is first a fever, but the sun is hot, the day is long; we
may need no more to cure it than a draft of small beer. Then there
is the vomiting – but who in London does not throw up their
guts from time to time? We are careful never to eat raw fruit from
the tree, but still the lurgy gets us. Every time we puke up in the
chamber-pot, we think we are victims of a poisoner's craft. But
there are signs, Lord help us, and, when these come, we know
the end is near. God preserve us from the swelling, for that is a
portent of the end indeed. And though there are those who live,
they are few, and strong. It starts like a strain, a pain that stretches
down an arm, or around the groin, but then focuses its evil into
one place. Which place is fixed to be a bubo, a sac of heavy poison
that will kill in moments if it bursts within your body. The ones
who live are those whose buboes split outside their skin, so the
fluid may be drained off. For whatever humour you may have
– phlegmatic, sanguine, choleric, melancholic – none blends
happily with this vile contaminant.

It is early summer. I am sitting at my hearth place, reading. Joan is standing at the doorway, looking out into the street, with that look of sour enjoyment with which she likes to greet disaster.

'It's a merry do,' she says. 'The dead outnumber the living all over the City. Heaven and Hell are bulging at the gate. St Bride's yard is full, and St Olave's. If it takes us off now, we shall be buried in the ditch.'

'Thank you for those cheering words, Joan. If you can't say anything more uplifting, go upstairs and tell your beads.' Rosaries are forbidden by the law, but I know she has one hid beneath her bedstead in a casket.

She takes no notice of me. 'The City pageant has been cancelled.'

'I know it.'

'Jack Mellor, that ran amok yesterday with his sores all out, was put to death this morning.'

'I know.'

'Cruel, I call it.'

'He would have died anyway,' say I.

'I was talking to the dog-catcher at St Margaret's, and he has killed more than five hundred hounds. Five hundred!'

'No wonder the streets are quiet.'

'Seventy-two parishes infected, Mistress Flood told me. And there are nine houses boarded up in Westminster, and eleven souls are newly dead. It stalks us close.'

I put my book down. 'For pity's sake, Joan! What do you want of me? Henry is kept from school. The house is full of onions and garlic. We have sweet herbs in every room: the physick garden is bare. And we pray.'

'I know it, mistress. We are taking every care we can.'

'What more can I do? Shall I lie down and weep in the fireplace? Shall I fill my hair with ashes? We are not dead yet. We shall sit it out.'

'Says who? Has the Almighty sent you word?'

'Don't be insolent. You are my servant, not my keeper.'

'Oh, and are the two so very far apart? Who would keep you, if not old Joan? Not your popinjay husband, that's for sure.'

This is quite enough. I get to my feet, ready to strike her. But she says, 'Mistress, you know I would do everything in my power to help you.'

I let my hand fall. 'Yes.'

'But what I can offer . . . my skills and remedies . . . they won't save us.'

'No.'

'There is something evil here.'

I have tried not to think of the witches, but they are never far from my mind. 'Joan – there is something that I want to ask you . . .'

Alfonso rushes in at this worst of moments. Back from the palace, and breathless with his own importance.

'The new King has called for the consort.'

'But the King is not here – not yet crowned . . .'

'Precisely. We are leaving London.'

'Praise be to God!' says Joan.

'Praise indeed!' I say. Is it possible that for once Alfonso has been useful? But – of course – there is a guilty look upon his face. I see how it will be without the need to ask. 'This *is* good news,' say I, falsely smiling. 'All the family will be saved. When do we go, husband?'

He looks down at his feet – fine shod in French boots, elaborately pointed. 'I . . . it is the musicians who are needed. At Cambridge, at the pleasure of His Majesty.'

'So be it,' says Joan. 'I will see to our preparations.'

'Preparations for what?' he asks, uneasily.

'Why, for the journey sir.'

'To *mine*. To my . . . preparations. Not to yours, Joan, or my wife's.'

'Nor to Henry's either?' I feel a surge of anger, even though this is no surprise. 'You will leave us, then. To live or die. And see what remains of us when you return.'

'This cannot be so, master,' says Joan. 'More people die each day. The pest house is full. They are digging graves out at Tothill Fields – graves as big as caverns . . . They lime the dead when their bodies are still warm . . . You could not leave your little son to that.'

Alfonso twists his hands together, his long, perfect fingers. 'It is not my choice, Joan. I am the master here, but merely a servant to the King.'

'Then you can pay for us to follow.' Her voice is quiet, but I have never known her so outspoken. 'You have gold, don't you? Or, if it is gambled, you have your fine Court friends, who will lend you a ducat or two to save your wife and child.'

'Get out!' says Alfonso. 'This is not a matter for you.'

Joan climbs the stairs, silent with rage.

I stare into the fire. I can see that this unmans him more than the tirade he was expecting. I watch the flames, thinking that each lick of heat is a like a human life, flaring up for an instant, and then gone for good. My calm is aided by my knowledge of my husband – expecting nothing is an excellent preparation for receiving it.

After a while he clears his throat. 'I am sure you will be safe.'

'Surely.'

'It will die out soon. Everyone says so.'

'Indeed. "Everyone" has such confidence that they are packing up their goods and chattels, boarding up their houses and heading for the hills of Kent.'

'The doom-sayers.'

'The wealthy. And the wise.'

'We have seen the plague before. Every year, it comes and goes.'

'Not like this,' I say. 'Not for years. If you insist on being a snivelling coward, then kindly have the grace to be an honest snivelling coward.'

'I shall be soon be back. With money. And preferment. A certain position, with the new King. I am doing this for all of us – for our future.'

'Alfonso?'

'Yes, my chuck?' He smiles, uneasy.

'Go.'

And so he does, with some clean linen in a bundle, and Joan's last impudent accusations following him down the street.

That night, I keep Henry in my bed, so I can will the plague away from him. His habit is to throw himself at an angle across the mattress, muttering and kicking, so the eiderdown comes off me, and there is no way I can lie straight. I lie there, sleepless. Much as I despise my husband, there is no doubt we are worse off without him. There was little hope of help before, but now no escape is possible. We can't flee the City like the wealthy and well-born. Money isn't all you need. Not only can the rich afford to hire carriages to remove their goods, they also have country estates to move to, with vast gardens, far from London. What's more, they have the legal right to run away. Each has a certificate of health, a pledge that they are clean of plague and not carrying the pestilence. Without this, if you flee, you may be hanged for your pains. When I lived at Court, we removed to Windsor Castle during one outbreak. The Queen had a gibbet put up on the village green. Poor souls who fled the City were put to death at her command. Horses supped water from the trough as these innocent subjects kicked their last.

At last I fall asleep, but I am prey to such dreams and nightmares! *I see them kill my father again, a circle of dark figures. I walk up behind him, and at first his steps are light and*

hurried, then slow and burdened, then they stop. Again he turns, and I see his silent scream. Again I reach out and my child's hands are in front of me. But this time they are botched with gore. I scream myself, but my screams are still silent.

There is a voice.

'Yet who would have thought the old man to have had so much blood in him?'

Then I see Lord Hunsdon, as he was the very last time I set eyes on him, in the promenading crowd at the Royal Exchange. Old and frail, and half-turning in the square, as if he wants to speak to me, but then I am pulled away by his companion. It is Lettice, all got up like a Globe whore touting for a groundling fuck, breasts like twin peaches. But then I see, it is not Hunsdon, it is Will. And we are not in the Royal Exchange but on the stage, and the audience is buzzing below us, angry and unhappy with our show.

Then I see Death, peering out of the Queen's bed at me, laughing. The Queen is with him, and laughing merrily herself, quite back to her old form. Her forehead is blooded, as it was on the days she came back from hunting. For all I know, the stag is in there too, in a state of equal high spirits . . . but then I wake. Or do I? It is a moment before I know what must have happened. My old affliction has returned, caused by dreams so violent they drive me from my bed. Night-walking.

I am not wrapped in blankets with my son. I am outside, in the plague-ridden street, bare-foot in my nightgown. I slap my wrist and pinch my skin to see if I'm still sleeping, and the pinches hurt, and my feet are cold, and I can smell the stench of putrefying flesh from the plague-house that is boarded up next door. I am awake, that is for sure, and abroad. I turn, too quick, to get back to my house, but for a second my head spins and I fear that I will fall. I stop for a moment, and put my hand upon the wall of the plague-house. From inside, I suddenly hear a dread cry, like the shriek of the damned.

'God help us! Help us! Give us water, show us pity! I have children! I have a baby! Help me!'

Two sotted prentice-boys appear. Staggering along the road, laughing and doing a little dance. They are tossing a flat cap between them, and tussling to reach it when it falls to the ground. When they see me, with my hand upon the plague-house, in my nightgown and with my muddy feet, they take me for one of the unfortunates who live there.

'What's this – you have escaped to spread your pestilence?' says the first, a great big lad with a mass of black hair. 'Get back inside!'

'You disobedient witch!' says the other, who is smaller, and has a scuff of brown beard 'Go indoors, and stay there till the Devil takes you.' They grab my arms and began to push me towards the door, though how they intend to get me through it I don't know, as the boards are nailed down sound, and there is no way in any more than there is any way out. I try to speak, and wrench myself free, but cannot, and a nauseous dark descends.

I dream of my father again.

We are on the stage with his consort; the boards stretch away in all directions, to the four corners of the earth, which are trimmed with heavy wainscots. To the east, these are carved with Chinamen and pearl-fishers; to the west with natives with feathered heads; to the south with Moors and minarets; to the north with wolves and mountains. Father is sitting cross-legged, holding his recorder. His lifts the pipe as if to play it. There is a dagger in his chest.

I sit down beside him. 'Father,' I say. 'You aren't dead.'

He looks up. 'Why should I be dead?'

'You were killed when I was seven.'

He laughs. 'I never died,' he says.

'Then where are you?'

'In Purgatory,' says he. 'Playing all my sweetest tunes.'

Then I look up and see a demon standing next to him. Its head is a thousand charnel-skulls, grinning rottenly; its eyes are empty graves. It is wearing a magician's gown of cloth-of-gold. My father produces a vial of scarlet notes and throws them upward. And the air is filled with the music of rubies, ascending and descending in filigree formations.

'Father!' I cry. 'Father, what happened to you?'

But he has climbed on to a giant viol, which is a tomb.

Scene V

'What is – ?'

'Hush. Keep your foot still – Lord knows what you have stood in. Fox shit, most likely. It's the worst of all, unless you ever step in the leavings of a wild boar.'

I am in the kitchen. My feet are in a bowl of warm water, scented with rosemary and orange peel, and Joan is squatting down before me, rubbing at my filthy toes with a piece of cloth.

'Night-walking again! I thought you were all done with that.'

'So did I. It's been years . . . not since . . .'

'. . . Henry was born, God bless him.'

I have only the vaguest memories of that dreadful time. Left on my own with Alfonso, who was rarely in the house, I was at first content to watch my belly grow bigger and bigger, waiting to be delivered of my baby. I ate well, and had a good serving girl who baked me apple cakes and brewed small beer. But, as the birth-date drew nearer, I began to sicken. Gall rose in my throat and would not clear, so I had to sit upright every night. Then my whole body swelled up to match my distended belly: my face and hands were so round and tight they might have been pregnant with their own progeny, and about to spill forth little newborn limbs. After a few days of this, I was struck down with a blinding head-ache, and I had a violent fit.

I remembered Joan's words when she gave me the potion in her apothecary shop. So I sent for her, and she came and saved me. All through the howling horror of the birth I was blind with

pain and my head seemed to be stuck inside a dark box. What kept me sane was the sound of Joan's calm voice, urging me on. And at the end of it, she gave my perfect son to me, with his blunt and folded face and his curled hands, and he opened his mouth and began to suck, and I would not have him taken from me, and I would not have a wet nurse, but fed him from my own breast and everybody marvelled at the way he thrived. When at last I emerged from my chamber, ready for churching, it turned out that Joan was now my servant, and my old one had vanished away. I never questioned this, being so pleased to have her there. Joan said little enough about it, only that her apothecary shop had been burned down by a mob, and they had stolen her herbs and simples before they torched the thatch.

She is looking at me now, her eyes bright. 'You're a good pupil, mistress. You have the makings of a wise woman, if not a sensible one.'

'Thank you.'

'So maybe you would like to help with a new concoction.'

'What is it?'

'An ugly brew.'

'What is it *for*?'

'It is a plague-juice.'

'An elixir? A cure?'

'No. For some, not all, it may work as a preventative.'

'How do you know it works?'

'I don't. But I made it once, long, long ago, and it saved my village.'

'From the plague?'

'We called it the Black Death back then. Only a few of the people caught it, but those that did all died.'

'Shame it's not a remedy.'

'Once you have the contagion, mistress, it is time to pray.'

'Pray? I do that every night. Dr Forman must know more than you do.'

Joan is quiet for a moment. 'If he has cured himself of plague, then he has bargained with the Devil himself. I told you – the Devil tempts the scholar just as he does the crone.'

'Perhaps he found a means through science and knowledge.'

'Maybe so. But all science comes from somewhere, and all knowledge has its price. All finished now – they're nice and clean.' I lift my feet out of the water, and she wraps them in a linen cloth. 'You aren't as strong as you think you are,' she says, drying them gently. 'The spirit is willing, I'll say that for you, but flesh is just flesh.'

'It's not my fault the plague has come.'

'No. But you are pitting yourself against it.'

I shrug. 'Who else can help me? Almighty God? I don't see much hope for this life coming from Him. All *His* promises are to be fulfilled when we are dead souls in Heaven. Then I shall be grateful. Now I am afraid.'

Joan ignores my blasphemous talk. 'That pamphlet for Mr Tottle,' she says. 'What'll you get for that?'

'Two shillings. I've given half to Inchbald, anyway.'

'Should you want another way to make a penny or two, you could always give him the recipe for my plague-juice.'

'There is a *recipe*?' I almost laugh. I think of plum pies and stuffed swans, of simnel cake and peacocks poached in wine.

'You need the brain of a plague corpse to make the paste, for one thing. A palmful of that. And a mandrake root. And various other – items.'

'What sort of items?'

'Gibbon blood can be hard to come by, unless you know the right apothecary. Not so difficult for someone with my history, of course.'

I watch her as she dries my feet, patting them gently with the towel. Joan can make a poultice of ointment flowers, read a urinal of piss, and brew up the most powerful of purgations. When Henry was teething, she soothed his sore gums with the brain of

a hare, and knew a cure for shingles made from earthworms and pigeon dung. Once, when Alfonso had been poisoned by a rival at the gaming-house, she cured him with a potion of rue, figs, walnuts and powdered Narwhal tusk. No more and no less than you would expect from a good apothecary. Yet there is something truly sinister about this plague-brew. She is a wise woman, and a faithful servant. What else do I know of her? And what don't I know?

Her hair is loose and hangs around her shrivelled face. Her skin is dun, her hands withered like the talons of a bird of prey. As she works she sings to herself. I don't recognise the tune, or understand the words.

'How old are you, Joan?' I ask.

She is drying the skin around the great toe of my left foot. Her grasp is firm; the cloth is rough and ticklish. She doesn't look up. 'Five hundred years,' she says. 'Or thereabouts.'

'*What?*'

She folds the towel, and straightens up, using a stool to lever herself on to her feet. 'Five hundred years,' she repeats. 'Time enough to learn all I needed.'

I'm not sure Methuselah lived so long. 'Joan, are you a witch?'

'What does it matter what I am?'

'I want to know. I believe I have a right to, being both your mistress and your friend.'

'I am a cunning-woman, who knows more than most.'

'A woman? Just as I am? And you have lived to such an age?'

'Remember, mistress, you are still learning. You know less than little, even now.'

'Joan, I have something to tell you. I should have told you this before, no doubt, but I thought you would take it for one of my night-fancies. If I tell you about this thing, will you tell me, in return, what you really know of witchcraft?'

Her face is shrewd. 'I might say a little more, but not enough to put you in the way of harm. Tell me your story, mistress. Does it concern the witches? I can see them standing by the Tyburn Tree.'

So I tell her the story of the meeting, and what they said about Baptiste and the plague, and how they showed me the bed with Henry dead upon it.

At the end she says, 'We must pray.'

'Pray! Will God help us, who helps no one when the pestilence comes?'

Joan hangs the towel over a chair to dry. 'God bless you, mistress, and give you strength.'

'God bless us all,' I say, testily. 'Now, Joan, what is this you say about being five hundred years upon this earth? Did God play a part in that?'

She crosses herself. 'Do not speak lightly of Our Lord, Aemilia. I was a witch once, and I did many things that I cannot bear to think of, and I have lived for many years beyond my span through the use of my craft. But I have repented of it now. They shut me in a nunnery, and I escaped it, and resolved to do my penance in this world, not in some stone prison. And so I am here. I have come to you. So you must believe me when I tell you that some matters are the will of God, and His will only. I have some experience in these matters.'

'But five hundred years!' I say. 'That is not possible.' Anne says there are rumours that Joan is mad, and I have always thought this to be a foolish piece of gossip. She is strange, yes, and possessed of far greater knowledge than most wise women. But . . . perhaps she is out of her wits after all? She hands me a pair of woollen stockings and I pull them on. I remember the two young ruffians who threatened me.

'What happened to those boys?' I ask.

'What boys?'

'Outside. They thought I had escaped from the boarded house.'

'You were dreaming. I saw no boys.'

I go to the door. It is a dank day with a dull grey sky. A dead-cart has stopped outside the plague house. The carter is adding two fresh occupants to his load. But they aren't boys. They are street-hounds. Their grey tongues are dangling from their open mouths. One is black with shaggy fur, the other brown, a bearded collie-dog.

Even Paul's Churchyard is quiet in this time of plague. The shops stand empty, their open fronts showing here a solitary printer proof-reading a chap-book, there a determined play-buyer, scrutinising a bill. When I reach Cuthbert Tottle's shop and look inside, at first it seems deserted. All I can see is the monstrous printing press, filling the room almost to the ceiling. Then I see Cuthbert, sitting alone, head bowed, hands folded as if he is praying. He is dressed in black.

'Mistress Lanyer,' he says. 'I bid you a good day.'

'And the same to you.'

I stand, waiting for him to demand a cheerful pamphlet, or one with two-headed monsters or demon births. But, after smiling at me vaguely, he returns to the contemplation of his hands.

'I have the cross-gartering pamphlet that you asked for,' I say. I've little confidence in this. I have rarely seen a thing so dull. But I hand him my pages and he peruses them, pushing his little spectacles up his nose. I see that it is wet with tears, which set his glasses sliding down again, and what I thought was prayer is grief.

'How is Mistress Tottle?' I ask, as he reads. 'I don't see her in the shop today. I hope she is well?' Of course, I fear the worst.

'She died on Sunday.'

'Oh, God rest her!'

'It took her off in two days. I was away at Cambridge, or else I would be boarded in our house, to await the Maker with her.

On Friday she sat over there . . .' he indicates her habitual place '. . . setting a psalter. She was as perfect . . . as perfect as . . . Well. I can't bear to see the half-done words.'

I frown. 'Mr Tottle, the pamphlet I have brought in is a very poor thing. I don't think I should trouble you with it any further.'

Grief has not affected his head for business. He hands it back to me. 'I can't find fault with your description. It's not worth sixpence,' he says. 'Nor even a farthing. At least your Lilith poem had some amusing passages, I seem to recall. I mean to say, they seemed amusing then . . .'

'I am sorry for your loss . . .' I hesitate. 'I do have something else. Something useful for these dreadful times.'

He rises from his seat and stands awkwardly, dwarfed by the printing machine. 'Hmm,' he says. 'If you can help us to survive the plague . . . I think I can vouch that there is an audience for that.'

'There is this,' I say, and give him a sheet of paper. It is Joan's recipe for plague-juice. 'It wards off the pestilence,' I say. 'It doesn't cure it.'

'Isn't that what we all want? Better avoid the smallpox than survive it, with the face of a pitted toad. Better avoid the plague than dance with death.'

'Then we might do business.'

He reads it, front and back. Then he turns it over, and reads it once again. His face brightens. 'Very interesting. I like this. I like it very much. It needs a little background – where you found this cure, why it works, why this is the best protection known to Man. That sort of thing.'

'I can do this.'

'When can you bring it to me?'

'Give me some paper and I will write more now.'

'Would that all the pamphleteers and poets could match your industry.'

'Would that I could match their sex.'

He brings me new paper, virgin-white. I stare at it for a moment, almost frightened to ruin its purity. But then I shake my head, sit down and write for two hours. I find that I can recall almost all of Joan's lore and a fair bit besides. Scraps of rumour, homilies from Anne, stories of strange cures and spontaneous recoveries. A little touch of Plato adds a scholarly flourish. When I have finished, Tottle takes the pages to the window and reads my words. Finally, he says, 'This is worth three shillings of anybody's money.'

He pays me in silver coins and I look down at them, not sure if I have been rewarded for words or witchcraft.

Scene VI

There is a rat on the kitchen table, bold as you please, eating cheese off Henry's trencher.

'Be off with you!' scolds Joan, thwacking it on the head with a poker. The creature barely seems to notice, but jumps off the table, a large chunk of cheese bulging out of one cheek. Its great earthworm of a tail flops into a bowl of small beer as it lollops on its way, finally disappearing into a hole in the wainscot.

'What's ailing Graymalkin?' I ask. 'Are we overfeeding him, or has he lost his taste for rat-flesh? There are more than ever this summer, I swear.'

'On account of the weather being so warm,' says Joan. 'It's not natural. I pray for rain, and a wholesome north breeze.' She fans herself with a pamphlet I had been reading to distract myself. (The title is *Jane Anger: Her Protection for Women to defend them against the scandalous reports of a late-surfeiting Lover, and all other like Venerians that complain so to be overjoyed with women's kindness*. Nothing about cross-gartering there, you will observe.) 'Flaming June indeed. We are burning up.'

'It's the sort of weather that makes a boy want to run out and play!' Henry is sitting at the table, grinding a knife into its side. 'No one else but me is stuck inside, with their old serving-maid, and nothing better than rats for playmates!'

'You stay here, where it's safe,' says Joan. 'There's another plague-house in this street, Lord save them. We must do all we can to stay away from the sick, Henry. It's a terrible illness, and a cruel end.'

'I don't care,' says Henry. 'If I did get the plague, I wouldn't notice any difference, seeing I am a prisoner already.'

Joan crosses herself.

'The difference would be that you would be purple-limbed, racked with pain and burning up with fever,' I say. 'Instead of missing the open fields, you would have a most sincere wish for Death. And stop sawing the table.'

'Well, I wish for Death now, if I can't go out,' says Henry, sawing harder. 'I want to watch the dead-carts! I want to see a plague-pit! I want to see them pour the lime! It's not fair!'

I smack his hand, and the knife falls to the floor. Joan crosses herself again. 'Dear Lord,' she says. 'There is no reasoning with the child. Say your prayers, Henry. You are tempting Providence.'

'I care nothing for Providence,' says Henry. 'I care for running and fighting and . . . falling over in the mud. And tree-climbing, and throwing stones at ducks and mallards, and making footballs out of dead frogs. And stealing eggs and blinding cats. All the normal things that boys must do.'

Joan shakes her head at him. 'These are not normal times. People are dying in hedges and on the highway. They say half the prisoners in Newgate died in one night, still chained to the walls. In any case, the bells of St Sepulchre's never stop their tolling. No wonder the new King is shut up at Greenwich and keeps out of the City.'

'Joan is right,' I say. 'And it's not just an illness, it's a madness too.' Sometimes the sick run mad through the streets, driven by witless spite to try to infect their fellows. They cast down their ruffs and cuffs and handkerchiefs as they go, wishing to spread contagion.

'I care for none of that. I am not a coward.'

'It is not a matter of cowardice, but of wisdom.'

'Then let me help you with the plague-potion. I am wise enough for that.'

'No, Henry,' I say, picking up the knife. 'It's as disgusting as anything you could get up to with those urchin friends of yours. We are using the brain of a plague corpse . . .'

'How good! Wait till I tell Tom!'

'Which is too much of a risk for a young boy. And tell no one. We came by it by means that not everyone would approve of, least of all Father Dunstan, so don't go blabbing on to Tom. Now, be off with you, and we will get on.'

'Stay in, but be off with me? Be off where?'

'Go into the vegetable garden. Or up the stairs.'

'You are a wicked gaoler. I shall go up to the attic and look out at the sky, and watch the kites and learn to fly.'

'So be it. Go away, you cheeky little hound.'

He runs up the stairs, in a great commotion of clumping feet.

Joan smiles wryly. 'You've made a rod for your own back,' she said. 'The child does as he pleases.'

'Yes, well, it's too late now. He is what he is, and I must take the consequences.'

We set to with the potion, and Lord above, it is a filthy business. When we have done, we scour our hands clean. Then we sit at the table, drinking ale. The plague-brew is simmering on the hearth, belching out its foul odours.

'Fetch Henry down for something to eat,' I say to Joan.

But she comes back shaking her head. 'He's hid himself somewhere,' she says. 'There's always something with that boy.'

'What's he up to now?' I sigh. 'I'll soon find him.'

But the bedchambers are empty, and he isn't in the wardrobe on the landing, or in the space under the eaves, or hiding on the balcony over the street. I climb the ladder to the attic. There is no sign of him there either. All I can hear is the rustling of rats in their nests, and the sound of their babies squeaking. Could he have climbed out upon the house-top, to look at the sky as he had promised? I open the window and see that a rope has been flung

across to the open window opposite, above the narrow street, to make a bridge. The house belongs to Anne Flood.

'Henry! I call. I half-expect his head to appear at their window, but no. There is no reason for him to stay at Tom's once he has made his escape. He could be anywhere.

We search both houses, from top to bottom, with Anne exclaiming over Henry's bad behaviour, and assuring me that Tom could have nothing to do with it, as the players have been summoned to a meeting at the Globe, which has been closed due to the plague. 'I shall send word to Tom,' she says. 'Heaven help us! We must tell him Henry has fled.'

'He'll soon turn up,' say I. But I am sick with fear, for there is no denying it: Henry has disappeared.

'The Lord has taken him,' says Anne. 'Oh, my heart goes out to you, Aemilia!'

I turn away from her. 'He has run away, off to play somewhere. He'll be back by dusk.'

But dusk falls, and there is still no sign of him. Fear takes hold of my body with an uncanny coldness. My limbs are heavy with dread. Yet at the same time it is impossible to stay still for one second, and I pace the house, up and down, ceaselessly, endlessly mounting the stairs, searching each chamber, looking under the beds, climbing up into the attic and sticking my head out of the window. I even go to the outside privy several times, as if he might have found himself some cranny to hide inside that malodorous place. At last I can bear it no longer. I set out, torch in hand, leaving Joan to wait for his possible return.

In the City, bells toll, marking not the hour but the passing of the dead. The evening is close and airless. A raven flies over my head, giving out its strange, throaty call. *Prruk-prruk-prruk.* An ill omen, if I needed one. Where can I look? Where might he have gone? If Tom has been at the Globe all day, there is no reason to think that Henry is with him. In any case, the Globe is on the other side of the river. Going by the Bridge is too far round, and

he doesn't have money for the wherryman. He would be more likely to head for the fields and woods. But then, he also likes to frisk along the outer walls of Whitehall Palace, fencing with himself and shrieking out in mock agony when the invisible blade strikes home. I can almost hear his high voice. 'Ooh! Aargh! Have at thee, knave! I bowel you – dead man!' My little Henry, wandering alone in the plague-ridden City.

Oh, Lord! Curse the boy! Or rather, bless him, protect him, deliver him from harm! I walk, as fast as I can, along Long Ditch and towards Camm Row, my breath heaving in my chest. If this is God's way of punishing me as an unfit mother, then it is roughly in proportion to his other punishments – an eternity of hellfire for a life that mixes sin with sorrow. From time to time I call Henry's name, in an agony of rage and pain.

I hold my crackling torch high against the dark sky, and what I behold looks like one of the old church wall paintings of the Dance of Death. I see a blasted, empty place. Deserted houses, blind and shuttered. An old woman, on her hands and knees, puking into the stinking kennel in the middle of the street. A skinny boy, carrying a limp baby. Here is a dead-cart rattling by me, loaded with corpses. Some are bundled in sheets; others are naked, mouths gaping open like landed fish.

I call out to the carter, 'You haven't seen a little boy, have you sir? A boy of ten or so. Yellow-headed and skittish.' My voice sounds unreal in this weird place. I meant 'haired' not 'headed', and in my mind I see Henry-as-monster, skull gold-painted.

'Not if he's alive,' says the friendly fellow, hunched and faceless. 'I deal in Death. I don't see the living.'

'You might have seen him running along somewhere. You can't miss him. He's – bold and bonny. Noisy. You'd be sure to remember.' I'm smiling at him, as if this might encourage him to recall my child.

'Take a look in the cart if you've a mind,' he says. 'I've got all sizes in there. Might be one of about that age, if you're lucky.'

I turn away, too brimful of horror to answer back in my normal way. The house before me is boarded – not a plague-house, but a grand merchant's home, left in a hurry. A sack of flour is spilled across the doorway, evidence of the hasty departure of the occupants. Against one of the wood-shuttered windows, a pamphlet has been posted. It is a warning from the City fathers, recounting a litany of causes of the plague. The fault lies with *'runnygate Jews, thrasonical and unlettered chemists, shifting and outcast pettifoggers, dull-pated and base mechanics, stage-players, pedlars, prittle-prattling bawds, toothless and tattling old wives'*, and many more. I read the words in a trance-state close to despair. I can't stop looking. But where should I go? The very ground hungers for corpses and sucks them in, nameless and unshriven. I say a prayer, a wordless, secret prayer, for my mind is blank of proper thoughts.

Then, I remember Henry's words – he wanted to see a dead-cart, and a plague-pit. Of course he did. Though the streets are empty and the populace lives in terror of this cruel distemper, gawpers crowd round the rims of the mass graves to wonder at the twisted faces of the dead. So, as I have no idea where to find him, I will follow the dead-cart to its destination.

I walk some distance from the cart, keeping it in view as I follow it along the road. From time to time the driver calls out, 'Cast out your dead! Any dead bodies to bury? Cast out your dead!' But the houses are silent.

Then, behind me, another shout goes up. 'Have you any more Londoners to bury, hey down a down dery, have you any more Londoners to bury, good morrow and good day?' I turn to look, and see two fellows behind me. The first is shabbily dressed and with a beard somewhat wild and untrimmed. The other is thicker-set, and looks more prosperous. His face is shadowed by his feathered hat. I quicken my pace, even though all there is to protect me is a cart loaded with corpses.

'Madam,' a voice calls out. 'A fine night for barn owls, and cut-throats. Not so fine for the likes of you.'

I answer without slowing down. 'A fine night for finding my son, I hope.'

'You look to find him in a grave? You will be lucky.'

'I look to find him above ground. He is not ill, he is merely disobedient.'

'Ah, the disobedient roaring boys! London would not be the same without them. Myself, I pray they live forever. For if London's underworld is the map of merry hell, then they are the dancing devils sent to please us.'

'Shush, Dekker, shush!' says the other man, grasping his arm. 'It is she.'

I know that voice only too well. The cart has lumbered to a halt, and the driver has gone into a house. I stop and wait till the two men catch up with me, knowing now that I have nothing to fear from them. No danger to my life, in any case. And I realise, as they come closer and our three torches make a bright space in the night, that I know both of them. The first is Thomas Dekker, a boy actor with the Lord Chamberlain's Men when I was Hunsdon's mistress, who has now turned his hand to writing. An eager, lively fellow, who is smiling now even in this earthly hell. I know the other fellow better, even when he hides behind his cloak and keeps his head bowed in the guttering torchlight.

'This is a strange time to be out,' say I. 'Did you come to take the air?'

'Aemilia,' says Will. 'Forgive me, but Tom Flood told us your son was lost. And I wanted to . . . It seemed fitting to come to see where he might be.'

'I assure you, sir, I have no need of help from anyone.'

'You are white as alabaster,' says Will. 'The poor child! God bless him.'

'Indeed, madam, you do not look well,' says Dekker. 'We will escort you, and I am sure we shall find this naughty son of yours.

Why, the whole City is running mad, but there is no need to fear for one quick boy who can outrun the pestilence.'

I know this is untrue, but I'm grateful for his cheerful tone.

'We will search with you, whether you like it or not,' says Will.

The flames illuminate his dark eyes and I see his fear, and I remember how he stared at Henry at the Globe. There is no mistaking the similarity between them.

Dekker's spirits seem unaffected by our two drawn faces. 'It's a pretty place, indeed!' he says. He gestures around him, as if to include the silent houses, the red crosses daubed on the doors and the weeds that grow on each side of the kennel. 'I am tired of being a poet to whores and strumpets. So I am writing a pamphlet on the plague.'

'A gloomy subject, as I am sure Mistress Lanyer will testify,' says Will.

We walk on together. My mind is so fixed on finding Henry, and the fear of not finding him, that I accept Will's presence as part of the nightmare chaos that surrounds me.

'Never was a vile contagion so badly run,' says Dekker. 'The Corporation hires women to keep their eye upon the sick and dying, and insists they are all sober and ancient. But instead they are a bunch of blear-eyed, drunken night-crows.' He lowers his voice. 'As for the likes of that one up ahead – I swear they hire these carters from Satan's own stable-yard. Nasty, foul-mouthed breed. Too brute and slovenly to make recruits for hangmen.'

'How long has . . . Henry been gone?' asks Will.

'Hours past. Hours and hours,' say I. 'I thought he was in the house – he might have been running amok since midday.'

'He might have been among the plague-pits these last ten hours,' says Dekker. 'Boys do love these places.'

My voice cracks. 'Dear God!'

'Show some sympathy for this poor lady, will you?' says Will. 'For pity's sake, she's at her wits' end. Her son is gone!'

'Not gone,' I say, quickly. 'He is mislaid.'

Dekker smiles. 'There is no one in London who doesn't run the risk of catching this disease,' he says. 'And most of us will live to tell the tale. I certainly hope I shall, for there is money in it. I plan to call my pamphlet *A Wonderful Year*. Satire,' he says quickly, catching Will's eye and clearly wanting to avoid another reproof.

'Look, Tom, go up ahead and see where that cart is heading,' says Will.

Whistling cheerily, Dekker obliges. We watch his torch move forward in a jaunty fashion through the darkness.

Then Will says, 'Aemilia, the boy – '

'He will be near, and we will find him,' I say. 'Have no fear of that.'

'He has such a look of Hamnet.'

'It makes no odds to us now, does it? We are estranged.'

'I know he is my son.'

We walk in silence for a moment.

'You have eyes to see: so be it,' I say. 'But he calls Alfonso "Father".'

He turns to look down at me, and holds the torch higher so that he can see my face. 'Do you wish to punish me?'

'Who has punished whom?' I ask. 'What am I – a foul-breathed Lilith? A demon succubus, come to corrupt you? I still have those poems you wrote – some strange respect for Art prevents me from burning them to ash. If there is a distinction in inspiring a poetry of hate, then I can claim it.'

'Aemilia – those poems – the words I used against you . . .'

But then Dekker returns, breathless. 'I have found the pit,' he says, all levity gone. 'There's no mistaking it. God save us all.'

We have reached the end of the lanes of Westminster, and come to open fields. Ahead of us, on the brow of a hill, a bonfire burns, lighting up the shapes of a crowd of people. There are smaller figures – children – among then. The cart has stopped at

the bonfire, and the driver is climbing down. Will pulls my arm and we step back into the shadow of a hay-barn.

'What a terrible place,' says Dekker. 'Jesu. I have seen nothing like it.'

'Aemilia – let Tom and I go up ahead and see if he is there,' says Will. 'You will be safe here.'

'It's not fit for a woman,' says Dekker. 'Truly, madam.'

'I would not think of staying behind,' I say. 'I would go into Hell to save my son. A plague-pit is nothing to me.'

Scene VII

The two men walk ahead of me and I follow, silently. I still carry my torch, and am at once grateful for the glare it casts on the rough and tussocky ground, and fearful that we will catch the attention of the watchers ahead. But no one notices us. And, when I reach the pit, I see why. The carter has backed his cart close to the open gash in the earth, so that it is hard up against the drop. Now, he stands beside it, like a showman at a Fair. All around the edge, illuminated by the flames of the crackling bonfire, stands a motley group of citizens such as I never wish to see again. They are like the walking dead themselves, battered and bedraggled beyond humanity.

'Show us your wares!' shouts one, an old man with bullfrog eyeballs bulging from his skull.

'Yes, do your worst. Let's see what ingredients we can put into our pot!' shouts a young bawd, pale and hollow-cheeked, with a baby at her breast and a small child clutching at her skirts with its skinny arms. The bawd is swaying, and shaking, and I suspect it will not be long before she tumbles down herself. I look into the grave, and at first can see nothing, for the pit is twenty or thirty feet deep, and the fire casts little light into its depth. But when I look closer I see that what at first seemed like gravel and stones in the shadows is a muddle of hands and feet and faces, piled and confused and tangled. The bawd is right: the grave is a cauldron, and this is human stew.

'Now then, now then, ladies and gentlemen, babes and children, all,' says the carter, clapping his filthy hands to win the

attention of the crowd. 'This is a good night, and good business. Sixpence I get for each of these deadmen, which you are about to see before you. The more of them, the better my breakfast. The Lord God is truly shining his light upon me.'

'Praise God in his wisdom,' shouts some ague-addled fool.

The carter goes to his plague-carriage and fetches the first corpse. It is the body of a big, wide-set man, of maybe twenty years or so. It is hard to tell, as its face is grey and twisted, and corrupted with sores.

'Here's a fine fellow,' says the carter. 'Wave at your attendants, good sir!' He flops the hand of the deadman at the watchers. 'We all know that worms need no apparel, saving only winding-sheets. So – let us take off what needs to be taken off.' He drops the corpse down, removes the doublet, and feels inside the pocket. 'Oh, indeed, my Maker blesses me once more!' He waves a leather bag before us, and drops the contents into his palm. 'Seven pieces of silver! I am near as rich as Judas! Thank you, sir!' And, with that, he kicks the poor fellow into the grave.

Next, he produces a naked baby. 'Nothing to speak of this small fry,' he says, holding it up by one leg. 'And I can see it has no pockets.' He tosses it into the pit, grinning as he does so.

I glance at Will. His face is clenched, as if he is willing himself to stay silent. I think this wise. The dead are dead, and God himself will deal with this man when he meets his end.

But here is something different, and which seems to interest the fellow more than either of the first two bodies. He lifts a young girl from the cart, aged sixteen or seventeen years. She is a veritable Juliet, with long, pale hair, as dainty and beautiful a young virgin as you could wish for. And she is still dressed in a fine gown, the ruff standing half-off, like a torn petal.

'O-ho,' says the carter. 'O-ho, again the Lord has showed me favour! What form of patient goddess have we here? Death is greedy. He takes this plump peach for his own and ravishes it like any hungry lover.' And with this he turns the girl round, so her

head and shoulders flop down and she is bent double before him, then he lifts her skirts and pretends to hump her from behind. There are calls and cheers from the crowd.

But he has not finished yet. 'Let's have a look at her fine titties,' says the carter, dropping the body down. 'Would she had been so pliant in life. Would that I could have tiptoed into her bedchamber, and fucked her while she breathed. Never mind, I'll have her now.' With this he begins to unlace her bodice, but, finding it stiff, he tears at the fabric, muttering to himself. After a moment, he hauls her to her feet, facing us, with her small breasts revealed. 'Who wants a lick of these fine dugs?' he calls. 'Come on, I'll make my price on this excellent bitch. Sixpence for one lick, a shilling for two. Or – '

Out of the night, out of nowhere, a figure comes rushing towards him.

'Aargh – you shall die, you stinking Devil!' screams a voice. I know that voice! I know it! There is a mighty roar from the carter, and the dead virgin drops into the pit.

'He bit me! He bit me, the demon!' shouts the carter, falling to his knees.

'Henry!' I shriek. 'Henry, in the name of God!' I rush round the edge of the pit, wielding my torch like a pikestaff and pushing the watching ghouls out of my way. But Will runs faster, waving his sword, and pulls the sobbing Henry away.

'Henry! Stop this at once!'

'Henry!' I scream, and catch him in my arms.

'Now fly – go!' shouts Will, and he and Dekker face the carter, swords and torches in hand. But the rabble, deprived of its sport, is shouting and coming closer. The carter lunges at Will, who thrusts the burning torch at his beard. It catches fire and flames leap up around the carter's blackening face. The crowd begins to run at us, and we all turn and flee towards the cart. I am clutching Henry's hand as we run. Dekker gets there first, and then we throw ourselves upon it and he whips up the old mare and she

lurches forward. Before the crowd can reach us she has lumbered to a canter over the uneven grass.

Dekker laughs wildly and cries, 'My God, we've escaped Hell, my friends! We've seen Death, plain as a pikestaff, and cheated him!'

But Will says nothing. His eyes are fixed on Henry.

When I dare to look behind me, the bonfire is growing smaller in the distance, and the cries of the crowd are fading, and I hold my son so tightly in my arms that they begin to ache.

Scene *VIII*

Henry sleeps till noon the next day, eats some bread and drinks some ale, then sleeps again till evening. When I go up to see him, he is lying in my bed, eyes open, looking thoughtfully at the embroidered hangings.

'I shall be good from now on,' he says. 'Biting the carter is the worst thing I will ever do.'

'Indeed, I hope so.' My throat is dry – why is he such a madcap child? *Please Lord*, I pray. *There was goodness in his heart. He was avenging that poor girl.*

'I shall fit myself for Heaven.'

I shiver and close the window. 'You have plenty of time for that,' I say. 'Year upon year. You will be an old man, all bent, with a white beard hanging down to your knees.'

Further along the street they are closing up another plague-house. The carpenters are smoking tobacco pipes and leaning planks of wood against the house front. A topless cross of St Anthony is painted in red on the wall to the right of the front door. The carpenters work calmly and slowly, as if taking pride in their craft.

'I shall fit myself in any case.' Henry smiles at me, so sweetly. 'I would have killed the plague-man if I could, so it's good I wasn't able to, else I would be a murderer.'

'It was very good we stopped you. Now, would you like a gingerbread man? Joan has been baking.'

'I'm not hungry.'

A spasm of fear in my guts. Henry is always hungry.

'Just a little?' I say. 'Just a tiny bit? I could break you off an arm or a leg?

'No, I will sleep again now.'

'Good.' There are tears behind my eyes. 'Good boy.' I smooth his brow, and he closes his eyes.

When I go back, half an hour later, with a cup of small beer, I touch his forehead, the little scar above his eyebrow where he had fallen from the window while trying to skewer a raven on his sword. He is slightly warm. Perhaps he will be well by morning, running into the kitchen demanding bakemeats and a farthing.

I stroke his face, and kiss his closed eyelids. Not a single lash shall be harmed; not a grubby toenail. I will stand between him and all that could threaten his safety. I will turn the plague from my door. I will face down the spectre of the Reaper, and cast it out, and it will limp away down the road, dark robe flapping, till it vanishes. My head aches, and when I shut my eyes I can see the Reaper's crow-form, black on red. I get into bed beside Henry and begin to pray, mouthing the words silently so that only God will hear them. But something is wrong: my mind is blanked with dead walls, and the ache of my head beats against them. The prayer I want will not come, only the litany:

'*O God the Father of Heaven: have mercy upon us miserable sinners.*' And then the response from the congregation. A thousand whisperers in my head, beneath the bed, behind the wainscot like black rats: '*O God the Father of Heaven: have mercy upon us miserable sinners.*'

I try again, seeking the prayer against the pestilence. But only say, '*O God the Son, Redeemer of the world: have mercy upon us miserable sinners.*' And there are the voices again, but this time I can only hear the rats: '*O God the Son, Redeemer of the world: have mercy upon us miserable sinners.*'

The tears run down my cheeks. Where is God? How can He hear me, down among the carrion and filth? '*O God the Holy Ghost, proceeding from the Father and the Son: have mercy upon us miserable sinners.*' The rats are ready for me: '*Have mercy upon us miserable sinners.*'

I raise my head, and listen. Silence, all around me, save for the rasp of Henry's breath. There is another verse – what is the verse? I close my eyes tight, tight, so there is no space for the Reaper, and bunch my hands together so the nails dig into the backs of my hands. '*Remember not, Lord, our offences, nor the offences of our forefathers; neither take thou vengeance of our sins: spare us, good Lord, spare thy people, whom thou has redeemed with thy most precious blood, and be not angry with us for ever.*'

And then come the rats: '*Spare us, good Lord.*'

Then I sleep, and in my dreams I feel the flames of Hellfire, rising up from the plague-pit and licking the feet of the watchers. They flock like patterned starlings against the roaring sky. When I wake, with a start, the flames still burn me, and I shrink away from the heat. My hand touches Henry's arm – flung out on the top of the covers – and I gasp, for his skin is burning hot. I bend to look at him. His eyes are half-open, and his breathing shallow. I push back his hair, and it is soaking wet.

'Mother,' he says. His voice is clear but small.

'What, my little one?' I touch his cheek with trembling fingers.

'Take my head away.'

'How can I, silly boy, when it's stuck fast to your neck?' There are tears on my face, and a raging pain behind my eyes. Is it his pain, or mine?

'It aches me. It's grown too big. You could tear it off and take it to the Bridge, and spike it up high, and the wind and air would cool me.'

'Don't speak of such – '

'I could see all the orchards of Kent, and the village ponds, and the hop fields and the apple trees going on and on till they reach the sea.'

'Henry! My love, my little love . . .'

'And then I could see the wild waves, and mermaids, and then France, and Venice after that, and then Constantinople and Ethiopia, where the dragons are ten fathoms long. My head is no good here.' He looks at me, and starts. 'But you're not my mother.'

'Yes, I *am*, dearest chuck. For good or ill, you have no other.' I gather him to me, and hold his quivering form against my chest.

'But you are old,' he whispers. 'My mother is young, and beautiful.'

'My sweet boy, I am still your mother!' I wonder where my light tone comes from, when I am brimful of fear. I talk as if the fairyland he describes is real, and the open grave of London just a dream.

'No.' His eyes close. I rock him, as I did when he was a baby. For this child I have lost everything: Will's love, Hunsdon's protection and my place at Court. I have sacrificed wealth and position and the only life I knew. And I have never wished it otherwise, not for one second, no matter what befell me. He is my son, my only child. There is no transaction to be made with such a love. I wish I could pass all the goodness and strength in my own body through to him. Save him, Lord! Save him! I search again for the right prayer, and this time come upon the words, '*Deus, Deus meus,*' then the Latin fades to English and I cry out, '*My God, my God, look upon me; why has thou forsaken me: and art so far from my health, and the words of my complaint? O my God, I cry in the daytime, and in the night season also, I take no rest . . .*'

There is a blank, then I try again.

'*All they that see me laugh me to scorn: they shoot out their lips, and shake their heads, saying, She trusted in God, that would deliver her, let Him deliver her, if he will have her . . .*

O go not from me, for trouble is hard at hand, and there is none to help me!'

But my voice rises to a monstrous wail, a she-wolf howling at the moon. This is not the prayer I need. Where is the prayer I am looking for, the spell that will summon the Lord? I stare up at the carved roof of the four-poster bed, and the brightly coloured waves and fishes heave and shift.

Then I see that Henry's eyes are fixed on me again. 'I've learned my lessons, Mother, don't beat me!'

'My son, what are you saying? *Who* beats you?'

His eyes are blank and staring. 'I've learned it well, the lesson. That all things have their situation, and must remain in that place. All things in Creation, fixed, like stars.'

'Rest, sweet baby; it doesn't mean a jot.'

'Of fish: carp, cod, dace, dog-fish, shark, eel, gudgeon, herring. And then the porpoise.'

'Henry – '

'Of creeping things – worm, serpent, adder, blindworm, slug and snail. And then the lizard and the gilded newt.'

I open my mouth to speak, but can make no sound.

'Of flies . . . house fly, blue-bottle, flesh-fly, louse and sheep tick. And then the . . . merry flea.'

He closes his eyes and I kiss his fluttering lids. 'That is enough now. The schoolmaster will be pleased with you. All God's Creation. In its place.'

He sits upright. 'But Mother, I have not done the dogs! The dogs must take their places! Let me do the dogs!'

'Do the dogs, my child. Yes, please do the dogs.'

He lies down again, and speaks precisely, checking the words off on his damp fingers. 'First the three ranks: game dog, house-dog, toy dog.'

'Well said.'

'Of game dogs: spaniels and hounds. Of hounds, eight kinds: harriers, temurs, bloodhounds, gazehounds, greyhounds,

lymnes, tumblers and thieves. Of spaniels, the water spaniel and the land spaniel, for falconry.'

Joan is standing at the doorway.

'You should have called me,' she says.

I scramble out of the bed and run to her, tripping and staggering. I put my hand on her thin shoulder to steady myself. 'He has a fever. That's all. A touch of fever. We must give him something from your physick store. A draught – to take away the heat.'

But Henry is not yet done. 'Dogs of the homelier kind. Are either shepherd's curs, or mastiffs, which can be . . .' He seems to drift, then comes back, his voice louder. 'Barn-dogs. Tie-dogs. And watchdogs.'

Joan stares at him, her eyes wide with sorrow.

'And then . . . the toy dogs. Of the sort which lick a lady's lips . . .'

His voice fades, till I hear the faintest sound of growling. 'The mastiff is a proud dog. Three can match a bear, and four can eat a lion.'

Joan looks at my torn gown and tangled hair. 'Lord save us,' she whispers. 'God help the little fellow.'

Her tone is kind, but I hate her hopeless words.

'*We* must help him,' I say. 'We must soothe the fever. Come now, you are the one with all the knowledge.'

'Mistress, I will help you all I can. But we must be brave. We must be ready. Half the people in this street have buried babes and children.'

I close my eyes, to will her voice away.

She grasps my hands. 'The Flemish family – four doors down – had fourteen girls and buried nine. You know this as well as I do. The plague is not even the worst of it. Sweating sickness, drowning, hunting-dogs, the pox. Five infants died in the baker's fire just one week past. You can't guard Henry against every danger, for all your care. But – God willing – he

may yet live for threescore years and ten. Put your trust in the Lord.'

I pull away. 'Bring me what you have to cure him!'

'Willow tea might soothe him a little. But for the pestilence itself there is no physick.'

'God's blood, Joan, I thought you were a wise woman! What wisdom is this? What about the plague-juice, the recipe you made?'

'Mistress, your worry is numbing your mind. It's for *prevention*,' she says. 'Not for cure. Only God in his mercy knows how to cure the pestilence.' And – so suddenly that I first think she has fallen – she sinks down upon the rushes. She puts her hands together, ready to pray.

I run barefoot from the chamber and down into the kitchen. The still-room is next to the cupboard on which I keep what is left of my pewter. It is lined with shelves, and barely big enough for a single person to stand up in. There Joan stores not only her potions and libations, but clear cakes of gooseberry, rose-hip conserves, syrups of green quince and melon, pickled nasturtium-buds, ashen keys, radish-pods and broom-buds – all stored in pots and capped with leather. Every manner of thing, in short, which Henry loves. I search the shelves, my breath coming in queer sobs. Each pot has been labelled in his best italic hand: he and Joan work together, she calling out the name, and Henry writing it down. I grab at the pots and bottles, and fling them on to the trestle table. A jar of moss-powder rolls over the edge of the table, and smashes to pieces on the stone-flagged floor.

'Calm yourself, you'll do him no good that way,' says Joan.

I turn to face her, my head full of aches and murmurs. 'I thought you had given him up for dead.'

She takes down a jar of hemlock. 'That's not what I meant.'

'What did you mean, then?'

'There is always the hope of a miracle.'

But God does not love Henry as I love him! Other children are dying, so why should He save mine? I need some other power, some other lore. There is one man who might help me in this enterprise, and, if the price of his power is a so-called 'halek', then I will fuck him for his knowledge just as Anne Flood fucks Inchbald to keep a roof over her head.

'I'm going out,' I say, putting on my cloak.

Joan looks up, startled. 'What, and leave Henry at such a time? And where to, in Heaven's name?'

'I will find a cure for him. You will nurse him well, I know.' I fasten my shoes.

'You're going alone?'

'Of course. Mind Henry, and, if he asks for me, say I will be back before he knows it.'

She looks out of the window. 'I pray to God you are true to your word. Be careful, mistress, and be quick.'

Scene IX

As I hurry on my way, the sky is lowering and I pull my cloak closer round me. The silent streets are grey and cold. As I pass Foul Lane, I see a kite, pecking at the corpse of a turtle dove. Its beak is crimson with blood. When I approach, it rises up, squealing, and flaps its giant wings, and I shield my eyes as it flies over my head.

Simon Forman lives at Lambeth. I know the place – a handsome new house on the outskirts of the village. Fortunately, it is on the river shore almost directly opposite to Westminster. Unfortunately, both the weather and the plague are against me. At the riverbank, I stop, looking up and down at the silent boatyards. The quays are usually a riot of noise and activity, crowded with boatmen and eel-men, shoutmen and shipwrights, trinkers and mariners. But now the quays are silent, and the only noise I can hear is the wind rattling in the rigging of the empty ships. I hurry along to the stairs, where the wherrymen are usually for hire. There is a single boat moored there, and a figure humped in the bows, hood pulled down low. The rain is lashing down now. I stumble along to the stairs, and make my slippery way to the boat.

As I approach, the hooded figure looks up. It is a young woman, with a white face, perfectly beautiful except for her cheeks, which are holed and pitted with smallpox scars.

'I am looking for a wherryman,' I say, unsure what she is doing there.

'Then you have found one.'

'Is your husband . . . ?'

'Dead, and my children will follow him unless I earn some coins. Let me help you in.' She stands up with the sureness of any boatman, and hands me into the craft.

We set out for Lambeth Stairs, and, as we go, I wonder about this woman, sensing that she is as desperate as I am. 'How many children do you have?'

She is rowing strongly with her thin arms. 'Six. The eldest cares for the younger ones. They are good children.'

'And did your husband die of the plague?'

The current is faster now, and she pulls for a few strokes before replying. 'No, mistress. He was murdered.'

'Lord above! I am sorry to hear it.'

'Not I.'

Have I misheard her?

'Not who?'

'Not I. It would be a false sorrow, and I am not a false woman.'

She rows in silence for a while. She is not one for the wherryman's patter. As the southern shore grows near, my curiosity gets the better of me. 'Do you know who killed him?'

She laughs, and looks me in the face for the first time. 'I should say so.'

At the steps, I pay her fivepence. She gives me another curious look and says, 'False, he called me. False, and I bore his children, and baked his bread and worked my life away for him. That great sotted oaf. If I'd lain with half the men he said I had, I'd be the biggest whore in Whitehall.'

'They see their own faults in us,' say I.

She stares, and I see a shimmer of insanity in her face. 'When I washed my hands, I knew it was all finished. It was just a little deed, and quickly done. It's only when I sleep that they are all dripping scarlet again, and I wash them and wash them – and the Thames runs red. I see the carp and salmon choking in his blood.'

She smiles. 'So I stay awake. I watch the moon go from one side of the sky to the other. Then the dawn comes, and blinds me with its light.'

The plague is driving us all mad. I turn and walk into the storm, barely able to see my way, slipping and sliding over the stones of the path. My rain-heavy cloak pulls at my shoulders, and my hands are frozen. I look around me, wishing I had a guide to show me the way. And then, I see it. A dark building looms out of the rain. It is surrounded by trees, waving and crashing in the wind. I wade through the mire and beat upon the door. The sound is unnaturally loud. A shock of lightning flames the sky.

No one answers. I look up at the black windows, hoping to see a light. I knock again, hammering louder this time. Perhaps the pestilence has reached Lambeth? Perhaps the doctor and his family are dead? No, no! I knock a third time, then stop and listen for the sound of footsteps on the other side. Silence. I go round the side of the house, half-blinded by the wet strands of my hair. There is a door in a high wall. It opens into an orchard. The high walls give some protection from the wind, but none from the rain: the neat pathways between the apple and apricock trees are flooded like Venetian canals. I squelch across the grass, mud sucking at my feet, till I reach one of the latticed windows. I pick up a heavy stone from the path and hurl it against the window. It crashes through the glass, shattering the stillness.

A moment later, there is a glow of candle-flame at the window above. The window opens and Dr Forman's voice calls out, 'Who's there?'

'It's me. Aemilia Lanyer.'

But the storm drowns out my words.

'What? Who? Be off with you!'

I shout louder. 'It's Aemilia! I have come to see you! I need your help – please let me in!'

Now he puts on a quavering tone.

'If it's Simon Forman you are after, he is gone to Cambridge. Go away, or I will call the Watch.'

'Then call them, you poisonous toad! If they'll come as far as Lambeth. Tell them a bastard whore is smashing up his house.'

With that, I pick up a second stone, as big as a fist, and throw it at another window. The leaded glass crashes into tiny pieces, and inside the room something falls. I pray it is the heart of a unicorn preserved in a pot, or some other precious item.

'Stop that! Stop it!' Now he sticks his head out, and his beard blows sideways. 'Come to the side door – see it? Down there, in the corner. Unseemly baggage! And come *quietly*.'

'Quietly? Satan himself can't hear me in this storm.'

'Shush! Shush! Lord help me! There is a price upon my head.'

Simon Forman looks thinner and yellower than he was when I saw him last, and he has exchanged his flowing necromancer's gown for a stout doublet and plain hose. He looks angry and ill at ease. 'Really!' he cries. 'House-breaking and wanton destruction! Whatever would Hunsdon have said?'

'I believe he would have applauded me,' I say, wiping rain from my eyes. 'He was a soldier, after all.'

'God's teeth! I shall send you the bill! Whatever is the matter?'

'Henry has the plague. I know you cured yourself of it. How did you do that?'

'Let us say I have strong nerves, and much knowledge.'

'Through necromancy?'

'I cannot say.'

'Through conjuration?'

'That is information that I will never share.'

'I need to cure my child, and I don't mind how I do it, or what I do to find the knowledge.'

The doctor seems to have no sense of urgency. 'No one knows how it is spread, though I, for one, do not believe it is the vapours,' he says, in a scholarly manner. 'I put my money on *Rattus rattus*, the common rat.'

'I don't care if it's spread by Gabriel and all the ministering angels. Please help me.'

He closes the wooden shutters over the broken windows before drawing the heavy curtains.

'Did you come alone?'

'Yes.'

'Were you followed?'

'I don't think so.'

'You told no one your destination?'

'Not a soul. Why?'

He pokes at the embers of seacoal till they spark into life. 'The College of Physicians is trying to murder me. They've hired assassins. They nearly had me – twice. I've sent my family out of London. I am leaving myself in the morning.'

I must say, this strikes me as ridiculous. The august body of good doctors, paying murderers to finish off this poor old goat! Men, and their precious knowledge. All the world is upside-down.

'I am sorry about your windows,' I say. 'But I had to see you.'

'Well. You certainly know how to put yourself in harm's way.' He draws up two chairs, and sits down by the fire. Reluctantly, I join him. I am anxious to find out what I need to and return to Henry's side.

'As to the power to stop the plague, did you read the pamphlet I gave you?' Forman asks.

'Every word. It is an account of the degrees of witchcraft. I understand what it is saying. And I know what I want to do. I need something more tangible – a spell for conjuring.'

'For the conjuring of what, precisely?'

'Of a demon that can help me – what else would it be?'

He looks at me thoughtfully. 'Are you really prepared to dabble in that Art?' he asks. 'To conjure evil?'

'Yes, I am,' I cry. 'If God won't help me, then I will settle for the other side.'

He thinks for a moment. 'It is true that it may be an efficacious way of dealing with the curse.'

'What curse?' I think of the witches, and the foul visions that they called up.

'That is what I saw in your future when you came to see me. I believe there is some old score to settle. An unpaid debt, something owed by your father.'

'Such as his soul – can you owe such a thing?'

'Each of us is possessed of that mysterious entity. When you see a man die, you see him shrink and lighten as it leaves. If a soul may be owned, *ergo* it may be owed. That would be the logic of the matter.'

I say nothing, my mind confused and all my thoughts on Henry.

Forman pokes the fire and watches the spark flare up the chimney. 'I have discovered something rather interesting. You were not the first person in your family to visit me, Aemilia. When I looked at my old case notes, I discovered this fact.'

'No? Who else have you seen?'

'Your mother, Margaret Johnson. A clever but unlearned woman, and not anything like as beautiful as you.'

'She came for your predictions?'

'She wanted my advice – she was ill and knew her death was coming soon. She told me all about your father, and his mysterious end. She said that when he came from Venice he was a good musician but not a brilliant one, and there were others in his family who had more virtuosity. He was the youngest of six brothers, and always felt that he was in their shadow. Then, he was lost in a storm one winter night, up Tyburn way. When

he came home the next day, with his clothes torn and his eyes starting from his head, he claimed to have no memory of what had happened. But, after that, he played the most extraordinary tunes, composed, sang, arranged – his talents seemed God-given. And then, after one year – exactly one year – he refused to play again.'

'He stopped playing? Why did I never hear of this?'

'She told no one.'

'But . . . I remember him playing all the time! So well! So wonderfully!'

'That may be because he was murdered just one full moon after he'd ceased playing. Murdered in cold blood, by assailants who vanished like ghosts, and were never seen again.'

'Oh, Jesu!' I say. 'I saw it happen. Did he break his bargain with the witches?'

'Who can say? Murderers are skilled at disappearance, such is their modesty about their craft. They may have been as corporeal as you or me.'

'But my mother didn't think so?'

'She was afraid. She had him buried quietly, and told no one of his violent end. No one but myself. It's a strange tale, certainly.'

'What I do know is that these witches have some grudge against me, and have sought me out.'

'Perhaps they believe the debt has yet to be settled.'

'Can such things happen? One soul traded for another?'

'I have heard of it. But all these things are beyond our realm. It is hard to have an illuminating discussion with the dead.'

'And now my child has the plague.'

'God protect him,' says Forman.

'Supposing God has other business?'

Forman looks uneasy. 'Proceed with care, Aemilia,' he says. 'I've known men driven mad by demon-summoning. One student ran babbling in the streets, stark-naked, and when they went to

his room they found a demon as big as an oak tree wedged inside, with its wings pressing against the ceiling and its tail up the chimney. Amateur necromancy is dangerous.'

'I'd die for Henry, a thousand times.'

He sighs and goes to his writing table and picks up a heavy volume. 'Cornelius Agrippa – now, there is an interesting fellow,' he says, opening the book. 'You have heard of him?'

'No.'

'He believes the woman to be – in *some* respects – superior to the male. He cites a great list of those favoured by God, from Eve to Mary Magdalene. Strange, strange views.'

'He sounds like a sensible man to me.'

I follow him to the table, my skirts wet and flapping about my legs, hungry to see this book. The writing is plain and clear, as if it were written yesterday.

'I'm sure he does,' says Forman. He turns a few pages. 'Now, were I to share such opinions, I could pass on what I know to you. All my knowledge, all my secrets. The wisdom of Paracelsus, the learning of Dr Dee. All over Europe, great men are lost in alchemical research, and I would appraise you of it, just as I tell a new maid how to lay the fire.'

'Does he know how to summon demons? Could he help me call down their power?'

'He may help a man who knows enough. If he has sufficient learning.'

'And a woman? As learned as myself?'

'I do not speak of women. I do not share his view of them.'

'Why? Because a woman is for haleking, and nothing more?'

'Now you are insulting me. You know I have always respected your intelligence. However, a woman can no more become a cunning-man that she can become a priest. It is not my doing; it is the natural order of things.'

'But supposing the natural order of things is wrong?' I ask. 'Supposing – with our God-given minds – we can see where nature

can be improved upon? If we were to accept what *is*, without question, why cure disease? Why seek to better anything?'

The doctor looks irritable. 'It is a matter of degree.'

'Good. Because I don't want to be a necromancer. I only want to save my child – as natural a desire as anyone could wish.'

'I do not see how I can help you.'

'If you cannot, then who can? You are my last hope!' I twist my hands together. 'What am I to do? I loved a man who damned me for a whore. Where am I to go? I am not allowed to be a lady, nor a poet, nor free, nor safe from the plague. How shall I go on? I am not allowed to do anything, in this stinking City of ours. Where does that leave me? My sole treasure is my beloved son. I will go now, since my sufferings mean nothing to you.'

The doctor shakes his head. 'You always did get the better of me. So be it.' He takes a bunch of iron keys from a hook by the door, and leads the way out of the consulting room and across the stone-flagged hall. 'I will show you the secret of my cellar,' he says.

'What?'

'If you wish to interfere with life and death, then you must see what is at stake.' He unhooks a rush lamp from the wall. 'There is a reason why such powers are those of gods, not men. Carry this, and light our way.'

I take the light from him.

'No matter what you see, do not drop this lantern,' says Forman. 'Otherwise we will never get out. It's dark as the pit of Hades down there. And, to my knowledge, there is nothing to match my discovery west of Constantinople.'

He unlocks the cellar door with the largest key. The heavy door swings into blackness and reveals a flight of stone steps, descending into the void.

Scene X

I follow him down the steps, my bare feet chilled by the damp stone. The torchlight shines on the scuffs and stains on his old doublet, and on the looped cobwebs on the dusty ceiling close above us. At the bottom of the stairs, the cellar opens out. There is space around us on all sides. It is deathly cold. He places the candle on the ground, and opens the chest. I peer inside. To my surprise, it contains yet another flight of steps, hewn out of the earth. There is a soft, cool scent: the smell of turned soil.

'What! Do you plan to bury me down here?'

'I wouldn't dare,' he says. He climbs over the side of the chest, and begins to descend. 'Whatever do you take me for? Come along! Follow me.'

I scramble down quickly, slithering on the earth steps. When I reach the bottom, I find myself in a narrow chamber, barely big enough for the two of us to fit inside. It is cramped, and filled with so many glass jars and parchment rolls and brass instruments and all manner of weird objects that I am forced to keep my arms close to my sides. Unlike Forman's public consulting room, which is neatly furnished and handsomely appointed, this is slipshod and disordered, as if this is where he lets his mind run free. There are all manner of cups and vessels, made of metal, stone or glass; a round oven, topped with a brass alchemist's kettle; and next to it, suspended from the ceiling like a great globe, a cow's swollen bladder, smelling sickly-sweet.

The doctor goes over to a desk crammed against one wall and spreads out a roll of parchment, pushing sundry oddments out

253

of the way. These include the shrivelled corpse of a half-grown mouldiwarp and what looks like the beak of a little duck. There is also a mirror, of polished black obsidian; a jar of loose teeth; a crystal ball, big as a smith's fist, and a dismembered thumb resting in a glass. (Quite pink, as if newly severed.) I hold up the torch and try to see what he's reading.

'Magicians are earthbound, human, lumps of clay,' he says. 'Ordinary beings, for all our talk of necromancy, all our books. Diseases – like the plague – can carry us off, just as easily as any other mortal. We might as well be stool-boys or dairymen. Yet . . . we can call on some higher state – call upon the planets and the stars – whose sublime powers might influence our sublunary world.'

'They could cure the plague?'

'If one were to find the philosopher's stone, it could cure all diseases, as well as transmute base metal into gold.'

'But you have not found it.'

'Not *quite*, no.'

'But a demon might do the same task? Don't they say so?'

'You wish to learn how to summon a demon. I am reluctant to give you the means to accomplish such an end.'

'I wish to save my son,' I say, again, dogged and determined. 'I will do what I must.'

'For a price, a demon might do anything you ask. But this is dangerous and difficult. You know what happened to Faustus.'

'Faustus was foolish.' I look down at the mass of signs and symbols. 'Show me.'

He covers the numbers with his hands, though he needn't be so cautious, as none of it makes any sense to me. 'It is perilous, Aemilia. There is devilment here. This knowledge is not like some simple tincture, applied to a seeping wound. Remember, we are going above our station. Entangle your spirit with an angel in the heavens, and you will be consumed in fire by their burning righteousness. Tamper with the power of demons

and God help you. Or rather, He will not. Such a direct contact would destroy your fragile body, and imperil your immortal soul.'

'So – all your studies have led to this conclusion? That it's dangerous to take a single step?'

'Quite the reverse.' He shakes his head, fiercely, as if my dullness is too much to bear. He closes his eyes and begins again. 'A man's learning is the distillation of the thinking of a great institution, the riches of the libraries of Oxford or Cambridge or Tübingen.'

'A man! So be it. Perhaps a woman may be more whole-hearted.'

'Will you *listen* to me, Aemilia? Will you *hear* me?'

'My son might die this night for all I know. I have no time for lectures on philosophy.'

'This is no lecture, mistress. This is the stuff of wisdom. Agrippa, that great genius, used the natural elements to tell the future. Earth, fire, water, air. The manufacture of objects – talismans, potions and rings. The summoning of angels and demons to work miracles on his behalf . . .'

'So summon me one! Quick! And I will bear it home to serve me.'

He sighs. 'There you are, you see? Your impatience is proof of your weakness. You grabble after small things, won't wait to be wise. A woman cannot think as a man can think. She is of her nature ruttish, light-minded, and with one eye on her looking-glass.' He points to the obsidian mirror, and there I am, staring out at myself, wild and woebegone.

My hand twitches: I would like to strike him. But I keep silent, watching as he rifles inside a wicker basket before producing another clutch of parchment rolls. He unfurls one, flattens it out on top of the other documents on his desk, and proceeds to examine column after column of tiny black calculations, intricate numbers piled one on top of the other, till they sprout more

numbers and still more, like lamp-black frogspawn. Forman touches the numbers lightly, as if they might sting.

'Theophilis and Cyprian gambled with their immortal souls in the quest for knowledge of this kind,' he says. 'As you will know, being a woman of education and much reading. Death is not the worst we have to fear.'

'Don't lecture me as if I were an infidel! Hell is as real to me as a garden gate.'

He pulls out another page, and bends close to look at it. 'The ignorant seek miracles. Priests, in their expedient wisdom, seemed to bestow as much. There's many a country church with an ass-bone on the altar, said to be the lost rib of a broken saint. Before Good King Henry swept away such falsehood, this land was steeped in lies and incense.'

He seems to have found what he was looking for. He stares at a long calculation, takes two vials of liquid and pours them into a long glass retort, thin as a reed at one end and spherical at the other. The two substances seem to hold back, one from the other, till they mingle with a sullen hiss.

'There is scarcely a town in the realm that could not offer its good burghers a blood-weeping Virgin or a sweetly nodding martyr. No surprise to anyone that the little fish swam shorewards to hear the preaching of St Anthony, or that the Virgin at Saragossa could make half a leg grow whole again.'

He breaks off.

'Magic, you see, Aemilia. *Magic*. Whereas what I'm about is *science*. If I show you what I have hidden here, you must swear that you will never tell another soul.'

'I swear.'

'Good. Because nobody would believe you anyway. This is the last night my discovery will remain here.'

'Why?'

'You are asking me to help you summon a demon.'

'Indeed, I am more than asking you! I am begging you!'

He pulls a stout chest out from underneath the desk and unlocks it. Very carefully, he lifts out a long, narrow object, shrouded in a black velvet cloth, embroidered with a pattern of silver stars. 'The point is, my dear, that the giving of life is a heavy responsibility. Just as any mother knows.'

'What's this?' I whisper. Something prickles my neck, as if a spirit walked. I glance at his little alchemy oven. 'Have you turned base metal into gold?'

'Almost,' says Forman. 'Or, you might even say that this achievement is the greater, since there is one thing in this world more precious even than gold.'

He rests his trembling hands on the draped velvet.

'Diamonds? Rubies?'

'Life itself.' He pulls the cloth aside.

My hands fly to my face and all the breath goes out of me. The cloth conceals a tube of glass, about a foot in length, and no wider than my wrist. I strain to see – my mind is chasing its own horrors – I see rats in the roof-thatch, plague-corpses in the street, a young virgin falling into Hell's pit. My child, running through this Hell towards me. A child. Oh, Lord God! What is the doctor doing? I stumble closer, catch my foot and fall upon the ground, which flames with stars. I come to myself – the doctor is so absorbed by the sight before him that he pays me no attention. I struggle to my feet. My belly is cold. Forman's body blocks my view. But, in the glass, I can see liquid and a little foot.

'What foul sorcery is this?' I whisper.

'Not sorcery, though fools will think it so. It is the higher magic – the crown of an alchemist's craft.'

'You *made* him?'

'Indeed.'

'But . . . I don't understand how this is possible. You are either God himself, or you are . . . the father of this manikin.'

'As you say, I made it.'

I stare at Forman.

'It's monstrous – terrible. Who will rear him? Who will suckle him? How can this be the crown of *anything*?'

'This required great study, let me assure you.' The doctor is studying the newly mixed liquid as it shivers and shifts at the swollen end of the retort. 'The creature is the fruit of a mandrake root and the semen of a hanged man's last ejaculation.'

'So that's what you are: Satan's midwife!'

'The root was dug up before dawn on a Friday, by a black dog bred for the purpose. I washed it and kept it in a pot of milk and honey. Each day I dripped in the blood of a stillborn and the hanged man's seed. And the creature grew and grew – to this.'

'God above! Can he speak, think, pray? Is he a man?'

'It is a homunculus.' Forman lowers the retort. 'I feed it on earthworms and lavender seeds.'

'May heaven forgive you! This is your science?'

'I have my natural children, through the pleasures of the flesh, and now I have this, through the power of my thinking.'

I think of my little Henry, when he was newly born, his tiny wrinkled face and elvish hands. I fear that, being so new, he might go back from this earth to wherever he had come from, and stay there for another eternity. And now . . . now that eternity is perilously close.

'Oh, most noble and erudite scholar! Most respectable philosopher! The Devil himself could not concoct a more vile experiment than this.'

'This is my brain-child.' The doctor frowns, drawing down his ginger brows. 'My invention.' He is distancing himself from his creation with cold words.

I press my hands to my mouth, feeling bile rising in my throat. 'Dear Lord, what are you saying? This is wicked, wicked blasphemy!'

Forman's face is set into a mask of disapproval. 'Do not upset yourself, Aemilia, please. This is merely an experiment in knowledge.'

'An experiment, you say?' I turn to him, shaking. 'You call him your "brain-child". So you are his father, and his mother too.'

'Only in principle.'

'But he is your own son!'

'Who is it, Mistress Lanyer, that wishes to summon demons to do her will? Ah, I forget myself. It is you! You cannot affect such squeamishness as this.'

I swallow acid-tasting puke. 'I want to call up some power that could aid me, so that I can save a life!'

'Very modest.'

'No, sir, not modest, but rooted in maternal love.'

'There is no link between "maternal love" and my vial-grown manikin,' says Forman. 'You see – your female logic is askew.'

'Jesu, sir! If you made him, then you must take care of him.'

'No.'

'Why not?'

'I am neither mother, nor father, to this manikin. I am its Creator.'

'Dr Forman! Hear yourself. Do you put yourself so high? You'll bring damnation on your head.'

He tears his gaze from the glass and looks at me. His eyes shine with determination. 'No. I will not be damned. Your theology is even weaker than your logic. What I have made is mine to destroy.'

'Isn't our Lord the God of Love? *Amor vincit omnia* – isn't that what we were taught? Love conquers all. *Love*, not philosophy. Not science.'

Forman frowns, his face set into stern lines. 'It's all very well to speak of love. Latin can be quoted in any cause. I might just as well say – *vita incerta, mors certissima*. Which has the virtue of being beyond dispute.'

'Oh, brave philosopher! "There is nothing certain in life but death." What thoughts of genius are these! I believe my cat knows as much.'

'In this brute world, men die each day upon the street, faces black with plague. Infants die before they learn to speak their mother's name.'

'Yes – but you can save him from such uncertainty! You can be a merciful God, not a cruel one!'

'And risk my own safety, and that of my family? No, Aemilia. Don't you see? Those who accuse me of necromancy might find this little experiment interesting indeed. Now I know that I can create such a thing, I have no need to preserve it. My work is done.'

'You truly mean to kill him?'

'I want to show you that meddling with life and death has consequences. And they are immense and terrible.'

'If you kill him, you do so because you choose to. You are sick in your soul, sir. Why do such a thing?'

'If the physicians find out what I have done, they will have their proof that I am not a respectable practitioner of medicine but a cozener, a conjurer of spirits.' His face twists to a smile. 'In short, no better than a witch.'

He lifts up the tube.

'Like Drake, and Ralegh, I am sailing to the furthest reaches of what is known. But I have no craft to bear me; my craft is my cunning. Those brave explorers must contend with pirates, ice-floes, sea monsters and the raging oceans. I must fight with vain physicians, caught in their staircase world of weasel tricks and pompous place-men.'

'What torments do beset you, sir! This is all vanity, nothing but self-seeking vanity!'

'They will kill me if they can, do not doubt it.'

My head is spinning with all this. 'You wouldn't murder your own child! Listen, Dr Forman – Simon – I implore you! You should feed him buttermilk and sweetmeats, see where his tastes lie! What does he hear? He might make music the like of which has never been heard in all of time, not even in the Court of Solomon . . . Your discoveries are only just beginning . . .'

'Silence!'

He comes closer. I can see the blood-threads in his eyeballs. I take a step backwards, and press my body against the cold wall.

'Aemilia Lanyer, you come here, breaking my windows, assaulting my privacy, when I am in fear of my life. This is my warning to you. Challenge the natural order if you must, but expect to pay the price.'

'What price?'

The liquid in the retort shimmers against the glass. It is the colour of a cat's eye, yellow flecked with topaz. 'The high magic has its own logic. I gave the creature life . . .' He picks up the glass and tilts it, then empties the liquid out of the retort and into the open top. Eventually, the glass tube brims with the golden liquid. 'And I will take it away.' He thrusts a cork into place, sealing the tiny fellow into his translucent prison. I hear a dread sound, like the aching wind that shakes the house above.

'For pity's sake!' I scream. 'Spare him!' I lunge towards him, but Forman knocks me to the ground. Inside, I can see something which squirms and writhes, then beats against the glass bird-fisted. Crouching like a dog, I spew forth bile. There are no Bible words for this. The doctor uncorks the tube, picks up another glass jar, and tips in the contents. This time the brew is a dark porridge, noxious as the shit in a ditch. It has an odour of incense mixed with the visceral stink of humankind. As the sick brew swirls into the amber liquid, it gurgles and bubbles, churning into black vapour.

I snatch up a candlestick and run back up the first flight of steps – into the vast cellar – and then the second, stumbling over my wet skirts. I run into Forman's study. I can hear his footsteps coming up the stairway. Looking around me, I see Cornelius Agrippa's grimoire, snatch it up and hurry through the hall. Then I unbolt the door and run headlong into the stormy night.

Scene XI

When I return, I run up the staircase to Henry's room and fling myself down beside his bed. He is tossing and turning, with his nightshirt pushed from his shoulders.

'Mother! Help me! I'm burning. I'm freezing . . .' His face is flushed dark, and his breath is foul. He stares at me foggily before his eyes roll backwards and he faints away.

'Henry!' I cry. 'Henry! My darling boy!' I hold him tightly. The whites of his eyes shimmer under his lashes.

Joan pulls the sheets back. 'There, see? Top of his leg. Tucked in the crease.'

A boil, blood-red.

'Plague-sore,' says Joan. She crosses herself and picks up the grimoire, which had fallen to the ground. 'I have heard of such a book, but never thought to see it,' she says. Her face is still. 'I don't need eye-reading for this.'

'What do you mean?' I scramble up and take it from her. I see that the words which were as plain as day at Dr Forman's have now formed themselves into indecipherable squirls and curlicues. '*Eye-reading*? What other kind is there?'

She touches the words on the cover. 'It's called *Pseudo-monarchia Daemonum*. A Bible of the purest evil. Is this what you have brought to cure him?'

I lie down on the bed next to Henry and kiss his hair. The room is swaying; the walls are pale with fever. Sweat is running down my back and Henry's body throbs against mine.

'Death is here! Death is in the house!' Henry starts up, and

is staring at something behind me, just as the Queen had done. I turn to look, half-believing that the grinning spectre might indeed be gazing down at me. There is nothing, except a wall-hanging showing good Susanna and the elders. The two old lechers leer at her over a garden wall. She is draped, white and naked, against the steps down to the blue water. I try to say, 'It's just a fever, my love. You will soon be well.' But I'm drowned out by the sound of a woman sobbing. I realise that the sobs are mine.

'He's come for me! He's come for us all!' cries Henry. And with that he vomits up all down his skinny chest and over my wet chemise, and such a stench I never knew. He rages and pukes, and soon there is nothing left inside him, only bile. We wash him clean, and lay him down again. I change into a clean nightgown, and I can't remember a single prayer, not one, beyond 'Our Father' and then silence.

I lie next to him, my eyes wide and dry now, watching, watching. I hardly know if I live or die, only that he is beside me, and I must guard him, hold him close to the earth with my eyes. Joan scatters rose leaves and bathes his body in sweet waters, and applies a poultice to his brow. She might as well sing him nursery rhymes and do a hop, skip and a jump for all the good it does him. He writhes and tosses and jabbers wicked-sounding words. I hold his hand tightly in mine, in case he runs mad and naked into the windy street. After many hours, he falls into a twitchy stupor, talking to himself.

At the darkest hour of the night, Joan gives me a cup of ale. I prop myself on one elbow and glug it down, wondering at its strange and bitter taste. She rests on a stool by the bedside and drains her own cup to the dregs. The blackness of the night seems to press against the candle-flame. I hear a mournful howling outside. Each long-drawn-out note seems more doleful than the last, and grows ever louder, till at last I say, 'Go and throw something at that hound, I cannot bear it.'

Joan gives me one of her looks. 'Don't you know what that is?'

'A dog, Joan, howling in the night.'

'There are no dogs left. They've all been hanged and skinned for purses. The creature outside is not a thing of flesh and bone.'

'Haven't we troubles enough, without these old tales?'

There is the howl again, most dreadful. It seems to echo inside my aching head. I run to the window and throw it open. There is a bright half-moon, and enough light to see the street by. The wind is blowing hard, flattening the weeds and grasses growing among the stones. But there's not a soul in sight. And no dog, either.

'It's a portent of Death,' says Joan, as I close the casement again.

'Oh, surely. With you, my bold and cheerful servant, everything is a portent of Death. The humming of a bee, a blossom laden tree, the scent of green apples. Death, Death, Death, every time.' But my sharp words tire me, and I lie down next to Henry once more.

Joan stands up. 'I'm going out,' she said. 'Since your errand brought us nothing useful.'

'What?'

'To fetch Father Dunstan.'

'That miserable old Papist! What for?'

'He knows the old religion. The old magic, that some would like to strangle with the law. He'll call St Roth to help us.'

I must have slept, curled round my son. When a great rapping comes on the front door, I rush to answer it, half-falling as I go. But it isn't Joan. It is a man, broad-shouldered, his face hidden in a black mask. He is dressed for a journey in stout boots, a leather doublet and a velvet cap. I know him even before he lifts his mask to look at me.

'Aemilia – Mistress Lanyer – you are safe,' says Will.

'I am alive.'

'And . . . the boy?'

'He lives too.'

He smiles and raises his eyes to Heaven. 'Thank God! Thank God!'

'What do you want?'

He is staring at me so intensely that he seems surprised to hear me speak.

'Can I come in?' he says, urgently.

'Why? What do you *want*?'

'To speak to you, and – '

'Then speak.'

He sighs. 'Come, let me pass.' And somehow he is in the hallway, standing much too close, and I have the sensation of the world falling backwards behind me. He glances around, with his familiar quickness, and more than his usual air of impatience. Taking in my face, my nightgown, the pot of plague-juice on the table, and the cat, gnawing at the hind legs of a coney by the smoking fire. I take a step, and stumble. He catches me, and I look down at the lampblack on his fingers, shocked by their familiarity.

'I hoped not to find you here. I hoped to see your house empty, and you and your brave little Henry gone to the country for safe keeping.' He speaks quickly, yet almost unwillingly.

'Henry is very ill,' I say.

'The King's Men are off to the country,' he says. His voice is rough and throat-sore. I have the feeling that he has rehearsed these words and is determined to say them to me, no matter what. 'To Coventry, Bridgnorth and then – as we hope – to Bath. We're touring the country till the pestilence is over.'

'Henry has a fever.'

'You can't stay here. You must come too.'

'*What?*'

He clears his throat and gives a slight bow, as if he was speaking from the stage. 'Aemilia – I beg you. I am afraid for you. I don't mean to . . . Our association has . . . I know what's gone before. But you would be safe with me. Come, quickly, out of London.'

If I weren't so anxious I would laugh at his confusion.

'We can rent you rooms, apart from the players, in each town that we visit. You'll be away from the infected air and filthy streets.'

'Henry is too ill.'

'No. We can care for him. He can come in a prop-cart. We will keep him warm.'

'I don't think so.'

There is a pause.

'You will both be safe with us,' he says. 'He will not die. You cannot remain in London.'

'It's too late, Will.'

'What?'

'For God's sake, Will! You are not listening to what I say!' I clasp my head in rage. 'Henry has the plague. The *plague*! The very contagion that the bold players flee from – how can I come with you? How can he? What is the purpose in leaving London, if you carry the foul contagion with you? I wish it were not so! I pray I am mistaken! But I cannot go. We must stay here, my son and I, and see it out together.'

He stares at me sadly. 'I see,' he says. He reaches into his bag, and hands me a heavy purse. 'Madam, please. Henry will be well again, I am sure of it. If you won't come, then take this. You might still find a carrying-coach and a man to drive it.'

I give it back to him. 'Don't insult me, sir.'

He looks down at the purse. His hands are shaking. 'When did he fall ill?'

I hesitate. Will frowns, and pushes past me. Before I can stop him, he is upstairs and in my bedchamber. I follow him, dizzy

and confused. Henry is breathing painfully, propped half-upright on his pillows.

Will sits beside him and touches his cheek.

'He has such a look of Hamnet! I knew it. I knew it, when I saw him in the plague-cart. My God . . .' He strokes Henry's sweat-soaked hair. 'When Hamnet died, he was just . . .' He stops. He is staring at Henry with an expression of intense sadness. 'He was eleven, so he might have been . . . taller than I remember. I hadn't seen him for a year. Such a merry little soul. And bold, like this one . . .'

He leans over and kisses Henry on the forehead, crosses himself and rises to his feet. His eyes are full of tears. 'God protect and save you, child,' he says. Then he whispers harshly, 'I always knew he wasn't Hunsdon's.'

I can't speak.

'Those sonnets were written from my heart,' he says. 'With love and hatred entwined within them. To one who changed my life, and then destroyed it.'

'What's done is done,' I say. 'We are older now, and it's all long past.'

He stares down at Henry. 'For pity's sake, Aemilia, take the money. For the child's sake.'

'No.'

'I want to help you. More . . . Or, that is, I should rather say . . .' He wipes his eyes with his sleeve like a child. 'Aemilia . . . He is our son.'

'Please – go.'

Then, another thought seems to strike him and he unhooks a bunch of keys from his belt. 'Take these – the keys to my lodgings at Silver Street. The house is empty – my landlord has taken his family out of London. A friend of mine would be a welcome guest while we are away. You can go there.'

'I live *here*! Is this house not solid enough for you? Goodbye, Will.'

'The poor child has the plague,' he says, flatly. 'If the City councillors hear of it, you will be boarded in for forty days. You know this.'

'Goodbye.'

'I will pray for him,' says Will. He hesitates. 'And for his mother, too.' And then he's gone, leaving the keys upon the bed-table.

Henry makes a strange sound, halfway between a moan and speaking, and I crouch down beside him and my tears pour out at last.

Scene XII

It is the hour before dawn. Footsteps come skittering up the stairs.

'The *parson* is here,' says Joan, in a warning voice.

I don't look at her, but at Henry's matted hair. The word 'parson' strikes me as odd, but not odd enough to jolt me from my misery and fear. 'Then let him pray for my son. He is a good boy and will soon be well. He'll be at church on Sunday.'

'Then repent now of your pride,' says a strange voice.

I see this is a new man, a young fellow, not Father Dunstan. I realise that I had put some faith in the old priest's Catholic magic, and was looking forward to touching the beads of Joan's forbidden rosary and smelling incense.

'Where is Father?' I ask.

'Dead,' says the young man. He has a hard, high voice, which makes simple words sound like sermonising. 'The plague took him off two nights ago. I have come to oversee his parish.'

He is no more than a youth, thin-faced and vinegar-skinned. His eyes seem hollowed into his skull. There is no flesh on his bones and his robes hang on him like dying-sheets.

'And who might you be?' I ask, holding Henry tighter.

'I am Parson John,' he says. 'A Cambridge man, of Sidney Sussex College. I abhor Papism in all its incarnations and I bring the Word of God to the common man.'

I take against him straight away. So much so that a glimmer of life returns to me. It is not hope that renews my spirit, but anger.

'The Word of God was here before you,' say I.

'The Word can be misunderstood.'

'By some, Parson John, but not by me, you will find. I can read it in the Latin.'

'Then be fearful of the sin of pride.'

'Say a blessing for this child, if you will. But we need neither priest nor parson. Go back to your flock. Some of them might yet be grateful for your sour-faced sermonising.'

But then Henry's eyes flicker open. 'Mother!' he screeches. 'Don't let him take me! Death is here! Death is in the room!' And he lets out the most terrible cry, worse than a murderer crushed under a pile of stones.

'Hush, child! Hush!' I say.

The parson glares. 'There speaks Satan's voice!' he cries. 'You see? This pestilence is God's punishment, and evil-doers suffer. That child will go straight to Hell if he is not blessed before he dies.'

Henry frees himself from my grasp. In doing so, he wriggles right out of his nightshirt, and stands by the bed, naked and dribbling with sweat. Parson John raises his hands above his head. I'm not sure if this is because he is calling on his Maker, or because he fears to touch my fever-ridden son.

'Pray for him, for pity's sake!' I cry. 'Speak to God, and ask him to spare my child. It is not his time! Tell the Lord this boy is innocent.'

'There are many mothers who could make the same plea. I see them by the score, Mistress Lanyer. You must accept the will of God. Do you forget that he sent ten plagues down on the people of Egypt? And the last of these *alone* killed every first-born son?'

'Mistress, you must save his soul,' says Joan. I look at Henry, and see that his limbs are covered with a rash of purple spots, dark as blackberries.

'No!' I scream. 'No! It cannot be.'

'It is God's will,' says the parson. 'Say your prayers.'

'By God, I swear I will not give up my child!' I scream. 'Get out of my house, you prating fiend!'

The parson's eyes widen, and he presses his hands together as if in prayer. 'Woman! How dare you speak in this manner to the servant of the Lord? Do you *defy* me?'

But I can no longer stop myself. 'I do defy you, sir! Yes, I do.'

'Then you are evil.'

'I defy you, and all who deny us hope.'

'Mind your words, mistress. For this, you will burn in Hell, for all eternity, with your son beside you.'

'Get out of my house!'

'You will exist in mortal agony, blistered and contorted in the flames, but never consumed. Your throat will cry out for water, but will crack like a desert. On Judgement Day the Lord will cast you out once more, into the eternal emptiness that lies beyond our understanding. Is that your wish?'

'If you call my son a sinner, who must be punished by this dreadful death, then I stand by every word I say, Parson John of Sidney Sussex College. I defy God himself, and all his angels. My son will *live*.'

'O-ho, mistress! You are not in your right mind. Remember who and what you are. A slip-shake pike, sliding through the twisting Thames, is only slightly less than you. A lowing heifer, chewing her cud on Chelsea Green, is your dull sister. By Heaven! I never heard an honest woman speak so!'

'Then honest women are fools.'

'Do *you* determine who will live or die? Are *you* the architect of your earthly fate? Fie on you for a witch and a most unnatural whore! There is something evil in you, I swear it, and in your kind, and the Lord will only forgive you if you bow down now and seek humble and profound forgiveness for this vile rebellion, this pustulating canker of the soul.'

I bend close to Parson John, so I get an unholy whiff of boiled onion on his breath.

'Leave this house,' I say. 'Get out, you scripture-spouting, fish-cold arse-wart. Or I'll call down a curse which'll curdle the guts in your belly.'

'Witch!' he hisses back at me. 'Evil succubus! Hear the Word of our Lord – *There shall not be found among you anyone that burns his son or his daughter as an offering . . .*'

'Spindle-shanked God-botherer!' I shout. 'I want to save my son, not burn him – '

'. . . *anyone who practises divination, a soothsayer, or an augur . . .*'

'Would you like to know what I predict?' I cry. 'That you will die in mortal agony, grabbling the air in your final madness, and Almighty God won't give a farthing . . .'

'. . . *or a sorcerer, or a charmer, or a medium, or a wizard, or a necromancer . . .*'

'Such a one as me? The fair and feeble sex? A wizard *woman*? Whoever would believe it?' I shove him hard, towards the door. 'I'll broil your brain in its shallow skull! Mangle your preachifying words into Bedlam babble, and corrupt your skin into a thousand worm-infested sores! I'll make you pray for Hades as a respite from your pain! And I'll twist your mind to such distraction that you'll tear off all your limbs to find relief and sanity! Do you hear me, you pox-groined, foul-nosed turd-stain?'

The parson takes a step backwards, eyes round with horror. And then Henry, who has been staring at the parson all this time, steps between us.

'Cure me, if you are a man of God,' he says.

The parson turns his startled gaze to the boy.

'Cure me, I command you.'

'Hell's progeny!' cries Parson John. 'Vicious, misbegotten whelp! Thou shalt not command a priest!'

And Henry spits a great gob of phlegm right at the holy man, and it lands on his yellow cheek and slides down slowly, leaving a shining trail behind.

The fierce insanity which loosened my tongue departs, and all I can see is blackest pandemonium, till at last I am crouching down on the floor, in the hall downstairs, with Henry shaking and spewing all down my chemise. It is dawn. I look up, and there is the figure of Joan, towering above us, wrapped in her black cloak. She seems taller and straighter than before, and her face, shadowed by the folds of cloth, strangely ageless. Her eyes, fixed upon me, are sorrowful.

'I hope I have served you well, mistress,' she says.

I stare up at her distant face wondering, in my feverish state, why she stands upon such high ground. It seems to me that I must be in an open grave, while she is standing on turned soil above. But I realise that I am lying on the stone flags of the hall, prickled by strewing-herbs. I am in my own house, after all.

'Until today you looked after me well enough,' I say.

'The parson could have helped you, if you'd let him. For all he is a Puritan, he serves the same God.'

'Serve! Serve! Why use this word so often?' I shift Henry's weight, and wipe his face. 'I am finished with service. Catholic, Puritan, parson, priest – I don't give a pigwidgeon for any of them. I will *not* serve.' I pick up a stand of dried marjoram and smell it, thinking of quiet herb gardens and meadow daisies.

'Beware of this ungodly pride, mistress. For I must leave you now, and, next time I see you, I hope it's in a better place than this.'

I toss the marjoram on to the floor. 'Abandon me now, in this house, with my sick son and the beadle doubtless on his way to board us in? A loyal and faithful servant indeed! Shame on you.'

She bends down and gives me something cold which jangles: Will's bunch of keys.

'You will need these,' she says. 'Listen to me, Aemilia Lanyer. In all my life, you are the finest woman I have ever known, and the boldest. But you are not the wisest. I have loved you dearly, as I have loved your son. From the moment I first set eyes on you, all fire and no sense, I knew that I must help you. I was a penitent, but had not served my penance. In you, I saw a kindred spirit, someone who needed help, and yet would never seek it. A brave soul adrift in a cruel world. I burned my shop myself, so there was no going back, and I became your servant. And I am your servant still.' Her voice is softer now, yet there is nothing of the servant in it.

Outside, I can hear the distant sound of shouting. Unusual now, in streets which are normally so silent. The beadle, of course, with his merry men, summoned by the good parson. The boarding-up of houses often lures a crowd.

'Now, go,' she says.

'Go? What do you mean? Where shall I go?'

There is a knock on the door, and she opens it. Tom Flood is standing there, blushing in his finest velvet.

'Joan – Mistress Lanyer – I . . .'

'Hurry,' says Joan. 'Tom has a cart, at the end of the lane. Full of costumes for the tour. John Heminge is holding the horses but he grows impatient.'

Tom stares at her.

'Take my mistress to the Mountjoy house, and be on your way,' says Joan. 'But be careful. The boy has the plague. There is a hand-cart by the door.' Mysteriously, there is.

Tom looks confused. 'Mistress Lanyer . . . ?'

'Help me,' I say, getting to my feet. Between us we wrap Henry in a bed-sheet and lay him gently on the cart. He is sleeping uneasily, and his eyelashes flutter as if disturbed by nightmares.

Joan follows us out. 'This is a brave deed, child,' she says, touching Tom's arm. Then she turns to me and hugs me tightly, and when we break apart she gives me Simon Forman's grimoire. 'You'll need this,' she says, 'if you are set on saving Henry.'

'But I can't . . .'

'But you will. God bless you, Aemilia. Now, hurry.'

We trundle the cart slowly forward till we are halfway down the street, the shouting of the crowd growing louder and louder behind us. There are yells and chants and the noise of pipes and drums. I look back, wondering again how Joan could leave me at such a time. She is standing with her back towards us, facing the oncoming noise. Why is she waiting? What is she doing?

'Hurry,' says Tom, face set with fear. 'We must get on.'

'Why did you come for us?' I ask, as we set to pushing the cart again. 'You could be halfway to Coventry by now! Such kindness, Tom!'

Tom is more flushed than ever. 'Henry is my dear friend,' he says.

'Pray God you are rewarded for your good heart.'

The end of the street is in sight, and there is the carriage and John Heminge, just as Joan had said.

'Thank God,' says Heminge. 'How does the boy?'

I can't speak. We lift Henry from the hand-cart and settle him in the carriage among the masks and head-pieces. The sound behind us has reached a pitch of fury and I am sick with fear for Joan. Then there is a hideous scream, long and piercing, followed by wild cheering. 'Wait,' I say. 'I will only be a moment.' And, before Heminge can stop me, I run back towards the shouting mob.

The crowd has formed a wall of backs, making a neat circle. I push my way forward, but my view is still obscured by those who have fought for a good viewing place. Even so, I can see

a dark-robed figure is standing in the centre, its face obscured by a black hood. The ringleaders are cat-calling and shouting filthy names. There are sixty or seventy people in the rabble: plague-followers, apprentices, vagrants, beggars and idiots. All of them are ill-dressed and ill-favoured. Some have the dazed stare of passers-by who have been sucked into the fray. Others – with their shrivelled faces and tattered clothes – look as if they spend their life on the road. I examine their contorted, shouting faces, wondering at their rage and hatred. A thin boy with a drum is beating out a gallows tattoo. An old crone with a twisted mouth wields a pitchfork. A young girl with a fair white face and filthy, tangled hair holds a firebrand above her head.

A clod of earth falls on the ground followed by a rain of stones and pebbles. Most fall short, but some find their mark and the figure winces and trembles at each blow. Then a heftier stone hits home, the hood falls back and the face of the victim is revealed.

'Joan!' I shout. 'Joan!' But no one hears me.

'What – would you hex a holy man?' screams one worthy, a wide and burly fellow twice Joan's size.

'Would you curse a parson?' cries another voice.

'Unruly, venomous bitch!'

The young girl thrusts the brand towards Joan. 'You stinking witch, we'll peel your skin from your body while you still live, and pin it up on the church door! The wrath of God is upon you! We'll do His will.'

Cursing the parson? What does this mean? Are they torturing her for *my* crime? 'JOAN!' I scream. 'For pity's sake, why don't you tell them? Tell them who cursed the parson! Tell them it was me!' I turn first one way and then the other, to see a fat matron screaming gutter-curses and a young lawyer squealing with rage. 'It's me you want!' I cry. 'It's me!' But the thunder of their joined cries is deafening. No one hears me.

The mob shifts, and I have a better view. Joan is almost unrecognisable as the upright figure from the hall. Her cloak has gone, and her dress is torn and bloody, half-ripped away from one shoulder so I can see where her flesh has been torn. Her hair is loose and her arms are scratched and bleeding.

'Witch's blood,' calls the crowd. 'Witch's blood! Bleed the witch and save yourself from her sin!' A boy runs forward – he is no older than Henry – and slashes at her face with a knife. She makes no sound, just looks from face to face without hope or fear. A stone hurtles towards her, smashing her on the temple. Another follows, then another, and suddenly the sky is filled with missiles and the crowd roars with blood lust. Joan grunts as she falls to the ground. The crowd closes in.

'Joan!' I scream again. I force my way forward. The crowd is dancing now, in a fashion, stamping in unison, first with the left foot and then with the right, and clapping out a slow rhythm. It has become one creature, one deliberate, remorseless behemoth. 'My God! Help me! Joan!'

The mob yells with one voice, 'Kill the witch! Kill the witch!'

Another boy throws a rope over an oak tree. Turtle doves fly from it, and he makes a noose and puts it round Joan's neck. Her eyes meet mine, and, although I long to, I can neither move nor speak. I open my mouth to call her name, but something is holding me back. And a voice speaks inside my head. '*Aemilia. I told you. Go now, in God's name.*'

The noose around her neck is pulled tight, and she grasps at it, her eyes bulging. They drag her towards the tree. With a 'heave ho' and shrieks of laughter they lug her upwards, so she stands on tiptoe. A heavy stone is flung towards her, smashing her mouth into a bloody hole of broken teeth. Then a burly man runs forward, and slashes her across the belly with his knife, and she grunts again, and all her guts spill out of her. Inside my head, I hear such a scream as the damned must scream, and I pray hard, hard, asking God to take her. I remember how Charles Blount and

his men had pulled at Southwell's legs when he dangled from the gibbet and how they broke his neck and saved him from his final torture, and I long to do the same, but am still spellbound. There is another banshee scream. And then the voice again, from inside that dreadful sound. '*Go, Aemilia! Go from here! God speed. My service is finished.*' Joan's voice is stern and powerful.

The crowd laughs and whoops to see the blood, and the pale girl holds her nose, making fun of the stench of Joan's snaking innards. I squeeze my eyes shut, willing her to die. They pull her up higher, and her arms flail and her bare feet kick thin air as she dances her life out. I think of those clever hands, that saved my son, of her good sense and acid tongue, that have preserved my sanity a thousand times. *God help her*, I pray. *God help us all.*

Then, suddenly, everything stops. All is silence, and Joan is still. The crowd falls back. I cannot bear to look at her dead face. Her cloak is lying on the ground. I pick it up, then turn and flee.

Silver Street is a good road, wide and well-kept, off Cheapside, in sight of St Paul's and west of the low arch of Cripplegate in the City walls. Like the rest of London, it is filled with a strange quiet, a plague-quiet. As we make our way inside, the silence rings in my ears after the noise of the crowd. I keep my gaze fixed on my son's face, and do not weep for Joan's sacrifice, but determine to make it worthwhile.

Heminge carries Henry to an upper chamber, and gently lays him on a four-poster bed. 'This is Will's room,' he says. 'He is praying for you, Aemilia. So are we all.'

I don't like the way he looks at Henry, as if all hope has gone. 'Thanks, Mr Heminge, for all your pains, and your great patience. Now you can be on your way,' I say. My calm voice sounds false to my own ears.

He takes my hand and bows, very grave. 'I wish you luck, and God's blessing.' Tom is watching with tears on his face.

When they have gone, I lock the street door behind them, and tend to Henry as best as I can. His whole body is raised and black with plague-sores, and they smell most horrible. It is the scent, I suppose, of poisoned blood. The nails of his hands and feet are of the same colour, as if he has rubbed them with dark river mud. Each breath sounds like a knife scraping on a skillet, and his chest trembles with the effort. Though sweat rolls from his body, his limbs are freezing to the touch.

I am swim-headed. The room swerves and shifts around me. I feel that I am flying through the air. Here I am, in Forman's little cell once more. I am on the floor, and looking up at the good doctor working at his bench. He lifts a cloth from a tube of glass. There, lying peacefully inside, is a little man. Not an infant, but an adult, full-formed male, well-made and (for his scale) well-hung. Naked as Adam in the Garden of Eden. His limbs are as pale as the moon, the little muscles of his body all most perfectly aligned. He is sound asleep, his head resting on the crook of one arm for a pillow. Then his eyes open, and he gazes at me. And he looks down at his naked dangling parts, and covers them with his hands, as I've seen Henry do when he was bathing and fancied Joan could see him. Lord God! I could not save him.

And then I pray – some words come to me at last – hoping God might yet turn his face in my child's direction, even though I am hell-bound myself: '*O God, the Father of heaven, have mercy upon us miserable sinners. Remember not, Lord, our offences, nor the offences of our forefathers; neither take thou vengeance of our sins: spare us, good Lord, spare thy people, whom thou hast redeemed with thy most precious blood, and be not angry with us . . .*'

I turn to look at him, weary and empty. Henry's eyes are half-open. But I know he can see nothing, not the carved bed-roof, decorated with bright, leaping porpoises, nor my face as I bend over him.

'Henry?' I put my hand against his cheek. 'Can you hear me, little one?'

His breath comes in a rasping sigh. I know that sound. When Death is near, the watchers wait in the eternity between each breath. In the end, they witness the final rattle as the soul departs. The waiting is over, and the mourning begins. That rasping sound has the rattle of death in it. *My little boy, my precious one. Henry Lanyer, my only child. All my world, in this small frame. What will I be without you? How shall I live? What shall I do?*

But no. He is not ready. I am not ready. His life still lies before him. I will not serve. God has deserted us. It is time. Time to set myself apart from wise women and cunning-men. Time to see how far magic will take me. If a witch must call on demons, then so be it. If demons are in the service of Beelzebub, then I am willing to take the consequences.

Scene XIII

I pick up the grimoire. My hands are stiff and trembling. I fumble with the pages, not certain what I'm looking for. A sign? A clue? There are demons hidden here, in these queer hieroglyphics and tables, figures like amulets instead of letters, pictures of chariots and scrotums, serpents and priestesses, the sage hierophant and inverted Hanged Man. How can I unlock a spirit from these strange inscriptions? I close my eyes and think of Joan, hanging from the tree. I see her eyes, fixed on mine.

When I open my eyes, the room is writhing and spinning. I can see Henry, but he seems far away, on a shore I can't reach. Black mists drift between us. I stretch out my hand to touch him. Pustules like bilberries cover my arm from wrist to elbow. *Holy God. Holy God. He has the plague and now I have it too.* I close my eyes again, but this time I see Joan's face close to, angry and accusing. It seems as if she wants to speak to me. But I don't know what she wants to say. What does she want to tell me? How can she help me now?

I grasp the bed-post and haul myself upright. Nausea and pain flood my body. I stagger backwards, then notice a tumble of darkness on the floor. I touch it – rough wool, coarse against my fingers. But there is something else – the slightest tremor, like a living creature. An animal would be warm – but this fabric cools my hot fingers. It is Joan's black cloak.

I put it on, and it falls around me in deep, whispering folds. I pull the hood over my head and the whispering continues, like the wind in the bulrushes, like the beating of a raven's wing. I can

hear Joan's voice, as if it is coming from a long, long way away. I can hear words – what is she saying? *I am a penitent witch. I am a penitent witch.* I see her putting a newborn child into my arms. I hear her words: *You'll keep it.*

Then I hear her voice say, '*Draw a circle.*'

I hesitate, not knowing if I have the strength.

She repeats, '*Draw a circle.*'

I find a lump of white chalk in the pocket of the cloak. Falling to my knees, I scrabble on the floor, pushing back the rushes with feverish hands. Then, breathing hard, I draw a great circle, nine feet across. '*Very good,*' says Joan. '*The space you have made is outside creation. Demons and spirits may enter it. You must stay on the outside. Do not cross the line. Do not listen if the demon tempts you.*'

I pick up the grimoire once more. My head is hot and heavy and I want to lay it down, to lie upon the frozen Thames in winter and become as one with that white cold.

'*Open the book.*'

I do so, and the mist slowly parts. First, I see only:

Τηεψ σαψ τηατ τηε ποωερ οφ ενχηαντμεντσ ανδ ϖερσεσ ισ σο γρεατ, τηατ ιτ ισ βελιεϖεδ τηεψ αρε αβλε το συβϖερτ αλμοστ αλλ Νατυρε. Απυλειυσ σαιτη τηατ ωιτη α μαγιχαλ ωηισπερινγ, σωιφτ ριϖερσ αρε τυρνεδ βαχκ, τηε σλοω σεα ισ βουνδ, τηε ωινδσ αρε βρεατηεδ ουτ οφ ονε αχχορδ, τηε Συν ισ στοππεδ, τηε Μοον ισ χλαριφιεδ, τηε Σταρσ αρε πυλλεδ ουτ, τηε δαψ ισ κεπτ βαχκ, τηε νιγητ ισ προλονγεδ.

But then the signs begin to wriggle and squirm, and I see that they are turning into words, the very words I needed to find.

They say that the power of enchantments and verses is so great, that it is believed they are able to subvert almost all

Nature. Apuleius saith that, with a magical whispering, swift rivers are turned back, the slow sea is bound, the winds are breathed out of one accord, the Sun is stopped, the Moon is clarified, the Stars are pulled out, the day is kept back, the night is prolonged.

This, then, is what I was after! What verse, though, what simple verse could unmake plague? I search back and forth through the incense-scented pages. Then I read these words aloud:

'Her with Charms drawing Stars from Heaven, I
And turning the course of rivers did espy;
She parts the earth, and Ghosts from Sepulchres
Draws up and fetcheth bones away from th'fires,
And at her pleasure scatters clouds i'th'Air,
And makes it Snow in Summer hot and fair.'

Is it snowing, or summer, now? My head is hot, but my hands have turned cold. I look down at them: they seem far away from me. I pull the cloak tighter around me, and feel a sick languor overwhelm me as I read the second verse:

'At will, I make swift streams retire
To their fountains, whilst their Banks admire;
Sea toss and smooth; clear Clouds with Clouds deform.
With Spells and Charms I break the Viper's jaw,
Cleave solid Rocks, Oakes from their seizures draw,
Whole Woods remove, the lofty Mountains shake,
Earth for to groan, and Ghosts from graves awake
And thee, O Moon, I draw –'

A Creature comes forth from the darkness, forming itself in the circle, so that shrouds and filaments of shadow are

woven into a formless shape. There is a wind around me, and a terrible stench, of rotting flesh and plague. There are sounds, like twisted weeping and the screams of babes. Yet unlike, too. The stench and the sounds are relations of what I can recognise, but not their copy. A band of pain wraps itself around my head, tighter and tighter and tighter. I clutch my forehead, but I stay in my place, holding some inner part of myself quite still. I have summoned Evil, there is no doubt of that, and it is growing and twisting in the circle, burgeoning out of itself, deforming as it grows. I listen for Joan, but I can't hear her. The sound of rushing air and weeping fills my ears, my mind, my body. I lower my arms and lift my head and look directly forward, at the Creature in the circle. For it has formed now, and is folded and hunched within its allocated space, and it has fixed me with its yellow eyes.

Thunder and lightning. The light shrieks over a blasted heath. Rocks are piled like plague skulls; the ground is running with rain and stones. A figure, bent double against the gale, walks towards me, a blacker shape against the dark sky. I turn to run, but my feet are broken tree-stumps, rooted in the frozen earth. The shape comes closer and I open my mouth to scream; my cry is noiseless and the creature grabs my hand. Its hood falls back.

'Fair is foul, and foul is fair,' speaks a bloody hole of broken teeth. Two horsemen are galloping towards us, two soldiers, bloodied with the battle.

'All hail, Macbeth,' shouts a young virgin selling sugar-plums. 'Hail to thee, Thane of Glamis.'

'All hail, Macbeth. Hail to thee, Thane of Cawdor,' says the beak of a raven.

'All hail, Macbeth, that shall be King hereafter,' I cry.

The men have fallen to the ground; their faces look up at us, the faces of children.

Knock, knock! Simon Forman shuffles to the door, a great gate the size of St Paul's. He shudders and shakes, aping frailty. 'Here's a knocking indeed! If a man were Porter of Hell-Gate, he should have Old Nick turning the key. Knock, knock, knock! Who's there, in the name of Beelzebub? Oh, come in, equivocator! Knock, knock. Never at quiet! What are you? But this place is too cold for Hell. I'll devil-porter it no longer: I had thought to let in some of the professions, that take the primrose way to th'everlasting bonfire . . . Anon, anon!'

Over the battlements, the wind rips my hair from my shoulders. The castle is stone and sky. I watch and wait for my Lord Macbeth. I have the spells and potions set around me. Poisoned entrails, toad-venom, dog-tongue and blind-worm's sting. The finger of a birth-strangled babe, ditch delivered by a drab. A charm of fell-gruel, hell-broth – wolf-tooth and hemlock digged in the dark. 'Glamis thou art, and Cawdor, and shalt be what thou art promised.'

For I can conjure what God will not; if Fate is tardy, I am always to the clock. The child lies in the dark room; the curtains are drawn around him; I tear them back. His face is black; they are calling him. The merry devils dancing in the fire and snow. The sepulchre is opening by his bed; all it needs is a little tumble – so – and there he goes! Down, down, to the place we all must end. Heaven and Hell are pulpit words; our station is in the ground, where the worms are, where the bee sucks.

'Hail to thee, Macbeth! Thou would'st be great, art not without ambition, but without the illness that should attend it. Would'st not play false, and yet would wrongly win.'

Here are the daggers. I would have killed the King myself, if he had not resembled sweet Bassano as he slept.

His hand is warm in mine. He towers above me. The tunes are angel voices, curling and rising in the air. His tales open out the seas

and skies; I float over the Grand Canal and see high-tailed boats decked out with cloth-of-gold, and masked princesses, their pale hands trailing in the water. Blood curdles the still reflections; their scarlet fingernails make the green one red. They come behind us, silent. I hear nothing, only feel the wind of their bodies as they rush at us, and we are falling, falling. His hand is torn from mine; his scream is pig-like. Fly from here! His dear body, riven with blood, the stench of it, on my hands, my face. Here's the smell of the blood still. Father! If I could call him back – would I? He would be a dead thing, then, the bloody and disfigured spectre of himself. If charnel-houses and our graves must send those that we bury back, our monument must be the belly of a crow. Dare I?

Glamis thou art, and Cawdor, and shalt be what thou art promised. Then screw thy courage to the sticking point, and we'll not fail.

I run along the battlements. London is on the one side: the plague-carts rattle, the ale-houses are singing, there are flames on the horizon and there, far off, I can see the King and all his courtiers, watching Twelfth Night. *See the boys upon the stage! Graceful Viola, with Tom's fine leg. Safe from me, from my contagion. But this is Scotland: see how the Viking sea rolls and storms, see the mountains and the mist and there is Scone, where they will crown you, my lord. Far away.*

The witch has black hair and the wings of a gryphon and the body of a serpent, twined around a tree. She is angry, and her forked tongue is made of fire. They strung Joan up; I could not save her. I held my hand out to her. I called her name, but no one heard me. She died for us. I will smirch their faces with the King's blood, if it helps this cause. There is no stopping-place for me, for there can be no punishment that is worse than this. Look – my hands are your colour, but I would scorn to wear a heart so white. What need we fear who knows it, when none can call our power to account?

The witch holds me with her woman's arms, and presses me to her breast. Her heart is beating, and her wings tear at the sky. The wind blows harder as she carries me higher, and I see it all below me, and it is a perfect pattern; I understand everything. I am GOD.

The Creature shifts and settles, malevolent and silent. It is a Winged Serpent, green and glittering, with the face and torso of a woman, white and cold. Is it female? I think it is. Her head is covered with black hair, which curls and coils to the ground. Her skin is bone-white and her arms are corpse-thin with narrow, spindle-fingered hands. Her yellow eyes have no pupils, merely snake-slits. There is no mercy in them. The great wings are folded; they are bone and gristle and cloud. They press against the ceiling and shift against the plasterwork as if the room cramps them. Fragments of white dust fall from above, and speckle the restless emerald tail.

'Who are you?' I ask.

'I am Lilith, Wife of Adam and the slayer of his children.'

Of all the demons of the air, I have called this one. Removed from Eden, she set out to kill one hundred babes a day. Of all the demons of the air, I have called the cruellest Serpent Queen of witchcraft. But she is in my circle, and I have the spell-book, and I must control her.

'I want you to save my son,' say I. 'You cannot have this child. He's mine.'

Her tail lashes towards the perimeter of the circle. 'He is dying,' she hisses, unblinking. 'He is at our gates.'

'You can have my soul instead of his.'

'The soul that's owed?'

'Yes. I will die for him, and gladly.'

'And burn in Hades? Until the Day of Judgement?'

'I will do anything.'

Lilith looks at me, full of poison to the brim. 'There is another way,' she says. 'There is a service you can do us, and keep your petty life.'

A cauldron forms from the air, and Lilith fills it with smoke-vapour and a vial of ruby liquid. She catches the light from the room in her fingers and presses it into her palms, forming it into a tiny orb, so the room is dark and the orb its candle. Then she drops it into the cauldron, and all is black.

'Do we have a bargain?' she says, in the darkness.

And I say, 'We have a bargain.'

'Go into the plague-pit,' she says, 'and bring me the head of a child.'

I see it is there before me – the pit and the stench and the human stew. Lilith gives me a stinking knife, smirched with gouts of blood. So I climb down into the plague-pit – down a flight of steps, carved out of the earth, smelling of soil and the ends of roots – and I find a homunculus lying in his glass, but he is a little boy. I carve his head off; the blade cracks through bone and sinew, and his eyes open to stare at me.

Across the rooftops I run, over the blasted spire of St Paul's, here I come, to Cripplegate, to my little one. Ah, my pretty boy! I have given suck, and know what it is to love the babe that milked me. And I am he, the dying child, and through my closed lids I can see infinity. I will lay my hand on my own forehead, so. I will call my own spirit back into itself. I am all things, and all people, all deaths and all life. Henry Lanyer, return to this place. Lord God, it is not his time. Restore him, Lord, restore him!

I open my eyes. I cannot tell if it is morning or evening, but the room is in semi-darkness. I look around me. My head still aches, but I no longer feel confused – the fever has left me. How long have I been here? Above my head, I see a blue ocean. Azure

waves chase each other across the upside-down seascape, and whales and porpoises and swordfish leap among them. The water is every shade of blue from navy to bright turquoise. The fish are grey and green and silver, painted bright upon the foaming spray so I can see each neat scale. I lie still and look at these for a while, not knowing who or what I am.

Then I remember.

'Henry?' I cry out. 'Henry?'

And I struggle up on to my elbows, and look, and there he is, lying next to me. He is quite still. His gold hair is matted against his cheeks, and he is half-turned away from me, so all I can see is one pale cheek.

'My love!' I scream. 'My little one!' I grab his body and hold him. 'Do not go away from me! Stay with me! God help us! Help us!' And I sob bitterly, drenching his tangled hair with my tears.

'I *am* with you,' says a muffled voice.

I hold him still closer, stunned and confused.

'Mother,' says the muffled voice again. 'You are squeezing me to death. Why are you crying?'

If I live as long as Joan I will never know such joy again. Henry wriggles out of my grasp. He looks up at me, pale but smiling. He is Henry, exactly and completely Henry, my merry son.

'Look!' he cries, lifting his nightshirt. I see that the vile plague boils have shrivelled up. Some are half-healed scabs, others nothing more than faint bruises. 'I am cured!' he says, eyes shining. 'I am immortal, Mother. You can let me do anything now, for God will protect me, have no doubt of it.'

'A clever thought, Henry, but we will dispute this later,' say I, kissing him on his cheek and hugging him again. 'My angel boy! Oh, Henry! Praise God! Oh, praise the Lord in Heaven!' I look at my own arms, and see that they too are clear of the inflammation. Miracle or magic, some wonder has surely taken place.

Now Henry sleeps, a deep, rosy sleep, like the first settled repose of a newborn. I lie next to him, looking at him, still dazed with shock and disbelief. Finally, I begin to drowse, but am jolted awake by Lilith's voice. *'The pages,'* she says. *'You must go and find your pages.'* I sit bolt upright, eyes wide open, and look around me. I notice, for the first time since Henry's recovery, the chalk circle on the floor. There is no sign of Lilith: it's as if she was never there at all. I look up at the ceiling, and the plaster has flaked off in places, but there is nothing to suggest that a demon's wing was the cause.

Then I see that the floor is covered with crumpled pages. I scramble out of bed and pick up one of the sheets. It is covered with writing – my writing. I peer at it, confused. It appears to be a record of my weird hallucinations: the castle and the lady and the fires of London. *'This is our bargain,'* says Lilith. *'Write up these notes and make a play of them. Write a play the like of which London has never seen.'*

I get up early and sit at the table by the bedroom window. On the table are some sheets of clean foolscap, a quill and a glass of lamp-black, as if Will were just about to sit down and start work on his next play. My mind is at once disturbed and clear: both filled with images and memories and quite empty. I pick up the quill, and dip it into the ink. I think of the wild castle and the strange creatures who live in it, and the blood seeping across the stone floor. I write the words: *The Tragedie of Ladie Macbeth.* And below it I add: *By Aemilia Bassano Lanyer.*

And then my fingers close more tightly around the quill, and I dip it again and began to scratch across the parchment. My hands move quick, as if I had written all this before. My queer dreams fill my head, the poems I have struggled to form make new and easy patterns, and the words of Holinshed whirl around me.

The raven himself is hoarse, that croaks the fatal entrance of Duncan under my battlements. Come, you Spirits that tend on mortal thoughts, unsex me here, and fill me, from the crown to the toe, top full of direst cruelty! Make thick my blood, stop up th'access and passage to remorse; that no compunctious visitings of Nature shake my fell purpose, nor keep peace between th'effect and it! Come to my woman's breasts, and take my milk for gall, you murth'ring ministers, wherever in your sightless substances you wait on Nature's mischief! Come, thick Night, and pall thee in the dunnest smoke of Hell, that my keen knife see not the wound it makes, nor Heaven peep through the blanket of the dark, to cry 'Hold! Hold!'

I write all that night, with the wind beating against the windows, till the sun comes up over the City walls and its clear light fills the room.

Scene XIV

Henry and I live happily in Will's house in Silver Street. The months pass quickly. In the daytime, I must teach or entertain my son. He is Henry, just as he was, hale and happy and silly and full of life. My greatest task is to keep him from the streets. He is allowed to come with me to buy food once a week, as long as he keeps close to me. I suspect he could not catch the plague twice. But I will not take the risk, so we live like hermits. I pray and pray and pray, and offer up my thanks to God.

However, when Henry sleeps at night, I return to my pages and improve them, taking out dead words and putting in live ones. It's a candle-tale, put together bit by bit in the guttering half-light. After many changes, I see that I have indeed written something that might be called a play. It seems to have drawn on fear, and horror of the plague, as well as something of Lilith's diabolic craft. It is plague-play, I suppose. I am so happy and so blessed that my son lives that it is strange to have written something so dark and sinister. And yet it is a celebration too, of the darkness of the human soul.

Who can say which stories will last and which will fade away? Old women crouch together round the fire, their figures humped against the flaming logs of oak and apple wood. They tell tales. Anyone can stop and listen. The servant girl carrying an empty flagon; the hunter sweating from his reckless ride; a young boy leaning against a sleeping wolfhound. Beyond the listening circle, the dark night shrouds troll caves in the mountains and forest creatures half-seen among the clustering

trees. Wolves, spirits, urchins, centaurs, satyrs, changelings and hell-waines.

This play may be one survivor. At the moment, I am its midwife and its mother. I must stay here, in this house, till London is safe again.

One breezy spring day, Henry calls out from his perch at the window. 'Oh, look, what a sight is this?' he cries. 'A horseman, at full gallop!' I can hear the sound of hoof-beats hammering on the road outside and a horse whinnying as it clatters to a standstill. 'He has a feathered hat,' says Henry. 'His cloak is scarlet – Lord above! Oh! Who is it? He is at the door, Mother. He is coming in! Who can it be?'

I hear the sound of footsteps pounding up the stairs. The door flies open and Will stands there. He looks at me, and then races across the room and kisses Henry. 'You are well, little man! You are recovered!' he cries.

'Unhand me, fellow!' shouts Henry, struggling out of Will's grasp. 'Of course I am well.'

I send Henry to play in the solar. Will is by the fire, pulling at the feather on his hat. I realise with a jolt of some emotion that he looks just like his son. I am used to seeing the resemblance the other way, but here is a grown-up Henry, fidgeting.

'You will ruin that feather,' I say.

'What if I do?' says Will. 'It is a feather, merely. It represents "nothingness" with such neatness that one might almost put it in a play to fill that function.'

'What function?'

'The representation of nothingness. Only its very neatness would preclude it. Surprise is all.' He pauses. 'Or . . . almost all. Audiences can be obtuse.'

'What are you *talking* about?'

He looks up at me, and his gaze is so intense that I look down at my open book, jolted by memory.

'I rode two days and two nights to get here,' he says. 'The rest of the party are some way behind me – as far as I could put them, making speed and almost killing my poor horse.'

'Why did you . . . ?'

But he has come to sit beside me. 'We don't have long,' he says.

'We?'

'You and I. Before your husband gets here. That fool Alfonso joined the players! His consort accompanied our plays . . . He was carousing late into the night, not knowing if you lived or died! What kind of man is that? How can he be so ignorant of his great fortune?'

'Alfonso has no fortune that I am aware of. Unless he has been lucky at the tables for once in his life.'

'I mean, his great fortune in having such a wife.'

I stare at him, perplexed. 'You have a wayward memory, William Shakespeare. I have your written words, and those in here . . .' I tap my forehead. 'The words you spat at me the day you found me with that plague-boil Wriothesley.'

'Yes, I want to speak of this – '

'Love is not immutable. It can be stifled at birth, or slowly suffocated, or killed, stone-dead.'

'No! I – '

'And you killed my love, in those dreadful verses, which I did not deserve, and will not forget, even if *you* have put your wicked cruelty from your mind. Perhaps it was of no account to you, but it was everything to me.'

He takes my hands in his and looks down at them. 'It was this matter – this matter of Wriothesley that I wanted to speak to you about,' he says.

'I cannot think what you have left unsaid.'

'I wanted to . . . I have meant to speak of this before.'

I am silent.

'He asked to see me before the old Queen died.'

'Oh?'

'He said he had something to tell me.'

I nod, biting my lip.

'So I went to see him in the Tower.'

He stands up suddenly and walks across the room. For a moment, he watches his horse drinking from a trough below the window.

'He said that it was his fault. He said that he admired your looks, but not your manners. He wanted to get the better of you . . . He said that he desired and disliked you. He didn't see why a mere concubine should be so proud, nor why an old man like Hunsdon should monopolise you. So when he saw a weakness in your situation . . . that you seemed to like me – '

For a moment I forget myself. '*Seemed to like*! God's teeth . . .'

A flash of rage crosses Will's face: the rage I saw after he found me with Wriothelsey, all those years ago. Then he shakes his head, as if he is calming himself. 'Just let me speak, Aemilia, for God's sake,' he says. He searches my face with his dark eyes. 'Will you bear with me? It's not a pretty story.'

I am silenced, by his seriousness and my own curiosity. 'Very well. Say what you have to.'

'When I saw Wriothesley, Essex had already been executed, and the headsman had done his task badly. He'd slashed poor Essex across the shoulders, ripping bone from muscle but leaving his head still set upon his neck. The scaffold was a waterfall of blood, and he was screaming in agony when the second blow fell. That, too, failed to find its mark – it was the third that sent him safe to God. Wriothesley knew of this. His normal cheerful humour was gone. He knew his charm was worth nothing.'

'Charm! Ha!' I say.

Will seems not to hear me, his mind fixed in the past. 'His earldom had been stripped away and now he was plain Henry Wriothesley, his possessions confiscated, his estate set to be divided among his rivals. And he was ill: his legs were swollen, he had the ague and for many months he had been refused visitors. He was pale, and fretful, nothing like the cocksure young rake I once knew. He was very low in spirits, and still believed the Queen might have him put to death. He had been no favourite of hers, after all, while she had treated Essex like a son.'

I look down at my fingernails, thinking of my last conversation with the Queen. This is indeed a sorry tale, but I feel no pity. Wriothesley surely deserves such a fate, if any man does.

Will is staring over my shoulder as if he can see the scene before him. 'He mentioned your name almost as soon as I arrived. I know this may be no comfort, but he truly seemed to want to do penance of some kind, make an honest confession about the . . . the commerce that there was between you.'

I cannot look at him. 'Lower your voice, Will! I . . . these are things I never speak of. Think of the child.'

He drops his voice to a whisper but can't seem to stop. 'And of course, being pregnant and cast off, you were weaker still . . . He admitted this. He said as much.'

Outside, his horse is shaking its head and blowing water from its muzzle.

'I could hardly think or speak,' Will says, 'but I managed to ask how the . . . the act itself had come about. And he told me that he had blackmailed you, and forced you. It could not be called a rape, he said, but it could be called a "wilful abuse of power". Those were his words. A wilful abuse of power.'

'I'd call that rape,' I say. 'But doubtless I am alone in that, as in so many other things.'

'I realised . . . I realised that I never . . . that I . . . that I should have listened to you. The pain . . . your rejection had already made

me partly mad. When I saw what I thought I saw, I thought I was just your fool.'

I feel my face flush scarlet. 'You saw what you saw, Will. As you have said quite plainly. I have no wish to talk of this now, with Henry close by. We are estranged – so be it.'

He searches my face, his eyes dark with feeling. 'Do you have nothing else to say about this? Nothing at all?'

'Only that I have tried to tell you, and you gave me no chance. And now it turns out you believe this cocksure braggart, when you would not listen to me! Do you think men are more honest than women, or that lords are more truthful than cast-off whores?'

'Aemilia, please listen to me. I see – perhaps because I am older now – I see I was mistaken.'

'Handsome of you, who damned my name to Hell.'

'I see that you were trapped.'

'Wise poet! Do you want a prize for such an insight? It was ever thus.'

'My prize would be your forgiveness, the greatest prize I can imagine.'

'I have lived my life trammelled in by circumstances. This is a woman's fate.'

'Forgive me, dear Aemilia. Forgive me for those sonnets, or that part of them which was bilious and vile. Forgive me for the things I said, when all the world seemed blackened and obscene because of what I thought you had done to me.'

'Blackened and obscene – good words. You should put them in a poem.'

'Please, my lady. I am sorry.' He takes my hands.

'You wrote as if our love itself disgusted you. Our great love!'

'I wrote what I felt then. It is not what I feel now.'

I pull my hands from his. 'God will forgive you, I expect.'

'And you?'

'I don't know.

'Aemilia! Please!'

'Come a little closer,' I say. 'This is what you think of women, sir.' Then I whisper these lines to him, from his own sonnets.

'Two loves I have, of comfort and despair,
Which like two spirits do suggest me still:
The better angel is a man right fair;
The worser spirit a woman coloured ill.
To win me soon to hell, my female evil
Tempteth my better angel from my side,
And would corrupt my saint to be a devil,
Wooing his purity with her foul pride.'

'Forgive my hot words!' says Will, twisting his arms around me at last. 'Madam, there is no cure for our affliction! Not in this life or the next.'

I push him away. 'Do not insult me, sir,' I say. 'Do not come creeping here, like a whipped dog, all sneakish and colluding, in the hope that you can fornicate with me in secret once again! Don't speak of love, when you have mashed my heart to butcher's pulp! Do not speak of "sorrow" when my love is cold, and spoiled and dead! What do you take me for? What do I care if an aristocrat, your mighty *patron*, cants his little secrets to you, so you want to lick his arse? Shall I lick yours, in turn? Shall I let you have me, once again, all addled and unmade, as once I was? I will speak of an affliction, sir, and my affliction is your company! Go forth, go from me, and never bother me again!'

'What's going on?' says a voice I know too well. Alfonso is at the doorway. One arm is resting on his sword. Henry, goggle-eyed, is beside him.

'Mother?' says Henry. 'Why are you shouting?'

Will and I spring apart, quite as guilty as if we had been naked among the rushes.

Alfonso smiles, rather coldly, but comes over and kisses me on the lips as if he has bought me at a fair. 'Come, Aemilia,' he says. 'You must quit this place. The plague is over.'

Act IV

Philosophy

Scene I

Weſtminſter, December 1605

It is Holy Innocent's Day, the fourth day of Christmas, and the snow lies thick upon the ground. This year the Thames has frozen over so thick and solid that people crowd on to it, making all kinds of sport. From Southwark to the Temple there are stalls, sideshows, merry-go-rounds, puppet plays and even donkey rides. (The miserable creatures trundle up and down the ice with straw slippers tied to their hooves to stop them skidding.) Fire-eaters and clownish acrobats slide this way and that, tumbling from their stilts. The City fathers have no jurisdiction over any of these frolics, as the river lies beyond old London's walls, and they view it all with much begrudgery. The prentice-boys are quick to fill their snowballs with sharp stones and all manner of disagreeable items. Pigs and swans are roasting over crackling bonfires, and songs and laughter ring sharp against the aching air.

From my stool by the fireside, I can see through the diamond-mullioned window. The stars are points of ice over the frosted roofs and twisted chimneys. Cold creeps through the walls of cob and timber, freezing my back even as I warm my feet.

Alfonso reclines in his coffer-chair, his shapely legs sticking out in front of him, his recorder resting across his knees. He contemplates the glowing Yule log from beneath his drooping lashes. Henry sits at his feet, quiet for once, stroking Graymalkin. The cat is purring as he stares at the roast goose on the table. By

the hearth is a pitcher of winter toddy, bubbling pleasantly to a woolly white top. Our new servant, Marie Verre, has laced ivy into the idle spokes of her spinning wheel. She's a foolish girl, seventeen years old, brimming with crazy laughter and tall tales, mostly of old France. (For she is the child of Huguenots who came from Paris after that foul Massacre on St Bartholomew's Day.) In spite of her silliness, she is a quick worker, and between us we have put together a table that wouldn't shame Whitehall Palace itself – though we could not match the quantity laid out for courtly gluttons.

A tap on the window. Henry jumps up and yells, 'Tom Flood! Tom Flood! All hail, Tom Flood!' Outside, a clear voice sings:

'Lully, lullay, Thou little tiny Child,
Bye, bye, lully, lullay.
Lullay, thou little tiny Child,
Bye, bye, lully, lullay.
O sisters too, how may we do,
For to preserve this day
This poor youngling for whom we sing
Bye, bye, lully, lullay.'

'It is Tom! What a voice he has, finer than any fey chorister!' says Henry, running to the hallway and flinging open the door. And Tom it is, and Anne Flood too, and a blast of Christmas wind and snow. Tom carries on singing while his mother shivers in her fur-edged tippet, her eyes popping with pride.

'Herod, the king, in his raging,
Charged he hath this day
His men of might, in his own sight,
All children young to slay.
That woe is me, poor Child for Thee!
And ever mourn and sigh,

For thy parting neither say nor sing,
Bye, bye, lully, lullay.'

'Isn't it pretty?' says Anne. 'Robert Armin taught it to him. The mummers sing it at Coventry.' I must say, it doesn't strike me as a pretty carol, or a merry one.

I point to Anne's lavish ermine trim. 'Surely they can put you in the stocks for wearing that?'

I finger the mottled fur, and she slaps me cheerfully.

'It's just a bit of Yuletide flummery,' she says. 'But it suits me, do you not think? Besides, an ermine is no more than a winter stoat.'

'I'm sure you have royal blood in you somewhere.' I wonder how many times she's sucked off Inchbald to earn enough to buy such an extravagant gewgaw. Or perhaps he gave it to her in fair exchange, for services rendered. Oh, Lord, now I can see her lips, pulsing away at his groin! And the white crumbs of her face powder, dusting his curly pubes.

She gleams with gratitude. 'And you can see it in Tom. He's more of a gentleman than any of those preening clowns at the Inns of Court.'

'Most decidedly,' say I, though this is scarcely saying much. Cross-dressing Moll Cutpurse herself is more gentlemanly than most young men of the law. 'Come along inside, and let's eat.'

'Indeed, I am hungry as a winter wolf!' says Tom. 'Ravenous, Mistress Lanyer, and sorely ravaged by thirst.' Spending time with the players has certainly improved his feeling for the drama when he is off-stage.

'Really, Tom!' says Anne. 'Have you forgot your manners?'

'I agree with Tom,' says Henry. 'I am dead with hunger. Let's stuff ourselves with greasy goose and Christmas pudding till we burst like rotting gibbet-men!'

So we sit round the table and fall to with a vengeance, finishing off the meal with coffin-shaped mince pies stuffed

with currants, cloves and saffron – thirteen ingredients in all, in honour of Our Lord and His Apostles. We only stop when our bellies stick out roundly, though I am pleased to say that not one of us bursts open.

The drink makes Anne maudlin. 'This day always makes me nervous,' she says, making moon-eyes at her empty cup.

'Oh, Anne, be more cheerful!' say I. 'Don't just sit there maundering on. You can be miserable for Lent.'

'Those poor Holy Innocents! I cannot bear it, the thought of losing a child.'

'Poor indeed,' says Tom. 'The young are not always lucky.'

'Indeed not,' agrees his mother, dabbing off a tear.

Tom flushes deeper, anxious to be understood. 'Not everyone is as fortunate as Nathan Field.'

'Why is he so fortunate?' I ask.

'Only because everyone says he is the new Burbage!'

'Is that so terrible?'

'First he is the Queen of France! Oh, ladies, sirs, bow down before him! Then mad Ophelia, then love-sick Juliet – all in a fortnight!'

'You are doing well enough,' I say, 'dressed like a jack-pudding every afternoon.'

'They don't take enough note of his talent,' says Anne. 'It galls me, but of course I am the last one who should speak up for him.'

'Well, you are luckier than I am,' says Henry. 'My life is a vale of suffering, I swear! We are whipped and tortured and forced to speak dog Latin. There is no mercy for a schoolboy. I would rather be at the theatre, even if I were playing a joint-stool or half a slug.'

'Henry, don't be such a clodpate,' I say. 'Without Latin you will get nowhere in this life.'

Anne's thoughts are still on Herod and his death-dealing soldiers.

'Such little children slaughtered so cruelly,' she says, as we gather close around the fire and Alfonso fills her cup. 'To think of it! The screaming and the grief. You would run mad, would you not?'

I pat her knee. 'Let's not speak of such things now,' I say. 'We have survived the plague. We are together, warm and well and safe from harm.'

'Amen to that,' says Anne.

'Amen, amen!' says Henry, sagely. He is growing into a boisterous, impudent boy, and some say my softness to him has made him wayward. He has a habit of blurting out memories that I had thought long buried, as if he's brooded on them till he is ready to unleash them on the world.

He picks at a mince pie with his fingers. 'Mother wrote a play,' he says. His voice is sly. 'I found it.'

Tom's eyes shine.

'What's it about?'

'Witches,' says Henry. 'Witches and kings.'

'Henry, what do you mean by this? Sneaking around and purloining my poetry! How dare you read my pages?' I am glad I locked the grimoire in my safe-cupboard.

He pops the piece of meat into his mouth. 'You can hardly blame me for wondering what comes of all that scribbling you do.'

'I don't "scribble" nearly enough, and thank you for making it sound like childish nonsense. Without my "scribbling" I'd go mad.'

'It's good,' he says. 'A most excellent piece of work. For a woman.'

'The King has written a book on witchcraft,' says Tom. 'I have heard them speak about it at the Globe.'

'Then he will find my story of blood and sorcery very foolish,' say I. 'Besides, Henry is wrong. It is not a tale of kings, but of queens.'

Alfonso begins to polish his recorder with his sleeve. 'Queens! God preserve us!'

'It concerns the tragedy of Lady Macbeth.'

'Lord, wife, will you never learn?'

'Don't "wife" me, sir! Did we not have the best Prince who ever lived, in the guise of our departed Sovereign? Is her Scots cousin even half the man she was? Drunk all day, and dull all night?'

Alfonso frowns. 'Hush, Aemilia! Mind that tongue of yours. They'd hang you, just like Guido Fawkes, for saying so much!'

'Oh, dear Alfonso!' shrieks Anne. 'How can you say so? They wouldn't *dare*!'

He ignores her and stares at me thoughtfully. 'But witches, now, that might . . .' He blows some notes, making them sound like the whistling wind.

'A little magic always pleases, on the stage,' says Anne, looking down at her ermine trim as if she were wearing Titania's gown. 'Does it not, Tom?'

'I heard tell that one Agnes Sampson, a witch in Scotland, told His Majesty of matters which only he could know of.' Alfonso's tone is light, but I can tell that he is delighted to be so well informed.

I look up in surprise. 'What "matters"?'

'Secret words of love which he whispered to Queen Anne on their wedding night, when they were newly come from Denmark. Which he swore all the devils in Hell could not have discovered.'

Now I laugh in good earnest. 'My dear husband! I had no idea you were such an authority. Is this what His Majesty confides in you, when you've done amusing him with jigs and ditties? He acquaints you with his pillow-talk and curtain-whispers, and describes his horror of the instruments of Satan? Why, soon you will be Duke of Long Ditch and we shall all be dressed in cloth-of-gold!'

'It is *said*, Aemilia, it is *said*. Of course I have not heard it from the King directly.'

'They say His Majesty is very wise,' Anne declares, sipping her toddy. 'He should be a doctor in a university, not a king.'

Alfonso shifts irritably in his chair. 'From this awful meeting sprang his interest in demonology.'

I poke the fire. 'What nonsense,' I say. But, as the flames dance, I can see Lilith the Serpent and her yellow stare.

It is true – I have hidden my play away, for what am I supposed to do with it? It could not be staged, being woman's words, so I can only put it from me, and continue with my verse. The party is over now, and everyone is asleep. So I read it by candle-light, safe in the knowledge that it would take all the fires of Hell to rouse Alfonso once he has had a bellyful of wine. I am surprised, if I am honest, that the words chill me to the marrow. When I have finished, I lock it up with the grimoire, to keep it from prying eyes.

Scene II

A serving boy comes knocking with a letter. To my surprise, it is from Richard Burbage.

> *My dear Mistress Lanyer,*
>
> *We have heard from young Tom Flood that you have written some Lines. There being a Hiatus in our Programme pertaining to some particular items that are likely to be pleasing to His Majesty, in brief, a thing which has some Occult infusion, some Conjuration in its design, and, further, which conceals about its person some reference to the union of the Scots and English, to make our Good King feel that the Scots and English are bed-fellows, we are seeking an engagingly Horrid drama. To cut it short, we are in need of some new Words.*
>
> *This being so, and knowing that you are a Woman of sound phrasing and a pithy way with Fools, we thought to ask you if we may see these Lines. In short, if you might give the bearer some notion of when you can fix to meet with us at this Theatre, we might arrange some Business to the benefit of all.*
>
> *Your most respectful,*
> *Richard Burbage*

Now, this puts me in a dilemma. If a woman's words can't put on the public stage, then what use can they make of my play? And yet . . . perhaps it could be performed before the King.

I would hardly dare to hope for this, but it does deal with a subject that I know will interest him. I haven't seen Will since the day he came to see me after the plague, and have heard little about him since that time, saving only that he prospers, which is bad enough. After all he has said, and written, he thought a brief explanation about Wriothesley's confession would be enough to make amends! Perhaps even sow the seeds for renewed passion. More fool him. What riles me most is his readiness to believe everything spoken by His Lascivious Lordship, and his reluctance to believe me. Or even give me a proper hearing. And, if he truly cared, surely he would try to speak to me again. I know Will well enough: that which he wants, he will strive for to the utmost. He has forgotten me, as his star has risen at Court. The Globe's players are the 'King's Men' now, and nothing seems beyond them. Why would he want me, in any case, ageing, penniless, stuck in my little house? I am no longer the 'Dark Aemilia' of his poetry, or his memory.

But these are scratching, irritating thoughts. Must I be humble? Must I be obedient and obscure? Am I just a housewife now, a dowdy work-drab? No. No one would ever say that of me. If Burbage has seen fit to invite me to the Globe, then I will go, and see what may come of it.

So I set off, alone, disguised in that old cloak of Joan's, which makes me look twice the hag I am, and get half the looks from passers-by. Its strange scents have faded, perhaps because Marie keeps it in the scullery, next to the hanging game, which gives off a pungent blood-scent as it ripens for the pot. It is February and still freezing: it's the hardest, whitest winter I have ever known.

When I go into the street, the air is full of cries of bewilderment and fright. I see that the neat tracks of a cloven-hoofed creature are marked out in the glistering snow. They seem to have been made by a two-legged being, striding like a man. It has crossed streets and gardens, dunghills and the frozen kennel. Looking about me, I see its tracks even march up the side of an old hay-

barn and over its pitched roof. How is this possible? Has some Beast marched over all things standing in its way? I shudder to imagine some black hell-wraith, perched upon a roof-stack, seeing all. I summoned Lilith – God alone knows what other demons fly among the roof-stacks, called up by those who know even less than I do. They say that Hades burns bright red, the city of eternal flame, but supposing it is froze blue-white, like winter? I say Hell is cold, the furthest distance from the Sun.

There is no need to hire a boatman: I walk across the frozen Thames, which is as black and smooth as an obsidian mirror and so clear that I can see a vast pike, frozen solid, several fathoms down. The booths stand in a disorderly muddle, not yet open at this hour. Dogs run hither and thither, cocking their legs and sniffing at littered bones, while sea eagles skid slush as their talons hit the ice. An apothecary sorts bottles inside the first booth I pass. Close by, a cobbler is selling leather shoes from a basket. 'Stout shoes for the frost!' he shouts, waving a pair before me. But I press on.

It starts to snow again, and the white flakes blur my sight. There is a strange light, as if the sun were shining from the river's edge. For a moment I feel confused and unsure of my way. I think of the pages I'm carrying with me. What am I doing, stepping out alone to visit a theatre in the Liberties? This is madness. What would Aristotle make of this, who saw Woman as some error in creation?

But I'll have none of this. I straighten my back, and walk more boldly. There it is, ahead, set back from the south shore: the Globe.

I study it as I reach Blackfriars Stairs. It rises like the castle of an enchantress above the surrounding trees. Midway up the walls is an encircling row of windows, no bigger than the arrow slits of the Tower prison. To the west of the building is the gabled roof of the stage and tiring-house, and pointing just above this a little cupola. It reminds me of the minarets of Richmond and Nonsuch: an Eastern oddity among the common homes and

stews. This fake opulence is of a piece with the gilt and foolery within, since every inch of this great palace is made from wood, not stone, and it has been carried, post by post, from its old home at Shoreditch. This temple of varieties has no more permanence than a widow's shack; yet it thinks itself well above its station. Over the entrance is a crest displaying Hercules bearing the globe upon his shoulders, and the dubious motto: *Totus mundus agit histrionem*: the whole world is a playhouse.

I knock on the door: no answer. I bang harder: but there is only silence. So I push it open, throwing all my weight against it. It groans as it yields, opening just a crack, and I wriggle inside. I'm standing in the dark passageway between the lowest tier of seats, facing the stage itself. There's no sound, save only the cry of the kites, flapping on the roof thatch high above me. I look around, bemused by the emptiness of the place, having only been there as part of a boisterous crowd. The pit, open to the grey, snow-burdened sky, stretches before me. The great stage is deserted. I walk over to it, looking around me uneasily.

Someone laughs, loudly, from far above. I climb the steps on to the boards.

'Hello?' I look up. 'Mr Burbage?'

Another laugh, very merry.

'Who's there?' I call. I narrow my eyes, scouring the entrances to the tiring-rooms, and the musicians' gallery which is just above them.

'She can't see us,' says a familiar voice.

'Aemilia!' This is a louder, richer accent. 'Aemilia, look higher!'

I look around me, flushing with anger. 'I can't see you,' I cry. 'Come out, and stop fooling with me.'

'Higher!' calls the rich voice. 'Even higher!'

Finally I spy them. Two heads, peering down at me, from the topmost point of the Heavens, half-hidden behind a painted wooden cloud.

The cloud-space proves to be a narrow platform, like a hidden stage, just below the cupola. It is reached by a series of steep flights of steps. Burbage and Will are bending over a chart on a small table. They present an odd contrast: Burbage short and stout, with his walrus nose and doleful eyes; and Will, taller, well-made, tapping his foot in time with some rhythm that beats in his own head. Both are dressed in heavy coats with black coney collars, and fine kid gloves, with long patterned cuffs. They could be two wealthy merchants, discussing a consignment of new kerseys from Halifax or a cargo of pepper from the Levant.

Burbage kisses my hand, bringing off his trick of being mocking and gentlemanly at once. 'Mistress Lanyer, we are honoured. And you are looking so *well*.'

'Thank you, sir.'

'I hope the climb did not tire you?'

'I am not in my dotage yet.'

'Indeed *not*. You have not changed one jot since the first day I saw you. Still as comely as a maid.'

I bow. 'I am sorry to see that you are busy with Mr Shakespeare. I had thought we had arranged to meet at this hour.'

'Oh, no matter, we will be done with this in no time,' says Burbage. 'It's just some hare-brained scheme of Will's.'

'It is *business*, Dick, I wish you'd give it your proper attention,' says Will, not looking at me.

'Business, man? Our business is the play, upon the stage.'

'Indeed,' says Will. 'I am aware of it.'

Burbage straightens his back, pushes out his chest and seems to grow a foot taller. Stepping back from the table, he declaims:

'Blow, winds, and crack your cheeks! Rage! Blow!
You cataracts and hurricanoes, spout
Till you have drench'd our steeples, drown'd the cocks!
You sulph'rous and thought-executing fires,

Vaunt couriers of oak-cleaving thunderbolts,
Singe my white head! And thou all-shaking thunder.
Strike flat the thick rotundity o'th'world,
Crack Nature's moulds, all germens spill at once
That makes ingrateful man!'

It is a splendid speech: he seems both aged and magnificent in the making of it.

'You see?' says Burbage. 'The words are all. Not dandling players like newborn babes.'

'I agree that they are *most* significant, since I wrote them,' says Will. He has not looked up from his study once.

'What do you mean?' I ask. 'What "dandling"?'

'Will sets out to make men fly,' says Burbage, extending his arm with regal generosity. 'As if he were Icarus.'

'Daedalus, if I may correct you,' say I.

Will looks at me for the first time, almost as if he is about to laugh. 'They've done it at the Fortune,' he says. 'Our competitors.'

Burbage makes another expansive gesture, as if dismissing Greek legends in their entirety. 'Ah, yes, Daedalus is the inventor. Of course, of course. Icarus is the son, who fell. As did two men at the Fortune, and broke their backs.'

Will appears to be making some sort of calculation on a piece of foolscap.

'Do you not think of that?' I ask him.

'I think of divinities and angels, descending from above,' says Will, after a moment. He seems to consider the empty air in front of him. 'I think of the heavens, riven by the radiance of a suspended goddess. Strapped safely in a chair.' Quite suddenly, he turns and flashes a glance at me. 'Come, Mistress Lanyer, look . . .'

I go over, lips pursed. The diagram shows a strange construction consisting of a pivot, a long arm and a chair. It reminds

me of the Wheel of Fortune, that most double of the Tarot cards, which can foretell great luck or dire calamity.

'You see, this is the stage we stand upon.' He indicates the outline of the diagram. 'We have enough space for windlass, drum and strong cordage. And – here – for the player to be readied for his flying seat.' He is looking down again, pointing to the next diagram. 'And here – with some little refinement to the plan, the whole business will be done in one sweeping movement – just a slight upward thrust so the chair can clear the edge of the platform – and then forward and downward. On to the stage. You see?'

I make as close a study of the diagram as I would if I were the carpenter myself. I dare not look up. At last I say, 'What do you want with my play?'

Will sighs and folds up the chart. 'You must discuss all that with Dick. It is nothing to do with me.' He disappears down the stairs, his dark cape flying out behind him.

Burbage, on the other hand, is smiling, all avuncular. 'Come, mistress, sit down,' he says, coming over to the table. 'Don't mind Will. He has a sore head. He has been doing the accounts again – it's best left to Heminge.'

'I don't mind him at all. I do not think of him.'

He smiles in a manner which annoys me. 'Please – sit down. I have a proposition to make, which I think will interest you.'

I sit.

'Have your brought the play with you?' he asks. 'I should like to read it, if I may.'

I pull it from my bag, but withhold it when he tries to take it from me. 'Sir, I should like to know *why* you wish to read it? Since a lady's work cannot be played upon a public stage.'

Burbage beckons me closer, lowering his voice and rounding his shoulders in a stage approximation of urgent secrecy. 'Can we speak in confidence? Up here, where none can hear us? Might I depend on your discretion?'

'I would not be alive today if I did not know how to be discreet.'

'Quite.' He shifts his chair closer, so I can see the smallpox pits on his great nose. 'To be frank with you, we are looking for something new. Fresh ideas, to please and reassure the King. He is distracted, sees an assassin in every corner and fears the Catholics will try again. He is not a happy man.'

'He can't be blamed for fearing plotters. Since they came so close to blowing him to Heaven.'

'Of course not. Daggers, poison, even curses might undo him. Or, like his own father, he might yet be ripped to pieces by a conspirator's bomb.'

'So why can't . . . Mr Shakespeare turn his hand to this?'

'Will is busy. His daughter is to marry, his wife wants more money to spend on her fine house, and he insists his next piece will be set in Ancient Egypt. I cannot for the life of me see a Scottish theme emerging there. We've looked at other plays – including three from Dekker – but none of them will do.'

I have to swallow hard at the mention of Will's greedy wife. 'No, I can see that would be difficult.'

'The King is . . . well, he is a scholar one day, and a sot the next. In his books, he is the wisest man I ever met. In his cups, the most foolish. I don't know what to make of him.'

'You are the leader of the King's Men. The Royal company, in his pay. What's there to worry you?'

'We are his appointed company now, but, in time to come – who knows? We must work hard to keep his favour.'

'Doesn't he like what you have done for him so far?'

'Well enough, I'm told. Though he's not as fulsome as the late Queen. Scots, you see. Uncivilised.'

'So what did you do last?'

'Madam! How can you ask such a thing? It was my greatest part so far. My King Lear!'

'The foolish dotard Prince? I saw it done at Court, years ago. I never understood it.'

He frowns, offended. 'What, a woman of your superior understanding?'

'Must Kings be told to keep hold of their kingdoms? I should not have thought so.'

'You must see the new play! We are staging it again in spring. No one remembers that hoary elder version now – Will's telling is quite new, and vastly better.'

'But you haven't changed the story?'

'No. Why should we?'

'The King divides his kingdom between his three daughters, and suffers the consequences.'

'That is the sum of it.'

'What King ever lived who acted in such a way?'

'In Will's hands, how could it be otherwise than great? An instructive, yet crowd-pleasing fable.'

'Crowds are not always right.'

'He always does so well with the *words*.'

'I've no doubt of it.'

'Also, there are some scenes of excellent torture, his best since *Titus*.'

'Now torture *is* a crowd-pleaser, that I certainly recall.'

'But . . . I don't know. The King seemed distracted, low in spirits when he was watching it. *Tired.* At least he woke up for my great speech, on the blasted heath. Which I just gave a flavour of.'

'So now you think . . . a Scottish play, with hags?'

'Indeed!' says Burbage. 'Blood and hags! We need a play to please the King, and to please the King, it must have murder in it, as he was nearly murdered, and that murderer must be most direly punished.'

'I see, but – '

'We must include the intended destruction of a kingdom – '

'Which I have – '

'The undermining of the good by the diligent deception of the evil. As our King was undermined – d'you see it? – by the traitor Fawkes and all the rest.' Burbage spreads his hands. 'And we need plots – which can be woven in, don't fear this. And equivocation, but we can do that in one speech.'

'Assuredly.'

'But most of all,' says Burbage, taking my hand in his, 'most of all we must have witches.'

'Why?'

'Marston has them in his *Sophosha*, and Barnes has his *Devil's Charter*. And Dekker's done one, which comes as no surprise, since he works like a thousand demons.'

Will has returned, with more rolls of paper, which he spreads out upon the table, using pewter mugs to flatten the corners.

'And what is Dekker's play called?' I ask.

'*The Whore of Babylon*,' says Will, his back still turned. He speaks with peculiar vehemence.

'So you see,' says Burbage. 'What you have wrote is well-nigh perfect.'

'But what's my reward for this?'

Burbage crosses his legs as if to make himself more comfortable in his seat, then recrosses them. 'Well . . . it would partly be this much: knowing these were your lines, of course, performed before the King of England. Few men can claim so much.'

'Few men. And no women. I should like my name to be heard.'

'Heard?'

'If my play were done before the King, this might be possible. As if it were a noble lady's closet play, put on at some great house.'

Burbage raises his eyebrows. He looks at me as he might have done if a black rat had addressed him from the wainscot. 'Give me the play, my dear, and we will talk about the terms – if it is good enough,' he says.

I consider this. 'I suppose it would be foolish to say no.'

Burbage smiles, and looks down at the first page, on which I have written: *The Tragedie of Ladie Macbeth, A Scottish Queen.*

'An excellent title, certainly. Leave it in my hands, and I will see what shall be done.'

Scene III

Something ails Marie. Never the most sensible of serving girls, she appears to have turned quite mad since Christmas, and at first I cannot think what can be the matter. She forgets to do the linen on washday, so that Alfonso has to wear a soiled shirt to the palace when he is called to discuss a new trip to the Indies with Sir Robert Unwin. Yesterday, she moaned so much over the drying of ruffs on wood sticks that I was forced to beat her about the head, giving her a thick blobberlip. Which I regret, as I am somewhat tender-hearted. After that, she was in such a state of woeful discontent that she spoiled the soap, burned the bread, spilled the milk, dulled the pewter and cried when I asked her to comb out my hair.

Today brings the latest of her blunders. She has failed to brush my best wool dress, so a great moth flitters up into the air when I shake it out to wear to church. The blind insect has feasted till the cloth is full of holes, and now it is only fit for wearing in the house. When I tell her of this, she is half-crying, half-laughing, and so distracted that I fear I might lose her to Bedlam. In fact, I have ceased being angry, and am afraid of what she might do next: set the house on fire or jump into the river.

'What's the matter with that simpleton Marie?' I ask Anne as we cross the fields towards the distant spire of St Mary's Church. Marie is ahead of us, walking along with Henry. I frown as she falls over a running pig, which Henry had the sense to side-step.

'Can't you guess?' Anne looks at me queerly.

'If I could, I would have said so.'

She smiles, hard-eyed. 'It's love. She feels the pangs of *love*.'

'But whom does she love?'

Anne regards me as if it was I who were the half-wit, and not my silly servant. 'Why it's Tom!' she says.

I give a scream of laughter. 'But he is just . . .'

She lays her hand on my arm and I see that Marie has turned to look at us. 'Just a babe in arms, I know,' she whispers. 'No more than a child in his ways. And besides, when he is of an age, he will most likely marry into the theatre, not waste himself on some little drudge.'

'To think of it!' I say. 'Of course, he cannot love her in return. Such a useless dizzard of a girl.'

'Of course not,' says Anne, sticking her chin out. And I see from the jut of it that he is utterly enslaved.

'Oh, Lord above!' I cry. 'Whatever shall we do with our misbehaving children?'

Anne stops and looks at the calm steeple of the church, cutting into the sky. She is weeping. All around I can hear the bleating of sheep in the winter sunshine.

'Marie is going to have a child,' she says.

'Dear God,' I say. 'So that is what it's all about!'

Anne wipes her eyes. 'He doesn't even know who else she's been with. Why should he marry the little slattern? She threw herself at him the minute she set eyes on him.'

'It was ever thus.'

'He could be great, Aemilia. He has a talent, you know. Now he wants to tie himself to that shameless trollop, and her unborn child.'

'Let us go to church,' I say, 'and pray. You have your son's foolishness to burden you. I have my idiot spouse.'

Inside St Mary's, we lower our heads and pray, most devoutly. 'Please God,' I say silently, deciding not to trouble with the Scriptures. 'Let Marie's womb-blood flow tomorrow, and let Sir Robert Unwin take Alfonso on his next sea voyage. Let him go

to the Americas, and preserve our fortunes. And my virtue, what is left of it.' I stand, head bowed, for some time.

'I do not want to fornicate with Inchbald, Lord, if this can be avoided.'

I stand longer, before my Maker.

'Forgive me, Lord, for being so bold.'

God answers one of these prayers, but not both. Alfonso is given a commission by Sir Robert that very day. Of Marie's womb blood I hear nothing, but she burns the bread each morning.

The letter I have been waiting for finally arrives. What I receive is not – as I had expected – a slender folded document. It is a bundle of messy pages. My pages, I see at once. And yet the note itself is brief enough.

> *Madam,*
>
> *We regret that these words, though Admirable in one of your Sex, are not of the Quality or Kind which will make a Show upon the Stage. For this reason, they did not inspire that Passion in us which we must feel in order to transform your Thoughts into Theatricals.*
>
> *Might we thank you for your Interest and wish you every Success with your future Experiments in Fabrication.*
>
> *Your most humble,*
> *Richard Burbage*

I do not breathe – I think I might not breathe again – but scrabble through the pages as if looking for reassurance, desperate to soothe the fizz and fury in my head. A speech springs out at me: Lady Macbeth, at full height.

> *Was the hope drunk, wherein you dressed yourself?*
> *Hath it slept since?*

And wakes it now, to look so green and pale
At what it did so freely?

I close my eyes, not needing to see the rest, as I could hear it clear. A voice that echoes between Lilith's and my own.

Art thou afeared to be the same in thine own act and
valour as thou art in desire?

I speak aloud, my eyes still shut. '*Would'st thou have that which thou esteem'st the ornament of life, and live a coward in thine own esteem, letting "I dare not" wait upon "I would"?*'
Cruel, duplicitous Burbage! To trip off this shoddy letter, when he has seen what I had put. I sink down to the ground, and the pages flutter around me, and I bury my head in my hands and I sob. I cry because I know now they will never hear me. This is it, and this is all of it, this house of thirty oaks, this board with its crooked stools, this fireside, the ham, the pots, the dirty skillet. I am hemmed in by walls of wattle, and by hours of life. There will be no breaking out, no second chance, no late reward. I am a spent whore, and that is the top and bottom of it. The best I can hope for is to keep the roof above us by licking Inchbald's little cock.

I cry till my throat aches, and after that there seems little purpose to it. For I have my son to think of. So I wipe my eyes, and look around me, and think. I can't sit sobbing here for ever more. What shall we eat? Who will do the shirts? And I pick up the pages and sort them into a tidy pile, in the order in which they were written.

That done, I begin to sweep the kitchen. I remember, looking at the uncleared table and the dirty wooden trenchers, that Marie has been gone from the house for the whole day. Since Anne told me she was pregnant, I have realised that I was foolish not to notice. She's fattened up like a cooped goose, week after week,

so that even her little wrists are now thickened, and her swollen breasts rest upon the table when she leans forward to sop up her pottage with her bread. What's more, her belly sticks out plainly now. And she and Tom are always whispering, and conniving, when they get the chance. Anne can do nothing with Tom, and I can get no sense from Marie.

But here she comes! Has she grown bigger in a single day? She waddles in from the street, sweating and with her dress loosened, even though the wind is still so bitter. Looking at her, I wonder how many months she's gone. More than seven? If so she must have been already with child at Yuletide, the little minx. Her belly is bigger than mine has ever been, and Henry was a porker of a baby, the biggest Joan had ever seen.

'Whatever are you thinking?' I say, straightening from my work. 'Are you turning vagabond and stalking the highway? Do you shun your mistress, and run out among the common doxies?'

'What is that you say?' She wipes her forehead with her kerchief. I may as well have spoken Latin.

'Street scum, that's what they are, with no home to go to and faces brown as privy slop.'

'I can't run anywhere,' says Marie. This is true, given she can barely walk. She lowers herself slowly on to a stool, using the table for support.

I frown. 'Shall your babe be born under a hedge? Or at Tothill Fields?'

'I don't know,' she says. Her face is white and set with tiredness. I feel a stab of pity for her, in spite of myself, this silly girl whose lustfulness has led her to child-bed so young. What fools we women are. I pour her some ale.

'Thank you, mistress. You are kind.'

'Kind!' I have to laugh.

'You are to me. I have been a bad servant.'

'I fear you have.'

'But I will pay for it.'

'You will have a child. *Then* you will pay. But you will also have your reward.'

Henry comes in from school, as if summoned, and throws his bag on to the floor. I draw him in and hug him, then push him from me. 'Begone, Henry, our talk is not for you.'

'Nor would I want to listen,' says he. 'Women's idle chatter. Of dull babies and fine dresses and . . . stupid slimy *kisses*.'

He makes a face, picks up his catapult and runs outside again.

I sit down opposite Marie, and pour myself a drink. 'You will still be my servant,' I say. 'The child – it won't prevent you sweeping, I hope, or stirring the stew.'

She looks at me, her eyes great with tears. 'No, mistress.'

I set down my cup. 'Then why are you so miserable?'

She rests her head on her arms and begins to sob.

I stare at her. 'Marie? What is it? Thomas is no worse than any other lad! Marie, tell me. What is wrong?'

At first she says nothing, just cries and cries, till I think I must get on and turn the mattresses. Then she stops, quite suddenly. 'There is something terrible,' she says, her face hidden.

'What do you mean?'

'Something is wrong.'

'*What* is wrong?'

She raises her head. 'Something is wrong with the baby.'

'Oh, for shame! You are young! It will pop out like a plum from a pie. You'll have another dozen before you're done.'

She rubs her bloodshot eyes with her wet fingers. 'I have dreams.'

'Dreams.'

'Dreams such as . . . such as I have never known.'

I sigh and pile up some dirty trenchers. 'And what do you dream of?'

Her gaze fixes on me, her eyes grow wider and wider as if she saw her nightmares in my face. 'I dream of monsters. Horrid

midnight creatures. Demons, misbegot, that stalk us when the sun has gone.'

'Nursery fears, which you must soon grow out of.'

'I dream there is a monster growing inside me. My mother used to tell me an old French tale, about this very thing!'

This child is too fanciful for her own good. 'Marie, you are trying my patience. There are a thousand tales like that one.'

'But why?' she says. 'Surely it's because such things are common? When monsters are born, I mean *really*, the midwives keep it quiet.'

I say nothing. The girl isn't quite as foolish as she looks. Many years ago, I attended a birth with Joan. It was a hard delivery, which lasted for two days and two nights. And after all her travail the poor woman had little enough to show for it. The babe – of no gender – was born with one great eye in the middle of its forehead. A sexless Cyclops. Joan swaddled it, and sprinkled it with holy water. But when the father saw his child he swore, grabbed it by the feet and bashed it against the wall till he had beaten out all its brains. The infant's screams were the worst I ever heard; no witch, nor gibbet-rogue, nor half-bowelled recusant, could make such a sound. Unshriven, that malformed babe went straight to Hell.

It's true, we kept it quiet, saying only that the child had died.

And of course, now that Alfonso is off cavorting on a ship somewhere, my landlord soon gets wind of it, and here he is. I am cleaning out the jakes when he comes up behind me, quiet as a river rat.

'Mistress Lanyer.' He removes his hat with a flourish. It is a new one, by the look of it. Bright scarlet, with a yellow ostrich feather: colours which are all the rage at Court.

'Mr Inchbald, shorter than ever. Good day to you, sir.'

'Your servant let me in, I hope I am not intruding.'

I make a lot of business of pouring a pot of piss into the maw of the privy. 'I fear I am somewhat busy. Hard at my chores, as you can see.'

'Such a lady as yourself should not be mired in . . . these matters.' He is looking at his feet. A turd has dropped on to one of them. I pretend not to notice.

'I am not fit for entertaining. Can't you come another time?'

He kicks the turd into the air with surprising skill. 'The rent is due, sweet lady.'

'Ah, the sweet rent.'

'I'll wait while you wash your hands, and perhaps we can share a glass of something from your larder.'

'Very well.' My mind is working quickly. I have one last item of some value, which might buy him off.

'Excellent. The workmanship is most careful. Quality, Mistress Lanyer, most admirable quality.'

The dwarf is examining a little silver pomander, shaped like a galleon. I am offering it to him in lieu of rent – and fornication. We are standing by the walnut cupboard in the kitchen in which I keep the few things of value that I have left.

'It's made in Nuremberg. See the mark?' I say. I point with a long arm, keeping my distance. 'The figures there are meant to be my dear husband, God bless him, and my good self.'

'Though they could be anyone,' says Inchbald.

'You can keep condiments and salt cellars beneath the deck.'

'Most . . . elegant.' His eyes have not left my bosom once.

I decide my attention should most usefully remain on the pomander. 'Fill it with rose-water, and you can use it to ward off foul vapours and disease.'

'Why, it's almost a shame to take it from you.'

'Almost, yes. But think on this – if you were a just a fraction shorter you could ride on it yourself.'

'Your wit is well known, mistress, but it can sometimes mar your perfect beauty.'

'Shame. Stop staring at my dugs, please, Mr Inchbald.'

He puts his hands behind his back, as if this was the only way he could stop them wandering towards my breasts. 'I'd still sooner have a suck, for all it is a handsome piece of work.'

'Take it, or take your leave.'

Disgruntled, Inchbald wraps the pomander up in a linen cloth and stores it in his leather satchel. He bows gracelessly, and I turn away and set about cleaning a candlestick, hoping he will leave. There is silence for a moment, then he says, 'It is a shame that you are so ill-disposed towards me, madam. I was intending to invite you to the theatre, as my most honoured guest.'

'Well, you do surprise me.' This is true. None of Inchbald's other ladies is taken out to town. It strikes me that Anne would think it most annoying if I were rewarded for my virtue with such a treat.

'There is a lot of talk about the latest work the King's players are staging at the Globe. They say they put it on at Whitehall and the Queen fainted right away.'

I have been standing with my back to him, scraping at a gobbet of dried porridge on the kitchen table with a carving knife, but now I stop and look at him.

'Queen Anne fainted?'

'Indeed. Quite the horridest play that she had seen in all her life. So I have been told. She thought there was black magic in it. Just like *Faustus*.'

I drop the knife. 'What is it called?'

He taps his forehead, tutting with irritation. 'Oh, do you know, I quite forget. Something odd-sounding. Something of the north.'

'Scottish?'

'Scottish! Yes! I have it now. It's *The Tragedie of Macbeth*.'

* * *

What's in a name? What indeed. Macbeth is a good one. Perhaps it is just the title they have filched. It is not feasible, not likely, that these seasoned players have stole my work. And yet I cannot sleep for thinking of it. The sun sinks, the night blackens, the sun rises again, and I do not so much as blink. For three days, and three nights, this is my rest. Would they do this, and say not a word about it? I can't face going to the theatre to see it for myself. No, I will ask Tom Flood.

I decide to seek him out at the Anchor at Southwark. It is a good spot for actors, for when the talk runs flat they can amuse themselves by watching the pirates hang at Execution Dock, and so learn how to make their stage-deaths true to life. A gaggle of prentice-boys is standing outside, laughing together and drinking ale from their leather black-jackets. They call out when I pass, cocky as you please. I stare back stony-eyed, and all three of them look nervously away. Inside, darkness and a roar of talking. Narrow booths contain half-seen groups of drinkers and bawds: a man kissing a white-armed girl; an old doxy, sitting astride a red-headed sailor-boy; a group of law students, opining in the Latin.

A thin man with a twisted lip comes hobbling towards me. 'Mistress, can I be of help?' He speaks with false gentility.

'I don't think so, thank you.' I look around the crowded inn.

'We don't see many married ladies here. Who do you seek?'

'Tom Flood, a player.'

'Ah, well. He is engaged. Occupied, or *occupying*, if I am to be precise.'

'I see. We are speaking, if I am right, of fornication?'

'She's not the youngest, nor the comeliest, but she is the . . . well. She *accommodates*.'

'A gamesome old jade, I am sure.'

'Else he'd be throwing away a good sixpence.'

'Indeed. Take me to him, will you?'

'Are you sure you wouldn't like to wait? We have the finest apple cider, the old Queen's favourite tipple.'

'Drank in this doghole often, did she?'

'Slept here, mistress, on each progress.'

Of course she did, and feasted on broken hog meat. 'Then by all means bring me some cider.'

When he's gone, I hasten up the stairs. I knock on the first door I come to. 'Tom Flood?' There are little panting shrieks from within. Yelping, rapid, rhythmic. It reminds me of the time I heard the old rogue Ralegh at his game of forest hide-and-fuck, a sport he was most fond of. I heard him having Bess Throckmorton against a tree. At first she was all coy decorum: 'Sweet Sir Walter, will you undo me? Nay, sweet Sir Walter!' But as her pleasure and excitement grew all she could squeal was, 'Swisser swatter swisser swatter.' And the branches shook as if brave Sir W. were pleasuring the trunk itself.

This is a seamier setting by far. I bang on the door once more. 'Tom?' I try again. But the bullish roar which rips out next sounds more like the come-cry of the Beast himself than any sound that Tom could make. I try the next door. A Blackamoor opens it a crack, and peers out at me, suspicious. 'Is Tom within?' I ask.

The Blackamoor disappears. 'Are you called Tom?' I hear him say. He returns. 'No Toms here.'

At last I come to a door at the end of the passage. I bang on it with the flat of my hand. At first there is no answer. But I can hear the gentle rattle of a snore. Pushing it open, I see Tom, sleeping softly. Next to him sits a raddled whore of at least my age, with dangling naked dugs. She is eating from a little dish, and red wine streaks her chin.

'Who might you be?' asks the whore, mouth full. 'Not his mother, are you?'

'What's it to you if I'm his wife? Get out, you filthy drab!'

After she has gone, I sit down on the bed and look at Tom, with his white skin and his curling, matted hair. His breath rises and falls sweetly with each snore. The stench of ale comes off him like a river fog.

'Tom,' I say. I touch his hand. 'Wake up.'

He makes a noise like a puppy nosing for his mother's tit, a hungry little whimper. Then he opens his eyes. With a cry, he sits upright, clutching the covers to his groin. 'Aemilia! Mistress Lanyer – Lord above! What is the matter?'

I fold my arms. 'I have a question for you.'

'God's blood!' says Tom. 'Has my mother put you up to this?'

'You've been drinking.'

'A little, madam.'

'And whoring too, it seems.'

'Well . . .'

'No way for a leading lady to go on. But that's not the worst of it.'

'What?' Now there is panic in his eyes. 'Marie! Is she ill? Has it come? I must go to her . . .' He leaps out of bed, naked as an earth-worm, and begins to dress himself.

'Tom – stop. Marie is not ill. And I doubt the baby's ready – though it's twice the size it should be.'

He stops, half in his shirt, and looks at me. 'What, then? Why do you pester me?'

'Pester? *Pester*? And your mother thinks it's *Henry* who is spoiled! I've come here for some information. Some facts. No *equivocation*, please. I know you have the answer.'

He starts buttoning his shirt. 'I don't know what I know which is of any use to you, but ask me what you like.'

I stand up and walk to the other side of the room, trying to set my mind straight. 'What's this about a Scottish play? The next one you're doing at the Globe?'

He frowns, as if trying to remember lines. 'It's a secret. They've told us to keep it quiet. This play will startle all the town.'

'Why so secret?'

'I don't know.'

'So who do *you* play?'

His fiddles with his shirt.

'Your *part*, Tom, what is it?'

'Lady Macbeth,' he says, looking at me with a sudden glint of pleasure. 'Later the Scottish Queen.'

'I know who Lady Macbeth is, you buffoon.'

He smiles, uneasy. 'Nathan Field is only Lady Macduff, and then a serving woman with hardly any lines. He was most put out when Burbage told us.'

'Is yours a little part, or long?'

'Littler than I would have liked. But the greatest boy's part, by some way.'

'How long?'

'Long enough.'

'What kind of woman is she?'

'What do you mean?'

'What is her nature?'

'In some scenes, she's a better man than her lord.'

'She leads him into wickedness?'

'She eggs him on, to kill the King. Then falls into a most excellent madness, walking in her nightgown like an unquiet spirit. This part is worth a thousand Juliets.'

'So.' The tale was written down by Holinshed, but some of this is mine. I breathe deeply, imagining Will's head, and that of Burbage, high above the Bridge, upon a spike. Par-boiled with cumin seeds, and dipped in tar. 'Do you happen to have your pages with you, by any chance?'

Tom takes a wad of paper from his doublet and hands it to me. 'They are brutal lines,' he says. 'But bold.'

I read them, and the blood beats in my brain when I see how they have cheated me. 'Who wrote these?' I ask, as if even now all might be somehow mended.

'Why, Will Shakespeare, of course,' says Tom. He is dressed now, and looks around him, then picks up his hat. 'Who else would it be?'

Just as he has finished speaking, the door opens, and who should walk in but Will himself, neat as a character in a play? He too is buttoning his shirt-front. I wonder if it was his voice I heard, roaring his pleasure a few moments ago? The room sways as if we were all at sea, and I recall how he would look at me when it was me he rode, and loved, and rejoiced in.

He is saying, 'Tom, we must go, for it's . . .' Then he catches sight of me and turns pale. 'Aemilia!'

I bow my head.

'What are you . . . ?'

'A woman, sir, more's the pity.'

'I mean – what are you doing in this place?'

'Business.' I look him up and down. 'And you? Pleasure, I if I heard you right.'

Oh, God! It is a summer's day again. I'm in his arms and he is fucking me in bright sun. When he comes he throws his head back and calls my name: 'Aemilia! Aemilia! Aemilia!' We are born again, one flesh, one love.

'Business?' He is staring back, then looks down at himself in dismay. 'I am on business myself, though I expect you will think otherwise.'

'It is no business of mine where you go a-whoring,' I say. 'I have other things to think of. I heard word about a play.' I nod towards Tom. 'From my young neighbour.'

'Of course. The play.'

'What is it called?' I ask, keeping my voice innocent.

Will smoothes his hands over his hair. 'It's – well. The title is *The Tragedie of Macbeth.*'

'The King's story, rather than the Queen's?'

'Quite so.'

'And therefore, different from the play I left with Burbage, which fell sadly short and which he returned to me. As you will recall.'

'Oh – very different! Utterly different! An India to your Kent,

as it were. A chasm of difference between your . . . musings and this finished work. Yes.' He looks unhappier still. 'That is the way of it. Plays are adapted, from many, many sources.'

'And yet – here are Tom's pages, and nearly all the words are mine.'

'Yours? Surely not.'

'I wrote them, and I know I'm not mistaken. And what about the witches? And the murder of Macduff's wife and her little ones? All thrown out – or some of this included?'

'All are there, aren't they?' says Tom. 'It's a fine, dark thing, and will set an audience trembling.'

'These things are there,' says Will, blinking. 'And more besides. I mean – new things, beside these . . . others. Come Tom, let us go.'

I step into the doorway, so they cannot pass. 'I hear it is highly thought of, this great, new, secret production.'

'There is no secret – we waited till it had been approved of by the King,' says Will. 'And now he has seen it, and admires it, and all is well.'

I look from Will's face to Tom's and back again. 'It's a poor business,' I say. 'Is this greatness, or littleness, I wonder? Is this genius, or common theft? Tell me, sir, you are a man of many words.'

'We call it poetry,' says Will. 'We call it Art.'

'Oh, shame on you,' say I. 'You and your kind.'

'What "kind" is that?'

'Filthy players, sir, and twisted poets and your frilly little helpmeets in their skirts.' Tom looks behind him when I cast a look in his direction, as if I could not possibly be referring to him.

'Aemilia, listen to reason, will you – ?'

'Reason? Heaven help us! Reason? Is this the best that you can do? You . . . men! Cock-heavy, brain-light, and brimful of your own importance? The apex of Creation? God aimed too low!'

I turn and hurry down the stairs, through the crowded tavern and out into the street. The sun is low over the roofs and chimneys, and it will soon be nightfall. My head aches; my heart beats fast. What hope do I have of getting anything, in this City? I will end up starving in the Cage with the other drabs and vagrants. But I have not gone far when someone seizes my shoulder.

Will is breathing heavily. 'Aemilia – there is something I need to say to you.'

I shake his hand away and keep walking. 'What is there to say? Unless you will admit that you have robbed me.'

He half-runs, half-walks to keep up with me. 'I will *not* say so, because it isn't true.'

I look along the street and cross over, heading for the Bridge. 'You have played me false, you and your conniving tribe.'

'Not false, Aemilia – this is how it is done. No play is made by one man alone. You don't understand this world. You mistake your place in it. Look, mistress, slow down, please . . .'

'My place? Would that I had one!'

'Aemilia, no, you are mistaken . . .'

I try to outpace him but he matches me step for step. I skip over a dog turd and turn to face him. 'Don't you see it? If a man had written that play, and it were put on with some changes, and he were one of your company or a tavern friend, like Dekker, all would be well.'

'So . . . what is the difference?'

'Lord save us, Will! I am a woman! I will get nothing if you don't acknowledge what I have done. Nothing. I'm not Mary Sidney, or some other clever lady of the manor, who writes her hobby-lines and is fêted by her little retinue. I am alone. I am that turd.' I point at it. 'I am nothing.'

He takes a purse from his belt and holds it towards me. 'Here is gold, if it will help you,' he said. 'Once, you said that you could not be with me because of my lowly station. But now I am a gentleman. I have a coat-of-arms . . . and houses.'

'Always trying to pay me off! I don't want your cursed coin. I want to be a poet myself.'

'The world is not run according to my wishes, any more than it is to yours! You are confusing me with Almighty God!'

'Oh, go and play bare-arses with the rest of them! Every one a cozener and a cheat.' I push past him and walk on.

'Aemilia!'

I keep walking.

'Aemilia!'

I quicken my pace.

'Aemilia!' *Oh, Lord, there is that scene again: pale flesh, bright sun; his rapt face; the white light in my head.*

'My love . . .' His voice breaks upon the word, and stops.

I look back. 'Your . . . *what?*'

'I must see you! I need to see you!'

'Well, here I am. Solid as a dead sow.'

'What I mean is . . . I must talk to you! We must . . . God! Where are all the words, the *words*, when I need them most?'

'They cheat you, sir, as you have cheated me. Perhaps there is some justice in Creation after all. Your words came easy enough when you wanted to strumpet me, and whore me and harlot me, and falsely accuse me of fornicating with all and sundry. "The bay where all men ride"! God's blood, what a phrase! From your so-called love to those foul insults. How great was the distance? You made the change quicker than a viper slips its skin.'

'Jesu!' He stares at me hopelessly. 'What have I done?'

'What?'

'I thought that I could exorcise you, if my lines were cruel enough. But . . .'

'But . . . what?'

We stare at each other across the muddy street.

'I wanted to believe the worst of you. If you wouldn't have me, then, in my madness, it was easiest to call you whore.'

'Ah,' I say. 'Now we have it. Now I believe you.'

'But, even in the midst of writing those lines, I never could destroy the passion that tormented me. That is the essence of them. They are love sonnets, from my heart.'

'Oh, Will,' I say. 'You are such a fool.'

He smiles, a strange, sweet smile, and says, 'And now . . . now I fear it is too late.'

The sun is low in the sky. 'I fear so. Henry will wonder where I am.'

'What are you doing tomorrow morning?' he asks, abruptly. 'There is something . . . I must tell you something.'

'I'm praying at the tomb of my lord Hunsdon,' I say, flushing.

'You still pine for that old place-man?'

'He was kind to me. None kinder.'

'I'll meet you there.'

I laugh. 'What a fitting arrangement! Perhaps his lordship will rise up from his grave and beat you round the head for leading me such a dance.'

'I cannot bear this . . .'

He looks so woebegone that I almost pity him. 'I'm going to the Church of St Peter early,' I say. 'Six of the clock, when it's still quiet.'

'I'll be there.'

I'm startled by his burning eyes. 'I must go,' I say, like some awkward, untried maid. 'My son . . .'

'Say that you will meet with me tomorrow.'

I stare.

'Say it, Aemilia, I beg you.'

'I . . .'

'Please, sweet lady.'

'If you want.'

'I do want. I want to see you more than anything.'

'Then I will meet you.'

Scene IV

For the rest of the day I run hither and thither like the silliest virgin, to stop myself from thinking. I swear, the house was never half so clean, before or after. Marie and I fetch water, scrub floors, air counterpanes, scour knives and clean plates with shave-grasse – what would normally take me three days takes three hours. She complains at first, but she soon gets to it, and while I do the hardest tasks – such as sweeping out the green rushes from the floors and casting down new ones – she toils away with a good grace. Too good a grace, as it turns out.

At last, she comes into the hall, where I am folding linen and placing it neatly in the great oak chest. I look up, and notice Marie's drawn face. 'For Heaven's sake, sit down, girl. You have done enough.'

She sits down on a hall stool, and rests her head against the wall, eyes closed. 'Truly, I am dog-tired,' she says. 'And the babe is jumping.'

'A good sign,' say I. 'It is when they're still that there is cause for worry.'

But when I look up to see why she hasn't replied. Her face is contorted with pain. 'Marie – what is it?'

'A feeling like the curse but stronger,' she says. 'Oh, mistress, it is like a knife! I couldn't stand it worse than this! I am not ready! I am not strong!'

'It is likely just a false alarm,' I tell her. 'Go and rest, and it will ease.' But I have to help her up the stairs and into bed, for she is heavy with fatigue.

As I turn to go, she grabs my hand. 'Did you see him?' she asks.

'See who?'

'Tom. When you went to the Anchor.'

I hesitate.

'Did you, mistress?'

'Yes, I saw him.' I think of telling her about the whore, but find I can't. 'He was snoring and in his cups. You are better off without him, child. Don't put your trust in players.'

'He loves me. He says he loves me.'

'I am sure he does, my poor Marie.'

I wake at the dead of night. Did I hear a scream? I open my eyes and stare up into the thick dark, listening hard. Silence loads my ears; blackness presses upon my eyes. A dream, a night fear. My mind at its old tricks again, and now there's no Joan to guard me. I am lucky to find myself safe and warm under my eiderdown, instead of out in the cold streets in nothing but my smock.

Then I hear it again, a scream that rips into the night, tearing the silence, louder, louder, then collapsing into agonised sobs. I push back the bed-clothes, light a candle and wrap myself in a woollen shawl. Then I climb up to the garret. Shivering, I open the door.

'Marie?'

She is naked, kneeling on her bed, with her head hanging down. All I can see is her loose hair, which hides her face. It is swinging to and fro as she rocks in pain. Then I notice, in the shifting orange of the candle-flame, that the sheets are smeared with blood.

I set down the candle. 'Dear Lord! How long have you been like this?' But she only grunts. 'Marie?'

'Umbstone. Umbstone.'

I throw off the shawl and kneel beside her. 'What? What is it?'

'Umbstone.' She lifts her head and points to the amulet which hangs around her neck. It is an eagle stone, a talisman to ward off miscarriage. The baby will not come till she takes this off. I unfasten it and set it down on the straw mattress where she can see it.

'I must fetch the midwife,' say I. 'I won't be long.'

But then she grips my hand. There is a look of terror in her eyes. 'Don't leave me, mistress. Stay!'

'Marie . . . I have no skill in this!'

'*You* will birth my child. *You* will save me.' Her grip tightens. 'Please.'

'What foolishness – you need someone who knows how to aid you in your travail . . .' But then I see myself, as Marie is now, as clear as if a mirror had been held up in which I could view the past. The night Henry was born and Joan saved us both. I see myself, crying out and clutching the birthing stool, and I see Joan, gentle, patient, always calm. While she was with me, I helped her with the births of several children in the parish. In truth, I can remember what she did: how she rubbed the women's flanks with oil of roses, fed them with vinegar and sugar, and eased the pain with powdered ivory or eagle's dung.

'If you want me, I'll stay, but don't forget I am not a midwife, nor do I have anything to recommend me.' The night watch calls outside – one of the clock. 'Do not lie down when the throes come; walk gently about the chamber. Keep warm, but don't take to your bed.'

I bank up the fire, so it gives out a good heat.

'I don't have child-bed linen or anything else for my poor baby!' she wails through her fallen hair. 'I thought it would be weeks from now!'

'Hush, calm yourself, I will see what I can fetch. I have a store of linen downstairs. Don't fret yourself. There is not a man or woman in this world who hasn't come into the world this way. Think on that, and breathe easy.'

341

I run down the stairs and rush into my room. Sure enough, I have a neat pile of forehead cloths, caps and belly-bands. And some open-fronted shifts which Marie could use for breast-feeding when it is time. Then I fetch the birthing-stool from the kitchen. I also get a pound of butter, a bowl of lavender water, some juice of dittany and my sharpest knife. Returning to the garret, I help the whimpering Marie on to the low seat, so that she is leaning against the back, legs wide. Then I stop up the cracks in the chamber walls with rags and blow out the candles, so that the roaring fire is our only light.

'Too much brightness can drive a mother mad,' I tell her.

She says nothing.

'Here, eat a knob of butter,' say I, cutting her a slice.

She groans and dribbles, but most of it goes down.

'I cannot bear it, mistress! I cannot cope! I swear there is an Oliphant inside me.'

I give her a drink of dittany juice, and then feel carefully inside for her cervix, and discover that she is beginning to open. Pressing against the widening space I can feel a round shape, covered in a waxy layer of vernix. Pray God it is the top of her baby's head and not some other part of its anatomy, for I cannot recall what to do if it is a breech birth, or there is some other mischief.

'I can't do it, mistress!' shouts Marie. 'I can't do it! I don't dare to, and I'm not strong enough! It will tear me in two. I can feel it. Oh, God, help me!'

'You'll do very well, a fine girl like you,' I say. I soak a cloth in the lavender water and wipe her brow. 'Keep cheerful! Don't waste your strength by calling on your Lord, when He has better things to do than mind a child-bed. Do you hear a mare in the field lamenting and crying as she pushes a gangling foal into the world? Save yourself for what must be done.'

'Lord help me! Our Lady, save me!' screams Marie, and her hands clench around the arms of the birthing-chair as another spasm takes hold of her. She is not an apt pupil. Poor creature, I

am beyond my own knowledge and experience, but not so much as she. I cannot see how such a flimsy thing as she can bring to birth the great protuberance that she's been carrying inside. I rub the tight barrel of her belly with butter, speaking soothing nonsense to her all the while.

'I will help you all I can,' I say. 'But you must also strive to help yourself.'

But now another seizure is upon her, and she screams and writhes in the chair, and it is all I can do to stop her thrashing in the rushes in a fit like Legion. When she has done, there is a great pool of blood all around her, so the chair is an island in a scarlet lake, but there is no sign of the baby. The limits of my scant knowledge being already reached, I mop up the blood with the bed-clothes and say my own prayers to God.

'Mistress,' whispers the child. Her eyes are tight shut, and her breath comes shallowly. 'Will my baby come?'

'In its own time.'

'So it could not stick inside for ever?'

'Of course not.'

The watch calls out again. Two of the clock. Time enough, time enough.

But then time contorts to nightmare, and it is as if some demon comes down and takes possession of Marie. The throes come faster and stronger – as they will – but her fear is greater with each contraction, and soon it isn't God and Mary that she calls for, but the Devil and his minions instead. I find myself shouting back at her, afraid that this can do no good, yet shout she will. To my horror, she leaps up from the chair and runs against the walls, tearing at the bloody shreds of her nightgown, roaring and yelling all the while.

And I swear she sounds more like a damned soul than a serving girl. 'By Satan! By the Devil in all his names! By Apollyon, Beelzebub, Diabolus, Lucifer, the King of Hell! Did I ask for this?'

I grab her by the shoulders. 'Marie! Marie! Stop it!'

'The walking spirits of the Earth do not feel pain as I do!'

'Come back to yourself . . .'

But it is as if she is in another world. She puts her head back and howls, then spouts the vilest gibberish, which sounds like the language of lost souls.

'Marie!' I cry. 'Stop this terrible noise! Do not speak of Satan at such a time! Say your prayers!' Still she rages on, scratching her own flesh with her nails.

I pray for her, hoping to limit the power of her wicked thoughts. She seizes my arm and, using me for purchase, pushes and screams, legs half-bent, eyes rolled back into her head. Then she falls down on the ground, and a torrent of blood comes belching from between her legs and there is the most fearful stench, and I am afraid that she has died. But when I feel the pulse in her neck the blood is still beating fast, so I take some more old sheets and press them between her legs, and mop up all I can of the blood and matter. Then I see that a baby's face is sticking out.

'Marie!' I say. 'Your prayers are answered! The child is coming.'

Marie only groans, and speaks more of her strange language.

'Be quiet now, and don't push out for a little while. Let it come gently.' I cradle the little head in my hands and gradually a tiny shoulder follows. Then comes the other, and then the top part of its body. I feel in its mouth, scrape out the dark mess that is there, and it coughs and splutters and begins to cry. 'It is good Marie, it's good, you have a child . . .'

I bend closer, wanting to release its legs, but they are stuck fast. I try to ease the infant out, but can't. So I grease my hands with more butter, and feel inside her, to see what ails it. I feel a rounded shape, a blockage. But then, with a terrible wail, Marie begins to push once more. Blood oozes out around the half-born baby.

'Don't push too hard now; let the child take its time,' I say, though I don't know if she can understand a word I say. There is another contraction and out slips the baby's legs. Yet there is still something wrong. The baby seems stuck to its mother's body by some hidden protuberance, and I can't free it. Its cries grow faster, and I look around me, wondering what I should do next. I see the sharp knife lying on a stool. I had thought to use this to cut the cord, but I know that sometimes Joan would cut the woman's skin to ease the progress of a birth. (It is part of Eve's punishment that babies are born with large heads, so that the agony of birthing is more severe.) I grasp the knife, and screw up my courage. Then I cut her taut skin, so that she is ripped wider. Thick gore gushes forth around the baby's protruding head. It seems Marie is indeed being torn in two. And then . . . a second pair of legs comes kicking out, a mirror copy of the first. Then slithers forth another child, a perfect twin. But then I scream myself, hardly able to believe what I see before me. The two infants are one flesh. It is a double-child, a hellish freak, joined at the hip. I shrink back from it, trembling, and the creature wriggles and mewls, crying out with its two mouths and flailing its four legs and four arms in the air. Creature? It? I must say 'they', for there are two souls here, two mortals bound together for eternity. Separate but whole. I cry out and take a step backwards, turning away, my hands clutched to my head. Turning back, I see the malformed creatures squirming and crying in a sea of blood. A hellish punishment indeed. A blot on nature, hideous and misbegotten. I think of the father who smashed his one-eyed child against the wall, and, looking down, I see that I still have the knife clenched in my hand.

I walk slowly back to the birth-bed. Marie is lying still, eyes shut. Her babies are crying with double force. Praying all the while, I cut the cord and tie it, then wash the infants with milk and water and wrap them tight. Then I put a biggin-bonnet on each of the two heads, with a compress under each to protect their soft spots. Then I swaddle the poor things on a board. And

there they lie, in an unbreakable embrace, arms locked around themselves. The two heads match exactly: black-haired and fairy-faced. Sweeter, prettier monsters you could not imagine. I hope that they will quietly die, and bless them, wishing I had holy water instead of just my scented bowl.

Of their mother I have little hope. Her breaths are shallow and uneven and she is deathly white. I fear she might not last till daybreak. The linen cloths that I have used are turned bright red, and my hands and dress are of the same colour: I feel like a murderer, not a midwife. I strip the bed and change the sheets, then begin to sweep the scarlet rushes from the floor. Outside, someone calls out the time. But I can make no sense of it.

Marie is stronger than she looks. After I have washed her and sewn her wound as best I can, she wakes. Her eyes blink open, and I see that the madness has left her.

'Where is my baby?' she asks, looking round the room. 'Does it live? Is it a boy or a girl?'

I hesitate.

'Mistress, is my baby well?'

'You have two babies, Marie,' I say. I lift the swaddled infants from their cot, and place them in her arms.

'Two babies?' She smiles down at the two faces, which are pressed tight together. 'Twins!'

'Twin girls.'

'What a wondrous thing.' She stares down at them.

'Every birth is wondrous,' say I. (This is lying, plain and simple.)

'But why are they swaddled to each other? Don't they need their own bands?'

I want to find a way to tell her why they are bound together, but I can't. She sees it in my face. 'What's wrong, mistress?'

I turn away.

346

'There is something terrible! Please tell me. What's happened?'

I shake my head sorrowfully.

Her voice rises up to a wail. 'Tell me what it is that ails them! I beg you!'

'I cannot say it. I am sorry, but I cannot say.'

With shaking hands she undoes the linens so that her malformed babies are revealed. Four-legged, four-armed, two-headed . . . two bodies linked by flesh and bone. She screams and flings them down upon the bed, and they wake, and wave their freed limbs in the cold air and wail with her. 'Alair! Alair!' Such a sorrowful sound that it tears at me; the sound that Henry made when he was tiny, and Joan put him in my arms for the first time. And I feel such pity for them.

I pick up the joined infants, and wrap them tight once more. Their cries quieten. Marie's do not. She screams and screams and screams, half in English, half in French. Sadly, I understand both languages: her words are more evil in that foreign tongue than in our own. Wilder and madder and louder she shouts, calling for the lynching of Our Lady, an end to Time, the emptying of Hell and sundry other changes to the proper order of things. Until at last she spews green bile upon the floor – a dreadful stench. I clean it up. I am starting to tire of skivvying for my own maid. After that – silence. The rage has passed. It is as if Marie has puked out some evil in herself. She sits hunched up in the bed, a shawl pulled round her shoulders, staring ahead of her, contemplating nothing.

After a while, she wipes her mouth with her long hair and says, 'I have committed a mortal sin. God has sent this to me.'

'We are all sinners,' I say. I sit down beside her. 'What you did with Tom is no more than a thousand girls have done before you. A thousand thousand! You fell into bed before you made a marriage vow. You are more fool than sinner.' I take one of her hands in mine. 'I will fetch a wet nurse.'

'What wet nurse will suckle *that*?' she says. She nods in the direction of the cradle. 'She'll run from the very sight of it.'

'Yours is not the first freak born in Westminster, nor will it be the last. It is "they", not "it" – and they must be fed. Just like other children.'

'But they are not like other children,' she says. 'They are joined! They are doomed!'

'We don't know what their fate will be. There's an old tale of twins joined like these two, who lived in Kent, in Biddenham, and were born to a good family. They lived for more than thirty years.'

She isn't listening. 'What shall I tell Tom?'

I shake my head, pick up the infants and begin to feed them with a horn of watery gruel.

After this I must have slept. I wake to find that I'm curled beside Marie on the bed. I rub my eyes and look out of the window. The sun is high in the sky. The hour to meet with Will is long gone. I stand up, unsteadily. Marie is watching me. Her eyes are calm. The joined twins are fast asleep, snuffling in their cot.

'Give them to me,' she says.

'What?'

'My babies.'

I gaze at her, confused. 'I was going to fetch a wet nurse.'

'I don't need one. Give them to me.'

I stumble to the cot and pick up the joined twins. She takes them from me. And she sticks her little finger into the mouth of one of them, waking it, then gently probes her teat into its mouth. I've seen many women struggle with this first suckling, and their babies fall away from the offered breast. But this child knows well what it needs and drinks greedily, eyes creased closed, one hand clasped around the white orb of her dug. The second infant rests its cheek upon it.

The door opens a crack. Henry's face appears in it, bright and curious. I hurry over to block his view. 'Is she alive?' he asks. 'I heard such screams I thought she must be dead.'

'Of course she is alive, you dolt!'

'And is the baby born?' He cranes round me to get a better look.

'It is . . . all done, yes.'

'In that case, praise to God,' says Henry.

'Indeed.'

'And hurrah!' says a loud voice, and in bursts Tom before I can stop him. For a moment he stares at the frozen scene: the pile of blood-soaked rushes, the disordered bed, Marie, clasping the tiny freaks. One head feeding from her breast; the other waiting, round eyes fixed upon her face. Though they are swaddled again, it is clear that something is strange. But Tom, young as he is, seems puzzled rather than afraid.

'Marie – you have your – children!'

'Oh, Tom – go away!'

'Don't you want to see me?'

'I do – but not now. Get out please, Tom, my dearest love.'

'But – *I* want to see *you*!'

'Not now, Tom, no, you must go.'

Henry, with his skill of slipping where he isn't wanted, has made his way to the bedside.

'Why don't you put one of them in the cradle,' he asks, 'while the other feeds? Doesn't it get tired of watching?'

'Is it – twins? Our children?' Tom's voice is uncertain.

'You heard what Marie said to you – get out,' I say. 'This is no place for you, and beyond your understanding. And Henry, come away from there!' I seize his arm and pull him roughly towards the door.

Tom looks at me, suddenly frightened. 'What is there to understand? She is my love, and we will marry – and these are my children! There is nothing strange in that.'

'Marry? What's this? No one is marrying without my consent.' Anne bustles in, bare-headed and wearing her shabbiest dress and oldest ruff, which droops down at one side.

Tom wheels round. 'Mother, you cannot forbid me to wed Marie. We are promised to each other already. Burbage oversaw the handfasting.'

She glances at the bed, seeming to notice the twins for the first time. 'Handfasting? Handfasting? How dare you even use such a word to dignify your sport? And with such a common little bitch as this? Handfarting, more like. She is a servant girl, nothing but a silly strumpet. There is no more reason to believe these . . . twins are yours than that they are the spawn of any other Tom Fool who came knocking.'

'Mistress Flood,' says Marie, 'please stop.'

'Stop? Why should I take note of you, that's laid a trap for my dear son?'

'Forgive me, but I think I can put him straight. These aren't your babies, Tom. I had a strange dream one night, and I believe I was ravished by some demon.'

Tom laughs. 'What? Marie, you are mad.'

'She's lain with another man, is the truth of it,' says Anne. 'More than one, I'm sure. Half the prentice-boys in the City have been up those skirts. She's a skittish, shameless doxy.'

'Marie, is that true? Have you been with another man? If so, tell me now.'

She looks up at him. Then she unwraps the twins. Anne screams and prays to Our Lady. Tom stares, as if the demon she had spoken of were sitting right in front of him.

Anne is still praying, eyes tight shut. 'Lead me from this place of sin,' she says. 'Lead me from it, and do not ask me to return.'

'Anne,' I say. 'This is cruel! Such things do happen, in the normal way of things. No demon needs to creep into a virgin's bed. God's creatures aren't all perfect – you can see that every time you walk down the street. Have pity on the girl.'

'Take me from here, Tom,' commands Anne, blindly holding out her hands. But Tom is still looking at his lover, as she quietly fastens one of her babies to her breast. Her movements are small and neat, and she has never looked so pretty. He kneels down and bows his head in prayer.

'Tom?' says his mother. 'Tom?'

'It is my fault,' says Tom. 'Get down on your knees, Mother, and pray to God to be merciful.'

'What?'

'May God forgive me, I have lain with whores. I have not been true to Marie as I should have been. This is my punishment. Pray for her, and pray for me. For we are man and wife, and nothing will divide us.'

I close the door and run, my head bare, hair flying. I am too late to meet Will, of that I am sure. But this is the only thing that I am certain of. It is as if all the times we ever met, or lay together, or quarrelled, have been broken into tiny pieces and tossed into the air, and mixed up with all my dreams of him, and his sonnets, and his burned letters. Everything has always conspired to keep us apart, and now this. Yet how could I have left that child, in her dark labour? I am human, after all. And what was it that he wished to say to me that has not been said already? Words joined and divided us. Words and the world. I think of Wriothesley and feel sick with rage. The great lord. His word against mine. I think of my play, that tumult of wild emotion, put to work at the Globe without my name upon it. I think of that wife, sitting Stratford-smug, counting his money.

But . . . there was once such a bond between us that it seemed that we could best them all, make our own world, and let them keep their lesser one. And there is still Henry. Oh, Lord. If Marie had given birth the day before, or the day after, all might have been . . . What? My mind is so full, it seems it must break

351

open. All I can see is that last look I had from Will. My memories swirl; my thoughts are frantic – I can't tell truth from tale. I run full-tilt, heading for the Church of St Peter, my breath tearing at my chest. When I see the great stone structure rising up ahead of me, I stop and hold my side and weep, because I know there is no reason for this hurry. Too late! The bells are ringing. Twelve tolls. Twelve knells. I walk up to the church door and push it open.

This is the church where I worshipped with Lord Hunsdon every Sunday, unless the Lady Anne was visiting, which was seldom. A royal church, and royally magnificent as befitted the rulers of England. They have dissolved, destroyed and cruelly disfigured much of what once was, yet this great building seems as permanent and vast as any fortress. In the lofty nave the air is cold and still. Sunlight shifts in through the jewel-coloured window panes, illuminating the flat glass faces of the saints.

Unsteady, and still breathing hard, I make my way down the passageway towards the chapel of St John the Baptist, where Hunsdon has been laid to rest. I look around me, filled with wonder in spite of everything. I have been excluded from the majesty of Whitehall and the other palaces, but not from the splendour of this House of God. The gold and silver working of the high altar and the rich embroidery of the altar-cloths are bathed in soft light. Behind the altar at the far end of the nave, a polished brazen screen glows brightly. Above my head, the stonework has been carved with such marvellous skill that it seems to hang in the air, as light as cobwebs.

The chapel of St John the Baptist opens off the north transept. It is a little enough space, fenced off from the main church with a high grille. Anyone entering is confronted by Lord Hunsdon's vast tomb, which takes up most of the space on the wall opposite. I pause and look at it now. Such a monstrous and ungainly lump of marble-work you never saw. There is no sleeping statue of my Lord Hunsdon here: no, it is as if he were a guild rather than a

man. His sarcophagus is decorated with black and white cheque-point, surmounted by what looks like a colonnaded fireplace. The man I knew is trapped behind a prison wall of weapons, armour and prancing bulls. It was his proud wife who built this hideous monument in his name, with money given to her by the Queen. No woman who loved her husband truly would erect a tomb that looked like Nero's privy.

My lord died in debt. Some say his taste in mistresses added to his woes. They used to say that I had put up with his aged passion for the sake of my fine gowns and the suite of rooms I had in Whitehall. There was a joke that I would make him hump me three times nightly in the hope that it would see him off. They did not know what we were to each other. He was a tender lover and a true friend, and I was happy with him. Until I fell in love with Will.

I sit down and rest my head in my hands. Twelve of the clock. There is no reason to expect that he would wait so long. I try to pray, to calm myself, dizzy with images of two-headed infants and splurting womb blood. Like a Puritan, I address myself direct to God, as if he were sitting next to me on the chapel step.

'Oh, Lord, please show me what should be done and give me the strength to see it will be . . .' My mind trails off again, seeing the knife slashing at poor Marie's pudenda and a face peering out from within.

'Oh, Lord,' I start again. 'I am sorry for wishing that Will would come, and I thank you for giving me the chance to help Marie and her baby. Her babies . . .' Now a vision of Will as I last saw him comes to me, and I stop again. It's not a prayer I remember now, but lines of Marlowe's: *Come live with me and be my Love . . .*

How beautiful these lines are! Why have I never lived straightforwardly? *And we will all the pleasures prove . . .* Why has my life always been such an unseemly muddle? I am blighted, like Eurydice, who died from a snake-bite on her wedding day,

and was followed by faithful Orpheus into Hades. But there is no Orpheus for me.

'Oh, Lord . . .' But this time I can think of nothing else, excepting only, 'Why?'

I open my eyes and look around me. The silence in the high church, with its sunlit windows and its soaring stonework, is complete. *That Hills and Valleys, dale and field, and all the craggy mountains yield.* If my passion could have found its true expression, I would conjure Will now, and bring him here before me. Solid flesh. Ink-stained fingers. Leather doublet. And his questioning, relentless gaze. To see him, to feel the weight of him, to sense his fingers touching mine. My hand flinches, as if he has reached out from my mind.

The pews gape. Empty, empty, empty. I feel my feebleness and littleness as I never have before. *You are old, Aemilia,* I think. *You are weary.*

And then I think, *Will. Come.* I summon all my passion, all my woman's power, and wish him, wish him to come before me. I close my eyes and plead with him, so hard that my head aches. He has slandered me, and dishonoured me, but that was long ago. Can I forgive him? I don't know. But I yearn to hear his voice.

When I open my eyes, for a moment I think that someone is standing in front of me. I look up. 'Will?'

But there is no one. I can conjure evil spirits, but I cannot conjure my lost love. Yet . . . I do notice something, lying on the raised shelf at the bottom of the huge sarcophagus. A book – a little book, prettily bound. With a strange feeling of apprehension, I pick it up. It is a collection of sonnets. The title reads *Sonnets to the Dark Lady.* I stare at in horror. I know full well who this Dark Lady is. And I now know why Will was suddenly so eager to talk to me. He has a guilty conscience. He knows of the existence of this vile thing. He probably commissioned it himself. I open it, and look at the title page, and sure enough: his name is on there.

Oh, Will. As if you hadn't done enough. Is this the 'love' you spoke of, when you called after me? My God, what duplicity! You even believe your lies yourself.

Turning the pages, I read one of the verses, one I already have by heart, and which is now for sale in this foul City, for anyone to see.

> *Past cure I am, now reason is past care,*
> *And frantic-mad with evermore unrest;*
> *My thoughts and my discourse as madmen's are,*
> *At random from the truth vainly express'd;*
> *For I have sworn thee fair and thought thee bright,*
> *Who art as black as hell, as dark as night.*

Then I notice that the book fell open at this page because there is a marker in it. A letter. I unfold the single sheet, and read these words:

Aemilia –
You did not come. I told you that I could not bear this, which is the truth. I will not be tortured by your lies, and double-ways, and cunning. My desire, my dreams, my waking thoughts have been distorted by your image for too long. I have a life, a wife, a place, a future, and no space for you within it.
I tried to apologise to you, seeing that Wriothesley was lying when he bragged about his conquest of you, and that the sight I had – which haunts me still – was not all that it seemed. But you would not forgive me. You are too proud. Perhaps your pride is all you have. Your pride, and little Henry.
These poems are my finest work. I see no reason why they should be hidden from public view, as you have spurned me and still spurn me, and keep me from my son. You have him. I have my Art. To spare him, your name

does not appear in this little book. There are those who will speculate about your identity; there are some who know. It is an ending, in any case. An end to my last hopes that we still loved each other even slightly; that there was something left to say. I wanted to warn you, but I have given up hope of any kind of commerce between us. So there you have it.

Do me one last service, if you will, madam. Do not come to me, or tempt me, or beguile me with your look. Do not bewitch me with your words. Do not think of me again, and I will not think of you.

Will

I fold up the paper, this way, that way. Again. And again. Dry sobs rack my body. I feel hatred and anger roaring through me; my veins are boiling with bad blood. Now the letter is shaped into a point as sharp as any dagger. You can kill with poetry. You can murder with a pen. I have been grievously injured, in the past, and in the present moment. I have been cast out, and ridiculed, and made invisible. My gender is nothing of itself – we are sought by men, loved by them, fucked by them; we are made pregnant with their seed, we mother them and then we die. In these functions, we may be solid. In any other, we are insubstantial as thin air. Give me the crow-scragged garb of witchcraft any day. Give me a witch's power; give me her ill-wishing, her night-spells, her terrifying potency. Give me the work of Hecate and of Lilith. As black as hell, am I? As dark as night? Well, I will take him at his word.

Scene V

The Tragedie of Macbeth rules all of London. There is talk of it everywhere, in the streets and taverns, at the docks and cook-shops. Prentice-boys run wild along the riverbank, affecting to be Macbeth in pursuit of Duncan. A chap-book is printed, which apes the play and puts King James in Macbeth's garb. A quick-thinking pie-man has starting baking Macbeth pies, pricked with an 'M' for Macbeth and for Murder. The streets seem transformed into the Globe's dominions, so each corner rings out '*I come, Graymalkin!*' and every window shouts, '*Out, damn spot, Out I say!*' The worst of it is that Henry's head is quite turned with it, and, far from thinking that this has anything to do with the play I have written, he is entranced by the Globe and the players and the genius of Mr Shakespeare. It is madness. It is Bedlam. It must stop.

And now I have a plan. Simple in its conception, though not in its execution.

For the plan to work, I must have solitude and secrecy. So one balmy day, I set out across the river. The water laps and gleams in the fitful sunshine. Flimsy clouds hasten across the sky. The waterman sets me down just by Deptford Creek, and I look around me. I am standing between two worlds. Down the river are the flags and cupolas of Greenwich Palace. Across the water is the Isle of Dogs, where thieves and cut-throats lurk among great banks of mud and stranded river-filth.

After asking the way, I walk along a dirt road passing through Deptford Strand. Much of the land is taken up with sheds and

store-rooms, but open fields still stretch away to one side. At last I reach the place I am looking for. It is a sturdy, stone-made building, most unlike the top-heavy wooden houses that line the London streets. Sheep graze on the sward of smooth grass before its front door, and next to it is a pretty garden, dense with medlar and rambling rose-bushes and bordered with sweet william. Beneath the trees there is a row of straw beehives, sheltered by a stout roof. No one knows me here. No one will comment on my coming, or wonder at my going. I can wreak revenge in peace.

I have taken an upper chamber in this quiet inn for one night. It is a small chamber, but large enough for my purpose. I set my bag down. My hands are trembling, but I know what I must do. First I take out my Geneva Bible, noting its holy weight. Heavy to carry, but I dare not be without it. Next comes an equally weighty book, Cornelius Agrippa's grimoire. And a piece of chalk, taken from Henry's toy box. Last of all, a vial of holy water. I range them on the long oak table, in a tidy row. My heart is jumping in my chest and my throat is dry.

I cross to the window and look out. Fragile rose petals drift past the window in the quickening breeze. The sun lights up the patchwork view of roofs and fields, paths and dock-sides, stores and timber yards. Shaking violently, I lie down on the bed. After a while I doze, and dream of Simon Forman. He is following me down a steep stairway into Hell. I wake with a jump, as if I have missed my footing on the stair. The room is growing dark, so I light a candle and open up the grimoire.

Sweat is sliding down my neck as I sprinkle holy water and make a sign of the cross. It is so dark I cannot see beyond the flame.

I wait. There is more noise outside: men are shouting at the fighting dogs. I hear a woman's gurgling laugh. A cart rattles past, wheels squeaking unevenly. I lick my lips, wondering how long to leave it before I give it up, read some good words from the Bible and tumble into bed.

The night is growing colder. Though I would not have thought it possible, the darkness deepens, and with it comes a weird silence, muffled by a thickness that was neither mist nor solid. I hug myself, trying to quell my ague of trembling. I can barely remember how it was when I summoned the demon before. I remember Joan's voice: was that my imagination, or did she really help me? I listen hard, trying to hear her. But there is silence. Before, I was fevered, desperate: Henry was dying in front of me. This time I am fuelled by cold anger. Yet one thing is the same: I have no choice. I must do this thing if I am to keep my sanity.

Lilith is the female demon of the night. Lilith was Adam's true equal, his twin soul. This was how we started – man and wife; woman and husband. Lilith was cast from Eden because 'she would not lie beneath'. She demanded that Adam should treat her as his equal: in their sexual dealings and in their life. She demanded this because she *was* his equal. If there is any demon, in any firmament, who will understand my plight, it is this evil Lilith, this snake goddess. The one who wanted me to write this turbulent play.

First I draw the chalk circle on the ground. Then I pour the holy water into a glass and place it by me, for my protection. I know the rules – the demon must stay within the circle. The circle is a place outside creation. If the demon stays within that place, then all should go well. I open the grimoire and turn to the summoning pages that I used before. I read them loudly, then shut my eyes and summon all my courage. 'Lilith!' I cry. 'Lilith, I call on you!'

There is silence, but I feel it listening. I feel the evil more sharply now. There is no plague in me, only fear.

I screw up my courage once again. 'Lilith, I call on you to do my bidding!'

A rustling now, fainter than my own breathing. A change in the layers of the air. Someone laughs, far, far away. A thick band

of pain begins to grip my head, just as it did before, but this time it is stronger and my nausea is overwhelming. And this time there is a shifting and heaving within my belly, a movement of my innards that causes me to lose my breath with sudden shocks of pain. The voices and screams that gather come from outside me – from cold air, from distant stars, from the riverbed. But they are also deepening and thickening and strengthening inside me, and I let out a mighty scream and a flying shape vomits from my mouth. It is as big as a dragonfly. It has landed in the middle of the circle, and the night air seems to feed it, and it grows and grows and grows. It is assembled from bone and shadow, from the webs of spiders, from my own saliva, from the sex-cries of the people in the next room, from a catfight in the street, from the keening of a beaten child, from the night-sounds I cannot hear. And yet, it is like a blurred reflection, steamy and half-seen. There is a vastness in front of me; the circle is filled, but the Entity is vapour and vacuity. This is the best description I can find for something that has never, I think, been fixed with Christian words.

Then I hear a voice, cold and distant, like the memory of ice.

I clench my sweating hands.

'Who calls Lilith?'

It is a physical voice this time – not human-sounding, but my ears can sense it.

'I do – Aemilia Bassano Lanyer.'

'Mother of the plague-child?'

'Yes.'

'Daughter of the recorder player, he who bartered his soul for greatness, then turned back to God at the last, defaulting on his blood-sealed bond?'

I feel a chill go through me, top to toe. The truth I have sought, revealed. 'Yes.'

Silence. I am straining so hard to hear the demon's strange unvoice, and make sense of its murky shadow-tones, that I feel

myself swaying and try to control my movements: I must not fall into the chalk circle.

'We have done your bidding,' says the voice. 'Why call Lilith twice?'

'I have been wronged.'

I listen again. I can hear a cruel sound now, many-voiced and violent, like a great crowd shouting at a bear baiting.

'We asked you for something,' says the voice, a little louder now. 'There was a bargain. Are you an equivocator like your father?'

'No! I wrote a play. I wrote down all the odd things that I had written in my . . . my malady. In the madness of the quest to help my son. Lady Macbeth and the witches and all the rest of it. I wrote it all down, and I made it into something, and they stole it from me.'

The figure in the circle is now full size, and looks as solid as the nightstand by the bed. Lilith's yellow eyes are fixed on mine, and their black slits look like the cracks of Doom. I don't want to look into those eyes, but I cannot look away. Her voice is so loud in my ears now that I wince when she says, '*Who* stole it from you? Who did this?'

I lick my lips. 'It was Shakespeare – William Shakespeare and the King's Men . . . Dick Burbage and – Tom Flood.'

'Men,' says Lilith. 'Men took it from you.'

'Yes.'

'It was ever thus,' she says. 'And so it shall be for many years to come. But they shall pay. We shall have revenge.'

'I . . .' My words must come, even faced with an agent of the Beast. 'I don't want . . . I just want you to unmake the play. To stop it. You helped me write it; I wanted to call you so that you would stop it . . . To see if you would *end* it.'

Lilith's eyes seem to have swelled up to the size of the circle, to the size of the room. Through those snake-cracks I can see Hell now, and the people in it. Little ant-ish figures, consumed

in flame. In Hell, there are no half-measures. 'We shall have revenge,' says Lilith, beginning to shrink again. 'Have no fear of that. The play is cursed.'

The room is colder than ever. I fold my arms, shivering, as Lilith begins to fade from sight. But then I notice that the holy water is red and bubbling in its vial. Then I see for the first time that the ground around her feet is strewn with tiny corpses – the bodies of babes and little children, still and rotted and wormy-eyed. I scream and stagger, and I lose my balance. Then I fall into the circle.

Scene VI

Henry is playing chess with Tom by the fireside, their faces drawn and intense. Tom's joined twins sleep beside them in their cradle. I am washing my face in a pail of water. The cold liquid seems more real than demons, and is washing away the black mist that is blurring my brain after my night in Deptford. Then, for an instant, I see Lilith watching, sitting in the shadows.

'Out – spectre!' I cry, and the two boys look at me in surprise.

'Mother?' says Henry. 'Whatever is the matter?'

'Nothing!' I say, turning away. And indeed, there is nothing there. Only Tom's cast-off jerkin and plumed cap.

'You will wake them,' warns Tom, pushing the cradle to a gentle rhythm with his foot. 'Hush now, Mistress Lanyer.'

'*Hush now. Hush now,*' says another voice, inside my head. Lilith's voice. '*I will do your bidding. Never fear it. I am to Silver Street, this night, to fix that thief Will Shakespeare for good.*'

The house is ordered and familiar. The pot simmers on the skillet. The goose hangs, waiting to be plucked. There is dust on the mantelpiece and the milk is on the turn. These are ordinary things with actual substance. The spirits haunt my mind, not the dinner table, nor the haberdasher's, nor the cowshed. But then I recall that voice, that nausea, the folded succubus before me. My own ignorance of these matters makes me more afraid. I do not know what I have done, or what the outcome might be. Like

Lady Macbeth, I have rushed to action, and must now deal with the consequences. But Lilith's voice and promise make me ill with fear. I called her once to save a life; this time I only wanted to save my feelings. This was wrong. I must go to Silver Street, and warn Will.

I slip through the Wall at Cripplegate just before the trumpets sound the curfew. As darkness falls, I make my way along Silver Street and towards St Olave's Church – a neglected, lichen-covered building – which is close to Will's lodgings at the Mountjoys' house. I still have the set of keys he gave me. Should I go in? Or should I knock, and ask to speak to him? My legs are heavy, and my heart thumps. I sit on a stone bench, my mind chasing round in circles. I can hear the calls of children playing in a nearby garden, and the shouting of the watch as they begin their patrol of the City streets. A fox slinks between the gravestones, with a chicken clutched in its black muzzle. The stone bench chills me through my skirts, and the grass beneath my feet begins to dampen with night-dew.

At last I stand up stiffly, and make my way across the street, taking the keys from the pocket inside my skirts. This must be done. As I approach, I see that the windows are dark, and not a chink of light shows anywhere. I knock on the door, and the sound echoes in the dark house. There is no one in. Still, I knock again, harder this time. Shall I return home? The curfew has sounded and the watch are doing their rounds. No, I will go in and wait.

I unlock the door and step inside. It opens on to a costume workshop. Of course, this is his landlord's trade. I light a wick-lamp and stare around me, distracted, in spite of myself, by the bales of satin, taffeta and gauzy lawn, each glowing with bright colour, the piles of silvered silk. When I came before, they had fled the plague and all this was packed away. Lifting my lamp higher, I see baskets of seed-pearls, glimmering on the shelves around the room, and golden gauze like fairy wings. Oh – what's

this? A dark mass of human hair spilling across the workbench? It looks like Lilith's snaking tresses. But it is only a headpiece, set upon a workbench, made of coloured beads and pitch-black feathers.

Protecting the lamp-flame with my hand, I tiptoe up the stairs, and cross the solar to Will's room. I enter, and close the door silently behind me. I look around his chamber, breathing sharply. It is quite empty, and exactly as I remember it. In the centre is the great curtained bed, its heavy velvet hangings drawn shut. Piles of books sit on the desk, and on the floor around it. There is a walnut chest by the fireplace. I raise the lid, wincing as it creaks. It is filled with neatly folded shirts, and two doublets, arms crossed.

Just then, I stiffen. Something has fallen, downstairs, in the empty house. I pick up the lamp, and go to the door, listening. I hear a soft voice: '*Men have taken it. We shall have vengeance.*' Lilith! Oh, Heavenly Father! My hand flies to my mouth, and perhaps the gust of air this makes extinguishes the candle. Or perhaps it blows out for some other reason. I stand for a moment in darkness. Then, almost without knowing what I do, I draw back the curtains and climb on to Will's bed.

I listen, as hard as I can, from inside the curtain, and I can hear the sound of whispering, and the swish, swish, swish of a Serpent's tail. After a moment, I notice how warm it is within the drawn curtains. Then I catch the gentle sound of breathing. I stare into the dark, my own breath still. I notice a familiar body scent. Once it would have had me reeling with desire. Then, sightless, I stretch out my hand, and another warm hand grasps it.

'Aemilia?' The familiar voice is taut.

'William.' What else? What else can I say? Here I am, within his own bedcurtains. I wonder he does not strike me. To say 'Lilith is here,' seems a strange beginning.

'What in God's name is going on? Am I dreaming?'

'I fear you are awake.'

'And you are in my bed? In plain fact? What *is* this?'

'It is I. It is Aemilia.'

'Christ's blood.' His tone is as harsh as any blow. 'What kind of witch are you? First you haunt me in the whore-house . . .'

'I was looking for Tom Flood.' My lips are blunt with shock.

'Then I wait all day for you, and you don't come . . .'

'My servant was in labour.'

'Your servant? You think more of her than you think of me?'

'She nearly died.'

'And, when I give you up, you come!'

'I am . . . I wanted to see you,' say I. For what else can a woman say who has crawled into an old lover's bed? And God forgive me, it is true.

'You have maimed me, woman. I told you to stay away.'

'Maimed you! What have *you* done to *me*? Have I written slanderous verses? Have I damned you with false accusations, lies and abominations? Have I stolen your words, and claimed them for my own? Have I done any of these things to you? Or have you done them all to me?'

'I have loved you,' he groans. 'Loved you to madness and beyond.'

'Ay, madness is the word!' I cry.

'I wanted to make amends. I see now that it cannot be done.'

I feel the night's cold at my back, and begin to shiver. 'Will – there is something that I need to tell you . . .'

He squeezes my arm. 'You have bewitched me, Mistress Lanyer. So much so that I can't untangle what is actual from demons and nightmares.'

The black night seems to bind us like a spell.

'Will – it's that matter of a demon that I . . .' He holds both my hands now, so tightly that they hurt. As I look into the blackness

I hear the bedroom door creak open. 'Who's there? Who is at the door?' I whisper.

'There is no one. Have you never done?' His breath is on my face. 'Your scent, lady – what is it? I remember it so well, like the musk of old Egypt.'

'Will . . .'

'Are you corporeal, or spirit?'

'I'm Aemilia, real and breathing . . .'

'Then let me have you once again – and again and again – as I have each night in my dreams and nightmares! Oh, my lady! Let us stay together, in the darkness, and have done with words forever. Let us be flesh, flesh, and nothing but.'

He lets go of my hands, and I feel his fingers unlacing my bodice. A wave of horror and delight rushes over me. 'Oh,' I whisper, trying to control myself. 'Will – you must stop . . .'

He has pulled the laces apart, and I can feel my under-smock coming loose about my breasts. Now our bodies are pressed together in the fug of warm air within the curtain. My breath shudders, and my legs are running sweat.

'I have done something evil,' I say. 'I fear it cannot be undone.' But, even as I speak, I run my hands over his unseen form. With joy and nausea I feel his naked shoulders. I tear my shift down further, and take hold of him in my bare arms.

'What are you, Aemilia,' he says, 'but Circe, the enchantress? I am ensnared, and lost, and yours.'

Sightless, I find his hard belly, his soft neck, his salt lips. 'I summoned a demon,' I whisper, too scared to say her name. 'I drew a circle.'

'Then draw another,' says he, winding his arms tightly around me. 'And let's go to it for an eternal night.'

There is a tearing sound as I rip myself free of my skirts and wrap my legs around him.

'You are a mystery,' he says, as the bed begins to heave beneath us. 'You are my witch.'

'I am not a witch, Will. I am a woman,' say I, as the night writhes. But I am not sure if he can hear me, or whether I have really spoken.

The night rears up, within us and around us, and we seem to leave the chamber and fly high above the roofs of London and dive deep below the City to the Underworld beneath. There is no sweetness, but there is ecstasy and pain so pure that it seems close to God. And there are no words, just flesh and lips and hair and panting, and wetness and darkness and a desperate pounding in my head and everywhere, till I hear him cry, 'Aemilia! Aemilia! Aemilia!' and there is a great violence inside me and my mind fills with perfection and white light.

We lie together, afterwards. Do I hear something? Is it the sound of the door closing? I raise my head, listening and wondering what I have done, and whether Lilith has played some part in it.

'What is it?' asks Will. He holds me closer. 'What is this supposed evil that you did?'

'It was, indeed, a sort of witchcraft.'

'To punish me?'

'To put an end to that *Macbeth*.'

I feel his body quiver. He is laughing.

'Don't you believe me?' I ask.

'I believe that you believe it, but I don't believe the Devil walks among us. There's evil enough in what men do.'

'What did I see, then?'

'That I cannot tell, my love.' His hand is stroking my face. 'I should have married you,' he says. 'A long, long time ago.'

My breath stops.

'Marry?'

'It should have happened. Fate did me wrong.'

'It was not God's will, so there's an end to it.'

'And yet we are twin souls, lady. There is no woman on this earth, not anywhere, who is a match for me, as you are. There is only you. A freak of beauty, and mind, and learning.'

'A freak! A fine compliment! Only the old Queen was allowed to call me that.'

He catches hold of me and we begin again, rocking in the bed in our rage to have each other and make darkness light.

Scene VII

It is dawn. Will is still sleeping, and I look down at his face. Just as I used to many years ago, when I was someone else. He is quite beautiful, so pale. I don't kiss him. I dare not. The room assaults me with its stark reality, all boxed and tight and quotidian. I get up, and pull my dress on. There are some papers on the desk, and I pick up a quill and dip it in the lamp-black. For a moment, my hand hovers over the page, but I don't know what to put. In the end, all I can write is: *I have loved you.* Nothing else makes any sense.

When I get home, I go up to my room and fetch down Forman's grimoire. I page through it, breathless, looking for guidance. Is there a spell, a form of words, which can undo a summoning? I have a nagging, sickened feeling. I am not sure what anything means. I hardly know myself. I poke the fire, seeing Lilith in the circle. Did I really summon her? Did it matter that I tumbled into the circle? Nothing seems right; nothing seems to be in my control.

With the cooking-pot simmering on the fire, and the cat sitting hump-backed by the scuttle, reality seems too solid for such wild fancies. I have not been in my right mind. I have walked at night, and my febrile nature has always been at odds with my strong will. This sudden night with Will is thrumming in my head, each touch, each cry. Perhaps my passion for him has broken some dark spell? I tip sea-coal from the scuttle and my spirits lift. I will have him. I will have my lover, every inch of him, night after night. Why should I not? Henry will not

suffer from my lying with his natural father. I can forgive Will for the sonnet book; I can forgive him for the play. What was I thinking of? Is God my master, or Lucifer and all the crones of Hell? I must go. I must go to the Globe, and see that play for myself, and hope to God that all is well.

Henry comes rushing in, bouncing a ball.

'Where have you been?' I ask, hiding the book in my skirts. 'Just because I am out on business, and Marie is resting, it does not mean you are free to run amok.'

'I have been playing football all around the town. You never saw such sport!' says Henry, sawing off a hunk of bread. 'We made the length of Long Ditch our pitch, and took on a score of prentice-boys and beat them soundly, though they bragged they'd trash us! What weakly, flap-eared knaves!' He stuffs the bread into his mouth all in one go.

'Those prentice-boys will stab you as soon as look as you, some of them. They're vile, rough creatures, who can't even spell their names,' said I, taking the ball up and keeping it. 'You should be safe at home, with Ovid and your hornbook.'

'Ovid!' says Henry, or something like it, through the bread. He pulls a goblin face. 'What does Ovid know? I saw a Serpent with a woman's face – where's *that* in your Ovid?'

'*What?*'

'She is not real, Mother, don't stare so! A fellow had a stall and charged us two farthings to have a look at his Lilith, Queen of Death. She is part woman, part Serpent. I touched her wings,' he says, modestly.

'Dear God! What "fellow" was this?'

'I don't know. His stall had "Lucifer" painted on the side, but I doubt that's the name he was born with. What is the matter, Mother? You are looking queer.'

I stand up, my head reeling. 'I am much put out and barely know which way to turn.'

He swallows the bread and pours out a glass of small beer.

'Because of Marie and her joined-up twins? Shall they always be such monsters? They are loathsome as all Hell!' He glugs back his drink with relish.

'No – because of . . . other matters. Things which do not concern you.' In truth, of course they do concern him. *I have just come from your father's bed, in which we fucked like werewolves.* How would that seem? Or, *I summoned the demon you saw today. Do not go out at night.*

Henry takes the ball deftly from me and begins to bounce it once again. 'Anyway, you need have no fear for me this afternoon. I am off to see a play.'

'What play?'

'Why, *Macbeth*, of course. If I miss it now, it won't be on for another month, and everyone else at school has seen it, and it's steeped in blood. And Tom says he will tell the doorkeeper to let me in for nothing.'

'*No!*' I say, startling even myself, such is the violence of my tone. 'No. You shall not go. I forbid it.' I must see this dark drama alone and Henry must remain here, safe from harm.

'But why? It is a most amazing play – everybody says so. And it's got fighting in it, and even some history, too.'

'I don't care. You must stay here and help Marie and her poor children.'

I pounce on him, catch his ear between my right thumb and finger, and twist it till he cries out. In this manner, I drag him into Marie's chamber, where she is sleeping, cradling her nuzzling twins. The spring sun is warm and heavy in the shuttered room, and a bee is buzzing drunkenly around her ale-jug.

'Mistress!' She jerks awake. Her face is drawn and tired. The babies begin to cry. 'What is it?'

'Henry will help you,' I say. 'Do you have need of anything?'

'No. Thank you.'

'Then will you lock the door when I am gone, and sit upon the key? And make sure he stays with you till five?'

'Till five?'

'Until the play is done,' says Henry, sulking. 'Mother, why do you persecute me so? I am not a child.'

'Is Tom playing today?' asks Marie. She picks up the twins and settles them into the cradle. 'Did he tell you, we are to marry next week?'

'That is good news,' I say, though my mind scarce takes this in.

'Don't tell Mistress Flood, lest she run mad in the street.'

It's hard to believe that I live in the same world as weddings and celebrations. How I wish that Will and I could begin again, stow away on some great ship and cross the ocean to a new world, far away. I would take Henry with me, but no other mortal, and we could be happy, somewhere, in a forest of tobacco trees. There would be no playhouses or print-shops, and no demons or deceived wives.

'Here is the key.' I give it to Marie, and wait outside till I hear it turn in the lock.

Why does my belly twist at the mere mention of the name 'Macbeth'? I'm not sure. But I suspect that Lilith might do us all most dreadful harm. I can see her yellow eyes so vividly, and, though I pray to God to let her sleep once more, I have no other power to rid myself of her foul presence. Yet I fear that God has matters to attend to other than righting misbegotten spells.

As I step out of the door, who should appear but Anne herself? All done up as usual, like the Queen of the May. She has a new ruff, all silvery like a fairy wing, and her eyebrows are plucked to nothing. Tom's misalliance has not distracted her from Fashion.

'My dear Aemilia,' says she. 'You are coming too? Well, then, we must hurry if we are to catch a boatman! All of London will be there.'

'Will be where?' I ask in confusion, with a sinking feeling.

'At the Globe, to see *Macbeth*! I would not miss this for all the world.'

'I thought you were angry with me.'

'I can't blame you for Tom's cock-brained foolishness! I am sure he will forget that girl in time. Now, come, quickly! It's a shame you look so poorly, but you will have to do.'

And so I consent to be dragged towards the river on her arm. The summer sunshine is bright and warm when we set out. But the weather changes suddenly. The sun disappears and rain is falling by the time we have climbed aboard a wherry, aided by an aged boatman. I throw my cloak over the two of us, for fear that Anne's finery will be washed away. When we reach the Globe, the storm is gathering strength. The wind crashes in the trees and rain is falling as if from a tipped bath. We sit in the second gallery, but it provides little shelter. Water streams between our feet, falling on to the heads of the groundlings below, who are slipping and falling in the mire. The covered stage, too, is awash with rain, blown inwards by the furious wind. I look up at the black sky and hear the first roar of thunder. No need for stage musicians for this performance – Nature is providing her own malevolent effects.

'They must call it off!' I shout to Anne.

'No, no,' she insists. 'If it is on the playbill, you can be sure that they will put it on. They have the public to consider.'

A dagger of lightning splits the sky. Three figures come on to the stage, and the trumpets blast out, calling for our attention. The trio gathers around the trapdoor in the stage, and up comes a black cauldron. I look hard at these three players – where have I seen them before? They are gifted boys indeed. One looks like an ancient crone, another like a middle-aged matron, and the third appears to be a beautiful young girl with a plait of yellow hair wrapped around her head. I narrow my eyes. It is hard to see anything clearly in this rain.

'When shall we three meet again?
In Thunder, Lightning or in Rain?
When the hurly burly's done,
When the battle's lost and won . . .'

The voices of the witches change, so that what first sounded like the newly broken tones of boy actors is first a keening banshee cry, and then a heavy-throated growl.

'Who *are* the witches?' I ask Anne. But she only grips my hand.

A heavy fog has rolled in from the river, and torches have been lit and set upon the stage, where they hiss and splutter. The crowd, subdued by the downpour, is silent. In place of heckles and cat-calls there is watchful quiet. In contrast, the voices of the three witches carry with a clear echo like words shouted into a courtyard well. There is a peculiar cold.

Lord Macbeth appears upon the back of a black destrier. The storm has upset the beast, and it is clattering round in circles, tail lashing, showing the whites of its eyes. Its hooves slip waywardly on the wet boards. Macbeth (who is Dick Burbage) is about to speak, but there is another flash of lightning, a livid fork above us, and the stallion screams. It rears up, pawing the air, and Burbage comes crashing down on to the ground. Dropping its head, the beast gallops from the stage, sending the players scattering. But none of this daunts Burbage. Not for one moment does his performance falter, and he gets back to his feet in an imperious manner, and regards the crowd calmly, hand on his sword.

And here is Lady Macbeth! You would never guess that she is only Tom, declaiming such evil words in her robe of gold and scarlet, crow-black hair hanging round her narrow face. Tom speaks his words with passion, and their meaning chills me more now than when they first spilled from my pen.

'I don't like this,' whispers Anne. 'It is unnatural.'

'That is the point of it,' I hiss back. 'Macbeth should know his place.' But, as I speak, there is a tightness in my head, as if the dead-cold of the theatre has clenched my skull. Whether through Will's alterations or because of this storm which is making night from day, my play now has a surfeit of evil in it. But I know that I *have* to watch it, for there is some rhythm in the story that draws me further and further in.

The scenes are rapid and the drama bloody – Duncan the King is killed, Macbeth takes his place, then murders Banquo and (as he hopes) his young son Fleance. Now the stage is set out for a banquet, with a trestle table, joint-stools and long benches. King Macbeth (as he has become) begins to speak of 'Noble Banquo' and to express the dissembling regret that his friend cannot be present at the feast. (Though he knows full well he is dead, having paid two murderers to slay him.) I know what's coming next, of course. The ghost of Banquo will appear, and Macbeth's posturing as King will be sorely tested.

It would have been simple enough to have the ghost walk out from behind one of the pillars. But of course they must use their latest effect: the crane. From above the Heavens, in the uppermost corner of the space above the stage, I hear the groan of the new contraption. Now is the moment for the flying chair to prove its worth. It cranks out into the audience's view, a suspended cradle with a seated figure strapped in place.

'Will Shakespeare himself is playing the Ghost,' says Anne, still gripping my hand. 'He will do it fearsomely, you can be sure.'

The creaking arm swivels slowly round. The figure is wearing a black cloak, and its face is hidden. There is something odd about its stance, something less than human.

'He always does the ghosts,' says Anne. 'There is almost nothing to it. He never had enough voice for a major part.' Her voice is tight with terror. Slowly, slowly, dangling in its seat, the chair creaks down towards the smoky stage. Macbeth's courtiers

carouse among the flaring lights as the cloaked form descends. Then there is a cracking sound, like stone breaking, and screams from the stage.

'What?' I say, trying to see more plainly. '*What*?' I stand up, in spite of the hisses and the cries of annoyance from behind me, and begin to push my way along the row. I can't see anything but the heads and shoulders of the audience; I can't see anything.

I reach the stairway and now the stage is spread before me – yet all is chaos there. Burbage is standing with his mouth wide open. Where is Tom? Where is his Queen? I stumble, amid a rage of protestation. The crowd roars. Everyone is standing. Something has happened. There is another terrible scream – I push this way and that way – I am blocked wherever I turn. What is wrong? What is it? At last I break through, hurry down into the pit and run squelching through the mire, shoving my way through the mass of people. A child cries, an old woman falls. But I keep on pushing till I reach the front, then force my way to the steps up to the stage. Panting, I reach the wet boards where the lights flare and the fog drifts. I'm half-expecting Heminge or another player to bar my way. But everyone is frozen, spell-bound. A dozen courtiers, faces mask-like in their paint, stand motionless. The crane has fallen: the great arm must have broken off and is lying across the stage. Burbage is bending over a figure in a scarlet dress, lying stretched out on the ground in a pool which is also scarlet. Tom. His wig has fallen off and his hair is splayed out all around him on the boards. His eyes are wide open, staring upwards. The arm of the crane has smashed into his chest, and pinned him to the ground.

Will appears, dressed in spectral black, his face daubed with stage blood, and kneels beside him.

'Help him, in God's name!' I say. 'What happened?'

'The crane fell – I didn't see . . . He is still; he isn't breathing!' cries Burbage.

'Fetch him wine!' calls Will, and a Scots lord hurries off.

But who's that, standing by the empty chair? A cloaked figure, immobile, head bowed. I look closer. I take a step towards it, and then it lifts its head. The face is bone-white, and translucent, fading in and out of my vision. There's no skill with stage paint that can ape such an effect. This is the creature I have summoned, cloaked in fog and falling rain. Lilith's yellow eyes regard the scene without expression, but her mouth is twisted in a smile.

'Thou, demon!' I shout. 'By God, why don't you go back to the place where you belong?'

The demon shifts, still looking straight at me, but doesn't speak.

'I did not want this! I didn't say that anyone should *die*!'

There is a voice in my head. '*I am Lilith. I am the taker of children. You said they stole your play – now you have your vengeance. This play is cursed.*'

'Go down to Hell, and leave us,' I scream. 'You have done your evil now.'

The spirit starts to move slowly towards Tom and I run between them, hands outspread. 'Leave him alone! Fiend! Leave the boy alone, and get thee back to Hell!'

Dick Burbage is sitting on the stage. He is weeping and stroking Tom's hair. Field is shouting, Heminge is running into the tiring-room. And Will is staring at me, eyes livid through the streaks of painted gore.

'What – Aemilia? What is this? Why are you shouting at thin air?'

The spectre moves slowly across the stage. Not walking, but moving like sea mist. It stops by the dead boy, and stares down at him.

I push Will away. The spectre looks at me again.

'Lilith!' I roar, so fiercely that I scrape my throat. 'Thou foul demon! Thou evil, hungry, wicked monster! Quit this place, quit it, I command you!'

'Tom? My Thomas?' There's another figure now, running across the stage, her fine clothes soaked and torn. 'Oh, my child!' she screams. 'Holy Mother! Mary! Spare him! Spare him!' She collapses on top of him, sobbing out half-lucid prayers. There is a crack of thunder and a spike of lightning and then I hear the shouts of the audience.

'What evil has been done?' cries one voice.

'The Devil is in this place!' calls another. 'Who called on Satan?'

Lilith is smiling.

'There she is!' I cry. 'Satan's agent! She killed Tom! She murdered him!' I look at Anne, weeping, prostrate, and at the dark crowd that heaves below me. I point at the shadowed figure. 'She – Lilith! Look! She has brought this curse upon the play!'

'*Lilith*?' says Will. 'A hag in a fireside fable? Are you *mad*?'

'What?' Anne's head swivels till she sees me. 'Why do you speak of black magic, over the body of my son?'

'She saw the demon!' shouts one of the voices from the crowd.

'That woman there – she spoke to it! She sees it still!' The dark faces are turned towards me.

'She conjured a demon!'

'Conjured Death!'

'Conjured the Devil! Foul, unnatural witch.'

'I did not call the Devil!' I turn to face the crowd, but can see only darkness and rain.

Anne leaves Tom's side and walks unsteadily towards me. 'What evil have you done, Aemilia? You saw it – you knew something was wrong! You saw it before Tom fell!'

'I saw Lilith.'

'Saw a *demon*? With my son?'

'I drew a circle,' I say. 'At Deptford.' As if that mattered. 'I made a spell.'

'What *spell* is this? What *circle*? Are you God Himself now, that can take a life at whim?'

'I meant no harm!' I scream, but Lilith is moving steadily towards me. 'Get thee behind me! Get thee behind me!' I shout, and I grab a flaming torch and lunge at her, but Will snatches it away.

Anne runs at me, her face riven with grief and rage. 'You killed him! With your wickedness and witchery and pride! You called on Satan and it was my son who took the punishment!'

'Anne! Listen to me ... Anne! I beg you ...'

'I'll kill you for this, you demon-loving bitch ...' With that she claws my face with her nails.

An almighty roar: thunder, or the crowd? I fall backwards, down into the dark.

Scene *VIII*

There is another flash of lightning. All is white light for an instant, and I crawl on all fours into the crowd, scrabbling through the filthy mud. Above me I hear voices shouting. The air is raging, and the mob has rushed forward, lured by the scent of death.

'Where is she?'

'Where is the witch?'

'She has turned herself into a bat!'

'She has made herself invisible!'

As soon as I dare, I scramble to my feet, drenched and slimed with mud. Out. Out. I must get out. Blindly, I make my way away from the noise.

'Seek her!'

'Find her!'

'Burn her!'

For a few moments I think this fury might work in my favour, for the crowd is shouting at the stage, as if expecting me to reappear at any moment. But as I reach the doorway the gatherer looks up from his pot of entrance coin.

'She's here – the one who called the demon!' he shouts, lunging towards me.

I slip past him, and pull the catch back on the heavy door. I feel a hand upon my shoulder, and bite hard till I taste blood. There's a scream of pain; the door opens. Rain and lightning. I kick off my pattens and I run. Helter-skelter I go, slipping in the mud, wading through deep-rutted puddles, my skirts clutched to my chest.

'She has called the Devil!'

'She is a witch! Catch the witch!'

My feet move faster, and I run as I have never done in all my life. But how can I outdistance a horde of burly men? I think of Henry and Marie, waiting for me. Oh, Lord God! What have I done? What have I done to Tom? Someone catches my skirt and it tears away; I run on in nothing but my soaking undershift. My hands and feet are bleeding. Sharp stones and brambles snare me as I run. But I will *not* die. I will *not*.

The ground is firmer when I reach the harbour, and the street that borders the river's edge. There are houses here, of the common sort, and candles burning in the windows. I smell the river-stench. The wind blows keener than before. I run down an alley and beat as loudly as I can upon the first door I come to, screaming and wailing, for no words will come.

A head appears from an upstairs window. 'Who's there?'

I find my voice at last. 'Aemilia Lanyer, a poor housewife! The mob are after me – please let me in!' I look back and see flaring torch-light at the far end of the alley. I run on, and beat upon another door.

'Away, witch!' shouts somebody inside.

I knock again. But there's no answer, just the rain. I run till I reach the end of the alleyway – the voices are louder, I can smell the torch-pitch as they gather in a crowd behind me. Then my hands meet a rough wall, and my torn fingers feel upwards and sideways. The wall is high and wide – it blocks the way. I look round, and see the faces in the spluttering firelight. My breath comes in shuddering sobs. This is it. This is Death.

For a moment the mob is silent. The people are afraid. Then a man as tall as a birch tree, a veritable giant, marches forward and says, 'Witch! You killed that boy! You called that demon!'

And the accusation is repeated by the crowd behind him, and a rain of heavy objects falls down upon me – rotted carrots, rat skulls and jagged stones. I shall die like Joan, with a cave mouth

for a face. I cover my head with my arms and turn my back, and hear my own scream as the missiles find their mark. A slippery rope is slung around my head; I feel it screwing tight into my neck as they pull me back with them along the alley. I walk silently, thoughtless, speechless, pissing with fear.

'Find a tree!'

'A Judas tree, and string her from it.'

I am pulled and shoved from all sides. Someone punches my belly, and when I look down I see I am wearing nothing but torn rags. Blood is pouring from my wounds. I feel nothing; I do not know what I am. The earth? The sky? The Beast? Looking up, I see the bright upper windows, and the heads of the watchers set black against the glow. There are little children calling questions and a babe in arms, dancing.

I see my father's face, bending towards me, his black eyes and his curled beard. I hear the sweet harmony of his recorder, making patterns in the air. I see my mother, laughing, in Lady Susan's garden. A swan, retreating from the green bank, creasing the silver image of the sky. Will, turning from a knot of players, smiling at the sight of me. Henry, bouncing his ball along Long Ditch in the sunshine. Tom Flood, lying dead upon the stage.

I call out, 'Lord forgive me! Lord forgive me! I have sinned and I repent of it! Mea culpa! Mea culpa!'

There is a sound. Deep in the earth, far above in the heavens, inside my head. What is it? I seize the noose with my hands, and struggle to loosen the rope around my neck. What is that sound? I know I have heard it before. Louder now, louder, like drumming.

'Here is the tree!'

'Here is the place. Hang her here.'

The rope pulls again, and I gag as it grips my throat. The sound is not drums but hoof-beats. *Those hooves are coming for*

me. A rescuer, or the Black Huntsman and his storm-dogs, sent from Hell? *I want to know.* I work my fingers between the wet rope and my neck. And then I find my voice, dry and sore.

'Why are you doing this?'

The giant speaks. 'To punish you for murder.'

Someone else says, 'To punish you for witchcraft.'

'For conjuring and evil.'

'Then take me to the King, and let him try me.' I cough and retch. My tongue cleaves to the roof of my mouth. 'He has studied witchcraft . . . Let *him* try me.'

'The King won't want to be bothered with the likes of you,' says the giant. 'A common witch.'

I can hear the hoof-beats more clearly now. Not of the air, or in my head, but on the ground. Yet between me and this sound there is a wall of bodies. In the rippling light of flares and shadows I see faces of every kind, some comely, some deformed, some scored with wrinkles. Each is distorted with the same murderous intent, more hobgoblin than human. Reason will not work with such a mob as this.

'If you kill me, what good will that do?' I ask, coughing and retching again.

'The good will be your death; no more is needed,' the giant shouts. 'String her up, there! String her up!'

But the rope stays slack. They are watching me. Words swim into my head, and I close my eyes and shout them out. '*Come, you spirits that tend on mortal thoughts, unsex me here, and fill me, from the crown to the toe, top-full of direst cruelty!*'

My voice is a raven-croak, sounding strange and terrible even to myself, but I am afraid to stop in case this breaks the spell.

'*Make thick my blood; stop up th'access and passage to remorse, that no compunctious visitings of Nature shake my fell purpose, or keep peace between th'effect and it!*' The words seem to warm me, and with each syllable, my strength grows.

'String her up!' shouts the giant again.

And someone says, 'I dare not!'

I grow taller and bolder as I speak. '*Come to my woman's breasts, and take my milk for gall, you murth'ring ministers, wherever in your sightless substances you wait on Nature's mischief!*'

'Slash her! Slit her open!'

'Use her guts to gag her!'

'We are afraid!'

I throw my head back, and scream at the sky. '*Come, thick Night, and pall thee in the dunnest smoke of hell, that my keen knife see not the wound it makes – nor Heaven peep through the blanket of the dark, to cry "HOLD! HOLD!"*'

The crowd falls back, and I hear sobbing.

'God protect us!'

'God save us, this is Beelzebub himself.'

With a roar of rage the giant leaps forward. The rope jerks and someone drags my hands away. The rope is pulled tight around my throat. 'Let it be quick, Lord,' I pray. 'Let me go quickly!'

'Ready, ho! Haul her up!'

My feet are lifted from the ground and all is agony and blackness. But the hoof-beats still come. There is a clap of thunder and screaming all around me. A horse squeals, men shout, there is a great crack, then the noise begins to fade.

Darkness, nothingness.

A swish of air above my head. I am falling. I am on the ground coughing and puking. I look up. The severed rope is dangling from the hanging tree. The black destrier from the Globe is rearing up against the bright house windows. There is a hooded figure clinging to it.

Satan has come to take me down to Hell. He lifts me from the ground and sets me on the saddle before him, then holds me tightly as the snorting horse gallops headlong through the mob. There are shouts and screams, hands clawing at me. The beast's back rocks beneath me as we charge into the storm.

Scene IX

Is this the road to Hades? If so, it's lined with the great houses of Camm Row, and the messy rooftops of Long Ditch. I look down, at the black-clad arm of the horseman who has saved me. It is the arm of a living man. We reach a small house, and the horseman halts his mount and jumps down. He reaches up and helps me to the ground.

Will's face is daubed with stage blood, and his eyes are rimmed with black.

'By God, Aemilia, what have you done?'

'I summoned Lilith,' I whisper. 'I drew a circle. I had a book.'

He wipes his hand across his eyes. 'Why, in Christ's name? Why dabble in such nonsense?'

'To stop the play! To end it! But not – '

'For pity's sake!'

'Not to do harm to anyone! Not to Tom!'

'What lunacy was this?'

I hide my face.

'What manner of falling off from what you were, and what you could be?'

'May God forgive me.'

Silence.

'Do you hate me so much?' he asks.

'No. It wasn't hatred that drove me to it.'

'What else could it have been? It surely wasn't love!'

'How do you know?'

'God in Heaven,' he says. 'If this *is* love, then we must leave it. Once and for all, and till we die.'

'Will . . .'

'You have driven yourself mad,' he says. 'You see what is not there, and are blind to plain truth.'

'No!' I cry. 'Lilith was there – upon the stage. She killed Tom. I swear it.'

'God rest that dear boy's soul!' says Will. 'He was the merriest, sweetest fellow I ever knew.' He pauses. 'The thing that killed him, Aemilia, was the falling crane. The crane *I* had constructed, so that we could have the best effects in London. If anyone is to blame, it's me. In this actual world.'

'Yes, but she was there! Lilith made it happen! She is the child-taker, and I called her, and she killed Anne's son!' I begin to weep, hopeless, tearless, grating sobs that hurt my chest.

Will puts his arms around me and holds for a long while. Then, very gently, he pushes me away. 'Let me say only this . . .' he begins.

'Don't twist the knife! I couldn't bear it!'

'Aemilia. Calm yourself. You are not a murderer.'

'I cannot calm myself! I cannot! Because I *am*!'

'Look at me. Look at me . . . Every evening, every morning, every moment – my love, my sweet girl. Aemilia, I think of you.'

'Will, no . . .'

'You have read my plays.'

'Yes.'

'Come back to this world. Come back to your true self. Didn't you see how it was? That all my heroines are versions of my Dark Aemilia? Black-eyed Rosaline, clever Portia, the Egyptian Queen who drove poor Anthony to madness – all you! All you. Each one.'

'Don't . . . don't say this.'

'I never was so happy, never so much myself, as I was when I was with you. When I loved you.'

'Will.'

'And you loved me.'

I hang my head. Rainwater swirls around our feet.

'Henry,' says Will. 'The boy – he is the two of us. I live in him, with you. It's only this that has sustained me. Only this, and writing. The recreation of my sweet lost lady in my words.'

'There is no . . . future for us, is there?' I say, my tears flowing from the sky. 'Only your words are left.'

Will says nothing. We embrace, and I know this is for the last time.

Act V

Poetry

Scene I

Aldgate, Spring 1611

I am a sinner, steeped in evil that is past, and I can never make amends. So it is now my habit to go to St Botolph's Church at Aldgate every morning for the matins service. It is a simple building, despite its gold-tipped spire. Today I feel ill and restless, and believe that the end of all this might be the madhouse. I have passed a disturbed night. The house echoed and stirred with malevolent spirits, and the air I breathed seemed odorous and distempered, infected by the demons that dwell among us. I could hear them whispering and gibbering in my ears, so I wrapped my head in the bed-sheet, sweating with terror. In the end, I crept up to the garret and sat upon a joint-stool by the window, waiting for the first rays of sunlight to drive the evil spirits away. Only when the rooftops and chimneystacks were gilded with the dawn did I dare to drowse a little, head sagging. I dreamed of Will, as I do most nights.

The last I heard from him was a short letter, sent to explain that the second publication of the sonnets was done without his knowledge. A volume was printed two summers ago: his hate-verse and the fulsome words he wrote to please Wriothesley. His note was polite, but there was no love in it. I keep it, with his poems.

Now I am sitting in the church, I feel as if I am lost in a dark mist, and the voices of my fellow worshippers seem far away. I sit among the other women, head bowed, ignoring their chatter,

waiting for the service to begin. Our usual prelate is not here. I don't see the new man when he enters, as I am busy with my prayers. But, as soon as he begins to speak, something in his voice and manner catches my attention.

'It has come to my notice,' says he, 'that this City is as full of Sin as Sodom, and as riven with Bawds and Strumpets as Gomorrah. There is a not a homily that addresses this Disease of London, so this morning I have written you my own, in plain words. May the Devil in you hear this, so you can cast him out.

'And you may ask yourselves – how did we come to this pass? And you may ask yourselves – how did we come to be cast out of the Garden of Eden, we whom GOD made in his own image, to have mastery over Creation and over all the beasts of the field, and all the birds in the air, and all the fishes in the sea?'

I shift my position. My knees are growing stiff. Where have I heard that rasping tone before? I clasp my hands tighter, and try to pray harder. But the voice is insistent.

'I can tell you how. I can tell you why. I have studied in the greatest universities in all of Europe, and I have looked most carefully at the cause. I have found our culprit, with GOD's help. It is Woman who has ruined us. First in the person of that weakest of vessels, Eve, and since then in the frail form of every woman born.'

I bow my head. 'Lord, forgive me. Jesu, have pity. *Mea culpa. Mea culpa.*'

But it is hard to concentrate on my own sin when there is so much of it about. And most of it the fault of my ignoble gender.

'St Thomas Aquinas has warned us of this wanton, wayward sex. "*A male is the beginning and end of woman, as God is the beginning and end of every creature.*" Man is made in God's image; Woman is a thing distorted from Man's rib. Her Latin name is "softness of the mind", but Man is called "*vir*" which we translate as "strength or virtue of the soul". Compared to Man, the Woman is an imbecile.'

It is no good. I open my eyes. The man standing at the wooden table in the centre of the church is my old adversary, Parson John. I stare at him, blinking, forgetting my own misdoing for the first time for many years.

The prelate is warming to his theme. 'What is lighter than smoke? A breeze. What is lighter than a breeze? The wind. What is lighter than the wind? A Woman. What is lighter than a Woman? Nothing. And yet, even in this lightness, she gushes most detestably, sullying all she touches with her womb-blood. Fruits do not produce, wine turns sour, plants die, trees lack fruit. The air about her darkens. If a dog should eat her vile blood, it will run mad.'

Lord above! Is this truly the Word of God? I glance around me, at the bowed and reverent heads of all the women.

'A woman is the cause of all our ill. Adam was deceived by Eve, and not Eve by Adam. The Woman summoned him to Sin. She lied and tricked him, and the whole of Creation was overthrown. So the female must pay. She must yield to the man as a reed bends in the wind.'

His words work a curious magic on me. They rouse me from my torpid, grief-stricken state. Dismissing Eve as being both weak and wicked has always seemed foolish and unfair to me. She was subordinate to Adam, more obedient than Lilith. And yet, she ended by looking beyond the life of a child, fenced in by our Maker. Her existence as a naked animal enthroned in flowers was not enough. She sought out Knowledge. Was that a bad thing? *Should* mankind be stupid? The Serpent may have been the agent of the Devil, but in truth human beings contain the impulses of Hell as well as Heaven. We are not angels. In order to defend Eve, it is necessary to think beyond the version of the Fall that Parson John proclaims. Must all women bear this burden of limitless guilt? Must we spend all our lives accusing ourselves of sin, and despising ourselves as second best?

393

I sit upright. I am thinking of the Cornelius Agrippa book that I stole from Simon Forman, and the thoughts that this wise philosopher expressed. He was a good Christian – just as much so as our revered parson – and yet he saw women in a very different way. Supposing that the Old Testament God of rage and plagues was not the God of Jesus and his disciples? Supposing Eden had been, not a paradise, but a prison from which humankind had to escape? With knowledge came freedom. I blink hard.

The service is over, and the parson stands outside the church, addressing the congregation with an air of chilly discontent. I walk past him, with no desire to speak, but can't resist giving him a sharp look I pass.

'I see we have a Jezebel among us, a copy of that wilful Eve,' he says.

'Do you remember me?'

'You are the termagant whose pestilent son was possessed by demons.'

The other churchgoers look at me askance. I must admit, I have not made it my business to be neighbourly, and they are already suspicious of me.

'I trust he died soon after,' says the pleasant parson.

The fear and self-loathing fall away from me. 'He lived, sir,' I said. 'And he is living still, praise God!'

'Then a miracle took place. God is good; he will save all sinners, even your diabolic son.'

'Yes. A miracle. And I would like to tell you that your view of women is quite mistaken. Eve is not the mother of our undoing. She has been much maligned.'

'It is not my *view*, mistress,' says the parson. 'I do not invent the Word of God. I am the mouthpiece of the Church.' He bends forward slightly, as if to direct his spleen more precisely. 'Ask forgiveness, and it may be that Our Lord will spare your soul.'

'I will not.'

'Will *not*, madam?'

'The Church is wrong.'

'Heaven protect us!' cries an old man.

'May the good Lord strike you down!' says his companion.

Parson John regards me coldly, a pillar of furious contempt. 'If you wish me to refer you to the City fathers for sedition, then I would be happy to oblige you. I will leave it to our Maker to offer a more long-lasting punishment, and broil your flesh for an eternity in Hell.'

'Punish me when I am printed, sir,' I say. 'Punish me when I set down the true story of Eve and Eden in a chap-book. Punish me when I have made a poem of it. Then I will be quite content.'

Scene II

My night fears have diminished. My wakefulness gives me time to write, and to think, and the shadows keep to themselves. I write and write, referring to the books upon my desk, and using the thoughts inside my head. I look upon the guilt and grief of other women, and I conclude that we have been the cursed receptacle for all the ills of mankind. In failing to be the Virgin Mary, we are Serpents every one.

It comes to me, as I write by candle-light and consider the darkness, that it is possible that poor Eve did not sin at all. She was not wicked. She was curious. I set out the words, and this time they are clearer and sharper than before. I see not only Eden; I see the truth.

> *Our Mother Eve, who tasted of the Tree,*
> *Giving to Adam what she held most dear,*
> *Was simply good, and had no power to see,*
> *The after-coming harm did not appear:*
> *The subtle Serpent that our Sex betrayed,*
> *Before our fall so sure a plot had laid.*

And if Eve is free of blame, then Adam must take the consequence. Now the words flow. I break a goose quill in my haste to get them down, and dip a new pen, greedy for the ink.

> *If Eve did err, it was for knowledge's sake,*
> *The fruit being faire persuaded him to fall:*

No subtle Serpent's falsehood did betray him,
If he would eat it, who had power to stay him?
Not Eve, whose fault was only too much love.

From the suffering of Eve came the suffering of the rest of us. Of guilty women, who must pay eternally for the Fall of Man. I remember the lines that had haunted me when Tom sang his sad song at Yuletide: of Rachel, crying for her children 'because they were not'. What is 'not'? The empty cradle. The folded nightshirts, put away for other babes. Tom's laughing face, his joy and foolery. So I write of that too, the love of all mothers, of which the love and grief of Our Lady is the highest expression.

Yet these poor women, by their piteous cries
Did move their Lord, their Lover and their King,
To take compassion, turne about and speake,
To them whose hearts were ready now to break.

I write at night. I write in the daytime. I write when the pottage burns. I write while the soap congeals. I write while the house-mice nibble the fallen cake-crumbs at my feet. I write.

It is a work of many months. Back and forth I go, repeatedly, until I have made a poem which praises the Bible women and puts their case, as if I were a lawyer at the Inns of Court. And, when I have done, I sit down and think of all the women of influence to whom I might dedicate it, and who might now give me patronage, and I write them all my thanks. I start with Queen Anne, and end with virtuous ladies in general. (Of which there are, as you will know, a substantial number.) Redemption is sweet. I find a printer and a seller. I do not go to Cuthbert Tottle, who has died of dropsy, but make a contract with Mr Valentine Simmes, a most enlightened fellow who sees no harm in women writing verse, and believes there is great merit in the case for

Eve. My book is sold in the bookshop of Richard Bonian in Paul's Churchyard.

I send a copy to Will, with my good wishes, but I hear nothing from him.

Scene III

Stratford, March 1616

Time passes not as a river flows, smoothly and ever onward, but as a mob seethes, wild and unpredictable. First walking, then running, then slowing to a stop, then starting to speed up again: faster, faster. Or this is how it seems to me. So I am standing here, on this bright, blustery spring day, and cannot believe that I am so old, or that the things that live in my memory happened so long ago. My chest aches with the pain of times past and loves lost. But I have Henry still, and my penitence, and this good hour.

Alfonso is dead, and I miss him more than I thought I would, though it is pleasant to have the whole bed to myself. (And to know how much money I have in the house from one day to the next.) I have a widow's freedom, to walk the streets and go about my business. The Globe was burned down, and then built up again, in brick. All were saved from the fire, and I hear the King's Men are doing well. Will is no longer with them – he retired after the blaze and came here to live the life of a fat gentleman with his wife. It is this wife – this Ann Shakespeare – who wrote a curt note to me. Summoning me here, to speak to Will. I would have ignored her message if I could. Why should I be told to jump to it by this queening country wife? But I have longed to see him for so many years.

Stratford is a busy, noisy place. Outside the inn, there is a bustle of carts, livestock and crowding townsfolk, blocking the

thoroughfare completely. There are plenty of beggar-folk as well, just as vile to look upon as their city cousins: doxies, vaga-bonds and all manner of hard-eyed beggars, displaying their deformities to tempt money from passers-by. And yet it's but a village compared to London's great smoking tumult. Around us is a rolling landscape of green hills and pleasant pasture. The trees that line the market square are beginning to put forth new leaves, and their branches whisper in the breeze. Stratford's most pungent odours are of the shippon, not the jakes.

I stare at the shop-fronts and at the cheery, bartering house-wives, trying to imagine Will buying a joint of lamb or a bolt of cloth. The houses are modest, built tight together, so that each shop counter, which juts out into the street, buts on to the next. A master tailor is sewing a shirt; a barber smoothes a linen cloth over his customer's chest; a baker flaps her hands at the flies that buzz around the sugar loaves.

'Somewhat small,' I say to John Heminge, who has come with me from London. 'Too small for *him*.'

But Heminge isn't listening; he is paying the horse-boy.

'Is New Place in this street?' I ask

He frowns, looking at his change. 'Close by,' he says. 'You'll have to wait, Aemilia. We don't know when he will see you yet.'

'Did *she* not ask for me to come?'

'Be patient. He is not the man he was. And speak fairly of Mistress Shakespeare. It was good of her to ask you here.'

That night, sleep deserts me again. I sit in my room, watching shadows, and light one candle from the next to stop them from haunting me. I think of my past, and wish that I could be a better sort of person. I think of my poems and wish that I could have made those better too.

I finally sleep, bolt upright.

I am a child in Bishopsgate again, walking with my father. The air is full of music, and we are walking past the walls of Bedlam, listening to the mad singing their angel songs.

My father tells me not to listen, and not to look through the keyhole of the great gate we come upon, which is so high that it reaches the clouds. I say I will not, and then he goes away. Then I look through the hole and there is a yellow eye.

I look at the yellow eye, and the yellow eye looks at me.

A voice whispers, 'Little girl.'

'What?'

'Little girl. I have been watching you.' It is a woman's voice. It has a sibilant hiss.

'I didn't do anything.'

'You have come here for a reason.' Now there is a wheedle in the voice. It wants something.

'I must go now. My father told me not to look.'

'You came because I called you, little girl.'

'I didn't hear you.'

'That is because I did not need to speak.'

New Place is built from solid brick and sturdy timber. It is a long building, which stretches along one side of Chapel Street, edged by a high brick wall. It has three storeys and five gables. Much of it is raw-coloured, where new bricks or wood have been used to patch and mend it. There a gate in the wall which leads to a grassy courtyard.

A great deerhound lopes across and welcomes Heminge as an old friend, wagging its tail and gently butting him with its head. Then he leaves me there and enters the house, pressing my hand before he goes.

I shield my eyes and look up at the plain glass windows, set in lead, wondering if Will is behind one of these, and whether he might be secretly studying me, as I am trying to catch a glimpse

of him. Nausea grips my throat. What will we say? How shall I meet his eye?

After a while, Heminge returns. He looks unhappy.

'Will is worse,' he says.

I frown. 'Worse than what?'

'He is very ill, Aemilia. I hope you understand that. It was no one's wish but his that you came all this way. Ann only tries to please him.'

'Then I must see him.'

'I don't know if he is well enough to see you today.'

'I am not going away till I have spoken to him,' I say. 'Even if it's only for five minutes.'

'She had better come in,' says a voice from the doorway.

I turn to see a woman standing there. I'm not sure what I expected in a neglected country wife, but it was certainly not this. A tall, upright woman, older than I am, but with fine, pale skin. Her eyes are grey, with long black lashes, like those of a young girl. She is dressed in a green velvet gown. She looks at me for a long moment, as if she was fearing the worst but I have exceeded it.

'I am Ann Shakespeare,' she says. 'The wife.'

'I am Aemilia Lanyer,' say I.

'The mistress.'

I nod.

'Come inside,' she says. 'I have been meaning to speak to you for some time.' I follow her to the foot of a wide oak staircase. It leads up to a long gallery, hung with bright tapestries. Behind her, a door stands open. I can see a physick garden, and hear children laughing.

We stand for a moment.

'We are alike,' she says, at last. 'I have heard that is often the way.'

'Yes, Mistress Shakespeare.'

'With some differences, of course.'

'I would expect as much.'

'Such as scruples, with which, I imagine, I have been better endowed than you.'

'I have scruples enough.'

'I dare say even a murderer has his limits.'

What has she heard? What has he told her?

'I won't stay long, Mistress Shakespeare, and I want to say how grateful I am that you have been kind enough to let me come. Ever since I heard about the fire at the Globe I have been anxious . . .'

'It was not your place to be anxious. He has people here who are anxious enough.'

'Of course. And then, I heard that he had left for good . . .'

'Not left. *Returned.*'

'After which, I heard that he was ill . . .'

'He *is* ill.'

'And then . . . then you invited me to Stratford.'

'He has become much concerned with giving things away. His books, for the most part, though I would like to read them myself. But, never mind – he had too many of them. I believe that he has something of this sort to give to you.'

A servant comes, and Ann speaks to her at length about drying malt, as if I were not there at all. Then the girl disappears. Ann stares at me in silence for a moment. 'You were beautiful,' she says, finally. 'I suppose there is at least some dignity in that.'

She takes me up the stairs, and leads me to a closed door. 'Here you are,' she says. 'When I open it, go inside and sit in the chair by the window. Keep your eyes down till I close the door again. Don't move from the chair till he has finished speaking to you. Do not go near him, and do not open the shutters. You will get used to the darkness when you have been sitting there a while.'

I go obediently to the chair by the shuttered window in the light of the open door. When it closes, I can see nothing. The room

smells of woodsmoke and peppermint. But after a while I realise I can hear the sound of unsteady, rattling breathing coming from the far side of the room. I think of the last time we lay together; the hot night in that other darkness.

I keep my eyes on the shutters and their cracks of daylight.

'Your wife told me that you asked to see me,' I say.

There is a break in the shuddering breathing and then it begins again. It pains me to hear it, and I find I am taking deeper, slower breaths, as if this might help. I want to touch Will again so badly that I grasp the arms of the chair to stop myself from flying across the room. 'I have come to pay you my respects, sir.'

Silence.

'I am very sorry that you are unwell.'

The breathing becomes faster, accompanied by the creaking of a chair. At length, a rasping voice says, 'Not unwell, Aemilia. Not unwell.'

'Then I am glad.'

'Dead, rather.'

'No! Do not say that!'

'Yes, for I am stuck here, away from the world, and I am not of it any longer. That is death to me.'

'The fire . . .'

'Ah, yes. The fire.'

I wait for him to say more, hardly daring to breathe myself, as each word seems to cost him so much.

'Did you hear what caused it?' he asks, then wheezes and coughs.

'No.'

'The effects! In *Henry VIII*. We launched a stage cannon outside, to mark the King's majestical entrance, and the thatch caught fire.'

'You over-reached yourselves.'

'Yes, we over-reached ourselves. Indeed we did. I should have learned my lesson from that cursed crane.'

404

There is another pause.

'I wanted to ask you about Henry,' he says quietly.

'He is well, sir. Clever and handsome. A fine young man now.'

'And . . . what I want to ask is . . . does he know me?'

'What do you mean?'

'Does he know that he's my son?'

I close my eyes. 'Yes. I have told him.'

'And . . .'

'He is glad. He is proud to have such a father.'

'Does he . . . what does he do?'

'He plays in the King's consort.'

'Ah.' He breathes heavily. 'My wife has a doublet and rapier downstairs for him. I have told her that he was a player at the Globe. I mean . . . she has no idea of his connection to me. It is a good doublet – I hope it fits him. She doesn't know the value of the rapier, nor that the grip and pommel are solid silver.'

Silence once more. I wait, listening so hard that my ears began to ache. 'I am sorry, Will,' I say at last, able to bear it no longer. 'I am sorry for all the pain and suffering I caused you. I am sorry if I was ever faithless, and I am sorry for doubting your love. But I am sorriest of all for summoning that evil demon, all because of my jealousy and spite, and my rage about the play.'

'No, no,' he says.

'Yes, it was my fault! I wanted to put a stop to it. I wanted to be avenged on you, and Burbage, and all the others. All the poets and players who are men, and look me up and down, and either see a strumpet or nothing at all. And then Tom died for it – for my revenge! I can never forgive myself. I am damned for it, damned for all eternity, no matter how much I pray for redemption. And so I should be, for I deserve nothing less.'

'Ah, my Aemilia,' he says, his voice faint. 'You are troubled with thick-coming fancies.'

I smile sadly. 'My words, or yours?'

'Yours, I believe. Poor Lady Macbeth.'

'They are thick-coming, certainly. But are they fancies?'

'Aren't they?'

I wait.

'I have read your poems,' he says. 'Or I should say, Susanna has read them to me. For I am . . . weak.'

'Your daughter?'

'Yes. She doesn't approve of your opinions. She thinks they are seditious.'

'And you?'

'I think it's excellent work. Most . . . polemical. You are right about the mistreatment of poor Eve. I saw . . . I saw how it might be. The other side of it. To be shut out because of your sex, by men and boys. And, *de facto*, by all the world. Not all maids can storm the Inns of Court by aping Portia.'

'No.' I am so happy to hear his words that I can think of nothing else to say.

'I once said – among many other cruel and angry things – that you would never be a poet.'

'You did, sir.'

'Well, you have proved me wrong. You *are* a poet, Aemilia Lanyer, and you are a good one, too. And you taught me much – remember that!'

'About Italy, and the ancients.'

'Ay, and about love.' Will is breathing heavily again. 'You must go soon.'

'I am so thankful to you. You are so . . . gracious.' These words are so feeble that I burst out: 'No one else's opinion is *anything* to me. No one else's words *exist*.'

'Think nothing of it. You have worked hard at your Art, and deserve much more than this. But . . .'

'But what?'

'Let me tell you something about the fire.'

'Only if you have the strength.'

There is silence again. Then Will speaks, and the rattle in his breathing fades and it seems almost as if he is talking to himself. 'It was a hot, bright day. Cruelly hot, so even the shadows sweated, and dogs lolled panting in open doorways. I was not at the Globe for the performance: I had business in the City. So the first I knew of the fire was black smoke, drifting over the house-tops as I hurried from St Paul's.' He pauses, and coughs again.

'As I reached Blackfriars Stairs, a cry went up. "The Globe is burning!" And I raised my head – for I was thinking of a verse that I was writing, and staring at the ground – and then I looked across the water and saw the flames, leaping into the summer sky. I paid the boatman half a crown to row quickly, and I ran from the south bank to the theatre door. What a sight it was! Like the Pit itself! The sun had crisped the thatch and dried out the walls, and the sound was terrible – the roaring of fire, and the crashing of timber. The heat smote me as I stood there, and I saw that the trees nearby were catching too.'

'Yet all were saved!'

'So Burbage told me. He came running up, with his shirt all soot-stained and his face as red as the flames. "We are all safe, praise God!" he shouted, tears pouring down his cheeks. "All safe, Will, every man!" But, as I looked at him, a thought came to me. I had been working on a play.'

'Was that so strange?'

He coughs again, and I can hear him struggling to find a clear way for his breath. 'That morning, I had brought it with me, to the tiring-room, because I wanted to get it done. Then I went off to see a printer at Paul's Churchyard, and I had left it behind, upon my table.'

He hesitates, and I wait. 'I have told no one of this but you, Aemilia. This play was to be the master-work that all my other writing led to – the play to end all plays. Such a piece that would always be remembered. Five hundred years – a thousand years

from now. The others might fade from memory, but this play . . . this one would last.'

'And so you ran into the fire.'

'Ah, you are the only one who understands insanity. Yes, I ran, shaking Dick off as I went. I hurtled through the entrance, into the pit. The lintel was burning red – I could see that it would fall at any moment. The pit itself was clear of fire, though the rushes were black and shrivelled and glowed beneath my feet. I ran over them, and up on to the stage. The canopy was flame; the Heavens were Hell. I felt my clothes begin to char and burn my skin. But still I went – into the tiring-room, where all the costumes burned like Catholics – and there was my table. And – lo! – the pages were still there. I praised God – then, as I ran forward, I looked up and the flaming roof timbers were falling down. I snatched the pages, and fled the room as it roared and crackled around me. Ran back across the pit, and into the open air. My clothes, my hair, my skin itself – all of this was flame. By some miracle, I got outside, and it was Dick who saved me. He wrapped a cloak around me and quenched the fire. I fell to the ground, clutching my papers, my breath coming like sword-shafts.'

'Dear God! But you saved your pages?'

The chair creaks.

'What of your pages? What of your great play?'

'All dust,' he says. 'All charred to nothing.'

He is making a strange sound. He is laughing again, after a wheezy fashion.

'Nothing left at all?'

'All that was left was one charred scrap of paper, with the title wrote upon it.'

'And . . . what was the title?'

'It was *Dark Aemilia*. The story of a great lady, and her fall.'

'Oh!'

'It was a fable, concerning love, and poetry and fame. But mostly love.'

I wipe my eyes. 'This was to be your great work?'

'I wanted to summon the spirit of our time together. Its passion and its madness and its joy.'

'Oh, my lord,' say I. 'My sweet, beloved Will.'

'My love,' he says, his voice weak and indistinct. 'We shall remember, shan't we? We have it still.'

After a moment, he says, 'Listen, I cannot speak for very much longer. I have three gifts for you. The first, most people might think was next to worthless, but I believe that you will see its value. As you are a poet.'

'I am overcome.'

I can hear him smile again. 'Wait till you hear what it is: you may think it a strange present. My foul pages. With all my crossings out and alterations.'

'Heminge said your pages are never blurred nor blotted.'

'That is because I keep my first draft to myself. Until now, that is. Now they are yours. You will be heartened by my short-comings, and perhaps you can learn from my mistakes.'

'Will . . . I . . . how can I thank you – ?'

'And also . . . also my bed.'

'Your *bed*?'

'Not the bed I sleep in now, which is of little value. No, the one where we last . . . went at it. Lord, what a night that was. It's still there – I could not bear to bring it back to Stratford, nor did I want to pay the fee the carrier wanted.'

I remember it well – the fug of love inside its curtains and its roof patterned with leaping porpoises.

'Aemilia?'

'Yes?'

'Still there – good.'

'Still here? I cannot bear to leave!'

'There is one final gift.'

'I don't need anything more. You have been kind enough.'

'I will put your name upon the play. Upon *Macbeth*. For, as

409

sure as anything, the meat of that strange piece is yours.'

'Thank you. But – no. It would be wrong.'

He sighs. A long, rattling sigh.

'Aemilia, you are many things. You are a troublesome, noisy, cock-teasing, cock-tiring, wild-tongued termagant . . .' He stops, as if to gather his strength. 'But you are not evil.'

'I *am* evil. Tom died because of me.'

'How do you know?'

'You were there! You saw it! He fell down upon the stage. The spirit cursed him, and the crane fell.'

'Yes, the crane killed him. We don't know why it fell, but it was the crane that brought about his death. Burbage and I built it, and it was me who pushed to have it. But I haven't spent all these years believing that I am evil! It was an accident. All life brings risk.'

'Is that what you believe?'

'Of course. You are no more guilty of his death than I am. Nor are you the evil strumpet of those sonnets. You are Aemilia. And I loved you better than myself.'

'Loved?'

'Love. I still love you. Nothing has changed that.'

'No. Nothing has changed it.' The tears pour out of me.

'Shall we forgive each other?' he asks. His voice is weaker still.

'Oh, Will!' I sob. 'If we forgive each other, then we are all done.'

'My love, we *are* all done,' says Will. 'Open the shutters.'

His face is dark from the sun. His eyes are full of sky. His lips are swollen red from reckless kissing. 'Let's not quarrel,' he says. 'Let's make love, and I'll teach you poetry that way.'

I smooth the hair back from his forehead.

'Am I your mistress, then? Am I all the things you wanted?'

'You are indeed, and I am your obedient slave.'
I look at him, eye to eye, to see if I can peer inside his head.
'Do you want me?' he asks, very serious.
Oh, I do. I do.
Afterwards, we lie together, sticky and naked in the long grass. 'Be silent with me now, my love,' he whispers.

She sits me in the hall downstairs, beside a smouldering log fire, and hands me a cup of wine. Quite kindly, compared to what has gone before.

'I am sorry that you had to see him so,' she says.

'I didn't know.'

'No one is allowed to speak of it.'

'I understand.'

'He ran back into the Globe. When it was burning. They tried to stop him, but he struggled free.'

'A brave act.'

'Brave indeed. He wanted to be sure that no one had been left inside.'

'Did he tell you that?'

'Why else would he have entered an inferno, if not to save a human life? He is a good man.'

I cannot say that he is more than good, and less. I sip my tear-thinned wine in silence.

'Poor Will! What an ending!' I say at last.

'The doublet and the rapier are beside you,' she says, nodding to an iron-bound box. 'And his foul papers with them. Take care of those in particular. They are the workings of his mind.'

'I'll put them in safe-keeping.'

'Safe! Where in London's pit of malice and foul-doing do you call "safe"?'

'It is safe enough, madam, I can assure you. I have a little house at Aldgate, though I am soon to move to Pudding Lane.'

Mistress Shakespeare looks at me blankly. I realise that London names mean nothing to her. 'I make a habit of reading the Scriptures when I can,' she says. 'I put my trust in God and his angels now.' She picks up the Bible that is lying next to her on the oak settle.

'So must we all.'

Opening the book, she reads for a moment, but she is crying. 'I wanted him to come back so much. I prayed for it,' she says, without looking up. 'And now these prayers have been most cruelly answered.'

I shake my head sadly.

'It won't be long before Will is with God,' she says. 'I try to see that. I try to bear it.'

The past is twisting in my mind, the greedy and illiterate country wife transformed into Patient Griselda. I try to think of words to comfort her – and me. But everything is muddled.

'I would like to ask one thing of you,' she says. 'Do not remember him as you just saw him. Remember him as he was.' She swallows and looks at me sharply. 'When you knew him. When he was young.'

'I shall.'

'He is a poet,' she says. 'And a magician. He is also my husband, but that is of less importance. I have learned to understand that, though I don't expect others to see it as I do.' Then, she closes her eyes. Is she about to pray? But no – she quotes these lines . . .

'I have bedimm'd
The noontide sun, call'd forth the mutinous winds,
And 'twixt the green sea and the azured vault
Set roaring war: to the dread rattling thunder
Have I given fire, and rifted Jove's stout oak
With his own bolt; the strong-bas'd promontory
Have I made shake and by the spurs pluck'd up

412

The pine and cedar: graves at my command
Have wak'd their sleepers, op'd, and let 'em forth
By my so potent Art. But this rough magic
I here abjure; and, when I have required
Some heavenly music, which even now I do,
To work mine end upon their senses that
This airy charm is for, I'll break my staff,
Bury it certain fathoms in the earth,
And deeper than did ever plummet sound
I'll drown my book.'

The words are so clear and bright that my neck pricks at their sound, and I sit there with my box of foul papers and stare at the sorcerer's wife in frank amazement.

I want to speak, of Prospero and love and endings. I want to say – our love was insubstantial, but magical. Like Ariel. But I can't. So I say, 'You had the best of him. A family, and a life here, and a home together.'

She stares at me. 'The best of him?'

'Yes.'

'What can you know of that? How can you presume to look into the minds or lives of others?'

'I don't presume to know anything, Mistress Shakespeare; you quite mistake me.'

'No, Mistress Lanyer, *you* mistake *me*. Of your own life you may be the witness, though no one knows when you are true and when you play false.'

'I am indeed the witness to it, mistress.'

'Of the rest of us, you can know next to nothing. Don't load us with your study, or your supposition. Do you *hear* me? Do you *understand*?'

We sit in silence. I watch a log glow red then crumble to a spume of fine grey ash. After a while, it falls to pieces in a rain of crackling stars.

413

Scene IV

The Globe, London, April 1616

Springtime, and the sky is streaked with fragile cloud. The meadows are white with lady smock and tender violets peer out from the hedgerow shade. Larks sing, cuckoos call, and a soft wind shakes the oaks which stand hard by the new-built Globe. The theatre is a splendid copy of its former self. But its roof is made from slate instead of thatch. God willing, this theatre will last longer than the old one.

'It's a fine thing,' says Henry, squeezing my arm. 'His work is born again.'

I cannot speak, but squeeze his arm in return. I have not set foot in the theatre since the day that Tom Flood died. Yesterday Ann Shakespeare sent me word that Will is dead too. He breathed his last while he was sleeping.

I am dressed in black. For Will would have his way, and this is his third present to me – a fine dress of ebony-coloured velvet. It was sent to me after I left Stratford, together with a caul of seed pearls. A single piece of paper was pinned to it, burned and charred so that at first the writing on it seemed illegible. Then I managed to make out two words: 'Dark Aemilia'. Now, I am wearing it on a bright spring day in a world in which he does not exist.

Henry persuaded me to come, full of pride for his dead father. He is wearing the Spanish doublet and the rapier is at his side. He is tall, and well-made, with thoughtful, shadowed eyes and a musician's ear for poetry. I could not bear a tragedy, or a

Roman rant, but the players are putting on *A Midsummer Night's Dream*, which I have never seen. A comedy for springtime, and for love, so Henry tells me, and the white flag that flutters over the theatre's cupola confirms that there will be no blood today.

We pass under the entrance, painted in myriad colours like the gateway to an ancient palace. Every detail of the old gate has been reproduced, even the likeness of Hercules with the world upon his shoulders. The world beyond the walls of the theatre is mutable and beyond our grasp. The world within is shaped and patterned for our understanding and diversion. We sit down in the gallery and Henry takes my hand. I look around at the pageant which surrounds me. The new pit is full to overflowing, and every seat on every tier of the gallery is taken. Those in the pit will find it hard to follow all the action, there is such a crowd of gallants seated upon the stage. The courtiers are rosetted and bombasted to the death, flaunting their warlike beards and girlish love-locks. The lesser folk are just as vivid in their cheaper finery, swarming together in a brawl of colour and vulgar show: yellow farthingales crushed by apple-women, stack-heels sinking in the mud. I wonder if the play-goers are wearing their finest clothing in Will's honour, just as I have put on my widow's gown.

The seething crowd is chatting, munching, singing, dicing, gaming, smoking, and swigging small beer. There are law students, strumpets, apprentices and oyster-sellers. Choirboys, pickpockets, servant girls and foists. I see a blur of movement; but also a multitude of London faces, looming and vanishing in the mob. A pretty Romeo and his pale Juliet, arms twined together. A handsome Moor and his whispering, rat-faced Iago. A stout and jocular Falstaff, drinking from an ale-pot, while a young blade laughs at his side. A student, in a black cloak, frowning deep as Hamlet as he reads his book. The sun shimmers on every button and scarlet pustule, every scar and cross-stitched codpiece, every tooth-stump and curling smile. So that the scene is as vibrant as a palace portrait, preserved in oils and distemper.

Here is Thomas Dekker, writing on his sleeve, head cocked to one side as if listening to the throng. Here is Moll Cutpurse, strumming her lute and singing out, full-throated. And see, there is my landlord Anthony Inchbald, propped high on one of the best seats, dressed in scarlet. Dogs run between the legs of the play-goers, snatching up the fallen chicken bones. The scent of tobacco smoke wafts into the balmy air. On the balcony above the stage, the musicians are playing. A nut-seller shouts for custom; a baby squeals; a drunk's song rages and stops.

And then I see them. A white-haired woman, overdressed in a tawny gown with a lace ruff. There is a younger woman next to her, with two little girls. They have black hair, wild and curly. The children are sitting side by side, so tight that they might be made of one flesh. I look closer. They *are* one flesh. It is Anne Flood, and Marie, and Anne's grandchildren, the joined twins. Anne leans close to Marie and whispers something to her, and Marie throws her head back and laughs.

I spring up, wanting to call to them, but Henry pulls me back into my seat. 'Mother! Sit down, sit down . . .'

Three trumpet calls blast out, to summon any latecomers. The musicians strike up a stately tune. Out comes Dick Burbage. He is head-to-toe in black: the only mortal here dressed as funereally as I am. His velvet cloak ripples behind him in the breeze. Behind him come two players. Oberon, in purple and cloth-of-gold, and his fair Titania in a gown of taffeta and *toile d'atour*. Their faces are painted white, their lips are scarlet, and the ostrich feathers in their jewelled crowns waft gently above their heads.

The audience is silent. Kites wheel to and fro in the blue sky, wing-beats rapid, then still as they soar upon the breeze. A bear screams from the pit next door, and the sound of cheering follows. Henry is smiling with tears upon his cheeks.

Burbage steps forward.

Further Reading

Historical Note

Dark Aemilia is a work of imagination, based on fact. I wanted to tell a story that was authentic and historically accurate. Equally importantly, I wanted to write about Shakespeare's London as if I was there. If a time machine had been available, I would have used it.

Historical fiction writers sometimes disagree about the extent to which people have changed over the centuries. It is certainly not accurate to suggest that a woman in the Elizabethan or Jacobean period would be 'feminist' in any sense that we recognise today. But the poetry that Aemilia Lanyer wrote shows her championing the cause of Eve, and drawing attention to the role of women in the Passion of Christ. Academics have referred to her poetry as 'proto-feminist'. So I felt I could work with that.

However, I believe that some aspects of human nature remain constant. Disease and death were part of everyday life in the past, but parents were still traumatised by the death of a child. There is certainly evidence for this, which ranges from the inscriptions and tombs in churchyards to the poem *Pearl*, a fourteenth-century allegory about bereavement and religious faith. And who can forget that most harrowing scene in all of Shakespeare – King Lear's lament over the body of Cordelia?

The starting point for this novel was the life of a real woman. Aemilia Bassano (later Lanyer) was born in Bishopsgate in 1569 and buried in Clerkenwell in 1645. She became the mistress of Henry Carey, Lord Hunsdon, in 1587. Six years later, she became pregnant and was married off to her cousin Alfonso, a recorder player in the Queen's consort. Her son Henry, born in 1593, is presumed to be Hunsdon's child.

There is no evidence that Lanyer was the lover of William Shakespeare, but she is one of the candidates for the shadowy role of the Dark Lady, the object of the later sonnets (127–154). However, there is no proof; only theory, opinion and the reinterpretation of existing facts. (The historian A.L. Rowse was one of the first scholars to suggest that Lanyer might be Shakespeare's muse.) In fact, there is no evidence that Shakespeare dedicated the sonnets to anyone at all, and many academics believe that the Fair Youth and the Dark Lady are symbolic figures.

We do know that Lanyer was one of the first women in England to be a published poet, and the first to be published in a professional way, as men were. *Salve Deus Rex Judaeorum* (Hail, God, King of the Jews) was printed by Valentine Simmes in 1611 and sold in Paul's Churchyard (the bookselling quarter of London) by Richard Bonian. Lanyer dedicated her collection, in a rather flamboyant manner, to a host of distinguished and wealthy women, starting with Queen Anne, the wife of James I.

Most of the surviving facts about Lanyer have been preserved in the notebooks of the physician and astrologer Simon Forman, who kept detailed accounts of his dealings with his clients. Forman was clearly fascinated by her, and hoped to seduce her. His notes indicate that, although he spent a night with her, she did not have sex with him. (Or 'halek', the word that Forman coined for sexual intercourse.)

Surviving church and court records provide the other information: her birth, marriage, death, the births and deaths of family members and her setting-up of a school at St Giles-in-the-Fields (1617–19). There is also a record of a legal dispute about her rights to Alfonso Lanyer's income after his death in 1613. We do not know if Lanyer's father, Baptiste Bassano, was murdered, but court records show that there was an attempt on his life a few years before he died.

There is no evidence that Lanyer wrote *Macbeth*, or any part of it. Forman does, however, mention that, on one of her visits to

him, she asked for advice about conjuring demons. The current consensus is that Shakespeare sometimes worked with collaborators, including Thomas Middleton and Thomas Dekker.

The dating of Shakespeare's plays is an inexact science, and one of the themes of the novel is lost stories and knowledge and the frailty of the paper trail to the past. There are websites that give 'exact' dates for his plays, but academics are more circumspect. *The Taming of the Shrew* was probably written in 1590. *Othello*'s dates are very uncertain; the play could have been written and performed as early as 1600, or as late as 1604. The key issue with *Macbeth* is that academics now believe it was written after the Gunpowder Plot of November 1605, because it is agreed that there are references to the plot in the play. The date I have given in the novel is May 1606. There is no record of a performance of *A Midsummer Night's Dream* at the Globe after the death of Shakespeare in April 1616. But it is plausible that such a production might have taken place.

One of the 'lost works' is the book of sonnets that Will has published in 1605 while he and Aemilia are estranged. The sonnets which have survived were not published until 1609, and they do not refer to the 'Dark Lady'. The title of the publication was simply *Shakespeare's Sonnets*, the publisher was G. Eld for T.T. and the seller was William Aipley. It is thought that the sonnets could have been written as early as the 1590s, and that they would have been circulated in handwritten form, as suggested in the novel. Although the 1609 collection bears the promise 'Never before imprinted', as was customary at the time, it is plausible that some of the sonnets had been published before, and this was the first imprint of the whole collection.

At the end of the novel, Aemilia tells Ann Shakespeare that Will's papers will be safe with her in Pudding Lane. As readers will know, fifty years after this conversation takes place, the City of London was devastated by the Great Fire of 1666. I liked the idea of suggesting that Will's spoiled pages were somewhere in

that huge conflagration. Just as an afterword, it is interesting to note that the Great Fire took several days to take hold, and the booksellers and printers of Paul's Churchyard and Paternoster Square stored their books, chap-books and pamphlets in St Paul's Cathedral for safekeeping. The building was stacked to the roof with paper. Three days later, it went up in smoke.

Historical Characters

William Shakespeare (1564–1616)

William Shakespeare was born and brought up in Stratford-upon-Avon. At eighteen, he married Ann Hathaway and they had three children: Susanna, and twins Hamnet and Judith. Few records of Shakespeare's life have survived. There is evidence, however, that Shakespeare worked in London as an actor and playwright in the late 1580s and early 1590s. (The first reference to him in London was made in the pamphlet *Greene's Groats-worth of Wit* published posthumously by his rival Robert Greene.)

Shakespeare became an actor, writer, and part-owner of the theatrical company the Lord Chamberlain's Men, which became known as the King's Men after James I came to the throne. Most of his surviving plays were written between 1589 and 1613. He is believed to have retired to Stratford around 1613 at the age of forty-nine, and he died there three years later. There is no evidence that Shakespeare was seriously injured in the Globe fire of 1613, but the theory has been put forward by Graham Philips and Martin Keatman in *The Shakespeare Conspiracy*.

Elizabeth I (1533–1603)

Elizabeth I was the last monarch of the Tudor dynasty, becoming Queen in 1558. The challenge with Elizabeth is that so much is known about her, and there have been so many fictional portrayals, that it is hard to find a new way of presenting her. I focus on her fragility and desperation at the end of her life.

The daughter of Henry VIII, she was born a princess, but was declared illegitimate after the execution of her mother Anne Boleyn. She had survived intense competition for the throne, and was imprisoned in the Tower for almost a year during her sister Mary's reign, on suspicion of supporting Protestant rebels.

One of her first acts as monarch was the establishment of an English Protestant Church, of which she became the Supreme Governor. This Elizabethan Religious Settlement later evolved into today's Church of England. It was a compromise between Catholicism and Protestantism.

Elizabeth I never married and became famous for the shrewd deployment of her virginity. In the novel, I make her the mother of Robert Devereux, Earl of Essex. The idea that Essex is not her lover but her secret, illegimate son links the themes of the novel together. It is a possible explanation for Essex's arrogance, his unreasonable behaviour and Elizabeth's inconsolable grief after his execution. There is of course no evidence for this, though there has been speculation that she may have had illegitimate children.

Alfonso Lanyer (1570s?–1613)
Most of what we know about Alfonso is taken from the notebooks of Simon Forman, and is based on his consultations with Aemilia. These state that Alfonso was her cousin and that he was a Queen's musician. Church records also show Alfonso and Aemilia were married in St Botolph's Church, Aldgate, on 18 October 1592.

It is known that the Lanyers were a French family, and that Alfonso was a profligate character. Aemilia told Simon Forman that he spent her dowry within a year. Even so, he does appear to have helped her in her quest for publication: the frontispiece of *Salve Deus Rex Judaeorum* includes a reference to 'Captain Alfonso Lanyer Servant to the King's Majestie'. We don't know if Alfonso actively assisted his wife, but his status helped her assert her respectability.

Alfonso Lanyer died in 1613. The cause is unknown.

Historical Note

Henry Lanyer (1593–1633)

Henry was the son of Aemilia Lanyer. His father is assumed to be Lord Hunsdon. Henry became a recorder player at the court, and died in 1633. Aemilia then bought up his two children.

There is no historical evidence that his father was William Shakespeare.

Baptiste Bassano (1520?–76)

Aemilia's father Baptiste is another obscure historical figure, and he only appears in the novel in Aemilia's memories of her childhood. As he is pivotal to the plot I think it is important to include a historical note which separates fact from fiction.

Baptiste came to England from Venice in the 1530s, and was certainly at Henry VIII's court in 1540, playing the sackbut (a kind of trombone) in the service of Edward Seymour, Earl of Hertford. He was the youngest of six brothers, who were originally from the town of Bassano del Grappa in the Veneto region. All of the brothers came to England, and only the eldest, Jacamo, returned to Venice. Henry VIII gave the brothers the right to live in apartments in the Charterhouse, a Carthusian monastery he had dissolved in 1537.

In 1563, conspirators Henry Dingley, Mark Anthony and a number of others were prosecuted for Bassano's attempted murder, and were sentenced to have their ears cut off and to be whipped, pilloried and banished for plotting to kill him. Nothing further is known about the incident. The murder that Aemilia witnesses is a fictional event, however; we do not know how Baptiste really died. In the novel, Margaret keeps it a secret, fearing for the rest of her family.

Baptiste was not formally married to Aemilia's mother Margaret Johnson, referring to her as his 'reputed wife' in his will.

In the novel, I make a reference to one of Margaret Johnson's cousins, Robert Johnson, who composed 'The Witch's Dance'

(the tune that Alfonso is humming in Act II, Scene V). I liked the fact that he shares his name with the African-American blues guitarist Robert Johnson (1911–38) who is alleged to have sold his soul to the Devil at the crossroads. Popular myth has it that this is how Robert Johnson gained his phenomenal musical skill. He died in mysterious circumstances at the age of twenty-seven. In my story, Baptiste makes a similar pact with the witches at the crossroads at Tyburn, and then reneges on the deal, repenting and giving up his music.

Simon Forman (1552–1611)
Simon Forman studied at Oxford University, and later set up a medical practice in London, providing astrologically based treatments and predictions. Demand for his services increased after he (apparently) cured himself of plague. He was in dispute with the College of Physicians for many years, and the College banned him from practising as a doctor. He was eventually awarded this title.

Forman is one of the few people to have accurately predicted the date of his own death. His papers are now in the Bodleian Library in Oxford.

The distinction between 'high magic' and 'women's magic' was not made explicitly at the time, but it is accurate to suggest that men developed the intellectual side of magic via experimentation, while women used old lore to cure common ailments for small sums of money. If you want to know more about the importance of 'magic' and its connection to belief systems during this period, I recommend *Religion and the Decline of Magic* by Keith Thomas, a truly magisterial tome.

Henry Wriothesley, 3rd Earl of Southampton (1573–1624)
Wriothesley (pronounced 'Rizley') is often identified as the Fair Youth of Shakespeare's sonnets, though this is not a matter of historical fact. In addition, there is no evidence that Shakespeare

and Henry Wriothesley were romantically or sexually involved, though many novelists have suggested this.

In the novel, I suggest that Wriothesley is bisexual, though not that he and Will are lovers. We have no information about Wriothesley's sexuality, though we do know that he was apparently happy with his wife, Elizabeth Vernon, and that they had several children. Surviving portraits of the handsome and highly elegant young man have been seen as evidence of his 'effeminacy' by some scholars, but his appearance could equally have been an expression of his interest in fashion, a widespread obsession at the Elizabethan court. Attitudes to sexuality were very different from today. Fulsome and seemingly romantic dedications, such as those made by Shakespeare to Wriothesley, were common. Young men were often physically affectionate towards each other. But male homosexuality was seen as a terrible sin, diverging from the natural order, and was a capital offence.

In the novel, I present Wriothesley as a young man intoxicated by his own power, who uses this to step beyond social norms. This is plausible, and fits in with the theme of over-reaching in the novel.

We do know that Wriothesley was involved in the rebellion led by the Earl of Essex in 1601, for which he was sentenced to death. Essex was beheaded – which Elizabeth apparently regretted – but after her death Wriothesley's sentence was commuted to life imprisonment in the Tower of London. He was released on the accession of James I.

Henry Carey, 1st Baron Hunsdon (1526–96)

Hunsdon was the son of Mary Boleyn, Anne Boleyn's sister. He was a blunt, outspoken man, a professional soldier rather than a courtier. As Lord Chamberlain, he was the patron of William Shakespeare's company from 1594.

Simon Forman's case-books record that Aemilia Bassano was his mistress for around six years (1586–92).

Hunsdon died in 1596 and was buried in Westminster Abbey. His tomb is indeed bizarre and ornate.

Ann Shakespeare, née Hathaway (1555/6–1623)

Very little is known about Ann Hathaway beyond a few references in legal documents, but her personality and marriage to Shakespeare have been the subject of a great deal of speculation.

Pregnant when she married William Shakespeare in 1582, Ann was seven years older than he was. Much has been made of this, and it has been suggested that Shakespeare was coerced into marrying her. We have no proof of this. Although Shakespeare worked in London, there is also no evidence that he disliked his wife.

Shakespeare famously bequeathed his 'second-best bed' to Ann. In my novel, he leaves his best bed to Aemilia. I feel that Ann has been poorly treated both by popular myth and (most) other fiction writers. Germaine Greer robustly challenges the idea that Ann was unintelligent or illiterate in *Shakespeare's Wife*; my version of Ann is inspired by Greer's book. Ann is as formidable as Aemilia in her own way. If you are interested in a ribald and witty fictional account of her life, read *Mrs Shakespeare: the Complete Works* by Robert Nye.

Thomas Dekker (1570?–1632)

Throughout his life, dramatist and pamphleteer Thomas Dekker had severe financial problems, and was imprisoned for debt several times. He is thought to have written about sixty plays, but only twenty have survived. Dekker wrote the city comedy *The Roaring Girle* (1610) in collaboration with Middleton. The heroine of this play, Moll Cutpurse, was based on the notorious London thief Mary Frith, who dressed as a man. His pamphlet *The Wonderful Year* (1603) describes London ravaged by the effects of the plague.

Moll Cutpurse (Mary Frith) (1584–1659)
Mary Frith (also known as Moll Cutpurse) was a cross-dressing fence and thief. She was mythologised even in her lifetime, and at least two plays were written about her. She smoked a pipe, played her lute on the stage, and swore. She lived into the time of Oliver Cromwell's Protectorate and is alleged to have fired a musket at one of his men. Her remarkable life story does indeed indicate that she enjoyed a level of personal freedom that was almost unknown among women at that time.

Richard Burbage (1567–1619)
Although Richard Burbage was a member of an acting family, his early career is poorly documented. Later he became one of London's best-known actors.

He was the lead actor with the Lord Chamberlain's Men, and a sharer in the company. Burbage played the title role in the first performances of many of Shakespeare's plays, including *Hamlet, Othello, Richard III*, and *King Lear*.

Background Events

1526	Birth of Henry Carey, Lord Hunsdon.
1533	Birth of Elizabeth I.
1569	Birth of Aemilia Bassano.
1576	Death of Baptiste Bassano, Aemilia's father, cause unknown.
1587	Death of Margaret Johnson, Aemilia's mother. The probable date of beginning of Aemilia's affair with Lord Hunsdon.
1591–92	Plague kills 15,000 people in London.
1592	Christopher Marlowe writes *Dr Faustus* (probable date).
1592	Aemilia falls pregnant and is married off to court musician (and cousin by marriage) Alfonso Lanyer.
1595	Robert Southwell, English Jesuit poet, hanged at Tyburn.
1596	Lord Hunsdon dies at Somerset House while still in office.
1597	Shakespeare's son Hamnet dies in Stratford.
1597	Aemilia visits Simon Forman for news about how her husband's 'business' will fare. This is the Islands Voyage trip to the Azores, 1597, led by Robert Devereux, 2nd Earl of Essex, the Queen's favourite.
1599	Globe Theatre built.
1600	Moll Cutpurse indicted in Middlesex for stealing 2s 11d. Two plays written about her in next ten years – *The Madde Pranckes of Mery Mall of the Bankside* by John Day, and *The Roaring Girle* by Thomas Dekker

and Thomas Middleton. Both dwell on the 'scandalous' issue of her dressing like a man.

1603 Queen Elizabeth dies.

1603 Alfonso is one of 59 musicians who played at Elizabeth's funeral. He is then employed by James I.

1603 King James 1 crowned.

1605 Gunpowder plot (known as the Treason Plot), November 5th.

1605–07 Probable date of first performance of *Macbeth*. Many scholars say that the play was probably written between 1603 and 1606. As it seems to celebrate the Stuart accession to the English throne, they argue that the play is unlikely to have been composed earlier than 1603, when James I was crowned. Others suggest a more specific date of 1605–06 because the play appears to refer to the Gunpowder Plot. *Macbeth* was first printed in the First Folio of 1623 and the Folio is the only source for the text.

1611 Aemilia Lanyer publishes *Salve Deus Rex Judaeorum*. She is one of the first women to be published as a poet in England, and the first to claim professional status for her work.

1611 Simon Forman writes first known review of *Macbeth* in his notebook.

1613 Alfonso Lanyer dies.

1613 Globe Theatre burns down during a performance of *Henry VIII*.

1614 Globe Theatre rebuilt (using brick rather than wood).

1616 William Shakespeare dies.

1645 Aemilia Lanyer dies, aged 76, a 'pensioner' therefore someone who has an income – not rich, but not a pauper.

Suggested Reading

If this story has made you want to find out more about the period, here are some suggestions for further reading:

Peter Ackroyd, *Shakespeare, The Biography* (Chatto & Windus, 2005)

Bill Bryson, *Shakespeare, The World as a Stage* (Harper Perennial, 2007)

Judith Cook, *Dr Simon Forman, a Most Notorious Physician* (Chatto & Windus, 2001)

Andrew Dickson, *The Rough Guide to Shakespeare* (Rough Guides, 2009)

Germaine Greer, *Shakespeare's Wife* (Bloomsbury, 2007)

Christopher Lee, *1603: The Death of Elizabeth I and the Birth of the Stuart Era* (Review, 2003)

Robert Nye, *Mrs Shakespeare: the Complete Works* (Sinclair-Stevenson, 1993)

Graham Philips and Martin Keatman, *The Shakespeare Conspiracy* (Arrow, 1995)

Lisa Picard, *Elizabeth's London: Everyday Life in Elizabethan London* (Phoenix, 2004)

Stephen Porter, *The Plagues of London* (Tempus, 2008)

Alison Sim, *The Tudor Housewife* (Sutton, 1996)

Keith Thomas, *Religion and the Decline of Magic* (Weidenfeld & Nicolson, 1971)

Susanne Woods, *The Poems of Aemilia Lanyer: Salve Deus Rex Judaeorum* (Oxford University Press, 1993)

Susanne Woods, *Lanyer: A Renaissance Woman Poet* (Oxford University Press, 1999)

Glossary

ale-pottle (noun) – beer bottle or tankard

bawdy (noun) – lewd or obscene talk or writing

bowelled – (adj) disembowelled

ceruse (noun) – a white lead pigment, used in cosmetics

chap-book (noun) – a small book or pamphlet containing poems, ballads, stories or religious tracts

cheat-bread (noun) – poor quality bread

coney (noun) – a tame rabbit raised for the table

coney catcher (noun) – a thief or trickster

the Corporation (noun) – the Corporation of London, the municipal governing body of the City of London

cozener (noun) – cheat or trickster (from verb, to cozen)

doxy (noun) – mistress or prostitute

dread-belly (noun) – Aemilia's own word, meaning stomach upset brought on by unwholesome food and/or anxiety about the Early Modern world

farthingale (noun) – a support, such as a hoop, worn beneath a skirt to extend it horizontally from the waist, used by European women in the sixteenth and seventeenth centuries

foolscap – (noun) paper cut to the size of 8.5 x 13.5 inches (216 x 343 mm) – traditional size used in Europe before A4 paper became the international standard

fribbling (adj) – time-wasting

grabble (verb) – Aemilia's own word: to catch at thin air in a desperate manner

gull (noun) – a gullible person, easily fooled or the victim of a trick (from verb, to gull)

Glossary

halek (verb) – Simon Forman's own word, meaning to have sexual intercourse

hell-waines (noun) – creatures from hell ('waine' is an Old English name for boy)

jakes (noun) – an outside toilet

kennel (noun) – a gutter along a street

kersey (noun) – coarse woollen fabric

kinchin-mort (noun) – a child used by professional beggars to gain sympathy

the Liberties (noun) – an area on what is now the South Bank of London which was outside the jurisdiction of the Corporation of London

Marranos (noun) – Jews living in the Iberian peninsula who converted to Christianity, many of whom practised Judaism in secret

mouldiwarp (noun) – a mole

pattens (noun) – outdoor shoes with wooden soles worn over indoor shoes

pavane (noun) – a slow processional dance common in Europe during the sixteenth century

pigwidgeon (noun) – an insignificant or unimportant person; something petty or small that is worthy of contempt

plague-mort (noun) – Aemilia's own word, meaning someone afflicted with the plague

pottage (noun) – a thick soup or stew

prentice-boy (noun) – apprentice boy

scragged (adj) – Aemilia's own word, meaning scraggy, skinny, lined

scrimmage (noun) – Aemilia's own word, meaning a mess and tangle of mucky things

shave-grasse (noun) – a plant with a brush-like appearance

shippon (noun) – cowshed

shittle-cock (noun) – shuttlecock, used in *Volpone* and *The Fox*, by Ben Jonson

simples (noun) – medicinal plants or the medicine obtained from them

slip-shake (adj) – Parson John's own word, meaning slippery and unwholesome

small beer (noun) – a beer or ale that contains little alcohol

solar (noun) – upper sitting room, common in most houses of the period

squibbling (to squibble) (verb) – Aemilia's own word, meaning the male habit of quibbling and double-dealing, being deceitful and emotionally dishonest

truckle-bed (noun) – a low bed on casters, often pushed under another bed when not in use. Also called a trundle bed.

virginals (noun) – keyboard instrument of the harpsichord family widespread in Europe during the sixteenth and seventeenth centuries

vizard (noun) – mask for disguise or protection, alteration of Middle English *viser* mask

wherry (noun) – a river ferry-boat

Acknowledgements

This book has been a joy to write, and many people have helped it along the way.

First of all, my heartfelt thanks to everyone at Myriad Editions, especially Candida Lacey, Linda McQueen, Holly Ainley and Vicky Blunden. It is inspiring and exciting to work with people who love books and writing so much, and are so meticulous about the publishing process.

I'm also indebted to the writers and historians who gave me the benefit of their considerable wisdom while I drafted and re-drafted the novel. Fay Weldon, Celia Brayfield, Elizabeth Evenden, Sarah Penny, Matt Thorne and Linda Anderson – thank you so much. Sincere thanks also to Ronald Hutton, Professor of History at the University of Bristol. The ideas, themes and characters in the novel came together after many fascinating meetings and discussions. Any mistakes or inaccuracies are mine alone.

There were times when my energy and determination flagged – the friendship and support of Martin Cox, Susanna Jones, Alison Macleod, Lisa Seabourne and Kate Wade have kept me going.

A special mention too, for Julie Burchill. After a long and boozy lunch party during a rather gloomy hiatus in my career, Julie gave me three books by Patrick Hamilton and said, 'I don't know why you don't write something darker and more historical.' I think this book fulfils the brief.

I am also grateful to Brunel University. The university's Isambard Scholarship gave me the means to study for a PhD in English and Creative Writing, and this novel is the main component of that research.

Acknowledgements

(Nearly there now.) I couldn't function without my children and (extremely patient) husband. Georgia and Declan, you are probably the funniest teenagers on the planet, and definitely the messiest. I don't know what I have taught you, but you have taught me what motherhood feels like. Noel, you are the best reader I could hope for, and please carry on telling me when my writing isn't good enough – even when you would rather have a quiet life. And thank you, Mum, the only person I know who is as forceful and unstoppable as Aemilia Bassano Lanyer.

Last of all – thank you, Aemilia. This book was meant to be about Lady Macbeth. Then I found you, threw away 30,000 words – and never looked back.

About the Author

SALLY O'REILLY has received numerous citations for her fiction, which has been shortlisted for the Ian St James Short Story Prize and the Cosmopolitan Short Story Award. A former *Cosmopolitan* New Journalist of the Year, her work has appeared in *The Guardian, The Sunday Times,* the *Evening Standard,* and the *New Scientist.* She teaches creative writing at the Open University and the University of Portsmouth in England. *Dark Aemilia* is her U.S. debut.

O'Reilly, Sally
Dark Aemilia